THE SOUL OF CLASSICAL POLITICAL ECONOMY

ADVANCED STUDIES IN POLITICAL ECONOMY

Series Editors: Virgil Henry Storr and Stefanie Haeffele

The Advanced Studies in Political Economy series consists of republished as well as newly commissioned work that seeks to understand the underpinnings of a free society through the foundations of the Austrian, Virginia, and Bloomington schools of political economy. Through this series, the Mercatus Center at George Mason University aims to further the exploration of and discussion on the dynamics of social change by making this research available to students and scholars.

Nona Martin Storr, Emily Chamlee-Wright, and Virgil Henry Storr, *How We Came Back: Voices from Post-Katrina New Orleans*

Don Lavoie, *Rivalry and Central Planning: The Socialist Calculation Debate Reconsidered*

Don Lavoie, *National Economic Planning: What Is Left?*

Peter J. Boettke, Stefanie Haeffele, and Virgil Henry Storr, eds., *Mainline Economics: Six Nobel Lectures in the Tradition of Adam Smith*

Matthew D. Mitchell and Peter J. Boettke, *Applied Mainline Economics: Bridging the Gap between Theory and Public Policy*

Jack High, ed., *Humane Economics: Essays in Honor of Don Lavoie*

Edward Stringham, ed., *Anarchy, State and Public Choice*

Peter J. Boettke and David L. Prychitko, eds., *The Market Process: Essays in Contemporary Austrian Economics*

Richard E. Wagner, *To Promote the General Welfare: Market Processes vs. Political Transfers*

Ludwig M. Lachmann, *The Market as an Economic Process*

Donald J. Boudreaux and Roger Meiners, eds., *The Legacy of Bruce Yandle*

Peter J. Boettke and Alain Marciano, eds., *The Soul of Classical Political Economy: James M. Buchanan from the Archives*

ABOUT THE MERCATUS CENTER

The Mercatus Center at George Mason University is the world's premier university source for market-oriented ideas—bridging the gap between academic ideas and real-world problems.

A university-based research center, the Mercatus Center advances knowledge about how markets work to improve people's lives by training graduate students, conducting research, and applying economics to offer solutions to society's most pressing problems.

Our mission is to generate knowledge and understanding of the institutions that affect the freedom to prosper, and to find sustainable solutions that overcome the barriers preventing individuals from living free, prosperous, and peaceful lives.

Founded in 1980, the Mercatus Center is located on George Mason University's Arlington and Fairfax campuses.

Papers and lectures included in this volume are used with permission from the Special Collections Research Center for the George Mason University Libraries, and, whenever possible, with additional permission from the authors.

Printed in the United States of America.

ISBN 978-1-942951-96-4 (hardcover)
ISBN 978-1-942951-97-1 (paper)
ISBN 978-1-942951-98-8 (electronic)

Mercatus Center at George Mason University
3434 Washington Blvd., 4th Floor
Arlington, Virginia 22201
www.mercatus.org

Cover design by Bill Pragluski, Critical Stages.
Editing and typesetting services by Westchester Publishing Services.

THE SOUL OF CLASSICAL POLITICAL ECONOMY

James M. Buchanan from the Archives

EDITED BY PETER J. BOETTKE
AND ALAIN MARCIANO

Arlington, Virginia

Contents

Foreword

When one thinks of researching an author's papers at an archive, the picture that may come to mind is a set of boxes with neatly titled folders listing the contents and dates, enhanced by a descriptive guide to the collection. Such an inventory does not yet fully exist for the James M. Buchanan Papers, and that makes the works included in this volume that much more precious and important to share. Professor Buchanan's papers have traveled thousands of miles from his days as a graduate student at the University of Chicago through his retirement from George Mason University in Virginia. The Buchanan archive itself continues on its own journey to achieve the complete organization and description that will make it fully accessible to scholars around the world from its home base at the George Mason University Libraries' Special Collections Research Center (SCRC).

This volume's editors, Professors Peter J. Boettke and Alain Marciano, are active supporters of the George Mason University Libraries and the SCRC, and they are ardent advocates for and users of the Buchanan archive held here. Both are eminent economics scholars, recognized by their colleagues in academia and the profession at large. As the director of the SCRC and the dean of the University Libraries, we can attest to their extensive use of this collection over almost a decade that contributed to this volume in the *Advanced Studies in Political Economy* series. We also appreciate their passion for sharing the knowledge of the Buchanan archive through their previous works. Indisputably, Buchanan is a seminal figure in political economics and public choice theory, and his papers hold a sizable cache of unexplored materials. The tip of this archival iceberg is reflected in what the editors chose to include as Buchanan's pivotal works. In his essay "Why Read the Classics in Economics?" Boettke (2000) noted the following:

> There is a case for reading the classics in political economy as a productive use of one's time in training to be an active research economist, and in fact, in engaging in the production of economic thought. Kenneth Boulding (1971) countered Samuelson's claims brilliantly in his essay "After Samuelson Who Needs Smith?" Boulding, in classic Contra-Whig fashion, argued that we all need [Adam] Smith because Smith is part of our "extended present." There are arguments and insights in Smith which remain unincorporated in our contemporary theory that once incorporated will improve our understanding of matters. The body of thought found in the classics retains intellectual evolutionary potential until the insights within are fully exploited. The "market" for ideas is not perfectly efficient—mistakes are made, intellectual resources are wasted, and as a consequence, there are indeed intellectual gems laying unexploited waiting for someone to grasp.

The James M. Buchanan Papers are such an intellectual gem waiting to be researched by students, scholars, and the general public. The archive in total contains the personal papers, books, and related materials belonging to James McGill Buchanan (1919–2013), economist and Nobel laureate, whose theories had a far-reaching influence on America's national life. In addition to Buchanan's extensive scholarship, the collection encompasses correspondence, memos, individual publications and offprints, photographs, audiovisual material, and other ephemera related to his life and impressive academic career. Spanning over 280 linear feet, this is the largest and most significant holding in existence of unique primary-source material documenting Buchanan's contributions to the field of political economics and his associated intellectual legacy.

This core Buchanan collection of original source materials is complemented by 15,000 books and journals from the libraries of Professor Buchanan, Professor Otto "Toby" Davis,[1] and the Center for the Study of Public Choice.[2] Combined, these resources make George Mason University a significant resource for historical aspects of economics research.

The impressive development of Buchanan's thought and academic career can be traced through his published works. This volume not only highlights those known achievements but also reveals selected (thus far) unpublished papers further documenting Buchanan's work in creating a world-famous research program in modern economics and his leadership in the rebirth of political economy. The archival collection at George Mason University includes evidence from Buchanan's time at the University of Virginia, where he and his colleagues originated what became known as the Virginia School of political economy. There is a wonderful set of posters in the archive from the late 1950s and early 1960s documenting the lecture series there, in which visiting scholars from around the world traveled to Charlottesville, Virginia, to present on and discuss political economy. In the spring of 1959, for example, the topic was "Economic Prospects of European Unification: Theory and Policy." Buchanan's initiative in sharing knowledge on economic topics of the day resurfaced in the 1980s as the Virginia Lectures in Political Economy during his tenure at George Mason University.

Buchanan's intellectual trajectory is also revealed in his correspondence with colleagues over the decades, along with other unpublished works and discussions with students and economists the world over. This type of material makes up the bulk of the James M. Buchanan archive and chronicles Buchanan's sixty-year academic career and beyond. Buchanan taught economics at a variety of institutions, including the University of Virginia; the University of California, Los Angeles; Virginia Polytechnic Institute and State University; and ultimately George Mason University, his academic home when he won the Nobel Prize in Economics in 1986 and for more than two decades after that.

Like most collections of such value and broad interest, Professor Buchanan's papers were highly prized and sought after by several prominent universities in the United States. The George Mason University Libraries were already in discussion with Professor Buchanan in early 2001, making recommendations for processing and cataloging these extensive holdings. These discussions continued for the next decade, with the University Libraries working with Center for Public Choice staff members to clarify what would be needed to make the collection safe and accessible in a professional archival setting. During that same period, the University Libraries partnered with the Center for Public Choice to host lectures honoring the work of Professor Buchanan on several occasions. James Buchanan died in 2013 and, through his will, gifted his papers, library, and other materials to George Mason University.

Over the next few years the Libraries worked with the Department of Economics to begin reviewing and organizing the Buchanan papers. The papers, books, and related materials were all held in the Buchanan House, originally the residence for George Mason University presidents. SCRC archivists, assisted by Solomon Stein,[3] then a PhD candidate in economics and a PhD Fellow at the Mercatus Center at George Mason University, began processing the main cache of papers according to archival standards. (Attempting to organize the papers *in situ*, over an extended amount of time and with multiple individuals working part-time on the project, was particularly challenging.) Between 2013 and 2016, the archivists completed initial processing work of about 145 linear feet of the collection. This part of the collection was then transferred to the state-of the-art SCRC facility, which is part of the newly constructed and expanded central library of the university (Fenwick Library).

In the fall of 2016, the SCRC staff members created an exhibition of documents, books, and ephemera from the Buchanan archive celebrating thirty years since Buchanan received his Nobel Prize in Economics. On October 25, 2016, the University Libraries hosted an event celebrating the exhibition and the archive. Titled "Celebrating 'Nobelity'—A Buchanan Retrospective," this event featured presentations by archivist Liz Beckman, Solomon Stein, and Professor Boettke. Boettke spoke on "What Buchanan Has Meant to Mason," outlining the Nobel laureate's influence on the theory of public choice and George Mason University's influence on political economy through its graduates and faculty.

In 2017, SCRC staff collaborated with the Libraries' Preservation Officer to completely remove all the Buchanan-related papers, books, journals and periodicals, posters, ephemera, and memorabilia—including graduation regalia, as well as the set of posters from the University of Virginia noted above—from the Buchanan House. Although the collection is not completely open to the public as of the date of this publication, researchers have been able to access a significant portion of the 145 linear feet of items originally organized at the Buchanan House. Professor Marciano's and Boettke's research forays began at the Buchanan House in the mid-2000s, and they are two of many researchers who have visited the collection or sought remote research assistance from SCRC staff.

The University Libraries have developed proposals, including grant applications, to secure the required funding (hundreds of thousands of dollars) to use the best archival practices in assessing and organizing the remaining materials, and then housing and describing the entire 280-plus linear feet collection.[4] The size of the collection, the breadth of topics addressed, and the number of decades covered in the papers require specialists, including a dedicated archivist, to concentrate solely on the Buchanan papers. Investing in the necessary human and financial resources and in the expertise, effort, and time to detail the contents of the collection will ensure that this research trove will be usable and useful to researchers for decades to come.

We look forward to readers of this book getting a new perspective on James M. Buchanan's work and intellectual legacy, and we welcome any and all to visit the George Mason University Libraries' Special Collections Research Center for research into previously unknown facets of his life and writings.

Lynn Eaton, Director, Special Collections Research Center
John G. Zenelis, Dean of Libraries and University Librarian
George Mason University

NOTES

1. Davis was one of Buchanan's students at the University of Virginia. He was a founder and second dean of the Heinz School of Public Policy and Management at Carnegie Mellon, and he was also a founder of the Public Choice Society.
2. The Center for the Study of Public Choice is part of the economics department at George Mason University. "Created in 1957 at the University of Virginia, the Center was initially called the Thomas Jefferson Center for Studies in Political Economy. In 1969, the Center was reconstituted at Virginia Tech under its present name. In 1983, the Center shifted its operations to George Mason University" (Center for the Study of Public Choice 2020).
3. Dr. Solomon Stein is currently a senior fellow in the F. A. Hayek Program for Advanced Study of Philosophy, Politics, and Economics and a senior research fellow with the Mercatus Center at George Mason University.
4. In spring 2020, the National Endowment for the Humanities (NEH) announced a significant grant award to the George Mason University Libraries, under its Humanities Collection and Reference Resources program, for the "Preserving the Legacy of James M. Buchanan" project. NEH Chairman Jon Parrish Peede said of the award, "NEH is pleased to support the processing of James M. Buchanan's papers, which will be accessible to scholars as a result of this project. In his lifetime, Buchanan received accolades including the Nobel Prize in Economics and the National Humanities Medal, and his work continues to have wide-reaching impact on American life." The press release can be found at https://www2.gmu.edu/news/584746.

REFERENCES

Boettke, Peter J. 2000. "Why Read the Classics in Economics?" Library of Economics and Liberty, February 24. https://www.econlib.org/library/Features/feature2.html.

Boulding, Kenneth. 1971. "After Samuelson, Who Needs Adam Smith?" *History of Political Economy* 3(2): 225–37.

Center for the Study of Public Choice. 2020. "About the Center." Accessed February 28. https://publicchoice.gmu.edu/about/about.

Introduction

PETER J. BOETTKE AND ALAIN MARCIANO

James McGill Buchanan was born in Murfreesboro, Tennessee, on October 3, 1919. Buchanan was educated at a local public school and then the local college, Middle Tennessee State College, where he earned a BA in 1940. He also earned an MS from the University of Tennessee in 1941. After being drafted into the US Navy in 1941 and serving through 1945 as a staff officer, he returned to school on a GI subsidy and earned a PhD in economics from the University of Chicago in 1948. After graduation, he taught at the University of Tennessee for three years until he moved to Florida State University, where he stayed until 1956. After 1956, Buchanan had three main professional associations with academic institutions in Virginia.[1] He spent thirteen years at the University of Virginia (or UVA, 1956–1968), where he founded the Thomas Jefferson Center for Studies in Political Economy (TJC), and fourteen years at Virginia Polytechnic Institute (VPI, also known as Virginia Tech, 1969–1983), where he became director of the Center for the Study of Public Choice (CSPC).[2] In 1983, he moved to the Public Choice Center at George Mason University (Mason), where he would spend the rest of his career. In 1998, he formally retired from active teaching at Mason and became professor emeritus. The same year, he was provided that status at Virginia Tech. Though "retired," Buchanan continued to lecture and write throughout the world and maintained an active presence at Mason, the CSPC, and the Buchanan House. He passed away at the age of 93, still an active scholar.

The Buchanan House was established in 1993 in the wake of Buchanan's Nobel Memorial Prize in Economic Sciences (commonly known as the Nobel

Prize in Economics). By design, it was both a place for active research, housing seminars and office space for visiting scholars, and an informal archive of the history of the Public Choice Society and of Buchanan's career, with displays of memorabilia from his service in the US Navy to his winning the Nobel Prize in Economics. Throughout the house, pictures and displays captured Buchanan's career at UVA, Virginia Tech, and now at Mason. In this and other capacities, the Buchanan House served as the physical base from which the Buchanan Archives were originally collected and stored. And in 2014, the Mason Library Special Collections began the preparation and formal archiving of the material and the relocation from the Buchanan House to Fenwick Library. As we hope this collection suggests, Buchanan's archive provides a unique window into not only James Buchanan the man, the scholar, and the teacher, but also into the fields of public choice and public economics. More generally, it helps us to understand what the rebirth of political economy within the economics profession post–World War II means.

A self-described "libertarian socialist" on his arrival at Chicago, Buchanan was "converted" to classical liberalism under the influence of Henry Simons and Frank Knight (see Marciano 2020). The libertarian values remained, but now Buchanan understood through Knight that the market (not government) was the institutional framework most consistent for the organization of those values. Knight became Buchanan's intellectual role model. Another intellectual model was Knut Wicksell, whom Buchanan also discovered at Chicago—more on that in the first section of this book. Indeed, Buchanan's work to a large extent can be summarized as the persistent and consistent development of the two intellectual influences from Knight and Wicksell. But one should also add a third influence on Buchanan: namely the Italian tradition of public finance that he was exposed to during a Fulbright fellowship year he spent in Italy (1955–1956). This tradition emphasized real as opposed to ideal politics and was the final piece of the intellectual puzzle that led to Buchanan's development of public choice theory.

From Knight, Buchanan got his basic economic theory framework and the idea that economics is not a science in the traditional meaning of that term. From Wicksell, Buchanan learned that politics needs to be understood in an exchange framework. Efficiency in the public sector would be guaranteed only under a rule of unanimity for collective choices. From the Italians, Buchanan learned that public finance theory must necessarily postulate a theory of the state, and that it would be best to reject either the Benthamite utilitarianism or the Hegelian idealism in postulating such a theory. In retrospect, once these three elements were brought together, the necessary foundations for Buchanan's contributions to the economics of the public sector were there. What remained was working out the implications.

By recasting the questions of public finance in light of this Knight/Wicksell/Italian connection, Buchanan was able to challenge the perceived wisdom of his day on several fronts. For example, the Keynesian theory of functional finance met perhaps its most fundamental challenge in Buchanan's *Public Principles of Public Debt* (1958). Buchanan challenged the Keynesian doctrine on methodological and analytical grounds. The level of aggregation in Keynesian fiscal theory, for example, strained imagination, violated the political norms of democratic society, and fundamentally misconstrued the nature of the debt burden. By confining their focus to the aggregate unit, fiscal theorists were unable to address the problem of who will have to pay for the creation of public goods and when payment will be made. The problem was an elementary one—the principles of opportunity cost and economic decision-making were ignored in the Keynesian analysis.

It is *The Calculus of Consent* (1962), Buchanan and Gordon Tullock's comprehensive examination of decision-making in politics and the interaction between politics and the economy, that deserves credit for shifting scholarly focus. Before public choice, it was commonplace in economic theory to postulate an objective welfare function that "society" sought to maximize and to assume that political actors were motivated to pursue that objective welfare function. The Buchanan/Tullock critique amounted to simply pointing out that (1) no objective welfare function exists; (2) that even if one existed, "societies" do not choose, only individuals do; and (3) that individuals within the political sector, just as in the private sector, base their choices on their private assessment of costs and benefits.

While he worked on constitutions and political institutions, Buchanan continued to work on public finance and on the question of the burden of debt. His analyses and the discussions and disagreements he had with other public finance theorists forced Buchanan to reexamine the conceptual foundations of economic science. This in particular led him to question the notion of cost used in economics. And this led to his slim but broad in implication volume, *Cost and Choice* (1969)—a book that Buchanan started to work on in 1964 and that was completed in 1967, as we evidence below. The consistent pursuit of the opportunity cost logic of economics would lead to surprising results on a broad range of issues, from the burden of debt to issues concerning the military draft to the problem of externalities to the choice context of bureaucratic decision-making.

Many of the major insights of modern political economy flow from these elementary propositions, including the vote motive, the logic of dispersed costs and concentrated benefits, the shortsightedness bias in policy, and the constitutional perspective in policy evaluation. Politics must be endogenous in any reasonable model of economic policy making, and political processes are not something to be romanticized. But the intellectual spirit of the age (the 1950s and early 1960s) was one of overly zealous optimism about the beneficial nature of politics. The Buchanan warning of democratic folly and the need for constitutional constraint was one that did not sit well with the intellectual/political idealists of the day. In the wake of the Vietnam War and Watergate, as well as the failed economic policies that have emerged from both Democratic and Republican administrations during the post–World War II era, it is now difficult to imagine a noncynical view of politics. This is not an endorsement of apathy and malcontent with politicians. Nowhere in the Buchanan body of work is it suggested that politicians are any worse than the lot of us. Rather, his work simply stressed that politicians are just like the rest of us—neither sinners nor saints, but a bit of both.

However, precisely because politicians, as any individual, may "sin," Buchanan preferred to start with the assumptions that they would indeed sin and behave as *homo œconomici*, being preoccupied by their self-interest in the narrower sense of the word. His objective was then to understand which rules would be the best ones to guard against "worst-case" scenarios in politics—that is, those *scenarii* that develop with "sinners." That was not an ontological assumption. To employ the assumption of economic man within politics, as it was used in economics, was not aimed at describing the motivation of any particular political actor, but rather as a modeling strategy in constitutional design. By postulating the revenue-maximizing bureaucracy, Buchanan was able to address the political rules of the game that would constrain the behavior of individuals within politics. In particular, if government officials are revenue maximizing, then the question becomes, What rules of the game are necessary to transform these behaviors from revenue maximizing into wealth maximizing? This is a question of constitutional design—one that affects the time preference of rulers and the range of policy choices at their disposal for pursuing their interests.

Buchanan dealt with these issues in the 1970s. In the early 1970s, he started to work on the *Limits of Liberty* (eventually published in 1975), which is his statement of the contractarian perspective in political economy. Then, in both his books with Geoffrey Brennan, *The Power to Tax* (1980) and *The Reason of Rules* (1985), Buchanan studied how to constrain politicians. One also finds these same ideas in most of the essays he wrote in the last two decades of the 20th century, which were gathered in volumes such as *Freedom in Constitutional Contract* (1977), *Liberty, Market and State* (1986), *The Economics and the Ethics of Constitutional Order* (1991), *Ethics and Economic Progress* (1994), or *The Return to Increasing Returns* (1994, a collection of essays coedited with Yong J. Yoon). Indeed, all these works exhibit one of the most important features that characterizes Buchanan's work: the remarkable unity in his research purpose throughout his career, since his early critique of social choice theory and welfare economics to his most recent writings on constitutional design and the 2008 financial crisis (see section 8). The basic propositions that guide his work can be summarized neatly:[3]

1. Economics is a "science" but not like the physical sciences. Economics is a "philosophical" science, and the strictures against scientism offered by Frank Knight and F. A. Hayek should be heeded.
2. Economics is about choice and processes of adjustment, not states of rest. Equilibrium models are only useful when we recognize their limits.
3. Economics is about exchange, not about maximizing. Exchange activity should be the central focus of economic analysis.
4. Economics is about individual actors, not collective entities. Only individuals choose.
5. Economics necessarily takes place within rules.
6. Economics cannot be studied properly outside of politics. The choices among different rules of the game cannot be ignored.
7. The most important function of economics as a discipline is its didactic role in explaining the principle of spontaneous order.
8. Economics is elementary.

Buchanan wove these eight propositions into a coherent framework for social theory and even for social philosophy. Indeed, he was a social philosopher. To be more precise, he viewed economics as political economy and political economy as a form of social philosophy. One of the major consequences of this approach was that he could not envisage a separation between the economy, economic activities, and the institutional framework in which these activities take place. He put this idea in terms of pre- and postconstitutional levels. During the preconstitutional stage, individuals define rules—the rules of the social game. At the postconstitutional stage, individuals play their game and adopt certain strategies and behaviors within the defined rules. That is how political economy should be understood, as the tacking back and forth between these two levels of analysis. That is how, according Buchanan, human societies were or should be organized and, in particular, how public policies should be elaborated. Hence, a successful application of modern political economy to the world of public policy demands that the analyst adopt such a *constitutional* perspective. In this regard, Buchanan introduces the vital distinction for applied political economy of "policy within politics" and the systematic change in the rules of the game. Lasting reform, Buchanan argues, results not from policy changes within the existing rules (or changes in people), but rather from systemic changes in the rules of governance. He made that claim in his early works (described in the first section) and repeated it during his career until his last writings about the financial crisis (described in the last section of this volume).

In what follows, we provide a more detailed discussion of the points suggested in this introduction. Each of the following sections corresponds to an aspect we find crucial in describing and understanding Buchanan's views on political economy as a social philosophy. For each of these sections, we illustrate Buchanan's views by using archival material—most of it being original and having never been published. We introduce this material and contextualize it to provide the user with a useful guide as they take a tour through the evolution of a scholar who actively published from the 1940s to the 2010s in the fields of philosophy, politics, and economics.

NOTES

1. During this period, the only moment he was not affiliated with an academic institution in Virginia was in 1968, when he was in California at UCLA. He was hired in January 1968—and effectively moved only in August 1968—and resigned one year later, in January 1969. See section 5.
2. The Center for the Study of Public Choice was established in 1968.
3. See Buchanan (1964).

REFERENCES

Brennan, G., and J. M. Buchanan. 1980. *The Power to Tax: Analytic Foundations of a Fiscal Constitution*. Cambridge, MA: Cambridge University Press.

———. 1985. *The Reason of Rules: Constitutional Political Economy*. Cambridge, MA: Cambridge University Press.

Buchanan, J. M. 1958. *Public Principles of Public Debt*. Homewood, IL: Richard D. Irwin.

———. 1964. "What Should Economists Do?" *Southern Economic Journal* 30(3): 213–22.

———. 1969. *Cost and Choice.* Chicago: Markham.

———. 1975. *The Limits of Liberty: Between Anarchy and Leviathan.* Chicago: University of Chicago Press.

———. 1986. *Liberty, Market and State: Political Economy in the 1980s.* Brighton, UK: Wheatsheaf Books.

———. 1991. *The Economics and the Ethics of Constitutional Order.* Ann Arbor: University of Michigan Press.

———. 1994. *Ethics and Economic Progress.* Norman: University of Oklahoma Press.

Buchanan, J. M., and G. Tullock. 1962. *The Calculus of Consent.* Ann Arbor: University of Michigan Press.

Buchanan, J. M., and Y. J. Yoon (eds.). 1994. *The Return to Increasing Returns.* Ann Arbor: University of Michigan Press.

Marciano, A. 2020. "The Origins of Buchanan's Views on Federalism, Chicago 1946–1947." *Journal of Institutional Economics* 16(3): 319–35.

SECTION 1

ETHICS, FISCAL JUSTICE, AND PUBLIC ECONOMICS

1.0 Introduction

PETER J. BOETTKE AND ALAIN MARCIANO

Buchanan was one of the founders of public choice, and it is usually, to say the least, from this angle that his analyses in public economics are presented—that is, from the perspective of the interaction between politics and the economy and how and to what extent politics influence the functioning of the economy. This is no surprise. It was the reason that was given to award him the Nobel Memorial Prize in Economic Sciences (commonly known as the Nobel Prize in Economics) in 1986. And it was also a central aspect of his work. Indeed, Buchanan was and, one may even say, was *always* a public choice theorist. In his first works, before he even graduated at Chicago—that is, in a master's thesis[1] and in his doctoral dissertation (1948)—Buchanan linked public economics and public finance with institutions; in his first published article, in 1949, he also insisted that public finance theories should rest on an explicit theory of the state (Buchanan 1949).

These are not, however, the aspects of Buchanan as a public economist that we are going to emphasize. Our focus here is not on what Buchanan said of the interconnections between the behavior of politicians and public policy or the role of governments and how decisions are made in the public sector. These views are well known. So well known, in fact, that they tend to obscure his less obviously "public choice" views on public economics, public finance, and market failures and how to solve them. This requires a discussion of Wicksell, obviously, but also of Samuelson and Tiebout. And, it is critical to see how his later, better-known views on public choice economics followed from his work in public economics, public finance, and market failure theory. There is a serious philosophical point that runs throughout Buchanan's work, and that is that any theory of public finance necessarily takes on board, either explicitly or implicitly, a political philosophy, because we are necessarily dealing with questions regarding not just the scale of government but the scope of government. So Buchanan urged fellow economists to be more explicit in order to encourage an honest and productive dialogue, whereas leaving these issues implicit and unarticulated by economists resulted too often in confusion and unproductive dialogue. In addition, methodologically, one can already see in these earlier conversations the beginnings of Buchanan's later full articulation of the critical importance of methodological individualism and of examining politics as exchange.

FROM WICKSELL TO FISCAL JUSTICE AND ETHICS

The obvious starting point to present Buchanan's public economics is his admiration for Wicksell. He was, as Geoffrey Brennan emphasized, "a self-declared Knut Wicksell disciple—or, at least, a disciple of the Wicksell 1896 habilitation thesis" (1967 [1999], ix), entitled *Finanztheoretische Untersuchungen* (Wicksell 1896). Indeed, it is Buchanan himself who created the myth of how and when he discovered Wicksell. It supposedly happened in 1948, after he had defended his own dissertation, that Buchanan found Knut Wicksell's unknown and untranslated dissertation of that title, buried in the dusty stacks of Chicago's old Harper Library. Buchanan (1986) viewed this find as one of the most exciting intellectual moments of his career.

Actually, certain parts of Wicksell's dissertation had been translated and were available before 1948. And, actually, Buchanan had read Wicksell earlier than he remembered. In the notes he took to prepare his term essay for Economics 362 (Federal and Local Taxation)—entitled "A Theory of Financial Balance in a Federal State"—one finds a reference to Wicksell written in Buchanan's hand, although he did not quote Wicksell in the essay. In his dissertation, "The Problem of Fiscal Inequality in a Federal State," which he defended in 1948, Buchanan cited and quoted Wicksell.[2] Whether these references concern the already-known parts of Wicksell or the unknown and untranslated ones he mentioned in his Nobel lecture is not important from a theoretical perspective. What really matters is that Wicksell's influence could not have occurred at a more important moment during Buchanan's years of formation. No wonder that Wicksell was one of the few intellectually fixed points in Buchanan's career. No wonder that he viewed his own approach to public finance as, in his own words, "an extension of some of Wicksell's ideas on fiscal theory to modern welfare economics" (Buchanan 1959, 124).

Buchanan extended and maybe twisted Wicksell's views[3]—how far is beyond the scope of this introduction—by starting with his *voluntary exchange theory*, which he found particularly appealing and which structured his views on public finance. One could not, however, stop at this technical level. There are more profound reasons that explain why Buchanan was so interested in Wicksell. After all, the latter was not the only one who had defended voluntary exchange in public finance. Buchanan himself was aware of that. In his early work, Buchanan mentioned the names of Erik Lindahl, Emil Sax, Adolph Wagner, and also the members of the so-called Italian school of finance, Antonio De Viti De Marco, Maffeo Pantaleoni, and Ugo Mazzola—important economists from the perspective of public finance and voluntary exchange who also influenced him.

Then why did Buchanan mention and cite Wicksell more than the others? Or why did Wicksell more than the others influence Buchanan? It was Wicksell's new principle "of *justice* in taxation" that Buchanan liked in particular (Buchanan 1987; emphasis added). It "gave [him] a tremendous surge of self-confidence" because it echoed what Buchanan already believed: Wicksell, "an established figure in the history of economic ideas . . . challenged the orthodoxy of public finance theory along lines that were *congenial with my own* developing stream of critical consciousness" (ibid.; emphasis added). Thus, Buchanan was attracted by the ethical content of Wicksell's analysis because he was already ethically minded, and this *then* led him to Wicksell's public finance.

FROM ETHICS TO PUBLIC FINANCE

Why was Buchanan so interested in justice in taxation, fiscal justice, and fiscal equity? An answer can be found in some—actually, a very few—of the articles published by Buchanan in the early 1950s. Those ideas and claims were already present in the essays mentioned earlier, which he wrote as a student at Chicago. Referencing these early works is important because they evidence that Buchanan's interest in public economics—and in Wicksell—has ethical foundations. It helps to understand that Buchanan was primarily interested in and concerned with fiscal justice in a federal regime.

His concern came from observation of what he named the "dilemma of federalism" (Buchanan 1947) or the "federal fiscal dilemma" (Buchanan 1948; see also his 1950 article): because of the differences in the fiscal capacities that exist between member states in a federation, individuals are treated differently because of their geographical location. They receive more or fewer public goods because they live in a more or less wealthy state. This is problematic not only for economic reasons—it leads to a misallocation of resources—but also for ethical reasons as well: equals are not treated equally. This meant, to Buchanan, a violation of fiscal justice. In effect, Buchanan adopted a principle of fiscal justice based on "equal treatment for equals" (Buchanan 1950, 587) or "equal treatment for persons dissimilar in no relevant respect" (ibid.). A principle "as old as Aristotle," "widely recognized," and "contained in every formulation of 'justice' in taxation from the latter part of the 17th century" (Buchanan 1948, 38), including those of Thomas Hobbes, Henry Sidgwick, and John Stuart Mill, meant that "the political units as a coercive force 'pressed' equally on similarly situated individuals in the economic structure if the tax burden of the similarly situated individuals were the same" (Buchanan 1947, 16–17).

It is a formulation that would be misleading if it were interpreted to mean that fiscal justice is a matter of taxes only. The *tax burden* he was referring to was net, including also the benefits received from the taxes paid. Buchanan was more explicit a few years later when he wrote, "The fiscal structure is equitable in this primary sense only if the fiscal residua of similarly situated individuals are equivalent" (Buchanan 1950, 588)—that is, if there is "balance between the contributions made and the value of public services returned to the individual" (ibid.). Thus, starting with a specific principle of fiscal justice, Buchanan was led to reason in terms of taxes *and* benefits. In other words, one should not discuss fiscal justice without taking into account taxes *and* the benefits received from taxation.

Another ethical dimension results from a focus on taxes and benefits rather than on taxes only. The economists who view taxes as a "burden" only or as "net subtractions from social income, never to be returned" (Buchanan 1949, 500) tend to define fiscal justice in terms of individuals' *ability* to pay or in terms of fiscal capacities. One corollary is that individuals do not pay taxes because they want to pay them. It may then mean that certain individuals will be coerced to pay taxes. This is why Buchanan viewed adherents to these approaches as "organicists" or holists: tax loads are determined by the state "acting for the society as a whole" (ibid., 496) and imposing those tax loads on individuals on behalf of the society. By contrast, seeing the two sides—expenditures and resources—of the fiscal process as interconnected implies viewing justice in terms of *willingness* to pay. From this perspective, individuals should pay taxes because they want to and are ready to pay them. No one imposes anything on the individuals. This perspective is "individualistic" (ibid.).

VOLUNTARY EXCHANGE AND PUBLIC FINANCE

In his mind, once Buchanan established that taxes and expenditures should be treated jointly for ethical reasons, he went on to study what it meant or implied for a theory of public government *finance*. Here, words matter. Buchanan was interested in public or government *finance* and not in public expenditures because it means taking taxes *and* benefits—rather than taxes only—into account. From this perspective, taxes cannot be disconnected from benefits. Taxes are a price paid to buy the goods and services supplied by the state. He insisted that "taxes or contributions paid are *exchanged* for services rendered by the political unit" (Buchanan 1948, 52; emphasis added) or are the "payment made by individuals out of their economic resources *in exchange for* services provided" (Buchanan 1949, 498; emphasis added). Taxpayers, in other words, buy public goods and services exactly as they buy private goods. As a consequence, no distinction can be made between a private transaction through which an individual buys a private good and the process through which an individual buys a public good. Indeed, Buchanan wrote, "the individual's financial relations with government are basically analogous to any private economic transaction; they consist of an exchange relationship" (Buchanan 1948, 51–52). And, more precisely, as is also the case with private transactions, transactions with the state are voluntary. Benefits are the reason why transactions with the government are voluntary: taxes are paid voluntarily *because* individuals receive benefits from paying them.

Certainly these benefits are difficult, to say the least, to evaluate for each individual—essentially because they are subjective. And accordingly, it will be "extremely difficult, if not impossible" (Buchanan 1951, 175) to determine the exact tax each beneficiary would have to pay in proportion "to his gain in subjective utility resulting from the free provision of the service" (ibid.). But this aspect of the discussion is secondary. One should not confuse a practical problem with a fundamental problem. In that case, the difficulty of evaluating individual benefits is not fundamental but simply empirical. What matters is that each individual gains something from paying their taxes. From this perspective, there is no doubt that benefits exist—Buchanan thus wrote that the individual's "satisfactions are increased by the government services provided him and theoretically this increase in utility can be reduced to value terms" (Buchanan 1948, 56). Indeed, his defense of benefits, and accordingly of "voluntary exchange," was not pure speculation but the logical conclusion of a reasoning without empirical dimension. To Buchanan, the benefit principle was not grounded in a philosophical conviction only. To him, it was a fact that could be empirically verified by observation. Indeed, to Buchanan, the very fact that individuals pay their taxes or vote for politicians who propose programs involving public expenditures and taxation proves that they benefit from paying these taxes. Otherwise—that is, if there were no benefits—one could not understand such behaviors. Later, in other works, he will also adopt the same reasoning for public goods. To him, individuals voluntarily pay for the public goods they consume—for instance, tolls in the case of highways (Buchanan 1952). Such confidence in individuals' willingness to pay is a fundamental—indeed foundational—feature that characterizes Buchanan's work.

This was rightly emphasized by Wicksell, Buchanan noted (1949, 500). Now, the very existence of benefits means that exchange is *voluntary*. To emphasize the voluntariness of the transaction with the state, Buchanan mentioned the names of Thomas Hobbes, John Locke, and Hugo Grotius (1948, 1949) and referred to the existence of a social contract between the individuals—the taxpayers—and the state. Buchanan wrote, "The so-called benefit theory of taxation arose as a direct result of the contract theory of the state first expressed by Hobbes, Grotius, and Locke" (1948, 43).

MARKET FAILURES AND THE PROBLEM OF SOCIAL COST

Thus, in the early 1950s, Buchanan believed in the voluntariness of those transactions between taxpayers and the state and, accordingly, in the voluntariness of contributions to the provision of public goods (1952). He nonetheless admitted that free markets could generate a misallocation of resources (see Buchanan 1950). A few years later—it was in 1954 (Buchanan 1954a and b)—Buchanan referred to a "problem of social cost" that would necessarily alter the functioning of markets. In the presence of externalities and when dealing with public goods, he somehow started to change his mind and wrote that markets will fail to allocate resources efficiently. The reason is straightforward: even if individuals voluntarily pay for what they privately consume, they do not take into account the interdependencies—in production or in consumption—that link them to other individuals. However, in the mid-1950s, Buchanan did not link those failures or the ignorance of these interdependencies to possible free-riding behaviors. Or to put it differently, in 1954 he discovered market failures, but it took him some time to mention the term or the possibility that individuals could free ride. This came later in his work (see Buchanan 1964 for a first mention; 1965 for a real discussion of the problem; also see Fontaine 2014).

Thus, Buchanan was perfectly aware that when there are interdependencies between individuals, the equality between each individual's marginal rates of substitution with the marginal cost no longer guarantees a Pareto allocation of resources. What would be the condition to satisfy or guarantee a Pareto allocation of resources?

One knows the answer given by economists to this question: when there are externalities or public goods, an optimal allocation of resources is guaranteed by the so-called Lindahl-Bowen-Samuelson condition axiomatized by Paul Samuelson in his 1954 article entitled "The Pure Theory of Public Expenditures" (Samuelson 1954). Most economists agree with Samuelson. Buchanan disagreed and proposed another condition. This condition is not easy to discover and not easy to connect to a criticism of Samuelson's ideas. In effect, this condition can either be found in works that are not related to Samuelson—for instance, Buchanan's work on externalities—or in an unpublished comment of Samuelson 1954. This is the comment that we publish here, a comment Buchanan wrote to express his disagreement with Samuelson.

PARETO OPTIMALITY AND PUBLIC GOODS: BUCHANAN'S CONDITION (CONTRA SAMUELSON)

Immediately after Samuelson's article was published, Buchanan felt that he disagreed with its content. There were two sources of disagreement.

First, Samuelson criticized and rejected the possibility to use decentralized mechanisms to optimally allocate resources in a situation with pure public goods. Complementarily, he defended the intervention of the state. More precisely, Samuelson linked market failures with the intervention of the state. To him, there could be no other possibility to solve market failures. To Buchanan, this was unacceptable not only because he defended Wicksell but also because he had already published his critique of the "fiscal brain" in 1949 (Buchanan 1949). He was prepared to challenge any efforts in economic reasoning that depended on reasoning the postulating of a benevolent and omniscient despot to make decisions in the public sector.

The second source of disagreement bore on the condition Samuelson put forward for an optimal allocation of resources. Buchanan thought that the condition was not sufficient to guarantee Pareto optimality. However, Buchanan, who was sincerely admiring Samuelson, could not simply disagree with him. He wanted to understand it and see how to make sense of it in his own Wicksellian, decentralized framework. He thus wrote a comment on Samuelson's paper that he first sent to Julius Margolis to check what the latter thought of it. Margolis did not understand what Buchanan meant (see more details in Marciano 2013). Despite Margolis's puzzlement, Buchanan sent his comment to Samuelson. This gave birth to a rather long correspondence, essentially fueled by Buchanan's long letters, aimed at reconciling Samuelson's views with his own.

Why was Samuelson's condition not sufficient? What was that condition that Buchanan suggested to add? To the first question, Buchanan answered by writing that, even if Samuelson's condition could guarantee that the costs of provision of a public good would be covered, it said nothing about the tax loads each individual would have to bear. It said nothing of how the tax burden would be split among individuals—a point that, as we have seen earlier, was crucial for Buchanan's approach to public finance. Hence, it could be said that Samuelson did not really integrate the two sides—revenues and expenditures—that Buchanan said should be united in a genuine theory of public or government finance. A genuine contribution to a theory of public or government finance, which was what Buchanan was trying to make, should not only guarantee that the costs of provision of the good were covered but also that the provision of the goods would not be made at the expense of some individuals. One should not let it happen that one individual be burdened with the entire tax load while the others pay nothing. Thus, Samuelson's condition guarantees that the Pareto frontier could be reached somewhere, but it did not say anything about the point at which that would be reached. Now, only one point was "consistent with the maintenance of the Paretian conditions" (Buchanan 1955, 4). Samuelson's condition did not take that into account, precisely because he was silent on the structure of financing public supply.

To correct this, Buchanan suggested the addition of an "individualist" condition, missing in Samuelson's approach, according to which "each individual must equate the marginal rate of substitution in consumption between any one collective and any one private good with the marginal rate of substitution between these two goods in production to *him*" (Buchanan 1955, 3; emphasis in original). When satisfied, Buchanan's condition means that *all* the individuals would agree with the provision of the public good and the tax structure chosen to finance it "in a Paretian way, that is, in such a way that no one is made worse off in the process of a reaching it" (Buchanan 1959). Hence, this was a Wicksellian condition through which unanimous consent could be obtained. Thus, with this condition, Buchanan had—or believed he had—found a way to reconcile Samuelson with Wicksell, two economists he admired. Needless to say, Samuelson did not agree with Buchanan.

The next step consisted in asking how the condition could be implemented. Wicksell, Buchanan reminded his readers, "apparently was willing to allow the give-and-take of representative assemblies to determine the final result" (Buchanan 1959)—that is, the financing of public expenditures and the corresponding tax distribution. But he did not seem enthusiastic—at least this is what can be guessed from what he wrote on how to finance the provision of public goods: he did not say anything on "representative assemblies." He rather focused on the arrangements that individuals could devise to share the costs of provision of public goods. From this perspective, the most important and central of his works is "An Economic Theory of Clubs" (Buchanan 1965). Clubs were proposed by Buchanan to solve the question of the provision of certain types of public goods, typically not pure public goods. Clearly, those cost-sharing arrangements are Wicksellian devices: the individuals who join the club pay a membership fee, which corresponds to the price they want to pay for a given good, and they benefit from a good *in exchange*. In addition, the exchange is entirely voluntary—only members benefit from the good, and no one can be forced to become a member of a club; as he wrote in the conclusion of the paper, clubs are mechanisms of inclusion and of exclusion. Therefore, there is a unanimous agreement among the members of the club on how to finance and how to share the costs of a public good.[4] If the provision of public goods could be based on clubs, fiscal justice could also be satisfied—something that Tiebout's approach did not address.

CLUBS: CONTRA TIEBOUT

Economists tend to not only assume that both Tiebout and Buchanan contributed to a theory of clubs but also that Buchanan's 1965 article formalized the claims made by Tiebout in his own 1956 article. Buchanan's 1965 article "was one of the first attempts to make rigorous the model informally presented by Tiebout (1956) in his seminal work on local public goods" (Conley and Dix 1999, 215; see also: Webster 2001; Casella and Feinstein 2002; Gugerty 2009). This rational reconstruction may make sense from a theoretical point of view but is not *historically* legitimate and accurate. Our claim is that Buchanan's clubs differ from Tiebout's communities (Tiebout 1956). More precisely, even if Buchanan could have had Tiebout's article in mind when he wrote his—he was perfectly aware of the existence of that article—he would not have written his article to "formalize" Tiebout's ideas. Buchanan disagreed with Tiebout. This is evidenced by the comment Buchanan wrote in 1957 to criticize Tiebout, submitted to and rejected by the *Journal of Political Economy*.

In this comment, Buchanan explained that Tiebout's demonstration is "marred by a serious oversight, the correction of which serves to limit severely the relevance of his conclusions" (Buchanan 1957, 1). The reason Buchanan gave was that, "in formulating his local government model, Tiebout makes the following assumption: '4. Restrictions due to employment opportunities are not considered. It may be assumed that all persons are living on dividend income' (p. 419)" (ibid., 1–2) And, this is precisely where the problem is: "I shall now show that this assumption must be modified in order for the Tiebout analysis to be fully valid. Specifically, the phrase, 'and income is equally distributed among individuals,' must be added" (ibid.).

Buchanan reasoned as follows. If one assumes that income is not equally distributed among individuals—and also if the different communities supply different public goods and services—then one of the consequences was that individuals would migrate from "the communities which do not satisfy their desires for public services and into communities which more closely satisfy them in this respect" (Buchanan 1957, 5). This is not surprising. But there was a problem that Tiebout did not see, namely that this would also lead individuals to move from relatively poorer communities to relatively richer ones, because they supply more public goods and services—which was a consequence of the fact that their fiscal capacities were more important than the fiscal capacities of the poorer communities. Although Buchanan did not use the expression, it can be said that he had in mind "spatial competition" between the different communities and that spatial competition was the result of the differences in fiscal capacities that exist in a federal regime.

Then, as a consequence of such spatial competition, there would be too many individuals in rich states in terms of the states' economic and fiscal capacities, and there would be too few in poor states. This would result in a nonefficient allocation of resources: "The demand for public services is not met in any 'efficient' manner since, to the individual, the real costs of providing public services differ among communities" (Buchanan 1957, 6). Hence, to Buchanan, "spatial competition" and mobility in a federal regime in which individuals have different incomes, far from being positive, would increase the interstate differences in fiscal capacities. It therefore differed from what Tiebout had written in his article but also from what would become known as the "Tiebout hypothesis" (Oates 1969).

That is not all. To Buchanan, mobility and spatial competition were problematic in terms of justice. As explained earlier, to Buchanan fiscal justice meant an equal treatment for equals. From this perspective, it was clear that the individuals who live in states with lower fiscal capacities are not treated like their equals in states with higher fiscal capacities. The difference between the taxes they pay and the benefits they receive, in terms of public goods and services—their fiscal residuum—is not equivalent. Then, by increasing the population of the wealthiest communities, individuals living with the rich one's mobility could not but increase fiscal injustice between the individuals living in poor communities. Spatial competition à la Tiebout was, to Buchanan, inefficient and not just.

The only means to avoid that spatial competition between states with different fiscal capacities—that is, the only solution to guarantee that Tiebout's conclusions were right or "for the Tiebout results to be attained," as Buchanan wrote (1957, 6)—is to adopt "a set of *inter-community real income transfers*" (ibid.; emphasis added). Interarea transfers were a necessity to prevent migration from poor to rich communities. And they would guarantee *fiscal justice*.

This was exactly the idea Buchanan had already put forward in previous works a few years earlier, in the late 1940s and early 1950s, to which he referred in his comment and that were devoted to the need for a rule of fiscal justice to prevent the detrimental effects of spatial competition in a federation. This is how he interpreted Tiebout (1956). To him, this article was about spatial competition—what would become later the Tiebout hypothesis—and, more than that, it was flawed because it was incomplete. It was not connected to a discussion about the provision of public goods and could not be connected to "An Economic Theory of Clubs" because of the Wicksellian content of the latter article. In effect, Tiebout was not favorable to Wicksell and voluntary exchange. And this is exactly what Buchanan realized when he read Tiebout's 1956 article and what he wrote in the comment he submitted to the *Journal of Political Economy*. Therefore, Buchanan was convinced that Tiebout was wrong and that their perspectives were impossible to reconcile when he wrote "An Economic Theory of Clubs." Even if the 1965 article was, to a certain extent, influenced by Tiebout, it nonetheless remains that Buchanan could not have written his article with the purpose of endorsing and formalizing Tiebout's views on mobility and the homogenization of clubs (for more details, see Boettke and Marciano 2017).

EXTERNALITIES: PARETO-RELEVANT OR PARETO-IRRELEVANT?

Besides public goods—which Buchanan defined as a form of externalities based on interdependent individual production functions—there exists a second form of market failures: externalities in consumption based on interdependent utility functions. Again, in his treatment of Pareto optimality in the presence of externalities in consumption, Buchanan disagreed with Samuelson exactly as he disagreed in the case of public goods/externalities in production. Actually, Buchanan demonstrated that in the presence of externalities in consumption, a condition should be verified to guarantee that an allocation be a Pareto optimum, and this condition is simply Samuelson's condition—Buchanan acknowledged it almost in passing at the end of his article on externalities (Buchanan and Stubblebine 1962) and in a footnote in another article on externalities (Buchanan 1966).

However, this condition is less important than a category of externalities introduced in the 1962 article, coauthored with W. Craig Stubblebine. Buchanan and Stubblebine distinguished between Pareto-relevant and Pareto-irrelevant externalities. An externality is Pareto-irrelevant when there is no way to remove the externality that would be beneficial to all parties. Pareto irrelevance implies, in the case of a negative externality, that the loss suffered by the "victim" of the externality is inferior to the benefit received by the "acting party" (the individual who creates the externality) from its action. It would not be Pareto-optimal to ask the acting party to stop its activity. The gain of the victim would be obtained at its expense. Symmetrically, an externality is Pareto-relevant when the loss of a "victim" of an externality exceeds the gain of the acting party. In that case, removing the externality would be Pareto-improving; both parties would gain from the modification of behavior of the acting party.

Buchanan did not only restrict the situations in which interdependencies between individuals could be viewed as a cause of market failures. He also explained that to identify the Pareto-optimal allocation of resources in the presence of externalities in consumption, two conditions should be satisfied: Samuelson's condition—which guarantees a Pareto equilibrium—and the Pareto-relevant condition—which guarantees that the Pareto frontier will be reached in a Paretian way, to paraphrase what Buchanan had written on public goods. Indeed, Buchanan's (and Stubblebine's) treatment of externalities parallels Buchanan's treatment of public goods discussed earlier.

Similarly, in his analysis of how Pareto-relevant externalities could be dealt with, Buchanan insisted on the size of groups and, more specifically, on the importance of small groups. One should note that those groups are not clubs in the sense of Buchanan's 1965 article. Clubs were envisaged only to organize the production of local public goods. Buchanan did not apply them to externalities in consumption. But the basic principle is similar. In large groups, if there are too many individuals involved in the interactions, negotiations become too costly and gains from trade diminish to the point that they disappear. It is only in small groups that individuals can bargain with one another and realize the potential gains from trade. Then, as a corollary, in small groups, externalities are spontaneously internalized, without the interference of the state, which is another major difference from Samuelson. The price individuals pay for those externalities corresponds exactly to what they want to pay. It also corresponds to what the creators of externalities want to receive. If those prices are viewed as a form of tax, then it can be said that taxes equate benefits. Once again, fiscal justice is satisfied.

NOTES

1. For his MS at the University of Tennessee, Buchanan (1941) wrote an essay on "Gasoline Tax Sharing among Local Units of Government in Tennessee."
2. Buchanan received from Knight in spring 1946 a reading list of books and articles that all PhD students are supposed to read before finishing at Chicago, and Wicksell's work is on that list—as is Mises's and Hayek's and, of course, Böhm-Bawerk's.
3. For example, see Johnson (2006, 2014, 2015) for studies on how Buchanan interpreted Wicksell and how far his interpretation differs from Musgrave's.
4. From the perspective of Buchanan's distinction between pre- and postconstitutional stages, unanimity is reached at the preconstitutional stage and delineates the size and scope of the club.

REFERENCES

Boettke, P. J., and A. Marciano. 2017. "The Distance between Buchanan's 'An Economic Theory of Clubs' and Tiebout's 'A Pure Theory of Local Public Expenditures.'" *European Journal of the History of Economic Thought* 24(2): 205–37.

Buchanan, J. M. 1941. "Gasoline Tax Sharing among Local Units of Government in Tennessee." Master's thesis, University of Tennessee. https://trace.tennessee.edu/utk_gradthes/2683/.

———. 1947. "A Theory of Financial Balance in a Federal State." Mimeo. Buchanan Archives, Buchanan House, George Mason University.

———. 1948. "The Problem of Fiscal Inequality in a Federal State." Mimeo. Buchanan Archives, Buchanan House, George Mason University.

———. 1949. "The Pure Theory of Government Finance: A Suggested Approach." *Journal of Political Economy* 57(6): 496–505.

———. 1950. "Federalism and Fiscal Equity." *American Economic Review* 40(4): 583–99.

———. 1951. "Knut Wicksell on Marginal Cost Pricing." *Southern Economic Journal* 8(2): 173–78.

———. 1952. "The Pricing of Highway Services." *National Tax Journal* 5: 97–106.

———. 1954a. "Resource Allocation and the Highway System." Mimeo. Buchanan Archives, Buchanan House, George Mason University.

———. 1954b. "Consumption Interdependence and the Interpretation of Social Cost." Mimeo. Buchanan Archives, Buchanan House, George Mason University.

———. 1955. "A Note of the Pure Theory of Public Expenditure." Mimeo. Buchanan Archives, Buchanan House, George Mason University.

———. 1957. "The Pure Theory of Local Expenditures: Comment." Unpublished response to Tiebout (1957). Reprinted in Boettke and Marciano (2017).

———. 1959. "Positive Economics, Welfare Economics, and Political Economy." *Journal of Law and Economics* 2: 124–38.

———. 1964. "What Should Economists Do?" *Southern Economic Journal* 30: 213–22.

———. 1965. "An Economic Theory of Clubs." *Economica* 32(125): 1–14.

———. 1966. “Externality in Tax Response.” *Southern Economic Journal* 33(1): 35–42.

———. 1967 [1999]. *Public Finance in Democratic Process: Fiscal Institutions and Individual Choice.* Indianapolis, IN: Liberty Fund.

———. 1986. “The Constitution of Economic Policy.” Lecture presented for the Sveriges Riksbank Prize in Economic Sciences in Memory of Alfred Nobel, December 8. https://www.nobelprize.org/prizes/economic-sciences/1986/buchanan/lecture/.

———. 1987. “The Constitution of Economic Policy.” *American Economic Review* 77(3): 243–50.

Buchanan, J. M., and W. C. Stubblebine. 1962. “Externality.” *Economica* 29(116): 371–84.

Casella, A., and J. S. Feinstein. 2002. “Public Goods in Trade: On the Formation of Markets and Jurisdictions.” *International Economics Review* 43(2): 437–62.

Conley, J., and M. Dix. 1999. “Optimal and Equilibrium Membership in Clubs in the Presence of Spillovers.” *Journal of Urban Economics* 46: 215–29.

Fontaine, P. 2014. “Free Riding.” *Journal for the History of Economic Thought* 36(3): 359–76.

Gugerty, M. K. 2009. “Signaling Virtue: Voluntary Accountability Programs among Nonprofit Organizations.” *Policy Sciences* 42(3): 243–73.

Johnson, M. 2006. “The Wicksellian Unanimity Rule: The Competing Interpretations of Buchanan and Musgrave.” *Journal of the History of Economic Thought* 28(1): 58–79.

———. 2014. “James M. Buchanan, Chicago, and Post-War Public Finance.” *Journal of the History of Economic Thought* 36(4): 479–97.

———. 2015. “Public Goods, Market Failure, and Voluntary Exchange.” *History of Political Economy* 47(1): 174–98.

Marciano, A. 2013. “Why Market Failures Are Not a Problem: James Buchanan on Market Imperfections, Voluntary Cooperation, and Externalities.” *History of Political Economy* 45(2): 223–54.

Oates, W. E. 1969. “The Effects of Property Taxes and Local Public Spending on Property Values: An Empirical Study of Tax Capitalization and the Tiebout Hypothesis.” *Journal of Political Economy* 77(6): 957–71.

Samuelson, P. A. 1954. “The Pure Theory of Public Expenditure.” *Review of Economics and Statistics* 36(4): 387–89.

Tiebout, C. M. 1956. “A Pure Theory of Local Expenditures.” *Journal of Political Economy* 64(5): 416–24.

Webster, C. 2001. “Gated Cities of Tomorrow.” *Town Planning Review* 72(2): 149–70.

Wicksell, K. 1896. *Finanztheoretische Entersuchungen: Nebst Darstellung und Kritik des Steuerwesens Schwedens.* Jena, Germany: Gustav Fischer.

1.1
A Note on the Pure Theory of Public Expenditure

JAMES M. BUCHANAN

Professor Samuelson's formulation of the pure theory of public expenditure (Samuelson 1954) contains within it a pure theory of taxation as well. Since the theory of taxation is confined to his third set of conditions, which also introduces the social welfare function involving interpersonal considerations, his approach seems likely to be misinterpreted by those who are not willing to move beyond the "narrow" or Paretian version of modern welfare economics. His first two sets of conditions may be interpreted as providing a pure theory of public expenditure independently of a theory of taxation, while keeping within Paretian limits. I shall show that an additional set of conditions that include a theory of taxation is required to provide such a pure theory of public expenditure.

I shall first restate Samuelson's first two conditions for optimality using the same mathematical notation.

$$\frac{u_j^i}{u_r^i} = \frac{F_j}{F_r} \quad (i = (1, 2, \ldots, s; r, j = 1, \ldots, n) \text{ or } (i = 1, 2, \ldots, s; r = 1, j = 2, \ldots, n). \quad (1)$$

These are the standard optimal conditions for the universe of private goods. They will tend to be produced by ideally operating competitive market forces, assuming, of course, the presence of the required side conditions.

It is in his second set that the pure theory of public expenditure is to be found.

$$\sum_{i=1}^{s} \frac{u_{n+j}^{i}}{u_{r}^{i}} = \frac{F_{n+j}}{F_{r}} \quad (j=1,\ldots,m;\ r=1,\ldots,n) \text{ or } (j=1,\ldots,m;\ r=1). \quad (2)$$

This states that the summation over all individuals of the marginal rates of substitution between any one collective good (denoted by the additive Σ script) and any one private good equals the marginal rate of substitution between the two in production.

Samuelson's third set of conditions introduces his social welfare function embodying interpersonal norms. This is not needed for the argument of this note. Notations (1) and (2) limit the discussion to the "narrow" welfare economics. They define the (s-1) fold infinity of points along a maximal utility frontier. Given any one initial distribution of relative welfare among individuals, these conditions may be interpreted to define a means of attaining the utility frontier in a world of both private and collective goods. And, since interpersonal utility comparisons are not introduced, these conditions may be misinterpreted as defining a means of attaining the frontier in the Paretian manner of making some individuals better off and no individual worse off.

I shall argue that (1) and (2) define necessary but not sufficient conditions for attaining the frontier in the "narrow" welfare economics, and I shall introduce the third set of conditions that is required for sufficiency.

The unique marginal rate of substitution in production of (2) bears close examination. This represents the physical possibility of substituting collective goods for private goods. It would appear to be uniquely determined by transformation possibilities in (2) just as is its counterpart in (1). In (1), the individual marginal rates of substitution in consumption are equated to the single marginal rate of substitution in production. The latter is made unique because prices or exchange ratios are made uniform for all individuals. That is,

$$\frac{F_{j}^{i}}{F_{r}^{i}} = \frac{F_{j}}{F_{r}} \text{ for all i.}$$

That the removal of price discrimination is a step toward Pareto optimality is a well-known proof. But the proof depends on the individuality or privateness of the goods, which allows each individual to adjust his consumption ratio to the price ratio facing him. In the universe where both collective and private goods are present, the relative "prices" of collective and private goods may not be uniform unless explicitly made so by a poll or head tax covering the cost of collective goods. But if this is done, it can no longer be shown that no one's welfare has been reduced. The very nature of collective goods prevents individual adjustments in consumption. Individuals cannot, even hypothetically, trade collective goods among themselves so as to reach a contract curve.

In the more general case, "prices" are not uniform, or

$$\frac{F^i_{n+j}}{F^i_r} \neq \frac{F_{n+j}}{F_r}.$$

The market analogy is discriminatory pricing; the unique "social" marginal rate of transformation does not represent a ratio of marginal cost to each individual. The relative "prices" of collective and private goods depend on the manner in which the real costs of the collective goods are allocated among individuals; that is, on the structure of the tax system.

In order that the movement to the maximal utility frontier be limited in the Paretian sense, (1) and (2) must be supplemented by (2a).

$$\frac{u^i_{n+j}}{u^i_r} = \frac{F^i_{n+j}}{F^i_r} \qquad (i = 1, 2, \ldots, s; r = 1, \ldots, n; j = 1, 2, \ldots, m). \qquad \text{(2a)}$$

Just as the function $F(x_1 \ldots x_{m+n})$ defines production possibilities for the whole economy in the Samuelson argument, the functions $F^i(x_1 \ldots . x_{m+n})$ define production or exchange possibilities for each individual, keeping in mind that movement along the individual possibility surfaces must be implemented collectively. F^i_{n+j} represents the marginal cost to the individual (his share of the aggregate cost) of an additional unit of the public good. The net (2a) states that for each individual, the marginal rate of substitution in consumption between any one collective good and any one private good must be made equal to the exchange ratio between those two *to him.*

If (2a) is not included, (1) and (2) are not sufficient to define a Paretian movement from a given position off the utility frontier to this frontier. Given a final distribution of welfare along the frontier, (1) and (2) define a point and a means of moving to this point. But (1) and (2) alone are of no use to the social calculating machine that does not also have (3) with which to work.

It is true that

$$\sum_{i=1}^{s} \frac{F^i_{n+j}}{F^i_r} = \frac{F_{n+j}}{F_r},$$

or that the summation of individual exchange ratios must be equal to the "social" exchange ratio. But this does not allow the individual differences to be neglected, since there are many possible ways of adding up.

Professor Bowen, in his treatment of the same problem (Bowen 1948), does not explicitly require that Pareto optimality be retained. If this requirement is presumed, his work may initially be subject to the same misinterpretation as Samuelson's. He defines the ideal output of collective goods as that determined by the equality of the summed marginal rates of substitution and marginal cost, essentially the (2) set. In his discussion of attaining this ideal by the voting process, however, he explicitly postulates a distribution of the real cost of the collective goods among individuals. In his example, this cost is covered by a poll tax. In Samuelson's notation, that would make (1) and (2) subject to the side conditions.

$$\frac{F^i_{n+j}}{F^i_r} = \frac{F_{n+j}}{F_r} \quad (i = 1, 2, \ldots, s; j = 1, \ldots, m; r = 1, 2, \ldots, n). \tag{2b}$$

This states that through the poll tax, the cost of acquiring the collective good is made the same for each individual. These are appropriate side conditions, provided one is willing to depart from the "narrow" welfare economics. It does serve to allow the expenditure side to be treated independently of the tax side, but it is only one of the many possible allocations of the tax bill that could be postulated. The set of conditions defined by (2a) is not restrictive in this sense. It allows the allocation of the tax burden to range at will, subject only to the individual equalities. In this sense, (2a) is similar to Samuelson's (3).

It is (2a) which states that only if taxes were levied strictly in accordance with the ideal benefit principle could Paretian optimality be retained. Of course, as Samuelson points out, there is no method of securing such allocation by individual choices since individual collective decisions involve elements other than discrete individual costs and utilities (Buchanan 1954). These "spillover" effects of individual choices on collective goods provided the great stumbling blocks in the path of Wicksell and Lindahl in their attempt to find the solution of (1), (2), and (2a). The fact that the solution cannot practically be attained does not, however, destroy the usefulness of its definition. We can just as readily conceive of a social calculating machine operating within this narrower framework as the broader Samuelson one.

I should repeat that (2a) is not needed in the Samuelson formulation. Notations (1), (2), and (3) provide a pure theory of public *finance* in the Samuelson welfare economics. Notations (1), (2), and (2a) provide a pure theory of public *finance* in the "narrow" or Pareto welfare economics.

SECTION 2

SUBJECTIVIST ECONOMICS

2.0 Introduction

PETER J. BOETTKE AND ALAIN MARCIANO

Buchanan was a rare radical subjectivist among elite post–World War II economists. To call him a radical subjectivist is to make both a strong and a vague statement. Subjectivity of value as well as choice on the margin and against given constraints have been defining characteristics of neoclassical theory since the 1870s. Yet, economic thinkers throughout that period have often sought to temper the implications of subjectivism by treating costs as objective at times or choosing to work with analytical tools that work only in situations where the subjective and the objective are perfectly aligned. These moves enable theorists to escape the implications of subjectivism. Buchanan throughout his career—and certainly after his visit to the London School of Economics (LSE)—sought not to escape but to embrace the implications of subjectivism for economics as laid out in his monograph, *Cost and Choice* (1969a), his edited volume with George Thirlby, *LSE Essays on Cost* (1973), and in various articles thereafter. When Buchanan utilized the term "subjectivism," he meant it, which is why we put the term "radical" prior, as his subjectivism was not merely the textbook version of the subjective theory of value. His was a subjectivism of value, costs, and expectations. But Buchanan suffered a sort of theoretical split personality because he fully embraced the implications of subjectivism if we want to study men as human beings, but he also insisted on the pragmatic value of studying men as "rats"—and thus his position of economics and political economy exists somewhere between philosophical understanding and predictive science.

In answering the question of where he would place himself on the wide spectrum of subjectivist approaches between G. L. S. Shackle and Ludwig Lachmann on one side and neoclassical orthodoxy on the other, he wrote,

> I'm certainly much closer to Shackle than I am to the mainstream. I've been tempted to go completely along with Shackle and become a very radical subjectivist. But I recognize that if you go all the way down that road you end up with a nihilistic position. I'm somewhere between von Mises and Yeager on the one hand and Shackle on the other. The person who comes closest to my methodological position is Jack Wiseman. (Buchanan 1987a, 3–4)

Buchanan's stated objective, rather than to defend radical subjectivism per se, was "to construct a bridge of sorts between the implied scientific nihilism in Shackle's position and the positivism that describes orthodox neoclassical economics" (1991, 218). It might be surprising that someone who, in *Cost and Choice* (1969a) and in "What Should Economists Do?" (1964b), among other works, criticized neoclassical economics and claimed that he was not far from Austrian economics would seek a bridge to orthodox economics. But this is an important aspect of Buchanan's work that must always be remembered. He was never comfortable with what he dubbed "the arrogance of the eccentric," and yet he constantly cautioned against being content to swim within the "dishwater of the orthodoxy"—which is from the title of a paper that we reproduce in section 4. His goal was always to bring the insights he found critical to press and, if necessary, prick a hole in the prevailing conventional wisdom, especially of the "establishment economics."

COSTS AND SUBJECTIVISM

Prima facie, it seems that Buchanan's thoroughgoing subjectivism was first displayed in *Cost and Choice* (the book was published in 1969, but a preliminary version was ready in 1967 and sent to some colleagues for comments, including Ronald Coase, Friedrich Hayek, and George Thirlby, among others; see Buchanan 1969a, acknowledgments). But actually, Buchanan started to work on costs and subjectivism much earlier. In particular he wrote, in the early 1960s, certain essays that would be modified and eventually included in *Cost and Choice*. There is evidence that Buchanan started to think of this book earlier. We publish here for the first time an essay that Buchanan wrote in 1964 that is entitled "The London Theory of Opportunity Cost," or "The London Theory of Cost" (Buchanan 1964a). About the same period, Buchanan wrote a two-page memo entitled "The Meaning of Cost." These works show that Buchanan was trying to connect his views on welfarism and positive political economy, already put forward in 1959 and early 1962, with costs and subjectivism. This would only become clear and explicit years later.

In another essay, "Notes on Cost and Welfare,"[1] Buchanan wrote that "the logical origin of cost is the economic problem itself" (Buchanan 1962a, 3). Buchanan carefully avoided referring to scarcity but nonetheless acknowledged that costs exist because individuals have to make choices. Indeed, because individuals cannot choose to do everything, they have to evaluate and compare various alternatives and reject some of them. This is precisely the basis of how one must define cost. Costs "reflect the value placed on the alternative that is considered to be available at the moment of choice but that is *not* chosen" (ibid., 3–4; emphasis added). As he wrote in the 1964 essay, "What is the meaning of opportunity cost? It is the alternative that is sacrificed" (Buchanan 1964b, 4).[2] Put differently, "the cost of anything is the sacrificed alternative" (ibid., 5). In other words, the cost is *not* what the individual will pay to obtain what he chooses. It is rather what the individual will not have. It is the pain that the individual anticipates from not choosing B because of choosing A.

Importantly, Buchanan did not speak of "disutility" or of "loss of utility" but instead utilized the term "pain" to convey a meaning that is closer to what he had in mind—a cost is "wholly subjective" (Buchanan 1962a, 4). Costs exist in the mind of the decision maker and only at the moment of decision. The reason is that cost is the value of an alternative to the decision maker that is not chosen. Once the individual has made the choice, the "actual or realized" cost no longer exists. As Buchanan would put it, "What happens to this cost once a decision is made? It no longer exists. It has vanished at the moment of decision" (Buchanan 1964b, 7). Therefore, and this is the main point, a cost "always exists in the mind of the chooser" (ibid.) and exists only before the chooser acts on their choice. It therefore cannot be known from the outside or evaluated by any external observer: a cost "is impossible for an external observer to measure. There is nothing observable to measure" (ibid.). This is the sense in which a cost, or an opportunity cost, is "purely subjective" (ibid.).

Thus, cost cannot be equated to the price the individual pays to buy the good that they chose to acquire. More precisely, the objective cost that is represented by the price paid by the individual only accurately represents the subjective costs in very specific circumstances: "When markets operate perfectly"

(Buchanan 1962a, 6). In those circumstances, the price reflects the subjective costs, the discarded alternatives. When economic forces have done all the work they are going to do and competitive equilibrium is realized, then—and only then—will the subjective assessments of the various participants in the market dovetail with the objective terms of market exchange. In that situation, there is no difference between the subjective and the objective costs. In perfectly functioning markets, subjective costs can be treated as objective costs. But it is only in this perfectly competitive equilibrium situation that the subjective elements in individual behavior can be neglected.

As we saw in the quotations from those 1962 and 1964 essays, in demonstrating that costs are subjective Buchanan made two claims: first, ontologically, individuals' choices have a subjective dimension; second, epistemologically and complementarily, the economic problem must be treated—except in specific circumstances—subjectively. It is this second claim that he develops at length.

SUBJECTIVISM AND THE ROLE OF ECONOMISTS

In "Notes on Cost and Welfare," Buchanan also derived, from the claim that choices involve a subjective element, implications for what economists could recommend in terms of public policies. Mainly, he criticized the standard Pigovian approach to welfare economics because its political recommendations are based on the possible divergence between *objectively* measurable private costs and *objectively* measurable social costs and, therefore they ignore subjective costs. But if it is the case that a difference exists between subjective and objective costs, then divergences between private and social costs are not sufficient for undertaking public policies. At best, the objective variables can indicate that a problem *may* exist and that political action *may* be justifiable. That is, in the words Buchanan used in another published paper, the economist can "presume" that a problem exists: "*Presumptive efficiency* is, therefore, the appropriate conception for political economy" (Buchanan 1959, 126).

But this presumption "cannot alone suggest specific policy steps," and more than that, it cannot "even imply non-optimality" (Buchanan 1962b, 21)—that is, we may not infer from the existence of divergences between private and social costs that the situation is inefficient. Indeed, what appears efficient to the economist, from his position as an external observer, may not be efficient and Pareto-optimal for the individuals involved in the choice. As Buchanan put elsewhere, any evaluation made by an economist is only "*his own estimate of his subjects' value scales*" (Buchanan 1959, 126; emphasis in original). Thus, a "specific change may be judged to be Pareto-optimal or 'efficient' only after it has, in fact, been proposed and the individual preferences for or against the change revealed" (ibid., 127; see also Buchanan 1962c). One can also find other occurrences of this very idea in later works. For instance, in his 1987 article "The Constitution of Economic Policy," Buchanan wrote, "The idealized agreement on the objectives of politics does not, however, allow for any supersession of individual evaluation" (1987b, 246). On the contrary, "improvement in the workings of politics is measured in terms of the satisfaction of that which is desired by individuals, whatever this may be, rather than in terms of moving closer to some externally defined, supra-individualistic ideal" (ibid.). This position led him to claim that economists should abandon the "omniscience assumption" on which their analyses rest and should replace it with a "presumption of ignorance" (Buchanan 1959, 126; see also Buchanan 1962c).[3]

More can be said in connection with Buchanan's conception of positive and normative economics. This is the object of section 3. What matters here and what is important about these "Notes" is that they reveal that Buchanan explicitly linked conclusions about the role of economists to subjectivism. To Buchanan, precisely because a subjective element in individual behavior exists and because economists cannot ignore it, the latter should abandon the assumed position of omniscient observers capable of predicting what individuals will do. Economics cannot be a "predictive science." It should be viewed as a moral philosophy.

WHAT SHOULD ECONOMISTS DO—A VERSION WITH SUBJECTIVISM

At about the same time as Buchanan wrote the notes presented in this section, he prepared the presidential address he was to deliver at the 1963 annual meeting of the Southern Economic Association and published as an article one year later. In this article, entitled "What Should Economists Do?," Buchanan studied another implication of subjectivism for economics, but importantly, he did so without using the term "subjectivism." Indeed, as in the papers mentioned earlier that Buchanan published around this time (1959, 1962b, 1962c) or in those published about the methodology of economics later in the 1960s, there is nothing explicitly mentioned about subjectivism. These papers were not only influenced by his subjectivism but are also crucial to understanding his subjectivism. This was made clear by Buchanan in 1976, in "The General Implication of Subjectivism in Economics," when he made explicit the connection between his conception of what economists should do and subjectivism. His views can be summarized by two propositions: first, "The subjectivist . . . is trying to explain . . . exchange. His is a 'theory of exchange'" ([1976] 1979,

83). Second, standard neoclassical economics is objectivist by focusing on the state of affairs that emerges once economic forces have done all the work and the end-state is achieved.[4]

Let us start with this second proposition. Standard neoclassical economists are objectivists because they view economics as the science of choice. Buchanan did not target the emphasis on choice per se. He, for example, was not ignorant of the agony of choice that confronts the individual in seeking to better their situation. His criticisms challenged the claim that economists should analyze choices. He criticized the standard approach to decision-making for assuming that individuals maximize *given* objective utility or profit functions and choose whatever quantities at which marginal benefits and marginal costs are equalized.

Certainly, constrained optimization for the individual *might* be useful within certain analytical limits, but this is not what a social science should study. Focusing on individual choice as optimizing removes the human in human behaviors. Indeed, there is not much choice left if the objective function, the constraints, and the choice set are given. The choice is "predetermined" (Buchanan 1969a, 40) and involves no uncertainty. The solution of the maximization problem preexists the problem. The only question that remains is to compute it or find it. As Buchanan wrote a few years later, "in a world of complete certainty, there is no decision problem. A computer can make all 'choices,' if indeed choices exist" (ibid., 89; see also Buchanan 1971). It is the case of Robinson Crusoe when he is alone on his island—his problem is "essentially a computational one" (Buchanan 1964b, 217). It is also the case of the "theoretical model of perfectly competitive equilibrium," in which "the individual responds to a set of externally-determined, exogenous variables, and his choice problem again becomes purely mechanical" (ibid., 218). But standard economics does not stop there. It moves optimization at the individual level to optimization at the level of the system. It also treats the market as an optimizing device aimed at allocating scarce resources as a way to answer how much to produce, what to produce, and for whom. This perspective is "organismic," to use the word Buchanan used to criticize public finance in the late 1940s (Buchanan 1948, 1949).

Once again, the preoccupation with equilibrium for the system, as the preoccupation for constrained optimization for the individual, *might* be useful and valuable scientific tools within certain analytical limits, but they are decidedly *not* the tools of *social science*. Any "social science" that purges capable but fallible human actors and the social ecology within which they interact is, in fact, "nonsensical social science" (Buchanan 1964b, 218). Buchanan would even refer to the perfect competition model as intellectual dry rot.

But why does Buchanan insist that these analytical tools result in objectivism? He does not mean that in the textbook treatment there is no subjectivity in the model of individual behavior, but rather that in equilibrium there is no difference between the subjective and objective dimensions of the behavior. Subjective behavior can be treated objectively. This implies, as a corollary, that under the assumptions made in textbook neoclassical economics, there is no need to consider that choices could be creative. Even creative choices are reactive. Thus, all choices can be treated as reactive—that is, as reactions to certain *given* conditions. Indeed, both Robinson Crusoe and any individual in a market are "reacting to an environment . . . to 'nature,' so to speak" (Buchanan 1965, 9). They treat other individuals as objects. Robinson Crusoe is, like any individual in a market, "alone" and "isolated." Both decide what they want, given whatever others do.

This is precisely why a subjectivist does not study choice but focuses on exchange between individuals. Creative choices can exist only when there are interactions between individuals and individuals recognize that there are interactions and interdependence. Thus, creative choices are possible only when Vendredi steps onto Robinson Crusoe's island or when individuals no longer treat others as objects, as part of nature. Then, the interaction between individuals—their *association* (Buchanan 1964b, 217)—"requires that a wholly different, and wholly new, sort of behavior take place, that of exchange, trade, or agreement" (ibid., 218). In those circumstances, when individuals interact with each other, aware of their interdependence, it is perfectly possible that they end up by doing something that they did not intend to do in the first place and, accordingly, that a new and original pattern emerges from the interaction. This is so because, in the interaction with others in the exchange process, individuals' preferences may change. Or, as Buchanan put it, individual utility functions cannot be assumed to be given and to exist independently from the act of choosing and also from interactions with others. On the contrary, individual preferences and the utility functions that represent them "do not, and cannot, exist independently from the choice action of [individuals] A and B in the exchange process itself" (Buchanan [1976] 1979, 87).

SUBJECTIVISM AND CREATIVE AND REACTIVE CHOICES

From what precedes, it is clear that Buchanan distinguished between two types of behaviors: choice when individuals are alone and choice in exchange—that is, "choice" and "behavior" (Buchanan [1969c] 1979, 40 and 42; see also 1969b or 1969d) or genuine choices (Buchanan 1969d). He also presented the difference between "choice" and "behavior" differently in a review article (Buchanan 1989) of one of Shackle's books, *Business, Time and Thought*. He introduced a distinction between "two mental events" (1989, 2) or "two quite separate conceptions of choice" (ibid.): "reactive" and "creative" choice (see also Buchanan and Vanberg 1991, 2002).

The ideas behind the words are simple but also relatively unclear. A choice is characterized as reactive when the chooser does nothing to modify or change the "conditions that had brought [a] new opportunity into realization" (Buchanan 1989, 2). It simply consists in responding or reacting to an external "stimulus" (ibid., 3) that can come from other individuals or from the "creative choices made by others with whom they may interact" (Buchanan and Vanberg 2002, 123). It seems that individuals who behave reactively cannot do otherwise than to make a predetermined choice. They face "stochastic determinacy" (1989, 3), and their choices are "at least probabilistically predictable" (ibid., 2). This implies, as we will see soon, that a reactive choice is not really a choice, since it is unavoidable. This is totally different, as one can guess, from a "creative" choice, which gives birth to something that did not exist before the choice and that could not be expected or predicted independently from the choice itself—that is, to "a sequence of events that did not exist prior to the choice and that were brought into being, literally, by the choice itself" (ibid.). Those choices or the behaviors that result from creative choices "are *not* probabilistically predictable" (ibid., 3; emphasis added). A creative choice is, as Buchanan insisted, *entrepreneurial* (ibid.).

The conclusion is clear: "Understanding how the economy works requires that we give due attention to both dimensions for choice, and neoclassical orthodoxy has surely neglected creative choice as the necessary complement to the reactive choice that must be its central focus" (Buchanan 1989, 3). The reactive choices are the "predetermined," perfectly objective choices, analyzed by orthodox (neoclassical) economists; the creative choices are the subjective choices individuals make when they interact with each other and try to coordinate with others.

We now understand how Buchanan was not a radical subjectivist: he did not argue that human choices could be entirely and only "creative" or "genuine." Individuals do not always behave as entrepreneurs. Sometimes they only react to what happens to them. Buchanan even noted that creative choices are not the most frequent ones as, for instance, when he spoke of "the *residual* aspects of human action that are not reducible to ratlike responses to stimuli" (Buchanan 1983, 17; emphasis added).

NOTES

1. This article is undated. However, from the list of references, it seems that it was written before 1962.
2. This is how he was to define "opportunity cost" in his Palgrave entry: "Opportunity cost is the value placed on the alternative that is rejected by the chooser," or "Opportunity cost is the evaluation placed on the most highly valued of the rejected alternatives or opportunities" (Buchanan 1987c).
3. We can note the connection with Buchanan's rejection of the idea he had put forward in his early work that there could exist a "fiscal brain" that would calculate all the taxes that should be paid by the individuals.
4. One must note here that the two propositions are not symmetrical. He did not argue that objectivism is incompatible with a theory of exchange. He gave the significant example of Adam Smith, who "after all . . . was no subjectivist" (Buchanan [1976] 1979, 84); later he would also mention Ronald Coase as one of those objectivist economists who could not be put in the same group as the economists who do other than what they should. And, conversely, mathematical economists could be subjectivists. His message was rather that being a subjectivist allows "a better understanding of the principle of spontaneous coordination" (Buchanan [1976] 1979, 82), which was equated with the study of exchange. From this perspective, "most of those who espouse a variant of Austrian subjectivist economics know what they are doing" (ibid., 91). In other words, a subjectivist approach may be helpful, but it is not necessary for economists to focus on what they should.

REFERENCES

Buchanan, J. M. 1948. "The Problem of Fiscal Inequality in a Federal State." Mimeo. Buchanan Archives, Buchanan House, George Mason University.

———. 1949. "The Pure Theory of Government Finance: A Suggested Approach." *Journal of Political Economy* 57(6): 496–505.

———. 1959. "Positive Economics, Welfare Economics, and Political Economy." *Journal of Law and Economics* 2: 124–38.

———. 1962a. "Notes on Cost and Welfare." Mimeo. Buchanan Archives, Buchanan House, George Mason University.

———. 1962b. "Politics, Policy, and the Pigovian Margins." *Economica* 29(113): 17–28.

———. 1962c. "The Relevance of Pareto Optimality." *Journal of Conflict Analysis and Resolution* 6(4): 341–54.

———. 1964a. "The London Theory of Opportunity Cost." Mimeo. Buchanan Archives, Buchanan House, George Mason University.

———. 1964b. "What Should Economists Do?" *Southern Economic Journal* 30(3): 213–22.

———. 1965. "Ethical Rules, Expected Values, and Large Numbers." *Ethics* 76(1): 1–13.

———. 1969a. *Cost and Choice: An Inquiry in Economic Theory*. Vol. 6 of *The Collected Works of James M. Buchanan*. Indianapolis, IN: Liberty Fund.

———. 1969b. "A Future for 'Agricultural Economics'?" *American Journal of Agricultural Economics* 51(5): 1027–36.

———. [1969c] 1979. "Is Economics the Science of Choice?" Reprinted in *What Should Economists Do?* Edited by J. M. Buchanan. Indianapolis, IN: Liberty Fund: 39–63.

———. 1969d. "Professor Alchian on Economic Method." Reprinted in *What Should Economists Do?* Edited by J. M. Buchanan. Indianapolis, IN: Liberty Fund: 66–91.

———. 1971. "Violence, Law, and Equilibrium in the University." *Public Policy* 19: 1–18.

———. [1976] 1979. "The General Implication of Subjectivism in Economics." Reprinted in *What Should Economists Do?* Edited by J. M. Buchanan. Indianapolis, IN: Liberty Fund: 81–91.

———. 1982. "The Domain of Subjective Economics: Between Predictive Science and Moral Philosophy." In *Method, Process and Austrian Economics*. Edited by Israel M. Kirzner. Lexington, MA: Lexington Books.

———. 1987a. "An Interview with Nobel Laureate James Buchanan." *Austrian Economics Newsletter* 1(1): 3–4.

———. 1987b. "The Constitution of Economic Policy." *American Economic Review* 77(3): 243–50.

———. 1987c. "Constitutional Economics." In *The New Palgrave: The World of Economics*, 134–42. Edited by John Eatwell, Murray Milgate, and Peter Newman. London: Macmillan.

———. 1989. "Shackle and a Lecture in Pittsburg." *Market Process* 7: 2–3.

———. 1991. *The Economics and Ethics of Constitutional Order*. Ann Arbor: University of Michigan Press.

Buchanan, J. M., and G. F. Thirlby (eds.). 1973. *LSE Essays on Cost*. London: Weidenfeld and Nicolson.

Buchanan, J. M., and V. Vanberg. 1991. "The Market as a Creative Process." *Economics and Philosophy* 7: 167–86.

———. 2002. "Constitutional Implications of Radical Subjectivism." *Review of Austrian Economics* 15: 121–29.

2.1
The London Theory of Opportunity Cost

JAMES M. BUCHANAN

Last spring, I conducted an experiment with my colleagues and advanced graduate students at the University of Virginia. I propose to commence the discussion by doing the same thing with you, and I have here some copies of the mimeographed sheet that I distributed at Virginia. Perhaps if you will merely look these over and make a mental response, this will be sufficient for our purposes here. You may use this current response for later reference in toting up your own score on what, at first glance, surely seems to be a very elementary lesson in price theory.

I might add, at the outset, that, at the University of Virginia, we claim a fair degree of sophistication in old-fashioned and rigorous price theory. We may be faulted, I suspect, for our failure to keep up to date with currently fashionable macroeconomic growth models, but we do not normally admit our error or ignorance in the elements of economics.

But, having said this, how did my colleagues and graduate students make out on this simple experiment? Of course, response was not mandatory and a good share of possible respondents feared a trick. But the response that I got was sufficient to provide me with confirmation of the hypothesis that I was testing, insofar as we can confirm hypotheses. (I should have said corroborate,

Draft dated January 15, 1964.

not confirm.) Economists do not really understand the meaning of opportunity cost. Fourteen of the respondents clearly indicated such a failure; three or four gave replies that were impossible to classify; only four respondents gave what I consider to be rather clear evidence that they understood what opportunity cost really means.

By saying that most economists are confused about costs, I am not being necessarily critical. Because, in my usual way, I only know this because I know that I was myself terribly confused on all this until I came up squarely against the prevailing theory at London. Until I tried the experiment, I simply did not know whether this was merely an awesome gap in my own understanding, unique with me, or whether it was also widely shared by American professionals. I now conclude, as a result of my experiment, that I was not alone in my misunderstanding. I think that I really learned cost theory not from Frank Knight but only between 1960 and 1962, when I spent some time around the London School of Economics (LSE), and, more importantly, when I was forced to think critically and had time to think critically about some of the contradictions that seemed to arise in trying to define cost in relation to the public debt controversy that my 1958 book had helped to generate. It was only after my "discovery," so to speak, of the "proper" theory of cost that I began to inquire around, and I found out that the theory has really been a part of the oral tradition at LSE since the 1920s. Written statements do exist, by Hayek, by Robbins, by G. F. Thirlby especially, by Ronald Coase, and by Jack Wiseman. And my colleague, Coase, tells me that some of it is in Wicksteed and Knight. These written statements are, however, almost always presented in such a way that the elemental meaning of cost escapes those who are trained, as we are, in a different oral tradition.

So much by way of introduction; I must get to the point, and I shall do so by starting with definitions. How shall we define opportunity cost? In the orthodox sense, opportunity cost is defined as the alternative product that could have been produced with the resources employed in the production of the particular commodity or service in question. This cost, presumably, is measured by the dollar value of payments to resource owners. And I suspect that, initially, you would have responded to my questionnaire by saying that costs need not equal total receipts. Cost covering and profit maximizing need not be equivalent behavior patterns, except insofar as mere survival in the competitive process forces firms to bring the two things into equality. In situations not characterized by long-run competitive equilibrium, I suspect you would have added, the two statements are not merely different ways of saying the same thing. Again, I merely say that this is probably what I should have said three years ago.

I now think that this "orthodox" or standard view of opportunity cost is wrong, and I accept fully the validity of the quoted statement in the questionnaire, which is, incidentally, taken directly from a 1938 essay by my colleague Ronald Coase, himself a member of the London group at that time. Let us look again at the question: What is the meaning of opportunity cost? It is the alternative that is sacrificed. On this, we all can agree. But what is the alternative? Surely, any profit opportunity that could have been taken but is not taken is itself a cost of taking the decision that is taken. Any failure to maximize profits is, therefore, failure to cover a genuine opportunity cost. Looked at in this way, the statement cited appears to be obviously valid and also extremely simple and elementary.

You may ask, as one of my colleagues did, why I seek to depart here from ordinary and accepted usage. Traditionally, we have not included profits forgone, rents forgone, as costs. There is surely some advantage in going along with the usual terminology, and there is little point in confusing things merely to insist on clarifying the language here. There is something in this, of course, and I should not seek to stir up these long-stagnant waters of elementary theory were it not for the fact that there are dangerous methodological crocodiles lurking beneath the surface. I hope to be able to demonstrate to you that this flaw in elementary cost theory has led important economists, and indeed almost the whole profession, to make analytical errors in at least three respects that have significant policy implications.

Let us return again to definitions. The cost of anything is the sacrificed alternative. This we accept. To what is a cost-benefit calculus to be applied, however? Is it appropriate to talk about the cost of a unit of commodity or service as we usually do? I think not. What we are ultimately seeking to explain is choice, decision, and this is what is relevant when we talk about costs and benefits. To each decision there can be attached a cost on the one side and a benefit on the other. In many cases, a unit of commodity or service can serve us well as a shorthand representation of "the decision to purchase or to sell a unit," but the *decision* framework is the essential point to be kept in mind, and the shorthand should never be allowed to confuse this.

What is the opportunity cost of a decision? When choice is confronted, the individual, as a potential chooser, faces *alternative* lines of action. To be confronted with genuine choice between course A and course B is the same thing as being able to select either course A or course B. Now let us examine the individual's mental process in making this choice. What are the ingredients in the mental calculus that takes place before choice is made? For each possible alternative, some sort of cost-benefit comparison must be made. What are the anticipated benefits from adopting course of action A? What are the *anticipated* costs? The individual must estimate the two sides of the account here. What are the costs of A? We may be inclined to say B in the simple model here presented. In one sense, this is correct, but we require a more elementary explanation in order to clarify our meaning precisely. The cost of A, to the chooser, is the anticipated enjoyment that he expects from B, enjoyment that he cannot possibly ever get if he should choose A and that is forever forgone once he makes an actual decision to adopt A. This cost of A can never be the actual enjoyment of B since this is given up; it must consist wholly in the *anticipated* enjoyment of B in the mind of the chooser.

What happens to this cost once a decision is made? It no longer exists. It has vanished at the moment of decision. Opportunity cost, in this sense, exists solely as the obstacle to that decision, the negative side of choice, so to speak, which simply fades out of being once commitment is made.

Again, I apologize for the elementary nature of all this, since I am sure that this seems not only familiar but mundane. But I doubt that many economists appreciate fully the implications of these very simple propositions about opportunity costs. One of these implications is that cost is always a *subjective* phenomenon; it always exists only in the mind of the chooser, and it is impossible for any external observer to measure. There is nothing observable to measure. A second implication is that, temporally, cost occurs only at the moment of decision or immediately prior to decision. Cost in this purely subjective sense can never be postponed until after decision; it can never be a consequence of a decision. There is no such thing as sunk cost in this subjective sense of opportunity cost.

Economists, and others, talk a great deal about costs in some other sense than this. They do talk about sunk costs, and they do talk about payments to resources as costs, costs that, presumably, can be measured. And it is the main job of accountants to measure something that is widely referred to as costs. How is it possible to reconcile all this very familiar jargon with the elementary notion of opportunity cost that I have tried to outline?

Reconciliation becomes possible, I think, when we recognize that every decision involves two quite distinct and quite separate costs. One is the cost to which I have referred, the obstacle to decision, the anticipation of enjoyment that is forgone, that must forever be given up on taking a decision. I propose to call this *subjective cost*.

Once a decision is made, consequences occur. Decisions embody commitments that must be honored, and in economic transactions, one of these consequences is that something must be "given up" to get something else. "Given up" here implies something quite different, conceptually, from the anticipation of enjoyment sacrificed upon decision, as we shall see. Here, "given up" means the physical remission of resource services away from the control of the one who has made the decision. A measurable "payout" of resource services takes place, always consequent to decision. I propose to call this observable payout, or outlay, *objective cost*. It is this that accountants appropriately measure, and it is this, and only this, that any external observer can see. It is not at all subjective, and it cannot directly influence decisions at all.

Note also that, temporally, this cost occurs only and necessarily after decision. It is always "sunk," so to speak. It is always "put off" or "postponed."

Why have economists failed to make clear this essentially dual nature of cost? I think that there are three fundamental reasons, and I shall try to mention each. First of all, most of our theory has been developed in terms of commodities, goods and services, and not in terms of behavior, of decisions. This is true despite our pretended emphasis on the theory of choice. And if we do think in terms of goods—say, a coconut—it does not make much initial sense to talk about the subjective cost of a coconut. Once we begin to think about the cost of a decision to consume or to purchase a coconut, however, the subjective element becomes obvious. Secondly, and perhaps more importantly, most of our theory has been based on the idea that choice and consequences take place simultaneously. Again, this is true despite all of our pretended discussion to the contrary. Our conceptual framework assumes this basic simultaneity. To illustrate again with the coconut, our theory assumes that a decision to purchase implies payment immediately. We purchase and pay for a good at the same time. Thus, our theory, without us realizing it, assumes that all buying is really impulse buying and all selling is impulse selling. It is not at all easy for us to fit lags between decision and payment into our models. But what if we assume that a person decides to buy a coconut on Friday and he does not get to market until Monday? When is the cost incurred? In the purely subjective sense, sacrificed alternatives are sacrificed on Friday, while observed payout takes place on Monday. The example is more familiar if we turn it around and assume that the consumer chooses to buy the coconut on Friday but charges it until the end of the month. When is "cost" incurred if there is only one cost? This example makes clear that there are two quite separate things that can be called costs here, and we all recognize this when put to it.

A third and final important basis for our confusion has been our implicit assumption of continuous competitive equilibrium in our models. It is evident that, in a position of full competitive equilibrium, a person who *correctly* estimates the subjective cost of a decision can accurately represent this estimate in money terms. If I buy a coconut for 50 cents, then this sum accurately represents for me the alternative enjoyments that I could enjoy should I not purchase the coconut. But this is true only because I am able, continuously, to adjust my purchases of all commodities and services in such a manner as to make me indifferent to which particular alternatives are sacrificed. In any case, this adjustment makes any alternative worth 50 cents, and this value now assumes subjective meaning. And, in equilibrium, once I make my decision, I also find that I actually have to pay out 50 cents to get the coconut. I give up or pay out 50 cents worth of other commodities. Thus, my own subjective estimate, my own measure of opportunity cost in money units, turns out to be equivalent, in money terms, to the actual outlay that I have to make on the commodity. The two costs, while remaining distinct as before, take on numerical identity here. Because they do, economists have failed to sense the elemental difference and to see that the numerical equivalence of the two "measures," one subjective and the other objective, can take place only in full competitive equilibrium. Since economists deal largely with the behavior of individuals and firms as quantity adjustors to a set of externally determined prices, the need for making the distinction between these two fundamentally different conceptions of cost rarely arises.

Let us look, however, at a single choice situation where change is allowed. A person makes a decision, let us say, to fly to Atlanta tomorrow morning. At the time that he makes this choice, he incurs some cost; he anticipates the enjoyments that he could secure if he stays in Tallahassee and if he does not purchase the plane ticket. This cost is the only barrier to his decision, but, also having estimated the benefits, he chooses to go and makes his plans accordingly. The next morning arrives; our man boards the plane, and he encounters very rough weather in the flight. This is the objective cost of his prior decision, or a part of it in any case, and there need be no equivalence between this, or a monetary measure of this, and the monetary measure of the opportunity cost that served as the obstacle to his decision in the first place. Having made his choice, what he now observes to be an erroneous estimate of cost, the man will of course tend to readjust such estimates for future decisions. He will in this way perhaps grope for what may be called some sort of behavioral equilibrium, which comes about, if it does, precisely because of the divergence between the anticipated costs and the realized costs of action or between anticipated benefits and realized benefits.

There is nothing either new or even interesting at this point, except in reference to the confusion that the model seems to generate. Economists have been wont to say that human error can make costs ex ante differ from costs viewed ex post and that these differences disappear in the world of certainty. But this is simply wrong. What the world of certainty produces is an equality between the measures of two separate things, between the estimate of the cost that informs choices—the subjective opportunity cost—and the estimate of the cost that is consequent upon choices—the objective cost of outlay. There remain two quite distinct things being measured, in fact, with wholly different dimensions: one being subjective and the other real or objective. The first is, in one sense, the psychological reflection of the other, which may or may not be accurate.

In one important respect, the only relevant cost is opportunity cost, that which influences decision; that is, subjective cost in the terminology used here. However, there remains the question as to what we should call that which accountants measure, which is always after decision, and which cannot ever affect decision directly. It might, given carte blanche, be preferable to refer to this as *outlay* or *payout*, leaving the word "cost" to refer only to the subjective element. But accountants and economists do call outlay "cost," and we need to minimize the changes in terminology. It is for this reason that I propose to retain the "cost" usage and to separate subjective and objective meanings.

I hope that I have been able, in general terms, to convey to you some idea of what I think is an important distinction between what I have called "orthodox theory of cost" and what I have called "the LSE theory," as I interpret the latter. One of the problems here is that the central elements of the London view are intuitively obvious to us all, while at the same time we have not really translated these views into our everyday theorizing. But the proof of the pudding rests with the demonstration that some failure to follow through on the proper notions of cost has been the source of specific confusion.

Let me try, then, to discuss three separate areas of theorizing. G. F. Thirlby and Jack Wiseman, especially, have tried to show that the whole debate on marginal cost pricing, as a rule for the managers of public enterprises to follow, has been hopelessly confused because most of the participants have been employing improper conceptions of cost. Neither Thirlby nor Wiseman has been successful in convincing many people, and I may not be able to convince you, but I think that it is worth trying.

In the view of cost that I have suggested, all cost is marginal in the subjective sense, and all cost is sunk in the objective or outlay sense. What are we to make out of this as an appropriate rule for the operation of a socialistic enterprise? As Wiseman has put it, we should require that the time horizon for each manager be precisely specified if the so-called rule is to work at all. Suppose, however, the managers were told to operate on marginal cost principles and given their head in so doing. Then at the end of some arbitrary accounting period, it was proposed to evaluate their performance. How would it be possible to tell which of them has best followed the rules? There would be no possible way of judging from the accounting comparison of costs and receipts. The manager who was the most accurate in his decision-making may make large losses, ex post, whereas the worst of all possible managers may make profits. This may be the result of exogenous forces rather than sharp decision-making. But, even if we agree to judge these managers by their ability to make profits, what is there left that is unique about the marginal cost rule? We are back where we started with the competitive rule: try to maximize profits, not revenue, or in other words, do the best you can. Certainly, there is nothing left in marginal cost pricing as a set of rules to be followed by managers of socialized enterprises.

Let me now turn to a second area of great confusion, which is in part owing to the conceptual difficulties over cost. I refer now to the tradition that we might call Pigovian welfare economics, in which assessments of "market failure" are drawn when "social costs" are alleged to be greater than "private costs," due to the presence of external diseconomies. Once again, I cannot go into the details of the analysis here, and some of you may be familiar with the "Virginia" contributions on this by Coase, by Davis, by Buchanan-Stubblebine, and Buchanan-Kafoglis, but I may be able, through using a very simple example, to show that a part of the difficulty at least is due to the cost confusion I am emphasizing here.

Suppose I keep hound dogs on my property, dogs that bark at night. Suppose now that this is known to bother my neighbor and that you, as an external observer, know this. My action in purchasing an additional dog imposes a cost, an external diseconomy, on my neighbor. As a welfare economist trained in the Pigovian tradition, you say that the "market has failed." Called in to give advice, you now say that I should be taxed in the amount of the cost that my action imposes on my neighbor. Suppose that this is assessed at $50. Then, a tax of $50 per dog will ensure that I take the external cost that my action generates into account in making my decision.

But surely this is all confused. What is the cost of making a decision to purchase an additional dog? I also know that he will bother my neighbor, and a part of the subjective cost that I will take into account in making my decision in the first place will be the additional displeasure that he will suffer and to which I may not be at all indifferent. To the extent that I take my neighbor's displeasure into account in my own anticipation of foregone alternatives, I do, in fact, take into account the external cost of my action, despite the fact that once I take the action, you can still observe the additional dog's barking as adding to my neighbor's woes. But, to the extent that this is true, then any tax, computed in the Pigovian manner, would in fact prevent me from making decisions that are surely Pareto-optimal.

There are, of course, many confusions in Pigovian welfare theory and its implications, but it seems clear that, in the example here, an elementary error lies in a failure to see that the cost-affecting decision is a purely subjective one that cannot be measured externally. The only cost that can be measured externally to the decision maker is objective cost or outlay, and these may not be at all the same values that affect decisions. Yet any Pigovian correctives, such as taxes or subsidies, must, in fact, be computed on the basis of objective cost, not subjective cost.

Now let me turn to a third area of controversy, in which I have been able to reconcile at least several of the different views by this clarification in the theory of cost. I refer to the whole controversy surrounding the location of the burden of public debt, which was stirred up, in part, by the publication of my little book in 1958.

Again, I cannot elaborate the argument here, and I have written a whole paper on this topic recently, but perhaps by hitting the main points I can demonstrate the cost theory of relevance. Look at the position of the individual as he participates in the political process as a taxpayer-beneficiary-voter. He is trying to decide whether to finance some public project through the imposition of taxes currently or to finance it through the issue of bonds, the creation of public debt. In making a decision to issue debt, the cost side, in a subjective sense, of this decision is represented by the anticipation of enjoyments of income in future time periods that he could have but cannot if he must make debt-service payments. Thus, in this sense, all of the cost of the public expenditure that is debt financed, all of the "burden," so to speak, must be borne upon decision itself, and it is impossible to transfer or to postpone any part of this in time. This is true whether or not the individual correctly or incorrectly anticipates the future costs that debt servicing will impose upon him.

It is, of course, the objective cost of the public project that is postponed in time. This postponement is the essence of debt finance, be this public or private. The observed payout of resource services, from taxpayers to creditors, takes place only in the periods subsequent to decision to borrow. Of course, taxpayers who must pay debt-service charges may also feel some "subjective" burden of payment in these later periods. This is wholly apart from the subjective cost of decision, however, which is incurred only at the moment of decision.

Perhaps this is sufficient to indicate that the simple recognition that there are two separate costs, not one, involved with every decision allows several of the ambiguities to be cleared up with reference to debt theory. This is not to say, of course, that this clarification will explain all of the divergent viewpoints in the controversy that continues to rage. A good part of the difficulty lies in a much more naive mistake about opportunity cost than I have tried to discuss here. I do not, at this seminar, propose to go into detail about the many confusions that have dominated thinking about public debts.

I have tried to suggest three possible areas of confusion that are, to an extent, clarified by a "correction" of our elemental meaning of opportunity cost. There are, no doubt, many other areas where this clarification should prove equally helpful. I make no particular brief for my own preferred terminology with respect to subjective cost and objective cost. I do claim that a better understanding of these rather fundamental notions about cost is necessary.

Frank Knight once gave a final examination in a price theory class by coming into the room and putting on the blackboard, "Write an essay on cost." I should like now to see my paper that I wrote then, and I should, in retrospect, like to tear it up and, perhaps, use the manuscript of this seminar in its place.

SECTION 3

POLITICS AND MORALS

3.0 Introduction

PETER J. BOETTKE AND ALAIN MARCIANO

From early in his career, Buchanan insisted on three basic points. First, following Wicksell and the Italian public finance theorists, he argued that economists cannot, and must not, continue to behave as if they were offering advice to a benevolent and omniscient despot.[1]

Second, in analyzing human behavior and exchange relationships that are formed in human interaction, Buchanan insisted on *behavioral symmetry*—whatever behavioral assumptions the analyst makes must carry across institutional environments. This was critical to focus our analytical attention on how institutional variation impacts human interaction. Same players, different rules produce different social "games" or outcomes. Not, different players, different rules produce different games, as was often in essence the methodological practice at the time he was writing. Greedy people in the market, but saintly people in politics; uninformed and irrational actors in the market, but well-informed and prudent decision makers in politics seemed to be the approach followed by those who held a "Romantic" notion of politics as the corrective to our social ills. But to Buchanan, the idea was to do "politics without romance."[2]

Third, also in connection with Wicksell and the Italian public finance economists, Buchanan insisted that all work in public finance relies implicitly or explicitly on a political theory/philosophy. This was because, by necessity, theories of public economics address questions not only of the scale of government but the scope of government. And questions on scope of governmental activities must by necessity rely on a political theory/philosophy. What are the legitimate functions of government in a democratic society?[3]

Add all three of these basic points and you can begin to see Buchanan's breadth and depth, especially when one adds that Buchanan linked institutions to morals. This connection is crucial to understanding Buchanan's approach to politics. Our argument is that, in Buchanan's view, morals or ethics determine the need for and range of politics.

ANARCHY: MORALS (ROMANCE) WITHOUT POLITICS?

Buchanan was a contractarian. We mentioned that point in the introduction and in section 1. As a contractarian, he explained the origins and necessity of politics and political institutions by starting from a state of nature populated with individuals living independently from others and having no rights. However, Buchanan did not much use the expression "state of nature." He rather used the term "anarchy" to characterize a situation without institutions, rights, or politics.

Anarchy can take two forms. It can be ordered/well-ordered, or it can be chaotic/disordered. Buchanan studied the first form in his famous book, *The Limits of Liberty: Between Anarchy and Leviathan* (1975a), and described it as the "ideal," the "utopian world" of any individualist—such as himself. It is a situation without "politics," without rules or rights: "In *conceptualized* anarchy, there are no individual rights, human or property, because there is no law defining these rights and no government to enforce them once they are defined" (ibid., 4; emphasis added). We emphasize "conceptualized" to indicate that Buchanan clearly viewed this situation as a theoretical starting point that could be used to explain how institutions emerge and how politics become necessary. In "Politics as Tragedy in Several Acts" (2003), a presentation delivered in the Mancur Olson series at the University of Maryland, Buchanan described anarchy as a "benchmark" or even as a "dream," and noted that "a first principle of a 'hard' social science requires that such a dream be classified for the romance that it is" (183).

If Buchanan used words such as "ideal world," "utopia," and "romantic dream," it is because "well-ordered" anarchy's existence and functioning rest on a behavioral assumption that was precisely ideal, utopian, or romantic—namely, that human beings are "angels," a term he borrowed from Madison.[4] In *The Limits of Liberty*, he was more explicit, writing that "the anarchist utopia" is "peopled exclusively of persons who respect the minimal set of behavioral norms dictated by mutual tolerance and respect. . . . The persons who inhabit this utopia need do no other than respect their fellows, itself a minimal behavioral limit, at least on its face" (Buchanan 1975a, 2–3). As he wrote in other essays, in that case, individuals are quite close to being angels: they do not act out of "narrow self-interest." Thus, well-ordered anarchy, if it ever existed, was based on a moral rule and, to be more precise, on what he described as Kantian ethics—that is, as an ethic in which individuals act out of "mutual self-respect" (Buchanan 1965, 46). In effect, even if Buchanan did not explicitly refer to Kant when he described anarchy, this is exactly how he defined Kantian ethics elsewhere—that is, as an ethic in which individuals act out of "mutual self-respect" (ibid., 6). In other words, one may conclude that to Buchanan, well-ordered anarchy is possible if individuals follow a Kantian version of ethics.

One must also add—and this is important—that this well-ordered anarchy is a situation in which individuals do interact with each other and develop a social life. Buchanan never viewed anarchy as a world of Robinson Crusoes. To him, independent individuals "separately and individually existent would not long survive." A lasting society, even an anarchical one, involves a certain amount of socialization. Indeed, if human beings want to do more than survive, and if they want to improve their situation, to live better (more flourishing) lives and become wealthy, they need to interact with others: "The production of value in any quantity that remotely approaches that which we observe requires our participation in a network of specialization and exchange that includes persons far beyond our kin or ken" (Buchanan 2003, 183). This is possible under well-ordered anarchy because individuals follow moral rules and respect each other.

"Well-ordered" forms of anarchy are, unfortunately, not viable. They remain an ideal, an exception, and a benchmark. In its normal—that is, nonconceptualized, nonidealized, nonutopian—form, anarchy is disordered and conflictual, a situation in which life is "poor, nasty, brutish, and short," as Buchanan wrote, using Hobbes's words. And the reason is straightforward: human beings are *not* angels. From this perspective, one should not forget that Buchanan frequently referred to and quoted Dennis Robertson on "What Does the Economist Economize?" (Robertson 1956, 148; also quoted in Buchanan and Tullock [1962] 1999, 28), which is "love." For him, it is preferable to assume knavery rather than civic virtue and to build institutions for knaves.

The consequence is that we cannot assume that they follow moral rules—namely, Kantian ethics.[5] On the contrary, they are narrowly self-interested. There might be a certain confusion here about ethics, since for Buchanan, individuals behave ethically, follow moral rules, and behave as angels, but only on certain conditions or in certain circumstances. To Buchanan, it seems that ethics was a norm of behavior that individuals could choose to follow (or not). When they choose to behave ethically, then, anarchy is well ordered. When they choose not to follow these ethical norms, chaos sets in. Then it also becomes necessary to move out of chaos. Since, obviously, such a move will generate a surplus, there are gains to be made by moving out of a chaotic situation. As a consequence, politics and political institutions are necessary. Such a move out of anarchy—the "leap" from a chaotic, disordered, or Hobbesian anarchy to a civil society—"is accomplished only through the instantiation of political authority" (Buchanan 2003, 183). Alternatively, he wrote, "I am not suggesting that politics, or political authority, destroys value. Indeed quite the opposite; the marginal product of politics is the gargantuan differential between the miserably small value of life in Hobbesian anarchy and that which we enjoy under almost any operative politics. . . . The political game is massively positive sum" (ibid., 182).

A state of disordered anarchy shows those involved to be incapable of well-ordered anarchy, and knowing that, one also knows that only the imposition of political society can escape the Hobbesian jungle. Hence, "Politics is necessary because of our nature as human beings—a nature that prevents us behaving as we could ideally behave without violation of any physical law" (Buchanan 2003, 182).

Hence, this is precisely why institutions have to be designed with the assumption that human beings are not angels. Or, in other words, we need to find that set of institutions that does not require us to "love one another" for our system to produce social cooperation under the division of labor. This is also precisely why Buchanan makes use of the homo economicus assumption to build in the worst-case institutional robustness.

Now that it appears that politics is necessary, the next question relates to determining the range of politics, as well as the nature and forms of politics and of the institutions for collective action. The answer to the question also depends on ethics.

THE RANGE OF POLITICS IN THE CIVIL SOCIETY: MORALS, ONCE AGAIN

Once society has become a political society—that is, once political institutions have been established—many questions have to be raised about the nature of these institutions and their range—that is, the size and scope of the government. The range of politics clearly depends on the possibility of having situations of well-ordered anarchy within civil society. Then, in those situations, governments have no role to play. And Buchanan did believe that "many aspects of social intercourse are organized anarchistically" (1975a, 118). By contrast, in all the situations in which individuals—left to themselves—are not able to coordinate peacefully, governments and political institutions are necessary. Now, if one recalls that a well-ordered anarchy depends on the fact that individuals follow ethical rules, then it follows that the range of politics or the size and scope of government depend also on ethics.

How so? Let us start with the situations where individuals do not acknowledge the interdependencies that connect them to others. To be clear, this does not mean that individuals *are* independent—only that they have the impression that they are independent from others. Buchanan characterized these situations by the fact that individuals are unconscious of the secondary repercussions of their act of choice that serves to alter the allocation of economic resources. The individual tends to act as if all the social variables are determined outside his own behavior, which, in this subjective sense, is nonparticipating and therefore nonsocial (Buchanan 1954, 336).

It is an "unconsciousness" that leads individuals to behave nonstrategically. They take as a given that they cannot influence others' behavior, and therefore they do not adapt to what others do. They simply treat others as "objects" that are part of their choice environment or part of nature—or as constraints or "means" (Buchanan 1965). As a corollary, individuals do not take into account the positive or negative consequences of their actions on others. They do not express concern for or antipathy toward others. In terms of morals or ethics, this means that individuals behave *nonethically* or *nonmorally*. But that does not mean that individuals behave *unethically* or *immorally*. Independence regarding others is *not* immoral or unethical. It should be regarded as nonmoral or nonethical.

The distinction proves to be crucial. The upshot is that nonethical or nonmoral behavior is not necessarily problematic or inefficient, and hence it must not be viewed as antisocial and must not be repressed. The most obvious illustration of legitimate nonethical behavior is the kind of behavior individuals adopt in competitive markets: each buyer and each seller treats others as given, and this is certainly the most efficient way to behave. From this perspective, such behavior is nonethical but not unethical. In markets, individuals can behave without taking care of others; their interdependencies are perfectly internalized, reflected in the price of the goods that individuals exchange, and markets function efficiently. There is no need for political institutions—actually, one can even say that markets perform political functions.

By contrast, one must envisage the case when individuals are unconscious of their interdependencies but nonetheless exhibit concern for others. They choose to help others—to do "good"—but forget that their behavior affects others and forget that their benevolence will have consequences for the people they help. To Buchanan, those consequences are likely to be negative, as he explained in "The Samaritan's Dilemma" (1975b). In other words, charity is not always socially efficient. Buchanan said that individuals neglecting interdependencies within certain institutional forms are ethically irresponsible. It is a form of unethical or immoral behavior. In this case, political institutions are required.

Let us turn now to the case where individuals acknowledge interdependencies with others. In that case, each individual "is fully conscious of his participation in social decision-making" (Buchanan 1954, 336). Two subcases can be envisaged. First, although conscious of interdependencies, individuals do not take the effects of their actions on others into account. In that subcase, they do behave unethically or immorally. Political institutions are therefore required. By contrast, and this is the second subcase, individuals may take into account the effect of their behavior onto others in their private calculus. Individuals then behave, to use Buchanan's words, *strategically*, in that they adapt their behavior to the behavior of others. And they also behave *ethically* or *morally*, or act out of Kantian ethics. Hence, if individuals are ethically responsible, then the state can be minimized because there is no need for "political authorities." Indeed, there is no need for politics if individuals follow a moral rule, a sort of Kantian imperative.

Hence, to conclude, we are left with the following options: first, political institutions are required when individuals behave unethically. Second, there is no need for political institutions if individuals behave ethically or morally. Third, there are circumstances in which nonethical or nonmoral behaviors are not problematic (in the market, for instance). Morals determine the range of politics.

MORAL COMMUNITY, MORAL ORDER, AND MORAL ANARCHY

The options at which we arrived in the preceding section give birth to a triptych: moral community, moral order, and moral anarchy, which Buchanan discussed in various essays he wrote for lectures at the beginning of the 1980s.

Moral anarchy is a setting in which "each person treats other persons exclusively as means to further his own ends or objectives" (Buchanan 1981, 3), and this means that "it is a setting within which persons violate the basic Kantian moral precept that human beings are to be treated only as ends and not as means" (Buchanan [1981] 2001, 190). More precisely, moral anarchy corresponds to situations in which individuals should exhibit a certain level of morality or ethics—that is, following a Kantian rule of ethics and being ethically responsible—but do not. According to our classification, individuals adopt unethical behaviors. In other words, moral anarchists are those individuals whom economists call free riders and whom Buchanan called "parasites" in the 1970s—in "The Samaritan's Dilemma" and in other writings as well. In a situation of moral anarchy, "without the coercive power of the sovereign, life for persons is 'poore, nasty, brutish, and short,' to employ the language of Thomas Hobbes" (Buchanan 1981, 4). And he added, "order may be purchased at the price of a coercive state. Repressive government may emerge as a necessary condition in a society with many moral anarchists," and the "need for governance (for rule) is maximal" (ibid.).

By comparison, moral communities and moral orders are two settings in which the "need for governance" will be minimized because individuals do take the consequences of their actions into account. In both settings, individuals behave morally and ethically. But there is an important difference between them. A moral community implies a form of identification with the collectivity or with the group. Individuals do not exist as autonomous entities but as group members only and through the values they share with others. One implication is that local communities may well work without any explicit rules. But since individuals are first and foremost group members, interactions between individuals from different groups will likely be conflictual. We have the same kind of problem as in a moral anarchy, except that conflicts take place between groups. Another implication is that if we consider a large moral community—the size of a nation, for instance—governments may justify decisions and measures in reference to community membership, and individuals will accept them because they identify themselves with the community. Despite the existence of moral links among the individuals, political institutions may be strong and coercive.

This cannot happen in a moral order. In such a setting, there exists no "sense of identification with a collectivity" (Buchanan 1981, 2) or, in other words, "no necessary sense of belonging to a community or collectivity" (ibid., 4). Individual autonomy is preserved. Each person "treats other persons with moral indifference, but at the same time respects their equal freedoms with his own" (ibid., 2)—that is, with "mutual respect and tolerance" (ibid., 4). Thus, in a moral order, "individuals are related, one to another, only by the set of minimal abstract rules which they mutually acknowledge to provide general benefits" (ibid., 10). There is no need for a large and coercive set of political institutions. In a moral order, "the need for explicit governance is minimized" (ibid., 4), and the scope of governance is limited to "the provision of protective services that define the boundaries of the minimal state" (Buchanan 2003, 183). It is the most ideal form of social organization.

MORALS AND POLITICAL BEHAVIORS: POLITICS WITHOUT ROMANCE

There remains a last and crucial point to be examined to complete our presentation of the link between morals and politics: the behavior of politicians. Here we have the same kind of issue as the one discussed in the previous sections. Politicians are not different from other human beings. There is no reason to adopt specific behavioral assumptions for them—specifically, to assume that they are benevolent or acting out of concern for the public, if the same assumption is not made regarding the rest of the population. Buchanan sharply criticized this "rather naïve" (Buchanan 1962, 25) "assumption of behavioral dichotomy" (24), according to which "individuals respond to different motives when they participate in market and in political activity" (23).

On the contrary, one must assume "behavioral consistency" (Buchanan 1962, 24). Therefore, in terms of political institutions, the implication is straightforward: either one assumes that *all* individuals are angels—and then, as we have seen earlier, there is no need for political institutions—or one assumes that no individuals are angels, and therefore we need institutions, but we also need to take into account that those politicians are not angels. Politicians can even be moral anarchists. Hence, if it is necessary to move out of disordered and chaotic anarchies—to create a surplus for all the individuals—one must not forget that politicians are no angels. It is necessary to control their behavior. Decidedly, rules must be filtered by an analysis of knavery, both the arrogant and opportunistic varieties.

Having realized that politicians could adopt this kind of behavior also has consequences in terms of what political economy should be. A robust theory of political economy thus challenges both the assumption of omniscience and benevolence of politicians. In "Politics without Romance," Buchanan argues that "it seems to be nothing more than simple and obvious wisdom to compare social institutions as they might exist rather than compare romantic models of how such institutions might be hoped to operate" (Buchanan 1979).

MORALITY AND GENERALIZED INCREASING RETURNS

Following up on the work of Allyn Young (1928) and Knight (1944), Buchanan sought to explain economic progress as a consequence of the adoption of certain moral rules and the institutional environment that these moral and ethical rules help constitute and enforce. In making this argument, Young, Knight, and then Buchanan were offering a slight twist on Adam Smith's famous dictum that "The Division of Labour Is Limited by the Extent of the Market." As Young put it in his aptly titled "Increasing Returns and Economic Progress," "That theorem, I have always thought, is one of the most illuminating and fruitful generalizations which can be found anywhere in the whole literature of economics" (Young 1928, 529). Buchanan clearly perceived the importance of Young's article. As he notes in the "introductory summary" of his and Yoon's book entitled *The Return to Increasing Returns*, "Young explicitly revived Adam Smith's central proposition on the division of labor, and he sketched out the relationship between economic progress and the presence of economy wide increasing returns" (Buchanan and Yoon 1994, 7).

Unfortunately, Buchanan noted, because of the Great Depression and because of "the dominating influence of John Maynard Keynes" (Buchanan and Yoon 1994, 7), increasing returns disappeared from the economists' agenda. When they came back, in particular with the work of George Stigler (1951), the focus was put on resolving the technical difficulties of incorporating Smith's famous dictum into models of static *equilibrium*. The definition and demonstration of the existence of a static competitive equilibrium that became crucial with general equilibrium analyses after World War II played an important role in this history. Not only did these analyses implicitly assume that institutions are fixed and given, but they also assumed constant returns to scale—a "vulnerable assumption in the model of competitive adjustment" (Buchanan and Yoon 1994, 119).

What Buchanan suggested in his interpretation of Smith's theorem and his claim that we need to return to increasing returns is that, instead of focusing on static allocative efficiency, economists should focus on the *process* that generates economic progress. Without ignoring the technical aspects of refinements in the division of labor, Buchanan—but also before him Young, Knight, and a few others (see Buchanan and Yoon 1994, 9–11)—sought to draw analytical attention to *generalized* increasing returns and to link them with adopting particular institutions of governance.

Political economists, Buchanan argued, must stress the technical principles of economics that enable them to assess how *alternative institutional arrangements* either promote or hinder productive specialization and peaceful social cooperation among diverse peoples. To accomplish this, the political economist engages in two levels of analysis: the rule level of analysis and the analysis of economic interaction within the rules. The Stiglerian reading of Smith's famous dictum makes sense when the analysis takes the institutional framework as given. Buchanan's reading draws our attention to how changes in that institutional framework itself have consequences for economic performance. In short, any narrative of economic performance through time should recognize that there are both increasing returns to refinements in specialization and generalized increasing returns to institutions that give greater scope for productive specialization and social cooperation.

Then, economic progress emerges from extending the limits of market exchange. There exists a positive feedback loop between practices, institutions, and progress that undergirds Adam Smith's virtuous cycle in the historical movement from a subsistence economy to an exchange economy. And, according to Buchanan, this virtuous circle is infinite: "I want to argue in support of the basic principle that all members of the inclusive production-exchange nexus tend to secure gains as the effective size of this nexus expands and that these gains are inexhaustible. That is to say, increases in specialization are always possible as markets are extended, producing in turn increases in economic well-being for participants" (Buchanan 1994, 119). In other words, in contrast to what neoclassical economists assume, returns to scale are not constant. They are increasing. Hence, the important question to ask is "how can potential advantages of increasing returns be secured?" (Buchanan 1991, 167).

It could be the task of an omniscient central planner to identify the industry or industries in which such increasing returns originate. But such a person does not exist. The solution then lies elsewhere: in institutions and institutional change? Partly. Buchanan is not totally convinced that institutions may help to yield generalized increasing returns, to harness the creative talent and skills of individuals previously excluded from an extended market order. They certainly can "remove the perverse incentives" (Buchanan and Yoon 1994, 125) to work less. For instance, Buchanan gave the example of tax policy: an individual "who chooses to forgo income for leisure should be required to pay *more*, not less, in taxes" (1994, 125–26), as should be a landowner "who withdraws land from productive use to a purely private use" (126). Certainly, the protection of private property is important, but it should not be protected at all costs. Property rights should not be *too* strong (see also Yoon 2017).

To him, the genuine and main solution to allow increasing returns consists in the "instillation of a work ethic" (Buchanan 1991, 170) or what he also called a "strong work ethic" (Buchanan 1994, 5).[6] A work ethic is an ethic that acknowledges that the well-being of an individual depends on how much other individuals work: "The individual's choice to work more generates external benefits to others; the individual's choice to work less generates harms to others" (ibid., 25). Hence, choosing to work or to "loaf," to use Buchanan's word, is not neutral. Loafing, leisure, or idleness have a social cost. Without such a strong work ethic, it would be difficult, according to Buchanan, to internalize the negative external effects that leisure or idleness would have on others—"it would be extremely difficult, if not impossible to internalize or correct for resource use externalities by ordinary or political adjustments . . . such internalization that exists enters the calculus of choice makers by way of ethical constraints" (ibid., 125). Buchanan attributed the evolution of our societies to such a work ethic. So, once again, morals and ethics trump politics and institutions: without such a work ethic, no institution would be able to control individuals' tendency to loaf or to supply work in too limited a quantity.

NOTES

1. Which is another way of putting proposition 7 (economics is a discipline aimed at explaining the principle of spontaneous order).
2. A combination of propositions 3 (economics is about exchange), 4 (economics is about individuals), 5 (economics is about a "game" played within rules), and 6 (economics cannot be studied outside of politics).
3. A combination of propositions 1 (economics is a "philosophical" science) and 8 (economics is elementary).
4. In "Politics as Tragedy in Several Acts," Buchanan wrote, "James Madison said that if men were angels, no governments, no politics would be necessary" (Buchanan 2003, 181).
5. In this section, we discuss ethics or morals as the rules that individuals follow in their interactions with others. We use the terms "moral" and "ethics" as synonyms. Even if there are differences between them, we do not think that these differences matter for our discussion of Buchanan's views. Buchanan did not seem to distinguish between them. In addition, he equated ethics with Kantian ethics—or his own understanding of Kantian ethics. In other words, we claim that, to Buchanan, moral people, defined as people following Kantian ethics, are people who follow ethical rules (see Buchanan 1965).
6. This work ethic is not totally different from the Kantian ethics we were referring to earlier. Indeed, it consists in spontaneously internalizing the external effects that one's choice has on others: that is, to acknowledge the interdependencies that exist with others and to take them into account.

REFERENCES

Buchanan, J. M. 1954. "Individual Choice in Voting and the Market." *Journal of Political Economy* 62(4): 334–43.

———. 1962. "Politics, Policy, and the Pigovian Margins." *Economica* 29(113): 17–28.

———. 1965. "Ethical Rules, Expected Values, and Large Numbers." *Ethics* 76(1): 1–13.

———. 1975a. *The Limits of Liberty: Between Anarchy and Leviathan*. Chicago: University of Chicago Press.

———. 1975b. "The Samaritan's Dilemma." In E. Phelps (ed.), *Altruism, Morality, and Economic Theory*, 71–86. New York: Russell Sage Foundation.

———. 1979. *What Should Economists Do?* Indianapolis, IN: Liberty Fund.

———. 1981. *Moral Community, Moral Order, or Moral Anarchy*. Colorado Springs: Colorado College.

———. [1981] 2001. "Moral Community, Moral Order, or Moral Anarchy." In J. M. Buchanan, *The Collected Works of James Buchanan*, vol. 17: *Moral Science and Moral Order*. Indianapolis, IN: Liberty Fund.

———. 1991. *The Economics and Ethics of Constitutional Order*. Ann Arbor: University of Michigan Press.

———. 1994. *Ethics and Economics Progress*. Norman: University of Oklahoma Press.

———. 2003. "Politics as Tragedy in Several Acts." *Economics & Politics* 15(2): 181–91.

Buchanan, J. M., and G. Tullock. [1962] 1999. *The Calculus of Consent*. Indianapolis, IN: Liberty Fund.

Buchanan, J. M., and Y. J. Yoon. 1994. *The Return to Increasing Returns*. Ann Arbor: University of Michigan Press.

Knight, F. H. 1944. "Diminishing Returns from Investment." *Journal of Political Economy* 52(1): 26–47.

Robertson, D. H. 1956. "What Does the Economist Economize?" In *Economic Commentaries*, 148. London: Staples.

Stigler, G. J. 1951. "The Division of Labor Is Limited by the Extent of the Market." *Journal of Political Economy* 59(3): 185–93.

Yoon, Y. J. 2017. "Buchanan on Increasing Returns and Anticommons." *Constitutional Political Economy* 28(3): 270–85.

Young, A. A. 1928. "Increasing Returns and Economic Progress." *Economic Journal* 38(152): 527–42.

3.1
A Governable Country?

JAMES M. BUCHANAN

I.

I shall discuss *governability* by reference to three basic concepts: (1) *moral community*, (2) *moral order*, and (3) *moral anarchy*. Any society may be described empirically by the mix among these three elements. A society is made viable by some combination of *moral community* and *moral order*; its viability is reduced by the extent to which *moral anarchy* exists. The mix among these three elements will, therefore, indirectly determine both the *need for governance* and the *difficulty in governing*.

Before developing my central argument, however, I want to enter a disclaimer. I am reluctant to discuss the term *governability*, because my dictionary defines "govern" as "to control, direct, or rule." As a libertarian individualist, I react negatively to the whole notion of *governance*. Governing is an activity to be minimized, not maximized, and in my personal evaluation, the best society is that which requires least governance. The society that must be ruled is already, to an extent, past the limits of my own description of a desirable social order. My own Utopia is a society of free individuals who interact with each

Revised draft dated January 1981, prepared for presentation at the Suntory Foundation Symposium, "Japan Speaks," March 20–21, 1981, Osaka, Japan.

other within an established and understood legal framework. Such a society requires no "ruler," it is a society that is well ordered but not "well governed."

I shall now define the three concepts. A *moral community* exists among a set of persons to the extent that the individual members of the group identify with the collective unit, the community, rather than conceive themselves to be independent, isolated individuals. In one sense, moral community always exists; no person is totally autonomous. Each person will to some extent identify with some moral community (or communities) whether this be with the small family, the extended family, clan, or tribe, the set of locational, ethnic, or religious cohorts, the trade union, the business firm, the social class, or, finally, with the nation-state. Most persons will identify simultaneously and with differing degrees of loyalty with several moral communities, and the weights assigned to these will, of course, differ from person to person. I suggest, however, that it may be possible to characterize different societies in terms of the importance of *moral community* as an element of social cohesion among persons within those societies. It is possible to classify societies as more or less *communitarian*, as less or more *individualistic*.

A *moral order* exists in a social group when participants treat each other as *moral reciprocals* but do so without any sense of shared loyalty to a group. Each person treats other persons with moral indifference but at the same time respects their equal freedoms with his own. *Mutual respect*, which is an alternative way of stating the conception, does not require *moral community* in any sense of identification with a collectivity. Each person treats other persons as autonomous individuals, independently of possible group classification. In a *moral order*, it is possible for a person to deal with other persons who are *not* members of his own moral community if both persons have agreed implicitly or explicitly to abide by the behavioral precepts required for effective *moral order*. The emergence of the abstract rules of behavior describing moral order historically had the effect of expanding dramatically the range of interpersonal dealings. It is not necessary that both parties to a contract belong to the same moral community. There is no need that trading partners claim membership in the same kinship group. Under the rules of moral order, it is conceptually possible for a genuinely autonomous individual to remain a viable entity. I suggest that it may also be possible to characterize different societies in terms of the extent that the rules of *moral order* describe the observed relationships among the persons within each society. The rules of moral order may either supplement the sense of moral community as a source of social cohesion where the latter exists or substitute for a moral community where it does not exist.

Moral anarchy exists in a society (if it can remain a society) when individuals do not consider other persons to be within their moral communities and do not voluntarily accept the minimal requirements for moral order. In *moral anarchy*, each person treats other persons as *means* to further his own ends. He does not consider other persons to be his fellows (his brothers) in a community of shared purpose (as in moral community) or to be deserving of reciprocal mutual respect as autonomous individuals (as in moral order). In a real sense, moral anarchy negates both moral community and moral order. I suggest that it may also be possible to classify different societies by the extent to which *moral anarchy* describes the attitudes and the behavior of its members, one to another.

I can illustrate the usefulness of the three basic concepts in discussing the governability of a society by taking extreme examples. And allow me to change the order of discussion from that used in the earlier definitional discussion.

In a setting where many persons behave as *moral anarchists*, the *need for governance (for rule) is maximal.* Without the coercive power of the sovereign, life for persons is "poore, nasty, brutish, and short," to employ the language of Thomas Hobbes. Men who neither feel a sense of community with others nor respect others as individuals must be *ruled*, and individuals will sacrifice their liberties to the sovereign government that can effectively insure order and personal security. But those persons who act on behalf of the sovereign government may also be moral anarchists in a personal sense. Order may be purchased at the price of a coercive state. *Repressive government may emerge as a necessary condition in a society with many moral anarchists.*

In sharp contrast, now consider a setting where persons adhere to the precepts and behavioral rules of a *moral order*. Each individual treats other persons as deserving of mutual respect and tolerance, even though there is no necessary sense of belonging to a community or collectivity. In this setting, the *need for explicit governance is minimized.* Correspondingly, the liberties for individuals are *maximized*. Indeed, in the extreme case, where literally all persons behave as indicated, *there would need to be no government at all.* In a more plausibly realistic setting, where most but not all persons are expected to behave by the precepts and behavioral rules of moral order, government can be restricted to a *minimal state or protective state role.* Government may protect personal and property rights and enforce contracts among persons, but it need do no more. In one sense, government need not "govern," as such.

It is much more difficult to discuss my third concept, *moral community*, in relationship to the need for governance. The difficulty arises because of the many possible moral communities that may be required to describe the interrelationships among individuals in a society. At one limit, if all persons identify with the moral community that is coincident in membership with the inclusive political unit, the nation-state, the *difficulty* of governing is *minimized.* In this setting, all persons would act as if they share the same objectives, as members of the national collectivity, including those persons who act on behalf of government. Vis-à-vis other nations, this model of society might be a source of nationalistic adventure. But internally, governance is easy. Persons "obey" the sovereign state because they feel part of the larger unit; conversely, the sovereign also behaves as persons would have it behave. Persons, rulers or ruled, do not behave toward each other as separate interacting individuals. They do not really think themselves to be autonomous units.

At the other limit, there may be no sense of moral community over the membership of the inclusive political unit, the state, while at the same time persons may express and act upon loyalties to collective units classified in differing ways. Persons may identify with collectives (ethnic, racial, religious, regional, occupational, employment, class, etc.) while sensing no identification at all with the national unit. This society will, like that which contains only moral anarchists, require *rule* or *governance* by a coercive sovereign. The separate moral communities or collectivities may, in terms of their relations with each other, be "moral anarchists." The Hobbesian war of each against all may apply to the separate collectivities in this case rather than to individual persons.

In effect, moral community as a concept can satisfactorily be discussed only in two-dimensional terms. The first dimension involves the general *individualism-communitarianism* spectrum, discussed initially. The second dimension involves what we may call the *nationalized-localized* spectrum, described in the preceding two examples. A simple two-dimensional diagram (figure 3.1.1) will be helpful here.

A society located at Point 1 on figure 3.1.1 is largely individualistic, with little sense of moral community but with what there is limited to localized groupings (perhaps family or firm ties). A society located at Point 2 would be, in contrast, largely communitarian but also with the loyalties of persons largely limited to localized collectivities and with little or no sense of national community. A society at Point 3 would remain largely *individualistic,* like that at Point 1, but in this society there does exist some sense of national community. At Point 4, the society is largely *communitarian* but, also, the personal loyalties are largely concentrated on the national collectively; there is little sense of localized community.

Figure 3.1.1.

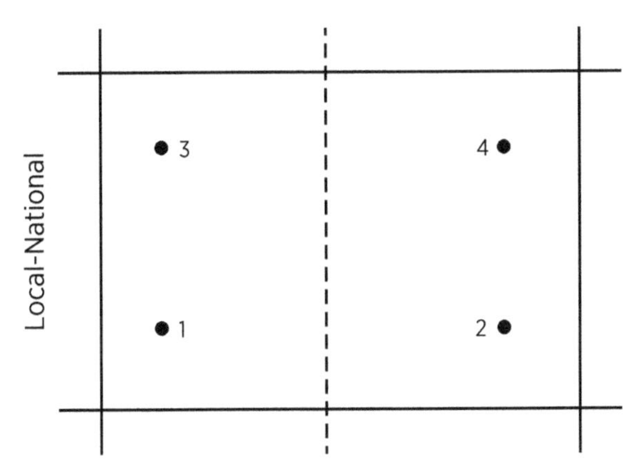

If we restrict analysis to the more basic concept, *moral community*, without reference to the national-local dimension, we can classify societies along the left-right dimension of figure 3.1.1 only. Any society classified to fall on the right side of the matrix would exhibit moral community as a relatively predominant characteristic.

Let me now return to further consideration of the differences between a society that exhibits a strong sense of *moral community* and that described as a *moral order*, differences that may be relevant for governability. And let me restrict analysis to the moral community that is *national* in scope rather than *localized*. For most persons, there is a sense of national community that is shared. As noted earlier, minimal governance as such is required in either one of these settings. In the moral community, persons share national objectives and need not be directed by the state. In the moral order, persons further their own objectives within a legal framework that requires no active interference by government. As we depart from idealizations of these two models, however, and as we allow for a potential threat of moral anarchy in each case, important differences arise. The necessary conditions required for the maintenance of tolerably effective social order are considerably more constrained in *moral order* than in *moral community*. The difference to be emphasized here lies in that between the *individualistic* basis of any effective *moral order* and the nonindividualistic or *collectivist* basis of any effective *moral community*. In the former, individuals are bound together in adherence to a set of abstract rules or laws, which are fundamentally *impersonal*, and which are grounded in the general recognition of other persons as cooperating "moral equals." The moral requirements placed on persons in such an order are minimal; the individual need not "feel" himself to be part of some inclusive collectivity. He need not exhibit feelings of benevolence or altruism toward any other persons, whether these be his neighbors or strangers. On the other hand, if he is expected to abide by the minimal behavioral precepts for such an order, to refrain from lapsing into the role of moral anarchist, he must think that the framework rules of the legal order are "fair" in the sense that all persons must be subjected to the *same rules*.

In an effective moral order, a government that discriminates among persons in treatment, that violates elementary precepts for "*fairness*" in dealing with individuals, will immediately face resentment and must ultimately expect rebellion. This predicted reaction follows from the very autonomy of individuals; each person remains a person and as such can claim entitlement to uniform treatment by those who administer the laws. There exists no overriding "community interest" within which individual interests are subsumed.

Let me contrast this setting with one properly described as *moral community* coincident with the national political unit. Here government may discriminate among persons without generating negative feedbacks in citizen discontent provided only that the discrimination may be justified or explained in terms of the *wider interest of the national community*, an interest that exists by definition of community as such. Since the individual person in such a setting thinks of himself as a member of the community rather than as an individual, he will more readily acquiesce in what would seem overtly "unfair" treatment in a moral order. In a setting best described as moral community, therefore, the whole set of issues involving "justice" or "fairness" as among separate persons, as such, really does not arise. It follows that government in a society described by national moral community will possess a *wider range of options* in taking any action than government under a comparable moral order.

The range and scope for governmental action is more limited in a society that locates its source of cohesion largely in *moral order* rather than *moral community*. At the same time, however, *such a society can allow for much greater flexibility and change in the attitudes and behavior of its individual members*. As noted, in an effective moral order, individuals need not share common purposes; they need only respect each other as individuals. From this it follows that individual attitudes and behavior may be widely varying, and may accordingly change widely, within the minimal requirements for orderly interpersonal dealings. In a very meaningful sense, individuals are *free* to select their own purposes in such a setting.

By contrast, consider the society that locates its source of social cohesion largely in a sense of *moral community* among its members rather than adherence to the behavioral precepts of *moral order*. This society is necessarily more vulnerable to shifts in the attitude and behavior patterns of persons that might reflect departures from the shared purposes of the community. Persons are tied one to another by their common identification with the collective, with the shared sense of nationhood, race, class, or ideology. The loss of this identification may involve an unavoidable plunge into *moral anarchy.* In the *moral order*, by comparison, individuals are related one to another only by the set of minimal abstract rules that they mutually acknowledge to provide general benefits.

II.

The first part of my discussion has been explicitly confined to a generalized analysis of the three basic concepts that may be used to describe social interaction: moral community, moral order, and moral anarchy. Any historically observed society will embody elements of each one of these concepts. Nonetheless, the mix may vary significantly among separate societies, and these differences may be important. In this second part of my discussion, I propose to apply the analysis to real-world societies. I shall try, first, to discuss my own country, the United States, in terms of these concepts. I do this not so much to analyze the United States as such, but rather to provide a basis for contrast and comparison with Japan. I shall then advance some suggestions about the application of my analysis to modern Japan.

In the United States of the 1980s, there is very little *moral community* that extends to the limits of the inclusive national unit, the nation-state, that embodies the central instrument of government. Individuals relate to and identify with communities larger than themselves (although clearly less so than the Japanese), but these communities tend to be of subnational sizes, both geographically and numerically. The national government, therefore, is unable to call upon or to exploit a sense of genuine "national interest" or "national purpose." Further, and importantly, those persons who themselves serve as "governors" possess little "national interest." Instead, these persons, like their cohorts who are outside government, identify with various subnational groupings if, indeed, they adhere to moral community at all in any relevant way.

By historical tradition, however, citizens of the United States have adhered behaviorally to the precepts of a *moral order*. There is a tradition of respect for adherence to the rule of law, for general rules, for promise keeping, for honesty in trading even of the most complex types. Voluntary adherence to rules laid down by government remains widespread, including voluntary payment of income taxes. With relatively few exceptions, government has not needed to become repressive.

For several decades, however, the moral order has been in the process of erosion. Larger and larger numbers of persons are becoming *moral anarchists* in that they are losing the sense of mutual respect for each other and the sense of voluntary adherence to generalizable rules and codes of conduct. To the extent that this erosion continues and accelerates, the *need for governance* must increase. If the social order is to remain viable, the potential excesses of the increasing number of moral anarchists must be *coercively constrained*. (The problem is exemplified in the observed increases in criminal activity, which must, with some time lag, result in more governmental coercion on all persons.) The voluntary limits on behavior must be replaced by governmentally imposed repression. As I have written elsewhere, if persons will not voluntarily abide by rules, they must themselves be "ruled."

Government itself is partially responsible for the erosion of the traditional moral order in America. As the national government has sought to take on a more comprehensive role, one that is necessarily coincident with the alleged or putative interest of the "national community," it has been unable to find moral support in any communitarian sense. "Governors" have exploited political office to advance their own individualized or group interests under the guise of a "national purpose" that does not exist. As this process has continued and accelerated, citizens have necessarily become more disillusioned with government and more attracted to the position of moral anarchy. Confronted with a government that legislates rules that command little or no respect, individuals quite naturally come to question long-standing rules that have traditionally commanded voluntary adherence. Restoration of moral order, or even a stop to the erosion process, requires a rollback of government, while at the same time the growth in moral anarchy suggests, for the reason noted earlier, an expanded governmental role in maintaining social order.

Somewhat paradoxically, as its traditional moral order erodes, the United States becomes increasingly *ungovernable* even while the share of resources commanded politically continues to increase and as governmental intrusion into the lives of ordinary citizens expands. There seems little or no prospect for a genuine emergence of a national sense of *moral community* that will channel individual behavior toward a set of shared or common purposes.

Let me now turn to Japan, with, of course, the necessary provision that my own knowledge about and "feel for" the society is limited in the extreme. Nonetheless, my suggestions may prove provocative for those who want to apply the three concepts to their own country. My purpose is to provide a conceptual framework for thinking about *governance* and *governability*.

There seems to be widespread agreement, both among the Japanese themselves and external observers, that there is a relatively strong identification of persons with *moral communities* beyond themselves, or, in my terminology, that Japan is less individualistic and more communitarian than the United States or Western Europe. The most important moral community for the individual Japanese may be local rather than national, but nonetheless, for racial, historical, and other reasons, there remains a relevant *national moral community*. As I have noted, this relationship between the individual and the national community, represented by government, surely makes governing easier, and, importantly, it allows government greater freedom in the formulation and administration of laws and rules than would be the case in a society more dependent on *moral order*. However, and for reasons already discussed in part I, the continuing stability of the society may remain critically dependent on the maintenance of the sense of national moral community. From this it follows that Japan may possibly be vulnerable to shifts in attitudes and behavior patterns on the part of individuals and groups who lose their identification with the nation. If such an identification is lost, such individuals and members of such groups may well lapse into positions of moral anarchists.

In this scenario, there might be no apparent means of recapturing national moral community short of possible international adventure. The question that emerges is whether or not a nation like the Japanese, faced with a possible erosion in their shared sense of moral community, can adopt essentially *Western* notions of *moral order* before moral anarchy assumes predominant importance and generates a breakdown in social cohesion. Can the Japanese citizen, circa 2000 or 2050, who may have lost his identity with the nation as a community, as a moral entity that commands his loyalty and respect, can he come to understand, appreciate, and live by the behavioral precepts of *moral order*, precepts that require him to grant fellow citizens mutual respect as moral equivalents and that give him criteria for evaluating governmental rules in some personal and noncommunitarian sense? Can Japanese governments, in their own right, keep within the limits of power that will allow a functioning *moral order* to evolve, and, further, can Japanese governments hold this stance as Western nations themselves are observed to sink further into the collectively dominated moral anarchy that now seems their fate?

In his recent writings, Professor F. A. Hayek has stressed that modern man's behavioral instincts are those that characterize what I have called moral community and that evolved over the ages in essentially tribal settings. He suggests that Western man very slowly evolved patterns of adherence to abstract rules that *he does not understand* and that really run counter to his instinctual proclivities (Hayek 1979). As applied to the Japanese setting, as I have described it here, one implication of Hayek's diagnosis would be that the Japanese people cannot explicitly replace *moral community* by *moral order*. For myself, I am much less *evolutionist* and much more *constructivist* than Professor Hayek. I should not exclude the possibility that the Japanese will come to accept explicitly chosen limits on individual behavior characteristic of moral order even in a setting of declining national moral community.

Western governments have failed to recognize that the moral order, described by voluntary adherence to these abstract rules of law, carries implications for the reach of governance. These governments have, accordingly, grown far beyond those limits that might sustain effective moral order, while at the same time they have failed to generate the effective moral community that might in turn justify or legitimate such extended governance. Indeed, the moral anarchists have used the instruments of governance to subvert both moral community and moral order as necessary to advance their own ends.

To exploit the limited sense of moral community as it empirically exists in Western nations would require that governments give up powers now possessed and, most importantly, that effective devolution and decentralization of political authority into smaller units be accomplished (Buchanan 1978).

Can we say that Japan has effectively bypassed or escaped from at least some part of the evolutionary process described by Hayek? I suggest that Japan may have been able to exploit a sense of national moral community in furtherance of modern economic potential without the slow evolution of patterns of behavior more descriptive of the moral order as it emerged in the West. This somewhat accidental historical sequence may have made Japan both *more governable* and *more productive*, especially since World War II, when economic growth came to be widely accepted as a shared national purpose. If this diagnosis-interpretation is broadly correct, Japan can sustain its momentum so long as it sustains the *moral community* among the Japanese that makes it possible. If this moral community is lost, I return [to] the questions posed earlier. I leave answers to my Japanese critics and to members of my Japanese audience.

REFERENCES

Buchanan, J. M. 1978. "Markets, States and the Extent of Morals." *American Economic Review* 68: 364–68.

Hayek, F. A. 1979. *Law, Legislation, and Liberty*. Vol. 3 of *The Political Order of a Free People*, 153–76. Chicago: University of Chicago Press.

SECTION 4

THE ORGANIZATION OF SCIENTIFIC ACTIVITY

4.0
Introduction

PETER J. BOETTKE AND ALAIN MARCIANO

Buchanan never directly wrote on the "organization of scientific activity," as Tullock did, for instance (Tullock [1966] 2004). But he wrote on education—and on how to organize education efficiently—and also recounted his own personal experience in academic entrepreneurship many times. Those works provide evidence or testimonies indicating what Buchanan thought about the organization of scientific activity. This is in particular the case of the chapter that is included in his autobiography, *Better than Plowing* (1992). Buchanan tells us his story of the years that go from 1957 to 1982. These are the years we focus upon in this section because understanding them helps us to understand how Buchanan put into practice his views on the organization of scientific activity in some of the most important places where he taught and worked: Charlottesville (University of Virginia), Blacksburg (Virginia Polytechnic Institute), and Fairfax (George Mason University).[1]

By choosing this specific period, we have also chosen to leave out of the picture what Buchanan did before 1957: his first position at the University of Tennessee, the years at Florida State University, the year he spent on a Fulbright scholarship in Italy, his stays in Cambridge and in London, and so on. This means we think that we learn more about Buchanan and the organization of scientific activities by studying what happened from 1957 to 1982 at the University of Virginia (UVA). But one must also note that Buchanan's tale is a summary and was meant to portray a broad picture. It is interesting because it provides a timeline. But some significant pieces are missing in his own narrative. Indeed, this story, Buchanan's story as he himself recounted it, does not mention some important episodes (the few months he spent at UCLA, for instance) and does not go much into certain details of other episodes. This is why we add additional articles and introductory comments that help to understand the story and his views of the "organization of scientific activity."

THEORETICAL ASSUMPTIONS ABOUT THE "ORGANIZATION" OF SCIENTIFIC ACTIVITY

What remains largely implicit in the story that Buchanan recounted—but what is certainly not surprising—is that Buchanan had an individualistic conception of scientific activities. It is perfectly consistent with his philosophical premises: everything starts with individuals, including academic research. This is stated explicitly in the article he wrote in October 1958 for the *University of Virginia Newsletter,* which aimed at presenting the Thomas Jefferson Center for Studies in Political Economy (TJC) and that he and Warren Nutter had just created: "Those studies which do come out of the Center—and we hope there will be many and important ones—are produced as a *result* of *individual* scholarly *effort*" (Buchanan 1958, 6; emphasis added). But don't be mistaken, as we are going to see, Buchanan also had a conception of academic research based on collaboration between individuals. That was crucial in the working of the TJC.

The origin of the TJC—and its scholarly mission—can be traced back to Buchanan and Warren Nutter's student days at the University of Chicago immediately following World War II. This mission can be put in a negative and in a positive way. It had two sides. From the negative perspective, the objective was "to counter the increasing technical specialization of economics and, for me, to keep the subject matter interesting when the discipline, in more orthodox hands, threatened to become boring in the extreme" (Buchanan [1961–1962] 1999, 26). Indeed, Nutter and Buchanan shared a concern that modern economics, as it was evolving after World War II, was becoming excessively formalized and accordingly hyperspecialized, with the consequence that it had "forced a separation" between philosophy, politics, and economics (Buchanan 1958, 5). Thus, according to Buchanan, very "few social scientists today have the competence or interest in studying broad issues of policy which is required for intellectual leadership" (ibid.). Economics was, to put it in other words, losing—hopefully not permanently—sight of the "grand tradition of political economy" that had characterized the discipline from Adam Smith to John Stuart Mill to Frank Knight. Hence, the mission of the TJC—put in positive terms—was to reestablish that tradition—that is, to reintegrate philosophy, politics, and economics. Buchanan summarized it as follows:

> Political economists stress the technical economic principles that one must understand in order to assess alternative arrangements for promoting peaceful cooperation and productive specialization among free men. Yet political economists go further and frankly try to bring out into the open the philosophical issues that necessarily underlie all discussions of the appropriate functions of government and all proposed economic policy measures. (Buchanan 1958, 5)

Even more, "to carry on the honorable tradition of 'political economy'" had to Buchanan a very important implication. This also implied to Buchanan the "study of what makes for a 'good society'" (Buchanan 1958, 5), a notion that Buchanan could not but associate with freedom. Thus, echoing Knight, Buchanan argued for the necessity of forthright and continuous discussion with a specific objective: "Political economists try to stimulate open and lively discussion of how a free society should be organized and preserved" (ibid.).

Then, to understand how the center should function to flourish and reach its objective, one may refer to the fact that Buchanan conceived of scientific and scholarly "exploration and discovery [as] a public good," as he wrote in "Social Choice and Freedom of Inquiry: The Internal and External Institutions for Decision-Making in Higher Education" (Buchanan 1973, 24). This means, first, that research is not the repeating of the already known but an exploration of questions yet unanswered—and oftentimes as yet even unasked. And second, it also means that it is crucial to cooperate and collaborate with other individuals to create new knowledge. To be clearer, it may be important to use an expression Buchanan applied when he worked on public goods, to have forms of collective action that combine with the individual dimension mentioned earlier. This is, once again, what he wrote when presenting the objectives of the TJC: "Research must come from the individual interests of the cooperating associates" (Buchanan 1958, 6). Thus, everything starts from individuals—an unsurprising individualist perspective—who generate a certain output by cooperating and collaborating with other scholars. There is no doubt that Buchanan believed that scientific research was a spontaneous process, starting from the bottom. Academic, scientific research cannot be constructed from the top. Or in other words, one—whoever it is—does not tell scholars what they should study. A research center should not try to "suggest or promote specific studies" (ibid.).

Thus, a university should be conceived "as a genuine 'community of scholars' characterized by an interaction system that produces spontaneous order from the private behavior of individuals and voluntary groups" (Buchanan 1973, 18).

This implies, as a necessary condition for the center to flourish, that in order to maintain the ongoing and integrated conversation across the social sciences and humanities that is at the core of political economy, scholars must be free to roam as they see fit. "Science should be organized with maximum individual freedom," Buchanan wrote (1973, 25). No one inside or outside the center—in particular at the university level—should try to "organize" scientific activity in any constructivist sense that this word could take. This means that no one, at the level of the center but also at the university level, should try to promote or suggest any specific study or approach. Within or outside the center, no one should interfere with what the members of this or any other center want to do. The university should be an ideology-free environment. Thus, a principle to promote rather than organize scientific activity was that research should be independent from any external—political or ideological—interference. The institutional infrastructure for cultivating the ongoing conversation must be established and maintained and, to whatever extent humanly possible, protected from corrupting influences. Later, Buchanan would explain that it would be necessary to introduce mechanisms of control in social sciences if and when certain scholars make an attempt at using the system to promote personal values—at least, this should be the case if the university is publicly funded.

The only—but evidently crucial—role that he could play was to create positive, favorable conditions that would motivate individuals. Or, in the words of Buchanan, the objective was to provide scholars "with an environment within which they will be individually motivated to undertake research" (Buchanan 1958, 6), to create "a community of scholars who share a common interest in social philosophy . . . [that] serves as a means of identification, of association, for those scholars" (ibid.). Concretely, this translated into an organization of research unique and different from how it is usually organized in academia, and certainly reflects a research and graduate education center that strove to be unique in the discipline of economics. The center invited a distinguished visiting scholar each year to UVA to deliver public lectures and conduct seminars with graduate students and research associates. Knight was the first scholar to be invited. He gave six public lectures that eventually became his book, *Intelligence and Democratic Action* (1960). Another of those early visitors was

Michael Polanyi, whose monograph, *History and Hope: An Analysis of Our Age* ([2017] 1962), was circulated as a TJC working paper.[2] Charles Lindblom and Ronald Coase were also invited. Also, the center sponsored lectures by invited guests and granted fellowships to graduate students and postdoctoral candidates, while supporting research projects by permanent members of the faculty.

NORMATIVE AND POSITIVE POLITICAL ECONOMY

At this point, we may make a detour via Buchanan's conception of science to legitimate this spontaneous-order approach to the "organization" of scientific activity. To him, a scientific approach in economics, what he called "political economy" and linked to Smith and *The Wealth of Nations*, has a twofold dimension. At the highest level, it is normative because it is guided by values such as freedom and democracy. However, to Buchanan these values were general and essential. They are the "comprehensive values of the society" (Buchanan 1973, 27), with which no one could disagree. They are more like a frame, or part of the frame, that allows individuals to pursue their own ends and values. They are normative but at a high, abstract, or constitutional level.[3] They are not personal values—the personal values of the scientist—and they do not imply much in terms of day-to-day implementation—that is, at the postconstitutional level.

This is precisely why Buchanan could nonetheless be considered a positive economist: because, although defending normative absolute values, he did not try to push his own values. Within this frame given by absolute values, the political economist remains "ethically neutral" (Buchanan 1959, 127). In this sense, the political economist had to stick to a scientific, nonnormative or "positive" role (ibid., 137). This was the major difference from the approach of, among others, Arrow, Pigou, and Samuelson. By using a social welfare function and by assuming the benevolence of the omniscient economist—or the omniscience of the benevolent economist—they tried to establish what *should* be done at the postconstitutional level and to tell individuals what to do to orient their behavior.

Now, if the political economist does not try to impose his or her own values, or in other words, if he does not try to establish truth judgments about public policy, what was he supposed to do? Buchanan explained that the political economist's role was only "that of diagnosing social situations and presenting to the choosing individuals a set of possible changes" (Buchanan 1959, 127)—what he called "formulating and testing hypotheses"—in order to "discover what people want" (137) by observing their behaviors:

> Propositions of positive economics find their empirical support or refutation in observable economic quantities or in observable market behavior of individuals. Propositions in political economy find empirical support or refutation in the observable behavior of individuals in their capacities as collective decision-maker. (Buchanan 1959, 128)

As Buchanan stated, "Political economy has a non-normative role in discovering 'what is the structure of individual values'" (1959, 137).

Later, in speaking of *The Limits of Liberty*, Buchanan insisted again on the same distinction, explaining why he "viewed [his] book, *The Limits of Liberty* (1975), as basically positive analysis, with ethical content squeezed to a minimum" (Buchanan 1979, 176):

> I did not want explicitly to advance my own private values; I did not want to and I refrained from spelling out just how society "ought" to be organized. I do not think that my values count for any more in this respect than anyone else's. But we must all recognize, I think, that the ultimate purpose of positive analysis, be it conceptual or empirical, must be that of modifying the environment for choices, which must, in some basic sense, be normatively informed. The ultimate purpose is the "ought," no matter how pure we stick positively with the "is." (Buchanan 1979, 176)

Therefore, political economists' work is "positive" because they cannot know in advance what policy would lead to a Pareto improvement. Buchanan refused to impose any a priori criterion of optimality, which he considered as a value judgment. Only the unanimous consent of citizens on a particular policy would reveal their true preferences and establish if the proposed changes would be Pareto-optimal. This process, moreover, ensured that freedom prevailed, because unanimity implied no coercion.[4]

One therefore understands easily that if scientists are not guided by personal values, scientific activity must not be "organized," and no interference should be tolerated.

THE ORGANIZATION OF SCIENTIFIC ACTIVITY IN REAL LIFE

The conditions we mentioned earlier that must be fulfilled to promote an efficient academic and scientific research program—the existence of a peaceful, cooperative, collaborative center of research at the university level—were fulfilled in the late 1950s, just after Buchanan and Nutter created the Thomas Jefferson Center at UVA. The people Buchanan and Nutter invited shared with them those fundamental values about freedom and democracy that a political economist should defend and also a conception of political economy similar to theirs. And the environment was cooperative and collaborative. At the higher university level, Buchanan also believed that norms of self-respect, tolerance, and independence applied among scholars. It is no surprise that he viewed "the university setting . . . as the most appropriate location for this effort" (Buchanan 1973, 24) at producing new knowledge. At least, this is how he would recall of the university in the late 1960s:

> The whole university-college tradition, the community-of-scholars notion, embodies an institutional arrangement in which individuals are expected to adhere to behavioral standards that are voluntarily maintained and changed only by a mutually acceptable adjustment process. . . . No laws existed, and none were needed as long as behavior was characterized by mutual self-respect and tolerance. (Buchanan 1971)

More specifically, he was convinced that UVA was "a proper setting" for scientific research and therefore for the TJC: a safe haven, a place where he could put his ideas about science and positive political economy into practice. The support from the administration of the university was constant and "enthusiastic" (Buchanan 2007, 94). Buchanan felt that he could develop his research project in total independence from external—political or social—pressures. Their independence was reinforced by the large five-year grant they obtained from the William Volker Fund (Buchanan 2007, 95; Medema 2000). They could go on inviting scholars they wanted to invite and develop their academic research as they pleased, with tremendous results in terms of core faculty research and the talented graduate students produced. The year 1962 was a particular high watermark for research, with the publication of *The Calculus of Consent* by Buchanan and Tullock, *The Growth of Industrial Production in the Soviet Union* by Nutter, and *In Search of a Monetary Constitution*, edited by Yeager.[5] The Thomas Jefferson Center was an outstanding academic success.

This blissful situation did not last. Quite soon, independence was threatened. The relationships with the rest of UVA—the administration, colleagues from other departments, and, at some point, also the students—deteriorated and ceased to be as cooperative as they were in the beginning. The story has been told (Medema 2009; Levy and Peart 2014). Buchanan's commitment to liberty was found "particularly objectionable" (Levy and Peart 2014, 44). He and the other TJC members were perceived as promarket right-wing economists. For instance, Ronald Coase recalled that his "wife was at a cocktail party and heard [him] described as someone to the right of the John Birch Society" (Gillespie 2013)—a conservative, anticommunist organization founded in 1958. Also, William Breit noted that, in the mid-1960s, outsiders associated the members of the center with far-right politics, and he even was once asked by an English professor whether he was a fascist (Breit 1987, 8). And, to say the least, neither the administration nor other faculty members liked the TJC's perceived politics. From this perspective, 1962 is an important year, a turning point indeed. It was the year when the administration of the university decided that it was time to start "changing or offsetting the 'political orientation' of the Department of Economics" (Medema 2009, 145) and began to build a committee—to be realized in 1963—to inquire secretly into the practices and political views of the members of the department.

But in 1962, Buchanan still believed—or feigned to believe—that the situation had not changed. In March, Frank Geldard, chairman of the Long Range Planning Committee, asked department heads for a candid statement of ideas regarding the academic future of the institution as a whole or of a particular school or department (see letter reproduced in this section). Buchanan replied with a note significantly entitled "We Must Dare to Be Different," which is reproduced in this section, in which he made exactly the same statements as he made in 1958 in "The Thomas Jefferson Center." The consistency of his claims about how to organize scientific activity is striking, as if UVA had not changed. But it had.

In 1963, the new president of the university, Edgar Shannon, and the dean of the faculty of the College of Arts and Sciences, Robert Harris, increasingly concerned about the reputation of the center, commissioned a committee to think about "ways of changing . . . the 'political orientation' of the Department of Economics" (Medema 2009, 145). Again, the conclusion underlined that the department was too supportive of a "particular viewpoint . . . described by its friends as 'Neo-Liberalism' and its critics as 'Nineteenth-Century Ultra-Conservatism.'"[6] Accordingly, attempts to interfere with the policy of the Department of Economics—by controlling the hiring of professors, for instance—increased. In fact, changes in American society and academia were making Buchanan's principles for how to organize scientific activity less and less realizable. He struggled a few years, won some battles, lost others, but ultimately became disillusioned and decided to move. In 1968, Buchanan left for the University of California–Los Angeles (UCLA).

UCLA: THE DARKEST OF THE DARK PERIODS

One period remains largely undiscussed in Buchanan's recollection of the 1960s and the 1970s—the few months he spent at UCLA (see, however, Fleury and Marciano 2018).

Buchanan was hired in January 1968 and moved to the West Coast in August 1968. He had great expectations about what it would be possible to do in California. It promised to be the same kind of environment in which he had worked at UVA in the late 1950s. Milton Friedman nicknamed the Department of Economics at UCLA "Chicago West." Chaired by William R. Allen, the department had a "core" (Allen 2010) of members who had a strong connection to Chicago—notably Armen A. Alchian, around whom the department revolved, but also Jack Hirshleifer, J. Clayburn LaForce Jr., and the young assistant professors Sam Peltzman (a former PhD student of George Stigler at Chicago) and Barry Chiswick (a former student of Gary Becker at Columbia).

However, the situation was not as pleasant as Buchanan imagined. The tensions between the members of the department, the students, and the administration were extreme and became even worse. The tense situation throughout the university and surrounding area was not any better. William Allen was threatened by students who were convinced that he did not want to open the Department of Economics to minority professors. A bomb was found at the entrance to the offices of the department. Scary as it was to the members of the department, including Buchanan, of course, it was nothing compared to the fatal shooting of two students on campus in January 1969. This convinced Buchanan that he had no alternative but to leave. He resigned on the spot. He had spent about six months in California.

Before leaving, he coauthored a book describing the problem in academia: *Academia in Anarchy* (Buchanan and Devletoglou 1970). He wrote, or started to write, essays or articles—including the one reprinted below—that complemented *Academia in Anarchy* and shed more light on his views about the organization of scientific activity. To Buchanan in the 1970s, the university was no longer what it used to be and what it should be. The intervention of the students in the functioning of the university was a mistake, precisely because it undermined the self-respect and tolerance necessary for any serious positive (scientific) research. But those who were really to blame were the other professors—the academic "liberals"—who did not resist the students or the politicization of academia (Fleury and Marciano 2018). In "Violence, Law, and Equilibrium at the University" (Buchanan 1971), Buchanan explained that the reaction of the academic liberals to the students' revolt—attempts at appeasement—would not solve the problem. The attempts made by the "hard-liners" would not solve it either. Laws, and more specifically constitutional provisions, were needed since the atmosphere was no longer that of mutual respect and tolerance. Academia was no longer a community of scholars, spontaneously ordered.

GOING BACK EAST: DIFFERENT CONTEXT, SAME ISSUES

In July 1969, Buchanan went back to Virginia, this time to Blacksburg at the Virginia Polytechnic Institute (VPI, also known as Virginia Tech), where he would be reunited with Gordon Tullock. Buchanan became director of the recently created Center for Study of Public Choice (CSPC). Originally, Buchanan and Tullock were optimistic about the opportunities in the hills of rural Virginia to build a world-class research center. Buchanan often stressed that his experience through the 1970s at VPI taught him that academic excellence could indeed take place outside of the academic establishment. As with the Thomas Jefferson Center, Blacksburg had a constant stream of visitors, a vibrant workshop, an environment of collaboration, and talented graduate students. But it also didn't take that long before trouble began to emerge between CSPC and the rest of the department.

Later in the 1970s, Buchanan would become increasingly frustrated and alienated with his situation at Virginia Tech. In discussing the experience that he and his colleagues had to face in pursuing a public choice research program in economics and political science, Buchanan invoked George Orwell's discussion of the true liberal's response to the "smelly little orthodoxies which are now contending for our souls" (Orwell 1946). Buchanan's essay (reproduced in this section) is titled "The Dishwater of Orthodoxies," and in it he argues that the orthodoxies he faced in methodology of the social sciences, the method of analysis in the social and policy sciences, and implications of that analysis for political economy and social philosophy, while not necessarily "smelly," were nevertheless dangerous. The reason why the orthodoxies he and his colleagues faced didn't smell is because they never were alive enough to actually stink. The orthodoxies Buchanan faced were "dull, dead, drab, dirty." But as Buchanan pointed out, one can drown in dull and drab dishwater nevertheless.

It is the dull, dead, drab, and dirty dishwater of social scientific orthodoxy mid-twentieth century that had to be resisted and effectively drained away so that a new science of association among free and responsible individuals could be developed. Those who held as sacrosanct the efficacy of majoritarian democracy or the necessary efficiency of modern bureaucracy had to be disabused of such notions. This requires disruptive intellectuals. Those who are comfortable in their academic life don't want to permit the methodological reevaluation required. They resist change and seek to cast out the heretic. But as Buchanan points out, when the only recourse left is dismissive name-calling, that means that the heretic has won because the opposition is out of genuine argument. "The genuine innovator-entrepreneur," Buchanan writes, "who seeks to challenge, to stir up the dishwater of the orthodoxy, must expect to counter resistance at every stage. At best, he and his fellow [heretics] can hope to find academic settings that are temporarily congenial to their efforts, settings that encourage those who dare to be different." To "dare to be different" was one of Buchanan's mottos.

Buchanan, a future Nobel laureate, was compelled to leave the University of Virginia and the Thomas Jefferson Center due to an ideological backlash on campus. He also left UCLA because of student unrest and inability of administrators to act appropriately, and he would later leave Virginia Tech because of a methodological backlash against the work at the Center for Study of Public Choice. There is no doubt that Buchanan was an academic entrepreneur both at the level of ideas and in terms of constructing institutions for the organization of inquiry around those ideas. In that process, he also experienced bumps and bruises as he took on the orthodoxy at a methodological, analytical, and ideological level.

In the early 1980s, Buchanan would relocate the entire CSPC to George Mason University (Mason) in the suburban area of Washington, DC. He would once again stress in this move independence of research (and the active avoidance of Potomac fever[7]), the importance of daring to be different and effectively challenging the prevailing orthodoxies, and finally the cultivation of a research community of political economists. Buchanan had long been arguing that the post–World War II counterrevolution to Samuelsonian economics was reflected not only in Milton Friedman's Chicago School monetarism but even more fundamentally in the microeconomic developments of property-rights economics, law and economics, public choice economics, and market-process economics. Rather than see these various schools as contending perspectives, Buchanan argued that they should form the basis of a conciliation into a coherent paradigm of a new political economy that could pick up that intellectual agenda as laid out in that *UVA Newsletter* quoted earlier.

Buchanan's move to Mason radically transformed its trajectory. His Nobel Memorial Prize in Economic Sciences (commonly known as the Nobel

Prize in Economics) in 1986 put the school on the map, and this eventually resulted in a set of moves by the school that transformed a largely commuter, regional university of roughly 10,000 students to the situation today, where Mason is an R1 international university and the largest research university in the state of Virginia, with over 33,000 students. A few other significant events happened besides Buchanan's move to Mason—such as Henry Manne becoming the dean of Mason's Law School and transforming it into a leading center for Law and Economics, Vernon Smith choosing to relocate his Interdisciplinary Center for Economic Science to Mason and then winning his own Nobel Prize in Economics in 2002, and finally the tremendous success of the basketball program throughout the first decade of the 2000s under Coach Jim Larranga, producing several postseason appearances, including a Final Four appearance in 2006. All of these events and others put Mason on a different direction than what was envisioned when the college was established in the 1950s as a branch of the University of Virginia. Mason became an independent university in 1972.

Buchanan's experience at UVA had alerted him to ideologically motivated critiques, and his experience at VPI had alerted him to methodologically motivated critiques, and so at Mason he was determined to help cultivate an environment in which neither of those rear-guard actions could undermine the "ordered anarchy" of a scholarly inquiry in the grand and honorable tradition of political economy at its finest.

We have yet to discuss the broader community of scholars that Buchanan helped cultivate with the Public Choice Society, emerging out of the Committee on Non-Market Decision Making, nor have we talked about his conscious effort—in cooperation with early founding fathers of public choice such as Vincent Ostrom—to cultivate a professional conversation on the constitutional level of analysis in political economy. Buchanan (and Tullock) through TJC and then CSPC supported the journal *Public Choice* and the Public Choice Society, and later Buchanan and CSPC supported the founding of the journal *Constitutional Political Economy*. These activities are worthy of serious examination as part of Buchanan's career as an academic entrepreneur and the organization of scientific inquiry (Medema 2000, 2009).

NOTES

1. Buchanan left Florida State in 1955 but only moved to Charlottesville in 1956, spending the academic year of 1955–1956 in Italy on a Fulbright scholarship.

2. History has a way of creating wonderful coincidences. Michael Polanyi's son, John C., won the Nobel Prize in Chemistry in 1986, the same year that Buchanan won the prize for economics. They were able to reminisce at the ceremony about Charlottesville.
3. Even these values are not *absolute*. To claim that they are absolute would imply that they are true. He was rather claiming that the constitutional values of a society are *relatively absolute absolutes* (see more details about this concept in section 6).
4. Political economy, to Buchanan (1959, 132), "applies to only one form of social change, namely, that which is deliberately chosen by the members of the social group."
5. Coase had already published "The Problem of Social Cost" in 1960. Also published in 1962 was Buchanan's "Politics, Policy, and Pigovian Margins" and Buchanan and Stubblebine's "Externality," as well as Davis and Whinston's "Externalities, Welfare, and the Theory of Games." Davis was a former PhD student of Buchanan's. All were significant papers in the emerging literature on comparative institutional analysis of government and the market.
6. Quotation from the University of Virginia's "Self-Study Report" about the Economics Department, Document Collection, Library of Congress, 1963.
7. "Potomac fever" is a colloquial term used to describe a "disease" peculiar to the greater Washington, DC, metro area that presents chiefly as an intense desire in the infected to be associated with the power and prestige of the United States federal government, particularly the Executive Branch.

REFERENCES

Allen, W. R. 2010. "A Life among the Econ, Particularly at UCLA." *Econ Journal Watch* 7(3): 205–34.

Breit, W. 1987. "Creating the 'Virginia School': Charlottesville as an Academic Environment in the 1960s." *Economic Inquiry* 25(4): 645–57.

Buchanan, J. M. 1958. "The Thomas Jefferson Center for Studies in Political Economy." *University of Virginia Newsletter* 35(2): 5–8.

———. 1959. "Positive Economics, Welfare Economics, and Political Economy." *Journal of Law and Economics* 2: 124–38.

———. [1961–1962] 1999. *The Demand and Supply of Public Goods*. Indianapolis, IN: Liberty Fund.

———. 1962. "Politics, Policy, and the Pigovian Margins." In Chennat Gopalakrishnan (ed.), *Classic Papers in Natural Resource Economics*, 204–18. London: Palgrave Macmillan.

———. 1971. "Violence, Law, and Equilibrium in the University." *Public Policy* 19: 1–18.

———. 1973. "Social Choice and Freedom of Inquiry: The Internal and External Institutions for Decision Making in Higher Education." In L. Erhard, K. Bruss, and B. Hagemeyer (eds.), *Grenzen der Demokratie? Probleme und Konsequenzen der Demokratisierung von Politik, Wirtschaft und Gesellschaft*, 387–406. Düsseldorf: Econ-Verlag GmbH.

———. 1979. "Notes on the History and Direction of Public Choice." In J. M. Buchanan (ed.), *What Should Economists Do?*, 175–82. London: Macmillan.

———. 2007. *Economics from the Outside In: 'Better than Plowing' and Beyond*. College Station: Texas A&M University Press.

Buchanan, J. M., and N. E. Devletoglou. 1970. *Academia in Anarchy: An Economic Diagnosis*. New York: Basic Books.

Buchanan, J. M., and W. C. Stubblebine. 1962. "Externality." In Chennat Gopalakrishnan (ed.), *Classic Papers in Natural Resource Economics*, 138–54. London: Palgrave Macmillan.

Buchanan, J. M., and G. Tullock. 1962. *The Calculus of Consent*. Ann Arbor: University of Michigan Press.

Coase, R. H. 1960. "The Problem of Social Cost." In Chennat Gopalakrishnan (ed.), *Classic Papers in Natural Resource Economics*, 87–137. London: Palgrave Macmillan.

Davis, O. A., and A. Whinston, A. 1962. "Externalities, Welfare, and the Theory of Games." *Journal of Political Economy* 70(3): 241–62.

Fleury, J. B., and A. Marciano. 2018. "The Making of a Constitutionalist: James Buchanan on Education." *History of Political Economy* 50(3): 511–48.

Gillespie, N. 2013. "Economist Ronald Coase Was Chased Out of UVA in 1964 for Supporting Market Solutions." *Reason*, September 4. https://reason.com/2013/09/04/economist-ronald-coase-was-chased-out-of/.

Knight, F. 1960. *Intelligence and Democratic Action*. Cambridge, MA: Harvard University Press.

Levy, D. M., and S. J. Peart. 2014. "Almost Wholly Negative: The Ford Foundation's Appraisal of the Virginia School." https://papers.ssrn.com/sol3/papers.cfm?abstract_id=2485695. Accessed February 22, 2020.

Medema, S. G. 2000. "Related Disciplines: The Professionalization of Public Choice Analysis." *History of Political Economy* 32(1): 289–324.

———. 2009. *The Hesitant Hand: Taming Self-Interest in the History of Economic Ideas*. Princeton, NJ: Princeton University Press.

Nutter, G. W., I. Borenstein, and A. Kaufman. 1962. *Growth of Industrial Production in the Soviet Union*. Princeton, NJ: Princeton University Press.

Orwell, G. 1946. *Critical Essays*. London: Secker & Warburg.

Polanyi, M. [1962] 2017. "History and Hope: An Analysis of Our Age." In R. T. Allen (ed.), *Society, Economics & Philosophy: Selected Papers*, 79–94. New York: Routledge.

Tullock, G. [1966] 2004. *The Organization of Inquiry*. Indianapolis, IN: Liberty Fund.

Yeager, L. B. (ed.). 1962. *In Search of a Monetary Constitution*. Cambridge, MA: Harvard University Press.

4.1 The Thomas Jefferson Center for Studies in Political Economy

JAMES M. BUCHANAN

The Thomas Jefferson Center for Studies in Political Economy was organized at the University of Virginia in 1957, and it is still in the early stages of its operation. This article will tell readers of the *News Letter* something about this center: the ideas behind its organization, its general aims and purposes, its administration, its operations to date, and its plans for the future. Those of us who are directly involved in the work of the center think that it should, and will, become an important part of the overall program of the university. But we recognize that the growth and the development of the center will depend upon support, not only from those on the grounds but also from many others in the community beyond.

WHY WAS THE CENTER ORGANIZED?

The Thomas Jefferson Center strives to carry on the honorable tradition of "political economy"—the study of what makes for a "good society." Political economists stress the technical economic principles that one must understand in order to assess alternative arrangements for promoting peaceful cooperation

Originally published in *The University of Virginia Newsletter*, October 15, 1968, XXXV (2): 5–7.

and productive specialization among free men. Yet political economics go further and frankly try to bring out into the open the philosophical issues that necessarily underlie all discussions of the appropriate functions of government and all proposed economic policy measures. They examine philosophical values for consistency among themselves and with the ideal of human freedom. Adam Smith was writing as a political economist when he composed *The Wealth of Nations*, and it is not surprising that this first great book in the field appeared in the same year as the Declaration of Independence.

In the century from 1750 to 1850, political economists were among the intellectual leaders guiding those political changes that had the result of removing many artificial restraints upon individual choice and initiative. The release of human energies made possible by such a widening of the range of individual choice produced something new in history; free society, as we now conceive it, was unknown three hundred years ago. Civilized society in the West was launched on a progressively accelerating improvement in material standards of well-being previously undreamed of, and, much more importantly, this improvement was accomplished by an expansion, not a contraction, of the freedom of individual citizens.

We live today, in the Western world, on the heritage of this greatest of all revolutions in human history. The earlier or "classical" political economists remain important to us because of their influence in laying the foundations for these modern institutions. And the reading of their works continues to be a necessary part of one's process of coming to understand the world in which we find ourselves.

But with the march of time come great social changes. As these changes have occurred over the last century, political economy and political economists seem to have become increasingly less influential. The increasing specialization of knowledge and scholarship has forced a separation between the economics and the political philosophy involved in particular issues. Economics and political science have become two separate academic disciplines. Students now spend their entire careers examining tiny areas within each of these broader fields. As a result, few social scientists today have the competence or interest in studying broad issues of policy that is required for intellectual leadership. Scholars totally absorbed in the minutiae of their particular disciplines can contribute to knowledge; yet it is essential that some scholars concern themselves with issues requiring broader examination.

A society is guided by its ruling philosophy—the prevailing conception of the "good" social order. Some political-economic philosophy must be the basis for intelligent social policy. Forthright and continuing discussion is necessary if this conception is to serve as a clear and coherent guide on numerous particular issues. Otherwise, statesmen and citizens will continue to lose their bearings amid the economic and social complexities of the mid-twentieth century.

Study of political-economic philosophy is the basic content of political economy. Political economists try to stimulate open and lively discussion of how a free society should be organized and preserved. And they go further. They examine and discuss the whole set of current policy issues in the light of some conception of the "good" society.

The fruits of Western civilization have perhaps been so bountiful that nations will not relinquish them voluntarily through orderly democratic processes. It is now widely recognized that the great appeal of Communism is largely limited to those areas of the world that have never really enjoyed the free society. But this reversal of Marxian predictions should not lull citizens of Western civilization into thinking that free social institutions, including the free economy, are more or less automatically guaranteed to us. There is, on the contrary, an ever-present danger that these institutions, which are vital to the preservation of individual liberty, may be undermined and eroded through an overly close attention to current minor irritations in the social fabric, accompanied by heedless neglect of larger issues of more lasting importance. Twentieth-century American democracy can well commit the irrevocable sin of "social carelessness," of allowing its institutions to be modified out of all recognition, of allowing them to be divorced bit by bit from their original intent and purpose in the social structure. Individual liberty or freedom remains the fundamental organizing principle of the free society, and the temporary pursuit of will-of-the-wisp current objectives at the expense of individual freedoms must be examined much more carefully and thoroughly than scholars and policymakers now seem willing to attempt.

Out of ideas such as these, the Thomas Jefferson Center for Studies in Political Economy was born. The center represents the institutional embodiment of an effort deliberately made to bring about a rebirth of political economy.

THE CENTER AND THE UNIVERSITY

It is particularly appropriate that this center should have been established at the University of Virginia. Although Mr. Jefferson's wide and varied interests and activities allowed him little time for the study of political economy in the specific sense, the ideas imbedded in his political writing parallel those of the "classical" political economists. The importance of Virginia and Virginians in the framing of the constitutional and legal structure of the United States is well known, but perhaps the importance of this structure itself in shaping the whole of the society that we enjoy is too often overlooked.

The University of Virginia appears a proper setting for a center devoted to reexamination of the whole political-economic structure, to a more broadly based approach to particular social issues, and to a hardheaded confrontation of modern institutional changes with underlying individual values.

WHAT IS THE CENTER?

Research is, of course, central to the program of the Thomas Jefferson Center. But it is not conceived primarily as a research organization in the more commonly accepted usage of these terms. Positive attempts to "buy research" in any specific area of interest seem questionable on several grounds. The Thomas Jefferson Center is conceived rather as a community of scholars who share a common interest in social philosophy. The center serves as a means of identification of association for those scholars. It tries to provide them with an environment within which they will be individually motivated to undertake research. But such research must come from the individual interests of the cooperating associates; the center does not, in any way, suggest or promote specific studies. Those studies that do come out of the center—and we hope there will be many and important ones—are produced as a result of individual scholarly effort.

Education is, of course, central to the center's total program. But again, the center is not primarily conceived as serving directly an instructional task. Political economy, as a discipline, contains few formal aspects that are not to be found in the institutionally organized disciplines of the social sciences. The technical competence of students and scholars must be gained by a study of those disciplines. The attempt to inaugurate a special curriculum in political economy would represent a still further step toward undesirable specialization. In accordance with these views, the center offers no courses; it grants no degrees. With its instructional as with its research function, the Thomas Jefferson Center serves as a means of identification, of association, for students and scholars. By creating an environment in which discussions and debate on fundamental issues can proceed, by providing intellectual stimulation for such discussion, and by encouraging individual participation in such discussion, the center aims at supplementing and enhancing the educational job accomplished through the acquisition of technical competence in the regular academic disciplines. In this way, the Thomas Jefferson Center hopes to accomplish the general aims set forth in its initial descriptive brochure, which was widely distributed in late 1957:

> The Center is organized to promote scholarly discussions of the basic ideals of Western civilization and of the solutions to modern social problems most in accord with those ideals.
>
> The Center is a community of scholars who wish to preserve a social order based on individual liberty. The Center will encourage students to see the philosophical as well as the technical issues entering into problems of social organization.

WHAT DOES THE CENTER DO?

What, specifically, does this Thomas Jefferson Center for Studies in Political Economy do? First of all, and perhaps most importantly especially during its formative years, the center brings to the university community each year a distinguished visiting scholar. This scholar is selected for his interest in political economy and social philosophy and for his demonstrated ability and competence. This scholar is widely known and respected. When he is in residence at the center, the visiting scholar participates actively in the intellectual life of the community; he delivers public lectures; he conducts small informal seminars with graduate students and research associates.

Secondly, the center sponsors specific individual lectures or seminar discussions by invited guests. These lectures and discussions fall outside the regular academic program of the university.

Thirdly, the center grants fellowships to graduate students and to postdoctoral candidates. These fellowships are awarded on the basis of ability and indicated interest in political economy, and they may be awarded to students in any of the social sciences. Graduate students who receive these fellowships must, of course, secure admission to the Graduate School of Arts and Sciences and pursue courses of study approved by the regular academic departments. Applications for these graduate fellowships are invited from all students in the social sciences interested in political economy as an integral part of their overall graduate program. Postdoctoral fellowships are awarded to young scholars who have demonstrated research competence. Through the postdoctoral fellowships, the center hopes to encourage young scholars to undertake research along the lines of its indicated interest.

Finally, the center acts as a clearing house through which independent research projects by permanent members of the university faculty are administered. Staff members become research associates of the center while the projects are being carried out.

PARTICIPATION IN THE CENTER'S PROGRAM

It has been stated earlier that the Thomas Jefferson Center is a community of scholars. It is a voluntary community, and from this it follows that participation in its activities is open, informal, and flexible. The center is dedicated to the idea that mutual advantages are to be gained from serious scholarly discussion of vital issues in social philosophy. This discussion may take the form of public lectures, seminars, forums, or written interchange of ideas; the forms themselves are flexible. Interested scholars at all levels both from within the university and beyond are urged to visit the center, to attend the announced lectures, and to participate even more actively in the smaller seminar and group activities. Indeed, one of the fundamental aims of the center is that of widening the community discourse, and it will not have served its purpose if, over the long run, participation is not extended.

HOW IS THE CENTER ADMINISTERED?

The Thomas Jefferson Center is administered by a director, an associate director, and an executive secretary. This staff acts with the advice and counsel of an Advisory Committee.

James M. Buchanan, who is also chairman of the Department of Economics, is currently serving as director. G. Warren Nutter, who holds a professorship in the Department of Economics, is associate director. Assistant Professor Leland B. Yeager is serving as executive secretary. The center has independent offices and a separate clerical staff in Rouss Hall on the Lawn.

The Advisory Committee currently is composed of the following members; the first three are ex officio: Colgate W. Darden Jr., president of the university; William L. Duren Jr., dean, College of Arts and Sciences; Lewis M. Hammond, dean, Graduate School of Arts and Sciences; Charles C. Abbott, dean, Graduate School of Business Administration; Hardy C. Dillard, professor of Law; and Rowland Egger, chairman, Departments of Foreign Affairs and Political Science.

HOW IS THE CENTER SUPPORTED?

Although independently organized, the center's whole program is complemented and supported by the regular academic program of the university. The staff members and the research associates of the center hold permanent academic appointments in the regularly constituted departments.

Financial support for the center has been provided by grants from foundations that have expressed by their confidence in the program contemplated by the center. This support finances the visiting scholars, the special lectures and seminars, and fellowship awards and provides for certain of the clerical and operating expenses resulting from the operation of the center as a separate entity. Foundation support has also been secured from independent research projects administered through the center.

OPERATION IN 1957–1958

The work of the Thomas Jefferson Center was seriously begun during the academic years 1957–1958. The first public lecture under the sponsorship of the center was delivered on September 20, 1957, by Peter T. Bauer, fellow of Gonville and Cauis College, and Smuts Reader in Commonwealth Studies at Cambridge University. Mr. Bauer, who is the author of several books on economic problems of underdeveloped countries, spoke on "The Political Economy of Compulsory Development." During the remaining months of the fall term, the center sponsored small seminar discussions by Professor Proctor Thomson of Claremont Men's College, Dr. R. N. McKean of the RAND Corporation, and Professor Carl Uhr of the University of California.

The inaugural visiting scholar at the center was Frank H. Knight, Morton D. Hull Distinguished Service Professor Emeritus of Social Sciences and Philosophy at the University of Chicago. Professor Knight is a world-renowned scholar, and he is recognized for his contributions both in economics and in social philosophy. He is the author of a classic work in economic theory, *Risk, Uncertainty, and Profit*, along with numerous other works. In December 1957, Professor Knight was awarded the Francis Walker Medal by the American Economic Association. This medal, given only once each five years, is awarded for outstanding contributions to economic science.

During his period of residence at the university, Professor Knight delivered a series of six public lectures on the topic, "Intelligence and Democratic Action." These lectures were well attended and they generated much discussion in the whole university community. In addition to this series of lectures, Professor Knight conducted a seminar for graduate students. The discussion theme of these seminars was the role of science in solving social problems.

Special lectures during the spring term of 1958 that were sponsored by the center included those by Professor Charles E. Lindblom of Yale University on "Adam Smith and Our Political System" and by Professor Ronald H. Coase of the University of Buffalo on "The Federal Communications Commission and the American Broadcasting System." A special visitor and lecturer who provoked much interest was Professor Josef Pajestka, member of the faculty of the University of Warsaw and of the staff of the Polish Economic Council. He discussed, both in a public lecture and in seminar, the problems of planning faced in socialist economic systems.

In addition to these special lectures, the center joined with the Woodrow Wilson Department of Foreign Affairs and the School of Law in sponsoring an address by M. Robert Schuman, former premier of France and a leader in the organization of the European Coal and Steel Community. M. Schuman spoke on "Problems of Western European Economic Integration."

PROSPECTS FOR 1958–1959

The center became fully operative with the beginning of the 1958–1959 academic year in September 1958. Eight graduate fellows and one postdoctoral fellow are directly associated with the center.

Dr. Overton H. Taylor of Harvard University will serve as visiting scholar for the first half of the 1958–1959 academic term. He will give a series of four lectures in the fall of 1958 on the general theme of economic theory and political philosophy.

Dr. Gordon Tullock, who has been trained in both economics and law, has been awarded the first postdoctoral fellowship to be granted through the auspices of the center. He will be in residence during the 1958–1959 academic term, and he will be at work completing his book on bureaucracy, which has been tentatively entitled "Inside Bureaucracy."

PLANS FOR FUTURE YEARS

The Thomas Jefferson Center for Studies in Political Economy is now a going concern. The program over an initial formative period has been deliberately limited, but as the center becomes a more permanent feature of the university community and of the intellectual community more broadly conceived, plans for selected, although still limited, expansion have been made. Some initial thought has been given to a series of publications under the sponsorship of the center, resulting either from the lectures delivered at the center or from research projects administered through the center. The possibility of summer seminars bringing together young scholars in the social sciences has been discussed. Other ideas for development are certain to present themselves as the center itself continues operation. We at the center will welcome suggestions and encouragement from members of the university and from the community beyond.

We hope that the operation of the center can be sufficiently flexible to allow for adaption and change to meet new conditions and to respond to new challenges, but the general aims of the center will endure, however. The effects of the Thomas Jefferson Center on the intellectual attitudes of the university community and upon the more general field of scholarship in the social sciences will be gradual, and they will be difficult to appraise. But, for those of us who have been instrumental in getting the center under way, there is an underlying confidence that it will have an impact and that the course of scholarship will be modified by the center's program, even if in a small and, at the present, wholly unpredictable way.

4.2
A Letter from Frank A. Geldard

University of Virginia
Charlottesville

March 1, 1962

Dear Colleague:

The Long Range Planning Committee is continuing its work and plans to submit a report to the president at the end of this session. Although attention is being given to a variety of administrative and nonacademic problems, the central concern of the committee, pursuant to its charge from the president, is with academic aims and programs—the intellectual life—of the university over the next ten to fifteen years. And in this all-important area the committee is anxious to gather fresh, stimulating ideas from among the university faculty. After deliberating on a technique for tapping a cross-section of thought among our colleagues, we decided simply to write this letter to those elected to the faculty between four and seven years ago.

We are thus asking you as one of this group to give us in writing any proposals you care to make concerning academic aims, ways of achieving those aims, and steps that might be taken to lift the intellectual horizons of the university. You might, for example, have ideas about interdisciplinary programs, the creation of new departments or the abolition or merger of existing departments, the creation of an area studies center or an environmental studies center, the introduction of entirely new fields of study, the use of closed-circuit TV, a "house system" for undergraduates, and so on. These are merely a few of the potential lines of inquiry. The committee would like to have a wide range of creative suggestions touching the academic future of the institution as a whole or of a particular school or department.

President Shannon has said that this committee's work is of signal importance to the university in the years ahead. We now call on you personally to help us with a candid statement of your ideas. A lengthy memorandum is not requested; we would, however, appreciate your putting your proposals in writing as concretely as you can and sending them to me within the next two or three weeks.

Sincerely yours,
Frank A. Geldard
Chairman, Long Range
Planning Committee

4.3 We Must Dare to Be Different

JAMES M. BUCHANAN

GENERAL STATEMENT

The university does not, automatically, assume a place among America's leading educational institutions. Nor does it, automatically, drop to a place among those of acknowledged second rank. Even more than most, the university's position in either the first or the second of these two groups depends on its own choices.

There are unique and attractive attributes of physical environment, of tradition, and of location. There are severe restrictions on financial resources, on research personnel, on top-quality students.

How best may the university ensure a position of leadership given the constraints within which it must operate?

I submit that it can do so only if it dares to be different.

THE LINE OF LEAST RESISTANCE

The line of least resistance for university policy, at all levels, is that of following trends and practices introduced elsewhere, notably at the acknowledged leading institutions. This line, if followed, must surely produce *mediocrity*, not distinction. For this reason, this policy line, at all levels, must be carefully avoided. Great dangers loom in the attempt to follow fads and fashions in education, to spread the product thin, and to refuse to have the courage of conviction.

CONCENTRATION AND SPECIALIZATION

The first implication for university policy to be drawn is that no effort should be made to cover all subjects offered by larger universities, or even all of the specializations within particular subjects. We must have the courage to make choices here, and we must concentrate on the areas of real and potential strength.

Total departmental offerings in the college should be reduced, not expanded, and new specializations within departments should be studiously avoided. No new schools or colleges should be established except on demonstrated need, and those existing should be required to continually justify their existence. The university cannot afford second-rate work. It is simply not large enough.

DISTURBING SIGNS

There is evidence that recent policy has been based on the line of least resistance, at least to some degree. Two years ago, for example, there was some discussion and some action taken to set up a program in non-Western studies. Why? Because this was being done elsewhere. I cite this not as criticism of the particular program in question but as an instance of the sort of thinking that should be avoided. When a new program is proposed, the fact that it is being done elsewhere should not be a negative nor a positive factor in its consideration.

THE TEACHING PROGRAM

The general philosophy suggested here should apply equally to all aspects of policy, including the teaching program, at both the graduate and the undergraduate levels. Teaching is now inefficient in that we both teach too much and too little: too much in the sense that we do not place sufficient responsibility on the individual student, too little in that the better students do not get the individual supervision that they deserve.

Here, too, we can dare to be different. The formal lecture courses should be modified drastically in content so as to include far fewer lecture sessions, perhaps covering not more than eight weeks per semester. This would leave ample time for reading periods, individual small-group supervision, preparation of papers, etc. The honors program should be expanded and strengthened in an efficient manner. This could be done by, first of all, ensuring that no mediocre students are admitted, preferably by rigid adherence to a three-point rule, and secondly by ensuring that all, or substantially all, top-level students are admitted.

The long-run return to the university is surely concentrated in the top 10 percent of its students. This should be more fully recognized.

GRADUATE PROGRAM

Graduate instruction is becoming an increasingly important part of the university program. The external influence of the institution must largely depend on its work through graduate and professional programs. Graduate programs proposed must be subjected to the intensity of critical evaluation that is suggested for other aspects of university policy.

Every effort must be made to secure state-financed support for fellowships. Advanced graduate students should be allowed wide flexibility in serving as teaching apprentices. Specifically, in this connection, arrangements should be made to secure apprenticeship teaching arrangements for graduate students in the university's branch of colleges.

AN ILLUSTRATIVE EXAMPLE

The philosophy of policy suggested here has been, to some extent, that followed by the Department of Economics during the past six years. Our best guarantee of mediocrity would have been an uncritical acceptance of drift, resulting in a departmental faculty that was unspecialized and unconcentrated, with individual members working singly and alone on the separate subdisciplines, with little genuine communication one with the other. Instead of this, we chose, deliberately and explicitly, to concentrate our efforts on the problems and methods that are summarized in the terms "classical political economy." The results have been, I submit, successful. Our product, measured in terms of graduate students, is now a differentiated one. A "Virginia" Economics Department is becoming a reality. Our strength lies precisely in the fact that it is different from other economics departments in its concentration. Only by daring to be different can small departments ever hold claim to positions of national recognition.

The difficulties that the Economics Department has faced in carrying out this policy suggest that the approach here indicated is not wholly empty. Daring to be different will, naturally, be opposed by those who fail to understand.

STRENGTHS AND WEAKNESSES

What are the university's strengths and weaknesses? No general answer can be given. Characteristics that are strengths in one sense and for one program may, at the same time, become weaknesses for alternative programs.

(1) First of all, the university is *southern*. This cannot be ignored or neglected, and it should be seized on as a source of potential strength rather than as an excuse for failure and something to be apologized for. Its disadvantages for certain programs should be acknowledged. This feature alone suggests that the university should not attempt to become a center for the training of foreign students, given the gross misunderstanding of the South generally in the foreign press, especially in the underdeveloped counties. But this characteristic can be employed to advantage in recruiting graduate students and staff from the southern region generally.

(2) Secondly, the university is *Virginian*, and not only in the sense of its support by the state. It is also Virginian by nature and tradition. This is, by and large, a conservative tradition, not a radical one. Again, this should be recognized and converted into a source of strength not weakness. Programs appropriate for North Carolina or Wisconsin are not wholly appropriate for Virginia but would be appropriate in the more "progressive" states. In the large, I think that the university has an opportunity here to fill an awesome gap in the American scholarly community. I simply refuse to think that, in university communities generally, it is always right to be left and wrong to be right.

(3) Thirdly, the university is *Jeffersonian*, not only in a historical-architectural sense, but also *philosophically*. Jefferson was an apostle of human liberty, of man's ability to choose and to adapt his own social institutions. This tradition can be uniquely valuable to the university, and it has been scarcely exploited at all.

The Thomas Jefferson Center for Studies in Political Economy represents but one among many possible steps that could be taken to fit the university progress to its heritage.

The highly successful Institute on Federalism, now a going concern at Claremont Graduate School, could have much more appropriately been set up at Virginia.

The Center for the Rule of Law, established at Duke, could have been more appropriately set up at Virginia. These are merely examples of the type of program for which the university possesses comparative advantages. And it should always seek to propose and to implement programs that exploit its comparative advantages, not its comparative disadvantages.

4.4
The Dishwater of Orthodoxies

JAMES M. BUCHANAN

Postdinner talks should be short and humorous. I promise you brevity; the humor will, I suspect, be present only for those of you who can stand bemused at what goes on about them, and who make a worse mistake than taking life too seriously, than of not taking it seriously enough. Despite the proper conviviality of this occasion, I want to be very serious with you tonight, but in such fashion that my remarks bear at least indirectly on this week's conference.

This conference is the sixth Liberty Fund Conference that has been organized through the auspices of the Center for Study of Public Choice. I hope it will not be the last. It is also the sixth conference that has been convened in Blacksburg. It will be the *last* Blacksburg conference, since, as you know, the center is shifting to George Mason University in Fairfax, Virginia.

It is this "last Blacksburg conference" and the prospective shift of the center that provides the theme for my remarks and the reason for my title as announced: "The Dishwater of Orthodoxies." What we have tried to do, from the outset, at these conferences is to offer a setting for serious and scholarly examination and discussion of *ideas* relevant for a society of persons who value liberty. In this effort, we have tried our best to follow in the patterns established

Remarks for Post-Dinner Occasional Lecture, Liberty Fund Conference, Blacksburg, VA, July 25, 1982.

by the organizers of the old Volker Fund conferences of the late 1950s and early 1960s, conferences that nostalgically stimulated both the Liberty Fund and the center to depart categorically from the *orthodox* conference format. Even in their very organization, therefore, these conferences break the bounds of orthodoxy.

A second emphasis has been our deliberate attempt to break out of the orthodox disciplinary boundaries and deliberately mix up economists, lawyers, philosophers, political scientists, historians, and sociologists, along with a few from still other disciplines. In earlier years, we have, I think, succeeded in preventing any in-discipline monopoly of dialogue from seriously inhibiting all-participants discussion. We have also tried to secure main speakers who, themselves, could scarcely be labeled as "orthodox" practitioners in their own parent disciplines. We have sought, first of all, *interesting* speakers with *interesting* ideas: Robert Nozick, Richard Epstein, Shirley Letwin, Jon Alster, John Passmore, Bill Niskanen, Doug North, Mike Parkin, Charles Plott, Dan Usher, Ken Minogue, John Hughes, Axel Leijonhufvud—I am not sure I have named them all. As these names suggest to you, none of these speakers fit an orthodox disciplinary mold. They have "dared to be different," and, in so doing, they have become interesting to those of us who have shared conference experiences with them.

In their quite different ways, and now speaking much more generally, both Liberty Fund and the Center for Study of Public Choice have "dared to be different," have tried to be *creative* in their choices and in so doing, I hope, have sent out flares that have attracted interest. I shall not discuss Liberty Fund's unique role in this respect, except to say that those of us at the center have been beneficiaries of the fund's unorthodoxy in the world of foundations.

However, I do want to talk a bit about the Center for Study of Public Choice and about some of the problems that we have confronted, because, in all of our work, we have challenged the orthodoxies in several respects. Recall that George Orwell referred to "the smelly little orthodoxies." By contrast, in the title of these remarks, I referred to "The Dishwater of Orthodoxies," because those that we have encountered do not have enough life really to stink; they are dull, dead, drab, and dirty. But let us never forget that one can drown just as readily in dishwater as in the freshes of a spring flood. And dirt is not as salt; it offers no flotation properties. But enough of such metaphor. The center's work, and public choice more inclusively considered, have challenged the orthodoxy of democratic socialist mythology. We are heretics to all those who hold as sacrosanct the efficacy of majoritarian democracy or the necessary efficiency of modern bureaucracy. And, despite our very considerable success in shifting ultimate academic and public attitudes, we have been treated as heretics have been treated throughout the ages. We have been excommunicated and reviled. In my own quite recent efforts to present the simple and straightforward case for changes in our fiscal and monetary constitution, for imposing new limits on the excesses of ordinary politics, I have, on more than one occasion, been charged with "intellectual fascism." (Perhaps, like Constantine Fitzgibbon, I should now write a book under the title "Confessions of a Fascist Hyena!")

Basically, however, I think that we have won this battle. The fascist slurs are clear signs of the absence of effective argument. And the socialist mythology cannot, I think, be revived, despite 1981 events in France, or despite John K. Galbraith, whom I heard today on *Meet the Press*. Nor can the ordinary politics of Speaker O'Neill rise to command the renewed respect that once was accorded to our Congress. The tax candy action of the Congress in 1981 was only confirming and corroborating evidence for a model of politics that has come to be well ensconced in the American psyche. Indeed, I fear sometimes that the destruction of the democratic-socialist mystique has gone too far, especially since we have not been very successful in generating a widely renewed interest in a new dialogue on constitutional rules.

Any modern scholar who dares to step even slightly beyond the mainstream and to challenge the dishwater of orthodoxies in his own discipline encounters even more formidable resistance in the totally nonmythological, nonideological, and nonpolitical organizational structure that describes the confined and sheltered groves of the academy. Those alleged practitioners whose intellectual capital is invested in "mainstream economics" or "mainstream political science" or like disciplines, and who either cannot or will not think for themselves, must, to protect their own private interest, strongly resist the efforts of all those who threaten methodological reevaluation, or even those who criticize the simplistic aping of allegedly mainstream research-educational fads and fashions. Those who seek only to travel the too-easy streets of the modern university cannot allow the entrepreneurs, in the 1980s or at any other time, past or future, to unmuddy or to undirty the dishwater. It is in the dull regimes that pure rents are best earned, and this is not a novel fact to those who are so disposed to seek them.

The genuine innovator-entrepreneur who seeks to challenge, to stir up the dishwater of orthodoxy, must expect to counter resistance at every stage. At best, he and his fellow workers can hope to find academic settings that are temporarily congenial to their efforts, settings that encourage those who dare to be different. But such academic innovators should never be lulled into complacency by their apparent external success in having a demonstrable impact on the world of ideas. They must always recognize that, back home, within the academic groves, external successes matter not one whit for those who seek only to maximize their rents. If those who challenge the orthodoxies allow a false sense of security to develop, the natural forces of bureaucracy emerge to empower those who seek to defend that which is and to keep the dullness of the dishwater as the protective shield behind which the rent-recipients may slumber on and on.

When such scenarios unfold, those who are the challengers must move on to still other academic settings that offer, at least temporarily, new congenial homes for their unorthodoxies.

Almost indirectly (or perhaps not so indirectly after all), I have sketched here for you a history of the Center for the Study of Public Choice, and, in a more personal sense, a history of my own academic career, not only here at Blacksburg and VPI, but much earlier at the University of Virginia. But let me end on a strongly upbeat note. The "Virginia School of Political Economy" still lives! Yes, Virginia, there is a Virginia School!

SECTION 5

THE VIRGINIA LECTURES IN POLITICAL ECONOMY

5.0 Introduction

PETER J. BOETTKE AND ALAIN MARCIANO

As David Levy and Sandra Peart have demonstrated (Levy and Peart 2013, 2014), the term "Virginia School" was coined in the early 1970s—in 1971, to be precise—by Mancur Olson and Christopher Clague (see Olson's "Why Is Economic Performance Even Worse after Communism Is Abandoned?" in this section). As Olson explained, when he delivered the ninth lecture in the Virginia Political Economy series,

> Chris Clague and I were concerned that many people at that time did not distinguish the Virginia School from the Chicago School. . . . If one thinks only ideologically, then it might be reasonable to classify the Virginia School and the Chicago School together. . . . But if one looks at scientific method and analytical insights instead of ideology, the Virginia School was and is very different indeed from the Chicago School. (Olson, section 5.9 in this volume)

To be more precise, it differs from what is now known as the "new Chicago School of economics" but has its roots in the "old" Chicago School of economics (on the distinction, see section 7.1 in this volume). Indeed, Clague and Olson stress, Knight was one of the "forebearers" of the Virginia School of Political Economy (Olson and Clague 1971).

Formally, the origins of the Virginia School of Political Economy date back from the creation of the Thomas Jefferson Center (TJC) by Buchanan and Warren Nutter. It emanated from the commitment Buchanan and Nutter bore when they were students at Chicago—that if they ever ended up in the same place, they would work together to "save the books" and "save the ideas"—and that was then brought into reality at the University of Virginia less than a decade later. In addition, it is important to note that this statement is not a rational reconstruction. The members of the TJC were self-identifying themselves and were all identified by others as forming a "Virginia School" (Levy and Peart 2014; Breit 1987).

The Virginia Political Economy Lecture Series was launched in 1985 and was sponsored by the Center for the Study of Public Choice at Mason. The objective was "to explore the origins, nature and contributions of the Virginia School of Political Economy" (see introduction to section 5.2). These essays help to get a clearer view of this school of thought, not only because some of the contributors gave testimonies as to how the school was established (Breit, for instance) or because they directly characterized the school (Mueller, Yeager, Mackay, Goetz), but also because they give instances of works that belong to this school of thought. The lectures illustrate Buchanan's influence and impact, and they are a particularly important complement to Buchanan's own work.

The 15 lectures are reprinted in this section as follows:

1. "The 'Virginia School' and Public Choice" by Dennis C. Mueller, 1985.
2. "Creating the 'Virginia School': Charlottesville as an Academic Environment in the 1960s" by William Breit, 1986.
3. "Getting More with Less, with a Notable Exception" by Dwight R. Lee, 1987.
4. "Ethics in the History and Doctrine of the Virginia School" by Leland Yeager, 1988.
5. "Winston Bush's Contribution to Public Choice: Anarchy, Politics, and Population" by Robert J. Mackay, 1989.
6. "The Tale of the Slave Owner: Reflections on the Political Economy of Communist Reform" by Geoffrey Brennan, 1990.
7. "Uncommon Common Sense vs. Conventional Wisdom: The Virginia School of Economics" by Charles J. Goetz, 1991.

8. "On the Political Economy of the Transformation of Political and Economic Regimes" by Peter Bernholz, 1992.
9. "Why Is Economic Performance Even Worse after Communism Is Abandoned?" by Mancur Olson, 1993.
10. "Virginia Virtue—Virginia Vice" by Hartmut Kliemt, 1994.
11. "The Public Choice Approach to International Economic Relations" by Thomas D. Willett, 1995.
12. "The Economics of Welfare Reform" by Edgar K. Browning, 1996.
13. "The Nature of Time in Economics" by Richard B. McKenzie, 1997.
14. "Will Johnny Read Next Year?" by Eugenia F. Toma, 1999.
15. "Economics and the Medieval Church" by Robert D. Tollison, 2001.

REFERENCES

Breit, W. 1987. "Creating the 'Virginia School': Charlottesville as an Academic Environment in the 1960s." *Economic Inquiry* 25: 645–57.

Levy, D. M., and S. J. Peart. 2013. *How the Virginia School Got Its Name.* Richmond, VA: Jepson School of Leadership Studies.

———. 2014. "'Almost Wholly Negative': The Ford Foundation's Appraisal of the Virginia School." https://papers.ssrn.com/sol3/papers.cfm?abstract_id=2485695. Accessed February 23, 2020.

Olson, M., and C. K. Clague. 1971. "Dissent in Economics: The Convergence of Extremes." *Social Research* 38(4): 751–76.

5.1
The "Virginia School" and Public Choice

DENNIS C. MUELLER

The title of this lecture contains two terms, both of which require definition. Let me start with the easiest of the two. I regard public choice as the economics of politics. Public choice uses the methodology of economics to study questions traditionally investigated by political science. The key ingredient in this approach is the assumption that political man, like his economic cousin, is a rational, self-interested being. The central role this assumption plays makes public choice, like economics, inherently individualistic and utilitarian. Both fields share this philosophical heritage, and this characteristic of public choice is important in understanding why the public choice approach often leads to radically different conclusions than its rival disciplines.

I favor a broad definition of public choice, one that encompasses what the literature in political science often referred to as "rational politics" and the literature in economics frequently referred to as "social choice." That is to say, I draw no distinctions based on degree of abstraction or analytic approach. Game theoretic and axiomatic analyses of political behavior are legitimately classified as parts of the public choice literature in that they build their analyses upon the assumption that individuals are rational and self-interested.

Prepared for the First Annual Lecture in the Virginia Political Economy Lecture Series, George Mason University, Fairfax, VA, April 24, 1985.

Given this conception of the public choice field, the question with which I am concerned today is what has been the Virginia School's contribution to the development of this field, and to some extent what has been the contribution of the field itself to our understanding of political institutions.

Before we can proceed, however, we must turn to the question of defining what we mean by the "Virginia School," or, more basically, determining whether it is even legitimate to speak of a Virginia School within the public choice field. Did Mancur Olson, whom Robert Tollison credits with having first used the term "Virginia School," fabricate an image for which no reality exists?

The appellation "school" is used surprisingly sparingly in the field of economics. Outside of the instance in question, I can think of only three, maybe four, other schools of thought in economics. There is, of course, the Chicago School, the most frequently used and widely known appellative of this sort. There is the Austrian School. There is the Cambridge School, whereby a place in England, not Massachusetts, is designated. And I think it legitimate to refer to a Marxist School. Some might object that this is too narrow a use of the term "school," and that one can also think of a Keynesian School, a Monetarist School, a post-Keynesian School, a Rational Expectations School, and so on. I reject these additional candidates to my taxonomy of schools for reasons that will become apparent as we proceed.

If we accept for the moment my claim that these are the only schools of thought in economics it is legitimate to differentiate, the question arises: What characteristics do they have in common, and does the Virginia School share these characteristics? While each appellation may connote different things to different people, I think there are three characteristics all schools have in common. Two of these will be readily acknowledged by all. First, each has its own methodology to some extent. Second, the writings of each school are colored by a distinctive ideology. I shall return to the third, more controversial characteristic these schools have in common after reviewing the first two.

Let us begin with methodology. This attribute is most clearly apparent in the Marxist and Austrian Schools. Marx was clearly influenced greatly by the writings of classical economics and incorporated some of its concepts into his analysis. Yet his writings were obviously meant in part as a methodological challenge to classical economics, and the distinguishing feature of Marxist economics to this day is the use of concepts and methods employed or developed by Marx and largely alien to the rest of the economics literature; for example, the dialectic approach, the concept of surplus value, and, most importantly, the substitution of class for the individual as a basic building block of the analysis. So different is the methodology of the Marxist from that of the modern non-Marxist economist, one might reasonably question whether Marxism is really a school of thought *within economics*. But if one is willing to classify as economists those individuals who study economic questions (the causes of poverty, unemployment, etc.) and/or are housed in economics departments around the world as economists, then there are many economists who employ the Marxist methodology, and Marxist economics is legitimately defined as a separate school in economics.

Austrian economics shares with Marxist economics an antipathy toward some of the fundamental methodological presumptions of the ruling orthodoxy in economics, although for the Austrians it is *neo*classical orthodoxy that is questioned. The Austrians' rejection of the use of equilibrium conditions and the importance they place on uncertainty and subjectivism can all be regarded as distinctive breaks with prevailing neoclassical analysis.

Of the four schools identified, the Cambridge School is perhaps the most amorphous. Methodologically, it is a mixture of Keynesianism and Marxism and is thus also critical of modern neoclassical economics, although it is not nearly as far removed from it as Marxist or Austrian thought. Ideologically, it shares with Marxist economics a distrust of the outcomes from the market and a belief in the desirability of government intervention, although the Cambridge School does not necessarily go as far as the Marxists in their espoused role for the government.

Where the Marxist, Austrian, and Cambridge Schools all are critical of orthodox economics methodology, the Chicago School embodies its quintessence. Chicagoans, more readily than most economists, are willing to extend the rational man assumption, as in rational expectations models, to the point where man is not only capable of behaving consistently when making choices but possesses powers bordering on clairvoyance. To assume that selfish, rational man might be motivated by altruism, ideology, or the like is to abandon economics for sociology in the eyes of most Chicagoans. While all non-Marxist, non-Cambridge economists share an appreciation for the potential benefits from market competition, this appreciation is carried, once again, to the extreme by members of the Chicago School. The notion that some product markets might not function well due to the existence of entry barriers is dismissed, since entry barriers, other than those created by government, do not exist in the opinion of most Chicagoans (e.g., Posner 1976, 92–93). Indeed, almost any criticism that is made of the efficiency of a capitalist market economy is answered by a Chicagoan by invoking an efficient market. Thus, for example, the potential problems raised by the separation of ownership from control in the modern, large corporation easily get resolved in a Chicagoan's eyes by the efficient working of the market for managers (Fama 1980). The Chicago School is distinguishable within the field of economics not because it rejects parts of the methodology or ideology of economics but because it epitomizes them.

I have slipped in that most abused word "ideology" in a couple of places already. Let me define it.

Webster's Third New International Dictionary (unabridged) presents the following definitions of ideology: "A systematic scheme or coordinated body of ideas or concepts, especially about human life or culture. . . . a manner or the content of thinking characteristic of an individual, group, or culture. . . . the integrated assertions, theories, and aims that constitute a sociopolitical program. . . . an extremist sociopolitical program or philosophy constructed wholly or in part on factitious or hypothetical ideational bases." Certainly, Marxist economics is an ideology on the basis of at least one if not all of these definitions.

I hope you will all agree with me that each of the other three schools I have identified is also an ideology by at least one of the above definitions, although we might disagree as to which of the several definitions best fits each school.

It is a pity that the word "ideology" has taken on a negative connotation, particularly among academicians. I suppose this goes back to the time in the fifties when, with some relief, it was popular to declare an "end to ideology" in the social sciences in favor of presumably more scientific and impartial social science research. It is understandable at a time when the world still vividly recollected the ravages wrought by fascism and was gripped by fear of the dangers of Communism that one would wish to free social discourse from the most fanatical manifestations of ideology, from "extremist sociopolitical programs(s) or philosoph(ies) constructed wholly or in part on factitious or hypothetical ideational bases." But in less extreme forms, ideology is to my mind an essential element or catalyst in most truly important research. To avoid the negative overtones of the word "ideology," let me substitute for it the German word *weltanschauung*. A good translation of weltanschauung is Webster's first definition of ideology: "A systematic scheme or coordinated body of ideas or concepts especially about human life or culture." Certainly this definition is more descriptive than the literal translation, "view of the world."

The work of the major figures in the development of each of the enumerated schools of thought was imbued with a clear weltanschauung. Perhaps the best reflection of a school of thought's Weltanschauung is not so much the answers it gives to questions but the questions it asks. Each school of thought has focused its attention upon a set of interrelated questions that distinguish it both from the other schools of thought and from the ordinary research of other economists and social scientists. Each has posed questions central to both our understanding of human life and our potential for improving it. Each has asked a set of questions, which either had gone previously unanswered or to which unsatisfactory answers had been given. Those who have been attracted to each school have been drawn by the belief that the questions their school is asking are the most important of the day in need of answering.

All of the great thinkers in economics have been first and foremost askers of important questions. Moreover, they seem to be driven by a curiosity that leads them to ask fundamental questions about aspects of everyday life. What separates the great thinkers from the average is their capacity to recognize which aspects of human behavior are capable of being explained by more general laws and their capacity to distinguish between the fundamental regularities in human behavior and the trivial. No reader of Adam Smith, Karl Marx, Ludwig von Mises, or John Maynard Keynes can come away from their writings without having gained the impression that these were astute observers of human behavior, who gained sustenance for their theories from their everyday observations of individual behavior and the operation of economic institutions.

While the great thinkers of all ages have in common a curiosity about their environment and a capability to observe and generalize about human behavior, they differ in both the questions they ask and the aspects of human behavior that attract their attention. Adam Smith was moved to inquire into the causes of the wealth of nations and into the possible impediment to the accumulation of this wealth the mercantilist practices of his day might constitute. Marx became obsessed by the misery of workers. What explains these different curiosities? Time and place? Social background? Religion? The answers to these questions I must leave to psychologists. Let me simply assert that it is here that an individual's weltanschauung plays its most visible and vital role. For some reason, different scholars of equal genius have had different conceptions of human life, which have led them to ask different questions about human life and to observe different aspects of it. These differences, these different weltanschauungs, have given rise to the different schools of thought.

Marx observed aspects of human life that many others feel that they, too, have observed, if only subconsciously. When these potential members of the Marxist School read Marx, a resonant chord is struck. A similar sensation is experienced by converts to Austrian, Cambridge, or Chicago economics upon exposure to the teachings of these respective schools. Moreover, the chords struck seem to resonate with a more vibrant sound than normally occurs when one reads a work in economics. Those won over to the teachings of each school seem filled with greater conviction as to the validity of their arguments, as to the rightness of their positions, and, by implication or explication, the wrongness of those opposed to the teachings of their school. This then is the third characteristic that the four schools have in common. Members of each school typically write and speak with more conviction about the teachings of their schools. A certain intensity is apparent both upon the written page and in the spoken word. Members of each school are filled with an enthusiasm for their work that goes well beyond the professional economist's normal interest in economic issues, an enthusiasm that even exceeds the fondness each of us has for his own ideas.

Let me now, finally, turn to the subject at hand. In what sense is it legitimate to speak of a Virginia School of economics or public choice? Is there a methodology and an ideology that is sufficiently identifiable that we can clearly speak of those who espouse it as members of a distinct group or school? Do members of the school have the same enthusiasm, the same passion for their work, as do members of the other schools?

So broad and fundamental were Adam Smith's insights into human nature and the workings of economic institutions that nearly every reader became a convert in part to Smith's way of thinking. Publication of the *Wealth of Nations* led not to the founding of a Scottish School *within* political economy, but to the founding of the field itself. Similarly, I think the Virginia School's methodological contribution to the evolution of scientific thought is not so much in developing a separate methodology within public choice as it is in contributing to the development of the public choice field itself. Of course, the early writings of the Virginia School were not the only works that one can legitimately classify as having led to the development of the field. Kenneth Arrow's *Social Choice and Individual Values* (1951); Duncan Black's early articles and subsequent book, *The Theory of Committees and Elections* (1958); Anthony Downs's *An Economic Theory of Democracy* (1957); and Mancur Olson's *The Logic of Collective Action* (1965) all appeared around the time Buchanan and Tullock's early articles and *The Calculus of Consent* (1962) appeared. But, Arrow and Downs failed to follow up their pathbreaking studies with further research on economic politics, and neither Black nor Olson appear to have produced many students of the subject.

In contrast, Buchanan and Tullock followed up their seminal writings with a stream of articles and books that continues uninterrupted up to today. In addition, and most importantly, the Virginia schools at which they have resided produced a large number of scholars who have chosen to work in the public choice field. The first meeting of public choice scholars was organized by Buchanan and Tullock and took place in Charlottesville, Virginia, in 1963. Soon thereafter, *Papers in Non-Market Decisionmaking* appeared, a journal devoted to the new field and forerunner to the *Public Choice* journal. The existence of both the journal *Public Choice* and the Public Choice Society can be traced directly to the early efforts of James Buchanan and Gordon Tullock. One can, with justification, question whether public choice would have emerged as a separate, well-defined field within economics and political science had Buchanan and Tullock not fathered the field they helped spawn with the degree of paternalistic care with which they did.

Today, those of us working within public choice are all members of the Virginia School, in much the same way that all economists are members of the "Scottish School" founded by Adam Smith. We are conscious that our methodology is somewhat unique only when we are in the presence of political scientists, philosophers, or other social scientists who do not employ this approach. That public choice scholars are a rather different breed is readily apparent at any interdisciplinary conference at which they are present. But at the annual Public Choice Society meetings, one cannot tell a member of the Virginia School without a scorecard. The Virginia School's methodology and the "public choice approach" are one and the same, particularly when viewed from the perspective of someone outside the field.

If the methodological approach does not distinguish the Virginia School from the rest of public choice, then ideology, or my third, less tangible ingredient, enthusiasm, must. Certainly, in the eyes of many, it is ideology that sets the Virginia School apart. But, in my mind, the third ingredient is at least as important.

I spent one year at the Public Choice Center in Blacksburg, Virginia, in the early seventies and have visited the Public Choice Center both in Blacksburg and Fairfax several times since. Upon each occasion, I have been struck by the level of interest of members of the Public Choice Center in questions of a public choice nature and by the intensity with which public choice issues are discussed, regardless of whether the issue is one upon which the individual is personally doing research. Chance meetings at the coffee urn, in the locker room, or in the cafeteria all become occasions for lively discussion of public choice issues. I have been employed at and have visited numerous other universities and research centers, but I associate with none of these the same level of enthusiasm and excitement for new ideas as I have always found at the Public Choice Center.

The importance of the existence of a center—that is, a place at which the public choice approach can be learned and public choice questions studied to the development of the public choice field and the Virginia School—cannot be overemphasized. Indeed, it is interesting to observe that three of the four schools discussed here are named after places: Austria, Cambridge, and Chicago. Why the choice of a place name in three cases and a single person's name in the fourth? The reason for the choice of a place name is that the body of research to which reference is made in each instance cannot be associated with the name of a single person. Rather, the research is the product of several scholars working over a number of years at the place that gives the work its name. But why are these places and these bodies of work singled out? Why is it that there exists no Belgian School, no Oxford School, no New Haven School? Certainly it is not because these places have lacked several fine scholars, who have produced much important research. Rather, it is because the research emanating from these and almost every other place lacks the methodological and ideological cohesiveness that allows one to identify it as being part of a school of thought, and it lacks my third ingredient, that extra degree of enthusiasm that makes members of the school excited about their own work and infects others with similar excitement.

If the leading luminaries of a school of thought are to be found at a given place, then those who read the work of the school and become enthused by it have a place to which they can go to study and mingle with those who share their weltanschauung. Moreover, if a school of thought is more or less associated with a given location, it is possible for the ideas of the school to evolve. By definition, the ideas of the *X* School are the ideas emanating from *X*. If *X* is a place containing several scholars studying different questions, then the ideas of this school will evolve as human behavior evolves and our knowledge of it accumulates. If *X*, in contrast, is a person, then only *X*'s ideas can be unambiguously defined as part of the *X* School, and once *X* dies the development of the school atrophies. This point is immediately underlined when one contrasts the Marxist and Chicago Schools. Since Marx was not associated with any university, there was no place to which his followers could go and study during his lifetime. When he died, no single place existed where Marxists studied and taught. There was neither a Pope, Marx being dead, nor a Vatican to authenticate the ideas put forward by disciples of Marx as legitimate elements of Marxist thought. The result has been that Marxism has by and large failed to evolve as an intellectual field. Both the methodology employed and the issues addressed (the misery of the working class, imperialism) are the same today as in the 19th century, even though blue-collar factory workers are a vanishing class, and all empires, except ironically the Russian Empire, have disappeared.

In contrast, because economists at the University of Chicago continue to share the same weltanschauung that has made "the Chicago School" readily identifiable, Chicago economics is an evolving body of thought. When an idea like rational expectations comes along, an idea which fits so comfortably into the Chicago weltanschauung as this one does, it can be incorporated into the litany without hesitation. For Chicago economics is what Chicago economists do, not some rigid set of principles. It is the Chicago economist's weltanschauung that provides consistency and ensures that only the "right" ideas are incorporated, not some set text to which reference must be made.

In much the same way that Chicago for so many years has served as a magnet attracting from around the world students and scholars in whom the Chicago School's weltanschauung has been kindled, the Center for Study of Public Choice, inexplicably but ineluctably linked to Jefferson's state of Virginia, has drawn from every corner of the globe those who share its weltanschauung, those interested in the basic questions of why governments exist and how they operate.

I come now to the issue of what public choice has contributed to our understanding of political institutions and what the Virginia School's share of this contribution has been. To appreciate these contributions, one must go back to, say, the 1950s and examine what the conventional wisdom within economics and political science was at that point of time regarding political institutions. Let us start with economics.

On the macro side, the Keynesian revolution was still in full swing. Theoretical and empirical work discussed how fiscal, monetary, and trade policies could be coordinated to control unemployment, inflation, and the balance of payments. A kind of macro-Walrasian counting of policy goals and instruments was popular, and a confidence existed that the former could be achieved if the government was free to vary all of the instruments potentially at its command. It was at this time that the Phillips curve came into vogue. A brief debate ensued over the impact of increases in government debt, with a consensus reached that it was largely of no economic consequence. In general, a mood of optimism regarding government's potential impact ruled on the macro front.

On the micro side, similar sounds were heard. Baumol's *Welfare Economics and the Theory of the State* appeared in 1952. It used the existence of externalities to justify government intervention on efficiency grounds. The classic papers on externalities and public goods by James Meade and Paul Samuelson appeared between 1952 and 1954. The whole literature was pulled together in the influential article by Francis Bator published in 1958, with the catchy title, "The Anatomy of Market Failure." "Market failure" was the watchword of the day, and the implicit assumption and explicit recommendation were that government could move to remove these market failures—and that it should.

Similar developments occurred in other branches of microeconomics. In industrial organization, for example, Joe Bain's classic *Barriers to New Competition* was published in 1956 and Kaysen and Turner's *Antitrust Policy* in 1959. These books provided arguments and evidence indicating that high industry concentration and entry barriers lead to high industry profits. They helped spawn a generation of research in the structure-conduct-performance tradition that advocated tough enforcement of existing antitrust laws and rationalized further tightening of the laws themselves.

Although his flamboyant generalizations often earned him the scorn of his more timorous professional colleagues, just as his elegant style elicited their envy, the writings of popularizer John Kenneth Galbraith during the fifties and early sixties are a fair barometer of the more staid "conventional wisdom" within the profession of the failings of the market and the promise of government action.

As representative of the thinking within political science at the time, let me focus upon a single work, Robert Dahl's *A Preface to Democratic Theory*, published in 1956, although mention might also be made of Dahl and Lindblom's *Politics, Economics, and Welfare*, published in 1953, in which the potential for government policy in a market economy subject to market failure is treated at length. But, *A Preface* is a clear and concise review of basic political principles by America's premier, nonpublic choice, political theorist.

Dahl takes as his point of departure James Madison's theory of democracy. Thus, Dahl does not base his analysis on a romantic view of the individual and his motives. The first hypothesis of the book is that, "If unrestrained by external checks, any given individual or group of individuals will tyrannize over others" (Dahl 1956, 6). Dahl goes on to analyze Madison's attempt to restrain the proclivities of individuals and groups to tyrannize through the introduction of checks and balances into the political process. Dahl concludes that Madison's model is "dearly inadequate" on both logical and empirical grounds (ibid., 31). Majority rule, at least as it has been defended in American Populist thought, fares even worse under Dahl's critical, analytic scrutiny (section 2), but, nevertheless, the American political system as it functions in reality winds up getting very high marks. The closing lines of the book read as follows:

> So long as the social prerequisites of democracy are substantially intact in this country, it [the American political system] appears

> to be a relatively efficient system for reinforcing agreement, encouraging moderation, and maintaining social peace in a restless and immoderate people operating a gigantic, powerful, diversified, and incredibly complex society.
>
> This is no negligible contribution then, that Americans have made to the arts of government and to that branch, which of all the arts of politics is the most difficult, the art of democratic government. (Dahl 1956, 151)

Thus, while leading practitioners in economics were busy demonstrating the need for government to achieve economic efficiency, the leading political scientists were demonstrating how well the American form of democracy did in fact work in practice. To these prevailing currents of thought, the pioneering contributions to public choice presented a stark contrast. Of the five major pioneering works cited above, only Duncan Black's *A Theory of Committees and Elections* (1958) sounds a uniformly positive note about the potential of political institutions. In this book, Black proves his celebrated median voter theorem. An equilibrium is possible under majority rule under certain conditions. Unfortunately, subsequent research has shown that these conditions are so unlikely to hold in practice that Black's important theorem stands, from the perspective of today, as a kind of special case illustrating the fragility inherent in majority rule committee outcomes.

Downs reproduced Hotelling's version of the median voter outcome and derived several other spatial model results (1957). Unfortunately, the Hotelling-Downs result gets overturned in precisely the same way Black's median voter result does, and the rest of Downs's spatial results are subject to similar criticism. The most original and lasting contribution of Downs's book is undoubtedly the idea of rational ignorance, the idea that the rather small probability of any voter making a difference to the outcome of the political process implies that rational voters will tend to remain uninformed. If one accepts Downs's reasoning on this point, then the issues of whether voters vote, or whether we can aggregate their votes rationally, become rather inconsequential.

No single work has driven home the message that political processes may aggregate information about voter preferences to produce outcomes with undesirable normative properties better than Kenneth Arrow's *Social Choice and Individual Values* (1951). A case can be made that the message has been misinterpreted and oversold. But three decades of subsequent research by countless scores of theorists dramatically attest to the captivating power of the theorem and the resiliency of the result.

Olson's first book (1965) is also full of gloomy notes. The free-rider problem is pervasive. Interest groups with small numbers of participants, like a producers' association for an oligopolistic industry, form more readily than do large member associations like consumers' unions. Olson's song does not sound any sweeter 20 years later, when he tells us of the causes of the decline of nations and stagflation (1982).

The Calculus of Consent (1962) also contains its discordant sounds. Gordon Tullock's classic article (1959) showing how majority rule can lead to an excessive expansion of government is reproduced as section 8, and in general the book is not kind to majority rule. But in many ways it paints the most optimistic picture of the potential of democratic institutions of the five major pioneering works discussed here. It comes close to defending logrolling as a method of revealing intensity of preferences, and it provides the normative raison d'être for a two-stage political process in which conflicts over voting rules, property rights, and other distributional issues get resolved unanimously and equitably in a first constitutional stage. It remains even today one of the most comprehensive and at the same time optimistic discussions of democratic institutions in the public choice field.

Subsequent developments in public choice have followed the pattern set by the early classics—some good news, but mostly bad news. Arrow's theorem has been reproved dozens of times. Logrolling does not make matters better but is symptomatic of the underlying cycling problem with which we began. The potential for cycles allows an astute agenda setter to maneuver a committee to almost any point in the issue space he prefers. New impossibility theorems have been added, like Sen's liberal paradox (1970). Government budgets grow large both because of the voting rules we employ (geographic representation, prevote screening by committees, seniority rules for committee leadership, the use of majority rule) and because we "purchase" government outputs from bureaucracies led by individuals bent on maximizing their budgets. Our legislatures sell bills to their highest bidders. The courts indemnify these sales through their interpretations of the laws. Voting with the feet is *not* a Pareto-efficient means for revealing individual preferences for local public goods, as we thought it was when Tiebout first made the suggestion in 1956. I could go on; the list is never-ending.

The bulk of the public choice literature is, like its half-sister economics, positive analysis. Positive analyses of an ugly world, if done properly, will paint an ugly picture. If the political world is truly ugly, then the positive public choice literature deserves high scientific marks for accurately reflecting this reality.

I have heard George Stigler quoted as having responded to the question of how his work differs from Milton Friedman's with the following answer: "Milton Friedman wants to change the world, I want to understand it." Forced to choose, most economists would associate themselves with Stigler's position, rather than the one attributed to Friedman. Indeed, many eschew entirely the posing of normative questions and profess with pride that they engage only in positive economic analysis.

Let me play devil's advocate and assert that the social scientist's objective *ought* to be both to understand the world *and* to change it. The first is, of course, a means to the second. To seek to understand the social world while totally disregarding the possible implications of one's research for improving it would be to allow one's research to be driven entirely by idle curiosity, by the whim of what questions struck one as interesting without regard to their importance. Such research is, alas, all too common in economics, but it is not the kind of research that, it seems to me, we as *social* scientists ought to be pursuing. If it is merely puzzle solving we seek, then certainly there are more challenging puzzles to be solved outside of the social sciences: the origins of life, of the universe, the existence of God. Finding an algorithm for aligning the colors on a Rubik's cube would involve more pure mental challenge than proving half of the propositions that fill the pages of the leading economics journals today.

If we date the founding of the Virginia School to the publication of *The Calculus of Consent* (1962), then the school's inaugural contribution was a blend of both positive and normative analysis. This comprehensive view of political issues may stem from James Buchanan's chance reading of Knut Wicksell's "Essay on Just Taxation" (1896) shortly prior to his departure from Chicago. In this essay, Wicksell clearly enunciated the reason why collective action outside the market is necessary and drew an analogy between the quid pro quo of a democratic process and the quid pro quo of the market. Wicksell's essay sketched an optimistic picture of the *potential* for democratic procedures, a picture whose outline has remained distinguishable in many of Buchanan's writings and those of others in the Virginia School.

That selfish people in a wicked world design institutions that produce wicked outcomes is not surprising. What is surprising is that so many political scientists and economists in the fifties and early sixties wrote as if this were not the case. But the news is now out. Public choice has played an important role in enlightening both academic and public discourse to potential failings of political institutions. But the payoffs to this line of research are significantly smaller than they were, say, 20 years ago. The big payoffs today are in explaining both why political institutions produce undesirable outcomes *and* how they might be redesigned to produce better ones. In my mind, public choice has been and remains an exciting field of research because it allows one to discover voting rules like the demand revelation process, which allows one to solve the preference revelation problem that has plagued public goods theory from the start. Public choice allows one to investigate how a federalist political system might be tailored to resolve externality and public goods problems at the differing geographic dimensions at which they occur. More generally, public choice has revealed the potential for designing constitutional constraints that might channel man's selfish interests in ways that we would all agree are acceptable. The Virginia School has had an important influence within public choice because it, taken as a whole, has always combined the analysis of political failure with the potential of political institutions.

The task of ensuring that the public choice baby survives and guiding it through its early years is now completed. Infancy and adolescence are over, and the Virginia School can be proud of the role it has played in the development of its progeny. Public choice has emerged from a period of rapid growth in which numerous important, exciting discoveries have been made. It stands today as a mature academic subdiscipline, whose future remains unchartered. It stands today at an academic crossroads.

The premium in academia today is on speed. The tenure decision is typically made during one's fifth year of employment, and this, combined with long queues at the journals, forces young scholars to pose questions that can be quickly answered. Habits acquired during the first few years of one's career often seem to persist throughout it. In a mature discipline, most of the "easy discoveries" have been made. One faces the choice between tackling difficult but important questions that require long gestation periods and have high risks of failure and executing less significant but safer extensions of the existing literature that can be completed quickly. The journals today are filled with ingenious answers to unimportant questions.

Public choice today stands in danger of following down this well-worn path. The welcomed growth of interest in the field has begun to show up in the numbers of scholars in economics and political science departments around this country and even in parts of Europe. The journal, *Public Choice*, has been joined by at least one other focusing exclusively on public choice research, and the leading journals in both political science and economics regularly publish articles in the public choice field. Significant diminution of the returns to researching some questions has been observed, however. The issue of whether the field will maintain its vitality as it matures is not an idle one. At this juncture, the Virginia School, guided by its weltanschauung, can serve as a beacon, with the Center for Study of Public Choice as a lighthouse, directing the young and not-so-young scholars of the public choice field away from the seductive sirens of inconsequential research, back to the basic issues of how self-interested individuals interact within political institutions and how individuals could design institutions that would better achieve their ends.

REFERENCES

Arrow, Kenneth J. 1951. *Social Choice and Individual Values.* New York: Wiley and Sons.

Bain, Joe S. 1956. *Barriers to New Competition.* Cambridge, MA: Harvard University Press.

Bator, Francis M. 1958. "The Anatomy of Market Failure." *Quarterly Journal of Economics* 72: 351–79.

Baumol, Williams J. 1952. *Welfare Economics and the Theory of the State.* London: Longmans, Green.

Black, Duncan. 1958. *The Theory of Committees and Elections.* Cambridge: Cambridge University Press.

Buchanan, James M., and Gordon Tullock. 1962. *The Calculus of Consent.* Ann Arbor: University of Michigan Press.

Dahl, Robert A. 1956. *A Preface to Democratic Theory.* Chicago: University of Chicago Press.

Dahl, Robert A., and Charles E. Lindblom. 1953. *Politics, Economics, and Welfare.* New York: Harper and Row.

Downs, Anthony. 1957. *An Economic Theory of Democracy.* New York: Harper and Row.

Fama, Eugene. 1980. "Agency Problems and the Theory of the Firm." *Journal of Political Economy* 88: 288–307.

Kaysen, Carl, and Donald F. Turner. 1959. *Antitrust Policy.* Cambridge, MA: Harvard University Press.

Meade, James E. 1952. "External Economies and Diseconomies in a Competitive Situation." *Economics Journal* 62: 54–67.

Olson, Mancur. 1965. *The Logic of Collective Action.* Cambridge, MA: Harvard University Press.

———. 1982. *The Rise and Decline of Nations.* New Haven, CT: Yale University Press.

Posner, Richard A. 1976. *Antitrust Law.* Chicago: University of Chicago Press.

Samuelson, Paul A. 1954. "The Pure Theory of Public Expenditure." *Review of Economics and Statistics* 36: 387–89.

Sen, Amartya K. 1970. "The Impossibility of a Paretian Liberal." *Journal of Political Economy* 78: 152–57.

Tiebout, Charles M. 1956. "A Pure Theory of Local Expenditures." *Journal of Political Economy* 64: 416–24.

Tullock, Gordon. 1959. "Some Problems of Majority Voting." *Journal of Political Economy* 67: 571–79.

Wicksell, Knut. 1896. "Essay on Just Taxation." In Knut Wicksell, *Finanztheoretische Untersuchungen.* Jena: Thoemmes Continuum. Translated by James M. Buchanan and published as "A New Principle of Just Taxation" in Richard A. Musgrave and Alan T. Peacock (eds.), *Classics in the Theory of Public Finance*, 72–118 (1967). New York: St. Martin's Press.

5.2
Creating the "Virginia School"
Charlottesville as an Academic Environment in the 1960s

WILLIAM BREIT

The universe of economics consists of a diversity of worlds. This lecture is about the creation of one version of a world, that which is identified with the name the "Virginia School." It is only in retrospect that I am able to discuss the formation of a new world version at Virginia. For when I arrived in Charlottesville in the fall of 1965, I was not aware that anything so dramatic was taking place. Neither, I think, was anyone else. However, with the clarity that hindsight allows, I want to discuss the Charlottesville environment in the mid-1960s because I think it provides important clues as to the reasons for the great success of the research and teaching program that was being carried out. Much of what I say is necessarily subjective and autobiographical. Although I was not present at the moment of conception, I was around and, to a slight extent, participated in the process of a world in the making.

I shall not attempt a summary of the technical content of the public choice tenets of the Virginia School. That task has been done admirably by

Prepared for the Second Annual Lecture in the Virginia Political Economy Lecture Series, George Mason University, Fairfax, VA, April 16, 1986.

my predecessor in this lecture series—Dennis Mueller. Rather I should prefer to say something about the environment in Charlottesville that prevailed during the period in which the Virginia School was established.

Not enough attention has been paid by economic historians to the question of environment and its relation to paradigmatic shifts within the profession. By environment I mean the physical geography, social relationships, and personalities that affect the style and content of academic discussion. As Harry Johnson has demonstrated, such factors were crucial in establishing the Keynesian revolution at Cambridge in the 1930s and determined the character of economics at Cambridge in the 1950s. The Charlottesville setting deserves similar attention because what transpired there in the period from 1957 to 1968 was a clear-cut paradigmatic shift—the creation of a new school of thought. Ideas generated in that environment became part of the received wisdom of economics under the rubrics "public choice" and "constitutional economics." But what was there about the milieu in Charlottesville that brought about this result?

Near the end of his volume on *The Department of Economics at the University of Virginia 1825–1956*, Tipton R. Snavely wrote, "James M. Buchanan, chairman of the Department of Economics at Florida State University, came as professor of economics to assume the chairmanship in 1956–57, and G. Warren Nutter, previously at Yale, accepted the position of associate professor. . . . These men took over leadership in the department and have pressed forward with fresh ideas and determined purpose toward a higher plateau of achievement in economic science" (Snavely 1967).

At the time Snavely wrote these words, a higher plateau had most assuredly been reached. In 1966 the American Council on Education published its influential assessment of quality in graduate departments in 29 academic disciplines. Economics was one of only four departments at the University of Virginia singled out for special mention as being among the country's leading centers in terms of the quality of the graduate faculty and effectiveness of the graduate program. In the two previous studies cited by Allan M. Cartter, the author of this report, the economics department received no such encomiums.

But it was not public choice or constitutional economics that attracted me to Charlottesville in 1965. Indeed, neither the terms "public choice" nor "constitutional economics" had yet been coined. Rather it was the emphasis on political economy. Political economy meant to me, as I think it did to most others within the department, a return to the basic principles of classical economics and in particular the application of economic theory to policy problems in the real world. Price theory was considered a powerful tool of analysis when applied to almost any problem involving exchange and decision-making in market and nonmarket settings. The importance of the rules and institutions within which the market order operates seemed to recapture the spirit of Adam Smith and other classical writers. What made Virginia unique on the national scene was an ideological and moral perspective that placed emphasis on market processes within specific institutional settings. As Buchanan put it years later, "We were convinced that the socialist arguments seemed persuasive only to those who were ignorant in economics."

I could understand this mood. In 1965 I had emerged from training within two important traditions. As an undergraduate at the University of Texas, C. E. Ayres made me into an institutionalist. From him I learned the importance of alternative institutions in affecting the manner in which individuals conduct their affairs. He taught that what were often perceived as differences in human nature were nothing more than different institutional settings within which individuals operated. However, Ayres had an unbreaking hostility to the market mechanism and the theory that explained its workings. He did not see it as a way of achieving beneficial outcomes in social interaction. As a consequence, he was attracted to central planning.

My second great teacher was Abba P. Lerner, when I was a graduate student at Michigan State University in the late 1950s. Methodologically, Lerner was the opposite of Ayres. He emphasized the beauty and elegance of price theory and welfare economics, but he taught these subjects as if theory existed in an institutional vacuum. The social and political institutions within which markets worked were all but ignored. Although methodological opposites, Ayres and Lerner were ideological partners. Lerner also supported government intervention into economic affairs under his program of "functional finance."

My arrival in Charlottesville was into an intellectual environment that seemed to bridge the gap between the formal analysis of markets and the institutional framework or rules of the game within which markets function. So I was most receptive to the teachings of my new colleagues in a way I might not have been had I not had such a split background.

To return to my main theme, the Charlottesville environment: I will start with the spatial relationships or the physical geography within which everyday work transpired. The Virginia economists were almost entirely housed in the basement floor of one building. Department faculty offices were in an L-shaped relationship structurally. One branch of the L housed the younger members of the faculty. At right angles, the other stem of the L housed the Thomas Jefferson Center for Studies in Political Economy. The stars of the faculty were found there. However, notwithstanding some age differences between these groups, there was no detectable rank difference as far as social relationships were concerned.

Upon entering the Thomas Jefferson Center, one encountered a small foyer. On the immediate right was a comfortable lounge that served as a department seminar room and also housed the faculty journal club's periodical collection. This room was also a commons room and an examining room for thesis and dissertation defenses. It was an area where a good deal of faculty and student contact took place. A narrow corridor led to a reception room where Betty Tillman, the secretary to James Buchanan and Gordon Tullock, presided. On her right was Tullock's office, on her left the more spacious quarters of James Buchanan. The other members of the center had offices that lined the hall leading to Betty Tillman's chamber. Outside the Thomas Jefferson Center a single staircase led to the floor above, which contained the department's main office where faculty members received mail and messages. As a result, department members came into frequent contact with each other, meeting often at the stairwell and in the central office.

Moreover, most of the academic community lived within a short driving distance of the university grounds, and on a given day a large percentage of the economics faculty would visit their offices. Coffee in the morning and tea in the afternoon at the faculty club on the Lawn were well-attended events. These informal social gatherings provided opportunities to discuss ideas, exchange viewpoints, and otherwise learn about the nature and progress of colleagues' research. There was much interaction between a relatively small group of scholars. Such was the physical setting within which the faculty worked and had its being.

The highlight of each day for me was lunch. Precisely at 12:30 p.m., a group began to gather in the basement for the short walk to the University Cafeteria, a private eating place directly across the main street that fronted the university. These lunches were an important part of everyone's education. Faculty members who "brown-bagged it" each day missed out on this interaction, and as a consequence few of them became full-fledged members of the Virginia School. Ideas were discussed, recent journal articles analyzed, and the present state of one's research criticized. Each lunch had the aspect of a seminar. The discussions were almost always energetic and vigorous and the arguments at the highest level. I think many of us felt that we were collaborators in the process of rediscovering political economy. This was conducive to a sense of mutual loyalty and a deep devotion to many of the ideas being espoused.

With this portrait of the stage setting in mind, I want to provide a sketch of the dramatis personae.

The cast of characters housed in the Thomas Jefferson Center, in addition to James Buchanan and Gordon Tullock, consisted of Leland B. Yeager, Alexandre Kafka, and G. Warren Nutter. Yeager was a specialist in monetary theory and international trade. He was a very shy person and aloof in his relationships with most other people. He did not dine in the caterer's sense of the term, preferring to take one meal only, usually rather late in the evening. As a result, he did not become part of the daily luncheon group I have described. But he was extremely popular with graduate students and served for a long time as director of Graduate Studies in the department. The students got what they called "perfect" sets of lecture notes in his classes. His written work was characterized by luminous clarity and an ability to cut right through to the heart of a subject and expose the hollowness at the core of many of the current orthodoxies. This was best demonstrated in his paper in the *American Economic Review* in 1954 that analyzed the then popular growth models of both Cambridge, England, and Cambridge, Massachusetts. He was a genuine pioneer in constitutional economics, as demonstrated in the 1962 volume that he edited, *In Search of a Monetary Constitution*, which contained lectures delivered at the Thomas Jefferson Center in the fall of 1960. Most refreshingly, he had a keen interest in philosophy and enjoyed discussing the then-popular ideas of Ayn Rand with a coterie of graduate students who sported dollar sign pins on their neckties and were ardent disciples of Ayn Rand's brand of libertarianism. Yeager was willing to spend a good deal of time after business hours in his apartment near the university arguing the finer points of objectivist philosophy.

Another impressive figure was Alexandre Kafka, who was department chairman my first year at Virginia. Although he was a citizen of Brazil, he had the demeanor of an aristocratic Czech, his home having been Prague. Kafka had once been a student of Ludwig von Mises in Zurich, and he had a keen mind and good grasp of economic theory, which he applied to the problems of international finance. Later he joined the International Monetary Fund as executive director. He was highly pragmatic in his politics and suspicious of any doctrine that he believed was too idealistic. Indeed, Kafka was the department's resident skeptic who looked on some of the excitement generated by the new ideas being espoused with detached bemusement. In spite of his exposure to the Austrian School, Kafka was never deeply attached to a free-market ideology. For example, he defended fixed exchange rates. But he was a thoroughly charming and civilized person who added a great deal of panache to the academic environment. He made a deep and favorable impression on me.

G. Warren Nutter was a rather dashing figure, a rough-cut Humphrey Bogart type of a man. Nutter, along with Buchanan, had founded the Thomas

Jefferson Center for Studies in Political Economy in 1957. Its purpose was, in the words of its original brochure, to establish a "community of scholars who wish to preserve a social order based on individual liberty." Nutter was really an inspiration. When he offered me a position at Virginia, he said that I was needed to come help "save the books." To an idealistic young man, those were heady words. I doubt if there was another economics department in the country where anyone was recruited with such a stirring challenge.

Nutter had established a wide reputation for work in comparative economic systems, price theory, and industrial organization. When I met him, his book *Growth of Industrial Production in the Soviet Union* had recently been published, and the controversy it stirred among Soviet specialists in the United States and Great Britain was still raging. In those days, there was great interest in the performance of the Soviet economy since it was held to be a prototype for centrally planned systems. The Soviet Union's own statistics showed an extremely rapid growth in industrial output, and, in comparison, the United States appeared in danger of quickly losing its lead. Many scholars in the West accepted this claim as a likely possibility.

Nutter's massive study for the National Bureau of Economic Research picked the Soviet economy apart. His conclusion, sensational at the time, was that the Soviet growth rate had been wildly overestimated. Moreover, he detected a tendency for the Soviet growth rate to decline in the later years covered by his study. He was almost alone among Western economists in so stating. History has shown Nutter's predictions to have been far more reliable than those of other scholars.

Nutter stands squarely in the Virginia School of political economy in that he applied price theory to real-world problems with a sharp eye on the institutional setting within which decisions were made. This interest in market process was, as I have indicated, a hallmark of Virginia economics. It had been instilled in Nutter, as in Buchanan, by Frank Knight, Henry Simons, and Aaron Director at the University of Chicago. This approach made Nutter observe the Soviet system from a different perspective than that of scholars from other traditions. For example, a roundtable discussion was held at Columbia University in 1965 to discuss Soviet economic performance in the light of its failure to grow at its predicted rate. As a result of that poor performance, Kosygin had announced that piecemeal reforms would decentralize the decision-making apparatus in the Soviet economy.[1]

The experts invited to the Columbia conference were almost all in agreement that such piecemeal reforms would help the Soviet economy grow at a higher rate in the future. Nutter was skeptical. His demurrer was informed by his understanding and appreciation of market process within institutional constraints. To quote Nutter,

> This approach that they're taking may mean that the cure is worse than the disease. Let's just take one area—the experiment in producing to order in some parts of the consumer goods industries. Now, this sounds very good and makes pretty good sense if we think in the context of an economy we're accustomed to, but suppose that we start, as in Russia, with shoes, and you let the shoe factory produce to order. How many orders it gets depends on how good a shoe it produces. Well, suppose that the shoe factory turns out very good shoes. The prices are fixed from above. Presumably its orders will increase. Now, if it has to meet its order, it has to get leather to produce the shoes, but presumably the leather isn't produced to order—it's produced to plan. And so you face the dilemma that the factory producing bad shoes presumably will still get its leather and the factory producing good shoes can't get the extra leather. The consumers cannot determine the price of leather, so shortages in good shoes will remain. There's a very grave question in my mind as to how possible it is to introduce these kinds of reforms piecemeal. (Nutter et al. 1966)

Of all the characters assembled in the Thomas Jefferson Center, Gordon Tullock was, in some ways, the most remarkable. Tullock was a rare bird, a generalist with the tools of a specialist. He wrote on any topic that captured his imagination, and he could build a solid theory on the merest whim. Tullock was one of the first economic imperialists. He could apply economic analysis to every nook and cranny of existence. Moreover, his work was characterized by a high degree of irreverence for sacred cows. He argued that voting and giving to charity were irrational acts and that inheritance of wealth could be justified on efficiency grounds. Worst of all, he argued that criminals should be punished. He was a pioneer in sociobiology, with an unpublished manuscript on social insects. A trained lawyer, Tullock was the first economist systematically to apply economic theory to law and was one of a very small handful to treat bureaucrats and politicians as if they were guided by self-interest and not as if they were selflessly dedicated to the good of all humanity.

Tullock's favorite weapon was the studied insult. One of my new colleagues at Virginia, a young Englishman named Ivan C. Johnson, told me of his arrival in Charlottesville. While he was unpacking the books in his office, Tullock entered and introduced himself with the words, "Oh, Mr. Johnson, I'm glad you finally arrived. I need the opinion of someone who is obviously inferior to me." Johnson felt at home immediately. Tullock's effect on impressionable students was not always salutary. He could talk them into almost anything and took pleasure in the result. Nutter once half-seriously proposed that a trapdoor be placed in front of Tullock's office and, when a student approached, Betty Tillman would be instructed to push the button at the appropriate moment.

Across from Tullock's office was James Buchanan's. I met him for the first time in 1964 when I came to Charlottesville to present a paper at a faculty seminar when I was being considered for an appointment. Buchanan had been an important name on my reading lists in graduate school. His book *Public Principles of Public Debt* was well known to me since it directly attacked the public debt theory identified with the name of my Michigan State teacher Abba Lerner. *The Calculus of Consent*, written in collaboration with Tullock, had already made its appearance but had not yet had its full impact. Buchanan's presidential address to the Southern Economic Association in 1963 had attracted a good deal of attention. It stressed the importance of voluntary processes of agreement among trading parties, in contrast to the influential view of Lionel Robbins that focused attention on the market as a mechanism for efficiently allocating resources. Buchanan's emphasis on process rather than on teleological end-states seemed a congenial way of viewing the world to this Ayres-trained institutionalist. Undoubtedly, Buchanan was the best-known economist at Virginia at the time. I knew that my performance that day in the Thomas Jefferson Center lounge would have to pass muster with him if I were to have any realistic hope of being asked on board. To my chagrin, almost immediately after I started my recitation, he closed his eyes and appeared to be asleep. My hopes sank. However, when my presentation ended, he opened his eyes and, from the questions he asked, it was clear that he had heard every word. On reflection, I might have been better off had he been asleep.

I have given this casual sketch of the Charlottesville cast of characters not for the sake of gossipy anecdote, but because I believe such information can teach something about the sociology of a discipline. The personality of a teacher or colleague performs an important social role in one's education. The idiosyncratic gifts as well as the ideological predilections of powerful personalities are transforming elements in that creative process of self-renewal that is part and parcel of the formation of a new world version.

My purpose, here, however, is not to propose an elaborate or rigid theory of the sociology of knowledge. But I would urge the explicit recognition of the importance of personality and style in our perceptions of reality. Unintelligent dullards do not gain the loyalty and allegiance of others.

In any event, the political economy group at Virginia made disciples in the best sense of the word. Students carried on research programs under the supervision of leading faculty members and began turning out articles and doctoral dissertations dealing with market process and political economy. The moral commitment to individual liberty that permeated the Virginia atmosphere was attractive to idealistic young people who carried the Virginia message elsewhere after taking their degrees. James Buchanan encouraged his students to publish. "Don't get it right, get it written" was his motto, by which he meant don't wait for the muse to strike: she can be an awkward bitch. Writing it down helps clarify what is, or isn't, in one's head. Students responded to this encouragement. For example, in 1968, *Why the Draft? The Case for a Volunteer Army* was published in a Penguin Books paperback format. The book was conceived and edited by James C. Miller III. Among the other graduate students who contributed chapters were Robert D. Tollison, Mark V. Pauly, Cotton M. Lindsay, David B. Johnson, and Thomas D. Willett. On the back cover were praises from John Kenneth Galbraith and Milton Friedman. What was striking about this work was the use of basic economic theory to understand the real costs of the draft and the probable consequences of a volunteer army. The students showed how conscription placed a tax-in-kind on the draftees and that a volunteer army would have the lowest real cost. Buchanan and Nutter couldn't have said it better, but were probably saying it as well in their classrooms.

In addition, students were writing dissertations on subjects quite different from those being reported in the annual list of dissertations published by the *American Economic Review*. For example, in 1965, Charles Goetz looked at tax preferences from the point of view of collective decision-making. Ogden Allsbrook in 1966 studied the aid to dependent children programs as a case study in multilevel bureaucracy. In 1968 David B. Johnson analyzed the charity market from the point of view of public choice. In the same year, Cotton M. Lindsay studied the public financing of medical care in the United States and its effect on the supply of medical services. I can only mention a few, but they should give a good indication of the Virginia product's uniqueness at that time and place.

There is another factor that must be mentioned in connection with the success of the Virginia School. I am referring to the establishment of a journal to promulgate its ideas and approach. The early issues of the journal were called *Papers on Non-Market Decision Making*. The first number appeared in 1966. Gordon Tullock's editorial preface sounded the clarion call. It stated that scholars who wished to apply intellectual tools drawn from economics to noneconomic phenomena had found it difficult to get published in the journals of social science. The new journal's rationale was to remedy this situation. "It would be hard to find a journal which would consider any of the articles printed here as directly in its field of concern," announced Tullock. The new journal would make it easier for scholars with such interests to keep abreast of new work and make them aware of one another's existence. In providing an outlet for those interested in applying economics to politics and other nonmarket phenomena, it would encourage others to pursue this new approach.

A year later, the second issue appeared with the announcement that plans for a third were well under way. In fact, the third issue was published in the fall of the same year, this time sporting an impressive editorial board and a separate book review editor. On the flyleaf, however, Tullock admitted that he was not fully confident of success. "The editors are not yet sure as to the supply of significant articles. In consequence the number of issues per year is not yet fixed." This was unusual and refreshing candor from an editor to potential subscribers.

There was another way in which the new review was different. Most professional journals are hard to get into. Tullock's journal was hard to stay out of. To my stupefaction, upon opening the third issue and looking over the table of contents, I found that I had a publication. Apparently, some casual remarks I had made to Tullock in the cafeteria line at lunch some months previously were turned into a "Comment" on a paper by Louis De Allesi. Moreover, there was a "Further Comment" by De Allesi. I searched with anticipation for my "Rejoinder." Alas, it did not appear. I must have missed lunch with Gordon Tullock at the appropriate moment. There was also a note by Paul Samuelson in that issue. I wondered if he was as surprised as I was in being there. In any event, it has taken tremendous will power on my part to keep that item from appearing in my vita.

The term "public choice" itself was coined sometime in 1968 when the journal's name was changed. Assigning such a crisp and pithy label to the journal was an inspired stroke. The name provided a mental filing system that helped sort out the sometimes inchoate and amorphous miscellany that fell under the old "nonmarket decision-making" and "collective decision-making" rubrics. The lead article in the fall 1968 number of *Public Choice* was by James Buchanan. It was titled, "A Public Choice Approach to Public Utility Pricing." Once the movement was named, it could be said to have "an approach."

Given the acknowledged success of the political economy program during its Charlottesville phase, one might imagine that the Economics Department would have been well thought of by the university's administrators, as well as by the faculty in other departments. However, that was not the case. Soon after my arrival at the University of Virginia, I had a disturbing encounter with a distinguished member of the English Department whom I met at a social gathering organized by students. When I was introduced to him as being a new member of the Economics Department, he gave me an icy stare and asked, "Are you a fascist?" I was soon to find out that his attitude was widespread.

The fact that Warren Nutter had taken a semester's leave of absence to serve as an adviser in the Goldwater presidential campaign was one source of this obsessive concern with the political views of the Economics Department among the liberal-left academics. But the negative attitude toward the department preceded Nutter's political involvement with Republicans. In 1960 the Ford Foundation had refused to provide a grant to the Thomas Jefferson Center, giving as a reason the statement in the center's brochure to the effect that the scholars involved wished to preserve a social order based on individual liberty. This was cited as evidence that the Virginia department was opposed to academic freedom. Kermit Gordon, the officer at the Ford Foundation in charge of grants in the field of economics, said the foundation could not consider making any grants to support work at Virginia until the Economics Department became as balanced politically as those at Harvard and Yale.

Moreover, in 1963 a secret self-study report on the Department of Economics was written by a Virginia faculty committee for examination by an external accreditation group. The department was neither consulted while the report was being composed nor informed later of its contents. This exceedingly interesting and revealing document came to light inadvertently in 1974 and shows that academic witch-hunting was alive at Mr. Jefferson's university during the 1960s. The report made the following recommendations, among others: (1) "Additions should be made to the staff of full professorial members of different 'modern' outlook"; (2) "Care should be taken in making or renewing non-tenure appointments, as well as those of higher rank, to avoid recruitment from the Chicago School."

This document helps make explicable some of the events that followed: the refusal to make a serious effort to keep Ronald Coase in the face of an offer from the University of Chicago in 1964; and the refusal to respond to the counteroffer from Purdue University to Andrew Whinston, one of the department's more able younger scholars, in 1966. Ultimately, the refusal to promote Gordon Tullock from associate to full professor on three occasions led to James Buchanan's resignation to accept a post at UCLA. In 1969, Warren Nutter took leave of absence to serve as assistant secretary of defense for international security affairs. A few of us who remained in Charlottesville continued struggling to keep the political economy orientation of the Virginia School alive. We soon found that a determined administration would have its way.

Here was a lesson I rediscovered in later years. In contests with the university administration, the trump cards are held by the bureaucrats. Nevertheless, this aspect of the Charlottesville period remains something of a puzzle. Why should university administrators care more about conformity to a respectable orthodox liberal doctrine than about academic excellence? I will not compensate for my uncertainty with an excessive certainty of statement. But I suspect the answer lies in the constituency of the university. At the University of Virginia, a state university in a small city where the business community has little power, there are only a few whose interests are adversely affected when a left-liberal administration decides to impose its ideological views on a department. In the case of private universities or state universities in larger cities with a more influential business community, the cost of indulging left-liberal ideological appetites is much higher. I am not sure about this. Perhaps one day a member of the Virginia School will produce a public choice model of universities that will explain the Charlottesville tragedy.

In his book *The New Economics and the Old Economists*, J. Ronnie Davis (1971) refers to Charlottesville during the years 1964 to 1967 when he was a graduate student as "Camelot." Is this hyperbole? Perhaps. Sometimes alumni, out of deeply felt nostalgia, have an idyllic view of their student years. Nevertheless, the character of the Economics Department and the style of the research that went on in Charlottesville in the period 1957 to 1968 did somehow give rise to an important movement in economics, one that proved enormously successful by all of the standards by which success is measured in academe.

In this paper, I have tried to set forth some of the criteria for that success in making a world. Public choice and constitutional economics were the creative outcome of colorful and intelligent personalities doing research and teaching within a favorable set of spatial and social relationships. Furthermore, the cogency and comprehensiveness of Virginia political economy were greatly aided by the organizing power of a journal and the compactness of thought that emerged from the rightness of the name, "public choice." I have only scraped the surface of this complex subject. But I hope I have convinced some of you that personality, environment, and circumstance are legitimate and even essential subjects for the historian of economic thought.

NOTE

1. Alexei Kosygin (1904–1980) was a Soviet statesman and Soviet premier from 1964 to 1980 (the editors).

REFERENCES

Allsbrook, Ogden Olmstead. 1966. "Aid to Dependent Children: A Grant-in-Aid Considered as Case Study in Multi-Level Bureaucracy." PhD diss., University of Virginia.

Ayres, C. E. 1944. *The Theory of Economic Progress*. Chapel Hill: University of North Carolina Press.

Breit, William. 1967. "Comment." *Papers on Non-Market Decision Making* 3: 90.

Buchanan, James M. 1958. *Public Principles of Public Debt*. Homewood, IL: Richard D. Irwin.

———. 1964. "What Should Economists Do?" *Southern Economic Journal* 30: 213–22.

———. 1968. "A Public Choice Approach to Public Utility Pricing." *Public Choice* 5: 1–17.

———. 1983. "Political Economy 1957–1982." The G. Warren Nutter Lectures in Political Economy. Washington, DC: American Enterprise Institute for Public Policy Research.

Buchanan, James M., and Gordon Tullock. 1962. *The Calculus of Consent*. Ann Arbor: University of Michigan Press.

Cartter, Allan M. 1966. *An Assessment of Quality in Graduate Education*. Washington, DC: American Council on Education.

Davis, J. Ronnie. 1971. *The New Economics and the Old Economists*. Ames: Iowa State University Press.

De Allesi, Louis. 1967. "A Utility Analysis of Post-Disaster Co-Operation." *Public Choice* 3: 85–90.

———. "Further Comment." *Public Choice* 3: 90.

Goetz, Charles John. 1965. "Tax Preferences in a Collective Decision-Making Context." PhD diss., University of Virginia.

Johnson, David Bruce. 1968. "The Fundamental Economics of the Charity Market." PhD diss., University of Virginia.

Johnson, Elizabeth S., and Harry G. Johnson. 1978. *The Shadow of Keynes*. Chicago: University of Chicago Press.

Lerner, Abba P. 1944. *The Economics of Control*. New York: Macmillan.

Lindsay, Cotton Mather. 1968. "Supply Response to Public Financing of Medical Care in the United States." PhD diss., University of Virginia.

Miller, James C. III (ed.). 1968. *Why the Draft? The Case for a Volunteer Army*. Baltimore: Penguin Books.

Nutter, G. Warren. 1962. *Growth of Industrial Production in the Soviet Union*. Princeton, NJ: Princeton University Press.

Nutter, G. Warren, et al. 1966. "Soviet Economic Performance and Reform: Some Problems of Analysis and Prognosis." *Slavic Review* 25: 221–46.

Samuelson, Paul A. 1967. "Indeterminacy of Governmental Role in Public-Good Theory." *Papers on Non-Market Decision Making* 3: 47.

Snavely, Tipton R. 1967. *The Department of Economics at the University of Virginia 1825–1956*. Charlottesville: University of Virginia Press.

Yeager, Leland B. 1954. "Some Questions about Growth Economics." *American Economic Review* 44: 53–63.

——— (ed.). 1962. *In Search of a Monetary Constitution*. Cambridge, MA: Harvard University Press.

5.3
Getting More with Less, with a Notable Exception

DWIGHT R. LEE

I am delighted to be back at George Mason, especially before such a distinguished group and in such an honored position. I genuinely miss George Mason University and the people here. It has not been that long since I left, and as soon as I did, George Mason began making spectacular progress. They would have been smart to have unloaded me a long time ago.

As soon as I left, Leonard Leggio and his impressive colleagues with the Institute for Humane Studies moved to George Mason. Within a month or two, feature stories on George Mason and the Center for Study of Public Choice appeared in the *Wall Street Journal*, the *New York Times*, and the *Washington Post*. Shortly after that, Henry Manne accepted the deanship of the George Mason Law School, bringing with him the prestigious Law and Economics Center. And, then, there was the Nobel Prize.

No one who has been associated with the Center for Study of Public Choice or George Mason University will ever forget that proud day of 16 October 1986,

Prepared for the Third Annual Lecture in the Virginia Political Economy Lecture Series, George Mason University, Fairfax, VA, March 19, 1987.

when it was announced that James M. Buchanan was the recipient of the Nobel Memorial Prize in Economic Science. I don't know if that was the highlight of Jim's professional career, but I do know that it was the highlight of mine. I honestly cannot think of anything within the realm of remote possibility that could give me more professional satisfaction than I experienced when Jim received the Nobel Prize. Now, I have to admit that part of this satisfaction resulted from the fact that I have coauthored papers with Jim. Before Jim received the Nobel Prize, my contributions to economics were unknown only in the United States. Now I am proud to say that my work is internationally unknown.

The Virginia School of Political Economy has for some time been exerting a growing influence on the perspective of academic economists. Only the most uninformed of professional economists are today unaware of the resurrection of political economy in its modern form of public choice. And with Jim's Nobel Prize, awareness of public choice and its contributions has burst beyond the domain of academic economists. Public choice can no longer be ignored, either inside or outside the academic community. But it can be misunderstood, and indeed it has been. It is one important area where public choice has been, I believe, persistently misunderstood that I wish to discuss in this paper.

It is widely perceived that public choice economics, as it has grown out of the Virginia School tradition, is negative toward government. The public choice paradigm is seen as motivated by a general hostility toward government, with the objective of public choice analysis being an attempt to establish that government is destructive of our freedom and prosperity. According to this view, public choice economists want to paralyze government with restrictions, making it impossible to accomplish most of the desirable things that well-meaning people want, and indeed have a right to expect, from government.[1]

This view reflects a fundamental misunderstanding of public choice economics. It is undeniably true that much of the writing that comes from the Virginia School is critical of government and of particular government programs. But this criticism is rooted not in the view that government is a negative force in society, but rather that it is an extremely positive force, with the potential for accomplishing even more than it currently is. It is James Buchanan who has persistently argued that government is the means for engaging in what he refers to as "complex exchange"—a process based on agreement to a set of political and economic rules of the game that, when followed, allow the prospects for all to be improved.[2] This positive-sum view of government is in marked contrast to the zero-sum (more realistically, negative-sum) view of government put forth by economists like Lester Thurow. Yet it is Thurow and those of his persuasion who are generally perceived of as having a positive view of government.

Though ironic, it is not difficult to understand why those who write in the tradition of the Virginia School are considered to be hostile to government. While public choice economists want government to accomplish more than it is currently accomplishing and are convinced that government is capable of accomplishing more, their approach to the goal of *more from government* is not in keeping with the standard orthodoxy. As opposed to the standard view that we can get more from government only by having more government, public choice economists are convinced that we can get more from government only by having less government. Instead of wanting to restrict government as a means of forcing it to accomplish less, Virginia political economists want to restrict government as a means of enhancing its power to accomplish more.

This *more with less* approach is not one that conforms naturally to our intuition. It requires explanation. Neither is the *more with less* approach one that appeals to our desire to identify specific problems and attack them head-on. Instead, it requires that we recognize the limits on what we can accomplish and acknowledge that it is only through a patient understanding of those limits that we can in the long run make full use of our problem-solving potential. Those who are impatient for action, who focus attention exclusively on the solution to particular problems, who are ideologically committed to expanding government, or who simply lack understanding will quite naturally tend to see the public choice approach of acquiring more from government as hostility toward government.

Before illustrating with particular examples the general validity of the view that more will be realized from government with less government, it is worth noting just how deeply the Virginia School of Political Economy is rooted in Virginia soil. The precursor to the Center for Study of Public Choice was established in the 1950s at the University of Virginia by James Buchanan and the late G. Warren Nutter (soon joined by Gordon Tullock) and was known as the Thomas Jefferson Center for Studies in Political Economy. The fact that the University of Virginia was founded by Thomas Jefferson is no doubt one of the reasons for the choice of this name, but there is another good reason as well. Jefferson was a master of expressing important ideas in a few well-chosen words. One of the best known of Jefferson's sayings, "*That government is best which governs the least,*" summarizes beautifully an insight that the Virginia School has grounded in sophisticated scholarship. It is this insight that I am discussing here as getting more from government with less government.

Even more than Jefferson, however, it was the Virginian James Madison who anticipated the modern scholarship of Buchanan, Tullock, and other public choice economists. Madison, our fourth president and the Father of the U.S. Constitution, articulated a coherent view of government that recognizes that government is on the one hand indispensable to our social well-being and on the other hand the greatest threat to that well-being. It was Madison's desire to frame a constitution that created a government strong enough to perform the important tasks that only government can perform. But Madison knew that this required a constitution that constrained government against the ever-present temptation to extend its reach beyond its grasp, an extension that reduces the good that government can accomplish. It should be noted that another famous Virginian, George Mason, was even more worried than Madison about the threat of an expanding government.

The important benefits that only government can provide are not provided directly. As was understood by Madison, Mason, and others of our Founding Fathers, the importance of government is not derived from its ability to convey particular benefits to particular people. Rather, the advantage of government is found in its ability to establish a legal and economic environment that provides general opportunities for people to benefit from their own efforts through productive cooperation with others. The threat of government is that its power will be captured by organized special interests, "*factions*" in Madison's words, and used to advance narrow objectives by imposing costs on the general public. To the extent that government becomes a vehicle for promoting special interests, it fails in its primary responsibility of expanding opportunities for all. Instead of creating opportunities for people to benefit through productive cooperation with each other, government will have created the illusion that people can benefit at the expense of each other. This illusion is a sure prescription for getting more government and fewer of the benefits that it is government's proper function to provide.

SOME SPECIFICS

The work that has come out of the Virginia School tradition contains many examples of getting less from government with more government. We now consider some of these examples.

It is almost universally accepted that specific government action is necessary if poverty is to be reduced. The private market is seen as a competitive arena in which self-interest participants make decisions with little thought as to how those decisions affect the general distribution of income. The income distribution that emerges from this competitive process will find many falling behind because they lack the skills necessary to compete effectively in the marketplace. It is widely assumed that government has the ability not only to alter the distribution of income but to alter it in accordance with some transcending social objective, such as narrowing the gap between the rich and the poor.

The public choice perspective is different. Transcending social objectives do not motivate and direct political action. Just like the private market, the political arena is seen as a competitive setting in which self-interested participants make decisions with little thought to how these decisions will affect the general distribution of income. Just as with market activity, the effect political activity has on the income distribution emerges as an unintended by-product of an interplay of competing forces. And while the skills that allow for successful competition in the political process may be different than those that allow for successful competition in the marketplace, there is no reason to believe that the distribution of political skills will differ much from the distribution of market skills. Certainly, there is no reason for believing that those people who lack the skills to compete successfully in the marketplace will have the skills to compete successfully in the political arena. It is for this reason that public choice scholars, such as Gordon Tullock, have questioned whether expanding government for the stated purpose of helping the poor will in fact help the poor. Long before one could question government welfare programs without violating accepted standards of good taste, Gordon Tullock was questioning both the motives behind and the effectiveness of these programs.

The evidence suggests that Tullock, whether in good taste or not, was correct. After adjusting for government taxes and transfers, the overall distribution of income has remained effectively unchanged in spite of the explosion of government spending on social welfare programs. The disincentives generated by these programs have, however, reduced the general productivity of the economy. So expanding government in the name of helping the poor appears to have reduced the size of the economic pie without increasing the percentage of the pie going to the poor. The unavoidable conclusion is that the poor have been made absolutely worse off. More government has resulted in less for the poor.

As a second example, consider that if government is to provide the setting in which the economic opportunities for all are expanded to the fullest, it is essential that government maintain a stable monetary unit. If the value of the dollar is subject to unpredictable fluctuations, the specialization and exchange upon which general economic prosperity depends is unnecessarily hampered.

Unfortunately, when the benefits from government are seen to come from its ability to provide specific benefits to particular groups, we get more government and less monetary stability. As an increasing percentage of our country's income is diverted into government activities, government finds it increasingly inconvenient to cover expenses with explicit taxation. Virginia School political economists have long pointed out that a politically attractive alternative to explicit taxation is hidden taxation in the form of inflation. As government has grown, so has the temptation to sacrifice the integrity of the currency to the demands of those pressuring for particular political programs and privileges. The inflation that resulted surely had much to do with the diminished productivity growth that characterized the U.S. economy throughout the 1970s and into the 1980s. With more government, we have had less stability in the value of the dollar and less opportunity to advance our interests through productive activity.

As of now, the prevailing view is that inflation has been brought under control, at least by comparison to the record of the 1970s, and the problem of inflation is a thing of the past. Don't count on it. It is precisely when the public begins believing that the price level will be stable and begins making commitments based on this expectation that government has the most to gain from another episode of inflation. When inflation is unexpected, it does the most to stimulate the temporary expansion in economic activity that serves to enhance the reelection prospects of incumbent politicians. When government has discretionary control over the money supply, the time to be worried about the threat of inflation is when people quit worrying about the threat of inflation.

Another example of getting less from government with more government comes from recognizing that one of the most important benefits government can provide is social harmony. Social harmony is best provided indirectly by enforcing the general rules of property and contract that form the foundation of voluntary market exchange. Market exchange offers the best means of harmonizing the conflicting goals and purposes of people who are necessarily in constant competition with each other for control over scarce resources. Success in market exchange requires appealing to the concerns of others, broadening the range for compromise, and seeking out areas of mutual interest. Increase the permissible scope of government activities, however, and you increase the opportunity for people to benefit at the expense of others through the exercise of political influence. Negative-sum plunder replaces positive-sum exchange and political combat replaces market cooperation. A large government sets the stage for what I have, in previous work, referred to as "Malice in Plunderland" (Lee 1982). With more government, we get less social harmony.

Consider one more example. Those who tend to favor an active government presence in the economy argue that government is needed to regulate business in order to keep it responsive to the interests of consumers. Virginia School political economists would generally agree that it is desirable to subject business to regulation and that this task requires government. But, as with so many functions of government, regulating business is best achieved indirectly rather than directly. A limited government with the power to enforce the general rules upon which the market process depends creates a competitive environment in which business is regulated effectively by the choices of consumers. Increasing government's power to regulate the details of business decisions results in less effective regulation of business because it is organized business interest, not the unorganized consumer interest, that will dominate the day-to-day details of government regulations. Give government agencies the discretionary power to impose regulations on the particulars of business decisions and you have created a power that business will exploit in order to protect itself against the regulation of free and open competition. With more government, we have had less regulation of business.

Additional examples of how we could be getting more from government with less government come readily to mind. Jennifer Roback's research on the history of racial relations in the United States has uncovered many cases where we would have had more integration and racial harmony with less government. Work by Robert Tollison on antitrust activities of government supports the view that more competition would result if government did less in the name of promoting competition. W. Mark Crain has received attention from the media, as well as the academic community, for research showing that we would likely get more—and certainly no less—automobile safety with fewer government safety inspections. John Baden of the Foundation for Research on Economics and the Environment at Southern Methodist University and Richard Stroup, Terry Anderson, and Peter J. Hill of the Political Economy Research Center in Montana have for over a decade been using the insights of public choice to analyze the effects of government policy on environmental quality. Their work has uncovered case after case in which more environmental quality would be achieved with less government.

Despite what many seem to believe, it simply is not true that public choice economists are callously indifferent to the social benefits that government can provide. Virginia political economists are no less concerned with helping the poor, with promoting social harmony, with expanding opportunities for all, with protecting our natural environment, and with the development of a social order that satisfies commonly accepted norms of decency and justice than are the most vocal advocates of bigger government social programs. No one has written more eloquently on the importance of a moral order in which people deal with each other with fairness and honesty than has James Buchanan. In unguarded moments, even Gordon Tullock admits to having charitable impulses. The difference between public choice economists and those who see every social ill as justification for expanding government is not a difference in moral vision. Instead it is a difference in understanding how government actually works as opposed to romantic notions as to how government should ideally work. No group of scholars has made a more systematic study of how it is that government actually works than have those working in the tradition of the Virginia School. It is this study that disposes most public choice economists toward less government, not because they want less from government but because they believe it is important to get more from government.

TO TURN THE TIDE

Despite the fact that more could be achieved by government with less government, the tendency has been toward a larger government. What explains this perverse tendency? A straightforward answer comes from the Virginia School perspective on political economy. It cannot be denied that a larger government can force particular outcomes that, when viewed in isolation, are desirable. And we can be sure that those who benefit from these outcomes will view them in isolation, because most of the costs will be borne by others. Even when the costs far exceed the benefits, as they commonly do, the costs will be so diluted over the general taxpaying public that they will be all but invisible politically. Furthermore, many of the benefits from expanding government programs are received immediately, while the costs are delayed, and the strong tendency is for political decision makers to dwell on short-run consequences while ignoring long-run consequences. As former British prime minister Harold Wilson supposedly said, "In politics a week is a long time." With expanding government making it possible to provide immediate and concentrated benefits to the organized few by imposing delayed and diffused costs on the unorganized many, it is easy to understand the tendency toward more government.

Can anything be done to moderate, and hopefully reverse, this tendency toward more government? At one level, the analysis that comes out of public choice economics is pessimistic. With the benefits from less government being spread over the general public and the benefits from more government being captured by organized interests, it is easy to conclude that the pressures that have pushed toward more government will continue to do so.

But the importance of the Virginia School would be grossly underestimated if its positive analysis of the political process was considered to lead to nothing more than a council of despair. Public choice offers reasons for being at least cautiously optimistic that government can be controlled.

The Virginia School is doing more than just examining the political process. The Heisenberg principle tells us that examining something necessarily changes it.[3] This does not mean that the changes are always for the better. Consider the Heisenberg principle in the case of the man who, at the bedside of his sick friend, asked him how he felt. The sick friend responded by saying fine, and the effort killed him. In analyzing the political process, public choice economists are necessarily changing that process. Fortunately, there are reasons for believing that these political changes are more beneficial than the one resulting from the inquiry of the bedside friend.

The excesses of government that have been the subject of so much public choice analysis suggest the possibility of correction. When undisciplined political discretion has made politicians the lackeys for organized special interests and these special interests have become the victims of their own destructive demands, the potential exists for all to benefit from self-denying limits on government. If politicians could honestly say to political pressure groups, "My hands are tied, so I cannot provide additional privileges to you by imposing yet more costs on the general public," then the potential for shortsighted political exploitation of one group by another would be reduced to the long-run advantage of all. The awareness that we could all do more if only government were restricted to do less is surely intruding, maybe vaguely, but intruding nonetheless, into the public consciousness. This intrusion is reflected in the fact that constitutional reform is increasingly being discussed and being seriously considered.

The best hope for bringing government under control is through constitutional limits on the political process. The Virginia School has generated important insights by considering how decision-making at the level of the Constitution differs from decision-making at the level of ordinary politics. *The Calculus of Consent*, the public choice classic by Buchanan and Tullock, is appropriately subtitled, *Logical Foundations of Constitutional Democracy*. Buchanan has, over the years, been particularly insistent that it is through their influence on the fundamental rules of the game—that is, the Constitution—rather than through their influence on particular policies, that political economists can make a genuine contribution. Attempting to control government by attacking separately each special interest policy will fail. However, with an increasing number of groups discovering that the value they receive from their programs is less than what they are paying for the programs of others, it becomes politically feasible to control government through constitutional changes that reduce the government's general ability to transfer wealth. Individual policy reform is analogous to fighting individual alligators. You lose when you do that. Constitutional reform is analogous to draining the swamp. By draining the swamp, you have a real chance against the alligators.

Obtaining agreement to changes in the political rules of the game is one thing. Making sure that people abide by those rules is quite another. Constitutions are not self-enforcing, and their effectiveness can easily erode over time. It is important that constitutional restrictions on government be enforced by a general public understanding of the need for those restrictions. With a return to the political understanding of the Founders, our Constitution, without explicit amendment, would once again become an effective barrier to government excesses. Without this understanding, our Constitution, no matter how amended, can be no more than ink on parchment. A constitution guards effectively against only those abuses of government that are widely recognized as abuses. If assaulted by public acceptance of particular government practices, constitutional barriers to those practices will soon be breached. As economist Henry Simons once observed, "Constitutional provisions are no stronger than the consensus that they articulate. At best they can only check abuses of power until moral pressure is mobilized; and their check must become ineffective if often overtly used" (Simons 1951, 20).

The best hope, then, for controlling government is found in the growing public disenchantment with government solutions. Much of this disenchantment has grown out of our experience with an expanding government that has promised more while providing less. But we do not learn from experience alone. As Samuel Johnson remarked when a friend of his married for the second time, "Another example of the triumph of hope over experience." Progress is made only when experience is accompanied by understanding. And it is the Virginia School that has provided the intellectual basis for understanding that the failure of past government programs is endemic to the political process. This failure cannot be overcome by reorganizing old programs, starting new programs, spending yet more money, or putting better people in charge. Public choice has changed the understanding economists have of the role of government in the economy. Only a few years ago, highly respected economists proceeded from the assumption that imperfections in the market could be easily corrected by government action. Policy analysis based on this naive assumption, when developed with sufficient mathematical refinement, was considered by most economists to be sophisticated scholarship. Today, only the most uninformed economists are unaware that government failures can be, and typically are, worse than market failures. And changes in the views of academics invariably lead to corresponding changes in the views of the wider public.

The ideas that become accepted in the academy do get transmitted. They get transmitted in the classroom. A generation ago, college students were learning that activist government policies guided by Keynesian prescriptions pointed the way to an economic millennium. Today's college students are learning to question not only the economic basis for this view but the political basis for it as well. The ideas in the academy also get transmitted through the media. Journalists can generally be depended on to protect their reputations by not straying too far from positions that are considered intellectually respectable. There are other avenues by which ideas travel from their academic source to the general public. The important point is that those ideas do get transmitted, and in the process they shape public opinion. The Virginia School analysis of the political process is gradually having an influence on public opinion and, in so doing, it is altering the environment within which political decisions are made.[4] In accordance with the Heisenberg principle, by examining the political process the Virginia School is changing the political process.

Consider the fact that it is almost impossible for a special interest, no matter how well organized, to obtain political privileges unless it is able to operate behind a facade of public interest rhetoric. It is for this reason that Gordon Tullock's favorite special interest program has never achieved political liftoff. Tullock's suggestion that the government increase the taxes of every person in the country by one dollar with the resulting $240 million being transferred to him certainly satisfies the conditions of concentrated benefits and diffused costs normally associated with political success. The only ingredient that Tullock's proposal lacks is a plausible pretense that it would promote the public interest. Penetrate the public interest rhetoric that glosses over the private interest reality of a government transfer program and that program is in political trouble.

This is not to say that the public interest rhetoric is easy to penetrate. Politically successful programs will always have some plausible connection with a worthy social objective, such as helping the poor, saving the family farm, increasing employment opportunities, or protecting environmental quality. Whether or not the programs actually promote these objectives, the private interests that are served by them will become accomplished at arguing that it is because of their programs that great good is accomplished and great harm is avoided. A rationally ignorant public will find it easier to accept these arguments than to uncover the fact that in case after case these programs help the few at the expense of the many while working against the very objectives they are supposedly advancing.

In spite of these difficulties, the private interest manipulation that lies behind government transfer programs is increasingly being exposed to public scrutiny. The private interest theory of government that has come out of the Virginia School has achieved a level of coherence and academic respectability that makes it difficult to ignore by those who communicate with the general public. An enormous volume of research by Robert Tollison, in collaboration with Mark Crain, Bill Shughart, Roger Faith, Gary Anderson, and others, has tied together a broad range of government activities with the unifying thread of private interest. The private interest theory of government has contributed to a shift in the ideological spectrum toward the view that we really do get more from government with less government. This ideological shift would be without political significance, however, if political outcomes really were determined only by private interests. Interestingly, the Virginia School, which spawned the private interest theory of government, also provides an explanation of how an ideological commitment to limited government can reduce the influence of private interests.

An individual who believes that government should be limited likely will vote against expanding government even though the expansion would promote his or her private interest. The reason for this anomalous result is understood by considering the benefits and costs associated with voting. We all derive a sense of satisfaction from expressing ourselves in favor of those things we support or against those things we oppose. Voting is an act of expression, and if someone has an ideological commitment to limited government, he will derive satisfaction from voting against expanding government. But what if the expansion in government would increase the person's income? Isn't the potential loss of that income a high personal price to pay for the satisfaction of advancing the public interest by opposing government growth? The answer is no, for the simple reason that no one vote is likely to be decisive in determining the outcome. It costs the individual nothing to vote in favor of the general interest, as he perceives it, and against his private interests because the outcome will be the same no matter how he votes.[5] It is with this in mind that Buchanan wrote over three decades ago, "It seems probable that the representative individual will act in accordance with a different preference scale when he realizes that he is choosing for the group rather than merely for himself. . . .

His identification will tend to be broadened, and his 'values' will be more likely to influence his ordering of alternatives, whereas in market choice his 'tastes' may determine his decision" (Buchanan 1954).

The Virginia School is exerting a restraining influence on government. The systematic study of the tendencies for government to grow is reducing the strength of these tendencies and increasing the strength of opposing tendencies. This is not to argue that the Virginia School has been the sole influence in this regard, or that government growth has been turned around. The influence of the Virginia School is only a part, though a very important part, of a wider set of influences that is working to restrain government. And it cannot be claimed that there has been a dramatic reversal in the tendency for government to grow. The claim has to be the more modest one that there have been marginal changes in public opinion that, if continued, have the potential for reversing government growth.

The progress that has been made in the battle of ideas over the proper role and scope of government, though modest, is not to be dismissed as unimportant. Think back to the intellectual environment that confronted Buchanan, Tullock, and Nutter in the late 1950s and early 1960s at the University of Virginia. Their situation at that time reminds me of the story of the little boy who answered the door and saw a stranger on the step. "I know you don't recognize me," the stranger said, "but I'm your uncle on your father's side." After thinking for a moment, the little boy replied, "Well, Mister, I still don't know who you are, but I sure enough know one thing. You're on the losing side." Buchanan, Tullock, and Nutter were unmistakably on the losing side when they began their intellectual journeys. They were part of a small band of intellectual dissidents who faced hostility within the academic community and indifference from outside that community. It may be premature to claim that Virginia School scholars are now on the winning side. But no one can deny that they now have their intellectual opponents on the defensive, or that their influence now extends well beyond the halls of ivy.

We owe a lot to the awesome intellectual horsepower of Buchanan, Tullock, and Nutter. And we owe even more to their character, to their refusal to bend to the demands of academic intolerance, or bow before the arrogance of petty power. Regardless of the personal cost, they did it their way. And they did it well. Thanks to them there is now a flourishing Virginia School of Political Economy. And, there are reasons for being optimistic that the success of the Virginia School will be instrumental in allowing all of us to realize more from government with less government.

The theme of my paper has been getting more with less. But you will recall that my title is "Getting More with Less, with a Notable Exception." It is now time to move to the notable exception, which is really the highlight of the program today. We are here to pay tribute to a wonderful lady whose contribution to the Virginia School of Political Economy through her devotion, love, and loyalty is being celebrated today. I am referring of course to Betty Tillman, who just so happens to be having a birthday today.

Betty Tillman is clearly the exception to the principle that we get more with less. The Center for Study of Public Choice, and all those who have been associated with it, have been blessed because Betty has always been more than a key member of the Public Choice Center. No one could have put in more hours, worked with more competence, and done it with more genuine graciousness and captivating charm than Betty. Because of Betty, the Public Choice Center has become much more than a center of academic excellence. The Public Choice Center has become an extended family, one that extends worldwide, and it is Betty, more than anyone else, who holds this family together.

It is hopelessly impossible to express adequately the special love for Betty Tillman that all of us feel who are fortunate enough to have been associated with the Virginia School and the Center for Study of Public Choice. But it is also impossible not to try. And there is no better time to try than tonight, on her birthday.

NOTES

1. For example, consider the comments of well-known political scientist Brian Barry (1985, 317): "The beauty of inflation is that it can be used as a rallying cry to sweep up people who might otherwise be chary of plans to cripple the ability of governments to make economic policy. A perfect example is James Buchanan's decade-long call for a 'constitutional counterrevolution' to undo the work of the New Deal and the Warren Court." I want to thank William Mitchell for bringing this quote to my attention.
2. Buchanan had emphasized politics as complex exchange in a number of articles and books. For a discussion of this view of government, see Buchanan (1975, chapter 2). Also see Buchanan (1986).
3. The Heisenberg principle is actually known as the uncertainty or, sometimes, as the Heisenberg uncertainty principle or even indeterminacy principle. It was made in 1927 by the German physicist Werner Heisenberg, and consists in saying that one cannot measure exactly at the same time the position and the velocity of a particle. It is sometimes confused with the observer effect, which seems to be what the author refers to here (the editors).
4. In considering the influence of economists, Herb Stein writes, "Where they do have influence, and I believe it is real influence, is in gradually affecting the climate of public opinion within which government officials feel they have to operate. See Stein (1986, 6).
5. This also explains why people will vote against their financial interest and support expanding government programs that they believe are socially desirable. See Tullock (1971).

REFERENCES

Baden, John, and Richard L. Stroup (eds.). 1981. *Bureaucracy vs. Environment: The Environmental Costs of Bureaucratic Governance*. Ann Arbor: University of Michigan Press.

Barry, Brian. 1985. "Political Ideas of Some Economists." In Leon Lundberg and Charles Maier (eds.), *The Politics of Inflation and Economic Stagflation*. Washington, DC: Brookings.

Buchanan, James M. 1954. "Individual Choice in Voting and the Market." *Journal of Political Economy* 62: 334–43.

———. 1975. *The Limits of Liberty: Between Anarchy and Leviathan*. Chicago: University of Chicago Press.

———. 1985. "Moral Community, Moral Order, or Moral Anarchy." In James M. Buchanan, *Liberty, Market and the State: Political Economy in the 1980's*, 108–20. New York: New York University Press.

———. 1986. "The Constitution of Economic Policy." Nobel Prize Lecture presented in Stockholm, Sweden, December 8.

Buchanan, James M., and Gordon Tullock. 1962. *The Calculus of Consent*. Ann Arbor: University of Michigan Press.

Crain, W. Mark. 1981. *Vehicle Safety Inspection Systems: How Effective?* Washington, DC: American Enterprise Institute.

Crain, W. Mark, Donald Leavens, and Robert D. Tollison. 1986. "Final Voting in a Legislature." *American Economic Review* 76: 833–41.

Crain, W. Mark, and Robert D. Tollison. 1976. "Campaign Expenditures and Political Competition." *Journal of Law and Economics* 19: 177–88.

———. 1977. "Attenuated Property Rights and the Market for Governors." *Journal of Law and Economics* 20: 205–11.

Faith, Roger, Donald Leavens, and Robert D. Tollison. 1982. "Antitrust Pork Barrel." *Journal of Law and Economics* 25: 329–42.

Lee, Dwight R. 1982. "The Political Economy of Social Conflict: Or Malice in Plunderland." International Institute for Economic Research, Original Paper 36, UCLA.

Roback, Jennifer. 1986. "The Political Economy of Segregation: The Case of Segregated Streetcars." *Journal of Economic History* 46: 893–917.

Simons, Henry C. 1950. *Economic Policy for a Free Society*. Chicago: University of Chicago Press.

Stein, Herbert. 1986. "Richard T. Ely Lecture: The Washington Economics Industry." *American Economic Review* 76: 1–9.

Thurow, Lester, C. 1980. *The Zero-Sum Society*. New York: Basic Books.

Tollison, Robert D. 1985. "Public Choice and Antitrust." *Cato Journal* 4: 905–16.

Tullock, Gordon. 1971. "The Charity of the Uncharitable." *Western Economic Journal* 9: 379–92.

———. 1983. *Economics of Income Distribution*. Boston: Kluwer Nijhoff.

5.4 Ethics in the History and Doctrine of the Virginia School

LELAND YEAGER

My talk has two parts.[1] First, I'll offer some personal reminiscences of the Virginia School. Doing so has at least two distinguished precedents: James Buchanan's Nutter Lecture of 1983, entitled "Political Economy 1957–1982," and William Breit's Virginia School lecture of two years ago, subtitled "Charlottesville as an Academic Environment in the 1960s." In the second part I'll try to follow up a remark that James Buchanan made to me at the Hutt conference in Dallas last September: He said that he, a contractarian, and I, a utilitarian, are really saying the same thing.

One link between the two parts is that both involve ethics. The first part concerns experiences and persons that have afforded me material for reflection on that topic. The second part concerns social or political philosophy, which is a branch or application of ethics.

I hope you will agree that economists can legitimately concern themselves with ethics. It is a topic that has fascinated economists at least since the time of David Hume and Adam Smith, including such prominent ones as John Stuart

Prepared for the Fourth Annual Lecture in the Virginia Political Economy Lecture Series, George Mason University, Fairfax, VA, April 5, 1988.

Mill, F. Y. Edgeworth, Henry Sidgwick, John Maynard Keynes, Ludwig von Mises, Friedrich Hayek, Henry Hazlitt, A. K. Sen, John Harsanyi, and James Buchanan. And rightly so. A prime concern of economists is the "spontaneous" evolution and functioning of social institutions that enable individuals to cooperate with one another indirectly as well as directly, exploiting their scattered knowledge and coordinating their decentralized activities, and thereby furthering their own and each other's diverse specific purposes far more fully than they could do in any other way. The market and ethics are two such coordinating institutions. I submit that economists are better equipped by their professional concern with social cooperation to shed light on questions of ethics than are, say, the theologians. An economist who occupies himself with such questions is not thereby claiming any special degree of personal virtue. He is merely claiming some degree of interest and professional competence.

REMINISCENCES OF THE UNIVERSITY OF VIRGINIA

James Buchanan recruited me from the University of Maryland to the University of Virginia in 1957. At the cocktail party after my job seminar in Charlottesville that spring, when asked what I would like to drink, I said, "bourbon and water," which, as Buchanan told me, was the correct answer. Reproductions of French impressionist paintings mounted on the walls of Rouss Hall helped convince me that a move to UVA would be a move upward in the academic world. When Virginia's Board of Visitors "elected" me as assistant professor, I was delighted with these bits of terminology used at my new base.

I recall with pleasure some of the visiting professors whom the Thomas Jefferson Center for Studies in Political Economy hosted at UVA in the late 1950s and early 1960s, including T. W. Hutchison, Overton H. Taylor, Maurice Allais, and Frank Knight. I recall one Saturday morning when Knight parlayed a particular bit of ignorance into a strengthened reputation for wide-ranging scholarship: He went from office to office in Rouss Hall confessing that he could not remember the date of the doctrine of Petrine Supremacy and asking, in vain, for instruction on that point. On another occasion, Knight entertained my neighbor Peter Goethals and me at a performance in Minor Hall of Samuel Beckett's *Waiting for Godot*. After a couple of hours, I was getting pretty exasperated with the lack of action and the banality of the conversation in the play ("Your feet stink," and the like). But Frank Knight leaned over to Peter and me and said, "Oh, isn't this wonderful? Doesn't the feeling come across perfectly of how utterly bored those two tramps are?" I could only agree: "It sure does."

While a visiting professor at Southern Methodist University during a providentially timed change of scene in 1961–1962, I had the great benefit of knowing Paul and Mathilda Homan, who helped me dispel a chronic blue mood. Back in Charlottesville, I enjoyed the flourishing of Virginia's graduate program in economics. (Buchanan's 1983 talk mentions some of our most distinguished PhD graduates.) Perhaps the most enjoyable single course for me was my Seminar in Political Economy in the spring of 1966. The students were Nort Buechner, Ronnie Davis, K. Ganesan, Umesh Gulati, Earl Good, Tom Ireland, John Ridpath, and Chip Seagler, as well as two undergraduates, Frank Forman and Gordon Heckel. Several of these students were followers of Ayn Rand, the novelist-philosopher. In and out of class they eagerly argued over her views and other strands of political philosophy. Amusing in retrospect but not at the time was an apparent threat made by a participant during one seminar session that somehow got reported to the Secret Service and resulted in cancellation of a talk by Senator Goldwater scheduled at the university, much to the annoyance of James Buchanan and Warren Nutter.

Another source of pleasure was the Political Economy Club of Virginia, whose charter members came not only from the Economics Department but also from other arts and sciences departments, the Law School, and the Medical School. Members or guests presented papers on topics ranging from technical economics to biography. Early meetings (in 1959, in the basement of Buddy's Restaurant, as I recall) featured talks by Rutledge Vining on his vision of political economy and by Ronald Coase, whose paper was published the following year as "The Problem of Social Cost." For a few years, as the club's treasurer, I had the responsibility of buying wine in Washington, DC, and bringing it, including our traditional port, to our monthly dinner meetings. The club came apart in the mid-1960s after an unfortunate misunderstanding over an election of new members. It was resurrected in the early 1970s, after Buchanan and Tullock had moved to Virginia Polytechnic Institute (VPI), under a new name with the acronym PEGASUS. After several meetings in Charlottesville and Blacksburg, the resurrected club fell apart again, this time because of the gasoline shortage created by policy bungles in the wake of the first oil shock of 1973–1974.[2]

ETHICS AND SOCIAL PHILOSOPHY

The episode supports, in my view, an insight that Moritz Schlick, Henry Hazlitt, and Mortimer Adler develop in their respective books, *Problems of Ethics*, *The Foundations of Morality*, and *The Time of Our Lives*: self-interest and the social interest tend to coincide with regard to heeding the ordinary precepts of morality and cultivating the sort of personal character that those precepts recommend. (The term "social interest" does not mean any supposed interest in society as a whole, transcending the interests of its individual members. It simply means the common good, the good that individuals prize in common. The "ordinary precepts of morality" are not mysterious either. They are pretty well covered by Thomas Hobbes's "laws of nature," which I mention a few pages later on, and by the University of Virginia's Honor Code, with its ban on lying, cheating, and stealing. The students are honor bound to enforce that code on each other, but, as I said, it is not enforced on faculty members and administrators.)

It is fairly obvious how honesty and so forth serve the functioning of society—serve "social cooperation," in the terminology of Herbert Spencer, Ludwig von Mises, Henry Hazlitt, and others—and thereby serve the happiness of people in general. But, according to the insight of Schlick, Hazlitt, Adler, and others, they also tend to serve the happiness of the individual person practicing them. One might object that the individual might fare best by cultivating a reputation for decency and indeed behaving decently the great part of the time while remaining alert to the rare opportunity for great gain from exceptional—that is, unethical—behavior. But such a person would have a different character from that of a person who behaved decently on principle and did *not* stay alert to opportunities to gain by secretly lying and cheating and stealing. Moral character is not the sort of thing that can be turned on and off as specific circumstances seem to recommend.

Furthermore, Schlick and others were referring to a mere *tendency* for morality to serve one's self-interest *in the long run*. Many examples can be found of people reaping a short-run gain by lying or stealing. Examples exist of criminals and crooked politicians flourishing over their entire lifetimes (although one may wonder whether many of them would not have flourished even better through more ethical employment of their talents and energies). Examples are also available of persons who have ruined or even lost their lives through honesty and decency. No guarantees are available in this world, no guarantees that morality will pay off. We have to go by the probabilities. As Schlick argues, however, the probabilities do recommend morality.

When Schlick and others say that morality tends to serve not only social cooperation but also the individual's own interest, they presumably are not forgetting that what an individual recognizes as in his own interest depends very largely on his upbringing and on the social environment. The character of a society and the characters of its individual members interact. This is one reason why social institutions—and the utilitarian comparative-institutions approach—are so important.

A generally accepted and generally observed ethical system is indispensable to social cooperation and a good society—so I could argue, though not in the time available today—and an ethical system could not prevail unless accepting and observing it did indeed tend to be in each individual's self-interest, at least in the long-run and probabilistic sense. There is no reason for wanting individuals to abide by an ethical code unless their doing so would be advantageous for society—unless it would serve the interests that individuals share in common—and it is idle to recommend an ethical code unless individuals would generally have good personal reasons for abiding by it. A prime requisite of an ethical system and of the related social and political system is that it would be *workable*, which presupposes that the individual find it to his own advantage, by and large, to abide by its precepts. An ethical system appealing not to self-interest but to self-*sacrifice* would not work and so would serve the interests neither of individuals nor of the aggregate of individuals called society. On this point, I agree with the teachings of Ayn Rand. I also agree with John Rawls (1971, section 29) that a workable social system must be able to withstand the "strains of commitment."

CONTRACTARIANISM AND UTILITARIANISM

By now I have shifted to my second topic for today. Following up James Buchanan's remark of last September, I am trying to find as much agreement as possible between his contractarian doctrine and the version of utilitarianism that seems persuasive to me. The most basic point of contact between the two doctrines is that both are applications of ethics to politics. Ethics is primary, and political philosophy derives from it; questions of political philosophy concern implementing or reinforcing ethics on the governmental level. As Brand Blanshard (1966) argues, "Political thought depends on ethics. . . . All political problems are in the end ethical problems." Political problems include "both the day-to-day problems faced by the legislator, and the problems of political theory, of how government itself is to be organized or justified." In the wide sense of politics, "any question about what a government should do is a political question. All such questions, or nearly all, are ethical."

Blanshard has elsewhere applied these insights to the question of political obligation (1961, chapter 14; I have tried to develop his insights in my 1985 paper, 280–85). Do citizens ordinarily have an obligation to respect the legitimacy of their government and to obey its laws? And if they do, why? (And why, under exceptional circumstances, does this obligation lapse?)

The obligation to support a reasonably decent government derives from ordinary ethical precepts. Scorning that obligation by arrogating special privilege to oneself, picking and choosing what laws to obey, and making exceptions in one's own favor tends to subvert a generally useful institution (which government is, even though perhaps only a "necessary evil") and so tends to subvert social cooperation. Respecting that obligation contributes to our own and our fellows' welfare—especially in view of the Hobbesian alternative.

Mention of Hobbes, who has influenced the thinking of James Buchanan, reminds me that he need not be interpreted as tracing political obligation to an actual social contract. Hobbes's fictions of the state of nature and the social contract may reasonably be interpreted as dramatic expository devices for emphasizing the great *utility* of acquiescing in government and in political obligation. The fact that Hobbes is widely classified not only as a contract theorist but also as a proto-utilitarian supports Buchanan's observation that the two doctrines really do have much in common.

Before ever discussing the supposed social contract, Hobbes describes the horrors of anarchy and of war of all against all. He stresses the importance of peace and states what he calls the "laws of nature," whose observance is conducive to peace. These are pretty much moral laws. They recommend a disposition to seek peace when it is attainable, a disposition to be accommodating, gratitude and forgiveness, fairness in dealing with others, forbearance from claiming special privilege, performance of covenants, and the like. Hobbes sees such ethical precepts as, in modern terminology, supporting social cooperation. Not until chapter 17 of *Leviathan* does he get around to discussing "a Commonwealth" as a means of reinforcing the observance of these precepts.

In short, morality comes first in Hobbes. It consists of behavior and dispositions conducive to peace and social cooperation. The rationale of government is to reinforce morality of this sort, which is the source of political obligation. Hobbes goes on to conceive of people behaving *as if* they had agreed among themselves to institute a sovereign and submit to his judgments. He does not say that governments derive their authority from an actual social contract, and he devotes little space to such a notion. It serves him as little more than an expository device.

I'd be surprised if any contractarians should try to base their political philosophy on the supposition of an actual contract *rather than* on ordinary ethics. But if any did, I'd ask them, "What would be significant about a contract unless it were binding? And how could it be binding except on the basis of already recognized ethical precepts?"

Contractarianism and utilitarianism agree, I believe, in accepting the points I used in shifting from the first part to the second part of my talk. Both doctrines recognize that a social system can function well only if it is perceived to serve the interests of the individual person, by and large. A good society is one in which the individual is raised to believe and correctly does believe that decent behavior and a decent character tend to be in his own interest. That belief is correct if society's institutions do tend to promote coincidence between self-interest and the general interest, as through operation of Adam Smith's invisible hand. (Institutions are unsatisfactory to the extent that they create tension between self-interest and general interest. Examples would be trying to fight inflation or cope with a supposed energy shortage by appeals to "voluntary restraint"; see my 1976 paper, 566–67.)

Contractarianism, on my utilitarian interpretation, is a way of emphasizing that the well-being to be promoted by ethical codes and social arrangements is not the *differential* well-being of named persons or of specific classes or generations. Instead, in the utilitarian formulation of John C. Harsanyi (1955, 276–77; 1976, 67) and F. A. Hayek (1967, 163; 1976, 129–30), it is the well-being of the person taken at random. This formulation is no doubt inexact. It is a mere stab at saying *who* the persons are whose well-being is the criterion of social institutions. One might want to specify the well-being of "everybody," except that no set of institutions can be better for literally everybody (including, say, privileged and sadistic agents of a tyrannical regime). As a practical matter, the exact articulation of the criterion is not crucial. Well-considered assessments of alternative sets of institutions would turn out the same regardless of what specific label is adopted for the persons, the "people in general," whose well-being forms the criterion.

This utilitarian formulation parallels the contractarian notion of unanimity of the "constitutional" (or even metaconstitutional) level: behind a suitably defined veil of ignorance, persons know they cannot forecast their own specific interests that might diverge even in the long run from the different interests of other persons; they know they cannot forecast the distinctive personal characteristics of their descendants and perhaps not even of themselves in the long run. Or, to use less fiction-ridden language, persons in the detached mood appropriate for philosophizing about the good society *disregard* possible divergences of their own specific interests from the common good. They recognize that they—or the individual considered at random—will probably lose from how some issues are settled and gain from how other issues are settled on the "postconstitutional" level, so they will acquiesce in ("conceptually agree on") arrangements likely to work out best on the average or on the whole.

Ideas about what arrangements might command agreement because they are thought likely to work out well must refer, at least implicitly, to some underlying criterion of the happiness, satisfaction, fulfillment—or whatever a suitable term might be—of individual people. (What alternative fundamental value judgment could one seriously avow? Performance of duty for its own sake? Observance of rights taken as axiomatic and incapable of being argued for? Implementation of the supposed will of God?) On several points, then, the contractarian approach and the utilitarian comparative-institutions approach resemble each other.

To suggest why someone discussing desirable social arrangements would probably adopt the detached, contractarian mood, I'll carry forward a kind of joke that Gordon Tullock has sometimes used. Tullock might want his own particular well-being to be the supreme criterion of social arrangements, regardless of how other persons might then fare. Or he might propose, as the supreme criterion, the well-being of polymath economists skilled in the art of the humorous insult. In either case, he would not be taken seriously. He would be hard put to answer the question of what is so special, even for other people, of the well-being of himself in particular or of the small distinct groups to which he belongs. To be taken seriously, he must propose a more neutral criterion, one from whose adoption he could expect to benefit *along with* other people, but not benefit differentially at the expense of others and especially not at the expense of identifiable individuals or classes of individuals.

When I speak of being taken seriously in recommending social arrangements and in expecting to benefit from them along with but not at the expense of other people, I am saying something that contractarians could claim, I believe, to be in the spirit of their own doctrine. If so, fine. Admittedly, I have criticized contractarianism in the past (e.g., my 1985 paper). I have expressed skepticism of philosophical positions that utterly depend on fictions and resist translation into straightforward language (though I have no objection to fictions used merely for stylistic or heuristic purposes). Today, however, I am performing an exercise in irenics. I accept the notion of contract as a device for cultivating the neutral mood usually thought appropriate for philosophizing about ethics and government. Utilitarians ask what arrangements are best for the person chosen at random, whereas contractarians ask what principles or arrangements could command consensus (or, ideally, unanimous agreement). These questions amount to pretty much the same thing, or so I am prepared to argue.

Contractarianism has a constitutional aspect: it distinguishes between decisions or judgments about fundamental principles and institutions of society and decisions on relatively specific issues. It emphasizes the importance of agreement (actual or reasonably to be expected) on the former, higher level, recognizing the futility of insisting on agreement on lower-level, day-by-day decisions. Utilitarianism shares a similar understanding. It, or its "rules" or "indirect" version, recognizes the need for appraising the desirability of rules, principles, institutions, and traits of character rather than confining appraisals to the merits of alternative actions in narrowly considered specific cases. Any acceptable version of utilitarianism rejects so-called situation ethics (see my 1985 paper, 274).

POINTS LEFT DANGLING

Time and space preclude dealing with all points of possible convergence between contractarian and utilitarian views. One issue left dangling is how adherents of the two schools react to Hayek's concept (actually, as Hayek says, 1967, chapter 6, Adam Ferguson's concept) of institutions and practices that are "results of human action but not of human design." My own reaction is that this concept of spontaneous evolution and natural selection can be highly useful in understanding how certain institutions (like ethics, law, and money) arose and flourished. It can even help counsel caution on the part of itchy-fingered reformers. But it is not, nor does Hayek claim it to be, an overriding criterion for the appraisal of institutions and reforms. Such a criterion must be fundamentally utilitarian or (as I say in my mood of today) contractarian.

Another issue for discussion with the contractarians is whether their doctrine and utilitarianism, or both or neither, countenance sacrificing some people for the benefit of others. The standard charge that utilitarians are ready to make such tradeoffs carries the tone that "I am nobler than thou" (I, the critic, would never countenance such shamefulness). Yet many such tradeoffs, plausibly so interpreted, are practically unavoidable. Allowing air travel, or even automobiles and superhighways, results in the early death of some people; yet allowing modern transportation is generally considered acceptable because it works out to the advantage of people in general or of the individual considered at random. A monetary policy of trying to stop inflation, like continuation of the policy that caused it, benefits some persons but harms others. Not carrying compulsory redistribution of income and wealth further than it is in fact carried might be said to harm those who would gain from still further redistribution, yet the exercise of some restraint in the degree of redistribution is deemed advisable for the sake of a well-functioning economy and thus for the well-being of the great bulk of the population. Having a capitalist rather than socialist economy works to the disadvantage of people who would get their kicks from the exercise of compulsion, yet utilitarians and contractarians generally prefer capitalism in the interest of people in general.

Is any set of institutions conceivable that would avoid such tradeoffs? Unless he can describe one, no critic of utilitarianism is entitled to his nobler-than-thou stance.

Some kinds of sacrifice of some persons for the sake of others, as in the hackneyed example of framing and executing an innocent person to pacify a raging mob, are definitely unacceptable. They are unacceptable precisely on utilitarian grounds. One reason is that the violation involved of the principle of honesty. Another is the question of the institutions required for deciding on and implementing such sacrifices.

Utilitarians insist, as I expect contractarians also would, on examining and comparing the institutions required for implementing one principle or another. Rutledge Vining, a leading figure in the Virginia Economics Department in its great days, has long insisted (e.g., in his 1984 paper) that legislators and constitution makers are not in a position to determine the specific results of social and economic systems, such as specific patterns of prices, resource allocation, production, industrial location, and income distribution. What they can do is to modify rules and institutions, with due attention, one hopes, to the probable operating properties of alternative sets of rules and institutions.

Robert Sugden, in a generally illuminating and praiseworthy paper (1989), reproaches utilitarianism for adopting a "synoptic" approach—that is, the viewpoint of an ideal spectator or ideal decision maker who sympathizes impartially with the pleasures and pains of all individuals and appraises alternative arrangements with a single, self-consistent social welfare function. Such a viewpoint, unlike contractarianism, supposedly does not take the diverse individuality of persons seriously enough. I welcome discussion on whether the version of utilitarianism I have espoused is open to this charge. I do not find Sugden's distinction between utilitarian and contractarian views particularly clear-cut.

Utilitarianism, as probably any social doctrine, comes in several versions, of which the worst are indeed reprehensible. The shallowest versions, whether documented or merely invented, constitute a favorite target for critics. I wonder what, except worthless triumphs, is to be gained by blowing down what are hardly more than straw men.

"Utilitarianism," as Hazlitt and other adherents of the doctrine have recognized, is an awkward and unfortunate name. History, however, has stuck us with it. A favorable attitude toward utility, broadly conceived, is indeed the fundamental value judgment involved. Abandoning the term "utilitarianism" would now seem like an unwarranted concession to superficial critics. "Eudemonism" (from Aristotle's *eudaimonia*) is a possible alternative, though I doubt that that name would fly. In conclusion, I submit that the version of utilitarianism I have espoused, a version deriving from the writings of Henry Hazlitt, Ludwig von Mises (see my 1987 paper), Moritz Schlick, and even Thomas Hobbes, reconciles quite well with the contractarianism of James Buchanan. Any differences are mainly ones of terminology and expository style. I am anxious to learn whether the contractarians agree.

NOTES

1. I am indebted to Roger Koppl for critical comments on an earlier draft, including warnings about passages to leave out or abbreviate. I am also indebted to questioners in my audience on April 5, 1988, and especially to Charles King. A long conversation with him that evening has influenced my revision of the paper.
2. Two sections of the lecture, dealing mainly with events at the University of Virginia from 1969 to 1979 and with lessons learned, are omitted here. Though those sections were appropriate for the live audience of April 5, 1988, the Center for Study of Public Choice has decided to leave their wider circulation to informal channels only.

REFERENCES

Adler, M. J. 1970. *The Time of Our Lives*. New York: Holt, Rinehart and Winston.

Barzun, J. 1968. *The American University*. New York: Harper & Row, 1968.

Blanshard, B. 1961. *Reason and Goodness*. New York: Macmillan.

———. 1966. "Morality and Politics." In Richard T. De George (ed.), *Ethics and Society*, 1–23. Garden City, NY: Anchor Books/Doubleday.

Breit, W. 1986. *Creating the Virginia School· Charlottesville as an Academic Environment in the 1960s*. Fairfax, VA: Center for Study of Public Choice.

Buchanan, J. M. 1975. *The Limits of Liberty*. Chicago: University of Chicago Press.

———. 1983. *Political Economy 1957–1982*. The G. Warren Nutter Lectures in Political Economy. Washington, DC: American Enterprise Institute.

———. 1987. "Economists and the Gains from Trade." Manuscript for the Hutt conference of September 1987 in Dallas. (And others of Buchanan's many writings on contractarian social philosophy.)

Coase, R. 1960. "The Problem of Social Cost." *Journal of Law and Economics* 3: 1–44.

Harsanyi, J. C. [1955] 1973. "Cardinal Welfare, Individualistic Ethics and Interpersonal Comparisons of Utility." *Journal of Political Economy* 63. Reprinted as selection no. 10 in E. S. Phelps (ed.), *Economic Justice*, 266–85. Baltimore: Penguin Books, 1973.

———. 1976. *Essays on Ethics, Social Behavior, and Scientific Explanation*. Dordrecht, the Netherlands and Boston: D. Reidel.

Hayek, F. A. 1967. *Studies in Philosophy, Politics and Economics*. Chicago: University of Chicago Press.

———. 1976. *Law, Legislation, and Liberty*, vol. 2. Chicago: University of Chicago Press.

Hazlitt, H. 1964. *The Foundations of Morality*. Princeton, NJ: Van Nostrand.

Hobbes, T. [1651] 1952. *Leviathan*. In *Great Books of the Western World*, vol. 23. Chicago: Encyclopaedia Britannica.

Rawls, J. 1971. *A Theory of Justice*. Cambridge, MA: Belknap Press of Harvard University Press.

Schlick, M. 1962. *Problems of Ethics*. Translated by D. Rynin. New York: Dover.

Snavely, T. R. 1967. *The Department of Economics at the University of Virginia, 1825–1956*. Charlottesville: University of Virginia Press.

Sugden, R. 1989. "Maximizing Social Welfare: Is It the Government's Business?" In A. Hamlin and P. Pettit (eds.), *The Good Polity*, 69–86. Oxford: Blackwell.

Vining, R. 1984. *On Appraising the Performance of an Economic System*. New York: Cambridge University Press.

Yeager, L. B. 1976. "Economics and Principles." *Southern Economic Journal* 42: 559–71.

———. 1985. "Rights, Contract, and Utility in Policy Espousal." *Cato Journal* 5: 259–94.

———. 1987. "Mises and His Critics on Ethics, Rights, and Law." Paper for a Mises Institute conference in New York, 16–17.

5.5 Winston Bush's Contribution to Public Choice

Anarchy, Politics, and Population

ROBERT J. MACKAY

On the morning of December 1, 1973, the then-infant field of public choice lost one of its brightest, rising stars. On that foggy winter morning, Winston Churchill Bush died in an automobile accident. His brief yet incredibly prolific and productive career was brought to an abrupt and tragic end. Many of us suffered a double loss when Winston died—the loss of a valued colleague and a unique and treasured friend. The second of these losses, of course, is the greatest and the one that fades least with the passing years. But that is not the topic of this lecture. Instead, my topic is the contribution of Winston Bush to public choice and economics.

It is right that Winston's work is the focus of an annual lecture in the Virginia Political Economy Lecture Series. As it stands today, Virginia Political Economy rests on a foundation built in part by his labor and the encouragement and

Prepared for the Fifth Annual Lecture in the Virginia Political Economy Lecture Series, George Mason University, Fairfax, VA, March 22, 1989.

support he lent to his colleagues and students. As evidence of this, his contributions in two areas—the theory of anarchy and the theory of bureaucracy and government growth—come immediately to mind.

The difficult question I faced in preparing this lecture was how I could best honor Winston and his work. I considered many alternatives, including tracing the effects of Winston's work on anarchy on later developments in public choice, such as James M. Buchanan's *Limits to Liberty*, Buchanan and Geoffrey Brennan's *The Power to Tax*, or Gordon Tullock's *The Social Dilemma*. I also considered sharing with you a sampling of "Winston Bush stories" collected from his friends, colleagues, students, and family. In the end, I decided that the best way to honor Winston, as a colleague and as a friend, was to honor his work. By presenting his work to you, I can allow you to hold it up to the light, examine it in detail, and see how his mind worked; you can see how he saw the fields of economics and public choice; you can see Winston, the craftsman, at work.

I realize that many of you did not have the good fortune to know and work with Winston and that many of us who did know him may have known only his work on anarchy or on politics but not his work on population. We may have read his easier pieces in any of these areas but never struggled with his more difficult, analytical pieces. My goals in this lecture, therefore, are twofold. The first goal is to show you the broad picture—the breadth of Winston's interests and talents. The second goal is to let you see in some depth how Winston thought, how he modeled particular problems, and how he extracted from the models he built whatever insight they might yield into human behavior and social and political institutions. To accomplish these goals, I will take you in some detail through several of Winston's papers. I will not do to you, though, what Winston so enjoyed doing to his students. You will not have to suffer through second-order conditions and derivations of comparative static results.

A BRIEF BIOGRAPHY

Winston was born on May 6, 1941, in Coffee County, Georgia, where he grew up and attended public schools. He graduated from high school in1958 and two years later married Mary Leitha Hobby. This marriage brought him two children, Paula Renee born in 1968 and Shari Leigh born in 1972.

In January of 1966, Winston began his undergraduate studies at Florida State University. He majored in statistics and graduated magna cum laude and Phi Beta Kappa in 1968. While in college, Winston worked full-time and attended classes year-round. Upon graduation, he enrolled in the Department of Economics at Washington University (St. Louis), having received a National Defense Education Act Fellowship. Winston completed his course work in two years and then became an assistant professor in the Department of Economics, University of Missouri at St. Louis, while working on his dissertation. His dissertation, "A Model of Family Size, Intergenerational Transfers, and Its Implications for Economic Growth," was completed in September 1971 under the direction of Ted Bergstrom.

Winston joined the faculty of the Department of Economics at Virginia Polytechnic Institute and State University (VPI) as an assistant professor in September of 1971. The following year he also became a research associate with the Center for Study of Public Choice. Winston was instrumental in organizing the center's Workshop on Anarchy during the academic year 1971–1972. This workshop led directly to the publication of two books, *Explorations in the Theory of Anarchy* and *Further Explorations in the Theory of Anarchy*.[1] Winston's paper, "Individual Welfare in Anarchy," is the lead article in the first book and provided the original focal point for the workshop. The workshop and Winston's work on anarchy also had a significant influence on at least two other books, Tullock's *The Social Dilemma* and Buchanan's *The Limits of Liberty*. The following academic year, Winston organized the center's Workshop on Bureaucracy. This workshop led directly to the publication of *Budgets and Bureaucrats: The Origins of Governmental Growth*, edited by Tom Borcherding.

To quote Gordon Tullock, these workshops were "outstandingly successful." For many of us, in fact, the period in which Winston was at VPI and organizing these workshops was the most exciting period in public choice. Much of this excitement was due to Winston's energy, creativity, and interest in ideas. And, of equal importance, it was due to his ability to spark the same energy, creativity, and interest in others.[2]

When he died in December of 1973, less than three years after arriving at VPI, Winston left behind a volume of work worthy of a much longer life. He left us twenty-one manuscripts dealing with such diverse issues as the determinants of income distribution in anarchy, the voting behavior of bureaucrats, and the interaction between family size and intergenerational transfers. Winston had seen five of these manuscripts reach publication. Seven more were published in journals or edited volumes after his death. Almost all of his work now has been reprinted or published for the first time in a memorial volume in his honor entitled *Essays on Unorthodox Economic Strategies: Anarchy, Politics and Population*, edited by Arthur Denzau and me. Table 5.5.1 provides

Table 5.5.1. Unpublished Writings of Winston C. Bush

"Two Fallacies in the Theory of Human Fertility." Summer 1971.*
"A Model of Family Size with Intergenerational Transfers and Its Implications for Economic Growth." Fall 1971.*
'The Hobbesian Jungle or Orderly Anarchy?" Spring 1972.*
"World Resource Distribution in Anarchy" (with R. J. Staaf). Presented at Midwestern Economic Association meetings, April 1973.
"Some Disturbing Aspects of Political Entrepreneurship." Spring 1973.*
"On the Expense of the Institutions for the Education of Youths: Adam Smith Revisited" (with R. J. Staaf). Winter 1973.
"Property Rights and Insurance" (with R. J. Staaf). Winter 1973.*
"A Collective Choice Analysis of the Growing Public Sector." Presented at Public Choice Society meetings, March 1974.
"On the Economics of Human Fertility" (with L. S. Mayer). Summer 1973. Final draft completed by L. S. Mayer in summer 1974.*

*These papers were all published in the memorial volume *Essays on Unorthodox Economic Strategies: Anarchy, Politics and Population,* edited by A. T. Denzau and R. J. Mackay (Blacksburg, VA: Center for Study of Public Choice, 1976).

a list of Winston's unpublished writings, including those that appeared only in the memorial volume. Table 5.5.2 provides a list of Winston's published writings and a citation count as of March 1989.[3]

Winston's work falls into three distinct groupings based on the topics addressed. These groupings are anarchy, politics, and population. His contributions in each of these areas are addressed in turn.

ANARCHY

Winston's work on anarchy provides a single analytical framework for viewing two distinct conceptions of anarchy—Hobbesian anarchy and the orderly anarchy of Proudhon. This unifying perspective is provided by a model in which individuals have initial endowments of commodities, and they must allocate their time to leisure, theft of other's endowments, and defense of their own endowments. The equilibrium of the predatory and defensive activities of all individuals yields a new distribution of income and welfare—the natural distribution. This is the equilibrium of Hobbesian anarchy. By its nature this equilibrium involves effort expended in theft and defense against theft. Since such effort is undesirable, there exist Pareto-superior redistributions, relative to the natural equilibrium, in which there is no theft. These redistributions

Table 5.5.2. Published Writings of Winston C. Bush

	Citations as of March 1989
"Individual Welfare in Anarchy," in Explorations in the Theory of Anarchy, edited by G. Tullock (Blacksburg: Center for Study of Public Choice, 1972).*	14
"Are Economic Journals Overly Quantified?" (with R. J. Staaf), Journal of Economic Education 4 (Fall 1972).	
"Review of Daniel Guerin's Anarchism" (with J. M. Buchanan), Journal of Economic Issues (March 1973).*	
"Population and Mill's Peasant-Proprietor Economy," History of Political Economy 5 (Spring 1973).*	3
"Review of Lester G. Telser's Competition, Collusion and Game Theory," Public Choice 16 (Fall 1973).	
"A Quality Index for Economic Journals" (with P. W. Hamelman and R. J. Staaf), Review of Economics and Statistics 56 (February 1974).	35
"Political Constraints on Contractual Redistribution" (with J. M. Buchanan), Economic Review 64 (May 1974).*	11
"Some Implications of Anarchy for the Distribution of Property" (with L. S. Mayer), Journal of Economic Theory 8 (September 1974).*	8
"The Effects on Public Spending of the Divisibility of Public Outputs in Consumption, Bureaucratic Power and the Size of the Tax-Sharing Group" (with T. E. Borcherding and R. M. Spann), in Budgets and Bureaucrats: The Origins of Governmental Growth, edited by T. E. Borcherding (Durham, NC: Duke University Press, 1975).*	24
"Public versus Private Sector Growth" (with R. J. Mackay), in Budgets and Bureaucrats: The Origins of Governmental Growth, edited by T. E. Borcherding (Durham, NC: Duke University Press, 1975).*	2
"The Voting Behavior of Bureaucrats and Public Sector Growth" (with A. T. Denzau), in Budgets and Bureaucrats: The Origins of Governmental Growth, edited by T. E. Borcherding (Durham, NC: Duke University Press, 1975).*	17
"Public Goods, Taxation, and the Distribution of Income over Time: A Collective Choice Analysis for the Case of Fixed Tax Shares" (with R. J. Mackay), Journal of Public Economics 6 (November 1976).*	6

*Reprinted in the memorial volume *Essays on Unorthodox Economic Strategies: Anarchy, Politics, and Population*, edited by A. T. Denzau and R. J. Mackay (Blacksburg, VA: Center for Study of Public Choice, 1976).

define the boundaries of the orderly anarchy of Proudhon. But orderly anarchy is a fragile equilibrium, potentially unstable due to coalition and enforcement problems.

Winston's work in this area reveals a steady growth in both the depth of his understanding of the problem and the rigor and sophistication of his analysis. His first effort, "Individual Welfare in Anarchy," presents the basic model of Hobbesian anarchy. The concept of the natural equilibrium is developed and conditions for its existence established. The existence of a Pareto-superior redistribution, relative to the natural distribution, is also established. That this equilibrium may be unstable without a scheme for the enforcement of property rights is a point that is recognized but not developed in any detail. In "A Review of Daniel Guerin's *Anarchism*," Winston uses the contrast between Hobbesian and Proudhonian anarchy to counter Guerin's uncritical acceptance of the Proudhonian conception of orderly anarchy. The enforcement problem is emphasized.

Winston's latter work on anarchy draws explicitly on game theoretic notions of equilibrium. For example, "The Hobbesian Jungle or Orderly Anarchy?" uses game theory notions to describe Hobbesian anarchy and the orderly anarchy of Proudhon as opposite extremes of the spectrum of individual cooperation. The natural equilibrium of Hobbesian anarchy is developed as the Nash-Cournot equilibrium of a noncooperative game. The orderly anarchy of Proudhon is developed as the solution of a cooperative game, and it is shown that an orderly anarchistic distribution that is stable against breakdown due to coalition formation may or may not exist. Furthermore, the instability of orderly anarchy is also developed and the resulting need for an enforcement scheme is emphasized.

The analytical culmination of Winston's work on anarchy is "Some Implications of Anarchy for the Distribution of Property." This paper contains rigorous proof of the existence of the natural equilibrium. The effects of increases in wealth and expanded individual abilities at predation on the level of conflict in an anarchistic society are examined. The β-core is shown to be nonempty and a subset of the orderly anarchistic allocations. In "Property Rights and Insurance," Winston applies the notions of the natural distribution and the instability of orderly anarchy to the argument for private provision of public goods by insurance companies.

This broad overview of Winston's work on anarchy cannot do justice to his contribution, nor can it adequately convey the way he thought and worked as an economist. The best way to understand Winston's approach to economics and to appreciate his unique talents is to roll up our sleeves and join him as he would have built a model of anarchy and worked the model to gain insight into human action and social institutions. The presentation that follows is based on "Individual Welfare in Anarchy" and "The Hobbesian Jungle or Orderly Anarchy?"

THE MODEL

Winston starts with a simple two-person, pure-endowment economy without defined and enforced property rights. Each individual receives an endowment or income of the all-purpose consumption good X. He works with the following definitions:

$$X_1^0 = \text{initial income of individuals.}$$

$$X_0 = \sum_{j=1}^{2} X_j^0 = \text{total income.}$$

X_i = natural income of individual "i" which equals his initial income plus or minus the amount transferred to or from him as a result of interaction with individual "j."

E_i = total effort expended by individual "i" in predation/defense.

a_i = a constant measuring the ability of individual "i" at predation/defense.

The preferences of each individual are given by a utility function:

$$U_i = U_i\,(X_i, E_i), \tag{1}$$

where $U_{i1} > 0$ and $U_{i2} < 0$ for $i = 1, 2$.

If individual "i" devotes E_i units of effort to predation/defense, he is able to capture a_i units of the consumption good from individual "j"; while if individual "j" devotes units of effort to predation/defense, individual "i" loses $a_j\,E_j$ units of the consumption good. Each individual's budget constraint is given by

$$X_i = X_1^0 + a_i E_i - a_j E_j \quad \text{for } i, j = 1, 2 \text{ and } i \neq j. \tag{2}$$

There is also a total time constraint, T, on effort devoted to predation/defense. That is,

$$0 \geq E_i \leq T \text{ for } i = 1, 2. \tag{3}$$

This model allows Winston to contrast two quite different conceptions of individual behavior and welfare under anarchy. Hobbes's conception of anarchy is one in which life is "nasty, short and brutish," since individuals, in the absence of government authority, find themselves devoting much effort to defense and predation at the expense of production and consumption. Proudhon's conception of anarchy is one in which individuals, once freed from the restraints of social rules, develop their natural talents, living in peace and harmony while voluntarily foregoing predation and without need of defense. In Winston's model, these two conceptions of anarchy are simply alternative equilibrium solutions lying at opposite extremes on the spectrum of cooperation, each with its own unique problems of existence and stability. Let's examine each of these solutions in turn.

HOBBESIAN ANARCHY

Given an initial distribution of income and no institutional or ethical barriers preventing one individual from preying on another, a redistribution of income is likely to result, leading to a modified distribution of income called the natural distribution. The natural distribution, as Winston shows, depends on the initial distribution, individual preferences, and individual abilities regarding predation and defense. To see this, consider an initial income for Mr. 1, X_1^0, and a level of effort on predation by Mr. 2, E_2'. Mr. 1 would choose his optimal level of effort and income or consumption so as to solve the following optimization problem:

$$\begin{aligned} &\underset{X_1\,E_1}{\text{Max}} \quad U_1\,(X_1, E_1) \\ &\text{s.t.} \quad X_1 = X_1^0 + a_1E_1 - a_2E_2' \\ &\qquad\quad 0 \le E_1 \le T. \end{aligned} \tag{4}$$

The solution to this problem is shown in figure 5.5.1, which depicts Mr. 1's optimal level of effort, E_1^*, income and consumption, X_1^*, and utility, U_1^*, conditional on his initial endowment, X_1^0, and Mr. 2's effort, E_2'.

Mr. 1's optimal level of effort devoted to predation/defense can be written as a function of Mr. 2's effort, Mr. 1's initial endowment, and the abilities of Mr. 1 and Mr. 2 at predation. That is:

$$E_1 = \tilde{E}_1\left(E_2, X_1^0, a_1, a_2\right). \tag{5}$$

If consumption is a normal good and effort is a normal bad, then

$$\frac{\partial \tilde{E}_1}{\partial E_2} > 0 \text{ and } \frac{\partial \tilde{E}_1}{\partial X_1^0} < 0.$$

A similar analysis can be conducted for Mr. 2's optimal effort, yielding

$$E_2 = \tilde{E}_2(E_1, X_2^0, a_1, a_2). \tag{6}$$

Figure 5.5.1.

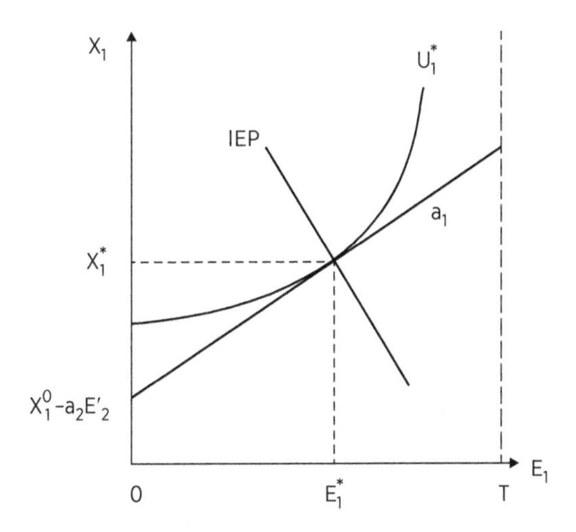

Figure 5.5.2.

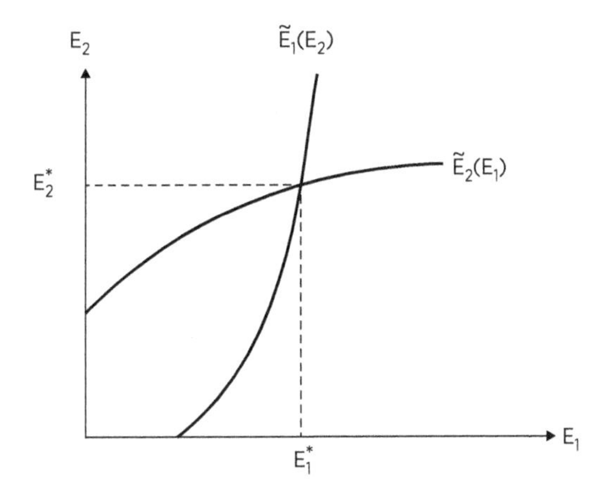

The optimal effort functions can be interpreted as reaction functions showing the best response for one individual to the choice of any particular level of effort by the other individual. The graphs of these functions are shown in figure 5.5.2.

If the individuals act independently of one another in choosing their levels of predation/defense, then the intersection of the two reaction functions gives the Nash-Cournot solution to this noncooperative game. That is, acting in a noncooperative or independent fashion, E_1^* is Mr. l's best response to Mr. 2's choice of E_2^* and E_2^* is Mr. 2's best response to Mr. l's choice of E_1^*. The equilibrium values are defined by the simultaneous solution of equations (5) and (6). That is,

$$E_1^* = \tilde{E}_1(E_2^*, X_1^0, a_1, a_2),$$
$$E_2^* = \tilde{E}_2(E_1^*, X_2^0, a_1, a_2).$$

Winston calls the Nash-Cournot solution the natural equilibrium and identifies it with the "ecological equilibrium" of Hobbes. He establishes sufficient conditions for the existence and stability of the natural equilibrium and examines its comparative static properties.

Winston also examines the comparative static properties of his model and establishes conditions under which

$$\frac{\partial E_1^*}{\partial X_1^0} < 0, \frac{\partial E_1^*}{\partial X_2^0} < 0, \frac{\partial E_1^*}{\partial a_1} > 0, \text{and } \frac{\partial E_1^*}{\partial a_2} > 0.$$

In words, an increase in the initial endowment of either individual lowers the equilibrium level of Mr. 1's effort devoted to predation, while an increase in either individual's ability at predation increases the equilibrium level of Mr. 1's effort. Similar results hold for the equilibrium level of Mr. 2's effort.

The natural equilibrium defines a natural distribution of income, (X_1^*, X_2^*), given by

$$X_1^* = X_1^0 + a_1 E_1^* - a_2 E_2^*,$$
$$X_2^* = X_2^0 + a_2 E_2^* - a_1 E_1^*.$$

Similarly, a natural distribution of welfare is given by

$$U_1^* = U_1(X_1^*, E_1^*),$$
$$U_2^* = U_2(X_2^*, E_2^*).$$

ORDERLY ANARCHY AND PARETO-SUPERIOR REDISTRIBUTIONS OF INCOME

The logic behind Proudhon's orderly anarchy solution can be seen by starting with the natural distribution of income. Since effort is an economic bad, there are Pareto-superior redistributions of income and effort that can make both individuals better off than they are in the natural equilibrium.

To see this point, consider figure 5.5.3, which shows Mr. l's situation in the natural equilibrium, labeled NE. Relative to the natural equilibrium, there are

Figure 5.5.3.

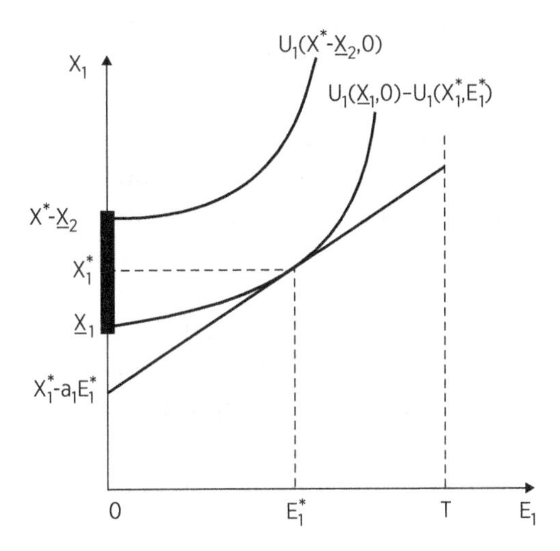

many possible Pareto-superior redistributions, all of which involve zero effort devoted to predation by both individuals and X_1 falling within the interval $[\underline{X}_1, X_0 - \underline{X}_2]$. Let's consider several of these points. At $(X_1^*, 0)$ Mr. 1 gets his natural income with zero effort devoted to predation. The same would be true for Mr. 2, and both individuals are clearly better off than in the natural equilibrium. At $(\underline{X}_1, 0)$, Mr. 1 gives up $X_1^* - \underline{X}_1$ units of income relative to the natural equilibrium (or $X_1^0 - \underline{X}_1$ units relative to the initial distribution of income). His effort, however, is reduced to zero, leaving him just indifferent between this outcome and the natural equilibrium. (This latter condition defines $\underline{X}_1$ and a similar condition for Mr. 2 defines $\underline{X}_2$.) With this redistribution, Mr. 2 is better off than in the natural equilibrium since he receives $X_0 - \underline{X}_1\ X_2^*$ without any effort. Finally, at $(X_0 - \underline{X}_2, 0)$ their roles are reversed. Mr. 2 is just indifferent between $(\underline{X}_2, 0)$ and the natural equilibrium while Mr. 1 is clearly better off, receiving a much greater income than in the natural equilibrium with no effort.

The precise final distribution of income in orderly anarchy cannot be determined. We do know, however, that the set of Pareto-superior redistributions as determined by the natural equilibrium satisfies the following condition:

$$E_1^F = E_2^F = 0,$$
$$\underline{X}_1 \leq X_1^F \leq X^0 - \underline{X}_2,$$
$$\underline{X}_2 \leq X_2^F \leq X^0 - \underline{X}_1,$$
$$X_1^F + X_2^F = X^0.$$

These equations, then, define the limits of redistribution.

In this two-person world, enforcement of an agreed-upon redistribution should not be a problem since both individuals know that the inferior state of Hobbesian anarchy will result if they do not abide by the rules defining property rights. Note that property rights do not emerge to preserve and justify the initial distribution of income. Instead, property rights define and enforce redistributions that depend on the natural distribution of income, which, in general, will be quite different from the initial distribution.

In a large-number setting, the stability of orderly anarchy is more problematic, as Winston points out, due to coalition formation problems and free-rider problems. Relative to the natural equilibrium with independent action, everyone can be made better off if they are allocated their incomes in the natural distribution while reducing their efforts to zero. But this outcome might be overthrown by the formation of a coalition that cooperated to maximize the welfare of coalition members at the expense of those outside the coalition. The search for stable orderly anarchy will have to look in the core for orderly anarchistic allocations such that no other coalition could be formed in which any of its members would be better off and no member worse off than the orderly anarchistic allocation. As Winston shows, an orderly anarchistic distribution may or may not exist that is stable against breakdown due to coalition formation.

Instability of another kind must also be addressed. If an individual knows that others are making no effort to protect their property because of an orderly anarchistic agreement, he could gain by accepting his own allocation in the agreement and then proceeding to steal income from others if detection is difficult or costly. Each individual would be aware of this incentive to violate the orderly anarchistic agreement and would take this into account in deciding whether to stick with the agreement or revert to Hobbesian anarchy. The larger the coalition, the more likely it is that the prisoner's dilemma would lead to instability.

POLITICS

Winston's work on politics is concerned primarily, to use Buchanan's phrase, with postconstitutional analysis—the study of the playing out of the political process under a given set of rules or structure. In this context, his work focuses on developing theoretical explanations of government growth. He draws on two different models of politics—basically a democratic and a nondemocratic model—in his search for insights into the causes of government growth.

The democratic model explains the growth of government expenditures as the outcome of a political process that fundamentally reflects the demands of the citizenry. Observed growth in the public sector is traceable to the demands of individual citizens for more services, concomitant with their willingness to pay additional taxes. Politicians and bureaucrats are essentially passive, simply reflecting and carrying out the wishes of the citizens as revealed through some voting process. In short, voters are sovereign.

The nondemocratic model explains the growth of government expenditures as the outcome of "government failure" to reflect and carry out the demands of the citizenry. The observed growth in the public sector is traceable to the behavior of those who derive direct personal gain from the expansion of government. Politicians and bureaucrats are no longer passive. Operating in an environment of diminished voter sovereignty, they actively pursue their own self-interest at the expense of ordinary citizens. In this model, objections to excessive government growth are objections to the use of governmental power by public sector decision makers to maximize their own wealth.

In two of his papers, Winston uses the median vote model to embed a democratic model of politics in a dynamic general equilibrium model of public and private sector behavior. In "Public Goods, Taxation and the Distribution of Income Over Time," Winston uses a median voter to aggregate individual demands for a public good in a two-sector economy. He studies the implications of alternative tax systems and, hence, distributions of tax prices for the distribution of income over time. The existence of a steady-state income distribution is established for regressive and proportional tax schemes. He then shows that progressive tax schemes exist that will reverse the ranking of the ordinal income distribution over time. In "Private vs. Public Sector Growth: A Collective Choice Approach," Winston extends this model, allowing for differential rates of technological progress in the public and private sectors. The resulting model is then used to analyze Baumol's propositions on unbalanced growth in an economy with an endogenous public sector, population growth, and capital accumulation. The equilibrium time paths for several measures of the relative size of the public sector are examined. In both of these papers, outcomes in the public sector are driven purely by demand-side pressures. Politicians and bureaucrats are passive players, responsive to voter demands as revealed through the political process. Public goods, like private goods, are provided at least cost.

In Winston's other work on the growth of government, bureaucrats and politicians are much more active, self-interested players with some discretion to pursue their own interest at the expense of the public. In "Some Disturbing Aspects of Political Entrepreneurship," he develops a model in which politicians are expected-income maximizers. They can trade off between vote maximization and political income—that is, salaries, perquisites in office, job opportunities afterward, and bribes. The income obtainable from these sources is assumed to be positively related to the size of the public sector. When politicians trade off decreased probabilities of reelection, voter sovereignty decreases and the size of the public sector increases. Political competition could restore voter sovereignty, but barriers to entry are important, thus lessening the degree of competition.

In "The Voting Behavior of Bureaucrats and Public Sector Growth," Winston develops a model in which bureaucrats, responding to a positive relationship between bureau size and their wage income, vote and lobby for a larger public sector than they otherwise would have. In this model, bureaucrats are active only in the sense of changing their voting behavior. In "The Effects on Public Spending on the Divisibility of Public Outputs in Consumption, Bureaucratic Power and the Size of the Tax-Sharing Group," Winston incorporates activist bureaucracies and mobile populations into the empirical median voter literature. The bureaucrats in this model are active in several ways: (1) they form voting blocs and also have high voting participation rates; (2) they make all-or-nothing offers to congressional committees given their monopoly on the supply of public goods; (3) through the civil service, they act as a mechanism for inhibiting reductions in program levels; and, (4) again through the civil service, they act as a cartel to limit entry and raise wages. Empirical evidence is presented to support each of these points.

In a paper reminiscent of his work on anarchy, Winston examines the interaction between the postconstitutional stage of politics and the constitutional stage. In "Political Constraints on Contractual Redistribution," he examines how anticipations about the outcome of majoritarian processes at the postconstitutional stage can limit agreement on redistribution at the constitutional stage. He examines, in other words, the time consistency problem for constitutional contract.

POPULATION

Winston's work on population addresses the economics of fertility and intergenerational transfers. He develops an integrated theoretical model of family choice involving the optimal family size, level of intergenerational transfers, and composition of transfers in terms of human and nonhuman capital. He characterizes the optimum of the family's choice problem and carefully examines the comparative static properties of the model—the effect on optimal family size and intergenerational transfers of increases in the cost of raising a child, the future earnings of a child, and the interest rate. His model of family choice is embedded in a growth model in which intergenerational transfers drive the capital accumulation process, and the population growth rate is determined endogenously.

More specifically, Winston develops the model of family choice described in "Two Fallacies in the Economic Analysis of Fertility" and uses the model to critique the work of Becker and Gardner on fertility. By recognizing that offspring may be assets, Winston is able to show that if intergenerational transfers are negative and absolutely greater than the cost of raising a child, parents will raise the maximum number of children. In other words, there is not a monotone relation between desired family size and wealth as is often asserted in the literature. He also establishes that with perfect capital markets, human capital investment in offspring is independent of the level of intergenerational transfers and the wealth of the parents. His paper "On the Economics of Human Fertility" continues the development of this model with more rigorous statements and derivations of the individual comparative static results. In addition, he studies individual behavior under different market institutions—under perfect capital markets and imperfect capital markets with no borrowing against future labor income. Under imperfect capital markets, desired family size is negatively related to the anticipated wage of offspring for low-income families and positively related for high-income families. The analysis of the composition of intergenerational transfers is more fully developed.

"A Model of Family Size and Intergenerational Transfers and Its Implications for Economic Growth" is based directly on Winston's dissertation and is the foundation for his other work in this area. The individual choice model is developed and its mathematical properties explored in detail. An aggregate growth model is constructed in which population is endogenous and savings for intergenerational transfers become the capital accumulation process. Necessary and sufficient conditions for the existence of a steady-state path are explored and its local stability established. In "Population and Mill's Peasant-Proprietor Economy," Winston applies the growth model developed in his earlier work to the study of population growth in a peasant-proprietor economy. The basic result he finds is that there will be no population growth in this economy because of decreasing returns to labor combined with parents' desires to leave their children at least as well off as they are.

Much of Winston's work on fertility and intergenerational transfers was unpublished at the time of his death. Partly this was due to a shift in Winston's attention and energy toward public choice, especially toward his work on anarchy. A careful reading of Winston's published and unpublished work on population, however, reveals major contributions to the economics of human fertility. He extended in important ways the work of Becker, Gardner, Lewis, and others. Most importantly, he explicitly allowed for the treatment of children as assets, as contributions to parents' income, and incorporated intergenerational transfers in his model, allowing them to take the form of human capital investments as well as cash transfers. In an important sense, Winston's work was ahead of its time. The focus on intergenerational transfers, so characteristic of Winston's work, became a part of the published literature in this area in the mid-1970s and transformed not only the analysis of fertility but also the analysis of savings and even fiscal policy.

The best way to appreciate Winston's work in this area is to work through his model of family choice. The presentation that follows is based on his paper with L. S. Mayer, "On the Economics of Human Fertility."

THE MODEL, PART II

Winston developed a two-period consumption model in which parents must choose the level of consumption during their working and child-rearing years, consumption during retirement, number of children to have, and the amount of wealth to transfer to each child. He works with the following definitions:

C = parents' consumption during their working and child-rearing period,

R = parents' consumption during their retirement period,

N = number of children parents decide to have, treated as a continuous variable ranging from 0 to $\bar{N}$,

W = wealth of each child during the period of his parents' retirement, which equals the child's earned income plus the wealth and return on the wealth transferred to the child by the parents,

S = parents' savings to finance retirement consumption,

T = amount of wealth transferred to each child,

e = anticipated wages of the child,

$\rho = 1/(1 + r)$ = discount factor where r is the rate of interest,

p = cost of raising a child, independent of any transfers to the child, and

w = wealth of the parents.

The choice variables are C, R, N, and W, while prices, e, r, and p, and initial wealth, w, are treated as parameters.

The preferences of the parents are given by the utility function

$$U = U(C, R, N, W), \tag{1}$$

where U_C and U_R, U_N, and U_W are the marginal utilities of the relevant variables and are all positive. Note that parents care about the number of children they have and the wealth of each child as well as their own consumption.

The multiperiod or present-value form of the parents' budget constraint is derived from the following single-period constraints. The parents' budget constraint during their working and child-bearing period is

$$w = C + S + pN + NT. \tag{2}$$

The parents' initial wealth, w, must finance consumption for the parents, C, saving for their retirement, S, the cost of raising N children, pN, and the cost of intergenerational transfers to N children, NT. The parents' budget constraint during their retirement period is

$$R = (1 + r)\, S. \tag{3}$$

Their consumption during retirement, R, is financed by their savings, S, and by the return on their savings, rS. The wealth of each child during his parents' retirement is defined by

$$W = e + (1 + r)\, T. \tag{4}$$

The child's wealth, W, equals their anticipated wages plus the transfer from the parents, T, and the return on the transfers, rT.

Rearranging equations (3) and (4) gives

$$S = \rho\, R \text{ and} \tag{3'}$$
$$T = \rho\, (W - e), \tag{4'}$$

where ρ is the discount factor defined as $1/(1+r)$. This formulation allows parents to make negative transfers to their children. The parents may do this by spending all of their resources before retirement, leaving the children to support them during retirement. In some cultures, parents may be able to sell their children into slavery or at least sell part of their earnings stream. Substituting equations (3′) and (4′) into (2) and rearranging gives the present-value form of the parents' budget constraint. That is,

$$w = C + \rho\, R + N[p + \rho\, (W - e)]. \tag{5}$$

The new term in the budget constraint is the last one on the right-hand side, representing the net cost of raising N children allowing for their future earnings.

Equation (5) can be rearranged by moving Nρe to the left-hand side so that it is in a form similar to that used by Becker in his analysis of the family. That is,

$$w + N\rho e = C + \rho R + N(p + \rho W). \tag{5'}$$

The left-hand side is the parents' full income, which equals their initial wealth, w, plus the present value of the earnings of all their children. This full income can be spent by the parents on their own consumption during their working and retirement years, on the direct cost of raising N children, Np, and on providing a wealth of W for each child, N ρ W. The total cost of a child is p + ρ W.

The parents' optimizing problem is given by the Lagrangian function:

$$L = U(C, R, N, W) + \lambda\,[w - C - \rho R - Np - N\rho(W - e)].$$

First-order conditions for utility maximization are as follows:

$$\frac{\partial L}{\partial C} = U_C - \lambda = 0; \tag{6}$$

$$\frac{\partial L}{\partial R} = U_R - \rho\lambda = 0; \tag{7}$$

$$\frac{\partial L}{\partial N} = U_N - \lambda[p + \rho(W - e)] = 0; \tag{8}$$

$$\frac{\partial L}{\partial W} = U_W - \lambda N\rho = 0; \tag{9}$$

$$\frac{\partial L}{\partial \lambda} = w - C - \rho R - Np - N\rho(W - e) = 0. \tag{10}$$

Equations (6)–(9) can be reduced to the following two conditions expressing the equality between marginal rates of substitution and relative prices:

$$\frac{U_C}{U_R} = (1 + r); \tag{11}$$

$$\frac{U_N}{U_W} = \frac{p + \rho(W - e)}{N\rho}. \tag{12}$$

The first condition is the standard one for a two-period consumption model. The second condition is the novel and more interesting condition. It says that the marginal rate of substitution between the number of children and the wealth of each child should be set equal to their relative price—the rate at which the number of children and the wealth of a child can be traded off in the market. Remember p + ρ (W-e) is the net cost of another child, holding their wealth constant, while Nρ is the cost of providing N children with another dollar of wealth. The complex interactions between W and N result in a budget set that is nonconvex.

Winston establishes the following comparative static results for his model:

- Holding ρ, p, and w constant, an increase in the anticipated wages of a child increases the optimal number of children if the wealth effect on optimal family size is positive.
- Holding ρ, e, and w constant, an increase in the direct cost of raising a child reduces the optimal number of children if the wealth effect on optimal family size is positive. Desired family size, in other words, is inversely related to the cost of raising a child.
- The effects of an increase in interest rates are quite complex. However, if the wealth effects on optimal N, W, and R are positive and if intergenerational transfers are positive, then an increase in interest rates increases the wealth allocated to the sum of N, W, and R, although the level of wealth devoted to any one or two may decrease. An increase in the interest rate, in other words, may lead to either a larger family size, a larger level of intergenerational transfers, or more savings for retirement or some combination of the three.

In Winston's model, parents can give negative as well as positive transfers to their children. If T is negative and greater in absolute value than the direct cost of raising a child, p, then the net cost of raising a child, p + T, is negative. Children are net economic assets with respect to family wealth. This leads to a corner solution in the model so that the optimal number of children is the maximum number possible. If the wealth effect on optimal family size and intergenerational transfers is positive, then the greater the resources of the parents the greater the transfers and the smaller the likelihood that children are net assets. From his theoretical work, then, Winston predicts a nonlinear or U-shaped aggregate relationship between family wealth and family size.

CONCLUSION

In the space of this lecture, I have been able to give you only a glimpse of Winston's work. Hopefully, this has been sufficient to let you see how Winston viewed economics and public choice and how he approached his job as a researcher. This brings us to the larger question: How are we to evaluate Winston's contribution? In this lecture, I have chosen to let Winston's work speak for itself and, to my mind, there is little doubt about the originality and importance of this work. When it comes to summing up Winston's contribution, though, Jim Buchanan has said it best:

> More than anything else perhaps, Bush had an ability to bring out the best in his colleagues, with "best" defined over more of the elements that enter the utility functions of economists. He was a man with an acute critical awareness who was intensely interested in ideas, both those of his own creation and those of others. But he had no sense of "property," and his willingness to help others with ideas was matched by his willingness to do chore work for his department, to help his friends in farming, and to buy beer for his students. Winston Bush forced an openness, an honesty, a frankness on us all, and the academic temptation to pretense could never have surfaced in his presence. I can be more specific. Without Winston Bush at least three and possibly four books would not have been written; without him two separate workshops would never have been organized; without Bush at least two young economists would never have stretched their own more traditional economist's tools to interesting aspects of public choice theory. All this within three short years. These are attributes that are easy to enumerate. Others are much more difficult to put into words. In retrospect, Winston offered us "solid ground," a point or place of reference, a haven from the artificialities and superficialities of academia, from the absurdities of the world in which we live and work. A discussion with Winston Bush made me feel much better about modern America, not because he offered hope at all, but because he recognized the alternatives. Winston Bush, along with my own mentor, Frank Knight, knew that life in modern academia is a "lot better than plowing." (Buchanan 1976, preface)

NOTES

1. See Tullock (1972) for a discussion of the seminars and the unique synergies that resulted from the way they were organized.
2. Based on an academic career that has taken me to such diverse and distant places as Tulane University, the University of Maryland, the University of California at Berkeley, and the Hoover Institution at Stanford University, I can attest that the intellectual excitement and productivity engendered by the Public Choice Workshops in the early 1970s were truly rare

events. This statement is in no way meant to be critical of the seminars I attended at these other institutions—the public economics seminar at the University of Maryland, the finance seminar at Berkeley, and the political economy seminar at Stanford were all first-rate intellectual experiences.

3. Those who would judge the importance of research by the number of citations would do well to study table 5.5.2. Winston's most highly cited article is far from being his most important article.

REFERENCES

Buchanan, J. M. 1976. Preface to Arthur T. Denzau and Robert J. Mackay (eds.), *Essays on Unorthodox Economic Strategies: A Memorial Volume in Honor of Winston C. Bush*. Blacksburg, VA: Center for the Study of Public Choice.

Tullock, Gordon. 1972. *Explorations in the Theory of Anarchy*. Blacksburg, VA: Center for the Study of Public Choice.

5.6
The Tale of the Slave Owner

Reflections on the Political Economy of Communist Reform

GEOFFREY BRENNAN

Let me begin by saying how pleased I am to be here, and how honored I feel to have been asked to deliver the 1990 Virginia Political Economy lecture. I don't say this merely to be polite. The Public Choice Center connection has been, and remains, a crucial part of my intellectual life. I owe the center a great deal, and I am grateful for the opportunity to maintain my various associations with it—and not least for this particular one.

I recognize that something of a tradition has emerged in connection with this particular lecture—that it has typically had a retrospective character, focusing on some aspect of the surprisingly rich history that the Virginia School of Political Economy has enjoyed (or suffered?) in the thirty-odd years since its birth. I want to break, this afternoon, with that tradition, and I should perhaps apologize to those whose expectations were otherwise. But I feel a compulsion to talk about matters very much in the present. The events over the past twelve months or so in Eastern Europe, Russia, and China have been so

Prepared for the Sixth Annual Lecture in the Virginia Political Economy Lecture Series, George Mason University, Fairfax, VA, March 14, 1990.

extraordinary and so central to the kinds of concerns that we as constitutional political economists profess that it seems to me that we have what amounts to a professional obligation to say something about them. At the very least, these were matters uppermost in my mind as I came to write this lecture.

The spectacle of country after country from the Communist bloc (or what we used to think of as the Communist bloc) outdoing its neighbors in some feat of liberal extravagance has been nothing short of dazzling. Central planning seems to be almost everywhere discredited; restrictions on freedom of movement both within and outside the Communist bloc are being removed daily; it seems not inconceivable that the Baltic states may be allowed to secede freely from the USSR; in most places, democratic elections are being planned and in some subset of those, there is talk of actually banning the Communist Party. Which of us would, I wonder, have predicted any of this as little as twelve months ago? We are living in amazing times. The parallel that some commentators have drawn between these events and those in France two hundred years ago seems to me apt, and the effects on world history may well turn out to be every bit as profound.

No less dazzling than the events themselves are the commentaries about them. Political journalists are having a field day; it is amazing how many commentators can explain just why what is happening had to happen and no less amazing how diverse those explanations are. Public choice theory ought to have something to add to this cacophony. This lecture is an attempt along such lines.

Unfortunately and somewhat strangely, there isn't much on the public choice shelf to take down and dust off. On the whole, public choice theory has focused on the analysis of the institutions of democratic regimes, not dictatorial ones. Apart from Tullock's book and a couple of interesting papers by Dan Usher (written, I may say, very much in the Virginia Political Economy tradition), there is remarkably little to guide the public choice scholar through the chaos of events that confront us. Should we be surprised at what is going on? If not, why not? And what aspects of the current situation should surprise us? What are our best guesses as to where it is all likely to end up?

In answer to these questions, I don't need to explain that I am no Soviet bloc expert. Yet I like to think that those of us within the Virginia School of Political Economy do bring some relevant skills to the table—and in particular an analytic tradition that generalizes certain significant facts about human experience relevant to the way in which institutions work and how they might be made to work better. We too have our giants, and they too have shoulders.

My specific object in this lecture is to make a modest start on a public choice theory of dictatorship. The points I shall make are for the most part simple and obvious ones. Yet I think these points make useful markers for discussion of the putative collapse of Communism, and I shall return briefly to current events at the end of my talk.

THE TALE

As my title indicates, the point of departure for my discussion is a parable, modeled on Nozick's famous "Tale of the Slave" (Nozick 1974). You will recall that Nozick's object is to show, by appeal to sequential analogy, that the lot of the citizen in a modern democratic welfare state is not significantly different from that of a slave in a slave-owning society. My parable has a similar message—though the object of my story is not so much to score a point against the welfare state as to score a point against despotism. But that will perhaps become clearer after the tale is told. It goes this way.

There was once a king who owned a rich land and was master over many subjects. This king was remarkably selfish. He was also remarkably greedy. He cared not at all for the adulation of his people; nor for wisdom; nor for honor. He feared neither God nor man. But he did desire to be the richest among all kings—to have the largest palace and the most opulent court and the most lavish treasury of all the kings of the earth. So he was a harsh king. He whipped his courtiers, who whipped his people. And all slaved long and hard to fulfill the king's desires.

Now there lived in a far province of this kingdom a man old in years and reputed to be wise beyond measure. And the king decided that such wisdom should be put to the test, so he demanded that the sage be summoned to appear before him.

In due course, the old man arrived for his regal audience, and the king addressed him thus: "Tell me old man, you who are so wise, tell me how I may become yet richer."

"Noble sire," the ancient replied, "you are known to be a harsh, and greedy man. I shall do as you demand—but only on one condition. It is this: that of every dollar in extra wealth you make, I receive one cent." And the king, who—though he had not (yet) heard of incentive structures, recognized a good deal when he saw it—agreed.

"Sire," said the old man, "you must assign rights in all persons to themselves. You must give away all the mines, forests, and lands to citizens—it does not matter to whom, providing that owners can subsequently buy and sell them freely. You must establish laws that will protect these rights—yea, even against your own power. You must allow your people to truck, barter, and exchange. And, in this way, the wealth of the nation will increase—and increase mightily."

"The wealth of the nation, perhaps," responded the king. "But what of my wealth?" (For, though the king was not of truly philosophic temperament, yet he possessed a certain native cunning.)

"Sire," responded the sage, "you must impose a tax on the transactions of all citizens. Of every dollar earned, you will take one-half. And of every dollar of profit made, you will also receive one-half. You will then share equally with your subjects in the wealth created. You will have unleashed the forces of the division of labor, and the entrepreneurial and creative energies of your people—and these forces will make you rich, and rich beyond measure." [Some histories record at this point some persuasive examples offered by the sage—including pin factories and conjectures of four-thousand-fold increases in productive capacity and suchlike pieces of collaborative detail, which need not here concern us.]

The king, though he had grave doubts, believed in the old man's great wisdom. And he did as he was bidden. And it came to pass—even as the old man had said. The king became rich beyond measure—the richest among all the kings of the earth. And his people prospered and honored him greatly—though, as to that, the king himself could not have cared less.

A GENERAL STATEMENT

Certain elements in my tale will be recognized as arbitrary—quite apart from the extreme age of the policy adviser. There is, for example, no particular reason why 50 percent will turn out to be the tax rate that maximizes government revenue. The king will be able to do better by selling off his mines and forests rather than giving them away in the initial period, providing that he can find someone with means to buy them. (Since his citizens will have negligible assets at the outset, the purchasers will have to be foreign; and we should note in passing that one of the notable features of the first phase of reform in many East European countries has been the selling of ownership rights in state enterprises to foreign capital.)

But these are all extraneous details. The central point is that the old man's advice is surely correct—at least if conventional economic theory has it anything like right. For the king's problem is really a monopoly problem writ large: he owns all the relevant resources, and his problem is to organize them in the way that will generate valued output most efficiently from his point of view. He faces a multiple set of principal-agent problems: the citizens are his "agents," because they have embedded in them the specialized knowledge and entrepreneurial capacities that require to be released; he is the "principal" because under the prevailing institutional order he has the power to appropriate all his subjects' product. As in all principal-agent problems, there are intrinsic informational and monitoring difficulties, for the king cannot know the necessary details to simulate the best (from his viewpoint) allocation of persons to tasks, or even know which tasks ought to be performed and at what levels. Some "profit-sharing" deal with all those agents seems certain to be the best feasible solution to this problem.

There are really two propositions at stake here. The first is the familiar Smith-Friedman claim that the wealth of nations is maximally promoted when people are free to choose. This is, I know, a debatable proposition in some circles, and probably calls for some minor qualifications. But it is not necessary for me to defend it before this audience, and to attempt any such defense would divert me from my main purpose. I simply take the claim as given. The second proposition is that wealth is only "semifungible": Wealth can in part be transferred via the fisc to the dictator (or to the "state" more generally), but much of it will necessarily accrue to ordinary citizens. It is the institutional order of private property and freely operating markets that generates the wealth, and that institutional order will tolerate only a certain amount of tinkering. Yet the wealth increment which that order makes available is so great that even when the dictator takes as much of it as possible, both the dictator and the citizenry are left better off than they would be otherwise.

It may be useful to depict the argument in terms of a simple diagram (I myself usually find it so). So, consider figure 5.6.1.

Here, A and B are any two citizens, and the axes denotes A's and B's wealths, respectively. The point A* corresponds to the point where A's wealth is maximized—where A is effectively assigned a property right in B, in short where A is king. Analogously, B* is the point where B is king. The initial point in our talc (when A is king) is depicted by N—this is the "no-markets" order (what we might loosely refer to as a Smithian state of Nature). The Nozickean "minimal state" is depicted by the outcome, M. Because of the "excess burdens" generated by the taxing process, aggregate wealth will be predictably greater at M than at either A* or B*: hence the convexity of the relevant frontier. At A*, both A (king/slave owner) and B (subject/slave) are much better off than they would have been at N.

The critical claim here—the one whose validity we will need to question and whose implications we will need to explore—is that all the Pareto-optimal points share certain significant institutional features. Those institutional features are, first, personal and property rights, guaranteed by the state against violation by other citizens acting in their private roles; and second, certain (arguably minimal) rights against the state itself. Clearly, I need to offer more by way of argument to justify these claims—and that will be part of my object in what follows. But it should at least be clear what my argument is: that under certain plausible conditions, it will be rational for the dictator to introduce such an institutional order unilaterally and that the institutional order so introduced will exhibit at least some of the features of the liberal economy.

Note that if all wealth were fully fungible—if, that is, the dictator could costlessly transfer all wealth to himself—then the proposition would be trivial. The maximization of the wealth of the nation would be pursued entirely independently of how it was subsequently distributed. The king would establish whatever institutional order was required to maximize aggregate wealth; and then the notorious fiction of the lump-sum tax would be wheeled in to redistribute that wealth at will. In this event, the relevant possibilities line in figure 5.6.1 would be the straight 135° line through M, and the relevant outcome (for A as king) would be where that line intersects with the horizontal axis. In this event, the institutional apparatus may indeed be that of a liberal economic order—but the normative consequences of that order would be very dubious. The citizen may have his personal and property rights protected in a nominal sense, but the full value of those rights would be lost to the predatory fisc and fully appropriated by the dictator.

I regard that possibility as hopelessly implausible—in all its various guises. The kind of total separation between institutional arrangements and distribution

Figure 5.6.1.

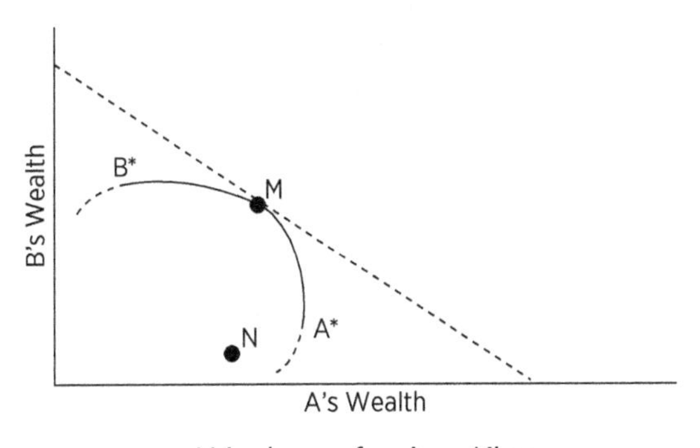

N is drawn for A as King

that the "lump-sum tax" assumption postulates simply cannot be entertained. Think of the fiscal problem for the dictator in terms of the generalized monopoly problem mentioned earlier. We might of course postulate a fiscal manager who is the analogue of the perfectly discriminating monopolist and can successfully appropriate the full surplus to be obtained from the economic system. But the informational demands required for such perfect discrimination must be recognized as wildly excessive: the fiscal manager would require knowledge of all the possible activities that agents might engage in were the system of rewards different—foreknowledge of exactly what the free market outcome would look like. It is of course exactly the point of Hayek's famous critique of socialism that such information is inaccessible to any single agent; and it is exactly Hayek's point I mean to take here.

In a rather different setting, public finance theorists always note, as a conceptual possibility, that there is a system of discriminatory lump-sum taxes that would achieve so-called vertical equity goals with no excess burdens but quickly move on to discuss something feasible like the personal income tax, where uniform rates are imposed over wide ranges of income. As Buchanan and I argue in *The Power to Tax* (1980), the presence of excess burdens from taxation imply limits on the state's revenue-raising power: the Laffer curve is the logical concomitant of distorting taxes. And it is the Laffer curve—the presence of natural limits on the power to tax—that ensures that citizens appropriate some of the available total surplus even under a revenue-maximizing Leviathan. Of course, some rough and ready kinds of discrimination (say between primary and secondary earners within families) may increase the fiscal take (or equivalently reduce excess burdens for any given revenue level), and such feasible forms of discrimination (applauded as they are by the optimal tax exponents) may well be precisely the kind of things against which the citizens will wish to guard under a fiscal constitution. The precise nature of that fiscal constitution is what Buchanan and I sought to explore in *The Power to Tax* and need not detain us. My point here is that, even in the absence of such a constitution, certain restraints on the revenue-maximizing Leviathan will be operative. Yet those restraints will not be sufficient to induce the revenue-maximizing fisc to jettison the basic institutional order of the market system.

To return to the diagram, the actual frontier of Pareto-optimal points under the liberal economic order is given not by the straight line thru M but by A^* MB^*, although for the purposes of the institutional move under consideration here, only the point A^* is relevant. It is the comparison between A^* and N that is critical, not that between A^* and some conceptually ideal minimal state M or between A^* and some other distributionally superior point on the

A* B* frontier. And in the comparison between A* and N, what is crucial is the necessary mutuality of gains: A must gain, since otherwise he would not institute the change; but B also gains (and possibly even more considerably), notwithstanding the imposition of the revenue-maximizing tax.

Before I go further, let me at least justify my implied attribution of the argument here to Adam Smith. Remember, for example, Smith's comparison at the end of chapter 1 of the *Wealth of Nations* between on the one hand the industrious and frugal European peasant, lodged in the network of complex market exchanges that characterized eighteenth-century Europe, and on the other the African potentate: "Compared indeed with the more extravagant luxury of the great, the accommodation [of the common man] must no doubt appear extremely simple and easy; and yet it may be true, perhaps, that the accommodation of a European prince does not always so much exceed that of an industrious and frugal peasant, as the accommodation of the latter exceeds that of many an African king, the absolute master of the lives and liberties of ten thousand naked savages" (Smith [1776] 1986). Or, note that the second of Smith's three references to the invisible hand (the first was in his essay on astronomy) referred to the distributional consequences of the market order. At the relevant point, Smith ([1776] (1986), 184–85) remarks,

> They [the rich] consume little more than the poor, and in spite of their natural selfishness and rapacity, though they mean only their own convenience, though the sole end which they propose from the labors of all the thousands whom they employ, be the gratification of their own vain and insatiable desires, they divide with the poor the produce of all their improvements. They are led by an invisible hand to make nearly the same distribution of the necessaries of life, which would have been made, had the each been divided into equal portions among all its inhabitants, and thus without intending it, without knowing it, advance the interest of the society. . . . When Providence divided the earth among a few lordly masters, it neither forgot nor abandoned those who seem to have been left out in the partition. (Ibid.)

Smith is not, of course, explicitly concerned with the conduct of the revenue-maximizing fiscal manager, but it seems to me that his reasoning bears. If the market order brings mutual advantage to both the economically privileged (the beneficiaries of centuries of accumulation of assets) and the economically dependent, then it seems likely that similar considerations will weigh in the case of the division of spoils among the revenue-maximizing dictator and his subjects. The central point in both cases is that it is extremely difficult—and almost certainly unprofitable—for the agent who is in a monopoly position to attempt to appropriate anything like the full surplus that accrues to others, and this will be so whether the monopoly in question is the conventional one familiar from economics textbooks or the more general fiscal monopoly embodied in the state's power to tax.

So much for Smith. Let me return to my central claim. It is not I think surprising that a rational income-maximizing dictator would provide for protection of his subjects and their property against the predation of other citizens. People and property are productive assets, in whose product the fisc shares via the tax system. To protect those subjects and their property is to protect the revenues they will produce once the subjects know they are protected. (And note that to ensure the maximum revenue, the assurance of protection may be even more important than the fact of it.) The provision of such protection is a natural result of enforcing the monopoly of revenue-raising power that the dictator is presumed to own. There is nothing perhaps too surprising here. But it is worth emphasizing that it will also pay the dictator to impose credible limits on his own activity, provided that some appropriate technology for imposing credible limits exists. That is, some elements of a fiscal constitution will emerge naturally.

Take, for example, the fisc's approach to capital taxation. At any point, it will be tempting for the dictator simply to appropriate all existing capital. Clearly, the threat of the dictator's doing so will mean that citizens will accumulate much less for the dictator to appropriate. If the dictator is to encourage the maximum value of the tax stream from the capital, the capital itself must be guaranteed. Put another way, if it is fiscally profitable for the dictator to provide assurance against threat of predation from other citizens, it will be no less profitable to provide assurance against predation from the state itself.

Consider, as a specific case, Leviathan's relations with some individual citizen, C. Suppose that C will live beyond his working life and will need to accumulate savings to consume through the period of his retirement. Presuming C can save, and if his accumulations out of net-of-tax income can be used to finance retirement consumption, he will rationally accumulate to the point of retirement and decumulate thereafter—providing his rights in his own accumulation are secure. But C must reckon on the prospect that once his contribution to total product becomes zero (as it does at retirement), Leviathan will have an interest in appropriating C's accumulated assets. Unless Leviathan offers a credible guarantee, C will simply not accumulate, and the capital stock will be at a level below that required to maximize Leviathan's revenue. The problem that faces Leviathan is how to make the required guarantee credible. For each knows that once the point arrives at which C is ready to retire, Leviathan will rationally revoke any prior commitment made to C and appropriate C's savings.

What could constrain Leviathan in this setting, however, is the presence of other agents, D, E, and F, and so on, who are not yet at the point of retirement and who are also in the process of accumulating for their own retirements. If Leviathan commits himself generally to refrain from confiscating retirement savings, he will find that revoking that commitment with respect to C's savings when C retires will have the effect of changing D/E/F's expectations as to Leviathan's conduct when they retire. If Leviathan does confiscate C's savings, D/E/F will alter their own accumulation levels, dissaving as quickly as possible, and the total level of capital will rapidly fall to zero. The cost of obtaining C's capital is the extra tax revenue (that is, the share in the increment to output accruing to Leviathan) that D/E/F's productive capital makes possible.

For this reason, Leviathan's commitments do become credible. Of course, one might remark that if the commitment is credible, Leviathan doesn't actually have to make it the public promise of someone to whom promises per se mean nothing; it is simply irrelevant. Insofar as citizens depend on promises alone, this is surely so. Words alone won't guarantee security: some institutional fabric will be required. It goes somewhat beyond the scope of this paper to discuss how the dictator's constitutional commitments might be enforced. In the case at hand, it may be sufficient to establish independent monitoring bodies that will reliably publicize violations of constitutional commitments: provided C is confident that when his assets are confiscated, D/E/F will immediately know, and C may perhaps be adequately assured of the security of his own assets. If so, the dictator will rationally provide some measure of "open government" and some elements of a free press. But I shall refrain from speculation more generally on the technology of constitutional constraints, beyond the observation that we do not require that technology to bind Leviathan totally—simply to increase the cost to Leviathan of constitutional violations. My point is that, within limits, if appropriate self-binding technology is available, the dictator will find it profitable to use it; and if appropriate technology is not available, the dictator will have an interest in its creation. In other words, we would predict the natural emergence of some elements of a liberal constitution.

If we can allow Smith to adumbrate Hobbes here, it is not merely that life in the state of nature is "nasty, brutish and short," it is also that we can reliably be assured that life under Leviathan will tend to be otherwise. And in this defense of our freedoms (limited though they may be), it is not to the benevolence of the dictator that we look, but to his self-interest!

THE ASSUMPTIONS

It should be clear that this construal of the self-interest of the dictator and the institutional fabric to which it gives rise depends on certain assumptions. I should enumerate three in particular. Firstly, the kind of general fiscal apparatus required for the appropriation of a significant share of total product must be feasible. It must, for example, be possible to monitor the transactions, incomes, and/or expenditures of the citizenry—something that itself depends on a well-developed complex exchange financial economy. In a context where most transactions are barter and/or where there is limited specialization (so that much of the individual citizen's consumption is self-produced), the problems of fiscal enforcement may be too great. And we know that fiscal systems that rely significantly on self-reporting depend on a widespread taxpayer morality, which cannot necessarily be presumed. To the extent that such taxpayer morality depends on a perception on the part of citizens that the state apparatus is legitimate, some investment in the "legitimacy" of the regime may be required to maximize revenue, and this may commit the dictator to actions in the citizens' interests beyond those involved in securing minimal, fiscally relevant freedoms. At some point, the fiscal apparatus may become so costly that the whole enterprise may not be worth the candle—at which point back to orders, whips, and the rack.

Second, the account does assume that the dictator is secure—that he can count on the fiscal rents his institutional innovations generate, at least for a sufficiently long period to make the deal worthwhile. Insecurity undermines the arrangement. For example, an institutional barrier that increases the cost to the dictator of appropriating the accumulated capital of citizens will not be sufficient to restrain a dictator whose future revenues come under threat. Moreover, the very deal that increases the dictator's rents also increases the capacity of other citizens to wage war on the dictator. If, for example, security for the dictator is a matter of his income relative to that of any subject, it will be perfectly rational for the dictator to spend resources to reduce the incomes of others (or to reject mutually wealth-enhancing trades that benefit others relatively more than himself).

Thirdly, the account does depend on the assumptions about dictator motivation that I have made, not, of course, the assumption of egoism. To the extent that the dictator is benevolent—to the extent, that is, that his utility function includes the standard of living of his subjects—then his enthusiasm for the institutional order of economic liberty that I have sketched will be increased. Rather, what is crucial is the particular form that the dictator's egoism (or benevolence) is assumed to take. The dictator must be concerned to maximize his income—either because of a simple personal greediness (in the case postulated) or because such income can be used to promote some other independent end (such as the promotion of artistic endeavor, as in Charles I Stuart of England, or of the Catholic hegemony, as in Philip II of Spain). The possible motivations for the dictator can, in other words, be quite rich and extensive—but not everything goes. The dictator may after all enjoy whipping his subjects; he may relish his relative superiority, even when no questions of security of tenure arise; he may have ideological or moral commitments that are themselves defined over the institutional apparatus that prevails. In these cases, it will simply not be rational for the dictator to introduce revenue-maximizing institutional reforms.

It is important to specify these assumptions because they point to the kinds of explananda that are at hand when we observe transitions, or what seem to be transitions, in institutional arrangements. Put another way, an obvious problem with the argument I have presented here (like many other attempted explanations of current events in the Communist bloc) is that it explains too much. That is, it begs the question as to why we ever observed the inefficient Leviathan in the first place. One can always beg off such questions with the response that an argument at this level of abstraction can only ever isolate tendencies—general trends that will eventually come to triumph over the vagaries of history. And I actually think that's not a bad response: distinguishing regularities from aberrations is a useful task. But more should be demanded of the model. It can be made to suggest a variety of possible "prime causes" for any institutional transitions we observe, and I should briefly gesture at such explanations. The prime causes may be the following:

1. A change in beliefs about (the fiscal revenues generated under) alternative economic regimes;
2. A change in the maximand of the ruling elite (from ideological purity, say, to simple self-interest);
3. An increase in perceived security;
4. A change in fiscal technology, rendering a general tax system more effective in revenue appropriation;

5. A change in productive technology, increasing the benefits of a spontaneous division of labor.

The possibilities are not, of course, mutually exclusive. What is interesting is that, although some kind of ideological transformation is often appealed to as an explanation of current events in the Communist bloc, much the same conclusions emerge from a rational dictator model, and that latter model offers a broader range of explanatory accounts. For example, it seems to me to be a suggestive fact that there have been some apparent changes in fiscal technology over the relevant period (i.e., say, the 70 years of Russian Communism): proportions of GNP currently garnered for public use in most Western countries were not garnered and probably could not have been garnered in 1917 or 1940.

But, for the moment, I want to set such speculations aside and simply assume that the relevant conditions hold or will eventually come to hold in most dictatorial systems. I want instead to ask what the implications of my general proposition are for the connection between economic, civil, and political rights and for the way in which libertarian arguments ought to proceed—questions more of political theory than of historical explanation.

IMPLICATIONS FOR POLITICAL PHILOSOPHY

I have argued here that, provided certain reasonably plausible background conditions apply, a form of social contract will emerge naturally between the dictator and the citizens over whom the dictator exercises control. It is an odd kind of social contract, since it is established unilaterally by the dictator: citizens will have no grounds to disagree to the terms, but they do not actually agree. Nor is such agreement required, de facto. (The conceptualization is a little like God's "covenant with his chosen people," in that the constitution is unilateral, though of course in my case the covenant does not issue from divine benevolence.) Whether mutually agreed upon or not, there is a naturally emerging constitution of a kind, and it is interesting to ask how this constitution (what I shall call the Leviathan constitution) differs from that which we might speculate would emerge from a genuine social contract among parties who are more or less equally positioned in the precontract situation (or some otherwise derived liberal ideal).

My claim is of course that the structure of rights to property and person are essentially the same. Economic rights—that is, rights to enter into complex exchanges—and the institutional undergirding to support those rights will be present in both cases. The conspicuous differences relate to civic and political rights. The Leviathan state will not "naturally" grant those civic liberties like freedom of association, freedom of speech, freedom of the press, and so on that do not enhance productive (and hence taxable) capacity (at least in any obvious way). And of course there will not be any analogue at all to the franchise—no right to form political parties, no legal opposition, no elections.

The absence of such political rights has potentially important fiscal consequences. Under any tolerable working liberal political system, we would presume that fiscal claims would be constrained by citizens' demands for public goods and for redistribution to those citizens who make ethically legitimate claims on the fisc. We would presume, that is, that both the aggregate size of fiscal claims and the uses to which fiscal resources would be put in a fully liberal polity would differ from those under a dictatorial one. Whether standard majoritarian democratic procedures will secure fiscal outcomes that do reflect citizens' demands tolerably closely is of course a matter on which public choice theorists have had a good deal to say. I have nothing to add on this matter here. I want to finesse the issue of what political and civic rights (or liberties) may be worth and simply focus for a moment on their absence.

There is a belief common among liberals of all stripes that there is a natural association between free markets and a free society/polity—that economic, civic, and political liberties are intimately connected; that, like love and marriage in the song, you can't have one without the other. Such an association springs naturally enough from a normative derivation of the liberal constitution. If, for example, we ask what constitution the typical citizen would choose (or what constitution rational individuals would agree on) in circumstances of appropriately constructed ignorance, then clearly the whole package of economic, civic, and political liberties (and protections against predation from other citizens acting in both private and state-agency roles) will be taken together.

But I take it that no one ever intended the social contract parable as an account of how the liberal order actually emerged historically. If it were so intended, then as Dan Usher insists in his paper "The Birth of the Liberal Society" (1990), it seems a hopelessly implausible account: historically speaking, the birth of the liberal society surely has to be understood in terms of the death of the autocratic one. And the purely descriptive, analytic question is not whether there is some natural association between the ideas of economic and political liberty al the level of nonnative theorizing, but rather whether it is possible to imagine an institutional arrangement in which one kind of liberty is present while the other is absent. I believe that it is. Moreover, I have argued here that this is precisely what the rational Leviathan will deliver. Those who assert that the Leviathan constriction I have postulated is intrinsically unstable will have to reckon with modern-day examples like Hong Kong and Singapore (where free markets exist alongside circumscribed civil liberties and, in Hong Kong's case, no franchise at all) and historical examples like Imperial China or, for that matter, eighteenth- and much of nineteenth-century Britain.

Of course, it might be argued that economic freedoms tend to generate a demand for political freedoms by virtue of some kind of cognitive dissonance that arises when the one is present without the other. This might be argued—but I don't find the argument convincing. Alternatively, one might argue that free economic institutions will generate a distribution of wealth among the citizenry under which some citizens will find it profitable to fight for the rents that Leviathan enjoys. I do not want to deny the possibility of such rent seeking: I simply deny that the rent-seeking process necessarily gives rise to the provision of widespread civic and political liberties. Or at least I deny that the case for that claim is direct and obvious.

Indeed, far from indicating much in the way of a positive association between economic and political liberties, constitutional political economy has, if anything, emphasized the extent to which those liberties conflict. There is, for example, a very natural sense in which the domains of private and collective choice are mutually exclusive. My economic liberty to determine my own consumption of bread unilaterally conflicts with my political liberty to participate in an electoral procedure that determines the consumption (and production) of bread by others. Exactly where the boundary between the domains of political and economic rights ought to be set has, of course, been for several decades the central issue in public economics, both in its orthodox welfare economics variant and in the public-choice-informed contractarian alternative. But wherever that boundary is set, we have wanted to insist that it ought to be specified constitutionally, rather than being left to emerge on a case-by-case basis under the operation of in-period majoritarian politics. In-period political process is a poor judge of its own proper limits.

Moreover, it is a characteristic feature of liberal regimes that there can be no security of political tenure: the possession of political power is determined by electoral fortunes, concerning which the current regime cannot have total confidence. The implications of such insecurity for political time horizons within a democracy are analyzed elsewhere (by James Buchanan and myself in *The Reason of Rules*, for example) and are, I think, well known. The shorter political time horizons characteristic of democracy will tend to encourage confiscatory wealth taxes, and more generally tax rates above the long-term revenue-maximizing levels; to encourage use of debt rather than tax financing; to discourage investment in public infrastructure—in short, to have lower regard for the long-term consequences of current policy choices than citizens consider ideal. Of course, the argument against democracy here is not decisive. Dictators may not expect to last forever; and they may plausibly predict that once unseated they are very unlikely to return to power (whereas a party defeated at the current election will have a reasonable chance of victory at the next).

Nevertheless, it is by means inconceivable that economic liberties may be more secure under a rational and reasonably secure Leviathan than under an inadequately restricted majoritarian democracy. This does not mean of course that life under Leviathan is necessarily to be preferred or that dictatorial institutions are normatively superior. One can't make that claim without some claim as to the value of economic liberties relative to political and civic ones. And of course constitutionally limited democracy may be deemed to be the best of all possible worlds. But at the level of political theory, we liberals may make things too easy for ourselves in assuming that economic and political liberties are natural bedfellows. And this is nowhere truer than in the transition to economic liberties under Leviathan—because if the dictator comes to believe that the natural concomitant of a more liberal market order is his own destruction, then such progress as might be achieved will be undermined. This is, I think, a case where the best may be the enemy of the good.

BACK TO THE FUTURE

What does all this imply about the current state of affairs in the Communist world? Should we be surprised at what is going on? What about it should surprise us? What are our best guesses as to where it is all likely to end up? These are the questions I began with: Can I now answer them?

In moving from abstract theorizing to speculations about currents events, I want to distinguish three cases: the Eastern European, the Russian, and the Chinese. For my purposes, the first is not too interesting. Once it became clear—as it did late in the Polish experience—that Russia was not going to intervene militarily in the domestic affairs of any of its erstwhile satellites (as it had done in Hungary 1956 and Czechoslovakia 1968), then the balance of internal power in those countries shifted dramatically, and resultant economic and political changes are not to be wondered at. In this sense, Russia is the prime mover. And China—always independent—is also a distinguishable case.

Now, the thrust of the general reasoning advanced here is, of course, that the strictly economic dimensions of Communist "reform" should occasion no surprise at all. Central planning is an inefficient institutional technology for wealth creation whether the object is to make citizens better off or to enrich the state (for whatever reason). In this sense, the Chinese case is perfectly consistent with the model. There seems to be no relinquishing of autocratic power, no concession in terms of political and civil liberties; there is merely a change in the institutional apparatus used for the generation and central appropriation of rents. While ever the political order in China remains tolerably stable, it seems to me that one could have reasonable confidence in the transition from a centrally planned to an economically liberal market order. Something perhaps rather like Hong Kong—though with rather higher general tax rates—seems to be a feasible endpoint to that reform process.

The Russian model is quite different. Although I have little doubt that the economic advantages of jettisoning central planning have been an important motivating force in the whole reform process, there seems to be a conviction that those advantages cannot be gained without simultaneous political reforms. Perhaps gestures toward political reform are seen to be the price that has to be paid in order to get general support for the abandonment of central planning. But the democratization of Russian politics still seems to me to be a puzzle: I can offer no plausible explanation for what seems to be a simple death wish at the center of dictatorial power.[1]

Moreover, in countries moving out of dictatorship, the critical move as I see it is the constitutionalist one of shrinking the domain of political decision-making, rather than that of extending the effective franchise within political decision-making. In fact, the semblance of democratic apparatus that is being put in place in Russia seems to me to be very thin soil within which to plant economic reform. Citizens need to have some confidence in the stability of the future in order to save, invest, take risks—in short, to set in place the activities needed for economic development. I cannot see that the Russian situation calls for much confidence in this respect. We know that things are likely to get worse for many people before they get better; we also know that populist democracy is not good at waiting.

In Canberra last week I met a colleague who had just returned from Russia. He told me that there is a story currently in circulation there. A Russian is asked by a visitor, "And how are things in Russia these days?" The Russian replies, "Well, there is Perestroika. It means higher prices and no job security. We are told things will get better—but we've been told that for 70 years. Then, there is glasnost. Its job is to wreck Perestroika."

Apparently, the Russians think this story is funny. I find it simply chilling. It may be my morbid imagination—but I cannot help remembering that if 1989 is the 200th anniversary of the French Revolution, the early 1990s mark the 200th anniversary of the Reign of Terror. If, as I fear, the Russian "reforms" are likely to establish an institutional arrangement that cannot deliver on its own promises, we—and more particularly they—have little ground for optimism.

NOTE

1. Unless Gorbachev is involved in some political maneuver that is aimed at entrenching his own power and the democracy talk on which Western commentators have focused is mere rhetoric. For a fascinating (though deeply pessimistic) account that hints at this possibility, see Z (1990). The identity of Z is currently a matter of speculation.

REFERENCES

Brennan, Geoffrey, and James M. Buchanan. 1980. *The Power to Tax: Analytical Foundation of a Fiscal Constitution*. Cambridge: Cambridge University Press.

Nozick, Robert. 1974. "Tale of the Slave." In *Anarchy, State, and Utopia*, 290–92. New York: Basic Books.

Smith, Adam. [1776] 1986. *The Wealth of Nations*. New York: Penguin Books.

Usher, Dan. 1990. "The Birth of the Liberal Society." Working Paper 770, Economics Department, Queen's University, Kingston, Ontario.

Z. 1990. "To the Stalin Mausoleum." *Daedalus* (Winter): 295–344.

5.7
Uncommon Common Sense vs. Conventional Wisdom

The Virginia School of Economics

CHARLES J. GOETZ

The "how to" books about speechmaking all suggest that one get off on the right foot with a little humor. But that's no easy task for an economist. Let's face it: most lectures about economics are as dull as dishwater.

I suppose all of us have heard economics derided as "the dismal science." People ask me why economists don't have more influence. I tell them, "That's easy: it's because economists all too often give answers that people just don't want to hear." Economists follow in the footsteps of Thomas Malthus. Economists naggingly talk about hard choices and the gloomy constraints of grim economic reality. We are fond of pointing out that "there's no such thing as a free lunch." In fact, some of my genetic coding to be an economist must have come from my Irish grandmother who was fond of pointing out that "you've got to take the bitter with the better."

Prepared for the Seventh Annual Lecture in the Virginia Political Economy Lecture Series, George Mason University, Fairfax, VA, March 19, 1991.

Whatever else economics is, you've got to admit it isn't very *funny*. Oh sure, we sometimes give it a try. There's the attempt at self-deprecatory humor that most of you have probably by now heard:

QUESTION: "Do you know what an economist is?"

ANSWER: "A person who would like to work with numbers but doesn't have enough *personality* to be an accountant."

Then there's the self-congratulatory humor: the bumper sticker or T-shirt that proudly proclaims, "Economists do it with models."

Still, as a later part of this lecture will echo, good beginnings are important. Perhaps because economists aren't often very lighthearted, I've always liked the story about how the late Charlie Tiebout reportedly once endowed his Principles of Economics course at Northwestern University with a sparkling good beginning. On the first day of class he strode in and, as the bell rang, commenced to lecture in a heavy Teutonic accent as he wrote long lists of German verbs on the blackboard. Well, as you can imagine, there was a great rustling while students pulled out schedule books, looked at their wrist watches, and checked the room number. Finally, a hesitant hand went up and a student holding aloft the schedule book asked, "Sir, isn't this supposed to be Principles of Economics?" The professor exclaimed, "Vaht? Vaht?! Chust a minute. Let me see dahdt!" Then, after checking the schedule, he exclaimed, "Vell, if it's Principles of Economics you vant, it's Principles of Economics you'll get," and started to teach economics.

Yes, it is true that "Well begun is half done." So, inspired by Tiebout's unconventional beginning, I want to stop right here. I want to recommence my lecture in a fancier format, or at least in the hope that fine feathers *do* make a fine bird.

[Speaker dons academic gown.]

Brothers and sisters . . . Hosanna! Bless you all! Gather together with me whilst I preach to you. I will expound tonight on a number of profound and inspired texts. And one of these is the following:

> I would that ye be either hot or cold. For if thou be but lukewarm, I will vomit thee up and spit thee out.

"He has," you will perhaps be thinking right now, "gone bananas, totally taken leave of his senses." Not so. Fear not. But I *am* here to preach to you in a very real sense. I will recount to you tales of prophets, of inspired writings, of the working of miracles, and, in general, the principles and canons of the "Virginia" economic cult that many if not most of the brethren gathered here tonight practice or preach.

Now, as many of you know, I have not stalked the front of an economics classroom for over 15 years. I am, I must confess, accustomed to speaking before audiences who find my economic messages both unfamiliar and uncongenial, if not even barbaric and pagan. When I was asked to give this lecture, my flush of pleasure was quickly followed by another gratifying thought: this would be, as the saying goes, a case of being able to "preach to the choir." It is worth remembering that in medieval times the "choir" was not just a group of believers who sang along at the services. Originally, the "choir" held the clerics, those who were bound by their vows to chant the Holy Office. The choir contained the reserved, upfront seats for the deeply committed: the novices, the monks, the cassocked clerics, the dedicated professionals and missionaries of the Word. No indeed, the choir was certainly not the abode of the lukewarm. In fact, among religious orders, those who have taken final solemn vows are called "professed." Note well the common etymological roots: professed, profession, professor. Well, I am a professor, and I am here to preach in my full vestments.

Likewise, most of you here are fellow members of the choir. As I look around me, I see an audience dominated by professionals or, like the novices of old, would-be professionals, waiting to be admitted to the full dignity of academic orders. Some of you are my own professors, some my colleagues; some from graduate school days, some from recent academic endeavors. Some of you are *my* students, some the students of others. Some of you, I know very well, others not at all. But many of us share a bond, a credo, a methodology that we practice and that we preach. What is it? What is the choir to which we belong and what economic psalms do we sing?

Many would, if they looked around this room, claim to identify a commonality among us: "These people are *Chicago School* economists. The place is *infested* with Chicago Schoolers." May their mouths be washed out with soap! The term "Chicago School" is one of those loose labels that seems to be applied—sometimes in the pejorative—to any economist who believes in the usefulness of price theory for policy analysis. Suppose that I asked everyone in this room who has been attributed to the "Chicago School" to raise his or her hand. I expect I would see a forest of such hands. *I* certainly have been so labeled. And the label, I confess, gives me considerable discomfort. Not that there is anything so wrong with our copractitioners of the Chicago persuasion. They are on the whole a good folk, even if sometimes said to be excessively fundamentalist. Still, I view myself as belonging to a different denomination. And so should most of you. We are Virginia School.

The colors on my academic regalia are orange and blue. They are traceable, of course, to the University of Virginia in Charlottesville where I received my doctoral degree. I hasten to say, however, that the Virginia School has no geographic significance except in a historic sense. Charlottesville is just where it started. Charlottesville may be like Mecca, but Blacksburg, Fairfax, and other locations are Medina, Karbala, and the other holy cities. The flock gathers in academic villages all across the land, far from the borders of the Old Dominion.

Why am *I* the person called to occupy this pulpit today? Perhaps my qualifications are not all that flattering. When I was a student I recall hearing someone say that nobody should be allowed to hold forth on the subjects of methodology or philosophy until they were at least 50 years of age. I have now achieved that qualification plus a little more. In fact, I was sobered to think that nobody can ask you to speak about the "good old days" unless you are—well—*old.*

Yes, I was there in those fabled primitive years as a student, a postulant, a novice, when gods and prophets seemed to walk the earth in Charlottesville and founded the Virginia School. I've been a pretty fervent practitioner for over 30 years. I was an early convert and a grateful beneficiary. Moreover, I have the advantages of a close personal perspective without any accompanying personal ego involvement. It's kind of like having been there in the Garden of Eden, but nobody could imagine me claiming any of the credit for the Creation. That's why, I guess, I'm here to tell you what's different about the Virginia School and how it got started on the track that I hope and believe that it still follows.

Why are we different? My first impulse was to say, "Well, we have Betty Tillman and the other folks don't." But there's more to it than that.

I am going to take us back to the "roots" of the Virginia School, to Rouss Hall in Charlottesville about three decades ago, the early 1960s. It will not surprise you to know that by far the three most important characters in the story are James Buchanan, Ronald Coase, and Gordon Tullock. Indisputably, these men occupy the *sanctum sanctorum* of the Virginia School. Nonetheless, it seems to me that Warren Nutter, Rutledge Vining, and Leland Yeager were, each in different ways, also key catalysts in the chemistry of those times. With apologies to other fine economists who also played supporting roles, I bow to the demand of reasonable brevity by concentrating on only the most venerable of the patriarchs.

The first observation to be made is that each of these men were very much hot or cold about the issues of the day, never lukewarm. They were all "mavericks" in the sense that they were, in one or more ways, willing to sail against the strong, prevailing winds of the economics profession in 1960. Indeed, they were prepared to challenge some of those prevailing winds as essentially gusts of hot air. It is helpful to describe a few items in the then-dominant conventional wisdom of the profession.

One strong current was the remarkable ascendancy of Keynesian macroeconomics of a type that would now be viewed as naive and highly simplistic. I remember Leland Yeager as, in stark contrast, one of the early adherents of the so-called neoclassical reformulation. At that time, there was little interest in what we would now call the microeconomic foundations of macro analysis. Macro theory and policy had yet to find room for common sense principles such as portfolio optimization and rational expectations. Microeconomic theory of any kind was, indeed, in generally bad flavor except at a few schools which, in addition to Virginia, included Chicago and UCLA.

Besides being a stubborn practitioner of traditional price theory, G. Warren Nutter also sinned against another of the sacred cows of the profession: It was virtually an article of faith that the Soviet economy was growing at an astonishing rate, that Russia would inexorably overtake and surpass the United States in economic power. Nutter took what was then a shockingly heretical view. It is perhaps almost understandable that Nutter's deviant position was maligned by most Soviet economy scholars at the time. A more bitter pill is that Nutter's work continued to be ignored by his detractors when eventually the emerging facts proved him correct.

The full array of the conventional wisdom of any profession is, of course, far too complex to describe in real detail. Fortunately, some of the quaint economic fashions of the 1950s and '60s are more relevant to my story than others. For what became the Virginia School, by far the most important piece of conventional wisdom was what I shall call the cult of "market failure." True, traditional economists had perhaps oversold the welfare-enhancing mechanics of markets, the benevolence and efficacy of the fabled Invisible Hand. If so, the pendulum had by 1960 swung far toward the other extreme: economists seemed to take great delight in gleefully cataloging all the reasons why markets sometimes run off the rails and yield pretty problematic results.

Understanding the reasons why markets sometimes fail is sometimes a very constructive and heartwarming business. Identifying the sources of market failure is particularly useful when the impediments to good performance are remediable. For instance, economists traditionally studied industrial concentration and collusive arrangements. "Let's get this wonderful market machine into even finer and more perfect tune than before."

But the market failure literature of the mid-twentieth century emphasized problems, such as information costs and externalities, that were thought to have no practical remedies. These were problems that just weren't going to go away. The common inference, then, was that "failed" markets should increasingly be replaced or supplemented by various forms of government action. In short, the welfare economics of the times tended to be a priesthood of interventionism.

I shall return in just a moment to the market failure movement. I shall argue that effective confrontation of the market failure thesis was the most important and distinctive thrust of the Virginia School. I tarry here, however, to make a different but related point. The leading thinkers of the early Virginia School were, in a variety of respects, quirky people who successfully took on the conventional wisdom of their day. Their weapons in this intellectual contest were surprisingly simple ones. Sometimes one "beats" the conventional wisdom by using complex analytical tools to disclose subtle and well-concealed errors. Other times, the errors lie more or less plainly before one's eyes if we would but have the courage to look. But people sometimes do not want to look, for fear of what they might see. Even if a thing is thrust before their eyes, many refuse to acknowledge what is plainly there.

I remember a college friend telling me about being caught, while on a date, in the classic scenario of The Girl's Parents Who Unexpectedly Returned Home. Having been discovered on the living room sofa in flagrante delicto, my friend beat a frantic retreat to the nearby bathroom in order to restore his pants to a more respectable position. Emerging in justifiable fear of verbal outrage, if not even the proverbial shotgun, my friend was flabbergasted to be engaged by the parents in friendly smalltalk as if nothing untoward had happened. Later life experience has taught me that what I then regarded as extraordinarily bizarre behavior is in fact remarkably common. I think that psychologists call it "avoidance." I leave it to you in the audience to extend the analogy to what I have to say here today about the state of economic inquiry three decades ago.

Of course, even one who does look must not become confused about what he is looking *for*. It's easy to fall into the old fallacy of muddling the forest and the trees. In reflecting about this lately, I was vividly reminded of the departmental economics seminars held every Friday afternoon in Charlottesville when I was a graduate student. Although I do not recall any dire sanctions for noncompliance, attendance by graduate students was supposedly mandatory. Quite frankly, *I hated* those seminars. Most of them were *just awful*. Still, those same tedious seminars were also in their own way quite wonderful. What a paradox! Let me tell you why.

Although some of the seminars were by local people, most of them were papers presented by eminent economists whose articles and books dotted the reading lists of the graduate seminars. The papers were all prepublication drafts at various stages of maturity, ranging from very early draft to almost ready to submit to a learned journal. The presenters, people whom I regarded as akin to Olympian gods, almost never failed to disappoint my lofty expectations. They typically stumbled and poked their way through disappointingly rare interesting points liberally interlaced with what seemed like ludicrous errors. It took me an embarrassingly long time to realize that this was part of the real educational value of the exercise: good scholarship does not spring fullblown like Athena from the head of Zeus. Good ideas must be winnowed from bad ones. And mere mortals do that winnowing. Thus, bad seminars by good people can be downright inspiring. Not "There but for the grace of God go I" but "There with the grace of God *can* go I. I can do it too." That was one good lesson from the Friday departmental seminars in Rouss Hall.

But the other lesson was perhaps more important, or at least more germane to this talk. At the close of every paper, there was a question period. Some of the papers involved extremely complex analytical models or sophisticated empirical analysis. Chalk dust flew and the blackboard was covered with hieroglyphics. It mattered not how technically complicated the model. It was a hallowed tradition that someone would always ask the presenter, "Could you summarize in just a few words the *economic common sense* of your results?" It was amazing to me how many people there were who, even if they had presented interesting *results*, could not describe the *economic insight* exemplified by the results.

I digress on this point for two reasons. First, it seems to me to be a part of the Virginia School tradition that the insights are the important thing, that form is not to be elevated over substance. Powerful mathematical and statistical methods of analysis are indeed used by Virginia School members, but models are not admired merely for their elegance and sophistication. I do not, incidentally, argue that complex models may not be worthy of admiration as clever artifacts, as veritable works of art. But a focus on modeling for its own sake is uncharacteristic of our tradition, and this has been so from the beginning. In the Virginia School, models are merely means to ends. They are the hammers and saws and bricks and mortar from which we build good economic common sense. Virginia School folks ask, "Where's the economic common sense?" If the economic common sense isn't there, the model is like a hamburger without the beef.

Secondly, I wish to draw your attention to the analytical simplicity of some of the core ideas of the Virginia School. Like many good ideas, the better they are understood, the more simple and obvious they seem, at least *in retrospect*. It is tempting, then, to disparage the value of simple insights no matter what their power. If these core insights sound simple or obvious to you as I discuss them in the next few minutes, ask yourself one question: Why were they so controversial when they were first raised? And I can give personal testimony that they were very controversial indeed.

An excellent illustration of this is the so-called Coase Theorem that emerged out of the Virginia School in these early sixties. The Coase Theorem has been so widely influential that it suffices for me to describe this work only very briefly. Coase's Theorem is encapsulated in his description of a railroad and the adjacent farm owner whose crops are injured by the locomotive's sparks. The law can, of course, assign the "property right" to control spark emission either to the railroad or to the farmer. Coase pointed out that legal rights were potentially transferable and that, to the extent such transfers were not barred by "transactions costs," efficient economic outcomes would emerge independently of the initial allocation of rights; just as any other goods, the rights would tend to find their way to the highest valued use.

In retrospect, this proposition seems like the simplest piece of common-sense economics. A key to the insight is merely to think of legal constructs as tradable goods. Initially, this was a surprisingly difficult pill for economists, and others, to swallow. It is well documented that Coase's first oral presentation of his draft paper at the University of Chicago was greeted with initial disbelief, even by leading thinkers of the Chicago School to whom the idea might have seemed most congenial.

Coase's creativity here was probably due in no small measure to his heritage as a student of Lionel Robbins: he was a stubborn opportunity coster, and I use stubborn in the complimentary sense. An unwavering opportunity cost perspective is, indeed, in my view one of the fundamental traits of the Virginia School. As Buchanan emphasized in *Cost and Choice*, opportunity cost has an inherently subjective element.

Part of the problem was that economists were not accustomed to thinking of legal constructs as in any way endogenous to the economic system. Among the few contemporary exceptions to the rule was UCLA economist Armen Alchian's work on property rights. Unfortunately, the Virginia department's attempts to recruit Alchian to Charlottesville were unsuccessful. Nevertheless, I have always thought we should claim Alchian as an "honorary" member of the Virginia School and try to take as much credit for him as we can get away with.

Meanwhile, Rutledge Vining's influence at Virginia was considerable, although not really evidenced in the sort of significant published work that would give Vining external name recognition. I remember Vining's wary characterization of models as description of "what tends to emerge." More important for our present story, however, I recall Vining's insistence on defining economics as systems of *rules*. He emphasized the difference between *variables* and *parameters* in an economic system. Although there is a legalistic sense in which Coase's tradable property rights can be called rules, such constructs are variables in the Vining scheme. The rules, the parameters of the systems, are things that single economic entities cannot adjust and, indeed, must adjust to.

The insight of the "rules" approach is extremely powerful but also insufficiently appreciated. Naive analysts focus excessively on *outcomes* of systems. Bad outcomes are taken as conclusive evidence of bad systems. In the real world, however, the instruments for changing outcomes are rules. But modifications of rules generally have systemic effects on a variety of variables, a variety of outcomes. In the real world, rules changes almost always have both desired and undesired effects. Policy changes require a comparison of alternative rules. Bad results do not imply a bad system unless you can show me a rule change that produces, on balance, *better* results. Bad results are, indeed, perfectly compatible with optimal systems. This is a counsel of humility in policy analysis.

Of course, economists—whether 30 years ago or today—should not be singled out for being especially susceptible to the bad-results/bad-system fallacy. Ironically, my daily experience in the legal profession bears this out. One might naturally expect policy analysis in law to be rigorously focused on rules rather than results. What are laws if not rules? Law students nonetheless find it extraordinarily difficult to distinguish between bad results and bad legal rules. Some find it an unpalatable pill that naive parties are held to written contracts that they did not really intend. Or they may bewail the occasional incongruence between moral obligation and legal obligation, such as when the law sometimes refuses to compensate individuals for serious harms suffered as a result of broken promises. Yet, these outcroppings of troublesome results can persuasively be defended as the workings of good rules that, unfortunately, inevitably yield a certain proportion of bad results. My grandmother was right; you *do* have to take the bitter with better.

Worse, it is not only the naive that err in this regard. For instance, the laws against insider trading—much in the news in recent years—are predicated on the perceived misuse of information by undeserving "insiders." What is little noticed is—the comparative results under the alternative rule which, as

George Mason Law School dean Henry Manne persuasively argues, is *even more* unfair. Manne, incidentally, is another early "honorary" Virginia School member who finally came "home" geographically to Virginia several years ago.

Opportunity cost and the "rules" approach merge in a common theme. That theme causes the Virginia tradition analysis always to ask, when something is claimed to be good or bad, "as compared to what?" I do not remember that slogan being used explicitly in those early Charlottesville days, but it was a bedrock implied principle. Doubtless it could sound better in Latin. But I now propose "As compared to what?" as the long-implicit motto of the Virginia School that should be inscribed expressly on our escutcheons. "As compared to what?" It may not be fancy, but it's powerful.

Coase's classic piece showed that marketlike processes could handle spill-over problems better than most people thought. And the classic Buchanan-Stubblebine piece on externalities followed that up by showing, in more traditional and formal economic language, that the persistence of externalities was not ipso facto a demonstration of market failure. Those of you who were not around at the time may be interested in knowing that the authors had a surprising amount of difficulty in having the externalities piece published.

To have known Coase at the time is to realize, however, that his Social Cost piece is now widely misunderstood by those who interpret it as merely a defense of marketlike processes in the unreal world of zero transactions cost. Coase knew that markets do fail and he was really fundamentally interested in the alternatives. Listen to what he said himself some years later:

> While consideration of what would happen in a world of zero transactions cost can give us valuable insights, these insights are, in my view, without value except as steps on the way to analysis of the real world of positive transactions cost. We do not do well to devote ourselves to a detailed study of the world of zero transactions cost, like augurs divining the future by the minute inspection of the entrails of a goose. (Coase 1981, 187)

Although Coase was interested in the implications of alternative institutions, including nonmarket institutions, he did not analyze where the alternative rules came from, who chose them, and why. That was the job of the Public Choice branch of the Virginia School.

You will note that I am many minutes into this lecture and have mentioned Buchanan and Tullock only in passing and public choice for the first time only now. Buchanan and Tullock, and their works, represent, of course, the full, finest and most distinctive roots of the Virginia School. I have been attempting to put these giants within their proper context as part of a professional symbiosis, a synergistic pool of ideas and talents in which we can all bathe—or at least dip a toe or two.

Buchanan and Tullock are the "as compared to what" boys par excellence. What they really did is to take on the conventional wisdom of market failure—and government intervention—on its own terms and beat it back into its proper proportions.

One reason for the ascendancy of the market failure paradigm in the mid-20th century was that the advocates of markets seemed to be adopting an untenable defensive posture. Externalities, public goods, informational distortions, and sundry other elements of market failure captured the imagination of academics. Would-be defenders of markets seemed to react to these difficulties in embarrassment. It was easy to argue that these were but minor ripples on the beneficent and placid stream of the market, that these were only minor tremors in the Invisible Hand. This bury-your-head-in-the-sand response was fundamentally evasive. I, and most other young people of my generation, didn't buy it. The world did seem to be getting more complex and markets did seem to be creaking.

The genius of the early Virginia School is that it did not evasively avert its eyes from externalities, free riders, prisoners' dilemmas, informational asymmetries, and the whole parade of horrors of market failure causes. These concepts were in fact actually embraced. But then they were applied *evenhandedly* to the alternative institutional arrangements, especially those of political control. In examining allocative institutions, most economists had forgotten to ask, "As compared to what?" At last, the early Public Choice theorists developed an anatomy of government failure to go along with the anatomy of market failure. For the first time, the policy arguments could now benefit from a consistent and balanced approach.

It would be tedious for me to try to list even the key developments in the emergent Public Choice literature. These developments are, in any event, quite familiar to most of you. Nonetheless, I do want all of you to appreciate something that some of you may have forgotten. Others, never having personally experienced it, will now find it difficult to believe: common sense is often a bitter pill that is not easily swallowed. That observation was surely true about the fundamental premises of Public Choice analysis. Public Choice insisted, after all, that *homo economicus* and *homo politicus* were one and the same animal.

Many economists who eagerly embraced the concept of the self-interested business manager were initially outraged at the notion that politicians and bureaucrats might be similarly self-interested (dare we say greedy?). The paradigm seemed to be that the "government servant" got up in the morning filled only with thoughts of what he or she could do to maximize the public interest. At a meeting of the Southern Economic Association in the early 1960s, I remember Buchanan being stridently attacked for "inappropriately applying marketlike motivations" to government decision makers. Of course, one does not need to be entirely cynical about the motives of any economic decision maker, but the converse notion that the typical business executive gets up in the morning infused with the ideal of selling the best possible product at the lowest possible price would have been greeted with derisive hee-haws. The conventional wisdom died harder than you might think.

Nevertheless, the Public Choice approach had a simple, brute common sense that ultimately was not to be denied. There was a miracle in the making, even if it took longer than one might now believe.

The distinctive flavor of the Virginia School influence in early Public Choice is apparent from comparing Buchanan and Tullock's *Calculus of Consent* to what, in my view at least, was the other great early classic in this genre, Anthony Downs's *Economic Theory of Political Action in a Democracy*. Downs brilliantly described the workings of political competition in a specific institutional setting, one similar to British parliamentary democracy. By contrast, Buchanan and Tullock focused on the implications of *variations* in the institutions. In sum, Downs worked out the behavior of the variables in the Public Choice supermarket while Buchanan and Tullock analyzed how the *parameters* came into play. I don't know whether Rutledge Vining took any vicarious pleasure from this or not, but he *should* have been happy.

Moreover, I think that the Virginia School has retained a distinctively institutionalist flavor growing out of the early Buchanan and Tullock work.

After the early breakthroughs on the fundamental insights, the basic ideas of Public Choice were expanded into a number of areas. Some of the expansion and consolidation was done by the "patriarchs" themselves. For instance, when I was a graduate student, our public finance classes dealt with the exciting ideas that were developed into Buchanan's *Demand and Supply of Public Goods*.

Meanwhile, Tullock had turned to the analyses of bureaucracy that figured so prominently in his later work. In retrospect, it seems odd to me that, immersed in the rules-oriented Virginia approach, the legally trained Tullock did not turn more quickly than he did to what we now know as law and economics. But I have discussed that topic in another place.

Before long, many of the rest of us in this choir began to play our parts in the consolidation and extension process. Dissertation topics, empirical tests, and theoretical extensions followed first in a trickle and then in a flood. These later contributions cannot, of course, rival the original insights. Still, the extension, testing, and consolidation of basic theories is what in the last analysis proves the real worth of the underlying principles: by their fruits ye shall know them. We had the basic recipes. Now there was a lot of scholarly pudding to be made and put to the test of the eating.

I hope now to avoid ensnaring myself on a two-pronged trap. One prong will impale me if I linger very much more on the highlights of the early Virginia School. Although it's nice to recelebrate happy high points, they can get to be pretty boring pretty quickly; everyone already knows about the dazzling highlights. Details, on the other hand, are less generally known. But for good reason: usually nobody cares about details. I am going, therefore, to switch gears a bit by moving from substance to what almost qualifies as "spirit."

I want to suggest to you that today's Virginia School has inherited from 30 years ago two distinct legacies that took root in Charlottesville. One is the legacy of content and the other is a system of what, for want of a better term, I shall call economic intuition. By "content" I mean the substantive ideas and insights that we are still mining, extending, and embroidering. I have talked about that earlier. The "instinct" element is a trickier idea that you may find less familiar. I am going to discuss the Virginia School's *teaching* roots.

Now, you probably think that I'm going to say that these guys were all, or at least predominantly, great classroom teachers who kept their students spellbound and sitting on the edges of their chairs. One could perhaps make that claim for Leland Yeager, but I would have to say that, as lecturers, the rest varied all the way from "pretty good" down to, well, not so hot at all. But there was a paradox here. Maybe there was not a lot of dazzling show biz in the classrooms, but there transpired something else ultimately more important.

For instance, I guess I've known a hundred—if not hundreds—of more polished classroom performers than James McGill Buchanan. Yet, I have on numerous occasions acknowledged that he is, by a very wide margin, the finest teacher I have ever encountered. I would make less extravagant statements about the other Virginia School patriarchs, but all did something quite special: they somehow taught their students how to think in uncommon ways; they taught uncommon common sense. Let me see if I can explain.

Most teaching is what I call the dispensing of information and of "ordinary" techniques of logically combining that information. Really original thinking sometimes apparently takes disorderly leaps. As a teenager, I remember being amazed by the account of how, in response to a question, Isaac Newton developed a series of complex and nonobvious scientific propositions within only a few days, but then required six months to work out the chain of reasoning that validated the answers he had already given. It seemed almost magical to me that Newton could instinctively or intuitively know the answers without yet being able to articulate the *path* to those answers. Later in life, I learned through a variety of experiences that this instinct is—albeit admittedly usually in less dramatic degree—characteristic of many people who have success in highly original analytic work. Perhaps it is impossible actually to create instinct, but the instincts that each of us have in some degree can at least be encouraged, nourished, and developed.

All of the teachers at Charlottesville, whether they were excellent classroom lecturers or not, made very heavy use of economic "puzzles" as teaching tools. Most of these were "trick" questions in the classical sense; each problem held some hidden "key" that unlocked the economic maze that one needed to traverse for the required answer. My students in recent years call these "hidden ball questions"—and they don't like them. When I was a student myself, I think I never got to like the frustration, but I sure did, over time, develop an increasingly good "nose" for where the key or hidden ball was probably hidden.

While I was a graduate student, Michael Polanyi came to Charlottesville and gave a lecture on the transmission of knowledge. He related a wonderful story, apocryphal I suppose, that gave me some insight into what was going on with all the puzzles. I now tell it to my own students when they grow frustrated with working puzzles. Some of you will have to listen to it one more time:

> It seems that an American antique dealer wanted to learn how to tell real jade from imitation. Now, the difference can easily be told by chemical analysis, but taking scrapings from priceless art objects is not a very desirable expedient. The American therefore signed up to take lessons from a Chinese antique dealer who was reputed to be infallible in distinguishing real jade just by its external characteristics. When the American arrived for the first lesson, the Chinese had tea ready and said, "Let's have some tea and get acquainted. While we're talking, take a look at this figurine. This is real jade." Well, that was fine, but each time the American arrived for a lesson, essentially the same scene was repeated: The Chinese dealer prepared tea, took a figurine off the shelf, and said, "Look at this while we're having tea; this is real jade." Well, the American began really pressing for more information about jade, but the Chinese would only smile and say, "Be patient, the ways of the Orient are inscrutable." One morning,

> like a revelation, the American realized that the Chinese had no real intention of ever teaching him about jade. Steam blowing from his ears, he marched into the Chinese antique office and started to angrily berate his faithless teacher, demanding a refund of all fees paid. "Calm yourself," the teacher said. "Why don't we have some tea and see if we can reach a reasonable accommodation. Meanwhile, here's today's figurine. It's real jade." The American took one look at it and said, "The hell it is!"

Many of us learned an essential part of our Virginia School economics in much the same way.

The pervasive teaching-by-puzzle technique even took the extreme form of professors asking exam questions that had no real answer; they just wanted to see how you attacked it. After exams, students commonly asked professors things like, "Was there an answer to question number 5?" straight-facedly and without even a hint of jocosity.

I was reminded of this when, several years out of graduate school, I stopped by Jim Buchanan's office with a draft manuscript in which I showed that a widely believed norm about the excess burden of excise taxes was untrue. He got all excited when he read my draft. "I knew it, I knew it. I knew in my gut that something must be wrong with that rule," he exclaimed. Pulling a folder out of the file cabinet, he showed to my amazement that, indeed, a question on his graduate public finance final exam five years earlier had asked the students what was wrong with the rule. Then came what I think is classic Buchanan: he shook his head and said wistfully, "Nobody got it right though."

Of course, asking diabolically good, mind-expanding questions was an essential feature of all of the formative figures in the early Virginia School, but Buchanan did do it best. Each week he assigned a question to be answered in about four or five typewritten pages. The answers were usually not so hard; it was figuring out what the question was really about that was difficult. My own average was about four and a half hours figuring out what the question was really about and only one and a half hours writing the answers.

Like me, I think most of my contemporaries in the graduate student pool decided that there was not only method in that madness, but there was actually magic. I can't prove it, but I think we developed unusual instincts about economic problems and a "nose" for interesting questions. Call it uncommon common sense about economics. In any event, many of us have tortured our own students with some of these same techniques, hopefully to their benefit.

I wish that someone would be able to tell me that the puzzle tradition of Virginia School teaching is alive and well, but I suspect it may be waning. The price it imposes on students is a level of frustration for which there is increasingly less tolerance. I am myself guilty of having become, in the past few years, more of an information dispenser and less of a puzzle purveyor. Information dispensing is so much easier, and the short-term student satisfaction is so much higher. The motto "No pain, no gain" seems to be in danger as the 21st century rolls in. I guess this is evidence for the proposition that "Yes, Virginia, there *is* market failure." Still, like the Prodigal Son, I am at least guilt stricken about my wandering from the tradition, and perhaps I shall yet make amends.

Speaking of guilt, I will not intrude on your patience much longer. My hymnbook has one final chorus. Admittedly, there is a thin and dangerous line that divides rationally based intuition from mere conditioned reflexes or, in the common parlance, "knee-jerk prejudice." I have described the Virginia School as a credo, a methodology, a set of traditions about analytic approach. With due deliberation, I have avoided the word "faith." Indeed, if there is an analogue to religion here, it is a rationalistic creed with *tested* beliefs rather than dogmas. Nor are there any immutable tenets. If the Virginia School's traditions have ripened over time into its own set of conventional wisdoms, then these beliefs are—and ought to be—subject to reassessment and evolution in the light of newly mined nuggets of uncommon common sense.

Thus, it irks me to have the Virginia School associated with an allegedly conservative political bias. For instance, I think of myself as a reformer, almost a radical, interested in institutional changes. But I always ask, "As compared to what?" Finding institutional improvements is, not surprisingly, harder than some would have us believe. That's the gospel I heard 30 years ago, and it still rings true today.

Well, I have strained mightily not to be too nostalgic. But, yes, Charlottesville in the early 1960s was a special time and place for a young economist. The ideas being developed were special. The teachers themselves were special and—dare I say it?—they helped many of us students to be a little bit special. I argued with and learned wonderful things from some of my fellow graduate students. I will not single out any special names; you all know who you are and what you did.

But, like the Garden of Eden or Arthur's Camelot, those halcyon days passed too quickly. Coase was gone by 1965, and for almost tragic reasons, Tullock and then Buchanan departed from Charlottesville in quick succession. While I cannot but view this diaspora with sadness, neither can I bring myself to dwell gloomily on who played the snake in Eden or Mordred to Arthur. However sad was the scattering of the flock, it ultimately may have been useful in spreading the leaven of new ideas.

There is a familiar saying that "What's well begun is half done." Perhaps it is just a half truth. The Virginia School was eminently well begun. I trust it can never be undone, undone in the sense of fading from view. In quite another sense, I hope and trust that the Virginia School is not half done, that it will never be done, its work never completed, that the horizons will only keep expanding as each answer gained reveals new and ever-interesting questions lurking beyond.

The Charlottesville giants are, of course, still at work. And their aging first generation of disciples like me are not ready to pack it in either. But the future of the Virginia School is, for the most part, in the heads of those who are not topped by gray. Let us hope that young scholars, in turn, rise to the challenge of finding the chinks in the conventional wisdom of now and of the future. You younger scholars need to attend bad lectures—although I hope that this will not be memorable as one of those. Work puzzles. Analyze rules rather than results. Always ask, "As compared to what?" And, above all, never be cowardly or lukewarm about scholarly inquiry lest the Virginia School "vomit you up and spit you out."

Amen, amen. My sermon for today is not half done; it's all done. Deo gratias! And go in peace.

REFERENCE

Coase, R. H. 1981. "The Coase Theorem and the Empty Core: A Comment." *Journal of Law and Economics* 24(1): 183–87.

5.8
On the Political Economy of the Transformation of Political and Economic Regimes

PETER BERNHOLZ

DEMOCRACY AND MARKET ECONOMY: ARE THEY DOOMED?

In this paper I will take up some problems that are intimately connected with the public choice approach and specifically with questions discussed by the Virginia School, a school that for several years not only extends to far-off Australia but also to Basel in Switzerland. The theory of party competition, of rent seeking, and of interest groups, given rational ignorance of voters, has explained the tendency of unrestricted democracy to move toward increasing government activity. It is well known that this takes place in the form of higher taxes and more regulations, of growing influence of special interests and redistribution, and that it leads to an erosion of the rule of law, to increasing inefficiencies, and to more and more restrictions on individual freedom. Many members of the Virginia School have contributed to these insights (e.g., see Buchanan, Tollison, and Tullock 1980) so that it is unnecessary to dwell on them any longer.

Prepared for the Eighth Annual Lecture in the Virginia Political Economy Lecture Series, George Mason University, Fairfax, VA, March 26, 1992.

Given these tendencies of unrestricted democracy, another important development of the theory of political economy—namely, constitutional economics—comes to mind. For, if a constitution for a free society agreed on at least conceptually by its members is discussed, then it must by necessity contain limitations on the domain of government, especially as a "productive state." From this insight it is only a short step to ask for constitutional restrictions on governments capable of preventing their steady expansion and thus to maintain a free society. Again, it is here that Buchanan and Tullock (1962), W. C. Bush (1972), and especially Buchanan (1975) have originated a promising and far-reaching development that is still winning momentum (see Gwartney and Wagner 1988), as witnessed, for example, by the papers published in the *Journal of Constitutional Economics*.

Still, in spite of the advances made in this field, we can probably agree that no final solution has been found to the problem of how to prevent a growing sphere of government and thus to maintain liberty, rule of law, safe private property rights, free markets, efficiency, the capability to innovate, and economic growth. Historically, all constitutional safeguards have been eroded or removed, at least after some decades, by supreme courts, constitutional amendments, by reinterpretations, and by changes of the written and unwritten constitutions. Recent theoretical developments may help to design new constitutional safeguards adequate to restrict government power for some longer period. This is not a mean accomplishment, but certainly not sufficient to maintain forever a free society once it has been established.

But if we admit this conclusion, then the prospects look rather dim for maintaining free societies and efficient and innovative economic regimes with stable property rights and free markets. On the contrary, as public choice theorists we have to expect a less and less productive and innovative interventionist economic regime with severe restrictions on individual freedom and prosperity, which, in time, may well lead to economic crises, widespread dissatisfaction, and civil unrest. And such a situation, we will argue, is not only a fertile ground for sensible reforms but also for ideological movements, dictatorship, and even totalitarianism.

THE RISE OF MARKET ECONOMIES AND OF DEMOCRACY

We have seen that market economies with democratic political regimes show a tendency to degenerate and to transform themselves into interventionist welfare states. But how can they originate? Are there forces working in favor of establishing efficient economic and political regimes with free markets, private property, rule of law, and democracy? Are there forces tending to reduce government regulation, intervention, and share in GNP?

Obviously related to these questions is the problem related to the conditions necessary for constitutional reforms to successfully implement the desired economic and political regime of a free society. I have personally taken up this question for the more limited problem of (re)introducing a sound monetary constitution in 1986 (Bernholz 1986). In response to this paper, James M. Buchanan rightly generalized the problem in his "The Relevance of Constitutional Strategy" (1986). Here I would like to move one step further and propose to look at constitutional changes toward a free society as events in a causal chain of evolutionary economic and political developments. In a later section, I propose to discuss the related puzzle of whether economic and political evolution leaves room for individual initiative to influence the process of regime change.

THE EVOLUTION OF THE PRESENT INTERNATIONAL SYSTEM

The present international system and its emergence cannot be understood without three major eruptions that took place in the 20th century: the two world wars, which destroyed the international balance of power of seven great powers that had dominated Europe and the world at least since the end of the Thirty Years War; and the downfall of the Communist Empire with its totalitarian regimes and its socialist planning utopia. The first events caused the emergence of totalitarian and imperialistic regimes because of the crisis engendered by World War I and led to the establishment of a bipolar international system after World War II in which two superpowers, the USA and the Soviet Union, confronted each other. The downfall of the Communist bloc and the Communist ideology allowed an end to superpower confrontation and opened the path for German unification and an institutional reorganization of Europe, since no big power striving for continental hegemony is left for the moment.

How have these eruptions, these crises in the original sense of the Greek word, come about? Let us recall that there are two different kinds of politics. The first kind are the political processes running within the given constitutional and institutional framework. Here politicians think that they are in control of the political processes and of their outcomes. This is true up to a certain point, though certainly not completely. For even day-to-day political actions have many unforeseen and unforeseeable consequences.

The second kind of political processes runs, as it were, subterraneously and is not perceived often for decades. Politicians and even statesmen are certainly only in control to a very limited, often even negligible extent. Here I refer to political processes that, in time, change institutions, constitutions, and the whole fabric of the political system, including the regime of international relations. The political processes of the second kind can be aptly compared to the subterraneous forces of geology, which lead from time to time to earthquakes and volcanic eruptions. According to the theory of plate tectonics, the continental plates are slowly moving subterraneously, building up immense tensions where they meet each other, tensions that lead after years or decades to eruptions and earthquakes. Geology can only predict that these events will eventually happen, but it cannot know at which time they will take place.

What are then the forces that work to undermine domestic and international political systems? Which factors have been responsible for the three eruptions of this century, namely the two world wars and the demise of the Communist system? Two such subterraneous forces can be identified: relative changes in populations, territories, and especially economic strength, which over time eroded the existing bases of relative military and political power of the great powers since the beginning of the 19th century. This development was reinforced by the second subterranean force, ideology, which led to the evolution of totalitarian supreme value societies that took power in several countries in the wake of World War I. The former force was correctly perceived by de Tocqueville already in 1835 and led to his famous prediction that America and Russia would once each dominate half of the globe (de Tocqueville [1835] 1945, vol. 1, 452).

There are at the present time two great nations in the world, which started from different points, but seem to tend toward the same end. I allude to the Russians and the Americans. Both of them have grown up unnoticed; and while the attention of mankind was directed elsewhere, they have suddenly placed themselves in the front rank among the nations, and the world learned their existence and their greatness at almost the same time.

All other nations seem to have nearly reached their natural limits, and they have only to maintain their power; but these are still in the act of growth. All the others have stopped, or continue to advance with extreme difficulty; these alone are proceeding with ease and celerity along a path to which no limit can be perceived. The American struggles against the obstacles that nature opposes to him; the adversaries of the Russian are men. The former combats the wilderness and savage life; the latter, civilization with all its arms. The conquests of the American are therefore gained by the plowshare; those of the Russian by the sword. The Anglo-American relies upon personal interest to accomplish his ends and gives free scope to the unguided strength and common sense of the people; the Russian centers all the authority of society in a single arm. The principal instrument of the former is freedom; of the latter, servitude. Their starting point is different. And their courses are not the same; yet each of them seems marked out by the will of Heaven to sway the destinies of half the globe.

The second, the ideological force, helped to make a restoration of the balance of power after World War II about impossible and exacerbated the bitterness of the Cold War between the two superpowers. It also led to the introduction of a more or less centrally planned socialist economic regime, dominated by a totalitarian government, a fact that had to lead to the third eruption of this century. I will return to the ideological forces later.

The third eruption took place during the last years with the breakdown of the Communist Soviet Empire. This third historical break was a consequence again of economic forces working and accumulating over decades. It was a consequence of the inherent weaknesses of planned command economies to innovate and to provide goods efficiently and in sufficient quality as compared to free-market economies with dominating private property. This breakdown of the Soviet system and the resulting erosion of its ideology has also been foreseen. George Kennan made this clear already in 1947, when he proposed as Mr. X the containment policy against the further expansion of the Soviet Empire (Kennan 1947).

In addition to this, we have the fact that Soviet economic development, while it can list certain formidable achievements, has been precariously spotty and uneven. Russian Communists who speak of the "uneven development of capitalism" should blush at the contemplation of their own national economy. Here certain branches of economic life, such as the metallurgical and machine industries, have been pushed out of all proportion to other sectors of economy. Here is a nation striving to become in a short period one of the great industrial nations of the world while it has no highway network worthy of the name and only a relatively primitive network of railways. Much has been done to increase efficiency of labor and to teach primitive peasants something about the operation of machines. But maintenance is still a crying deficiency in the entire Soviet economy. Construction is hasty and poor in quality. Depreciation must be enormous. And in vast sectors of economic life, it has not yet been possible to instill into labor anything like that general culture of production and technical self-respect that characterizes the skilled worker of the West.

It is difficult to see how these deficiencies can be corrected at an early date by a tired and dispirited population working largely under the shadow of fear and compulsion. And as long as they are not overcome, Russia will remain economically a vulnerable and in a certain sense an impotent nation, capable of exporting its enthusiasms and of radiating the strange charm of its primitive political vitality, but unable to back up those articles of export by real evidences of material power and prosperity.

Meanwhile, a great uncertainty hangs over the political life of the Soviet Union. That is the uncertainty involved in the transfer of power from one individual or group of individuals to others. And if disunity were ever to seize and paralyze the Communist Party, the chaos and weakness of Russian society would be revealed in forms beyond description. For we have seen that Soviet power is only a crust concealing an amorphous mass of human beings among whom no independent organizational structure is tolerated. In Russia there is not even such a thing as local government. The present generation of Russians has never known spontaneity of collective action. If, consequently, anything were ever to occur to disrupt the unity and efficacy of the Communist Party as a political instrument, Soviet Russia might be changed overnight from one of the strongest to one of the weakest and most pitiable of national societies.

Thus the future of Soviet power may not be by any means as secure as Russian capacity for self-delusion would make it appear to the men in the Kremlin. That they can keep power themselves, they have demonstrated. That they can quietly and easily turn it over to others remains to be proven. Meanwhile, the hardships of their rule and the vicissitudes of international life have taken a heavy toll of the strength and hopes of the great people on whom their power rests. It is curious to note that the ideological power of Soviet authority is strongest today in areas beyond the frontiers of Russia, beyond the reach of its police power. This phenomenon brings to mind a comparison used by Thomas Mann in his great novel, *Buddenbrooks*.

Observing that human institutions often show the greatest outward brilliance at a moment when inner decay is in reality furthest advanced, Mann compared the Buddenbrook family, in the days of its greatest glamour, to one of those stars whose light shines most brightly on this world when in reality it has long since ceased to exist. And who can say with assurance that the strong light still cast by the Kremlin on the dissatisfied peoples of the Western world is not the powerful afterglow of a constellation that is in actuality on the wane? This cannot be proven. And it cannot be disproven. But the possibility remains (and in the opinion of this writer, it is a strong one) that Soviet power, like the capitalist world of its conception, bears within it the seeds of its own decay, and that the sprouting of these seeds is well advanced.

Even more precise than Kennan, the German law professor and ordoliberal Franz Böhm expected already in 1952 that reform from above would be taken in the Eastern Bloc with the passage of time and that this would lead to chaotic consequences:

> If such a (centrally planned) system has once consolidated itself, then it is, moreover, extremely difficult, if not nearly impossible to remove it again. For in this system each citizen is a public officer. The leadership has destroyed for citizens all possibilities to set up and to realize private economic plans by abolishing private property of the means of production. . . . What shall he done and how shall the economy move on, if a centrally administered economy is removed revolutionarily? Who shall direct the plants when the authority of central government officials ends, but if, on the other hand, nobody owns the plant and its machines and tools; i.e., somebody able to keep these plants running and who could set up economic plans supported by this ownership? Exactly this is the curse of systems of exaggerated power concentration (Herrschaft), that their breakdown must entail complete chaos. In such cases a period of terrible and bloody struggles for power and social upheavals have to be expected, so that each counteraction is paralyzed by fear, and that the suppressed wish to renounce revolution and to kiss the hands of their oppressors. (Böhm [1952] 1980)

I am, however, inclined to believe that there exists besides war another possibility to get rid of such a system: namely, try to perfect the economic system of freedom in those parts of the world in which central planning has not yet been installed, especially to dissolve or to restrain with all means economic power concentrations; to prove the immense social, political, and economic superiority of this free system; but otherwise to help the centrally planned economies to raise the standard of living of the broad masses. For by increasing the latter, the tasks of central steering grow a hundred- and thousandfold and raise the demands of the governed concerning the art of steering by their rulers. The rulers themselves will feel forced to decentralize their tasks and make use of the automatic mechanisms of freer systems to facilitate them. Sooner or later they will introduce elements of the market system from above. But thus they create with their own hands the social base from which the rebellion can grow, which is impossible in the rough initial stages of a centrally administered economy. As soon as islands of market freedom have once been created, there exists a high degree of probability that the explosive power of the market system brings down central planning. It has, however, to be assumed that such a process will be accompanied by dramatic domestic power struggles. But after all, it is never possible to calculate in advance the ideological changes in a system dominated by doctrines; and a peace preserved with stubborn intelligence is not the worst weapon against a tyranny.

This predictive analysis of forces shaping future events by de Tocqueville, Kennan, and Böhm is, I believe, quite in agreement with public choice theory. If we take the political and military competition of the member states of the international system and the striving of at least some politicians for power and influence, then national leaders have to be quite concerned about a worsening relative power position of their nations.

But the relative political and military position is mainly dependent on the relative developments of the economies and, especially in former times, of populations and territories (Bernholz 1985, 1992). Thus either preventive war or domestic reforms will be deemed necessary, in time, by those leaders of the great powers whose rates of economic growth are lagging behind those of competing nations. But war to reduce the relative power of a quickly growing competitor is only an alternative if there exists a reasonable chance of winning. Otherwise, economic reforms are the only option and will be taken up by innovative politicians if they feel no longer bound by an ideological creed and have mentally grasped the situation.[1]

Finally, since market economies with strong private property outperform planned or strongly interventionist economic systems because of their greater efficiency and economic capabilities, a reform and thus a regime change of centrally planned socialist regimes seems to be only a question of time, if they do not succeed before in subjugating the other nations by war, revolution, terrorism, guerrilla war, or ideological conversion.

REASONS FOR THE EVOLUTION OF A FREE AND PROSPEROUS SOCIETY

Let us draw a more detailed picture of the rough sketch presented. As mentioned, it seems to be rather clear today under what conditions prosperity will develop in a society. But given an oligarchic, totalitarian, and/or despotic regime, why should the ruling elite agree to strong and safe property rights for everybody, to minimal state intervention and regulation, to a strong limitation of taxes, and thus of its own powers to command and to take away goods and resources at their discretion? This question is the more important, since despotic regimes have ruled for the greatest part of history in most countries—

and, in fact, even today. Regimes ruled by dictatorships, oligarchy, and despotism have been rather stable systems in the course of history. Freedom, rule of law, safety of property rights, and democracy have been the exception and not the normal state of affairs in history.

Fortunately, well-known historical explanatory sketches such as *The Rise of the Western World* by North and Thomas (1973) and other new economic historians are now available to answer our question (see also North 1981; Eric Jones 1981).

As Erich Weede puts it, "European disunity has been our good luck" (1987, 2). After the breakdown of the Roman Empire, feudalism with its many power centers developed and a split opened up between religious and temporal power (pope and emperor and kings). A strong rivalry arose between these powers or emerging states and their rulers to gain, to preserve, and to extend their powers. This forced European rulers to become interested in the well-being and loyalty of their subjects and, above all, in economic development to secure a greater tax base and thus stronger armies. But economic development in its term depended on the development of adequate property rights and on free markets. As a consequence, competition among states forced on reluctant rulers a limitation of their domestic powers. The development of competing legal systems and the rule of law, of property rights, and of due process of law was helped, not only by interstate competition but also by the separation of church and state, the preventing of a theocracy (Berman 1984). Limited government and pluralistic society were thus predemocratic achievements. They were not planned by anybody, but they emerged and proved to be successful. First capitalism and later democracy were their progeny.

The motivation of rulers to limit their domestic powers and to strengthen economies as a base of their power in the international system is present also today. It is highly probable that the efforts to decentralize and to move toward market economies in China since 1979 and recently in the Soviet Union and Eastern Europe have more to do with the aim of China and the Soviet Union to build up or to maintain a great power status than with the wish to supply the population with more and better goods or even to grant them greater freedom.

We can now understand why Gorbachev tried to move the Soviet Union to undertake far-reaching institutional and economic reforms. He obviously realized the inefficiency and lacking innovativeness of the Soviet economy. Before Gorbachev became secretary general of the Politburo, he already stressed the necessity for reform in the Soviet Union. According to the *Neue Zürcher Zeitung* of December 13, 1984, which referred to reports in the Soviet press, "The youngest member of the Politburo was the main speaker at a (Communist Party) conference on Ideology." The article reports that Gorbachev stated that

> it was inescapable to transform the Soviet economy and to raise its technical and organizational performance to a qualitatively higher level. The course, to increase productivity and to intensify work effort, was necessitated by objective factors. . . . No alternative existed. Only such a modernized economy could meet the necessities of the population, allow a strengthening of the position of the USSR on the international stage and make it possible for her to enter the new millennium as a powerful and flourishing state. . . . One could not learn from the presentation in which way the Soviet economic production should be modernized and which reform ideas Gorbachev would like to apply.

From this statement, the reasons for reforms from above seem to be obvious. Note also that only reforms by the rulers or their power holders seem to be possible in dictatorships and/or totalitarian regimes. For, as Gordon Tullock has argued convincingly (1974), a free economic and democratic regime are public goods, and the risks for life and family implied in a revolution or coup d'état far outweigh the possible gains for the ordinary person not in control of at least part of military or police power. Also the wish of rulers to grant more economic freedom to realize a more successful economic regime does not mean that the reforms are adequate and will be successful. On the contrary, the greater freedom implied by successful efforts to reach greater efficiency and higher growth rates soon comes into conflict with dominating ideologies and with the primary aim of the ruling oligarchy to preserve its dominance, an aim which may easily doom the efforts toward more efficiency. Given these problems, together with the vested interests of bureaucrats and functionaries to preserve their privileges and of the risk aversion of the general population, it is in no way sure that capitalism, rule of law, and perhaps even democracy will finally evolve. There exists a chance for such institutions to evolve, but its probability seems to be not too high, though it depends on specific circumstances of the country in question.

An example of a successful reform of the constitutional legal and economic regime is provided by Japan during the second part of the 19th century, a reform which, in a sense, was fully completed only with the new Japanese constitution introduced by General MacArthur in the wake of World War II. The Meiji Restoration of the 1860s was also a revolution from above, led by the nobility against the weakened power of the shogun and skillfully using the device of restoring factual power to the Tenno. The restoration was decisively shaped or even caused by the realization of the superiority of the powers of Western states after the forced opening of Japanese harbors to Western trade, beginning with Commodore Perry in 1854. "Thus the new slogan of the day became 'fukoku-kyohei,' 'rich country, strong arms'" (*Encyclopedia Britannica* 1962, 12:924). The reforms took the form of a wholesale adoption of Western constitutional, legal, educational, economic, technical, administrative, and military systems, which proved very successful in the long run.

If we turn to the cases of South Korea and Taiwan, it seems also that the foreign policy situation vis-à-vis North Korea and Red China may have been the most important consideration for the leaders to give capitalism a chance. It would thus be of interest to hear the specialists' opinion on the reasons causing the rulers of South Korea and Taiwan to allow and even to further a capitalist development, limiting their own powers and thus indirectly motivating their populations to ask also for more political rights and even for democratic regimes.

What other reasons exist for motivating the rulers in oligarchies or even in democracies to limit their own powers and to allow safe property rights, free markets, and low taxes? I am under the impression that only some kind of crisis can bring about such a response. First, the United Kingdom had fallen back behind France and West Germany for decades in its economic performance. This may have been more important for the Thatcher turnaround than the fact "that by 1979, the British had experienced the practical consequences of all the ideas propounded by the politicians in all the parties" (Seldon 1988, 19). Second, Hong Kong and Singapore faced the challenge to support a big inflow of refugees and of the separation from their hinterlands in China and Malaysia.

THE ROLE OF IDEOLOGY IN THE CHANGE OF ECONOMIC AND POLITICAL REGIMES

Until now I have mentioned only in passing the role played by ideology in influencing or bringing about the eruptions that may lead to changes in political and economic regimes. But ideology, until now rather neglected by public choice, plays a major part as a cause and as a beneficiary of such eruptions.

I have already discussed the tendency of democratic market regimes toward an ever-increasing intervention and/or welfare state. This development, however, leads in time to less and less efficiency, freedom, innovation, and productive investment and to a misallocation of resources and decreasing growth rates of GNP. As a consequence, in the end the political-economic regime enters a crisis because of widespread voter dissatisfaction. At the moment, Sweden seems to be experiencing such a situation.

Crises can also develop because of other reasons: wars, religious and ethnic strife, hyperinflations, depressions, and so on. Obvious examples are the consequences of World War I, especially for the defeated countries after the harsh peace treaties of Versailles, St. Germain, Trianon, and Neuilly. The Great Depression, beginning in 1929 and the hyperinflations in Germany, Austria, Hungary, and Poland in the 1920s, in China in the 1940s and presently in some Latin American countries are further examples.

Crises are obviously a fertile ground for reform plans designed to introduce new political-economic regimes. Crises are thus also fertile ground for the application of ideas or the success of ideologies purporting to have the right recipe for solving the perceived problems. For example, German neoliberals like Eucken, Böhm, Röpke, and Müller-Armack had already prepared their ideas or theoretical visions about a new free-market system during the Nazi regime and the war (Peacock and Willgerodt 1989). These ideas were available at the time of the currency reform of 1948 and were implemented by Ludwig Erhard, Müller-Armack, and others in West Germany. A regime change from the degenerating system of a planned economy to a free-market system was successfully engineered.

During other crises, different theories and ideologies competed with their proposals for problem solutions. By an ideology, I understand a worldview, a weltanschauung, trying to interpret major aspects of the world and its interrelationships. Usually such an ideology contains also supreme values that have to be pursued according to the creed to solve the problems of individuals and/or society. An ideology thus fulfills a latent human demand for spiritual goods, since the weltanschauung provides safety and meaning in an otherwise incomprehensible world. A sharing of this worldview with others offers a feeling of warmth and belonging, of safety in the womb of collectivity. Examples of ideologies of this kind are major religions, but also Communism and National Socialism.

It is obvious that ideologies become most attractive to disoriented and suffering people in times of crises, especially if they seem to propose through their worldview solutions to problems perceived by the masses. Thus it was during the crisis of the Great Depression in the wake of World War I that both the Nazis and Communists gained strong voter support in Germany (Frey and Weck 1981) after they had widely lost it with the end of the German hyperinflation in 1923. It is also not by chance that Lenin and his supporters gained power in Russia in the debacle of defeats and suffering brought about by

World War I. And we may also ask whether Mao and his Communists would have defeated the Kuomintang so easily in 1949 without the dismal economic plight, the corruption, and the ravaging hyperinflation in China.

We can conclude that ideological movements enjoy a good chance to grasp power during crises if they have an attractive belief system promising to solve the problems perceived by the masses of the population. Once having succeeded, such an ideological movement may then even turn the nation into a totalitarian state, if the supreme values of their creed seem to demand it (Bernholz 1991a). At the moment, however, we are interested in another trait of ideological movements. Their supreme values usually contain certain rules referring to the economic regime wanted. For example, Islam does not allow interest and Christianity forbade usury. Communism and Nazism imply a more or less centrally planned economy, the former additionally socialist or state property. Note that ideologies contain fixed, constitutional rules that are binding on everybody—even the leadership. For even Stalin or Lenin could not preach capitalism or introduce free markets except for a short intermediate period with the purpose of moving on toward socialism and Communism. There thus exists what I have called a "Constitution of Totalitarianism" (Bernholz 1991b). And as far as such a written or unwritten constitution contains comprehensive rules referring to the organization of the economy, the political success of an ideological movement necessarily leads to a change not only of the political but also of the economic regime. And this is exactly what happened in the Soviet Union, in Nazi Germany, in Eastern Europe, Communist China, Cuba, Vietnam, and Cambodia.

We all know that in countries in which the Communists came into power, the economic regime was changed to collectivized or state-owned property and to more or less central planning instead of markets. But it has already been mentioned that such a regime must, in time, lead to growing economic inferiority compared to free-market economies with strong private-property rights, because it cannot solve the informational and motivational problems implied by it (Pejovich 1987). The resulting weakening of the relative economic base of military and political power leads to increasing tensions that finally result in another major eruption, as witnessed by recent events in Eastern Europe.

CYCLES OF POLITICAL-ECONOMIC REGIMES OR BACK TO ARISTOTLE?

This analysis suggests the existence of a long-term cyclical movement from one economic—and perhaps also political—regime to another. Democratic free-market economies in time degenerate into excessive welfare and/or intervention states. The ensuing crisis allows ideological movements to grasp power and to transform the economic regime by introducing central planning and perhaps collective property. Central planning requires a central political authority, preferably a dictatorship. But the economic regime thus established leads, in time, to a deterioration of the relative power position in the international system of competing states. Finally, reforms from above are taken and a free-market economy with dominating private property is introduced or emerges from the chaos of reform. But economic liberalization requires political decentralization and promotes again the latter. Thus rule of law and democracy emerge. Here the cycle can begin again. Given these stylized relationships, it may be asked whether we are back to some kind of political cycle as already proposed by Plato (1965) and critically discussed by Aristotle (1965).

Though there are certainly forces working toward such a definite long-term cyclical movement among political-economic regimes, there are other factors that may push the process into other directions or cycles (figure 5.8.1).

An excessive welfare or intervention state may be reformed by cutting back government regulations, taxes, and redistribution, if only an opposition party with a corresponding reform program presents itself to the voters at the time

Figure 5.8.1.

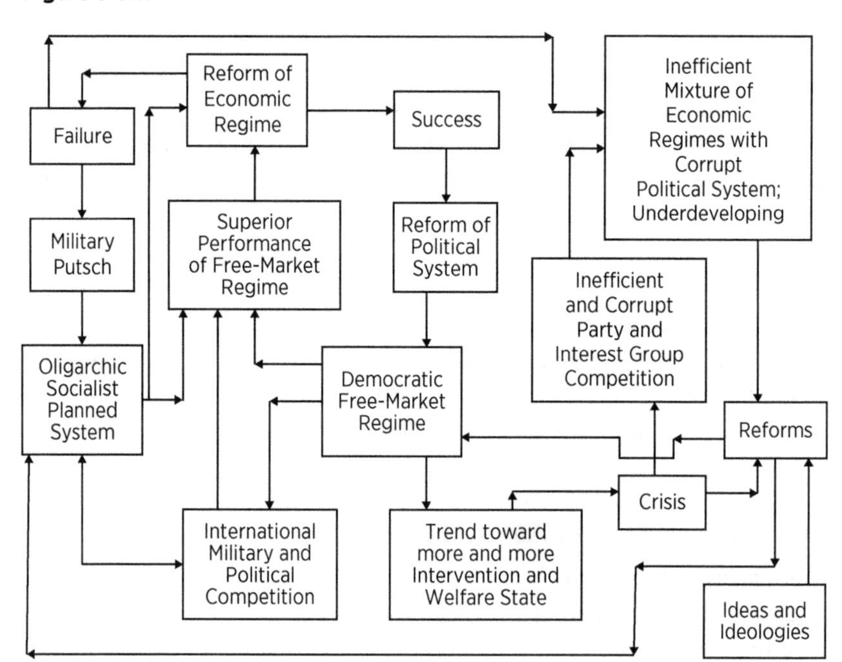

of crisis. Or neither such reformers nor an ideological movement are present during the crisis to recommend themselves as alternatives. In this case, the political-economic system may slowly degenerate and in time turn into an underdeveloping country like Argentina after the 1930s, with increasing budget deficits, corruption, exchange controls, and rising rates of inflation. The same may happen if inadequate or unsuccessful reforms are taken in formerly planned socialist economies. Or, if a strong economic deterioration results from the reform process, a military coup may move the country back to dictatorship and central planning. Recent events in the (former) Soviet Union from 1989 to 1992 especially show that the former alternative may happen with quite a substantial probability. And in fact, it is always much more difficult and politically dangerous to move from a less complex to a more complex economic system than vice versa.

In short, political-economic systems may not substitute each other cyclically in a fixed order, but shortcuts or moves back to the formerly ruling regime are possible. Also, the economy may move away in an unstable process from any stable economic regime and end up for a long period with inadequate and weak political and economic institutions, which imply an underdeveloped or underdeveloping economy. Obviously, economics broadly speaking and public choice theory specifically have still a lot of work to do to understand better the preconditions and the dynamics of these processes.

But let me end with another problem. Given the broad evolutionary perspective taken, is there anything left for fundamental economic policy or, for that matter, for economists trying to advise politicians on adequate strategies of how to introduce and maintain, let's say, the institutions of a free-market economy? I think what I have said allows at least one answer: namely, that if the right ideas are available at the right time in crises, they may prove successful if they win the battle with other ideas and ideologies. But how can we ensure that our ideas win this battle? True, we can point to the better empirical record of free-market economies with strong private-property rights. But is this sufficient to convince a power-hungry oligarchy or a badly informed population and their feelings? Feelings may be influenced by ideological fanatics and by the intellectuals of the mass media who are mostly hostile to a free-market economy and to private property (Schumpeter 1943, chapter 13). Do we perhaps need a religion or ideology incorporating the tenets of a free-market economy among its supreme values to solve these problems? Max Weber's *Die protestantische Ethik* (1965) seems to point in that direction.

It seems that we do not have an answer to this question. And it may be even more difficult to solve the problem of how to maintain the rule of law and a free-market regime. I think we have to be modest and to try patiently to solve some of these open questions. To be able to learn requires humility, the humility to admit that there are so many things that we do not understand. Public choice theory and constitutional economics have been very successful undertakings during the last decades. Especially the Virginia School can be rightly proud of its accomplishments. But to move on in the future requires humility—humility allowing us to take a fresh look at reality ever and ever again.

NOTE

1. Kammler (1990) argues similarly (especially on p. 57). He also points out correctly that the possibility of the population to compare their own political and economic regime with superior foreign regimes erodes the domestic consensus.

REFERENCES

Aristotle. 1965. *Politik*. Nelly Tsongopoulos and Ernesto Grassi (eds.). Franz Susemihl (trans.). Hamburg: Rororo Klassiker.

Berman, Harold J. 1983. *Law and Revolution*. Cambridge and London: Harvard University Press.

Bernholz, Peter. 1986. "The Implementation and Maintenance of a Monetary Constitution." *Cato Journal* 6: 477–512.

———. 1988. *The International Game of Power*. New York, Amsterdam, and Berlin: Mouton.

———. 1991a. "Notwendige Bedingungen für Totalitarismus: Hochste Werte, Macht und persönliche lnteressen." In G. Radnitzky and H. Bouillon (eds.), *Ordnungstheorie und Ordnunqspolitik*, 241–84. Berlin, Heidelberg, and New York: Springer.

———. 1991b. "The Constitution of Totalitarianism." *Journal of Constitutional and Theoretical Economics* 147: 425–40.

———. 1992. "The Economic Approach to International Relations." In G. Radoitzky (ed.), *Universal Economics*. New York: Paragon.

Böhm, Franz. [1952] 1980. "Wirtschaftsordnung und Staatsverfassung." In Ernst-Joachim Mestmacker (ed.), *Freiheit und Ordnung in der Markhvirtschafl*. Baden-Baden: Nomos.

Buchanan, James M. 1975. *The Limits of Liberty: Between Anarchy and Leviathan*. Chicago: University of Chicago Press.

———. 1986. "The Relevance of Constitutional Strategy." *Cato Journal* 6: 513–18.

Buchanan, James M., Robert D. Tollison, and Gordon Tullock (eds.). 1980. *Toward a Theory of the Rent-Seeking Society*. College Station: Texas A&M University Press.

Buchanan, James M., and Gordon Tullock. 1962. *The Calculus of Consent*. Ann Arbor: University of Michigan Press.

Bush, Winston C. 1972. "Individual Welfare in Anarchy." In Gordon Tullock (ed.), *Explorations in the Theory of Anarchy*. Blacksburg, VA: Center for the Study of Public Choice.

Encyclopedia Britannica. 1962. "Japan." In *Encyclopedia Britannica*, vol. 12. London: William Denton.

Frey, Bruno, and Hannelore Weck. 1981. "Hat Arbeitslosigkeit den Aufstieg des Nationalsozialismus bewirkt?" *Jahrbücher für Nationalökonomie und Statistik* 196(1): 1–31.

Gwartney, James D., and Richard E. Wagner (eds.). 1988. *Public Choice and Constitutional Economics*. Greenwich, CT: JAI Press.

Jones, Eric L. 1981. *The European Miracle*. Cambridge: Cambridge University Press.

Kammler, Hans. 1990. "Interdependenz der Ordnungen: Zur Erklarung der osteuropäischen Revolutionen von 1989." *Ordo* 41: 45–59.

Kennan, George. 1947. "The Sources of Soviet Conduct." *Foreign Affairs* 25(4): 566–82. Reprinted in *Neue Zürcher Zeitung*, December 13, 1988.

North, Douglass C. 1981. *Structure and Change in Economic History*. New York: W. W. Norton.

North, Douglass C., and R. Thomas. 1973. *The Rise of the Western World: A New Economic History*. Cambridge: Cambridge University Press.

Peacock, Alan, and Hans Willgerodt. 1989. *German Neo-Liberals and the Social Market Economy*. London: Macmillan.

Pejovich, Svetozar. 1987. *Socialism: Institutional, Philosophical and Economic Issues*. Dordrecht, the Netherlands: Kluwer.

Plato. 1965. "Politeia." In W. F. Otto, E. Grassi, and G. Plamböck (eds.), *Sämtlithe Werke*, vol. 3, *Rowohlt*. Friedrich Schleiermacher (trans.).

Schumpeter, Joseph A. 1943. *Capitalism, Socialism and Democracy*. 5th ed., 1952. London: Unwin University Books.

Seldon, Arthur. 1988. Paper Presented at the Meeting of the Mont Pelerin Society in Kyoto, Japan.

Tocqueville, Alexis de. [1835] 1945. *Democracy in America*. New York: Vintage Books.

Tullock, Gordon. 1974. *The Social Dilemma: Economics of War and Revolution*. Blacksburg, VA: Center for the Study of Public Choice.

Weber, Max. 1965. *Die protestantische Ethik*. Munich: Siebenstern Taschenbuch Verlag.

Weede, Erich. 1987. "From 'The Rise of the West to Eurosclerosis': Are There Lessons for the Asian-Pacific Region?" *Asian Culture Quarterly* 15(1): 1–14.

5.9 Why Is Economic Performance Even Worse after Communism Is Abandoned?

MANCUR OLSON

I.

This lecture is given on the evening of St. Patrick's Day.[1] Just as in the day we honored St. Patrick, so this evening we honor the Virginia School. I am glad to join in honoring the Virginia School. Like some others, I have been calling attention to the contributions of this school for some time—in my case, for thirty years. I also have a vested interest in the name "Virginia School": my colleague Chris Clague and I, in a 1971 article on "Dissent in Economics," seem to have given the "school" its name (Olson and Clague 1971).

Chris Clague and I were concerned that many people at that time did not distinguish the Virginia School from the Chicago School. Some people, both on the left and on the right, use ideological criteria to classify different tendencies in economics. If one thinks only ideologically, then it might be reasonable to classify the Virginia School and the Chicago School together. Perhaps for that reason, there was for a time no separate name for the Virginia School.

Prepared for the Ninth Annual Lecture in the Virginia Political Economy Lecture Series, George Mason University, Fairfax, VA, March 17, 1993.

Jim Buchanan and Gordon Tullock and their students were taken, by some opponents and also by some supporters, to be out-of-town members of the Chicago School.

But if one looks at scientific method and analytical insights instead of ideology, the Virginia School was and is very different indeed from the Chicago School. Though the Chicago School has other important achievements, the Virginia School started to analyze the incentives facing individuals in government and politics quite a long time before the Chicago School did, and some of the Virginia School's contributions are inconsistent with some well-known arguments of Chicago origin.

Jim Buchanan, Gordon Tullock, and other members of the Virginia School have not, of course, been the only people analyzing the incentives confronting individuals in governmental and political contexts, but they are distinguished by how much good work of this type they have done, and by their influence, both in this country and overseas.

Admittedly, my praise for the method of the Virginia School may be due in part to the fact that it is a method that I also use myself. This is also a method that is important to the work of my IRIS Center—Center on Institutional Reform and the Informal Sector—that Bob Tollison so kindly mentioned in his introduction. My partiality to the method that the Virginia School and I share will also show up in my talk tonight because I want to illustrate the use of this method on a problem to which it has not, to the best of my knowledge, previously been applied.

Since it is a point that I have been making for more than a quarter of a century, it would be unnatural if I neglected now to mention one suggestion or criticism that I have for the Virginia School. I have argued over many years that the Virginia School ought to put more effort into separating its scientific achievements from the ideologies and political movements with which they are sometimes associated. There are economists and also people in other fields who disagree with some of Jim Buchanan's or Gordon Tullock's political asides but who could, even at the same time that they disagreed, also profit greatly from using their insights. They may be kept from doing this by the understandable—yet profoundly mistaken—assumption that these insights are of no use to those with different political or ideological goals. At the same time, there are I think some others who accept the Virginia School for political reasons, without mastering or appreciating the analytical insights at its core.

In this lecture I hope to illustrate this profound difference between analytical insights and ideological creeds by examining a part of the world that is very far from Virginia, yet important for us all. This is the part of the world that fell under the control of Stalin. If my argument tonight is right, what Stalin called Marxist-Leninist ideology tells us almost nothing about why the Soviet-type economies were organized the way they were. To understand what happened under Communism and to help the formerly Communist countries make the right choices now, none of the familiar ideologies will do. We must instead use the analytical method that the Virginia School and I share. We must analyze the incentives facing individuals in political, organizational, and governmental settings in the Soviet-type societies and in the societies in transition today.

II.

The Communist economies ran down over time. Though those economies grew rapidly in the 1950s and in the early 1960s, they began to deteriorate in the mid-1960s and became progressively poorer throughout the 1970s and 1980s. The economic performance of the Soviet-type economies became especially bad in the time of Gorbachev. Unfortunately, now that Communism has collapsed, economic performance has become even worse—not only worse than in the salad days of Communism but also worse than in its decaying years.

Admittedly, the deterioration in economic performance after the collapse of Communism is often exaggerated. Some of the production that has been lost was not worth what it cost, so its disappearance was desirable. The statistics that depict the drop in output also omit the gains to the populations of the lately Communist countries from spending less time in queues. They also fail to capture the gains from the availability of a greater variety of goods. Conceivably, in some countries the level of real output did not really fall at all. Nonetheless there is an unmistakable and large drop in output in most of the formerly Communist countries, and this deterioration in economic performance is paradoxical.

Why, when a poor economic system is abandoned, doesn't economic performance promptly improve? It is easy to say that any change takes time and that a deterioration in economic performance is natural when there is a major transition. This comfortable explanation is really not satisfactory.

It is not true that fundamental changes in economic arrangements regularly bring on periods of poor economic performance. The liberalization that Deng introduced in China not long after the death of Mao promptly generated increases in output that have sometimes been more than 10 percent per year. The transitions in Germany and Japan after their defeat and dismemberment in World War II were also very rapid, but these countries had economic miracles rather than declines in economic performance. As brutal as the transition to Communism after World War II was in the countries that Stalin captured, this transition was not associated with at least any extended decline in output.

Some people say that the transition from Communism to the market is more difficult than the opposite transition. They say that "you can make fish soup out of an aquarium, but you can't make an aquarium out of fish soup." This metaphor is at first vivid and charming, but it doesn't survive examination. Note that many people say that for a thriving market economy, all you need is for the government to leave things alone—that you just need to "let capitalism happen." If this view were true, then the transition to a market economy ought to be automatic and painless. In fact, it is not true that all you need for a thriving market economy is to let capitalism happen. Still, there is no reason the transition to a market economy should be more difficult than the transition to any other type of economy. Why should it require more organization, planning, and time to set up a market economy than a Communist economy? So the puzzle remains: why is there such a large drop in economic performance after a bad economic system is abandoned? That is a puzzle that should not be concealed by erroneous generalizations about inevitable losses from transitions or by the false claim that creating markets takes a particularly long time.

III.

The economies in transition from Communism are a mix of two things: first, the new markets that have been added to those that existed in these economies all along; and second, what is left of the old system of state-owned enterprises. To understand this mix that is the economy in transition, then, we must analyze not only the motive force in the marketplace but also the motive force behind the Communist economy.

In particular, we must ask why the Soviet-type economy, inferior as it undoubtedly was, produced and mobilized as much output as it did. How did an economic and political system so flawed that it was ultimately not able even to survive nonetheless create a superpower? All over the world, the Soviet Union was taken to be a superpower that was more or less a match for the United States. The Reagan administration, for example, believed that the Soviet threat was so formidable that it required a considerable increase in US military expenditures. Though I personally believe that the power of the Soviet Union was less than was usually assumed, a vast amount of output had to be produced and mobilized even to make a country appear to be a superpower. So, even on the lowest estimate of Soviet output and power, there is definitely still a need for an explanation.

To the best of my knowledge, no adequate explanation has ever been supplied. Perhaps economists have not been ready enough to give the devil his due. Even the Roman Catholic Church recognizes that there is sometimes a need for a devil's advocate. We must assume that difficult role now.

Explaining why markets are superior to a Communist economy is, by contrast, an easy job; economists have been able to explain why a market economy is desirable—and to illuminate some of the pathologies of a centrally planned economy—for a long time. Familiar microeconomic theory has all along made it easy for economists to understand why a society gains a great deal from giving a considerable scope to markets, and virtually no skilled economists have ever been advocates of a Soviet-type economy. Even those economists who advocated government ownership of the means of production did not normally advocate centralized planning, and they attempted to devise means of mimicking the role of the price system in allocating resources within a market economy. Explaining why a market economy is superior to a centrally planned economy is also normally no longer even necessary: almost the whole world now knows which is better.

Thus the intellectually difficult task—and the task that has not yet been accomplished—is to explain why Soviet-type economies, given their repression of markets and their manifold inefficiencies, functioned as well as they did. This task is not simply of historical interest: it must be completed before we can understand how the inherited, state-enterprise part of the economy in transition works before we can understand why economic performance is even worse after Communism is abandoned.

IV.

To obtain a good theory of how the Soviet Union mobilized the resources needed to become a superpower—yet still was not able to survive—we need to use not only the standard neoclassical economic analysis of markets but also the modern theory of collective or public choice. Though this theory has often illuminated life in democratic countries, it has only lately been extended to cover autocracies such as the Communist countries.

I will attempt to show here that when the new collective choice theory of dictatorship is applied to the Soviet-type regimes, we immediately obtain one insight into why these regimes—as strong, stable, and absolutist dictatorships—became as powerful as they did. When we then elaborate the general theory of autocratic government to accommodate certain autocratic innovations pioneered by Joseph Stalin, we can see also why the Soviet Union and Communist China were so much more powerful than other autocracies. The same theory also shows why the Soviet-type regimes with central planning gradually decay over time. Once we understand the motive power behind the production and resource mobilization of the Communist autocracies—and why it weakened over time—we can also understand why economic performance is even worse after Communism is abandoned. This, in turn, points the way to new strategies for the economies in transition.

The Soviet Union and its satellites were, at least until their last years, certainly absolutist dictatorships rather than democracies.[2] Of course, many of the autocracies of the world do not have centrally planned economies, and no regime of any kind had such an economy before Stalin consolidated his power and ended the "New Economic Policy" at the end of the 1920s. But the general theory comes before the special case, and the general theory of autocracy immediately provides an elementary insight into the productivity and power achieved by the Soviet-type societies. Thus it is very important that we should first analyze autocracy in general and only later elaborate this model to account for Stalin's extraordinary autocratic innovations.

V.

One part of the general approach to autocracy that will be used here came to me by chance when reading about a Chinese warlord (Sheridan 1966). In the 1920s, China was in large part under the control of various warlords. They were men who led some armed band with which they conquered territory and who then appointed themselves lords of that territory. They taxed the population heavily and pocketed much of the proceeds. The warlord Feng Yu-hsiang was noted for the exceptional extent to which he used his army for suppressing bandits and for his defeat of the relatively substantial army of the roving bandit, White Wolf. Apparently, most people in Feng's domain found him much preferable to the roving bandits.

At first, this seems puzzling: Why should warlords who were stationary bandits continuously stealing from a given group of victims be preferred by those victims to roving bandits who soon departed? In fact, if a roving bandit settles down and takes his theft in the form of regular taxation and at the same time maintains a monopoly on theft in his domain, then those from whom he exacts taxes will have an incentive to produce what they lack when confronted by continual random plunder. The rational stationary bandit will take only a part of income in taxes, because he will be able to exact a larger total amount of income from his subjects if he leaves them with an incentive to generate income that he can tax.

With the rational long-term monopolization of theft, in contrast to episodic or uncoordinated competitive theft, the victims of the theft can expect to retain whatever capital they accumulate out of after-tax income and therefore also have an incentive to save and to invest. This increases the subjects' future incomes and the stationary bandit's tax receipts. The monopolization of theft and the protection of the tax-generating subjects thereby eliminates anarchy. Since the warlord takes a part of total production in the form of tax theft, it will also pay him to provide other public goods besides a peaceful order whenever the provision of these goods increases taxable income sufficiently.

In a world of roving banditry, there is little or no incentive for anyone to produce or accumulate anything that may be stolen and thus little for bandits to steal. Bandit rationality accordingly induces the bandit leader to seize a given domain, to make himself the ruler of that domain, and to provide a peaceful order and other public goods for its inhabitants, thereby obtaining more in tax theft than he could have obtained from migratory plunder.

Thus we have "the first blessing of the invisible hand": the rational, self-interested leader of a band of roving bandits is led, as though by an invisible hand, to settle down, to wear a crown, and to replace anarchy with government. The gigantic increase in output that normally arises from the provision of a peaceful order and other public goods gives the stationary bandit a far larger take than he could obtain if he did not provide government.

Thus, government for groups larger than tribes normally arises not because of social contracts or voluntary transactions of any kind, but rather because of rational self-interest among those who can organize the greatest capacity for violence. These violent entrepreneurs naturally do not call themselves bandits but, on the contrary, give themselves and their descendants exalted titles.

Any individual who has autocratic control over a country will provide public goods to that country because he has what my book on *The Rise and Decline of Nations* defined as an "encompassing interest" in the country (Olson 1982). The extent of the encompassing interest of an officeholder, political party, interest group, monarch, or any other partial or total "owner" of a society varies with the size of the stake in the society. The larger or more encompassing the stake an organization or individual has in a society, the greater the incentive the organization or individual has to take action to provide public goods for the society. If an autocrat received one-third of any increase in the income of his domain in increased tax collections, he would receive one-third of the benefits of the public goods he provided. He would then have an incentive to provide public goods up to the point where the national income rose by the reciprocal of one-third, or three, from his last unit of public good expenditure. Though the society's income and welfare would obviously be greater from a larger expenditure on public goods, the gain to society from the public goods that a rational self-interested autocrat provides is nonetheless often colossal. Consider, for example, the gains from replacing a violent anarchy with a minimal degree of public order.

History until relatively recent times has been mostly a story of the gradual progress of civilization under stationary bandits, interrupted by occasional episodes of roving banditry. From about the time that Sargon's conquests created the empire of Akkad in ancient Mesopotamia until, say, the time of Louis XVI and Voltaire, there was an impressive development of civilization that occurred in large part under stationary banditry.[3]

VI.

Though an autocrat is analogous to the owner of any productive asset in the sense that he has an encompassing interest in the productivity of that asset, he is also the monopolistic owner of all the wealth, tangible and human, in a country. The autocrat does indeed have an incentive to maintain and increase the productivity of everything and everyone in his domain, and his subjects will gain from this. But he also has an incentive to charge a monopoly rent and to levy this monopoly charge on everything, including human labor.

In other words, the autocratic ruler has an incentive to extract the maximum possible surplus from the whole society and to use it for his own purposes. Exactly the same rational self-interest that makes a roving bandit settle down and provide government for his subjects also makes him extract the maximum possible amount from the society for himself.

The consumption of an autocratic ruler is, moreover, not limited by his personal capacities to use food, shelter, or clothing. The main social costs of autocratic leaders arise mostly out of their appetites for military power, international prestige, and larger domains. We must remember that, as Shakespeare so nicely put it, "War is the trade of Kings."

Though the forms that stationary banditry has taken over the course of history are diverse, all ordinary (i.e., non-Soviet) autocracies can be analyzed by assuming that the autocrat gets all of his receipts in the form of explicit and nondiscriminatory taxation. The rational autocrat will devote some of the resources he obtains through taxation to providing public goods, but he will impose far higher tax rates than are needed to pay for the public goods since he also uses tax collections to maximize his net surplus. The higher the level of provision of public goods, given the tax rate, the higher the society's income and the yield from this tax rate. At the same time, the higher the tax rate, given the level of public good provision, the lower the income of society, since taxes distort incentives.

So what tax rate and what level of public good provision will the rational self-interested autocrat choose? Assume for the moment that the autocrat's level of public good expenditure is given. As Joseph Schumpeter (1991) lucidly pointed out, and as Ibn Khalduhn (1967) sensed much earlier, tax receipts will (if we start with low taxation) increase as tax rates increase, but after the revenue-maximizing rate is reached, higher tax rates distort incentives and reduce income so much that tax collections fall. The rational self-interested autocrat chooses the revenue-maximizing tax rate.

Though the amount collected at any tax rate will vary with the level of public good provision, the revenue-maximizing tax rate for the autocrat should not. This optimal tax rate determines exactly how encompassing is the interest of the autocrat in the society: in other words, it determines what share of any increase in the national income he receives. He will then spend money on public goods up to the point where his last dollar of expenditure on public goods generates a dollar's increase in his share of the national income. At this point, the gain to society will be the reciprocal of his share. (A detailed and somewhat formal statement of the optimization conditions facing a rational dictator, and various other types of ruling interests, is available on request from the author.)

Though the subjects of the autocrat are better off than they would be under anarchy, they must endure taxes or other impositions so high that, if they were increased further, income would fall by so much that even the autocrat, who absorbs only a portion of the fall in income in the form of lower tax collections, would be worse off. There is no lack of historical examples in which autocrats for their own political and military purposes collected as much revenue as they possibly could. Consider the largest autocratic jurisdictions in Western history. The Bourbon kings of France were (especially on the eve of the French Revolution) collecting all they could in taxes. The Hapsburg kings of Spain did the same. The Roman Empire ultimately pushed its tax rates at least to the revenue-maximizing level.

VII.

The foregoing theory immediately suggests two factors that help explain why the Soviet-type regimes were for a long while regarded as an economic challenge for the democracies of the West and able to mobilize enough resources to achieve superpower status.[4] The Soviet Empire was undoubtedly an autocracy, and therefore

(1) It was governed by an encompassing interest—the more productive the Soviet domain was, other things equal, the more resources were available to achieve the autocrat's objectives, so the first secretary of the Communist Party had a powerful incentive to make the society more productive;
(2) Its leader maximized the surplus extracted from the society to serve his political and other objectives, so that his regime obtained large amounts of resources to devote to increasing the military might, political power, and international influence of the Soviet Empire.

Though this is an important part of the story, we are not done yet. Until Stalin consolidated his control over the Soviet political system, no autocrat had ever organized his economy the way Stalin organized the economy of the Soviet Union. Why did Stalin impose on the Soviet Union (and later on the satellite countries) an economic system with almost universal state ownership and a large proportion of the prices and wages set by the regime?

The standard assumption—that the choice for a centrally planned economy was because of Marxist-Leninist ideology—is inadequate. Saying that the actions of autocrats are explained by their ideologies adds only a word rather than an explanation unless we can, in turn, explain what inspired that ideology and what reason an autocrat had for choosing that ideology rather than some other doctrinal or eclectic option. When a power-hungry autocrat is trying to gain power and he then espouses an ideology that is popular with the constituency or power base that he has to win over, we have an explanation of his use of that ideology. Thus, when Stalin was struggling to win dictatorial control over the USSR, it is not surprising that he joined the apparently stronger or pivotal Bolshevik faction that (like Lenin himself) had opted for the market-oriented "New Economic Policy" and had decided against the forced collectivization of agriculture.

Once he had unchallenged power, Stalin did not need to please any Bolshevik faction, and he then adopted policies that he had previously opposed: total state absorption of the economy with brutal collectivization of agriculture. We do not obtain much enlightenment from the notion that this was done for unexplained ideological reasons, especially when Stalin was not a consistent adherent of any one ideological position. Marx's writings also did not require the economic organization that Stalin imposed; Marx had focused on capitalism and said almost nothing about the organization of socialist or Communist societies. In time, because of Stalin's practice and propaganda, Marxism-Leninism ideology came to identified with the type of economic and political system he had imposed, but this later orthodoxy cannot explain the choices Stalin made when he initially obtained dictatorial power.

Especially in view of the inadequacy of existing explanations of the special economic system in the Communist autocracies, we need to extend the general theory of autocracy in the preceding chapter so that it can explain why the special economic system in the Communist autocracies was chosen.

VIII.

What limits the amount of resources that a typical autocrat can extract from his society? As was shown earlier, the rational autocrat chooses the revenue-maximizing tax rate. Is there anything he can do to obtain still more? One possibility to consider is the confiscation of the capital of his subjects. Another possibility is that the autocrat can start taxing real money balances by printing money for his own use in such amounts that unexpected inflation results. Another possibility is that he can borrow money and then refuse to pay it back.

Whenever any autocrat has a short enough time horizon, all of these possibilities can serve his interests. For example, whenever a dictator has a time horizon that is so short that the tax yield of an asset over that time horizon is less than its price, it pays him to confiscate that asset. Thus much of the dictatorship we observe is more nearly roving than stationary banditry. The account of autocratic optimization earlier in this essay implicitly assumed that the autocrat had a Barro-infinite time horizon. When the autocrat does not have a long planning horizon, his subjects are worse off than they are under the steady-state revenue-maximizing tax rate. (It is no accident that "Long live the King" was the preferred form of toast of a king's subjects, or that dynasties were thought desirable.)

The autocrat who expects to be around a long time, by contrast, will normally lose from confiscation, inflation, and repudiation of his debts. I hypothesize that Stalin, at least after he consolidated his power in the late 1920s, expected to be in office (as he was) until he died a natural death. For the most part, he did not engage in inflationary methods to obtain resources, and he scrupulously paid off the sums he borrowed from Western firms. In these respects, he was typical of intelligent autocrats who have a long time horizon.

Autocrats with a long time horizon usually also cannot gain from confiscating capital assets, because this normally means that there will be less investment and less income and therefore also smaller tax receipts in the future. So, it appears that expropriation of capital goods, because it reduces future investment and income, cannot increase the tax receipts of an autocrat over the long run. But there is one way that it can, and Stalin was the first one to discover this way.

Stalin confiscated all of the farmland and natural resources of the Soviet Union and all of the commercial and industrial property that had been privately held in the period of the New Economic Policy, and the rate of savings and investment increased substantially. In general, the Soviet Union after Stalin's innovations, and the other societies on which the Stalinist system was imposed, had far higher rates of savings and investment than most other societies. Stalin's innovation was to take almost the total natural and tangible capital stock of the country through a 100 percent wealth tax (i.e., an expropriation) and then to use these resources to produce a mix of output that was much more intensive in capital goods and other goods Stalin wanted than would otherwise have been produced.

By determining himself how much of the nation's resources would be used to produce consumer goods and by keeping this proportion much smaller than it was in most other societies, Stalin gave the Soviet Union an extraordinarily high rate of capital accumulation at the same time that he augmented his annual tax receipts by an amount approximately equal to all nonlabor income. In the long history of stationary banditry, no other autocrat seems to have managed this extraordinary innovation, nor succeeded in claiming so large a part of the social output for the regime, while at the same time greatly increasing savings, investment, and the level of output.[5]

IX.

Stalin and his advisers also had a second innovative idea about how to expand the autocratic budget constraint: if an autocrat has different tax schedules for individuals of different productivities, he can collect much more tax revenue. In the typical modern democracy, high-income people confront higher tax rates or brackets than do low-income people, but everyone faces the same tax law or schedule.

When everyone faces the same tax schedule, it is impossible to tax people more on their first hours of work than on their marginal hours of work and also to have very high tax rates. Obviously, if each of us was taxed heavily on the first four hours a day of work, less on the next two, and not at all on hours after that, then we would have an incentive to work a lot more. We would have a stronger incentive to work because, if we were taxed heavily enough on the first few hours of work, we would be poorer and the income effect of taxation would make us work more. If we were not taxed on our last hours of work, we would also have a greater post-tax reward for additional work, so a larger substitution effect would also make us work more. Economic efficiency would also increase. So, in some sense the Western democracies would be more efficient and productive if somehow it were possible for us to be taxed more on our first hours of work but not taxed on our last or marginal hours of work.

But that's not a real possibility when we all face the same tax schedule. Suppose that the United States decided to tax the first $5,000 a person makes a year at 99 percent, the next $5,000 at 98 percent, and so on, and to tax what each person makes above a certain level at 0 percent. This method—reversing the usual progression and regressively taxing lower incomes at much higher rates than higher incomes—would create a situation in which the least productive people wouldn't have even enough income to survive. The productivity- and efficiency-enhancing policy of taxing people highly on their inframarginal income but not taxing their marginal income is not only morally repugnant but also practically impossible when the same laws apply to everyone—when any society has the rule of law.

There is, however, a way that a cunning autocrat can tax inframarginal income at far higher rates than marginal income and thereby obtain great increases in both tax collections and national output. Somehow, Stalin hit upon this method and was power-hungry and ruthless enough to put it into practice. The method is to set the salaries and wages of each occupation and ability level in the society with the purpose of collecting the maximum income for the autocrat's purposes from every individual in the economy.

First, Stalin had the subordinates he put in charge of the economy set wages and salaries very low so that when people went to work they didn't get very much income, so they couldn't afford much leisure. Second, he established a system of high bonuses, of special rewards for people who were Stakhanovites or model workers, and of progressive piece rates—that is, piece rates that increased the per-unit payment with the amount that the person produced.

There is also piecework in democracies with market economics but not usually progressive piece rates. If you are picking fruit or selling insurance policies, you might be paid by the bushel picked or by the policy sold. But you are not paid progressively higher rates per unit for higher amounts for the obvious reason that that usually wouldn't be an efficient contract for a typical employer and a typical employee to make.[6] By contrast, Stalin's combination of bonuses, progressive piece rates, prizes for Stakhanovites, and special perquisites for other especially productive workers was a system that left people with a large proportion of the marginal output that they produced but at the same time implicitly taxed them very highly indeed on their inframarginal work.

This could be done only because the system implicitly had separate tax schedules—not simply different tax rates—for different individuals. In effect, Stalin's system of wage and salary setting had the effect of implicitly confronting individuals in different jobs or with different ability levels with a different tax schedule. This made it possible to impose higher average tax rates on the more able individuals who could produce a larger surplus over subsistence, while at the same time taxing the first hours of work severely and the last hours only lightly.[7]

Let us illustrate these points with two very simple figures in which leisure is measured along the x-axis and consumption on the vertical axis. Let's first suppose for simplicity that we have a flat tax and that the rate of this tax has been set, on traditional autocratic principles, at the revenue-maximizing rate. The total output of the individual is given by the pretax wage curve in figure 5.9.1. Instead of getting the full value of output, the individual gets the much lower revenue-maximizing post-tax wage depicted in figure 5.9.1. In the case shown, the individual chooses the amount of leisure OLF and obtains OA of money income. The autocrat obtains amount AB as tax receipts. Of course, since the revenue-maximizing tax rate has been assumed, the indifference map of this individual (or the opportunities they have in the informal economy) must be such that if the flat tax were raised a trifle, the individual would reduce taxable work time just enough so that the autocrat's tax receipts were unchanged.

How did Stalin improve on this simple and straightforward autocratic optimum? He set the person's wage or salary at very low levels and captured most of the value of the individual's output during the ordinary working day in implicit taxation—by keeping the profits of industrial enterprises, which were made far higher than they would otherwise have been because wages were set so low. If taken to the polar extreme, this means in effect that the person is faced with a lump-sum tax of amount CD = EF, but that the person isn't taxed on marginal income. Then the individual will, of course, take less leisure. The person now can't afford much leisure because of the high tax rate, and in addition the person has a greater reward for additional hours of work because there is no taxation of marginal income. This individual under the Stalinist mode of taxation will take an amount of leisure OLD, which will lead to much higher output. In this case, the state will obtain CD of output—much more than was

Figure 5.9.1.

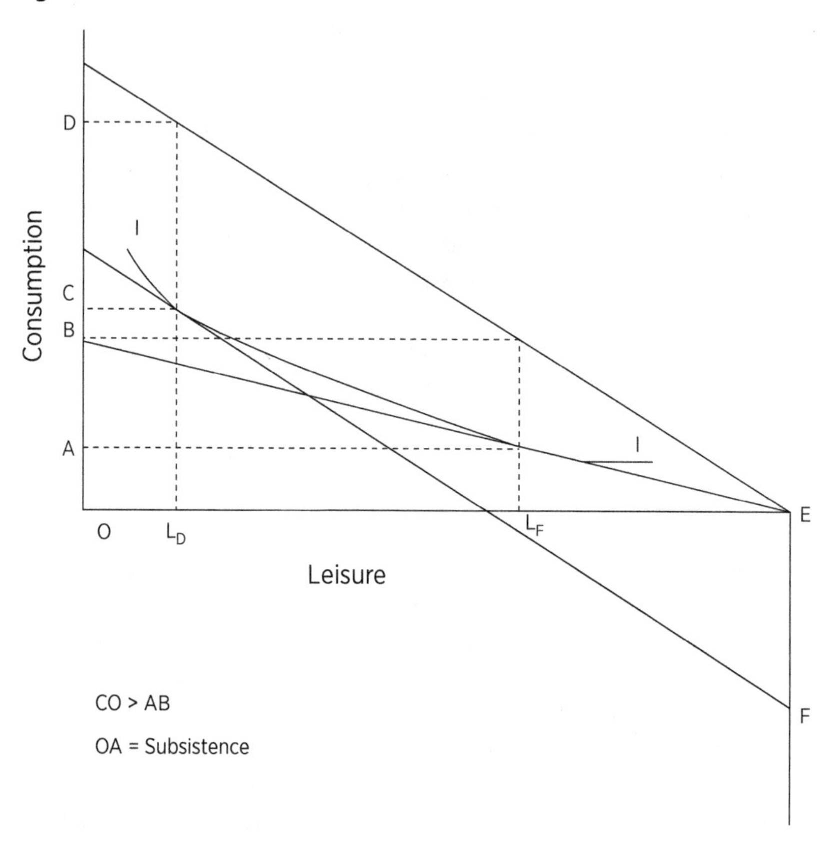

obtained by ordinary autocratic taxation at the revenue-maximizing rate. The individual gets the same level of utility as before (and more consumption), but the dictator gets much more revenue; with indifference curves of the normal shape, CD has to be larger than AB.

Let's now further suppose that OA is the subsistence level. If Stalin's system of making inframarginal tax rates higher and marginal tax rates lower (or zero) is used, it's possible to take still more than CD in taxes, and the person still will remain above the subsistence level. An essential feature of this system is tax-price discrimination: as we saw earlier when discussing taxes in countries like the United States, the same tax law cannot apply to everyone. If it did, and tax rates were high, the least productive would not have enough post-tax income to survive. The Soviet implicit tax-price system takes advantage of the larger surplus above subsistence produced by the more productive individuals.

So the more able person in a Soviet-type society is, in fact, confronted with what in a rule-of-law democracy would be called a different tax law with a different tax schedule, but which in that system appears to be only a different administrative decision about wage and salary levels. The basic or inframarginal salaries of the most able people who are chosen to be, say, factory managers, are set only a little higher than the inframarginal wages of unskilled workers, since they can generate a larger taxable surplus.

The small differentials in base or prebonus pay across occupations were sometimes said to be motivated by egalitarian ideology. In fact, Stalin set egalitarian ideals aside to maximize the incentive to produce—he was explicit and emphatic about this. The extra effort of the people in the most important and demanding jobs was elicited by having very low taxes on their marginal income—the bonuses, the allocation of housing, the distribution of scarce consumption goods at the workplace, the prizes for Stakhanovites, and so forth—and by keeping all inframarginal incomes so low that people could afford relatively little leisure. If an egalitarian ethic had been driving the system, the implicit taxes for the purposes of the autocrat would not have been so large and there would have been no progressive piece rates or other devices that made marginal income especially unequal.

For the autocrat maximizing tax collections, the ideal situation would be one where he could rely on each foreman and manager to provide complete information about the ability or potential productivity of each subject. Suppose for illustration that the autocrat's bureaucracy provided perfect information about what each subject could produce. The regime could then impose a different head tax on each person, and one that was so large that, after paying it, each person was exactly at the subsistence level. If there was at the same time no taxation on marginal income whatever, the autocrat would then have the largest possible tax revenue.

Though the information needed for an autocrat to reach the theoretical absolute maximum level of tax receipts was obviously not available, the Stalinist regime did know that it took more ability to be a factory manager than an unskilled factory worker, and it must have known roughly what ability and education level was appropriate for each major type of job. To motivate the more able people to take on the jobs needing more ability, Stalin had to make the total pay—including bonuses and other forms of marginal pay—for the more demanding jobs higher than the total pay for the less demanding jobs. He said explicitly that there should be such inequalities in pay, and these inequalities did, in fact, exist. So long as marginal tax rates were zero or very low, as they were, Stalin needed only small differentials in inframarginal rates of pay: the more able individual

Figure 5.9.2.

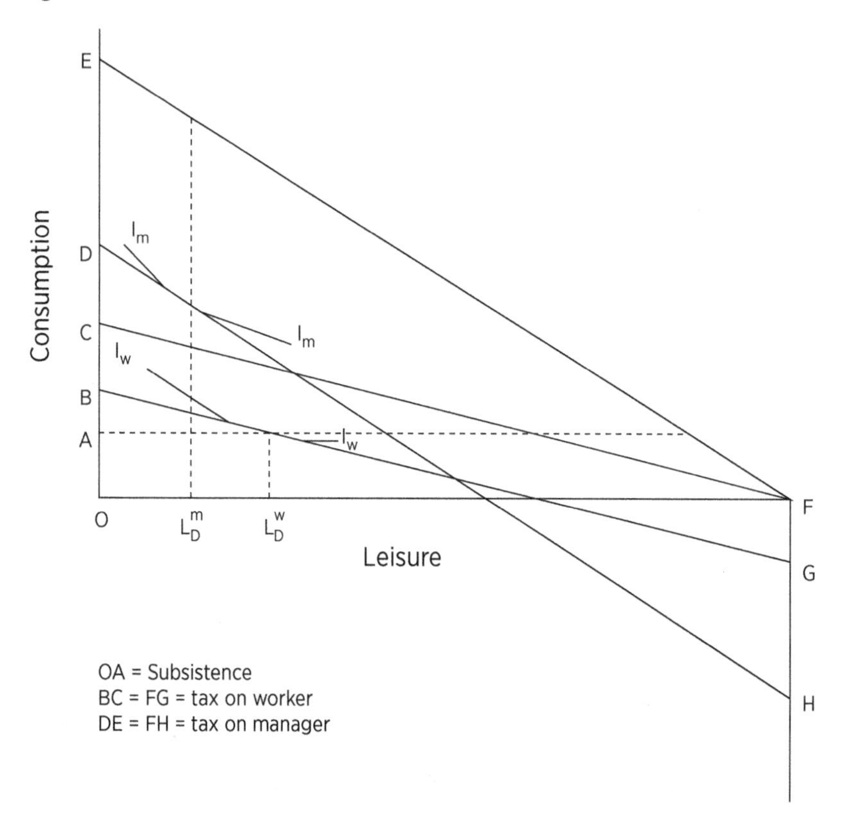

could earn much more in bonuses and other forms of marginal pay if he were in a job where he could be highly productive than he could at a humbler job. With wages and salaries that provided only austere levels of consumption, the higher marginal earnings in the more demanding jobs were made all the more attractive. In a job with higher productivity, the more able person also had an incentive to work harder than the less able person did, since with low taxes on marginal income he would have a higher post-tax reward for his marginal hours of work.

This is illustrated in figure 5.9.2, where OA again gives the level of consumption that each individual needs for subsistence. The less talented individual's (the unskilled worker's) total output is given by the line FC and the more talented individual's (the manager's) total output is given by the curve FE. The autocrat, by setting the rates of pay in each job far below the level of productivity but by leaving the marginal pay virtually untaxed, approximately achieves the effect of a lump-sum or head tax. By taxing the inframarginal pay in the more demanding and productive job more heavily than in the less demanding job—that is, by making the differential in the basic or inframarginal wage much lower than the productivity differential of the two types of work—the autocrat can obtain most of the larger surplus above his own subsistence needs that the more able individual produces. The tax on the manager is thus DE = FH, while the tax on the worker is BC = FG. The manager, if he has the same preference ordering as the worker, necessarily finds it in his interest to take even less leisure than the worker at the subsistence level. The only thing that keeps the autocrat from taking all of the surplus above consumption produced by the more able individual is the imperfection of the regime's knowledge of the exact ability or potential productivity level of the more able individual. As this knowledge improves, the autocrat can obtain more of the surplus above subsistence produced by the more able worker and in the limit take it all.

So the system of taxation that collects the most revenue is one that meets two conditions. First, it confronts more productive people with tax schedules different from those applied to less productive people. Second, given that the first condition is met, it is then possible (even with very high tax rates) to tax inframarginal income more highly than marginal income, so a tax system that approximates a lump-sum tax is the second condition.

Note that the familiar Western progressive income tax does not meet these conditions at all. Thus it is no coincidence that the Soviet Union, even as it attacked the market democracies for their inequalities of income, did not in any serious way use the progressive income tax (for a long time, the maximum rate of income tax in the Soviet Union was only 13 percent).

Thus I have explained the paradox that the degree of income inequality of the Stalinist system was restricted, but the incentive to work was greater than would be expected from the limited degree of inequality. The relatively high degree of equality in inframarginal pay but the lightly taxed or untaxed marginal earnings are precisely the conditions that maximize tax collections for the totalitarian leader. To paraphrase an old saying, it was "from each according to his ability, to the man in charge."

The proportion of income in the Soviet Union in Stalin's time that was devoted to personal consumption was lower than in virtually any non-Communist country, and that is exactly what the theory here predicts. Stalin was able to obtain a larger proportion of the national output for his own purposes than any other government in history was able to extract.

X.

The origins of Stalin's innovative system of tax collection showed up most starkly in agriculture. The Soviet Union was mainly an agricultural country when the Bolsheviks took over in 1917. Most of the national income was produced in agriculture, especially by the "kulaks"—the relatively larger farmers. Thus there was no way that the Bolsheviks could obtain a large part of the Soviet national income for their own purposes unless they could get their hands on most of the output produced in the rural areas. Most notably, they had to have a surplus of grain to feed their cadre, who were mainly in the cities. They also needed more people in the cities to man factories and to produce steel and armaments and more people in the military and government bureaucracy to do the work of the regime. So the Soviets wanted more food and could only obtain it from the peasants and kulaks.

In order to have the resources needed to build heavy industry, produce armaments, and to supply the party cadre and the army, the Bolsheviks first offered low prices to food producers, thereby implicitly putting a high tax on the kulaks and the peasants. Of course, the response of the farmers was to produce less, to consume more of what they produced at home, and to sell food privately and illegally. So the only way the Bolsheviks could obtain the food they needed would have been to pay the farmers enough to give them an incentive to produce more. But that would have used up much of the social surplus that the regime wanted to devote to industrialization, to the military, and to political and prestige projects. So the Bolsheviks had to work out a collection system that would get more of a taxable surplus out of the agricultural sector that was then the main part of the Soviet economy.

Before Stalin had consolidated his power, some of the more "radical" Bolsheviks argued that the Soviet Union needed "primitive socialist accumulation." This was the socialist analogue to Marx's "primitive capitalist accumulation"—the initial thefts and windfalls to which Marx had attributed the capitalists' initial accumulation of capital. In other words, some Bolsheviks argued that there was no alternative but to take the initial capital needed for socialist industrialization from the kulaks and the peasants. As we know, Stalin at first aligned himself with the moderate Bolsheviks who opposed any such seizure, but he adopted the radical program as soon as he had consolidated his power.

He then confiscated the agricultural land, livestock, and machinery of the country, imposing extraordinarily severe punishments on peasants who hid any grain or livestock. He dealt especially harshly with the kulaks, who had the greatest reason to resist this. Those assigned to each collective farm were made responsible for providing a given amount of grain or other foodstuffs to the state. Stalin set up a system in which there was a large enough number of people that collusion among them was difficult, yet monitoring was facilitated so that the implicit taxes couldn't usually be evaded. Separate organizations providing tractor services to the collective farms and Communist Party units helped prevent collective farms from escaping the implicit tax. Thus, Stalin's system was designed to make it easier to determine the amount that people had to supply to the state and thus to tax them as much as they were capable of being taxed.

I submit, then, that the collective farm was mainly an instrument of tax collection, not something that was ideologically required. The ideologically preferred system of organization was the "state farm," where the workers were paid a wage and the state was the residual claimant. But much of the output of the state farms was taken up in wages paid to the workers, so these farms did not provide much surplus for the regime. Hence Stalin chose collective farms instead of state farms and made the members of the collective farm responsible for supplying the amounts (the theoretical "biological yield") he demanded: the collective farms could not keep the resources needed to pay state-farm wages to their members. The collective farm, unlike the state farm, was designed to be "collective" in the sense of "collection," not as in "collectivist."

After providing extensive labor services to the collective farm, the farmers were allowed to use any leisure time for work on the tiny private plots that were allocated to them. As the theory here predicts, the income from these plots was not, in general, taxed.

From Stalin's point of view, the food collection system worked. During World War I, the Tsarist state (even though at times it also used coercive measures to collect food) was not able to provide enough food to people in the cities to maintain its control: the February revolution began as a protest over the shortage of bread. By contrast, during World War II, the Soviet regime had at its disposal a well-developed procurement system. Despite a disastrous fall in food production per head of the collective farm population, the share of total meat and grain output taken by the government rose. The collective farmer was left with a reduced share of a smaller total than before the war. Even before the war, the government attitude to the consumer needs of the farm population had been harsh and arbitrary. Military-style procurement campaigns meant that the confiscation of food from farm stocks became still more arbitrary in wartime (Gatrell and Harrison 1993).

XI.

In summary, Stalin's brutal and cunning innovations enabled his regime to

(1) Expropriate essentially all of the national stock of tangible capital, land, and other natural resources, thereby adding the yield of all of these assets each year to his tax collections.

(2) Avoid the collapse of investment that normally follows such expropriation by directly controlling the level of consumption and of investment, and thereby giving the Soviet Union a far higher rate of saving and investment than other societies.

(3) Raise taxes on labor income far above what had, under prior tax-collecting methods, been revenue-maximizing rates, partly by introducing tax-price discrimination that captured a larger part of the output of relatively productive individuals.

(4) Reduce the ratio of marginal to average tax rates, thereby increasing not only the proportion of labor income paid in taxes but also the amount of labor supplied both through the income effect (families could afford less leisure and home-produced output, so almost all women had to work outside the home) and the substitution effect (increasing the reward for marginal effort).

By the time that this system had been perfected, the Soviet Union had more resources for the purposes of the leadership than any other society in history.

XII.

Though Stalin was often considered the pope of Marxist religion, he was not, in fact, a sincere ideologue. Though ideology no doubt played a role in explaining some of his support, the hypothesis here is that Stalin was not blinded by—or even faithful to—what had previously been called Marxism. If Stalin had been a committed ideologue, he wouldn't have done many of the things he did, like kill off all of the people who had participated with him as initial leaders of the Bolshevik revolution, or purge those Bolsheviks who dared to defend their Marxist principles, or make the Nazi-Soviet pact. Stalin also did nothing whatever to bring about the withering of the state that Marx had predicted and advocated.

Yet he did a great deal to increase the size and power of the Soviet military and the industrial and scientific base that it required. Though the main features of the Stalinist system were not required by Marx's writings, nor by Lenin's example in the period of the somewhat market-oriented New Economic Policy, they are consistent with the hypothesis that Stalin wanted, above all else, the power that increased tax collections could give him.

XIII.

The foregoing theory is consistent with the history of the Soviet-type societies and, unlike the assertion that the Soviet-type of economic organization was due to ideology, it offers an explanation with genuine explanatory power. More than one theory can, however, be consistent with the historical facts and also meaningful, so we must ask what implication s of the theory offered here would expose it to further testing. If the theory offered here is true, the military or geopolitical power and the expenditures on projects that add to the status and prestige of political leaders should have been greater, in relation to the standard of living of the population, than in other societies—even other autocratic societies. Even a casual glance at the record indicates that this was in fact the case.

There have been many non-Communist dictatorships that offer instructive comparisons with the Communist countries. Since World War II, for example, there have been many dictatorships in Latin America, especially, that were not Communist. But none of these other dictatorships has been remotely as formidable or influential as the Soviet Union or Communist China. Most other autocracies did not, to be sure, preside over such large domains or such huge populations as the USSR or Communist China came to control. But this is not in many cases sufficient to explain why they were not as formidable.

Tsarist Russia, though much the largest country on earth, was not able to give a good account of itself in the Crimean War. Nor was it able to defeat even the then-backward island society of Japan in 1904–1905. Similarly, Chiang Kai-Shek's China, though it had the world's largest population, was militarily impotent.

Compare also Tsarist Russia in World War I with Stalin's USSR. In World War I, the gigantic empire of the Tsars was defeated essentially only by Germany,[8] even though the German army had its hands full fighting on a second front against the French and British from the beginning of the war and normally used only a small fraction of its forces against Russia. By contrast, in World War II, Stalin's Soviet Union was victorious against Nazi Germany, even though the Germans committed the great bulk of their fighting troops to the Soviet front: there was no "second front" until the Normandy invasion in June of 1944. Though German ground and air munitions production was

2.6 times as large in World War II as in World War I, Soviet munitions production was 24.5 times as high in World War II as the Russian Empire's munitions production in World War I (Gatrell and Harrison 1993, table 9 and 425–52).[9]

Whatever interpretation may be offered for the fortunes of the different Russian autocracies in World Wars I and II, there can be no doubt that after World War II the Soviet Union was universally accorded a superpower status that the Tsarist autocracy never achieved, and that the Tsars never managed an autocratic prestige coup comparable to the Soviet initiation of flight in space. When the Stalinist system was applied in China, Vietnam, and North Korea, it again made the Communist autocracies incomparably more powerful militarily and politically than other third-world regimes. We must in the same vein note that Communist China was never so inconsequential militarily as the autocracy it replaced. It was able (with North Korea) to fight the United States and its allies to a draw in the Korean War. There is also Communist North Vietnam's feat in forcing the United States eventually to abandon its objectives in the Vietnam War. Part of the story is that the United States commitment to the Vietnamese and Korean Wars was far from complete, that the United States was inhibited from using nuclear weapons, and so on. Still, when one compares the military and geopolitical significance of the Communist regimes in China, North Korea, and North Vietnam with predecessor regimes and with other third-world countries with similarly abysmal standards of living, my theory that the Communist economics were unprecedentedly effective systems of mobilization or tax collection is surely supported.

XIV.

Some of my audience may be troubled by my tiresome insistence that the Soviet Union's superpower status was an achievement that we have to explain and by my emphasis on the separation of science and ideology. A few may even think that what I have said is alien to the Virginia School. In fact, the method that I have used tonight is the method that the Virginia School and I (along with others) have shared from the beginning. In addition, there is also a substantive contribution from the Virginia School that is resonant with what I have said tonight.

Consider Jim Buchanan's *The Limits of Liberty: Between Anarchy and Leviathan* (1975), especially chapter 9 on "The Threat of Leviathan," and Geoffrey Brennan and James Buchanan, *The Power to Tax: Analytical Foundations of a Fiscal Constitution* (1980). There is some connection between these books and my argument tonight. The Virginia School books just cited consider the growth of government in modern Western democracies rather than in Soviet-type societies and suggest that, without restrictive constitutions, modern democratic governments can maximize tax revenues. Types of taxes that traditional students of public finance considered desirable, because they induce relatively little distortion, do not appeal so much to Brennan and Buchanan. They show, for example, that such traditionally favored types of taxes could lead to greater tax collections and to a greater expansion of government than other taxes.

This view surely has something in common with my argument tonight that Stalinism was a formidable evil precisely because it found implicit taxes that could capture an unprecedentedly large proportion of the national income, yet at the same time increase investment and participation in the labor force. Though other work of mine suggests that maximizing tax collections is not an optimal strategy for a president or majority party to obtain reelection in a democracy (see Olson 1993), there can be no doubt that revenue maximization and the Leviathan idea in Brennan and Buchanan fits autocratic governments. And, if there is any truth in the argument that I have offered here, the Leviathan idea fits Soviet-type regimes in spades. So my argument tonight is, I claim, consistent with the Virginia School traditions not only in method but also to some extent in substance.

XV.

Why, after becoming so formidable, did the Soviet-type systems decline and ultimately collapse? I have argued that the encompassing interest of Stalin and his special method of tax collection explained why the Soviet Union was as formidable as it was. We also need to use the same theory to explain why the system collapsed. Note that the system that I have described—in which everything is adjusted to maximize the amount of the autocrat's take—is entirely dependent on the regime's administrators. If an autocrat claims the full amount of what (in a market economy) we call rent, interest, and profits as tax collections each year, and if he also uses tax-price discrimination to maximize tax collections on labor income, he automatically eliminates a great many markets. If he eliminates so many markets, it follows that many more things have to be decided administratively and that he therefore needs an army of managers. These administrators need to exercise discretion, so he is highly dependent on their decisions.

In the early years, the Soviet autocrats, and Stalin especially, were able to use competition among bureaucrats to force the administrators to do at least approximately what the autocrat wanted them to do. When there was a lot of competition among managers and other bureaucrats, the Soviet-type system served the autocrat fairly well and helped generate fairly rapid economic growth. The center always had great difficulty in getting the information needed to design and implement a more or less coherent plan, and it was never able to get within light-years of a Pareto-optimal plan. Nonetheless, until the system decayed in the later years, the Soviet center obtained enough information to make the economy produce the outputs required of a superpower.

The information needed for a modicum of economic efficiency and growth could be obtained only because different bureaucrats competed with each other. It would take much too long to set out all of the ways in which bureaucratic competition ameliorated the information problem of a Soviet economy, but one example may serve as an illustration. Imagine an industry with five factories. With a Communist takeover, the factories are confiscated by the autocrat, and a manager who reports to a higher-ranking official is put in charge of each factory. If a manager understates the potential production of his factory, other managers in the industry may expose the first manager's falsification; if there is real bureaucratic competition, the other managers will have an incentive to report their colleague's understatement of how much can be produced, because they thereby help their superior and thus earn rewards from him. I suggest that bureaucratic competition, particularly in combination with Stalin's policy of punishing on suspicion, meant that Stalin's administrators usually did not deviate that far from what Stalin wanted them to do.

XVI.

What happened as time went on? Individual groups of managers in different industries or localities have an incentive to collude and to agree to reduce the amount of information that they provide to their superiors about how much they can produce. Specifically, they have an incentive to underestimate the amount that they can produce per unit of input. If all the factory managers in a given industry ultimately agree covertly (or even implicitly) that each of them will underestimate what his factory can produce, then the center will demand less output from (or supply more inputs to) these managers. The managers will then be able to use the surplus resources under their control for their own purposes.

Colluding to withhold information, in other words, generated a collective good to those in the group that was affected by the collusion. But the benefits of a collective good go to those who have not made any of the sacrifices needed to obtain the collective good as well as to those who have, so each member of the group will try to avoid the personal cost or risk associated with the collusion. Therefore, collective action is difficult and takes a long time to organize. Collective action is incomparably easier for small groups than for large groups (Olson 1965), and that made collective action in the Soviet societies emerge faster. On the other hand, such action is much more difficult when it has to take place covertly, and that made the collusions emerge more slowly.

As time went on, the covert collective action of subordinates—particularly those of high rank—led each of these small groups of subordinates to collude in underestimating what could be produced from given resource allocations. If subordinates don't give correct information to the people above them, the center won't have the information it needs, for there is normally no other source of information than those further down the hierarchy.

In fullness of time, the difficulties of covert collection action were overcome by more and more groups—even by subordinates of subordinates and sometimes even down to typical workers. The result was that much of the real power in the Soviet Union and in other Communist states was no longer held by the dictator, since (in the absence of bureaucratic competition) he had to go along, at least to a substantial degree, with what the coteries of subordinates (who monopolized the correct information) wanted.

XVII.

Recall that I argued earlier that an autocrat—and especially one who obtains such a large part of the society's output as the Communist autocrats did—has an encompassing interest in the productivity of his domain, and that this was an important source of the productivity and power of the Soviet-type regimes. What is the interest of the coteries of subordinates that eventually overcome the barriers to covert collective action?

The proportion of the society's income that would be obtained by each of these coteries was, of course, minute. If everyone in a coterie composed of the managers of an industry that represented (say) 1/1,000th of national output worked hard to increase the productivity of the Soviet Union, those in the coterie would obtain only a minuscule share of the benefits. But those in the coterie have to bear the whole cost of their extra effort to increase the Soviet society's productivity. Whereas the dictator has an encompassing stake in the productivity of his domain, each of the coteries of subordinates has a very narrow interest in the domain. That leads them to neglect the productivity of the whole system and to focus on the amount of the social output that they can, albeit covertly, control in their own interest; they maximize their perquisites, their turfs, their consumption, and sometimes even their theft. This system became so bad in the later days of Communism that collective action to steal—that is, theft in which coworkers participated in concert, sometimes with the connivance of their superiors—became commonplace.

Such aggregately perverse sets of incentives are exactly what we should expect from narrow groups that are able to collude or engage in other kinds of collective action. Over time, the Soviet Union and the other mature Communist countries developed a "red" version of the "British disease" of slow growth. That is, they devolved in the same way that (as I showed in *The Rise and Decline of Nations*) long-stable societies with market economies devolved; the main difference was that this devolution was not slowed in the Communist societies by the competition of imports and domestic substitutes nor by the feedback loop from the population that exists in democracies.

The statistical evidence (in spite of all its great inadequacies) shows that, as time went on, the Soviet-type dictatorships became less dynamic and less productive relative to other countries. In the 1970s and 1980s, their growth rates slowed considerably. Yet the Soviet Union and its satellites still had a huge way to go to catch up to the West and thus great opportunities for catch-up growth (Murell and Olson 1991). During the time of Gorbachev, when the center was more open and democratic and less severe, the problem in production became more serious, and there were at times even absolute reductions in output.

XVIII.

What should we expect when democracy is suddenly introduced into a Soviet-type system that has devolved into serious sclerosis? I've argued in the past that lobbies have to overcome the difficulties of collective action and that it takes a long time for a dense network of lobbies to emerge; that there is more lobbying in this country today than in the early 19th century, and more in a long-stable country like postwar Britain than in a country with mainly new institutions, such as Germany in the early 1950s. What is the pattern of collective action that we would expect in a newly democratic, formerly Communist country?

Though the new firms and, of course, the consumers won't be organized, these societies are dense with vested interests that were long ago organized by the old regime. The huge state enterprises are, especially now that the dictatorships are gone, organizations that lobby as well as firms that produce. Indeed, many of the state enterprises are much better at lobbying than at producing. They are also insider lobbies. As a part of the state, they are usually all the more powerful. They are especially strong in relation to the lobbies for new enterprises, which, because of the difficulties of collective action, mostly don't yet exist.

The institutions through which Stalin extracted so much with his system of tax collection—the state enterprises—are now often the most powerful institutions in the newly democratic societies. So now, instead of paying taxes, they demand subsidies. For lack of regular Western-type tax systems, these subsidies are normally supplied through inflationary use of the printing presses and the banking system. The large state enterprises lobby for protection and subsidy even though the economy would probably be more efficient if it relied mainly on new domestic and foreign firms that come in response to market incentives. As narrow interests, each of these state-enterprise lobbies has essentially no interest in making the country work—they have instead an interest in obtaining protection and other subsidies that they need to continue.

Thus they promote a set of policies that makes output even lower than it was in the late stages of totalitarianism. As it happens, in most of these new democracies there are no majority parties or other organized bodies with an encompassing interest. In most of these new democracies, any encompassing interests are relatively weak at the same time that the lobbies with a vested interest in the old and inefficient allocation of resources are relatively strong.

There are also other factors that we cannot go into now, but I would submit that we have here an important part of the reason why economic performance is often even worse after Communism is abandoned. The legacy of Stalin's system of tax extraction is a society filled with organized interests with incentives to lobby for policies that are inconsistent with economic advance in the new democracies. Although the new democracies are also enjoying gains from the emergence of new markets, these gains are much less than they would otherwise be because of imperfect property and contract enforcement rights. The increased output from the new markets is accordingly more than offset by the reductions in the useful output of the state enterprises. The state enterprises that were, in the heyday of Communism, required to adapt as needed and to generate a large surplus for the autocrats are often now not forced to produce or adapt by either the plan or the market. Economic performance is, accordingly, even worse after Communism has been abandoned.

XIX.

No doubt many will disagree with much of what I have said tonight. But everyone must, I think, concede that the method that I have used is a fitting and proper one to use to honor the Virginia School. Almost everyone in my audience will also, I think, agree that this method that the Virginia School and I share with an increasing number of scholars has not exhausted its usefulness. It can, as I have attempted to show, tell us something about the autocracy and Communism, as well as about democracy and capitalism.

NOTES

1. I am grateful to the US Agency for International Development for support of this research through my Center on Institutional Reform and the Informal Sector (IRIS) at the University of Maryland, to Jongseok An, Christopher Bartlett, Suzanne Gleason, Satu Kähkönen, and George Pavlov for their important roles in this research, and to Marie Seibel for secretarial help. The argument is mine alone and does not represent the views of any agency or institution. I am solely responsible for all of its shortcomings.
2. After Stalin, some of the Soviet-type regimes were to some degree tiny "politburo" oligarchies, but the number who shared the central power was so small that they could engage in small-group optimization of the kind described in my 1965 book.
3. Many of the more remarkable advances in civilization even in historic times took place in somewhat democratic or nondictatorial societies such as ancient Athens, the Roman Republic, the North Italian city-states, the Netherlands in the 17th century, and in Great Britain, at least after 1689. I have explained the disproportionate representation of nonautocratic jurisdictions in human progress in my paper, "Autocracy, Democracy, and Prosperity" (Olson 1991).
4. Part of the productivity of the Soviet-type economics was because they used markets much more—and gained much more from them—than is usually understood. I have discussed this in "The Hidden Path to a Successful Economy" (Olson 1992).
5. In the very short run, just after the collectivization of agriculture and other productive assets, there was apparently a period of "indigestion" and confusion when output may have significantly declined. But for most of the rest of Stalin's reign, the output that Stalin cared about was far higher than it had been before he imposed Stalinization on the USSR.
6. There are special cases, like fixed costs of each employee or the transaction costs for employers in hiring temporary employees, that sometimes generate such things as higher rate for overtime, and so on, in a market economy. But these considerations are presumably not of much relevance here.
7. I am grateful to Jim Buchanan for pointing out to me, at a very early stage of my work on the hypothesis that Stalinism was fundamentally a tax-collection system, that a communist tax-maximizing system would not only try to raise the ratio of inframarginal to marginal taxes but also try to take more taxation from those who were productive.
8. The army of the Austro-Hungarian Empire was also used against Tsarist Russia, but this army was often said to be poorer than that of any other combatant country in World War I, and it did not play an impressive role in the defeat of Russia.
9. Gatrell and Harrison (1993, 438) point out that "In World War I . . . only Germany's failure to disentangle itself from the Western front prevented the speedy victory over Russia which Germany intended. Even so, a small fraction of Germany's military power was able eventually to bring about Russia's defeat and disintegration. In the second war . . . the scale of Soviet mobilization, when combined with overwhelming economic superiority of the Allies, was sufficient to destroy Germany completely as a military power. . . . The USSR made a contribution . . . that was disproportionate to the size and level of development of the Soviet economy."

REFERENCES

Brennan, Geoffrey, and James M. Buchanan. 1980. *The Power to Tax: Analytical Foundations of a Fiscal Constitution.* Cambridge: Cambridge University Press.

Buchanan, James M. 1975. *The Limits of Liberty: Between Anarchy and Leviathan.* Chicago: University of Chicago Press.

Gatrell, Peter, and Mark Harrison. 1993. "The Russian and Soviet Economies in Two World Wars: A Comparative View." *Economic History Review* 46 (August): 444.

Kalduhn, Ibn. 1967. *The Mugaddimah.* Franz Rosenthal (trans.). Princeton, NJ: Princeton University Press.

Murrell, Peter, and Mancur Olson. 1991. "The Devolution of Centrally Planned Economies." *Journal of Comparative Economics* 15(2): 239–65.

Olson, Mancur. 1965. *The Logic of Collective Action.* Cambridge, MA: Harvard University Press.

———. 1982. *The Rise and Decline of Nations.* New Haven, CT: Yale University Press.

———. 1991. "Autocracy, Democracy, and Prosperity." In Richard J. Zeckhauser (ed.), *Strategy and Choice*, 131–57. Cambridge, MA: MIT Press.

———. 1992. "The Hidden Path to a Successful Economy." In Christopher Clague and Gordon Rausser (eds.), *The Emergence of Markel Economies in Eastern Europe*, 55–74. Cambridge, MA: Blackwell.

———. 1993. "Dictatorship, Democracy, and Development." *American Political Science Review* 87(3): 567–76.

Olson, Mancur, and Chris Clague. 1971. "Dissent in Economics: The Convergence of Extremes." *Social Research* 38 (Winter): 751–76.

Schumpeter, Joseph A. 1991. "The Crisis of the Tax State." In Joseph A. Schumpeter, *The Economics and Sociology of Capitalism*, Richard Swedberg (ed.). Princeton, NJ: Princeton University Press.

Sheridan, James E. 1966. *Chinese Warlord: The Career of Feng Yuhsiang.* Stanford, CA: Stanford University Press.

5.10
Virginia Virtue—Virginia Vice

HARTMUT KLIEMT

The old lord was dreaming that he was addressing his fellow lords in the House of Lords. And he was dreaming, and dreaming. . . . Suddenly, "Oops," he woke up, and there he was, giving a talk in the House of Lords! Well, that is roughly how I feel addressing "Lord Jim" and all of you this night. I am aware, though, that a philosopher's dream may be an economist's nightmare. So let me assure those among you who are somewhat shaken by the prospect of listening to a German philosopher that I came to your new world of economics as a fellow worldly philosopher.[1] Having my intellectual roots in the works of the British moralists, I feel naturally at home among Virginia political economists. Therefore, let me dare to adopt a "we" perspective henceforth.

There are those among us who intend to make the world a better place, and there are those who just want to understand and to explain what makes the social world go round. But we all draw attention to the same basic insights of our dismal science: insights related to scarcity and opportunity costs. To those who have seen the light, we talk of shadow or prices that are necessarily

Prepared for the Tenth Annual Lecture in the Virginia Political Economy Lecture Series, George Mason University, Fairfax, VA, March 23, 1994.

attached to the pursuit of values. We point out that in a world of scarcity, trade-offs must inevitably be made, and we insist that they better be made under general rules by those who have to bear the costs. Our ways of drawing attention to the unwelcome basic facts of life seem vicious to professional good men and women. But without paying due attention to scarcity and due respect to individuals, the rational pursuit of any overall project of a good life is hardly conceivable. Thus if you are dreaming that your alleged vices are in fact virtues, wake up. You are not dreaming: Virginia's vice is Virginia's virtue. So, why not let it rest with that and turn to the project of a good dinner?

Well, since we all used to say that there is no such thing as a free lunch, there neither should be a free dinner. Therefore let me exploit my transient monopoly and collect a price by making you pay attention to an exercise in worldly ethics. I will first generally speak of varieties or types of scarcity. The virtues and vices of what I regard as typical Virginian ways of dealing with the more dramatic types of scarcity will then be illustrated by addressing some increasingly important problems from the field of organ transplantation. Talking about what is under your skin might not get under your skin. But it may make even the hard-nosed understand better why showing the virtues of a Virginia political economist so often seems vicious to less worldly philosophers.

VARIETIES OF SCARCITY

Though scarcity is a universal fact of life, there are different degrees of scarcity, and the needs involved are of different urgency. Since we all have heard the saying that the boat is full, let me distinguish three types of scarcity by studying three boats or ships.

Type 1 Scarcity

Imagine a boat in which there are a hundred people. The boat is so crowded that it inevitably will sink if another person enters. Our intuition tells us that in this case the hundred who are in may refuse to let another one in. If the 101st were admitted, then 101 persons would die immediately, while under some principle of exclusion a hundred persons could be saved. Therefore rational people would decide on a principle of exclusion and against free entry no matter what.

But what of the single swimmer? He might not agree and point out that the insiders could dispose of one of their kind to let him in. Would selling a slot in the game of life to the highest bidder be an adequate procedure? Should wealthy swimmers be allowed to make promises for the time after the shore is reached? May all dimensions of value be included in the bargaining process and the measuring rod of money universally be applied if personal integrity and even lives are at stake?

Type 2 Scarcity

If our boat is not so crowded that it will inevitably sink if another passenger comes aboard, we tend to require that additional passengers be admitted. But, perhaps the boat is leaking badly. All those who are on board must already work hard to keep it afloat. Decreasing returns to scale prevail, and thus with every newcomer, all, including the newcomer, must work harder.

Still, according to the publicly expressed "rescue ethic,"[2] a human life is worth paying any price as measured along other dimensions of value. In particular, rescuing the life of one is of higher value than any decrease in the quality of life of all others. If we accept such a lexicographic preordering of saving lives,[3] we should also be willing to accept its implications for life on board. Increases of life expectancy of those who are newly admitted must just cancel out at the margin with decreases of the overall life expectancy of those who are on board already. All other tradeoffs would be irrelevant.

Such a view is fine for Sunday speeches in which altruism and solidarity between all humans can be praised, while selfishness can be condemned at zero cost. But is it at all likely that people who have to pay the price would want to organize life that way? Certainly not. In their private lives, all make their tradeoffs between life expectancy and other values. Still, people do tend to assume that values concerning personal integrity and mere survival have a special status.

Type 3 Scarcity

Life—at least in highly industrialized countries—is not like the struggle for survival in an overcrowded lifeboat. It is rather like a trip on a luxury liner. It may be that in the last resort we are on board another *Titanic*.[4] But it is yet a long way before we will hit the iceberg. The orchestra is still playing, and we are engaged in our several amusements rather than toiling all day to keep afloat. Once in a while we may even gather armchair economists and armchair philosophers for a panel discussion of what the upper deck passengers owe to those on the lower decks. Then tradeoffs are considered, but only those imposed by a mild third type of scarcity that does not touch upon individuals' personal integrity or lives.

Reasonable people accept that economic reasoning is applied to type 3 scarcity. But the same people regard it as almost self-evident that the economic approach to dealing with the more dramatic types of scarcity is of necessity grossly inadequate. I do not share the latter view. I rather think that quite the opposite holds good. Still, as always the proof of the pudding is in the eating. In our wealthy societies, extreme scarcity typically emerges in cases in which the provision of health services is involved. Therefore I will try to apply arguments from Virginia political economy to this realm. Let us look at some real and some conceivable rules or institutions for dealing with often tragic tradeoffs in view of extreme scarcity.

LIFE, LIMB, AND REASONABLE RULES

Classical Triage

We all know the example of triage in wartime or in the case of emergencies after catastrophic events. Those who need help are classified according to the urgency and the likely effects of assistance. In the first class, we have those who are only lightly, though possibly painfully, injured. They will survive even without any assistance. In the next class, we have those whose survival prospects are a decreasing function of time. They are severely injured but can survive in all or at least quite high likelihood if they receive some help immediately. A third class is formed by those who are so badly injured that their survival prospects are dim regardless. According to the triage rule, individuals from the second class should be treated with highest priority, for only their survival prospects depend critically on the time before help is received.

As Virginia political economists, we could try to defend triage with a standard contractarian argument: individuals who have a dominant preference for survival per se would prefer the rule that offers the highest expected number of lives saved. The constitutional choice of the triage rule maximizes their own survival prospects behind the veil of uncertainty. Therefore they will unanimously agree to adopt that rule.

Things get more complicated if we include expected length and quality of life. But I guess that the general interest in an extended discussion of the triage rule may not be very strong. The well-to-do will not tend to devote much time or effort to the study of apparently unlikely events of extreme scarcity. However, taking into account increasing wealth and its likely effects on technical progress in medicine, they perhaps should. Situations of extreme scarcity will in all likelihood more frequently emerge in the midst of our rich societies (cf. Buchanan 1990).

As recent efforts of the Clinton administration show, big government is already in business. But this should not keep us out of the business of reflecting on what is involved. Since it is always advantageous to have a specific example, let me try to address some of the issues in a discussion of organ transplantation.

Type 1 Scarcity in Organs

Organ transplantation is the tip of the iceberg of potentially extreme scarcity of medical resources necessary for securing survival and personal integrity. I do not presume that this iceberg will make the *Titanic* sink. But something big seems to be coming up. In the case of organs that are necessary for survival, type 1 scarcity clearly applies. Even if we assume that sufficient resources are devoted to transplanting organs, the organs themselves are still an extremely scarce resource in very inelastic supply. This is no surprise, since in the case of heart, lung, or liver transplants the ideal donor is an individual who, except for being dead, is healthy and thus somewhat hard to find outside the community of motorcyclists.

The scarcity of transplantable organs could be slightly alleviated if we would devote more resources to harvesting organs from cadaveric donors. But in the last resort, we must make decisions in which a donated organ is allocated to one individual while another one will not be treated and might eventually die on the waiting list.

The actual practices of allocation are quite close to a somewhat modified triage rule. If a patient's death whose life could in principle be rescued is imminent, he or she will tend to receive highest priority. The maximization of qualitatively adjusted life expectancies will at least implicitly play a considerable role, too. This becomes obvious from the fact that younger patients and those of generally superior health will tend to be treated with higher priority than older ones.[5] Again, a standard contractarian argument could roughly reach the same conclusion. It seems quite plausible that rational individuals who are not only interested in survival per se, behind the veil of uncertainty, would unanimously accept an institution that amounts to maximizing qualitatively adjusted life expectancies. In a way, this high degree of agreement in cases of type 1 scarcity is not surprising. The values between which tradeoffs must be made are more or less all of the same category, and preferences are interindividually quite similar. The more difficult and interesting issues emerge if we address cases of type 2 scarcity. In discussing them, I will focus on what is by far the most important case of organ transplantation: namely that of kidneys.

Type 2 Scarcity in Organs

Since renal dialysis is available, problems are less dramatic in the case of kidney transplantation than in other cases of organ transplantation. Renal dialysis can secure survival before transplantation. But dialysis is not only costly in monetary terms, it also severely impairs the patient's quality of life. Given the political commitment to dialysis, expanding the number of kidney transplantations is a kind of Pareto-superior move. In the long run, this treatment is less costly than renal dialysis and at the same time enhances the quality of life of the recipients.

Therefore, in industrialized Western countries, some efforts have been made to increase the yield of transplantable organs from cadaveric donors. For instance, some countries have simply shifted the burden of proof on those who are not willing to donate. Implicitly they thus adopt the collectivistic view that everybody is under a prima facie duty and presumably willing to help others in society. Not all countries are going that far. But almost all treat cadaveric organs as a common pool resource (cf. Ostrom 1990). In view of extreme scarcity, it is not acknowledged that former owners may freely decide whether they want to bequeath their organs to their heirs, the general public, or the worms. But if organs from cadaveric donors are treated as a common pool resource anyway, why not include the organs of the living in the common pool? It seems that within the collectivist mindset, such an institution could quite easily be defended as well.

We may feel that this is just another proof of the potentially vicious consequences of adopting the perspective of maximizing the common good. But one can construct a prima facie plausible contractarian argument in favor of such public demands on individuals as well. The quality of life of an individual who is dependent on renal dialysis is severely impaired, and his life expectancy is reduced. The quality of life of the living donor is not or only slightly decreased. Neither does donation considerably increase the risk of needing dialysis in the future. It is quite unlikely that the one remaining healthy kidney of a healthy donor will fail. Thus a slight increase of risks as well as a slight and mostly transient decrease in the quality of life must be weighed against a fundamental improvement of the quality of life and of life expectancy. As a further provision, it could be specified in an auxiliary rule that anybody who has served as a living donor and afterward suffers from terminal failure of the remaining kidney would have highest priority in receiving a new organ, or perhaps even several if retransplants should be necessary. Since the pool of potential donors is very large if a whole population of living donors is included, tissue match in all likelihood will be very good. As recent empirical studies show, the long-term survival prospects for a donated kidney are then very good, too (cf. Takemoto 1992).

Without going into further details, we could plausibly conclude that behind the veil of uncertainty everybody will be better off if organ sharing among living donors is implemented. At least from that detached point of view, gaining access to other individuals' organs seems worth paying the price of granting them access to one's own organs. Such institutions would meet the test of conceivable unanimous agreement. Therefore a contractarian seems to be forced to regard their implementation as justified. Still, at least I feel that the strength of the preceding argument is a vice of classical contractarianism rather than a virtue. It is actually hard to imagine a more collectivistic political institution than "mandatory kidney sharing among living donors." Taking resort to the classical contractarian argument from conceivable agreement may thus lead us to conclusions that are not in line with our otherwise individualistic vision of a well-ordered society and the good life.

Virginian contractarians seem not unaware of such problems, though. They therefore tend to treat the contractarian model merely as a heuristic. This amounts to the concession that the model of conceivable agreement cannot shoulder the burden of justifying actual policies. Implementation can be justified only by actual or real consent.[6] And any obligation of real people must be based on their actual rather than merely on their conceivable consent. This is a viable way to avoid the collectivistic trap. But it should not be overlooked that it restricts the applicability of the contractarian argument to settings that allow for clublike organizations. It must be feasible that the collective goods involved can be provided as club goods for a self-selected group of members rather than as political public goods for a predetermined collectivity.[7]

In the case of organ transplantation, clublike organization is feasible. Taking my inspiration from Buchanan's theory of clubs rather than his contractarianism, I have myself suggested in the German debate that one should resort to clubs for sharing organs from cadaveric donors (cf. Kliemt 1993a, 1993b). Individuals are entitled to receive an organ only if they have voluntarily joined the club of potential donors at a time when their own need for a transplant could not be foreseen yet. Behind the veil of uncertainty of one's own future health prospects, this provides a nonpecuniary incentive to donate in case of one's own death. Unlike the present arrangement, it excludes free riding on others' willingness to donate for the contingency of their death.

Individuals who join the club can themselves compare the potential gains of such an act with its costs and thus can make an autonomous value decision.

Turning to a club arrangement also shifts the perspective—or frame—from asking oneself the question, "What if I die?" to the question, "What if I want to live on and cannot get an organ myself?"[8] As economists, as well as psychologists, we should expect that this shift in incentives, as well as in perspective, would lead to an increase of donations. We could even empirically check this hypothesis since—as I recently learned—in the state of Singapore, a rule like this was actually enacted in 1988 (cf. Teo 1992). Though Singapore perhaps is not exactly the archetype of a system in which Western values rank highest, this specific institution complies very well with our ideals. Those who feel that the gains of joining the club are not worth paying the price opt out. They exclude themselves from the benefits, while others who feel just the other way round will join the club. It is all up to them.

And what of clubs of living donors? Even Singapore did not dare to go that far. But the classical contractarian heuristic suggests that it would lead to Pareto improvements if our legal orders would allow for and even facilitate the actual formation of organ-sharing clubs of living donors.[9] When such clubs are formed, the tradeoffs are not merely made in the abstract thought model. They are made in real-world negotiations for membership by the very same individuals who afterward are entitled and obliged under the bylaws of their clubs.

Not only can the classical condition of conceivable consensus be met, but the stronger consensus condition of club contractarianism can be met as well. Therefore, the Virginia political economist seems to be bound to accept such an outcome as legitimate and should consequently recommend the implementation of legal institutions that facilitates its emergence.

That a wider public might regard such suggestions as politically incorrect or even outrageous should be taken into account. It is relevant as far as political implementation is concerned. But it does not provide counterevidence against the argument as such. Moreover, even though I personally would be reluctant to join an organ-sharing club of living donors, the possibility that such clubs may form seems appealing to me. For I want to live in a society of individuals who decide these matters themselves.

This line of reasoning raises the obvious question why tradeoffs and thus exchanges should be restricted to agreements on in-kind transfers along one dimension of value only. Why not regard scarcity in transplantable kidneys as allowing for financial transfers and a market for organs? As long as agreements are voluntary, why should we as individualists object to "organs for sale?" On the other hand, human organs simply belong to another category than Wurlitzer's, and thus, perhaps, individuals should be somewhat restricted from trading them in for Wurlitzers (cf. Kass 1992).

I trust that most of us at least in our more unguarded moments can feel the appeal of the latter view. Thomas Hobbes may have expressed the truth, but certainly not our vision of the good society, when he stated that "the Value, or Worth of a man, is as of all other things, his Price; that is to say, so much as would be given for the use of his Power; and therefore is not absolute; but a thing dependent on the need and judgement of another" (Hobbes [1651] 1968, 151 ff.).

To avoid the sterile discussion of whether the rich would exploit the poor if organs were for sale, let us impose some minimum standard of wealth on the seller. Let us assume that the opportunity costs of not selling one's organs must not themselves be within the domain of extreme scarcity. Given this, sellers are not compelled by extreme scarcity to offer their organs. Therefore it seems clear that they, like in all other processes of free contracting, should be legally entitled to go ahead.

We may impose some checks against performing irreversible acts spontaneously under a misperception of long-run costs and benefits. For instance, even an otherwise quite radical proponent of individual self-determination like Wilhelm von Humboldt maintained that no present self should be in a position to enslave a future self (cf. Humboldt [1851] 1993). Incidentally, this is why he opposed marriage without divorce. Still, bygones are bygones, and thus all that we do is irreversible in a sense. The irreversibility involved in selling one kidney seems to be much closer to letting individuals ride motorbikes than to letting them engage in lifelong legal commitments. If we let them deliberately take such risks as riding a motorbike, why not let them take a calculated risk in selling their organs?

The general public is willing to accept the latter decisions anyway. According to a common understanding, it should be legal that human individuals may serve as living donors for their close kin. However, these donations are as irreversible as between nonrelatives. If we feel that present selves of individuals may make these decisions in favor of their kin, why should we forbid likewise well- or ill-considered decisions to trade one's organs beyond the limits of kinship? Maybe we should have some institutional checks securing that donating individuals are fully aware of the consequences of their actions.[10] But then the rest should be left to the individuals themselves. They should themselves decide and in the process of decision-making determine relative prices according to their values. Pushpin is as good as poetry as long as pushpin is what individuals want in clear recognition of consequences. If they regard dimensions of value as commensurable, they should be legally treated as commensurable.

Thus, if we feel inclined to go along with the club of living donors and the exchange of promises of mutual aid for future contingencies, how could we offer any reason to resist a market for organs? Is it not implied by our vision of the good life and by our ideal of self-restraint in imposing values on others that individuals should decide these matters themselves?

It should be noted that subjectivism and value skepticism as methodological norms do not imply the moral norm that the skeptic may not impose his values on others. Quite to the contrary, within his means-ends perspective the moral skeptic has good reason to impose his own values on others if this serves the skeptic's ends. But at the same time, the skeptic may pursue certain ideals. He may, as a matter of fact, want to follow Rutledge Vining and subscribe to "the moral principle that no individual should treat another simply as means to an end" (Vining 1956, 18).[11] If we adopt that principle, we can immediately ask whether this would change the conclusions reached so far in any substantial manner.

So let us look at whether the Kantian moral ideal has some cash value when applied to the issue of "organs for sale." As long as we do not base our argument merely on conceivable but rather on actual consent, there seems to be still no good reason against admitting the formation of clubs for organ sharing among living donors. People who join a club actually would express a common concern and a willingness to enter in a reciprocal mutual-aid relationship, granting certain rights in exchange for certain self-imposed obligations for future contingencies. Moreover, the potential donor is identical with the potential recipient. Tradeoffs are made intrapersonally along the same fundamental dimension of value and thus seem unobjectionable. Of course, members of the club of living donors pursue what they regard as their own long-run interests. But as long as they do it under conditions of mutual agreement, this does not contradict the Kantian ideal as expressed before. Seeking another individual's agreement to a mutually advantageous exchange is almost tantamount to respecting one's partner as a person who is pursuing her or his own ends. Therefore no degradation of human personal integrity seems involved.

The matter of subgame perfectness may raise some eyebrows, though. What would we do with somebody who has promised to serve as a living donor and is not willing to comply? Should we have a special police? In case of a monetary payment that would be made only after delivery of the organ, such problems, as well as Samaritan's dilemmas (see Buchanan 1975) and corruption in the enforcement of contracts, would actually be avoided. This seems to be an argument for introducing a market for organs. Again we must inquire whether its consequences would be in line with a quasi-Kantian norm of respect. The use of money in exchanges does not change their moral status as such. If mutual agreement expresses mutual respect, why not let people agree on exchanging money for organs? Within the ethic of mutual respect, money cannot be at the root of the problem, if there is any problem at all. However, contrary to the club of living donors model, on a full-fledged market for organs trade and mutual agreement are not restricted anymore to one dimension of value only. Individuals may make adjustments and thus coordinate for mutual gains along all dimensions of value. From the point of view of efficiency, this should certainly be allowed. Nevertheless, going beyond in-kind transfers in such matters like human organs might in fact change our self-perception as humans and our ways of social world making.[12] It is conceivable that we may gradually start to perceive each other not so much as persons but rather as a kind of natural supply of body parts if we start selling human body parts in markets. If that were in fact the case, it could lead to an erosion of support for legal institutions that respect individual rights.

The Virginia political economist who pursues the Kantian ideal of respecting other individuals by institutional means must agree that this line of argument against a market for organs can conceivably be compelling. But conceivability of risks is not a compelling argument as such. Like the contractarian consent, such risks must be demonstrated as being real rather than merely conceivable.[13] If a climate of mutual respect would in fact be threatened by letting people sell organs on the market, I would concede that the right to one's organs should be made inalienable. As the example of legally inalienable basic citizen's rights shows, such restrictions are not completely alien to the idea of a free society anyway.

CONCLUSION

In realms that in principle allow for clublike organization, the imposition of inalienability of rights is a kind of ultimate measure.[14] Organ transplantation is such a realm. Real consensus is possible and mutual agreement should reign. Therefore, within a non-Kantian as well as within a Kantian variant of normative Virginia political economy, there are no convincing general arguments against a market for organs. Institutional reform and policy measures are a different story altogether.

We should start with reciprocity arrangements for in-kind exchanges and then move on in a piecemeal way. At each step toward full property rights in organs, we must carefully evaluate all effects.[15] But in principle, it seems clear that the Virginia political economist's vision of the good life in a well-ordered society is at least compatible with a market for organs. It is up to you to decide whether this conclusion proves Virginia's vice or Virginia's virtue. Hopefully I have at least shown the virtue of not putting to sleep too many Virginia political economists this night. But if I was vicious in that regard and you are dreaming that this talk is over now, wake up, you are not dreaming—it is over and the good life can start again.

NOTES

I should like to express my gratitude to Olivier Binet, University of Basel, and Frank Forman, Fairfax, for drawing my attention to important literature, and to Manfred Tietzel, University of Duisburg, for inspiring discussions about "rationing" while queuing for scarce Austrian lift chairs. For "lifting" my knowledge of economics, I am indebted to the people at the Center for Study of Public Choice, and I am still queuing for that treatment.

1. Of course I am alluding here to McKenzie and Tullock (1975) and Heilbroner ([1953] 1983).
2. See Dworkin (1994) on that term. Though I otherwise very rarely agree with Dworkin, his criticism of the "rescue ethic" seems sound to me.
3. There should be no risk of confusing this with the concept of a "preordering" as used otherwise.
4. See Hegselmann's discussion of technical progress, the ethics of science, and life on the *Titanic* (1989).
5. Additional aspects like time on the waiting list are often taken into account, too, but seem to be of relatively minor importance in most countries. A somewhat more general if older account of the American situation can be found in US Department of Health and Human Services (1986).
6. See Buchanan's appendix on "Reading Political Philosophy" in Buchanan and Tullock (1962).
7. For a more general account of related problems, see Kliemt (1994).
8. A typical framing effect should be expected to emerge; see Thaler (1992), and with respect to social issues, see Lindenberg (1992).
9. Of course, the rules of the club would have to be worked out so that adverse selection effects could be controlled. It would also be necessary to design provisions for exiting the club, entitlements due to length of membership, for children, and so on.
10. Schelling-type "egonomics" might motivate this (Schelling 1984).
11. If this Kantian principle, as Vining (1956, 18) suggested, is regarded as constitutive for the universe of economic discourse in general, I have serious doubts whether the "new world of economics" is still among its territories.
12. I am borrowing Goodman's nice phrase here (1978); for an account of the effects of payments in the case of blood donations that goes beyond the often sterile a priori discussions of the "gift relationship," see Espeland (1984), and for a stimulating public choice discussion of related rent-seeking obstacles to markets for organs, see Binet (1993).
13. Otherwise we would have to take seriously as well the argument that sexual practices between consenting adults threaten society. Though I am willing to let people buy almost everything, I am not willing to let them buy that without further ado.
14. For a fine discussion of how clublike organization principles could be emulated even under compulsory membership in a "health insurance club," see Breyer (1992).

15. If we are primarily interested in increasing organ yield, it may well be good policy not to go for a market for organs. For the emergence of such a market can conceivably diminish the general inclination to donate for other than monetary reasons. But however we assess the empirical validity of the premises on which this argument is based, it should be noted well that it alludes to considerations of general welfare rather than to the aims of respecting and strengthening individuals' decision rights.

REFERENCES

Binet, O. 1993. "Das mangelnde Angebot an menschlichen Organen: Hintergründe und Auswege." Mimeo, Institut für empirische Wirtschafts-forschung, Universität Zürich.

Breyer, F. 1992. "Wahlfreiheit in der gesetzlichen Krankenversicherung: Eine wohlfahrtstheoretische Analyse." In G. Gäfgen (ed.), *Systeme der Gesundheitssicherung im Wandel*, 33–52. Baden Baden: Nomos.

Buchanan, J. M. 1975. "The Samaritan's Dilemma." In E. S. Phelps (ed.), *Altruism, Morality, and Economic Theory*, 71–85. New York: Sage.

———. 1990. *Technological Determinism Despite the Reality of Scarcity: A Neglected Element in the Theory of Spending for Medical and Health Care.* Little Rock: University of Arkansas for Medical Sciences.

Buchanan, J. M., and G. Tullock. 1962. *The Calculus of Consent.* Ann Arbor: University of Michigan Press.

Dworkin, R. 1994. "Will Clinton's Plan Be Fair?" *New York Review of Books*, January 13, 20–25.

Espeland, W. 1984. "Blood and Money: Exploiting the Embodied Self." In J. A. Kotarba and A. Fontana (eds.), *The Existential Self in Society*, 131–51. Chicago: University of Chicago Press.

Goodman, N. 1978. *Ways of World Making.* Indianapolis, IN: Hackett.

Hegselmann, R. 1989. "Die Wissenschaft, ihre Ethik und der Eisberg." In E. Meinel, E. Englert, and H. Kliemt (eds.), *Das Unbehagen gegenüber den Wissenschaften*, 65–82. Heidelberg: R v. Decker's Verlag, G. Schenck.

Heilbroner, R. [1953] 1983. *The Worldly Philosophers.* Harmondsworth, UK: Penguin.

Hobbes, T. [1651] 1968. *Leviathan.* Harmondsworth, UK: Penguin.

Humboldt, W. [1851] 1993. *The Limits of State Action.* Liberty Fund Classic. Indianapolis, IN: Liberty Press.

Kass, L. R. 1992. "Organs for Sale? Propriety, Property, and the Price of Progress." Bradley Lecture, American Enterprise Institute, Washington, DC.

Kliemt, H. 1993a. "Reziprozität und Versichertensouveränität als Leit-vorstellungen einer Neuordnung des Gesundheitswesens." In P. Oberender (ed.), *Institutionelle Erneuerung des Gesundheitswesens in Deutschland*, 9–31. Baden-Baden: Nomos.

———. 1993b. "Gerechtigkeitskriterien in der Transplantationsmedizin: Eine ordoliberale Perspektive." In E. Nagel and Ch. Fuchs (eds.), *Soziale Gerechtigkeit im Gesundheitswesen, Ökonomische, ethische, rechtliche Fragen am Beispiel der Transplantationsmedizin*, 262–83. Berlin: Springer.

———. 1994. "*The Calculus of Consent* after Thirty Years." *Public Choice* 79: 341–53.

Lindenberg, S. 1992. "An Extended Theory of Institutions and Contractual Discipline." *JITE* (*Zeitschrift für die gesamten Staatswissenschaften*) 148: 125–54.

McKenzie, R., and G. Tullock. 1975. *The New World of Economics.* Homewood, IL: R. D. Irvin.

Ostrom, E. 1990. *Governing the Commons: The Evolution of Institutions for Collective Action.* New York: Cambridge University Press.

Schelling, T. C. 1984. *Choice and Consequence*. Cambridge, MA: Harvard University Press.

Takemoto, S., P. I. Terasaki, J. M. Cecka, Y. W. Cho, and D. W. Gjertson. 1992. "Survival of Nationally Shared, HLA-Matched Kidney Transplants from Cadaveric Donors." *New England Journal of Medicine* 327: 834–39.

Teo, B. 1992. "Is the Adoption of More Efficient Strategies of Organ Procurement the Answer to Persistent Organ Shortage in Transplantation?" *Bioethics* 6(2): 113–29.

Thaler, R. 1992. *The Winner's Curse. Paradoxes and Anomalies of Economic Life*. New York: Free Press.

US Department of Health and Human Services. 1986. *Organ Transplantation: Issues and Recommendations*. Report of the Task Force on Organ Transplantation. Washington, DC: US Department of Health and Human Services.

Vining, R. 1956. *Economics in the United States of America: A Review and Interpretation of Research*. Paris: UNESCO.

5.11
The Public Choice Approach to International Economic Relations

THOMAS D. WILLETT

I. INTRODUCTION

The study of the political economy of international economics (or international political economy, as this field is usually designated by political scientists) has received increased attention from growing numbers of political scientists and economists in recent years. Furthermore, the perspectives from which both economists and political scientists view international economic policy issues have undergone substantial shifts, which suggests greatly expanded opportunities for the mutual enrichment of both disciplines.

A number of factors have contributed to this resurgence of interest in political economy by economists. Unlike in the 1960s and 1970s, one can no longer assume that an economics book or article with "political economy" in the title will be written from a Marxist perspective. Mainstream economists have come to realize that economic policies are implemented through a political process and consequently that the theory of optimal economic policy, even where its conclusions are unambiguous, often will fail as a positive guide for predicting or explaining the course of governments' economic policies. While it is

Prepared for the Eleventh Annual Lecture in the Virginia Political Economy Lecture Series, George Mason University, Fairfax, VA, March 15, 1995.

difficult to judge their relative importance, other crucial factors have been the widespread recognition of systematic policy failures at both the macro- and microeconomic levels, the development of public choice analysis, and the emphasis on anticipations of policy actions coming out of the rational expectations revolution in macroeconomics.

On the political science side, as the Cold War thawed and the high politics of international military strategy stalemated, economic issues moved to a higher place on the agendas of competing states, and international relations scholars took increased interest in such issues. Furthermore, a substantial shift in the theoretical orientation of researchers in this field developed as younger scholars began to gain prominence. Bruno Frey (1984b), in an influential survey of the public choice approach to international political economy, argued that

> Political scientists do not hesitate to claim international exclusive domain. *Power and authority*, and not market relations, are taken to be the central concepts with which to study the problems. . . . There is a marked tendency to reject economic theory. The rejection does not seem, however, to be based on an extensive knowledge of the literature. . . . From the public choice point of view, political scientists' international political economy is deficient in various respects. The most important shortcoming is its non-analytical structure. It lacks a well-spelled out theory of behavior from which to derive (non obvious) testable hypotheses. Rather, the approach is disruptive, historical and (sometimes) anecdotal. No effort is made to put up clear propositions and to subject them to empirical (econometric) testing. (9)

Until recently, Frey's assessment of the substantial majority of writings by political scientists on international political economy was, unfortunately, quite accurate. However, a new generation of international relations scholars, influenced in part by a small group of more senior scholars such as Robert Keohane and Stephen Krasner, displays considerable knowledge of the basic ideas of economic analysis. While often critical of particular aspects of economists' analyses, this new group of scholars' criticisms seldom arise primarily from ignorance. In fact, the technical sophistication of the analysis of some of these scholars in areas such as game theory and public goods theory has been quite impressive. There has been considerable growth in the number of both economists and political scientists using public choice analysis explicitly or implicitly in their study of international economic relations. Papers in the leading international relations journals frequently make use of public choice analysis, and at the meetings of the Public Choice Association there are a number of sessions on international public choice.

Unfortunately, misunderstandings about the nature of public choice analysis are still common. In part this occurs because public choice is often understood to consist of specific models of self-interested rent seeking by interest groups, vote seeking by politicians, or budget seeking by bureaucrats. This narrow view is wrong: public choice is an approach, not a specific theory, and it is capable of incorporating a broad range of considerations.[1] Specific theories differ both in their assumptions about the objectives of actors—for example, narrow economic self-interest versus allowance for ideological preferences—as well as about the weights given to different actors in the collective decision-making process—for example, the importance of direct lobbying by interest groups versus voting by the general public. There is substantial variety in the models used by public choice scholars, just as there is among the political scientists working in international political economy.

In my judgment, however, efforts to test the comparative explanatory power of specific public choice theories and to develop theoretical frameworks that explain the variations in explanatory power across different types of issues, institutional structures, and so on, are woefully undersupplied to public choice analysts. In this endeavor, economists can learn much from recent work by their more eclectic colleagues in political science.

As is reviewed in section II below, there are very serious problems with the organizational framework for international political economy initially emphasized in the political science literature, which focuses on liberal, Marxist, and realist or mercantilist views. Each of these views pays insufficient attention to the possible range of objectives that governments may seek to pursue and to the political pressures and constraints they may face. Especially lacking is attention to the rent-seeking activities of domestic interest groups, compared to much of public choice analysis. It is gratifying to note, therefore, that in recent years many political scientists have begun to emphasize the role played by domestic interest groups and institutional structures in shaping international economic policies.

In section III, I draw on this literature to analyze trends in US trade policies. While interest-group rent-seeking versions of public choice analysis are highly successful in explaining why we have protectionist policies, they have difficulty explaining why we do not have even more protection. The answer, I suggest, lies in considering carefully the institutional framework and applying aspects of the international relations scholars' theory of realism—but in a form that assumes liberal rather than mercantilist trade policies as the government's objective.

In section IV, I illustrate the use of public choice for normative analysis, in this case the design of national and international monetary institutions. The insights from public choice analysis on why governments may have incentives to adopt destabilizing rather than stabilizing macroeconomic policies has revolutionized the way most economists (and many policymakers) look at monetary policy issues. The adoption of a constitutional perspective has become much more common. On the international side, this has contributed to a resurgence of support for using pegged exchange rates as a method of enforcing monetary discipline. I argue that while the case for adopting institutional structures to promote monetary discipline is strong, the case for using fixed exchange rates as a general mechanism for this purpose is weak.

Much of the recent discussion of exchange rates as a nominal anchor has failed to distinguish sufficiently between genuinely fixed and adjustably pegged exchange rates, but this distinction is absolutely crucial for predicting the likely effects of particular exchange rate regimes. Furthermore, economic theory shows that the economic costs and benefits of fixed versus flexible exchange rate regimes vary systematically across countries. Thus the adoption of a fixed exchange rate regime may be a very sensible strategy for some countries, but for others it could be quite costly. In countries where fixed exchange rates are inappropriate, the focus should be on domestic institutional arrangements to promote monetary discipline. This issue nicely illustrates the need to combine political, economic, and institutional analysis in policy making—the hallmark of the public choice approach.

II. PUBLIC CHOICE ANALYSIS AND INTERNATIONAL POLITICAL ECONOMY

Following the influential formulations by Robert Gilpin (1975, 1985), early treatments of international political economy by political scientists often focused on three major contending theories or schools of thought: realism (also frequently called mercantilist, nationalist, or statist views); liberalism (sometimes labeled as "interdependence" or "sovereignty at bay" views); and Marxism.[2] As a description of significant differences in worldviews held by important actors in the global political economy, this trilogy is quite useful, I believe. However, as a basis for organizing inquiry into issues of positive political economy—that is, the attempt to explain why governments adopt particular policies rather than what policies they "should" adopt—this approach is seriously deficient.

One typical difficulty with work based on this trilogy is its failure to distinguish systematically between the positive and normative elements of these approaches.[3] Another source of difficulty is the frequent but misleading implication that these are not just three important approaches, but that they are the only three relevant alternatives. Gilpin (1987), for example, argues that

> Scholars and other individuals differ, however, on the nature of the relationships between economic and political affairs. Although many positions can be identified, almost every one tends to fall into one of three contrasting perspectives, ideologies, or schools of thought. They are liberalism, nationalism, and Marxism. . . . These three ideologies are fundamentally different in their conceptions of the relationships among society, state, and market, and it may not be an exaggeration to say that every controversy in the field of international political economy is ultimately reducible to differing corruptions of these relationships. (24–25)[4]

Such statements, however, are fundamentally misleading. As Tollison and I (Tollison and Willet 1982) have argued, a public choice perspective on the nature of domestic and international political relations is excluded or ignored from these three major approaches as they are typically described in the literature.

As users of the trilogy are usually careful to point out, the stylization of these three approaches can hardly do justice to the variety of thought encompassed within each school. For example, while for purposes of the trilogy Marxist and dependencia views are usually lumped together, there are indeed considerable differences of view both within and between writers in these two groups (see Gilpin 1987 and Staniland 1983). Likewise, while the standard summary of liberalism treats it as only being concerned with economic well-being, Adam Smith is famous for his dictum that "defense is more important than opulence."

With this caveat in mind, let me offer a brief summary of the trilogy of approaches as typically described in the international political economy literature. Realism, from a methodological perspective, is actually very similar to traditional economics as often practiced by international economists. It treats the nation-state as unified rational actor as is standardly done in much of international trade theory. If they do not come at it from a public choice perspective, many economists tend to look at trade conflicts among nations as conflicts of optimal tariffs instead of disagreements among domestic economic interest groups.[5] I remember being very heavily influenced by Leland

Yeager in an international economics class at the University of Virginia when he told us we should be wary of treating a nation as if it were a single entity. My experiences in government and what I have learned about public choice over the years have reinforced Yeager's observation and strongly influenced my approach to international economic relations. There are, of course, some important insights to be gained from taking a unified rational actor approach. As Milton Friedman taught us, we do not want to automatically toss out a theory because it has simplified assumptions, since simplifying is the essence of good theorizing. Nevertheless, we need to be very careful how we go about it. In analyzing many of the national security issues that have formed the traditional domain of international relations scholars, the "unified actor" is a highly sensible approach, but as one turns to issues of international economic policy, its explanatory power drops sharply.[6]

From the standpoint of public choice theories, the realist approach corresponds in one sense to the Leviathan model since the government is assumed to be autonomous from domestic societal pressures, and those who capture it pursue their own interests. However, in public choice applications such as Brennan and Buchanan (1980), the government is typically assumed to be rent seeking, while in the realist literature the standard assumption is that the government pursues some broad concept of national interests: that it is public spirited. Such public spiritedness stops at the national boundary, however, and interstate relations are characterized by conflict. Where conflicts arise, it is assumed that national security considerations will (and should) dominate economic concerns, and, in the economic area, the focus is on relative rather than absolute gains.[7] The major independent variable for this approach is the international distribution of power.

The Marxist approach offers a theory of government almost exactly opposite that of the realists. Government within the Marxist paradigm is endogenous, not autonomous. In public choice terminology, the traditional Marxist view rests on an interest-group rent-seeking model, but one with a very special formulation of interest groups. There is only one group that matters, and that is the capitalist class. To the Marxists, a focus on conflicts of economic interest is a big advantage. They do not assume that everyone shares a commonality of interest and that economic relations will be harmonious. But as public choice analysis demonstrates, even apart from the deficient positive and normative aspects of Marxian economic theory, the Marxists tend to look at all distributional conflicts in terms of homogeneous labor versus homogeneous capital. This misses the essence of many distributional conflicts. As Mancur Olson

(1965) points out so nicely, the free-rider analysis says we need to look at disaggregate costs and benefits to individual actors. This dictum applies as much when class is a unit of analysis as it does when looking at the unified rational actor models of realists as a theory of government.

The third school, the liberal approach, is basically an application of orthodox economics. Typical is Robert Gilpin's (1987) characterization that "the liberal perspective on political economy is embodied in the discipline of economics as it has developed in Great Britain, the United States, and Western Europe" (27). The idea of the liberal model is that the state is out to maximize national economic efficiency. It predicts that because, in the liberal view, if international trade is beneficial and trade restrictions are inefficient, there should be a trend toward free trade. This formulation of the liberal approach explains, or at least is consistent with, some of the broad developments in international trade policies for significant periods of time. For roughly a generation following World War II, there was a very decided trend toward trade liberalization in the industrial countries. Unfortunately, by the late 1960s or early 1970s this trend had slowed and began to be reversed. While tariffs continued to fall, the use of quotas and "voluntary" quantitative restrictions rose and the net incidence of protectionism began to increase.

In the literature on international political economy, one of the other names for realism is modern or neomercantilism. As trade barriers began to rise, many of the realist writers in international relations—for example, Gilpin (1987)—interpreted this as strong evidence for the relevance of their approach. I want to argue, among other things, that this interpretation is fundamentally misconceived.

Discussions of these three schools of thought typically do not make clear what positive theory of political economy underlies the predictions of free trade policies associated with the liberal view. An informed median voter model would give this prediction, but so would a Leviathan model if it is assumed that the government pursues the public interest by maximizing aggregate economic efficiency. Just such a public-interest theory of government actions was, for a long period, implicitly or explicitly held by many economists. This view of a disinterested government underlies the optimal policy approach to economic analysis that focuses only on aggregate efficiency effects and typically ignores distributional considerations and problems of implementation.[8]

If one's view of international economic relations is limited to this trilogy of approaches, one misses an awful lot of what is going on in terms of increased protectionist pressures in the United States and the world today. This occurs, in part, because analysis based on these perspectives is often founded on a misunderstanding (or perhaps ignorance) of public choice and basic economics. One key feature of the liberal approach, as it appears in the international political economy literature, is the assertion that there is no basis for conflict within the political economy. Frieden and Lake (1991), for example, argue that three assumptions are essential to the liberal perspective. "First, . . . that individuals are the principal actors within the political economy and the proper unit of analysis, . . . Second, . . . that individuals are rational, utility maximizing actors, . . . [and] Third, . . . individuals maximize utility by making tradeoffs between goods" (6). They incorrectly conclude that "These three assumptions imply that there is no basis for conflict within the political economy" (7). Likewise, Robert Gilpin (1987) argues that "In the abstract world of economics, the economy and other aspects of society exist in separate and distinct spheres . . . national boundaries are assumed not to exist. . . . A fundamental harmony of interest among individuals, groups, and states is assumed to underlie the growth and expansion of the market and of economic interdependence" (21–22).

Economists, with their emphasis on the potential for mutual gains from exchange, certainly do tend to see a higher ratio of harmony to conflict in life than do international relations scholars of the realist school. But seeing interactions as positive rather than zero-sum games does not imply that there is no basis for conflict. Even were one concerned only with one's own absolute gains, there are still incentives to maximize one's own share of the gains. Thus there are incentives both for cooperation and for conflict. Today, basic international economics texts are usually clear that the gains from trade discussed are net gains, so that aggregate efficiency increases in the sense that the gain to the gainers is sufficient that the losers could be compensated and everyone be made better off. As we all know, in the real world such compensation is seldom made. In truth, there are losers from international trade as well as gainers, and this generates distributional conflict. That this distributional conflict is highlighted with the standard tools of economics in modern international economics texts and is at the core of public choice analysis is often completely missed by political scientists writing general overviews of international political economy.[9]

Writers on approaches to international political economy now generally recognize that there is a public choice approach, but they frequently consider the public choice approach to be synonymous with the liberal approach (see Frieden and Lake 1991).[10] This characterization is quite right from the standpoint of the methodology used. The public choice approach applies economic methodology to politics and distributional conflicts. It is also true that most practitioners of public choice share liberal values. But in terms of worldviews of how the political economy operates, the public choice view differs fundamentally from the standard economics view because public choice analysis focuses on the distributional conflicts that can occur.

With its focus on methodological individualism, public choice analysis forces one to stop focusing only on aggregate economic efficiency. In this sense, the public choice approach is as much a critique of the optimal policy approach of standard economics as it is of realism. In each case, public choice analysis says you have to abandon the assumption that nations are unified rational actors in which all distributional conflict has been resolved. It forces one to focus on distributional conflict, not necessarily as the only factor in the analysis, but certainly as a very key factor. Thus public choice analysis agrees with the Marxist view that conflicts of economic interest have an important impact on government policy making, but it offers greater insight into the nature of these conflicts. It is not just aggregate capital versus aggregate labor.

A second deficiency in the early literature on international political economy that the public choice approach is helpful in highlighting was its tendency to reductionism to explain policy choices by a single factor. Sometimes accompanying the view that there are but three grand theories or approaches to international political economy was the idea that one of these approaches could explain most of what determined government policy. Fortunately, support for this view is rapidly breaking down under the weight of studies investigating the behavior of policy. Not only economists, but quite a number of political scientists have begun to do statistical analysis and carefully structured case studies of the influences shaping economic policies during different episodes, and a number of political scientists now emphasize the roles of domestic interest groups and institutions.[11] In the wake of this scholarship, it is clear that many different factors influence economic policy. Further, these different factors are important at different times for different types of policies and different institutional arrangements under different conditions. Any one of the grand theories has some important explanatory power, but each falls far short of complete explanation.

It did not take many months working in government for me to learn that the factors influencing international trade policy formulation were very different from the factors influencing international monetary policy formulation.[12] Interagency meetings on international monetary policy came very close to conforming to a unified rational actor model. To be sure, the Federal Reserve Board's views weren't always exactly in line with the Treasury's, but this typically was a relatively minor squabble. Here one generally was faced with economists from different agencies facing common problems and trying to figure out how to deal with them. There was little concern about the effects of policy on specific industries or congressional districts. Most of the analysis would be on how a policy would likely work in aggregate and whether we could sell it to other countries. Discussion of distributional considerations almost always focused on effects among rather than within countries.[13] In contrast, trade policy issues prompted negotiations within the government before we began any international negotiations. In trade policy meetings, the Labor Department would worry about the effects on domestic labor. The State Department would emphasize effects on foreign relations. The Commerce Department's arguments had a schizoid quality, as one might expect. They had one set of officials from the international business side who favored liberal trade and another set favoring protection for domestic business. The Council of Economic Advisers, Treasury, and Office of Management and Budget would generally try to advocate aggregate economic efficiency or consumer or taxpayer interests as the objectives. It was a completely different environment from the monetary one.

Such observations suggest that we need to develop a framework in which many factors affect policy. Just because there are many influences on government, we don't want to stop, throw up our hands, and say the whole process is so complex that we'll give up and conclude that anything can happen. There is considerable scope for analysis that systematically looks at the conditions, circumstances, institutions, and characteristics of issue areas that will make some factors more important than others. What are the conditions under which interest groups will be more important? What are the conditions under which the government is likely to be more autonomous? What conditions foster bureaucratic politics? One of the virtues of the public choice approach is that it gives us a systematic framework from which we can theorize at the multifactor level by looking carefully at incentive structures.

By systematically considering the costs and benefits of actions by different individuals or groups and the constraints they face, we can develop theoretically useful and potentially empirically falsifiable propositions. For example, adopting Steven Krasner's (1972) view that the president can win any confrontation with the bureaucracy if he really wants to but that constraints on his time and energy prevent him from controlling everything, we can develop systematic predictions about the factors that will influence the effective degree of autonomy of various bureaucracies on various issues. The less important the issue is to the president and the less likely are other influential actors such as other bureaus, domestic interest groups, and foreign governments to raise complaints, the more autonomy a particular bureau is likely to have.

Likewise, for a given level of presidential interest, the more complex the issue and the more difficult it is to ensure instructions are carried out, the more effective is the control that the bureau will have. Thus, for example, the votes cast by the US executive directors in the International Monetary Fund and World Bank on major loans are easier to control than the Federal Reserve Bank of New York's official interventions in the foreign exchange market (as long as such intervention is not entirely prohibited), which in turn is less difficult to monitor than whether the US delegation to the Law of the Sea negotiations was adhering to its negotiating instructions (which it often was not).

In developing a framework for the analysis of questions of positive political economy, it is important to move beyond stressing the importance of particular considerations. Such championing was very useful in earlier stages of the development of the modern field of political economy, but today the most valuable contributions to knowledge are more likely to come from the less glamorous task of studying the conditions that will lead to systematic variations in the relative importance of the various single factor explanations (see Dillon, Odell, and Willett 1990).

In this endeavor, it is important to recognize that the relationships among the various single-factor explanations will not always be linear; sometimes there will be important interaction effects. For example, in response to Arye Hillman's (1989) analysis, which posed a horse race between interest-group rent-seeking and public-interest-type conservative welfare function explanations of protectionism, I argued that there were often important interactions between these two factors. If you look at the incidents of major special trade protection in the United States over the last several decades, it certainly is heavily skewed toward the groups that are most successful in direct political lobbying. Thus the insights from the public choice models of interest-group rent seeking are clearly quite important. If you look at the timing of such protection, however, it is heavily influenced by the existence of adverse economic conditions for the industry in question. The ability to present an at least superficially plausible cover to the often large number of legislators who do not have a strong direct interest in the issue is frequently quite important in securing majority support for protectionist measures. Thus for cases of major special protection, it seems that high scores on both rent seeking and perceived conservative social welfare function criteria are typically both necessary conditions, with neither being sufficient by itself.[14]

III. THE POLITICAL ECONOMY OF TRADE POLICY: WHY DON'T WE HAVE MORE PROTECTIONISM?

Trade policy, especially the case of special protection for individual industries, is a perfect example of highly concentrated benefits and very diffuse costs from protection, so there are substantial incentives for interest-group lobbying. When one looks at exchange rate and international monetary policies, both the costs and benefits are usually highly diffused. Public choice theory predicts that these are instances where a government would have a good deal more scope for autonomy than in trade policy areas. Indeed, just such an analysis was recently provided by a political scientist, Joanne Gowa (1988). Her article is an excellent example of the public choice analysis being used in the international relations literature.

Another important issue is how we see the nature of the domestic conflicts of interest over international trade policies. Still one of the most prominent international trade theories today is the Hecksher-Ohlin factor proportions theory. In the famous 2 factors 2 goods 2 nations version of that theory, you have two countries, two goods, and two factors of production: labor and capital. Internal distributional conflict is formulated in terms of aggregate labor versus aggregate capital, exactly the distributional conflict highlighted by the Marxists. So as international trade theorists turned to political economy and public choice analyses, many examples of their formal analysis were exactly what one would expect from the Marxist tradition.

Such analysis offers important insights. If one is looking, for example, at the NAFTA debate, there was clearly a systematic difference between the positions of organized labor and the majority of industries (see Carlos, Kaempfer, and Layok 1996). However, while the labor versus capital conflict has important explanatory power, it also misses a lot. If one considers trade policy issues such as voluntary export restraints or special quotas, what is most often seen is labor and capital in the same industry coming in together and arguing for protection for their industry. To explain such behavior, one must turn to a specific factors model of trade.[15]

This is a powerful illustration that public choice is an approach, not a specific theory. It gives us a way of thinking about these issues. It emphasizes the need to look at distributional aspects, not just aggregate efficiency, and to consider carefully the objective functions of policymakers and the constraints they face, but it does not give us any one determinant outcome because we have a whole host of theories to work with. Predictions would vary depending on which specific model of the operation of the economy was used—specific factors versus Hecksher-Ohlin trade theory—and which model of the political process—interest group versus median voter models.

As a first cut, we would expect from the informed median voter model that free trade would predominate because the vast majority of individuals are going to benefit from free trade. If we have a median voter model where we are each voting our own interest, free trade should be the norm, not the exception. Why does this not hold? Key concepts from public choice of the rational ignorance of the consumer-voter and of differential incentives to organize and lobby explain the disproportionate influence of small, well-organized groups. Trade policy is a tailor-made laboratory experiment to explain these insights of public choice analysis. So if we consider, as did Bruno Frey (1984) a decade ago, that the chief task of public choice analysis of international trade policy is to explain why we have protectionism, we've done that hands down.

Interesting issues remain about the structure and forms of protection; for example, the use of tariffs versus quotas. In the industrial countries, while tariff levels have continued to fall, the incidence of quantitative restrictions has risen. To international trade economists concerned with economic efficiency, it appears that not only do governments give too much protection, but they also give it in excessively costly ways since quotas and voluntary export restraints typically impose greater aggregate economic costs than equivalent tariffs. At first look this appears consistent with the Virginia public choice view, which sees rational ignorance generating incentives to produce transfers in forms that are less easily visible even if more costly in contrast to the Chicago view, which assumes that the potential process will see through such fog factors so that transfers will tend to be effectual in ways that minimize efficiency costs.

On closer reflection, however, the evidence on this issue from trade policy experience is not so clear. While quotas tend to generate greater economic costs than equivalent tariffs, they also tend to generate greater rents for the interests protected, so that it is not clear that the efficiency costs of the quotas per dollar of rents transferred are always greater than for tariffs. Likewise, while it is correctly argued that voluntary export restraints tend to transfer rents abroad, this is not necessarily inefficient since it may be part of an implicit international compensation mechanism that reduces the likelihood of trade wars. The structure of international commitments under the General Agreement on Tariffs and Trade (GATT) and its successor, the World Trade Organization, have also likely played an important role in influencing the forms of protection adopted. The conflicting views of the Chicago and Virginia approaches on the forms of transfers in general, and in the trade area in particular, are an important area for further political economy research.[16]

Perhaps an even greater puzzle for public choice analysis, however, is explaining why we don't have a great deal more protectionism than we do. Why do we still have a basically liberal trading system despite lots of exceptions? On the spectrum between free trade and autarky, we are far closer to free trade than we are to autarky. How do we explain this?

Part of the answer can be provided within an interest-group framework when we remember that not all well-organized groups benefit from protection. Indeed, Helen Milner (1988) has argued that a major reason for the lower degree of protectionism in the United States during the economic strains of recent decades as compared with the 1920s and early 1930s is due to the substantially greater amount of lobbying today by export industries and multinational corporations as a result of increasing economic interdependence. (See also Dester and Odell 1987.) For a full explanation, however, I believe that we need to go beyond interest-group models and consider also the role of the foreign policy objectives of the executive branch and changes in institutional structures. This involves giving the realist model some credit. It ends up having far more explanatory power in combination with other factors than I had expected.

Like most economists, when I first started applying public choice analysis to trade policy issues, my focus was on the protectionist bias in the operation of the political system.[17] I was shocked when I started reading literature from political scientists talking about the liberal bias or the free trade bias in American trade policy (see Goldstein 1988). What in the world were they talking about? When I finally understood their terminology, it turned out that what they were arguing made a lot of sense.

In discussing the biases of institutional arrangements, you always need to be careful to specify the bias as compared with what alternative. Compared with the idealized norm of policies that produce aggregate economic efficiency, the political process clearly tends to operate with a protectionist bias due to incentives of well-informed and politically active special interests, as is highlighted in standard public choice analysis. But compared with the trade policy institutions that we had prior to the mid-1930s, today's institutional framework for making trade policy decisions does have a distinctly liberal trade bias. If you take simple interest-group models of trade policy, their predictions tend to look much more like the disastrous Smoot-Hawley tariff of the 1930s than the much milder incidence of protectionist policies that we see today.

With the increasing pressures for protectionism that have been generated in recent years, why has the actual increase in protection been so much less than in the 1930s? Part of the answer is that despite all of the complaints about the performance of the American economy, we are far removed from the horrendous economic conditions of the 1930s. But another very important part of the answer is that we operate under a fundamentally different institutional framework for trade policy making today then we did when Smoot-Hawley was passed. Major reforms were fostered by the debacle of the Great Depression and Smoot-Hawley.

These reforms reflected a basic shift in how trade policy was viewed. Previously, it was viewed almost totally as a domestic political issue. Smoot-Hawley is easy to explain in terms of rent seeking by interest groups, domestically oriented legislators, and a relatively indifferent executive branch.[18] While the depth of the Great Depression was hardly due entirely to Smoot-Hawley, the beggar-thy-neighbor trade policy it helped trigger was highly visible, and this temporal association gave important ammunition to liberal-trade advocates. Trade policy clearly could be seen as an important element of foreign policy, not just domestic policy. With the disaster of Smoot-Hawley fresh in mind, Congress proved willing to reduce substantially its say in the making of trade policy. The role of the executive branch in formulating trade policy was substantially strengthened by changes both in the institutional framework and in the ideological or conceptual frameworks of many of the participants in the policy process. Arguments for free trade became closely associated with broad US national security and foreign policy interests.[19]

Cordell Hull, the secretary of state during that period, was a key player in this process. He drew the lesson that the seeds of World War II were sown by the failure of postwar international economic planning at the end of World War I, which in turn contributed to the Great Depression. He was a firm believer in free trade, not so much for its economic benefits, but because this would be a major plank of US foreign policy to build a more secure world. US policy toward trade became dominated by the idea that whether it was in our immediate economic interests or not, fostering a liberal international economic system certainly lay in our foreign policy interest. Combined with reforms of the institutional framework giving the executive branch a much stronger say in making international trade policy, this shift of attitude generated a fundamental change in the policy process. In the early postwar period, these changes in domestic institutional structures were reinforced by international commitments under the General Agreement on Tariffs and Trade.

There is a wonderful irony in this analysis, because essentially what I am arguing is that the realist model of the unified rational actor of the state pursuing its perception of the national interest actually has substantial explanatory power with respect to US international trade policy in the postwar period, but that what it explains is liberal, not protectionist trade policies.[20] On this interpretation, the increased protectionism that we see in the United States today is a reflection of a decrease rather than an increase in the explanatory power of the realist model in terms of its focus on the autonomy of the state. When one looks at the structure of the increased protection, what one sees primarily is not a highly autonomous government undertaking increasingly active strategic trade policies based on maximizing the national interest, but rather a weakened and fragmented government that is forced to cater increasingly to a multitude of domestic political pressures. Increased import competition has increased domestic political pressure for protection. At the same time, but for a variety of reasons including the end of the Cold War, there has been a general decline in the strength of the executive branch relative to Congress. Both Democratic and Republican administrations have continued to advocate much more liberal trade policies than those favored by the typical member of Congress, but the political strength of executive branch arguments has declined. Though the power of executive branch support for liberal trade policies on foreign policy grounds is still substantial—witness the passage of NAFTA—it is substantially less than it was in the 1940s and 1950s.

In summary, I would argue that we have a relatively simple explanation for the current trend toward increased but still rather limited protectionism in the United States. Part of it is increased interest-group lobbying because of increased import competition. The traditional public choice analysis from an interest-group perspective has important explanatory power, but taken in a vacuum it would predict considerably more protection than is observed. Countering these pressures, we have the clout of a relatively strong executive branch with lots of institutional arrangements biased in the direction of giving us more liberal trade policy outcomes than would come out of a policy process dominated by Congress. It's the decline in the power of the realist model (in its liberal form) relative to the domestic interest-group, rent-seeking model that gives rise both to the particular incidents of discretionary voluntary export restraints, quotas, and so on, and that have also given rise to recent pressures to revise again our basic trade policy institutions, this time to reduce the power of the executive branch.

IV. MONETARY DISCIPLINE

Let me now turn briefly to an analysis of macroeconomics and international monetary issues. Here, public choice analysis has had a major impact. The vast majority of economists working on these issues do look at them in fundamentally different ways today than in the days when I was learning my international monetary economics at the University of Virginia. In those days, when considering reform of the international monetary system, almost everyone focused on the provision of a stable international monetary environment in a way that minimized constraints on discretionary macroeconomic policy making. In other words, we asked, How do we give maximum freedom to domestic policymakers? Even in those days there were some economists who were saying, no, we should really be focusing on discipline in monetary policies, that an unconstrained government would have an inflationary bias. But this was really a very distinct minority. Today this normative view is widespread, albeit not universal, among economists.[21]

The key insight underlying this shift in view is the recognition that governments cannot always be counted upon to operate in the public interest and to maximize aggregate efficiency. While substantial use is still made of optimal policy models, applied policy economists increasingly recognize the need to take into account the political pressures and incentives that governments face. The recent literature in money and macroeconomics is full of analysis of political business cycles and time inconsistency issues that can generate incentives for governments to follow destabilizing policies.[22]

In considering the design of international monetary regimes, one can draw very different types of implications from such analysis. One approach is to assume that there will likely be considerable instability in domestic macroeconomic policies and to adopt an international regime that will minimize the effects of this instability on international activities and other countries. This offers a powerful damage control argument for flexible exchange rates for larger countries.

At the other extreme, many have drawn the conclusion that such propensities for domestic instability increase the case for fixed exchange rates in order to force macroeconomic discipline upon governments and constrain such propensities. Over the past decade, this idea of using the exchange rate as a nominal anchor to constrain domestic inflation has gained enormous popularity.[23] The argument is certainly not without merit, but it has been greatly oversold.

There are two fundamental issues that have received inadequate attention by many advocates of this approach. One is whether the exchange rate will be an effective constraint on domestic policies. The second is whether it is the most appropriate type of constraint. These two considerations will, of course, interact. The more costly is the constraint, the less likely it is that it will remain in effective operation. What matters primarily for policy making are political costs. How these are affected by the distribution of economic costs and benefits from exchange rate policies has unfortunately been studied much less than is the case for international trade policies.

Contrary to the way the argument is often presented, discipline considerations do not present an independent argument for fixed exchange rates in general, although they may for particular countries. Granting the case for the adoption of institutional mechanisms to foster discipline, the question becomes whether such arrangements should be domestically or internationally based. There is, of course, a vast literature on the merits of different types of institutional arrangements designed to promote monetary discipline.[24] Potential problems have been identified with all of the approaches, so evaluation must rest on the comparison of various imperfect alternatives. Such evaluation must consider issues both of political implementation and of the economic effects of the alternative approaches. While the former issue is largely one for public choice analysis, standard economic analysis is relevant for the latter.

We can draw powerful implications from the theory of optimum currency areas.[25] This literature argues that there is no one right answer for all countries about the relative desirability of fixed versus flexible exchange rates. There are costs and benefits to each, and the balance may vary tremendously depending upon the characteristics of the country involved. A major conclusion is that on economic grounds, fixed exchange rates are generally more desirable for small, open economies and flexible exchange rates are more desirable for large economies. Intuitively, one can think of the issue as being whether, in the face of disturbances, the international sector should be adjusted to the domestic economy or the domestic economy should be adjusted to the international sector. Fixed exchange rates imply the latter strategy. For small, open economies like Austria, Estonia, and Hong Kong, this form of monetary constraint may make a good deal of sense.[26] For large economies like Germany, Japan, and the United States, it does not. In such countries, one should look to domestically based institutional approaches to provide monetary discipline.

Failure to recognize the differences in countries' economic interests with respect to exchange rate regimes was a major source of difficulty with the Bretton Woods international monetary system established at the end of World War II and a major cause of the collapse of its adjustably pegged exchange rate mechanism in the early 1970s. This is a failure that has been repeated in the recent political push for a European Monetary Union.[27]

A second lesson from the Bretton Woods system that still has not been universally learned is the fundamental distinction between adjustably pegged and genuinely fixed exchange rates and the difficulties of operating the former. For the exchange rate to serve as a genuine source of long-run monetary discipline, it must be extremely difficulty to change. Examples are parities under the gold standard and currency board arrangements, such as those in Estonia, which provide substantial institutional impediments to changing the rate. Often, however, discussions of exchange rates as nominal anchors refer to temporarily pegged exchange rates. In some circumstances, they may give an economy a beneficial short-term quick fix, but they should not be confused with more genuinely fixed rates that provide a long-run constraint on domestic monetary and fiscal policies.[28]

While unlikely to provide an important long-run source of discipline, such adjustably pegged exchange rates could, on economic grounds, provide a reasonable compromise between fixed and flexible exchange rates for some countries. This was one of the basic ideas of the Bretton Woods system. The general failure of this approach to operate well in practice is another illustration of the importance of public choice analysis. In designing economic regimes, we must consider not just whether a mechanism exists to deal with each type of major problem that may arise but also whether it is technically feasible and whether political incentives will permit its implementation. When I first studied the problems of the Bretton Woods system as a graduate student, I assumed that this was a typical example of governments adopting policies that conflicted with the advice of economists. To my surprise, I learned that Bretton Woods was designed primarily by economists, including John Maynard Keynes, who was the chief British negotiator. On purely economic grounds, it was a logically consistent system. The Bretton Woods system became inconsistent and eventually broke down in large part because political considerations kept the mechanisms provided from being implemented in a timely fashion.[29]

For an adjustably pegged exchange rate system to work well, exchange rate parities must be adjusted promptly in the face of emerging disequilibrium. There are considerable technical difficulties in identifying emerging disequilibrium, but an even greater problem is the political incentive to delay adjustments. While exchange rate adjustments will impose net economic costs on some groups and net benefits on others, the conventional wisdom of officials is that they will face more political heat from those who are hurt than they will reap in political gains from those who are helped. Furthermore, devaluations are widely considered to be an admission of the failure of a government's economic policies. This is compounded by the tendency of officials to try to calm speculative markets by publicly pledging that exchange rates will not be changed, thus increasing their political incentives to attempt to maintain the peg, even when they have increasing doubts about its long-run sustainability. Statements by top Mexican officials during 1994 provide a recent example of such behavior. Uncertainties about future balance of payments developments and their implications for equilibrium exchange rates contribute to the tendency for overly optimistic forecasts that pegs can be maintained. The interaction of these considerations resulted in the breakdown of the Bretton Woods exchange rate system after a series of increasingly large exchange rate crises. This was repeated with the breakdown of the pegged rates within the European monetary system in 1992 and 1993.[30] The Mexican exchange rate crisis in 1995 provides more evidence (see Willett 1995).

With all of this theory and history pointing to the problems of pegged rates, why have they retained such popularity among governments? The answer, at least in part, comes from the same source that creates many of the incentives for unstable domestic macroeconomic policies in the first place: the difference between short-run and long-run effects combined with the short time horizon adopted by many government officials. In the case of macro policy, unless policies are fully anticipated and wages and prices are highly flexible, the initial effects of changes in policy show up more heavily on output and less on prices. Consequently, expansions have more favorable effects in the short run than over the longer term, whereas just the reverse occurs with contractions. These considerations give governments perceived incentives to generate inflationary surprises and disincentives to bear the short-run costs of disinflation. (The substantial disinflation in most industrial countries during the 1980s suggests, of course, that these aren't the only considerations at work.)

Pegging exchange rates has a similar incentive structure. There may be considerable short-run benefits to establishing a pegged rate, while the prospective costs of having to deal with substantial exchange rate disequilibrium typically will not occur until well into the future. With luck, one may be able to buy some short-run anti-inflation credibility on the cheap by implying a strong commitment to the current peg or a limited rate of downward crawl, while retaining the option for future exchange rate adjustments if needed.[31] With the far-sighted actors assumed in most of our game theoretic literature, such a strategy of attempting to have one's cake and eat it too would not be expected to work. But, in the real world, such considerations do not seem to be sufficient to keep governments from sometimes trying. One can only hope that the recent failures of this strategy will provide a cautionary note.

The recent Mexican experience is quite instructive in this regard. It appears that in the short run, the Mexican adoption of a slowly crawling peg did help secure lower wage settlements and contributed to the extremely successful disinflation from triple to single digits. Surely the major cause of success, however, was the prudent monetary and fiscal policies the government followed. Unfortunately, by tying much of the credibility of their policy strategy to the exchange rate, the government put itself in a very vulnerable position. The emergence of strong indications of substantial overvaluation coincided with an approaching presidential election, so that there were particularly strong political incentives to delay adjustment. On top of this, it now appears that the disequilibrium was worsened by expansionary fiscal and monetary preelection policies. Over this period, instead of there being a discipline effect from the pegged rate system, it added to the incentives for preelection expansion. The old government managed to keep the emerging balance of payments crisis under control before the election, but a very heavy price was paid by the new government when the rapid depletion of international reserves caused by capital outflows forced a devaluation soon after it took office. Because of the emphasis on the pegged system in the government's policy strategy, what should have been the moderate economic effects of a needed exchange rate adjustment due to changing balance of payments conditions became instead a crisis of confidence in the government's whole economic strategy. This led to a substantial increase in inflation and inflationary expectations and a much greater depreciation of the exchange rate than would have been needed if an adjustment had been made in a timely fashion.

In summary, I believe that one should be very wary of efforts to use the exchange rate as a source of monetary discipline. While this can be effective in some cases—the hard currency pegs of Austria and the Netherlands to the German mark are examples—the nature of the pegging relationships involved must be carefully analyzed. The case for adopting institutional arrangements to promote monetary and fiscal discipline is strong, but for countries of substantial size, exchange-rate based mechanisms will typically not be the most effective approach and, indeed, are subject to substantial abuse. In general, we need to look to domestically rather than internationally based mechanisms for promoting discipline.[32]

V. CONCLUDING REMARKS

This lecture has touched upon only a few of the areas in which public choice analysis has been fruitfully applied to the study of international economic relations. Beyond the traditional focus of international economics on international trade and monetary issues, today there is also increasing interest in areas such as international environmental and resource management, international cost sharing of the provision of public goods, economic sanctions and security aspects of international trade, and the role of international organizations. Public choice analysis and the closely related approaches of the transaction cost economics and the new institutional economics have made important contributions in all of these areas as well.[33] The scope for such applications is far from exhausted. My hope (and expectation) is that public choice analysis will increasingly inform the work of international economists and political scientists specializing in international political economy, and that this, in turn, will have an increasing impact on the formulation of international economic policies and the operation of international economic institutions.

NOTES

The author gratefully acknowledges helpful comments on earlier drafts from David Andrew, Tom Borcherding, Bill Brown, Richard Burdekin, Benjamin J. Cohen, David Feldman, Yi Feng, Bruno Frey, Jürgen von Hagen, Eduard Hochreiter, Tom Ilgen, Bill Kaempfer, Steve Marks, Pamela Martin, Nancy Nieman, Lewis Snider, W. Craig Stubblebine, Edward Tower, Roland Vaubel, and Paul Zak.

1. Interestingly, while Frey (1984a, 1984b) mentions the stress on rigor as one of the main characteristics of the public choice approach to international political economy, Colander (1984), comparing the approaches to political economy analysis taken by international trade and public choice economists, describes the trade economists as formalists while arguing that "public choice theorists are nonformalists and integrate far more ideas into their implicit model" (7). He goes on to argue that there are significant potential gains from trade between these approaches. While it seems fair to say that, on average, the degree of rigor declines and breadth of ideas increases as one goes from the work of international trade economists to public choice economists to political scientists writing on political economy, a full spectrum of rigor and breadth is reflected in the work of all three groups. See Odell and Willett (1990). I have argued for the fruitfulness of taking a broad public choice approach to the analysis of the political economy of monetary policy (Willett 1990). For valuable characterizations of key elements of the public choice approach to analyzing international issues in addition to Frey (1994a, 1984b), see Smith (1991).
2. See also Barry Jones (1983) and the popular readers in international political economy edited by Crane and Amawi (1991) and Frieden and Lake (1991, 1995). Many of the major articles in international political economy have been conveniently collected in a series of volumes published by Edward Elgar. These include Baldwin (1993a), Cohen (1993), Grieco (1993), and Lake (1993).
3. In his book, Gilpin (1985) changes his label for these approaches from models to ideologies and argues that they are akin to different paradigms in the sense of Thomas Kuhn, in that they are not subject to empirical testing. This is likely a fair characterization of some of the normative elements of these approaches, but it does not apply to their formulations as theories of positive political economy. In places, Gilpin does use the distinction between positive and normative analysis, but he does not apply the distinction systematically to his analysis of the three approaches.
4. Frieden and Lake (1991) likewise begin their discussion of "Three Perspectives on International Political Economy" with the statement, "Nearly all studies in International Political Economy can he classified into one of three mutually exclusive perspectives: Liberalism, Marxism, and Realism" (5). In the latest edition of their reader, Frieden and Lake (1995) give considerably less weight to these three approaches and focus more on a four-way

classification based on the strength of states versus societal pressures and international versus domestic considerations. In my judgment, this is a much more productive framework.

5. Of course, there are also important noneconomic motives for tariffs, such as economic sanctions adopted for foreign policy reasons.

6. See Kaempfer and Lowenberg (1992) for a public choice approach to international relations from the perspective of one tool—namely, economic sanctions.

7. One of the strongest recent advocates of the primacy of realism over relative gains is Joseph Grieco (1990). In my judgment, Grieco substantially overstates the extent to which security considerations should generate a rational focus on relative economic gains and ignores the extent to which rent seeking by interest groups induces governments to behave as if they were pursuing relative rather than absolute gains. The focus in GATT on import liberalization as a cost is an example of this later point. See, for example, Finger (1991). For an excellent critical review of the recent international relations literature on absolute versus relative gains, see Milner (1992), and on the broader debate between neorealism and neoliberalism, see Baldwin (1993b).

8. I contrast the optimal policy and political economy or public choice approaches to international monetary analysis in Willett (1983).

9. See, for example, Lindert (1991) and Markusen et al. (1995). Other frequent mischaracterizations of standard economics and liberalism include statements that "Liberalism also assumes that a market exists in which individuals have complete information" (Gilpin 1987, 28) and that the "economic rationality" of the liberal perspective is "a notion which soon confirms rational choice is the maximization of only those objectives which can be satisfied through market exchanges and which therefore ignores (and ultimately legitimizes) all those other needs, wants, and desires which an individual may well seek to satisfy through his actions and choices" (Barry Jones 1983, 175). For further analysis of mischaracterizations in the political economy literature of modern economics and international trade theory, see Dillon, Lehman, and Willett (1990).

10. Frieden and Lake (1991) argue that "the principal Liberal approach known generally as public choice or rational choice thinks of the political area as a market place. . . . This view, closely related to long-standing theories of interest group pluralism, sees government action as the result of competition among politicians, and among their constituents" (7).

11. See, for example, Destler (1986), Destler and Odell (1987), Goldstein (1993), Gourevitch (1986), Katzenstein (1978], Milner (1988), O'Halloran (1994), Putnam (1988), Verdier (1994), and the contributions in Ikenberry, Lake, and Mastanduno (1988) and Odell and Willett (1990). Political scientists coming to international political economy from a background in comparative politics are much more likely to stress the importance of domestic political considerations than those coming from international relations theory.

12. During 1969 and 1970, I served as a senior staff economist at the Council of Economic Advisers. From 1972 to 1977, I worked at the US Treasury, first as deputy assistant secretary for International Research and Planning and then as director of International Monetary Research.

13. This was in the 1970s. More recently, especially with the strong dollar of the first half of the 1980s, concern with effects on particular economic groups appears to have begun to play more of a role in discussion of US international monetary policies. See Destler and Henning (1989) and Henning (1994).

14. The conservative welfare function formulation is concerned with reductions in income, which appear to be caused by adverse economic developments beyond the control of the group in question. This formulation can thus explain the relevance of public-interest cloaked arguments for support of steel and autoworkers with well above average worker incomes. Note that to be politically effective, public-interest cloaked arguments do not necessarily need to be economically sound. The public choice concept of rational ignorance has considerable explanatory power.

15. For a nice discussion of the distinctions between the Hecksher-Ohlin and specific factor theories, see the basic international economics text by Lindert (1991). For political economy applications of these theories, see Magee, Brock, and Young (1989), Midford (1993), and Rogowski (1987, 1989).

16. See the recent contribution by Cote and Morris (1995). Specifically on this issue with respect to the use of tariffs versus quotas, see the analysis and references in Kaempfer and Willett (1989) and Kaempfer, Tower, and Willett (1990).

17. Amacher, Tollison, and Willett (1979). For recent applications, surveys, and references to the recent public choice and political science literature on the political economy of protectionism, see Daldwin (1985), Cohen (1990), Conybeare (1987), Goldstein (1993), Hillman (1989), Nelson (1988), Odell (1990), Odell and Willett (1990), Oye (1992), Rodrik (1995), and Rowley, Thorbecke, and Wagner (1995). On the issue of tariffs versus quotas, see the references in Kaempfer, Tower, and Willett (1990) and Kaempfer and Willett (1989). While most applications have been to the United States and other industrial countries, there has been an increasing number of important applications to developing countries as well. See, for example, Krueger (1993).

18. See the analysis and references in Eichengreen (1989) and Ferguson (1984). The classic analysis of the role of special interests is by Schattschneider (1935).

19. For detailed discussion of these changes, see Destler (1986), Goldstein (1988, 1993), and Haggard (1988). For evidence that median legislator models explain changes in US tariff levers well before these institutional changes but not afterward, see Hansen and Prussa (1996). On the role of ideology in US trade policy, see also Baldwin (1985) and McArthur and Marks (1988).

20. Realist models of hegemonic stability theory are also used to explain the increase in protectionist pressures across the industrial countries as a function of the perceived decline in the United States' hegemonic power to impose a liberal trading order. Various versions of hegemonic stability theory stimulated by the initial work of Charles Kindleberger have been subject to considerable debate in the international political economy literature. For a sympathetic interpretation, see Gilpin (1987), and for a succinct critical survey of the key I use, see Gowa (1990). Of particular interest is the argument due to Conybeare (1984) that the Kindleberger version requires a public-interest or broader security-minded goal for the hegemonic government, since a narrow national economic-interest-maximizing hegemonic government would likely impose an optimal tariff.

21. For discussion and references on the discipline debate, see Willett and Mullen (1982).

22. See, for example, the analysis and references in Mayer (1990), Persson and Tabellini (1994), Sheffrin (1989), and Willett (1988).

23. For discussion and references on the nominal anchor debate, see Bruno (1991), Westbrook and Willett (1999), and Willett and Al-Marhubi (1994).

24. See the analysis and references in Dorn and Schwartz (1987), Wijnholds, Eijffinger, and Hoogduin (1994), and Willett (1988).

25. For surveys of this literature, see Talvas (1993) and Tower and Willett (1976), and for recent applications, see Sweeney, Wihlborg, and Willett (1999).

26. Hochreiter and Winckler (1995) argue that Austria did not fully meet the criteria for forming an optimum currency area with Germany when the Austrian hard currency policy was initiated, but that the strategy generated responses such as increased wage and price flexibility, which moved Austria closer to these criteria. For policy, what is most important for countries deciding to pursue a pegged rate strategy is that they not deviate too greatly from the optimum currency area criteria.

27. See Willett (1994). On the political motivations behind the push for a European Monetary Union, see also the contributions and references in Eichengreen and Frieden (1995).

28. It is often difficult to tell just how "fixed" a particular exchange rate regime is. While neither Austria nor the Czech Republic have formal legal obligations to maintain their fixed exchange rates, these governments' commitments to maintaining these pegs appear to be quite strong, and the political costs of abandoning them would likely be quite high.
29. On Keynes's tendency to assume that government policies will be determined by experts operating in the public interest, free from political pressures, see Buchanan and Wagner (1977). On the establishment and breakdown of the Bretton Woods system, see the analysis and references in Solomon (1982) and Willett (1977).
30. On the operation of the European Monetary System and the 1992 and 1993 crises, see Abegaz et al. (1994), Fratianni and von Hagen (1992), Portes (1993), and Wijnholds, Eijffinger, and Hoogduin (1994).
31. For a similar argument, see Cohen (1993).
32. On the recent interest in central bank independence and optimal contracting approaches to promoting monetary discipline, see Banaian, Burdekin, and Willett (1995), Burdekin and Willett (1995), Cukierman (1992), Gruner and Hefeker (1995), Lohmann (1992), and Walsh (1995).
33. See, for example, Eckert (1979), Gowa (1994), Kaempfer and Lowenberg (1992), Keohane (1984), Vaubel and Willett (1991), and Yarbrough and Yarbrough (1992).

REFERENCES

Amacher, Ryan C., Robert Tollison, and Thomas D. Willett. 1979. "The Divergence between Theory and Practice." In Walter Adams et al., *Tariffs, Quotas, and Trade: The Politics of Protectionism*, 55–66. Washington, DC: Institute for Contemporary Studies.

Baldwin, Robert. 1985. *The Political Economy of U.S. Import Policy*. Cambridge, MA: MIT Press.

——— (ed.). 1993a. *Key Concepts in International Political Economy*. Vol. I and II. Cheltenham, UK: Edward Elgar.

——— (ed.). 1993b. *Neorealism and Neoliberalism: The Contemporary Debate*. New York: Columbia University Press.

Banaian, King, Richard Burdekin, and Thomas D. Willett. 1995. "On the Political Economy of Central Bank Interdependence." In Kevin D. Hoover and Steven Sheffrin (eds.), *Monetarism and Methodology in Economics: Essays in Honor of Thomas Mayer*. Cheltenham, UK: Edward Elgar.

Barry Jones, R. J. 1983. "Perspectives on International Political Economy." In R. J. Barry Jones (ed.), *Perspectives on Political Economy*, 169–208. New York: St. Martin's Press.

Brennan, Geoffrey, and James M. Buchanan. 1980. *The Power to Tax*. New York: Cambridge University Press.

Bruno, Michael. 1991. "High Inflation and the Nominal Anchors of an Open Economy." *Essays in International Finance* 183 (June): 1–29.

Buchanan, James, and Richard Wagner. 1977. *Democracy in Deficit: The Political Legacy of Lord Keynes*. Cambridge, MA: Academic Press.

Burdekin, Richard C. K., and Thomas D. Willett. 1995. "Designing Central Bank Arrangements to Promote Monetary Stability." In Thomas D. Willett et al. (eds.), *Establishing Monetary Stability in Emerging Market Economies*, 115–26. Boulder, CO: Westview Press.

Carlos, Ann, William H. Kaempfer, and Gregory J. Layok. 1996. "Factor Interests in Lobbying for Commercial Policy: The Case of NAFTA." University of Colorado Working Paper.

Coate, Stephen, and Stephen Morris. 1995. "On the Form of Transfer to Special Interests." *Journal of Political Economy* 103 (December): 1210–35.

Cohen, Benjamin J. 1990. "The Political Economy of International Trade." *International Organization* 44(2): 261–81.

——— (ed.). 1993. *The International Political Economy of Monetary Relations*. Cheltenham, UK: Edward Elgar.

———. 1993. "The Triad and the Unholy Trinity." In Richard Higgott, Richard Leaver, and John Ravenhill (eds.), *Pacific Economic Relations in the 1990s*, 133–58. Crows Nest, Australia: Allen and Unwin (reprinted in Frieden and Lake 1995).

Colander, David (ed.). 1984. *Neoclassical Political Economy*. Pensacola, FL: Ballinger.

Conybeare, John. 1984. "Public Goods, Prisoners' Dilemmas and the International Political Economy." *International Studies Quarterly* 28: 5–22.

———. 1987. *Trade Wars: The Theory and Practice of International Commercial Rivalry*. New York: Columbia University Press.

Crane, G. T., and Abla Amawi (eds.). 1991. *The Theoretical Evolution of International Political Economy*. Oxford: Oxford University Press.

Cukierman, Alex. 1992. *Central Bank Strategy, Credibility, and Independence: Theory and Evidence*. Cambridge, MA: MIT Press.

Destler, I. M. 1986. *American Trade Politics: System Under Stress*. Washington, DC: Institute for International Economics.

Destler, I. M., and Randall Henning. 1989. *Dollar Politics: Exchange Rate Policy Making in the United States*. Washington, DC: Institute for International Economics.

Destler, I. M., and J. Odell. 1987. *Anti-Pollution: Changing Forces in United States Trade Politics*. Washington, DC: Institute for International Economics.

Dillon, Patricia, James Lehman, and Thomas D. Willett. 1990. "Assessing the Usefulness of International Trade Theory for Policy Analysis." In John Odell and T. D. Willett (eds.), *International Trade Policies: The Gains from Exchange between Economics and Political Science*, 121–54. Ann Arbor: University of Michigan Press.

Dillon, Patricia, John Odell, and Thomas O. Willett. 1990. "Future Directions in the Political Economy of Trade Policy." In John Odell and T. D. Willett (eds.), *International Trade Policies: The Gains from Exchange between Economics and Political Science*, 278–83. Ann Arbor: University of Michigan Press.

Eckert, Ross. 1979. *The Enclosure of Ocean Resources: Economics and the Law of the Sea*. Stanford, CA: Hoover Institution.

Eichengreen, Barry. 1989. "The Political Economy of the Smooth-Hawley Tariff." *Research in Economic History* 12: 1–43.

Eichengreen, Barry, and Jeffrey Frieden (eds.). 1994. *The Political Economy of European Monetary Unification*. Boulder, CO: Westview Press.

Ekelund, Robert, and Robert Tollison. 1981. *Mercantilism as a Rent Seeking Society*. College Station: Texas A&M University Press.

Ferguson, Thomas. 1984. "From Normalcy to New Deal: Industrial Structure, Party Competition, and American Public Policy in the Great Depression." *International Organization* 38(1): 41–94.

Finger, Michael. 1991. "The GATT as an International Discipline over Trade Restrictions: A Public Choice Approach." In Roland Vaubel and Thomas D. Willett (eds.), *The Political Economy of International Organizations: A Public Choice Perspective*, 125–41. Boulder, CO: Westview Press.

Fratianni, Michele, and Jürgen von Hagen. 1992. *The European Monetary System and European Monetary Union*. Boulder, CO: Westview Press.

Frey, Bruno. 1984a. "The Public Choice View of International Political Economy." *International Organization* 38(1): 199–223.

———. 1984b. *International Political Economics*. Oxford: Basil Blackwell.

———. 1996. "The Public Choice of International Organizations." In Dennis Mueller (ed.), *Public Choice*, 106–23. Cambridge: Cambridge University Press.

Frieden, Jeffrey, and David Lake (eds.). 1991. *International Political Economy: Perspectives on Global Power and Wealth*, 2nd ed. New York: St. Martin's Press.

———. 1995. *International Political Economy: Perspectives on Global Power and Wealth*, 3rd ed. New York: St. Martin's Press.

Gilpin, Robert. 1975. "Three Models of the Future." *International Organization* 29(1): 37–60.

———. 1987. *The Political Economy of International Relations*. Princeton, NJ: Princeton University Press.

Goldstein, Judith. 1988. "Ideas, Institutions and American Trade Policy." In G. J. Ikenberry, D. Lake, and M. Mastanduno (eds.), *The State and American Foreign Economic Policy*, 179–218. Ithaca, NY: Cornell University Press.

———. 1993. *Ideas, Interests and American Trade Policy*. Ithaca, NY: Cornell University Press.

Gourevitch, Peter. 1986. *Politics in Hard Times*. Ithaca, NY: Cornell University Press.

Gowa, Joanne. 1988. "Public Goods and Political Institutions: Trade and Monetary Policy Processes in the United States." In G. J. Ikenberry, D. Lake, and M. Mastanduno (eds.), *The State and American Foreign Economic Policy*, 15–32. Ithaca, NY: Cornell University Press.

———. 1990. "An Epitaph for Hegemonic Stability Theory? Rational Hegemony Excludable Goods, and Small Groups." Reprinted in Odell and Willett (1990, 55–74).

———. 1994. *Allies, Adversaries and International Trade*. Princeton, NJ: Princeton University Press.

Grieco, Joseph. 1990. *Cooperation among Nations*. Ithaca, NY: Cornell University Press.

——— (ed.). 1993. *The International System and the International Political Economy*. Cheltenham, UK: Edward Elgar.

Gruner, Hans, and Carsten Hefeker. 1995. "Domestic Pressures and the Exchange Rate Regime: Why Economically Bad Decisions are Politically Popular." *Banca Nazionale del Lavoro Quarterly Review* (September): 331–50.

Haggard, Stephan. 1988. "The Institutional Foundations of Hegemony: Explaining the Reciprocal Trade Agreements Act of 1934." In G. J. Ikenberry, D. Lake, and M. Mastanduno (eds.), *The State and American Foreign Economic Policy*, 121–50. Ithaca, NY: Cornell University Press.

Hansen, Wendy, and Thomas Prussa. 1996. "Congressional Decision Making and the Rise of Delegation: An Application to Trade Policy." Departmental Working Papers 199409, Rutgers University, Department of Economics.

Henning, C. Randall. 1994. *Currencies and Politics in the United States, Germany and Japan*. Washington, DC: Institute for International Economics.

Hillman, Arye L. 1989. *The Political Economy of Protection*. Reading, UK: Harwood Academic.

———. 1989a. "Policy Motives and International Trade Restrictions." In Hans-Jürgen Vosgerau (ed.), *New Institutional Arrangements for the World Economy*. Berlin: Springer-Verlag.

Hochreiter, Eduard, and George Winckler. 1995. "The Advantages of Tying Austria's Hands: The Success of Austria's Hard Currency Policy." *European Journal of Political Economy* 11: 83–111.

Ikenberry, G. J., D. Lake, and M. Mastanduno (eds.). 1988. *The State and American Foreign Economic Policy*. Ithaca, NY: Cornell University Press.

Kaempfer, William H., and Anton Lowenberg. 1992. *International Economic Sanctions*. Boulder, CO: Westview Press.

Kaempfer, William H., Edward Tower, and Thomas D. Willett. 1990. "Optimal Performance, Contingent Protection to Achieve Political and Economic Objectives." *Economics and Politics* (November): 261–76.

Kaempfer, William H., and Thomas D. Willett. 1989. "Combining Rent Seeking and Public Choice Theory in the Analysis of Tariffs versus Quotas." *Public Choice* (October): 77–86.

Katzenstein, Peter (ed.). 1978. *Between Power and Plenty: Foreign Economic Policies of Advanced Industrial States.* Madison: University of Wisconsin Press.

Keohane, Robert. 1984. *After Hegemony: Cooperation and Discord in the World Political Economy.* Princeton, NJ: Princeton University Press.

Krasner, Stephen. 1972. "Are Bureaucracies Important?" *Foreign Affairs* 7 (Summer): 159–79.

Krueger, Anne. 1993. *Political Economy of Polity Reform in Developing Countries.* Cambridge, MA: MIT Press.

Lake, David, A. (ed.). 1993. *The International Political Economy of Trade*, vols. 1 and 2. Cheltenham, UK: Edward Elgar.

Lindert, Peter. 1991. *International Economics*, 9th ed. Boston: Irwin.

Lohmann, Susanne. 1992. "Optimal Commitment in Monetary Policy: Credibility versus Flexibility." *American Economics Review* 82: 273–86.

Lombra, Raymond E., and Willard E. Witte (eds.). *Political Economy of International and Domestic Monetary Relations.* Ames: Iowa State University Press.

Magee, S. P., W. A. Brock, and L. Young. 1989. *Black Hole Tariffs and Endogenous Policy Theory.* Cambridge: Cambridge University Press.

Markusen, J. R., J. R. Melvin, W. H. Kaempfer, and K. E. Maskus. 1995. *International Trade: Theory and Evidence.* New York: McGraw-Hill.

McArthur, John, and Stephen Marks. 1988. "Constituent Interest vs Legislator Ideology: The Role of Political Opportunity Costs." *Economic Inquiry* 26: 461–70.

Midford, Paul. 1993. "International Trade and Domestic Politics: Improving on Rogowski's Model of Political Alignments." *International Organization* 47(4): 535–64.

Milner, Helen V. 1988. *Resisting Protectionism: Global Industries and the Politics of International Trade.* Princeton, NJ: Princeton University Press.

———. 1992. "International Theories of Cooperation among Nations." *World Politics* 44 (April): 466–96.

Nelson, Douglas. 1988. "Endogenous Tariff Theory: A Critical Survey." *American Journal of Political Science* 32: 796–837.

Odell, John. 1990. "Understanding International Trade Policies: An Emerging Synthesis." *World Politics* 43(1): 139–67.

Odell, John, and T. D. Willett (eds.). 1990. *International Trade Policies: The Gains from Exchange between Economics and Political Science.* Ann Arbor: University of Michigan Press.

O'Halloran, Sharyn. 1994. *Politics, Process, and American Trade Policy.* Ann Arbor: University of Michigan Press.

Olson, Mancur. 1965. *The Logic of Collective Action.* Cambridge, MA: Harvard University Press.

Persson, Torsten, and Guido Tabellini. 1994. *Monetary and Fiscal Policy: Politics.* Cambridge, MA: MIT Press.

Portes, Richard. 1993. "EMS and EMU after the Fall." *World Economy* 16(1): 1–15.

Putnam, Robert D. 1988. "Diplomacy and Domestic Politics: The Logic of Two-Level Games." *International Organization* 42(3): 427–60.

Rodrik, Dani. 1995. "Political Economy of Trade Policy." In Gene Grossman and Kenneth Rogoff (eds.), *Handbook of International Economics*, 1457–94. Amsterdam: Elsevier.

Rogowski, Ronald. 1987. "Political Cleavages and Changing Exposure to Trade." *American Political Science Review* 21(4): 1121–37.

———. 1989. *Commerce and Coalitions: How Trade Affects Domestic Political Alignments*. Princeton, NJ: Princeton University Press.

Rowley, Charles, Willem Thorbecke, and Richard Wagner. 1995. *Trade Protection in the United States*. Cheltenham, UK: Edward Elgar.

Schattschneider, E. E. 1935. *Politics, Pressure and the Tariff*. New York: Prentice Hall.

Sheffrin, Steven. 1989. *The Making of Economic Policy*. Oxford: Basil Blackwell.

Smith, Rodney. 1991. "Canons of Public Choice Analysis of International Agreements." In Roland Vaubel and Thomas D. Willett (eds.), *The Political Economy of International Organizations: A Public Choice Perspective*, 46–57. Boulder, CO: Westview Press.

Solomon, Robert. 1982. *The International Monetary System, 1945–1981: An Insider's View*. New York: Harper and Row.

Staniland, Martin. 1985. *What Is Political Economy?* New Haven, CT: Yale University Press.

Sweeney, Richard J., Clas Wihlborg, and Thomas D. Willett (eds.). 1999. *Exchange Rate Policies for Emerging Market Economies*. Boulder, CO: Westview Press.

Tavlas, George S. 1993. "The New Theory of Optimum Currency Areas." *World Economy* 16(6): 663–85.

Tollison, Robert, and T. D. Willett. 1982. "Power, Politics and Prosperity: Alternative Views of Economic Interdependence." *Annals of the American Academy of Political and Social Science* 460 (March): 21–28.

Vaubel, Roland, and Thomas D. Willett (eds.). 1991. *The Political Economy of International Organizations: A Public Choice Perspective*. Boulder, CO: Westview Press.

Verdier, Danier. 1994. *Democracy and International Trade: Britain, France, and the United States, 1860–1990*. Princeton, NJ: Princeton University Press.

Vosgerau, Hans-Jürgen (ed.). 1989. *New Institutional Arrangements for the World Economy*. Berlin: Springer-Verlag.

Walsh, Carl. 1995. "Optimal Contracts for Central Banks." *American Economic Review* 85 (March): 150–67.

Westbrook, Jilleen, and Thomas D. Willett. 1999. "Exchange Rates as Nominal Anchors." In Richard J. Sweeney, Clas Wihlborg, and Thomas D. Willett (eds.), *Exchange Rate Policies for Emerging Market Economies*, 83–112. Boulder, CO: Westview Press.

Wijnholds, J., S. Eijffinger, and L. Hoogduin (eds.). 1994. *A Framework for Monetary Stability*. Dordrecht, the Netherlands: Kluwer.

Willett, Thomas D. 1977. *Floating Exchange Rates and International Monetary Reform*. Washington, DC: American Enterprise Institute for Public Policy Research.

———. 1983. "The Functioning of the Current International Financial System: Strengths, Weaknesses, and Criteria for Evaluation." In George M. von Furstenberg (ed.), *International Money and Credit: The Policy Roles*, 5–44. Washington, DC: International Monetary Fund.

———. 1987. "A New Monetary Constitution? An Evaluation of the Need and Major Alternatives." In James Dorn and Anna Schwartz (eds.), *The Search for Stable Money*, 145–60. Chicago: University of Chicago Press.

——— (ed.). 1988. *Political Business Cycles: The Political Economy of Money, Inflation, and Unemployment*. Durham, NC: Duke University Press.

———. 1989. "Policy Motives and International Trade Restrictions: Comments." In Hans-Jürgen Vosgerau (ed.), *New Institutional Arrangements for the World Economy*, 303–9. Berlin: Springer-Verlag.

———. 1990. "Studying the Fed: Towards a Broader Public Choice Perspective." In Thomas Mayer (ed.), *The Political Economy of American Monetary Policy*, 13–26. Cambridge: Cambridge University Press.

———. 1994. "Some Often Neglected Aspects of the Political Economy of European Monetary Integration." In B. Abegaz et al. (eds.), *The Challenge of European Integration*, 205–18. Boulder, CO: Westview Press.

———. 1995a. "Guidelines for Constructing Monetary Constitutions." In Willett et al. (eds.), *Establishing Monetary Stability in Emerging Market Economies*, 103–14. Boulder, CO: Westview Press.

———. 1995b. "The Plunge of the Peso: The Dangers of Exchange-Rate Based Stabilization Policy." Claremont Polity Briefs No. 95-01. Claremont, CA: Lowe Institute of Political Economy.

Willett, Thomas D., and F. Al-Marhubi. 1994. "Currency Policies for Inflation Control in the Formerly Centrally Planned Economies." *World Economy* 17(6): 795–815.

Willett, Thomas D., Richard Burdekin, Richard Sweeney, and Clas Wihlborg (eds.). 1995. *Establishing Monetary Stability in Emerging Market Economies*. Boulder, CO: Westview Press.

Willett, Thomas D., and John Mullen. 1982. "The Effects of Alternative International Monetary Systems on Macroeconomic Discipline and Inflationary Biases." In Raymond E. Lombra and W. E. Witte (eds.), *Political Economy of International and Domestic Monetary Relations*, 143–56. Ames: Iowa State University Press.

Willett, Thomas D., and John Odell (eds.). 1990. *International Trade Policies: The Gains from Exchange between Economics and Political Science*. Ann Arbor: University of Michigan Press.

Willett, Thomas D., and Edward Tower. 1976. *The Theory of Optimum Currency Areas and Exchange Rate Flexibility*. Princeton Special Papers in International Finance, No. 11. Princeton, NJ: International Finance Section, Department of Economics, Princeton University.

Yarbrough, Beth, and Robert Yarbrough. 1992. *Cooperation and Governance in International Trade*. Princeton, NJ: Princeton University Press.

5.12
The Economics of Welfare Reform

EDGAR K. BROWNING

It is a great pleasure for me to have the opportunity to deliver the Twelfth Annual Virginia Political Economy Lecture. As some of you know, I am a Virginian, one of the few "real" Virginians associated with the "Virginia School." Moreover, I was an undergraduate at the University of Virginia in the 1960s when the as-yet-unnamed "Virginia School" of economics was in its infancy. Although undergraduates are often far removed from the intellectual activity in their major department, I was involved in a program that required me to take several graduate-level courses, something I would never have had the courage to do on my own. Consequently, I took five graduate courses from Drs. Buchanan, Yeager, and Nutter. I have often said that I learned most of the economics I know at the University of Virginia, largely in these five courses. My one regret is that I missed the influence of Gordon Tullock while at the university. If he were here, he would probably tell you that my lingering intellectual deficiencies can be attributed to that oversight.

I would probably not have gone on to specialize in public finance had I not taken Dr. Buchanan's graduate Public Finance seminar. Among other things, his course taught me how to write papers quickly. At the time, he required a

Prepared for the Twelfth Annual Lecture in the Virginia Political Economy Lecture Series, George Mason University, Fairfax, VA, March 15, 1996.

1,000-word paper approximately every other week. Confronted with the first assignment, which was on whether there was double taxation of saving under an income tax, I must have spent 20 or 30 hours searching the literature trying to find something intelligent to say. I was not too successful; I got a B– or C. As the semester wore on, I found less and less time to devote to these papers, but surprisingly my grades went up. By the end of the semester, I got an A on the final paper that I had written in two hours the night before it was due. There seemed to be a new economic principle operating here: the less work you do, the better the result. Since then, I have engaged in extensive firsthand empirical work trying to confirm this youthful insight into the way the world works, but for some reason convincing proof remains elusive.

I do want to assure you, however, that I did not write the paper I am going to discuss today in two hours last night, but you will have to decide whether that is a good or a bad omen.

HOW MUCH DO WE REDISTRIBUTE?

It always surprises me how many people believe that the United States does relatively little to help low-income persons. Conservatives, especially public choice scholars, seem inclined to this view, perhaps because it would then constitute yet another instance of "government failure." George Stigler was one of the first to make the case on public choice grounds in his discussion of Director's Law: "Public expenditures are made for the primary benefit of the middle classes, and financed with taxes which are borne in considerable part by the poor and rich" (Stigler 1970, 1). Lee and McKenzie, in their provocative application of public choice theory to redistribution, put it this way: "There is no *a priori* reason . . . for believing the distributional outcome of political activity will differ much, if any, from that of market activity. . . . Expanding government for the stated purpose of improving the relative position of the poor will almost surely fail to do so" (Lee and McKenzie 1988). Mitchell and Simmons echo this view in their public choice text: "The political process not only promotes inefficiency but is skewed to advance the interests of those who are better off. Those who do well in the marketplace also do well in the polity" (Mitchell and Simmons 1994, 81).

Despite the prevalence of this view, I believe the truth is the exact opposite. Given the complexities involved in trying to evaluate the overall distributional impact of all government policies, it is easy to adduce bits of evidence that seem to support the proposition that government doesn't help the poor. It is common, for example, to point to the virtually unchanged share of income going to the lowest quintile of households, or the lack of reduction in the official poverty rate in the last 25 years, as proof of the absence of effective redistribution. But these data are very misleading for several reasons, not the least of which is that they are based on cash incomes, and most redistributive spending does not take the form of cash transfers.

To suggest the magnitude of downward redistribution, note that in 1992 federal, state, and local governments spent a total of $290 billion on 81 programs which are means-tested; that is, with benefits that go only to persons with low incomes (Congressional Research Service 1993, table 1). This sum does not include social insurance spending, such as Social Security or unemployment insurance, since these programs are not means-tested. There are, of course, a number of other programs that also redistribute downward, but I will consider only two: Medicare and public schools.[1] If we assume that 20 percent of the total spending on these programs accrues to the benefit of low-income persons—a plausible assumption if we think of the lifetime effect—this constitutes another $90 billion going to those with low incomes, bringing the total to $380 billion, or more than 7 percent of net national product.

For a variety of reasons, this sum does not represent a net redistribution to low-income households. For example, the figures for government expenditures include the costs of administering the programs, which in themselves are no benefit to low income persons, but administrative costs rarely exceed 10 or 12 percent of outlays.[2] So let us assume that $50 billion, or 13 percent, is absorbed as administrative costs. Taxes are also paid by low-income households, but they are small enough to be ignored.[3] Thus, I suggest that about $330 billion in resources actually goes to low-income households. Most, but certainly not all, of these transfers go to households in the lowest quintile of the income distribution.

To provide some perspective on whether $330 billion is a "large" redistribution, let us compare it to the total income of all households in the lowest quintile of the income distribution. In 1992, the Census Bureau counted $141 billion as the total cash income of the lowest quintile of households. The only major programs included in the $330 billion figure whose benefits are counted as income by the Census Bureau are Aid to Families with Dependent Children (AFDC) and Supplemental Security Income (SSI). But if we reduce the $330 billion figure by subtracting AFDC and SSI, we get $288 billion in spending (net of administrative costs), and virtually none of this is counted in the conventional Census figures. Consider what this means: the lowest quintile receives $141 billion in cash income (three-fourths of which is government cash transfers) that is counted by the Census, but it also receives the bulk of

$288 billion in resources that is simply not counted. As a rough approximation, that means the true "income" of the lowest quintile is about three times the amount that is usually counted, and most of this income is in the form of government transfers. Overall, about 90 percent of this quintile's income takes the form of government cash and in-kind transfers; that is, it is a redistribution from the upper part of the income distribution.

I realize that this discussion—I won't dignify it by calling it an analysis—has a lot of loose ends. It largely ignores taxes, shifting and incidence of programs, general government spending, regulatory costs, welfare costs, rent-seeking costs, and the distinction between annual and longer-run, or lifetime, effects. I have considered these factors, and as best I can determine, they do not overturn the general proposition that I am trying to suggest: to wit, that there is in fact a large redistribution downward, at least large relative to the market earnings of those in the lowest fifth of the income distribution.

It is natural to consider what this means for the poverty population. In 1992, there were 36.9 million people living in households with incomes below their respective poverty lines. As mentioned earlier, total expenditures for means-tested programs (not counting Medicare or public schools) was $290 billion in that year, or about $252 billion net of administrative costs. This expenditure is enough to provide a transfer of $27,000 for each poor family of four, well above the poverty line of $14,335 in 1992. How can there still be 36.9 million poor people when we are obviously devoting more than enough resources to raise them all above their poverty lines? This familiar comparison is often taken as evidence that the poor don't get the resources intended for them because the welfare bureaucracy siphons off a large chunk. But we have already netted out administrative costs. Another interpretation is that this shows that the non-poor get the benefits instead of the poor. To a limited degree this is true, but the largest reason is, as before, that most of this spending is on in-kind programs that are not counted as income in measuring poverty.

Just how poor are families that are officially counted as living in poverty? No one knows with certainty, of course, but a growing body of evidence suggests that the poor are not as deprived of material resources as generally thought. To illustrate, let me describe a recent study by Kathryn Edin that sheds some light on the standard of living for a group of families with incomes counted by the Census Bureau as less than half their poverty lines (Edin 1995, table 1). (Although not widely known, more than 15 million poor persons, or 41 percent of the total poverty population, lived in families with incomes of less than half their poverty lines in 1992, according to the US Bureau of the Census [1993, table 17].) Edin conducted intensive interviews with 214 female

AFDC recipients in four cities spanning the range from very high to very low benefit levels. These interviews were designed to solicit detailed information regarding sources of income and spending patterns of these families. On average, these families had cash incomes—largely AFDC benefits—of $4,344 in 1991,[4] which compares to a poverty line of $10,860.[5] These families, in other words, would have been counted by the Census Bureau as having incomes equal to 40 percent of their poverty lines.

Edin's results showed that there was a lot of income received by these AFDC families that would not be counted by the Census Bureau. This uncounted income included the following. Food stamps and housing subsidies added about $4,152 in income per year, when counted at market value. The earned income tax credit provided another $36. In addition, the welfare mothers supplemented their welfare benefits with $1,308 in earnings in covert jobs—46 percent of the women worked, although they did not report these earnings. They also received another $2,328 in contributions from family, friends, boyfriends, or absent husbands. Again, these contributions were not reported to caseworkers to avoid reducing their welfare benefits. Combining this uncounted income with the cash, income that would be counted by the Census Bureau yields a total income of$12,168, which was 12 percent above the official poverty line and about 20 percent above the adjusted poverty line when corrected for the overstatement of inflation in the official consumer price index or CPI (i.e., when using the CPI-U-XI to update the poverty lines). Moreover, all AFDC families are eligible for Medicaid, providing benefits on average of about $3,380, which, if counted at market value, would bring their incomes to 43 percent above the official poverty line and more than 50 percent above the adjusted poverty line.[6] Note that, in this calculation, a number of other smaller programs, like Head Start and school lunches, are not taken into account, and of course public schools are not counted.

That families the government counts as having incomes 60 percent below their poverty lines actually have incomes 43–50 percent above (if Medicaid is counted), or have actual incomes almost four times their counted incomes, is, I think, astonishing. I don't mean to suggest that this situation is typical of low-income households, although it may well be for the 5 million families on AFDC. What it does graphically demonstrate, however, is the great gap that separates the money income measures underlying the Census estimates and the material resources actually available to many low-income families.

I have been trying to emphasize two general points that I think are important to recognize in any discussion of welfare reform. First, there is in fact a massive redistribution of income in favor of lower-income households in the United

States, most of which is not counted by the Census Bureau or by the numerous analysts of poverty and income distribution. Second, and closely related to this, is the fact that standards of living of low-income households, especially those on welfare, are much higher than is normally acknowledged. Indeed, our welfare system, whatever else it has done, has largely eliminated material poverty, but our accounting procedures don't record this achievement.

THE NEGATIVE INCOME TAX

When economists discuss welfare reform, the most common recommendation seems to involve the negative income tax. Agreement among economists on this issue is surprisingly high. In a 1979 survey of economists, fully 92 percent supported this proposition: "The government should restructure the welfare system along lines of a negative income tax."[7] Nor has this consensus diminished with time. Basically the same proposition was put to members of the National Tax Association in 1994, and 86 percent of economics professors agreed that we should move toward a negative income tax (Kearl et al. 1979, table 1).[8]

What exactly is this panacea? As you know, the negative income tax (NIT) is a program that provides cash transfers to households with low incomes, with the size of the transfer inversely related to the household's own income or earnings. An NIT is described fully by three parameters. The first is the income guarantee, which is the transfer received by those who have zero incomes of their own. Second is the marginal tax rate, or benefit reduction rate, which determines how the transfer varies with the household's income. If the marginal tax rate is 40 percent, for example, this means that a household that increases its earnings by $1,000 would receive $400 less from the NIT program. The third is the breakeven income, or the level of own income for the household at which the transfer would be zero when it is tapered off at the specified marginal tax rate. Of course, these parameters are not independent. The income guarantee must equal the marginal tax rate times the breakeven income. Thus, if the income guarantee is set at $10,000 and the marginal tax rate is 40 percent, the breakeven income will be $25,000, since reducing the initial transfer of $10,000 by $400 for every $1,000 earned makes the transfer reach zero at exactly $25,000.

Such a transfer program has some well-known disadvantages. Foremost among these, and the best known, is that it reduces the incentive to work for all families with incomes below the breakeven income. A related disadvantage is that the transfer program is likely to lead to a reduction in the total money income for families with incomes just below the breakeven income. In other words, for some recipients earnings will be reduced by more than the transfer received. It should, however, be recognized that there are at least two other important choices that are likely to be adversely affected by this policy. They involve family size and family composition. If the income guarantee in the program varies with family size and composition, it introduces financial incentives that can affect the relevant choices. For example, if the income guarantees were set equal to the poverty thresholds in 1992, a couple could increase its transfer by $1,743 if it has one child, by an additional $3,149 for a second child, and by $2,257 for a third child. Moreover, these incentives apply to all those under the breakeven income, not just to those with zero earnings of their own. In addition, a family unit can increase its combined income by separating into two units—for example, by divorce. The point is not that the financial incentives are large enough to encourage everyone to act on them, but only that the NIT will reduce the opportunity cost to recipients of having children and of family dissolution or nonformation. Given the importance attached to issues related to these behaviors in the current welfare reform debate, it is important to recognize that an NIT will inevitably have effects similar to those some attribute to current welfare programs.

In view of these disadvantages, what accounts for the popularity of the NIT among economists? That is a good question. The reasons why many economists favor the NIT have perhaps never been more succinctly stated than by one of its early proponents, Milton Friedman, in his *Capitalism and Freedom*: "The advantages of [the negative income tax] are clear. It is directed specifically at the problem of poverty. It gives help in the form most useful to the individual, namely, cash. It is general and could be substituted for the host of special measures now in effect. It makes explicit the cost borne by society. It operates outside the market. Like any other measures to alleviate poverty, it reduces the incentives of those helped to help themselves, but it does not eliminate that incentive entirely. . . . The total administrative burden would surely be reduced" (Friedman 1963, 192–93).

There is at least one other advantage of the NIT, at least in comparison with most other welfare programs: it makes apparent the difficult compromises that must be made in designing any welfare program. I am referring, of course, to the infamous tradeoff necessitated by the relationship between the income guarantee, marginal tax rate, and breakeven income of the program. Let me illustrate by considering how we might use an NIT to eliminate poverty as it is officially defined. Suppose we set the income guarantee(s) at the poverty threshold, which for a family of four is about $16,000. That is, after all, the only way to eliminate poverty as we define it, since there will always be a substantial number of families with no incomes of their own. Suppose further that we set the marginal tax rate at 50 percent, so that people can keep half of each additional dollar of earnings, thereby reducing but not completely destroying the incentive to work. But with these two choices, we have implicitly set the breakeven income at $32,000, so all families with incomes below this level will receive transfers and be subject to the disincentives of the program. This includes all the families with earnings between $16,000 and $32,000, who have incomes above the poverty line but will now be subject to a disincentive to work, as well as incentives encouraging procreation and family breakup. Moreover, such a program will be quite costly, since it will be providing transfers to perhaps 35 percent of the population (recall that median family income is around $40,000).

In fact, this program is likely to be even more difficult to implement than it appears. Even if we eliminate all other welfare programs, the recipients of this NIT will also be subject to existing taxes, and that can make the effective marginal tax rate on earnings even higher. Consider that a family with an income of $25,000 is today subject to a 15 percent rate from the federal income tax, another 15 percent rate from the Social Security payroll tax, and typically a 5 percent state income tax rate. Even before our NIT is implemented, the overall marginal tax rate for this family is 35 percent. The NIT would add 50 percentage points to the overall marginal tax rate, bringing it to 85 percent. Most would agree that this is dangerously high.

It is possible to get a lower marginal tax rate by increasing the exemptions in the income tax and introducing exemptions in the payroll tax, so that these taxes impose a zero marginal tax rate on those below the NIT's breakeven income, but this option has two undesirable effects. First, it means that we will be redistributing income to families with incomes well above $32,000, probably up to $50,000, implying that more than half the total population would have income redistributed to it. Second, increasing the exemptions means great reductions in the tax bases of these taxes. Consequently, we would have to substantially increase the marginal tax rates in those programs that apply to earners above $32,000. It would probably require an overall marginal tax rate in excess of 55 percent to finance this NIT in addition to other, nonredistributive government expenditures. In short, if we try to eliminate poverty with an NIT that preserves incentives to work for low-income families with an effective marginal tax rate of no more than 50 percent, then we must be prepared to impose marginal tax rates in excess of 50 percent on everyone else.

This lengthy discussion only hints at the difficulties of eliminating poverty as officially defined with an NIT. I count that as an advantage of the NIT: it forces us to face reality. But now consider the only alternative way to eliminate poverty with an NIT. Instead of a 50 percent rate on transfer recipients, we use a higher rate, say 80 percent, with the same $16,000 guarantee. This eliminates poverty by using a breakeven income now of $20,000, and financing it would be more feasible since a much lower marginal tax rate on incomes above $20,000 is required. But with this NIT, we have almost completely destroyed incentives to work for those who would normally earn anything below $20,000. Visions of a large dependent class of people are not farfetched with this program.

What other alternative is there? With an NIT, the only other real option is to go for a lower-income guarantee. We could, for example, use a guarantee of $8,000, a marginal tax rate of 50 percent, and a breakeven income of $16,000. This would be relatively easy to finance (we are already doing more than this), but it would not move a single person above their respective poverty line and would, in fact, mean reduced benefits for many families if we eliminated existing welfare programs—as we would have to if we wished to keep the effective marginal tax rate at 50 percent. Consider, for example, that it would mean substantial reductions in the welfare benefits received by the AFDC families I discussed earlier.

I have perhaps not made any of these options look very attractive, and that is the point: they do illustrate the sort of tradeoffs that must be made. Any welfare system modeled after the NIT must confront these sorts of unappealing tradeoffs. And at this point let me emphasize that the US welfare system is modeled after the NIT. Most actual welfare programs are variants of the NIT, and it is my contention that one can understand the difficulty of reforming the US welfare system best by thoroughly understanding how an NIT operates and the unattractive tradeoffs it forces us to make.

I would like to consider a bit further a very simple analysis that helps to emphasize the point that it is very costly to eliminate poverty through a negative income tax. It stresses the consequences for the marginal rate of taxation on taxpayers as well as on recipients. As you know, economists emphasize the marginal tax rate because it measures the distortion in relative prices that is produced by a tax or transfer. More to the point, the actual inefficiency, or welfare cost, of the program depends critically on the marginal tax rate. It is helpful to recall that the welfare cost rises more than proportionately to the marginal tax rate; in fact, the welfare cost rises more than proportionately to the *square* of the marginal tax rate.[9] What this means is that the economic harm of a 51 percent marginal tax rate is twice as large as that of a 40 percent rate, and a 63 percent rate produces twice the damage of a 51 percent rate and four times the damage of a 40 percent rate. That suggests there are very good reasons for focusing on the marginal tax rate and trying to keep it from becoming too high.

Now let's consider a type of tax and transfer program that is a special case of the NIT. It uses the breakeven income of the NIT as the exempted amount for a positive income tax. Moreover, we will design the program so that the marginal rate of tax is the same for taxpayers as it is for recipients; this particular type of tax and transfer program is called a linear income tax in the literature. For example, we might set an income guarantee of $16,000, a marginal tax rate of 40 percent for recipients of transfers so that the breakeven income is $40,000, and then apply a flat-rate tax with a rate of 40 percent on income in excess of $40,000 to finance the transfers.

This type of tax and transfer policy makes it easy to determine the marginal tax rate that will finance any given income guarantee—that is, the rate that will balance the budget. It turns out that the required marginal tax rate is equal to the income guarantee divided by average family income; in addition, the breakeven income always equals average family income.[10] This immediately tells us that if we want an income guarantee equal to 30 percent of average family income, which would be approximately equal to the poverty line, then the required marginal tax rate will be 30 percent for both recipients and taxpayers.

Of course, this example tells us only what the tax rate required to finance the transfer program is. To be a bit more realistic, we need to recognize that tax revenue is also required to finance other, non–NIT programs like national defense, Social Security, and interest on the debt. Suppose we assume that a 25 percent marginal tax rate on an income is required to finance these nonredistributive programs; I think this is a realistic, if rough figure. Then we know that if we want an income guarantee equal to 30 percent of average income, the combined required marginal tax rate will be 30 percent plus 25 percent, or 55 percent for everyone. If we want an income guarantee equal to half the average, the required rate is 75 percent.

This simple overview of the tax and transfer system suggests why it can be economically very costly to eliminate poverty or reduce inequality substantially. We can have an income guarantee of 15 percent of average income with a marginal tax rate of 40 percent; if we increase the income guarantee to 25 percent of average income, the marginal tax rate will be 50 percent. Recall that this approximately doubles the welfare cost of the entire tax and transfer system. Since the poverty line for a family of four is approximately equal to 30 percent of average family income, this analysis suggests that we must be prepared to impose marginal tax rates in excess of 50 percent on everyone to eliminate poverty through this type of tax and transfer scheme. Actually, the required rate may be higher if increasing the tax rate reduces the average income.

Obviously, this linear income tax does not exactly describe the much more complicated US system. But it does provide a lot of insight into how high marginal tax rates must be to establish substantial income guarantees. What the example shows is that a marginal tax rate of approximately 55 percent is required to eliminate poverty when we use a policy that imposes the same marginal tax rate on all people, recipients and taxpayers alike. But if we are prepared to impose a higher marginal tax rate on low-income households, we can finance the same income guarantee with a lower marginal tax rate on middle- and upper-income households. For example, we might be able to use an income guarantee of 30 percent of the average combined with a marginal tax rate of 75 percent on low-income families: This phases out the transfers at a lower breakeven income and permits us to use a rate that might be about 45 percent on taxpayers. There are two points to be made about this possibility. The first is that this, in a very rough way, approximates what we in fact do in the United States today, as I describe more fully later. Second, this option appears preferable to one that applies the same marginal tax rate to everyone. Even though it will impose severe disincentives for those with low incomes, they produce a very small part of national income. By using a 45 percent rate for middle- and upper-income taxpayers, the gain (reduction in welfare cost) in comparison to using a 55 percent rate will be substantial.

Thus, I am once again describing another sort of tradeoff imposed by an NIT type of policy. We can set an income guarantee close to the poverty line and impose very high marginal rates on recipients, producing severe disincentives for them. But what we buy with this option is substantially lower marginal rates on the upper three-fourths or so of the income distribution, and they produce more than 90 percent of all national income. Since economic growth and progress depend largely on productive incentives for those with higher incomes, this may be a good bargain—even though the welfare programs may produce a large dependent population.

These remarks about NIT-like policies are highly relevant to understanding the current US welfare system. The combination of welfare programs we have, in fact, operates very much like a negative income tax now, as I explain next.

THE US WELFARE SYSTEM

In terms of expenditure policies, the US welfare system is composed of at least 81 separate programs with combined expenditures of $290 billion in 1992, plus a number of nonmeans-tested programs like Social Security, Medicare, and public schools that also redistribute income downward. Even if we had the time, I do not have the ability to explain how all these policies operate and interact with each other. But I am going to try to give a rough overview of a large part of the welfare system by focusing on five of the 81 policies that together account for two-thirds of all spending. These five policies are Aid to Families with Dependent Children (AFDC), Medicaid, food stamps, housing assistance, and the earned income tax credit (EITC). I will also focus on two large groups of low-income households that are eligible to receive assistance from some or all of these programs. These two groups are single-parent families with children and very low or zero incomes, predominantly female-headed families, and low-income married couples and single-parent families with children. Approximately two-thirds of those officially counted as poor belong to these two groups. It is important to consider these groups of households separately because they are typically eligible for different programs. My basic contention is that the US welfare system can be thought of as two NITs, one for each of these groups.

Female-headed families comprise the bulk of recipients of AFDC, a cash welfare program jointly financed by the federal government and state governments. They are also automatically eligible for benefits from food stamps and Medicaid and will receive the EITC if they have earnings. In addition, approximately 30 percent of AFDC recipients receive some form of housing assistance. Thus, in describing the situation confronting the typical AFDC family, we must consider the interactions among the separate programs. That means it is exceedingly difficult to understand, but fortunately the House Committee on Ways and Means has done the work for us. It describes in the *1994 Green Book* the situation confronting a mother with two children in Pennsylvania, taken to be a fairly representative state.[11]

In 1994, this hypothetical family would receive AFDC plus food stamp benefits of $7,548 if it had no earnings of its own. It would also be covered by Medicaid, which spent about $4,000 on the average AFDC family. Thus, the income guarantee of the "welfare system" is about $11,500. (It would be about $4,000 higher if housing assistance is received; this policy is not incorporated into the *Green Book* example.) The combined effects of the various programs can then be described as an NIT but with an overall marginal tax rate that varies with earnings. For example, the effective overall marginal tax rate on the first $2,000 of earnings is 31 percent; the family keeps 69 percent of the first $2,000. If earnings are increased from $2,000 to $8,000, however, the effective marginal tax rate is 83 percent. If earnings are increased from

$8,000 to $10,000, the effective marginal tax rate over that range is actually 250 percent, which occurs because eligibility for Medicaid ceases when earnings reach $10,000.

Viewing the entire set of programs as if they were a single NIT, we could describe it as having an income guarantee of about $11,500 and a breakeven income at about the same level, implying an average value for the marginal tax rate of 100 percent. Economists are often horrified when they come to understand how these programs affect welfare mothers. It is no wonder, economists say, that welfare recipients work so little when there is virtually no financial incentive to work. And it is true that recipients work very little. Some 94 percent report no earnings at all; only 2 percent of AFDC adult recipients report full-time work. However, as you recall from my discussion of Edin's study, there are apparently a substantial number who engage in covert work and do not report their earnings, but even in this group the earnings averaged only $1,308.

The first reaction of economists, and most others as well, is that this is an insane program, and we need to change it to make "work pay" by lowering the effective marginal tax rate. I vividly recall watching CNN's *Crossfire* a couple of years ago when, in what must have been a unique occurrence for that show, all four panelists agreed that welfare mothers ought to be allowed to keep more of what they earn. Apparently, they had been listening to economists. But you already know the problem with that reform. If the income guarantee is kept intact, lowering the marginal tax rate raises the breakeven income, and that means many currently self-supporting female-headed families will be brought under the welfare blanket and will confront increased disincentives to work.

It is not even clear that a reduced marginal tax rate for those on AFDC now will lead to any substantial increase in work. Most of these families do not work (officially) now, even though they can keep 69 percent of the first $2,000 earned. Unless the reduced marginal rate raises their net wage rate above their reservation wage, they will continue to not work. There is evidence suggesting that this would be the common reaction. You may recall that between 1967 and 1982, the AFDC program was modified to reduce the marginal tax rate confronting recipients, and the evidence from that experience suggests it had little effect on the initial nonworkers (Moffitt 1992). In addition, we have an ongoing experiment now in which the effective marginal rate has been significantly lowered over the past several years. This is the result of the expanded EITC, which acts as an earnings subsidy with a negative marginal rate for those with low earnings. That is one reason why the marginal tax rate on the first $2,000 of earnings was only 31 percent in the example I discussed. Work already "pays" more now for AFDC recipients than just a few years ago, but there is as yet no evidence of substantial labor supply responses. Moreover, it is tempting to interpret the results of Edin's study, which found 46 percent of AFDC mothers engaging in covert work, as evidence of what could be accomplished with a zero marginal tax rate. Recall that these women averaged only $1,308 in earnings;[12] if that is the magnitude of response from a zero marginal tax rate, which these women effectively faced, lowering the marginal tax rate is not a very promising reform. It will simply confront female-headed families who are now self-supporting with incentives to reduce work without leading to much of an increase for those already on welfare.

From these remarks, you can begin to see the outline of a justification for this part of our welfare system, however horrific it may appear in terms of financial incentives to work. Welfare benefits are restricted to a set of needy families who are apparently not going to work very much under any circumstances, so the high marginal tax rates do little damage to their labor supply choices. Since benefits are effectively restricted to female-headed families, other low-income families are not subjected to the disincentives of a universal negative income tax. Of course, this argument is weakened by recognition of the fact that the number of female-headed families is not fixed; the welfare system encourages the formation of this type of family. Moreover, such a system can be characterized as unfair to poor families who do not qualify for benefits because they are not single-parent families.

That brings me to the welfare programs that are available for married-couple families and for single-parent families with earnings too high to qualify for AFDC. Among the major programs, there are basically two that provide benefits to large numbers of these families: the food stamp program and the earned income tax credit.[13] Let me briefly describe these programs as they apply to a family with two children. The food stamp program is easy to understand. It is a negative income tax, with only the qualification that the transfer is given as food stamps rather than cash. However, for most recipients, the restriction that food stamps be spent only on food is nonbinding, making the equivalence to an NIT nearly perfect. In 1994, the income guarantee was $4,500 and the marginal tax rate was 24 percent, so the breakeven income was $18,660.

The EITC is more complicated. It is a combination of an earnings subsidy for those with very low earnings and a negative income tax for those with higher earnings. To be more precise, in 1996 a family with two children receives a transfer equal to 40 percent of the first $8,900 in earnings. Thus, the marginal tax rate over this range of earnings is minus 40 percent, which raises the net wage rate for low earners. Between earnings of $8,900 and $11,600, all families receive the same subsidy, $3,560, so the marginal rate is zero over this range. Now the subsidy must be phased out at higher income levels; it is phased out with a positive marginal tax rate of 21 percent, implying the subsidy reaches zero at about $28,500. Thus, for families with incomes between $11,600 and $28,500, the program operates exactly like a negative income tax with a marginal rate of 21 percent.

There is probably no welfare program that has been more misleadingly described than the EITC. It is frequently called an earnings subsidy—true only for the bottom of its range of coverage—and is often said to "reward work." Those descriptions may be appropriate for those with earnings below $8,900, but they comprise only one-fourth of the recipient households; for the remainder, the EITC is like an NIT and discourages work. To put this another way, only about 5 percent of the total earnings of families eligible for the EITC occur at levels where the net wage rate is increased; 95 percent of total covered earnings fall in the range where the EITC would be expected to lead to reductions in work effort.

Exactly how large an impact on work effort the EITC, in combination with the food stamp program, will have is unclear. As you know, there were major expansions in the EITC enacted in 1990 and 1993, and the 1993 law phased in over a period of three years, reaching its full size only this year (1996). Moreover, it is difficult to understand, which may delay its full impact for several years. But you can get some idea of the potential consequences by examining how the marginal tax rates of families will be affected.

Just as was the case with the AFDC population, it is the combined marginal tax rate from all policies together that is relevant for the work incentives of families receiving food stamps and/or the EITC. To give an idea of what is involved, consider a family with earnings of $25,000. Even before the expansion in the EITC, this family confronts a 15 percent marginal rate on earnings under the federal income tax, a 15.3 percent rate under the Social Security payroll tax, and perhaps a 5 percent state income tax rate. Together, the effective rate is around 35 percent before the EITC. But with the EITC, the family also loses 21 cents in EITC benefits on the marginal dollar of earnings, bringing the combined marginal tax rate to 56 percent. Thus, the EITC increases the effective marginal tax rate from 35 to 56 percent, and that approximately *quadruples* the welfare cost of the labor supply distortion for this family (recalling how the welfare cost depends on the marginal tax rate)! Families with earnings lower than $25,000 who receive food stamps may confront an even higher marginal tax rate. Consider a family with earnings of $15,000, low enough so that no federal income tax is paid. At this level, there is the Social Security payroll tax of 15.3 percent, the marginal tax rate of 24 percent in the food stamp program, and the 21 percent rate of the EITC itself, creating a combined marginal tax rate of around 60 percent.

With the food stamp–EITC combination, we effectively have a negative income tax for most low-income families not covered by AFDC. It uses a relatively modest income guarantee, the $4,500 in the food stamp program, but still manages to impose marginal tax rates in the 50 to 65 percent range on about 7.5 million families with incomes up to almost twice the poverty line.[14] Although I have been emphasizing marginal tax rates and work incentives, it should not be ignored that the program also has incentives relevant to family size and structure, just as every NIT does. For example, a couple with two children and with each parent earning $10,000 can actually increase its disposable income by about $5,000 by divorcing and claiming to be two separate households, each with one child, for purposes of receiving EITC benefits.

To sum up, our welfare system can be thought of as a two-track system, and both parts are variants of the NIT. One track is aimed at nonworking female-headed families and has a high-income guarantee and very high effective marginal tax rates. The other track is available to working female-headed families and married couples with children. It involves a much lower income guarantee and lower but small substantial marginal tax rates; most significantly, it extends these marginal tax rates of 50 to 60 percent much higher up the income distribution. So we already have a system modeled after the NIT. Economists should be happy.

You will notice that I have not yet said very much about welfare reform. Partly, this is because we can't discuss welfare reform without first describing the current welfare system, and that is not easy. More importantly, it is because my primary contention is that once you understand that the current system is fashioned after the NIT and how an NIT operates, you already know much of what standard economics can contribute to welfare reform. You know the tradeoffs that are implicit in the relationship between the income guarantee, marginal tax rate, and breakeven income. We teach this in economic principles classes, and it tells us that hard choices have to be made and that any change is going to have some undesirable consequences.

Let me illustrate how this framework applies to one common welfare reform proposal: expanding childcare subsidies. Danziger and Gottschalk, in their recent book, *America Unequal*, propose expanding the existing nonrefundable Dependent Care Credit in the income tax and making it refundable. They propose this in a section entitled "Rewarding Work," noting that the intent is to "reduce the costs—of working for all families with children" (Danziger and Gottschalk 1995). In other words, the goal is to reduce the marginal tax rate. This is to be accomplished by paying a subsidy equal to 80 percent of childcare costs (up to a maximum subsidy of $4,800 for two children, on the maximum allowable expenses of $6,000) for families earning less than $10,000. This does have the effect of lowering the effective marginal tax rate for families earning less than $10,000, such as the AFDC population. Perhaps it would encourage some of these families to work more, although our experience with past reforms, including the EITC, makes this questionable.

But the problem with this proposal, as I am sure you recognize, is that the maximum subsidy of $4,800 payable at an income of $10,000 must somehow be phased out at higher income levels. Danziger and Gottschalk propose phasing out the subsidy by lowering the subsidy rate by 4 percentage points (e.g., from 80 to 76 percent) for each $1,000 earned in excess of $10,000. Although it may not be immediately apparent from this way of putting it, this implies that the phase-out marginal tax rate is actually 24 percent. Thus, those low-income families that are already working and have incomes above $10,000 will find their effective marginal tax rate increased by 24 percentage points. Recalling that marginal rates are already in the 50 to 60 percent range for incomes between about $10,000 and $28,000, adding this childcare credit would raise the effective rate to, roughly, between 75 and 85 percent. (This will again roughly quadruple the welfare cost for these families.) Danziger and Gottschalk do not mention this in the text, but in a footnote at the end of the book that is a model of understatement, they say, "One disadvantage of the tax credit approach is that phasing out the credits yields high cumulative tax rates for families with incomes between about $15,000 and $30,000" (Danziger and Gottschalk 1995, 163). They know the tradeoffs involved, even if they don't feel it necessary to make them apparent to the reader.

The lesson here, of course, was already clear from how an NIT works: you can't improve financial incentives to work at low-income levels without reducing the incentive to work at higher-income levels unless you reduce welfare benefits (the income guarantee). Whether it is desirable to improve incentives at the bottom at the expense of those higher up is a debatable point. For myself, I am greatly concerned with the dangers of extending work disincentives to millions of moderately low income, fully self-supporting families via the EITC, in the name of "making work pay" for those at the very bottom. I side with William Henry, who said, "The vital thing is not to maximize everyone's performance, but to ensure maximal performance from the most talented, the ones who can make a difference" (Henry 1994, 20).

WHAT DO WE WANT FROM WELFARE?

Proposals to reform the welfare system are usually predicated on some vision of what we would like to achieve with welfare policy. That vision is usually implicit, especially when economists discuss the issue because they take for granted a common paradigm. Thus, I did not have to explain in any detail why I focused on work incentives and marginal tax rates. But I think it is important to consider more carefully what the goals of welfare are. What exactly are we trying to achieve with these programs? Obviously, this is a supremely normative issue, and it is unlikely that we will all agree. I will argue, however, that the vision that animates most economic analysis is too narrow and may hinder us in considering welfare reform.

Let me first describe what I take to be the way economists evaluate welfare programs. The goal is taken to be to raise the utility, or well-being, of those with the lowest incomes and to do so at the least possible cost, in terms of utility, to those who are better off. Lump-sum transfers and taxes appear to be ideal policies in this view, but for a variety of practical reasons they are not feasible. Thus, we have to choose among distorting policies, and the goal becomes to minimize welfare costs insofar as possible. This involves basing transfers on behaviors that are inelastic in their response to financial incentives and trying to keep marginal tax rates low. Since labor supply and saving are inelastically supplied, income is a good base for transfers, especially since need is thought to be closely correlated (negatively) with income. So a negative income tax becomes the favored vehicle. Moreover, if it turns out that some demographic groups are particularly needy and they also have unusually low elasticities of response, we can do even better by restricting transfers to these groups. Thus, we may be able to give larger transfers to the disabled and single-parent families with small children at low welfare cost even though we use high marginal tax rates.

As I suggested earlier, this approach can be used to defend the broad outlines of our existing welfare system. But the extreme dissatisfaction with our present welfare system suggests something is missing from this vision.

An alternative goal might be to focus on the material resources, rather than the utility, of the poor. In other words, it is consumption and not leisure that we wish to raise. There is a lot of indirect evidence that many people view this as a major goal. For example, the fact that poverty thresholds are measured in terms of material resources—income—and not leisure is suggestive. To attach such importance to poverty counts based on this definition, as many do, certainly seems to suggest that leisure is not to be considered important.

If the goal of welfare is to increase material consumption, then we can view consumption by the poor as an external benefit, and according to standard theory it should be subsidized. In other words, a policy that raises the net wage rates of the poor is the optimal policy, and that requires the use of negative marginal tax rates. Practically speaking, such a policy is very difficult to implement, as the consequences of the EITC may suggest. Perhaps more significantly, NIT–type programs are decidedly the wrong kind of policy to use, as they discourage work and consumption instead of encouraging them. Put another way, the welfare cost of the current system is much higher than my remarks may have suggested, since the distortion introduced by the marginal tax rate must be measured as the deviation from the optimal negative rate and not from zero (which implicitly assumes that a lump-sum transfer is optimal).

To see that this goal is not sufficient to inform the welfare debate, I need only remind you of the results of Edin's study. Apparently, AFDC recipients do have material resources that place them well above their poverty lines. Why aren't we happy with the welfare system that accomplishes this? Of course, it could be argued that if people really knew that poverty, as measured by material resources, has been virtually eliminated, they would be content. And make no mistake about it: if poverty were measured accurately and according to the original standards, the poverty rate would surely be below 5 percent instead of the 14–15 percent rate that is officially recorded. But when I tell people this, I don't find that they suddenly become happy about the welfare system. We have won the War on Poverty, and nobody is celebrating.

The reason that nobody is celebrating, I conjecture, is that it is understood that material deprivation is not the real problem; it is only a symptom of the problem. This is the way the authors of *The New Consensus on Family and Welfare* put the issue: "Linked to poverty among an important fraction of the poor is a high incidence of dropping out of school, of failure to prepare themselves for future employment, of begetting children out of wedlock, of crime, of drug use, and of other visible disorders. Such persons . . . are the behaviorally dependent, since their need for help from others springs in significant measure from their own behaviors" (Novak et al. 1987, 4). In short, it is the dysfunctional behaviors that we associate with the underclass that are perceived as evidence of the failure of our welfare system. Note that I am referring to a very small subset of the official poverty population now, the so-called underclass, which is often defined in terms of dysfunctional behavior and constitutes perhaps only 10 or 15 percent of the poor. Whether such behaviors are caused by welfare programs is hotly debated, but no one argues that welfare programs have done much to diminish these behaviors. Welfare enables, to use Charles

Murray's felicitous term, these behaviors to flourish. And that is welfare's failure; its proper goal should be to diminish these behaviors that lead to welfare dependency.

When preparing this talk, I happened to watch for the second or third time the musical *My Fair Lady*. As you recall, Rex Harrison sings a song entitled "Why Can't a Woman Be More Like a Man?" It seemed to me that this was much like the lament of many people concerning the poor. The refrain would go like this: "Why Can't the Poor Be More Like Us?" I do not mean this frivolously. I think that for many people, a successful welfare system would produce a society with a smaller underclass, with fewer low-income people who engage in self-damaging behavior.

One could, I suppose, fashion this argument in the language of externalities: the nonpoor receive external benefits or costs from particular behaviors like illegitimacy or drug use. Not only is that very unhelpful, but it misses the point that the goal is to really help the poor lead more satisfying lives. A 14-year-old girl who has an illegitimate child and drops out of school is acting contrary to her own long-term interest, and certainly that of her child, regardless of what she thinks. In other words, the goal is avowedly paternalistic. We want a welfare system for at least some of the recipients (certainly only a small minority of the official poor) that manipulates their environment and incentives in ways that may not only influence their actions but also, hopefully, shape their character, according to our conception of what is good for them.

As an economist with libertarian leanings, I have a lifelong aversion to paternalistic government policies, but in this instance I think there is a pretty good case to be made. Consider that we all agree that a paternalistic policy is appropriate for children. The only question is who controls the necessarily paternalistic decisions. In the vast bulk of cases, we believe the best results arise from leaving the decisions largely in the hands of the parents. But in the case of the underclass, the parents by their very actions demonstrate that they are incompetent and irresponsible. For example, four out of five cases of reported child abuse are in welfare families (Magnet 1993, 54). Perhaps the best solution would be that these persons not have children, at least until they are more mature and able to give them a good home. Barring that outcome, the children may be better raised by taking a lot of the decision-making authority out of the hands of the parents. *An NIT is not the right kind of policy to deal with this problem.*

What kind of policy is called for by this conception of the goals of the welfare system? At one extreme is the solution associated with Charles Murray. Murray has argued that totally eliminating all welfare programs would reduce behavioral dependency and would actually be better for the children on balance. This is the ultimate "tough love" version of a paternalistic welfare system. More moderate reforms, but still far from the pale, have been suggested by Myron Magnet and James Q. Wilson. Magnet, for example, proposes a system of group homes for welfare mothers and their children, with the focus on the welfare of the children and not the job prospects of the mothers. In a similar vein, Wilson suggests that unmarried, pregnant girls be required to live in group homes as a condition of receiving welfare benefits.

I do not know whether such reforms would work—no one does. But I do think the concerns that motivate such proposals are legitimate and that economists should pay more attention to them. We should begin by facing the fact that lack of material resources is not the problem; it is the self-destructive (and other destructive) behaviors that most urgently require attention. Moreover, it is clear that the negative income tax model for a welfare system is inappropriate to address these issues; we already have a variety of NITs, and they have permitted, if not caused, behavioral dependency to grow. We need something radically different, and perhaps the best option we have is to encourage experimentation by states—or better still, local communities and private charities.

I hope it is clear that these last remarks are intended to apply to only a small part of our welfare system, principally the long-term AFDC population. That is the group most people have in mind when they think of the failure of welfare. For the remainder of the low-income population, it may be that the NIT is the best form of welfare we can design, and we need only be cognizant of the tradeoffs involved. On the other hand, the AFDC disaster has been produced by using a form of NIT, and so we should realize that there is a danger in extending that type of system to ever-increasing numbers of people, as we have recently done with the EITC.

NOTES

I would like to thank my colleagues, John R. Hanson and Morgan Reynolds, for helpful comments on an earlier draft.

1. I include Medicare but not Social Security cash retirement benefits here because Medicare is far more redistributive. For all (eligible) retired persons, Medicare benefits are the same regardless of how little was paid in taxes in previous years. Social Security cash retirement benefits, on the other hand, are higher for those who paid more in taxes, so it does not redistribute as much to low-income persons.
2. In 1992, administrative costs were 12 percent of total outlays on food stamps and 11 percent of total outlays on Aid to Families with Dependent Children. See Committee on Ways and Means (1994, 325, 761).

3. As we will see, about 90 percent of the income of the lowest quintile takes the form of government transfers, and these are usually exempt from taxation. In addition, exemptions and deductions under federal and state income taxes shield most of the income of low-income persons from taxation. Social Security payroll taxes do place a substantial burden on the "working poor," but they are only a small part of the lowest quintile.

4. Edin gives all income figures as average monthly values. I have expressed them as annual values.

5. This is the poverty line for a family of three in 1992. Edin does not give average family size for her sample of AFDC families, but in 1992 the average family size of all AFDC families was 2.9. See Committee on Ways and Means (1994, 325).

6. The $3,380 figure is calculated from table 18-19 in Committee on Ways and Means (1994) based on the assumption that the family is composed of one adult and two children.

7. I have combined those who "Generally Agree" (58 percent) and "Agree with Provisions" (34 percent) to arrive at the 92 percent figure.

8. Slemrod 1995, table 1. I have given the percentage of economics professors who responded "yes" to the question: "Should the government restructure the welfare system along the lines of a negative income tax"? A smaller percentage of other NTA members answered affirmatively.

9. The formula for estimating the welfare cost due to the labor supply distortion of a tax levied on labor earnings at a marginal rate of *m* is given by $0.5nYm^2/(l- m)$, where Y is labor earnings and n is the compensated labor supply elasticity. For a derivation and further discussion, see Browning and Browning (1994, 462–69).

10. For a more detailed explanation, see Browning and Browning (1994, 293–98).

11. The description that follows is based on table 10-3 in Committee on Ways and Means (1994).

12. This was the average earnings for all the surveyed women, not just the 46 percent who engaged in covert work. Thus, the average earnings among those who did work must have been around $2,800. However, presumably the 54 percent who did not work also confronted an effective marginal tax rate of zero, since they could have engaged in covert work also.

13. Some married couples participate in AFDC-UP or receive housing assistance and Medicaid, but the numbers involved are relatively small, and I shall ignore them.

14. This is the number of families estimated to be in the phase-out range of the EITC, where it imposes the 21 percent marginal tax rate. See Kosters (1995).

REFERENCES

Browning, Edgar K., and Jacquelene M. Browning. 1994. *Public Finance and the Price System*, 4th ed. New York: Macmillan.

Committee on Ways and Means, US House of Representatives. 1994. *1994 Green Book*. Washington, DC: US Government Printing Office.

Congressional Research Service, Library of Congress. 1993. *Cash and Noncash Benefits for Persons with Limited Income: Eligibility Rules, Recipient and Expenditure Data, FY 1990–92*. Washington, DC: US Government Printing Office.

Danziger, Sheldon, and Peter Gottschalk. 1995. *America Unequal*. Cambridge, MA: Harvard University Press.

Edin, Kathryn J. 1995. "The Myths of Dependence and Self-Sufficiency: Women, Welfare, and Low-Wage Work." *Focus* 17 (Fall/Winter): 1–9. The figures discussed here are based on Edin's table 1.

Friedman, Milton. 1963. *Capitalism and Freedom*. Chicago: Phoenix Books.

Henry, William A. III. 1994. *In Defense of Elitism*. New York: Doubleday.

Kearl, J. R., C. L. Pope, G. C. Whiting, and L. T. Wimmer. 1979. "A Confusion of Economists?" *American Economic Review* 69 (May): 28–37.

Kosters, Marvin. 1995. "Scale Back the Earned Income Tax Credit." *On the Issues* No. 28, American Enterprise Institute, Washington, DC.

Lee, Dwight R., and Richard B. McKenzie. 1988. "Helping the Poor through Governmental Poverty Programs: The Triumph of Rhetoric over Reality." In James D. Gwartney and Richard E. Wagner (eds.), *Public Choice and Constitutional Economics*, 389–90. Greenwich, CT: JAI Press.

Magnet, Myron. 1993. *The Dream and the Nightmare*. New York: William Morrow.

Mitchell, William C., and Randy T. Simmons. 1994. *Beyond Politics*. Boulder, CO: Westview Press.

Moffitt, Robert. 1992. "Incentive Effects of the U.S. Welfare System: A Review." *Journal of Economic Literature* 30 (March): 1–61.

Novak, Michael, et al. 1987. *The New Consensus of Family and Welfare*. Washington, DC: American Enterprise Institute.

Slemrod, Joel. 1995. "Professional Opinions about Tax Policy: 1994 and 1934." *National Tax Journal* 48 (March): 121–47.

Stigler, George. 1970. "Director's Law of Public Income Redistribution." *Journal of Law and Economics* 12: 1.

US Bureau of the Census. 1993. *Poverty in the United States: 1992*. Current Population Reports, Series P60-185. Washington, DC: US Government Printing Office.

5.13
The Nature of Time in Economics

RICHARD B. McKENZIE

In the movie *Student Prince* made in the 1950s, Mario Lanza sings of glorious student days gone by: "Golden days in sunshine of our happy youth, golden days full of gaiety and full of truth . . . Golden days, golden days."

As I thought about this talk, that refrain played over and again in my head. I did not remember all of the words, or else I would have recognized the song wasn't fully on the mark of my talk. After all, it is a love song. Nevertheless, I can't help but think of my time back at Virginia Tech as a time of "golden academic days." I do remember vividly those days when many of us shared a time, a place, and a common mission, to go where no mind had gone before, to think thoughts rooted in the received wisdom but, in the process of developing those thoughts, to alter forever the wisdom that would be received by the next generation of economists. Looking back through time and considering what has been accomplished by the people in this room, you must know that I could not help thinking, "Golden days, golden days."

As we gather here under the auspices of the Virginia Political Economy Lectureship, I suspect that similar refrains from several different songs are

Prepared for the Thirteenth Annual Lecture in the Virginia Political Economy Lecture Series, George Mason University, Fairfax, VA, March 19, 1997.

playing in everyone's head. We gather this evening not just to hear a lecture, but to remember and celebrate the making of a particular history of thought, the "Virginia School," a form of political economy that is rich in the traditions of an avowed free society and an undefined collection of academics who share a split and constantly dueling personality, one side of which is grounded in the finely tuned logic that individual ideas can't matter for much within the broad collective and the other side firmly committed to the irrational conviction that, in the end, ideas are all that matter. I am honored by your inviting me to give this talk and recognize that I, fortunately and fortuitously, have been a part, albeit a minor one, of that history.

I hope that I can justify the honor accorded me with a talk worthy of your time and attention. In fact, I intend to talk about *time*—not as in history but as a unit of measurement and perception that might, just might, be subject to variation from one person to another and across time itself. I hope to convince you that thinking in terms of the variability of time can yield constructive, potentially novel perspectives on a number of fundamental economic problems.

My comments, at times, must necessarily be speculative and brief, but I hope to avoid wasting your time with time. Indeed, my goal is to do what so many of you have done throughout your careers: challenge basic assumptions and come up with a totally new way of looking at the world. I will be proposing that the paradox of, for example, why the old save more than the young (or why the young's discount rates appear to be so much higher than market interest rates) may be unraveled by reference to the difference in their time frames. From the perspective I will propose, a country's rates of saving and investment—and, thereby, growth—may be explained by the variability of time across age groups, cultures, and ethnic backgrounds, which can have a physical (not fiscal) foundation. I plan to do all of that and more in a few short minutes.

TIME IN ECONOMICS

To make analytical progress, science in general and economics in particular often need either to ignore some factors or assume they are constant. We all acknowledge that simplifications and constants reduce the complexities of analysis to manageable proportions. Time in economics is the great constant, not subject to variation. An hour is an hour, no matter when or where or by whom it is experienced. Time is conventionally treated in economic theory as completely exogenous and totally objective, always considered from the perspective of some external unvarying measuring rod—an hour, minute, or time period. Treating time as a constant has probably been done not as a conscious choice, but as the simple thing to do, or what has always been done.

The treatment of time in economics, however, stands in sharp contrast with the discipline's treatment of every other factor of production, distribution, and consumption. Consumer preferences vary both in terms of what is wanted and in intensity. People can want more or less of a good, and they may want (i.e., desire) the amount they do at differing levels of intensity. Economists (especially those with an Austrian bent in this room) have no trouble acknowledging that any given good—for example, a painting in an art museum—can be viewed, evaluated, and appraised from different perspectives, all yielding different results. But, as yet, they have not acknowledged that time may be viewed similarly.

In economics, production varies with the resources used. Labor can be more or less intensely applied to production. Discount rates vary across individuals and through time. Even people's willingness to accept risk varies; that is, we think of people as more or less risk averse.

Static economic analysis is truly timeless, with time being assumed away totally. Thus, equilibrium is a balance of market forces that literally never have time to work, because equilibrium is achieved instantaneously, and disequilibrating forces have their impact on market outcomes without the passage of any time at all. This is often all to the good, however. Analysts/economists assume time is often nonexistent solely because they are interested in identifying the outcomes, not the processes by which the outcomes are achieved.

Granted, in economics, sometimes it is said that people have a "time preference" in consumption (which relates to the optimum timing of consumption), but even so, it is not necessary for time to pass before consumption is affected. Moreover, there is no hint that the "time" in the preference is anything but fixed at the unit level. Granted, in dynamic analysis, multiple time periods can be introduced explicitly with each period, identified in whatever units are convenient. Indeed, time is invariably assumed to be of one form, that which is measured by the ticks on an external, correctly wired mechanical, electronic, or atomic clock. The chosen time units of analysis are always assumed to remain constant—given, immutable, and unchangeable. Unlike clay (or steel or labor), the common assumption is that time cannot be manipulated—that time is the ultimate constraint that must be accepted for what it is. That is to say, when time periods are represented as t1, t2, t3, and so on, the units of time in time period t1 are implicitly or explicitly assumed to be fully equivalent to the same units of time in t2, t3, and all other time periods, whether in the future or in the past. Time is something to be worked with, not to be worked on or altered

Figure 5.13.1.

Hypothetical View of Segments of Time in a Normal
Expected Life Span with Equal Units of Time

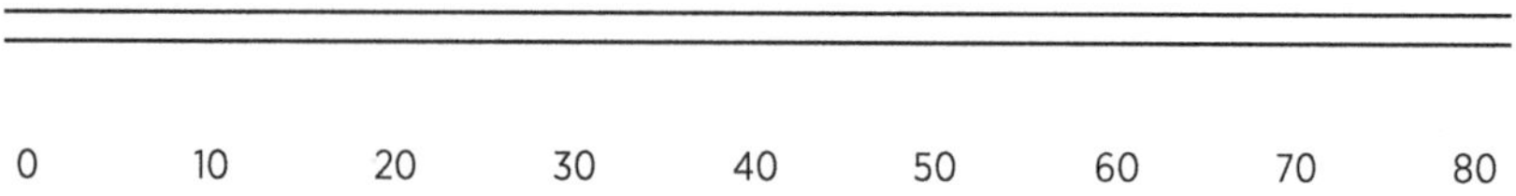

0	10	20	30	40	50	60	70	80

in its basic structure. That is to say again, time is invariant, with no regard for circumstance or even for time itself (time of day or time of life).

Visually, time is generally treated by economists as if it can be conceived to be one long, ever-unfolding continuum that can be divided into equal units, as shown in figure 5.13.1. In this figure, the hypothetical "time line" divides a person's life expectancy into equal portions. A ten-year segment of time at the start of the expected life span, under the conventional view, is no different (as represented by the length of the segment) than a 10-year segment of time at the end of the expected life span.

Economists' conception of time has not changed since the days of the venerable Adam Smith, who wrote in his classic, "Time both pervades our activities and makes us its profaner, its chains invariably constraining our actions. True liberation from its bonds is a hopeless endeavor, since opposition merely binds its subject ever more tightly" (1988, 1). Also, more recently the late Ludwig von Mises has noted, "Man is subject to the passing of time. He comes into existence, grows, becomes old, and passes away. His time is scarce" (1963, 101).

CONCEPTIONS OF TIME

The normal assumption in economics—that people see time in the same units—stands in contrast to, if not at odds with, the widely recognized different conceptions of time in other disciplines, which recognize the prospects of "biological time" (in which the relevant unit of time is not the ticks on an external clock but events in evolutionary development), "physiological time" (in which the relevant unit, for example, may be the required healing time for given-sized sores on people of different ages), and "psychological time" (which may be measured more by how much is experienced)—as well as "physical time" (which is the usual form of time, the time of classical mechanics, which relate units of time to the rotation of the earth).[1]

The economist's usual conception of time also stands in contrast with people's self-acknowledged differences in their perceptions of time. People recognize that they can do things more or less intensely within any given time frame and that they can pay more or less attention to what happens over the course of time.

But is the economist's conception of time reasonable? Clearly, time is not always viewed the same at all times and in all circumstances by all people. People (even economists) have been known to work with such focus and concentration that time no longer appears relevant in their decision to continue working.[2]

People have no trouble acknowledging that "time" spent at anything depends critically on what the "thing" is. Einstein once quipped, "When a man sits with a pretty girl for an hour, it seems like a minute. But let him sit on a hot stove for a minute—and it's longer than any hour. That's relativity." Almost all people past high school graduation readily report that time speeds up as they have grown older, and the speeding-up process appears to continue into old age. A year of time at age 20 goes by faster than a year of time at age 5, and a year of time at age 70 appears to go by with much more rapidity than at age 20, or so few dispute.

That is to say, as opposed to a person viewing life as divided into equal segments, he or she may see life in diminishing segments, as is drawn in figure 5.13.2. A person's life span may not be the same "length" as the "expected" one pictured, but what is important to note in the illustration is that each ten-year segment gets shorter with age, which means that, as seen in figure 5.13.2, the ten-year segment from age 70 to age 80 is approximately one-fifth the length of the segment for representing years 0 to 10.

People who have used computers for years and have moved gradually to faster and faster microprocessors confess that their conception of time has changed. Once they thought of some tasks in terms of the minutes they took to accomplish, but now they are disturbed and irritated if their instructions are not completed in their much shorter time estimates—seconds or nanoseconds. Indeed, some fret about having to watch the hourglass icon, which appears on computer screens operating Window-based programs when there is the slightest delay. They have, in effect, been moved by technology into a different

Figure 5.13.2.

Hypothetical View of Segments of Time in a Normal Expected Life Span with Diminishing Units of Time

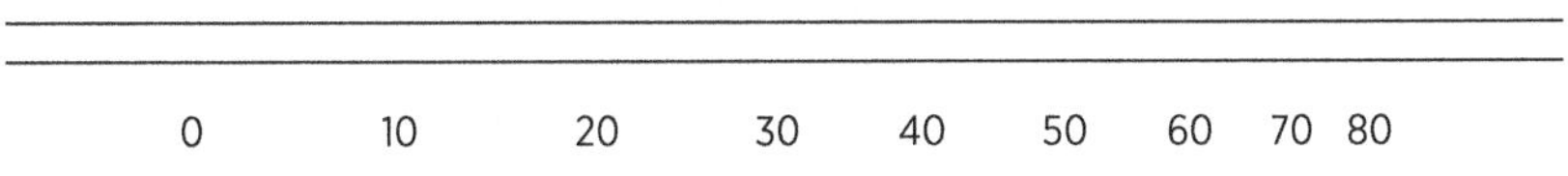

0 10 20 30 40 50 60 70 80

conception of time, or "time warp." What I find interesting is how few people on the streets of Blacksburg in the early 1970s would have ever heard of "nano-seconds." Now, few are surprised to hear talk of such minuscule units of time.

In fact, it may not be unreasonable to claim that people see time in widely varying units. To see how that can be, a metaphor, albeit imperfect, is required. Individuals may conceive of time in terms of units; for example, in bits and pieces, or in "time frames," much like those on a roll of film. Differences among individuals can be thought of as differences in the number of frames each individual can detect, evaluate, and act upon during any given period of time, externally evaluated. Some people might see time pass at a rate equivalent to that of old homemade movies, eight frames per second, while other people may see time go at rate experienced in movie theaters, 24 frames per second.

Frames might have nothing to do with the length of the film as it is measured by some external time standard, but the number of frames may determine the actual "length" of time people ascribe to an experience, as well as how far removed from their present lives a future event is. That is, an event at the end of one roll of film that runs at eight frames a second may be, when measured by some external measure of time, equally far removed from the beginning of the film as the same event captured on another roll of film that runs at 24 frames a second. However, to two people who experience the event, the event may not seem equally far removed. The one whose film runs at eight frames a second may indeed experience a different amount of time, because he or she will observe fewer frames (absorb less information) than the person whose film runs at 24 frames per second. What seems paradoxical is that the person who "sees" more frames go by (and is more intensely involved in what he or she is doing) tends to report a mere rapid passage of time. If this be so, the two would not necessarily be expected to evaluate the future event the same and should be expected to act differently with regard to the anticipated futures.

The point I'm struggling to make here is that time may not be "something" in and of itself. It may only be "something"—that is, exist—*because of what we do.* Time may be nothing more than the means by which we understand and record experiences in the brain, as some psychologists suggest. Time is the consequence of events that pass in sequence. Seen from this perspective, time may be more of a mental-internal "something" than a physical/out-there "something." Seen from this perspective, time does not pass; it is created, so to speak, as we experience events sequentially. And its conception may be partially a product of how we choose to sequence events in our lives.

Do people experience time as a constant? In preparation for this talk, I took an informal survey of the several hundred MBA students at my university.

I simply asked the students five straightforward questions by way of e-mail about the changing relative speed of time. More than 90 percent of the respondents agreed that time passed more quickly now than when they were children. The students, whose ages ranged from 21 to 53, figured that an hour in class today felt, on average, like 37 minutes of an hour-long class when they were eight (with range extending down to as little as 5 minutes and the median and mode equaling 35 and 30 minutes, respectively). Moreover, as a general rule, the older the student, the shorter an hour today felt (although the relationship appears weak, which might be attributable to the crude survey instrument I used).[3] More than 70 percent also expected time to continue to speed up as they aged, and practically all (95 percent) professed that time tended to pass more rapidly when they were doing interesting and absorbing things.

I understand that my survey was not "scientific." I may be on some less-than-firm theoretical ground with my claim about the variability of time, but I submit that the ground I wish to explore is far and away more firm than the traditional ground claimed by economists, defined by the heretofore unquestioned assertion that time is constant, no matter what.

EINSTEINIAN TIME

Economics is certainly behind the times—at least if economists' conception of time is compared to physical scientists' conception of time. Economists remain mired in the Aristotelian physical world in which time was the great constant around which everything else in the universe varied. Still the captive of an Aristotelian view of the universe, Newton never imagined how the force of gravity that he identified could possibly affect time.[4]

Close to a hundred years ago, Albert Einstein put an end to the Aristotelian world by proposing that time, too, is a variable, dependent on place, circumstance, gravity, and speed of moving bodies.[5] Physicists now consider it natural to talk in terms of "space-time," often written as one word, as though the two concepts are inseparable, as physicists believe they are.

A key to understanding the variability of time is to recognize the consistency of the frequency, given the energy level. Indeed, a second is defined as 9,192,631,770 vibrations of the microwave radiation emitted by a caesium-133 atom during a specified atomic rearrangement, and time can, in fact, be either sped up or slowed down by the absorption or release of energy. Following Einstein, we can see that energy levels can be affected in very precise, predictable ways by the forces of gravity and speed. That is, the greater the gravitational force and speed, the slower the time. Hence, when in 1971 American physicists sent caesium atomic clocks around the Earth aboard airplanes in opposite directions, they predicted that the eastbound clocks would lose 40 nanoseconds while the westbound clocks would gain 275 nanoseconds when compared with stationary earthbound clocks. The estimates of such a difference between the clocks in the planes and on the ground were explained by the fact that the clocks on the ground are subjected to a stronger gravitational force than the ones in the air, and the difference between the eastbound and westbound clocks is explained by the fact that the eastbound clock had to move against the natural rotation force of the earth. The eastbound clock actually lost 59 nanoseconds while the westbound clocks gained 273 nanoseconds, with the discrepancies between the predictions and observed time changes attributable to the imprecision of the instruments.[6]

The variability of time under such circumstances is not a matter of a physical illusion (as even some physicists who followed Einstein wanted to think) but as a matter of the impact of gravity on the rate of atomic reactions within the molecular structure of the atomic clocks. In the same way, the biological clocks of humans would also be affected by gravity: the greater the gravitational pull, the slower people's biological clocks—the slower time passes.[7]

In the Einsteinian world, acceleration has the exact same effect on time as does gravity, and for the same reason: atomic reactions—within both atomic and biological clocks—are slowed by the exertion required to neutralize the force of gravity and to achieve any given speed. The special theory of relativity implies that a person's biological clock could be slowed by the person flying off into space in any direction, and the slowdown would not be an illusion (or delusion). The greater the speed, the greater the exertion and the greater the slowdown in the body's clocks, a deduction that has led physicists to conceptualize time differences in terms of the "twins paradox." If one twin were sent off into space at a very high speed while the other one remained on Earth, the astronaut twin would find his or her biological clock slowing down, although he or she might not recognize the change unless he or she communicated with the earthbound sibling. When the astronaut twin returned, he or she would be younger than the earthbound sibling. How much younger would depend upon the speed and length of the space travel.[8]

Several years back, a public television documentary concerned with Einstein's physics explained the concept of relative time by going to the Swiss city where Einstein lived and worked as a clerk in a patent office. The program's host walked along the street that Einstein took to work by way of a trolley. Atop a tower that was at the beginning of the street Einstein took to work each morning was a large clock. The host asked listeners to envision Einstein on a trolley riding away from the clock and imagining that he was riding not the trolley but a beam of light that had been reflected away from the surface of the clock.[9]

Theoretically, from Einstein's own theory of relativity, it would have been impossible for anybody or anything, with any mass at all, to reach the speed of light. Nevertheless, imagining such a trip would enable Einstein to deduce that if he were on the light beam, time for him would stand still, given that all light travels at a constant speed and that no other light beam reflected from the clock could catch the beam he imagined riding.[10]

Einstein's fictitious travel on a light beam is helpful, because it enables us to imagine how, at the speed of light, time loses its relevance (because time never passes) and how speed and time are functionally and inversely related—which is a more important insight for our purposes. Close to the speed of light, time still remains relevant, although it passes very slowly. A person moving at close to the speed of light may act no differently in terms of motivations and planning horizons (given the time frame) than an identical person standing quietly beneath a clock on earth. Both could evaluate present and future events identically, in that it would be possible for them to appraise future events at a given future point in time (for example, one year hence) in the same way and to give them identical values. There is no reason for the high-speed traveler to know or believe (unless he or she has been steeped in relativity theory or had contact with earthbound people) that his or her biological and atomic clocks have slowed. Everything around the high-speed traveler would be in the same time warp; the laws of nature relevant in Earth's time warp would be fully operational in the high-speed time warp (even light would move away from the traveler at the same speed).

In this regard, the assumption of relative time might not make any difference—but that is the case only when looking at each individual separately within their separate time contexts. The high-speed and stationary persons might, indeed, save and invest the same amount over the same period of time—as they separately measure time by their internal biological clocks and by the external atomic clocks close at hand. Accordingly, their growth rates per unit of time—given some fixed measure of time (a year)—would be identical (or no different than they would have been had they both been in the same time frame).

However, the concept of variable time can make a great difference when the behavior of the two people is compared and evaluated by someone who does not imagine that the two people's time frames are radically different. Identical people—one traveling close to the speed of light and one fixed in place below the clock at the end of the street—cannot be viewed as acting identically by an external observer/analyst/economist. Indeed, an external observer who is imbued with economists' predilection toward time might totally miss the extent to which the two people's behaviors are the same unless he or she recognizes that the two people are operating within different time frames.

THE DIFFERENCES TIME CAN MAKE

An assumption of constant time may not make much of a difference to many economic discussions. Much analytical progress has been made in the discipline, not in spite of the assumption of constant time, but because of it. The assumption has, as mentioned at the start, kept the discussion simple. Besides, even if time varies, it might vary very little, so little that nothing much in the way of accuracy is lost by assuming time is constant. It may be that time passes more slowly with greater gravitational pull, for example, at the equator, than in the temperate zones on Earth, but the difference is so small that nothing much is gained or lost by changing how time is perceived.

On the other hand, there are at least three nontrivial problems with the assumption of constant time. First, the standard assumption may be descriptively inaccurate. Time may not be constant. An assumption of constant time may be no more analytically valid than an assumption of constant utility for given consumption levels across individuals and across time itself.

Granted, the impact of gravity and speed may have little to do with the variability of time across individuals, given that gravity and speeds vary little (when compared to the speeds envisioned in the twin's paradox discussion). But I am not so sure that the long-term effects are necessarily "small." The economic consequences of any difference in the impact of gravity at the equator and temperate zones on people's conceptions of time might be minute on a year-to-year basis, but when compounded over the millennium, "minute" effects might add up to something worthy of attention, given the connection between time frames and saving and between saving and growth rates. Also, I suspect that the concept of variable time might mean economists could, conceivably, help astronomers in their search for "advanced" societies in the cosmos.

I would be the first to admit that connections between gravity and speed and time conceptions might prove to be inconsequential. Still, how people *perceive* time could conceivably vary enormously, so much so that behavior could vary materially because of the differences in the conception of time. Again, my thoughts are necessarily speculative, but they are tendered because, if nothing else, my survey respondents confessed to seeing time in widely varying "lengths."

Second, and more importantly, the assumption of constant time may block an understanding of otherwise inexplicable behavior; for example, why the old save more than the young, and it may lead to ascribed causes—the young have a higher discount rate than the old—that are simply wrong.

Third, if we assume *time* is constant, we may never search for (potentially novel) explanations for why time might vary across people, places, and time itself. That also means that we might never fully understand why growth rates differ, given, again, that growth rates depend on the rates of saving and investing and those rates depend crucially on how *time* is perceived.

HOW TIME CAN MATTER: LIFE-CYCLE SAVING PATTERNS

Does it make a difference as to how we think about time? Naturally, I think it makes, potentially, a very big difference. Frankly, it has always made a difference to the people here and everyone else who investigates issues in public choice and constitutional economics. An abiding interest of public choice economics has been to alter permanently people's time frames. My time frame was definitely and irreversibly altered when I was a student at Virginia Tech. I change my time reference from individual policy issues to a time reference that allowed for a sequence of policy issues to be considered under a given set of decision-making rules. Constitutional economics essentially forces a more expanded time frame, one that covers the development of rules—for example, majority rule—under which policies will be considered. I submit that those shifts in time references are far more important to what we do than the particulars of the models conceived under any given time frame.

Moreover, it is widely acknowledged that young people tend to save less (as saving is normally viewed as "nonconsumption") than older people, even after adjustments are made for income differences. Young people also take more life-threatening risks than do older people (as is evidenced by the relatively greater amount of reckless driving and bungee jumping among the young). However, by saving earlier in their lives, people would have to save less—that is, postpone less consumption—than is necessary when saving is postponed until later in life. Young people, on average, have more years of life left (if nothing else) than do older people. For that matter, their expected lifetime incomes are, on average, greater, given their expected life spans and given some growth in the economy. In these senses, they have more to lose from death in traffic or bungee-jumping accidents than do older people. If economists' natural presumption that "more is better" is true, younger people might be expected to save more and to be more cautious than older people.[11]

Economists have found differences in the saving-rate behaviors of young and old something of a puzzle that, admittedly, can be partially explained by relating saving and consumption to expected or permanent income streams, as have Modigliani (1963, 1988) and Friedman (1957).[12]

However, as researchers who have evaluated the life-cycle saving and consumption theory have observed, "For all its elegance and rationality, the life-cycle model has not tested out very well" (Courant, Gramlich, and Laitner 1986, 279–80). Instead of making decisions based on a consistent discount rate that comes close to market interest rates, people exhibit varying interest rates that are upward of 30 percent and depend on the size of the potential award and when the award is received. Friedman (1957) estimated consumer discount rates at between 33 and 40 percent (several times the going market interest rates), which implies that they have planning horizons of three to four years, a finding that is roughly equal to the discount rate observed by Hall and Mishkin (1982). Thaler (1981) reports that when he asked students to consider several levels of awards and how much they would have to be paid to delay the award for one, two, and three years, he found that the respondents required higher discount rates to delay small awards than larger awards and that the required discount rates declined with the length of the delay, findings that he notes are consistent with the work of others (Benzion, Rapoport, and Yagil 1989).[13]

Economists have set aside these unresolved puzzles by assuming that differing discount and saving rates that exist among groups—for example, young and old—are the consequence of some groups being poorly informed of market interest rates and risks or, if informed, are more reckless (less risk averse) than older people. Moreover, some groups, that is the young, are said to have higher internal discount rates (more intense time preferences) that can be explained by the "psychology of perception" (Lowenstein and Prelec 1989), "mental accounting" (Shefrin and Thaler 1988), and "debt aversion" (Thaler 1992, 100).

Such explanations are not without merit. After all, time (in almost all of its possible forms) is *duration* that can only be understood when the past, present, and future can be distinguished; and some groups of people, especially older people, have had more time and other resources to become better informed on the value of saving and the detriment of risks than younger people, and a person's conception of time does appear to be related to memory (Sorokin 1964, 166). Should it be surprising, then, if younger people who were intensely educated on the benefits of saving and the risks of various forms of behavior still take more risks over the course of some measured time period than do older people? Would we not expect older people, who may have had little education on the risks associated with various forms of behavior, to act more cautiously than younger people? Similarly, should we be surprised that older people save more, after adjusting for income, wealth, and other differences, than younger people (until, at least, some age at which older people start to dissave)?

What makes the difference? Differences in the internal discount rates of the old and young might be the only "right" explanation. But such an explanation has a hollow ring, at least to the extent that it fails to explain the differences in the discount rates used by young and old and why, on the margin, the discount rates of young and old are not identical and equal to market interest rates.[14]

Might not the differences in the discount rate (which may not be differences at all) be explained by the differences in the two groups' conceptions of time? Young people's basic unit of time is much longer than older people's unit of time. The old may perceive a reward to be received as being only two years removed, but to the young, using the same time yardstick, the same two years may appear equivalent to ten years to the old. This is what the survey findings mentioned earlier seem to suggest.

Figure 5.13.3 represents a hypothetical illustration of the ways a "young" person (at, say, 20 years of age) and an "old" person (at, say, 60 years of age) see their respective futures. At their respective points in life, each can appropriately discount future events (having both costs and benefits), but at some point (described by the ends of their lines in figure 5.13.3), the present discounted value of a far-removed event approaches zero and is no longer economically relevant. In the illustration, the relevant time horizon for the young person is three years, while the time horizon for the old person is thirty years.

Figure 5.13.3.

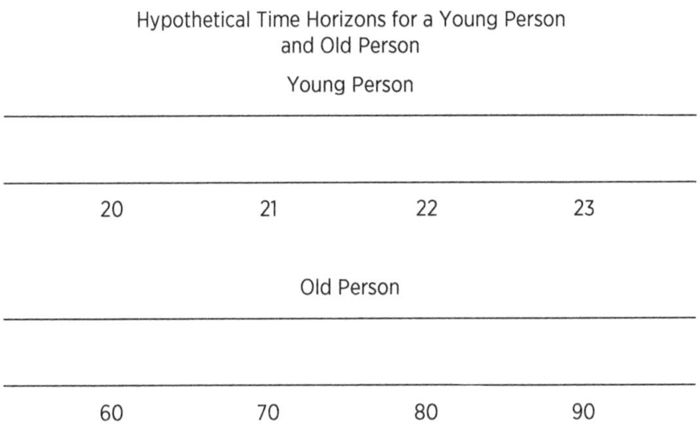

Hypothetical Time Horizons for a Young Person and Old Person

Young Person

20 21 22 23

Old Person

60 70 80 90

Granted, alternative partial explanations abound. It may be that people save more as they age simply because the age at which they expect to retire and to start their dissaving grows closer, an important inducement to start thinking more seriously about having the funds for their dissaving phase of life. Retirement, in other words, comes within the person's relevant time horizon. However, such an admission does not deny the validity of what has been said about the changing nature of time. It may be that the aging person's inducement to save is compounded by the actual or perceived shrinking units of time extending toward retirement, which means that the rewards from saving become ever more immediate for two reasons: first, the number of units of time until retirement shrinks; second, the "length" of each relevant time unit shrinks progressively as they extend into the future.

The young person (imbued, let us say, with fully rational expectations and with perfect information) may also understand that his or her future time units will shrink. However, many of those time units will be outside his or her relevant frame of reference. The discounted value of the time units will be zero, or close to it, and therefore they will be ignored. Put differently, a young person may be inclined to save less and may take more risks simply because many of his or her expected years of life are so very far removed that they appear unworthy of consideration (that is, their discounted value approaches zero). To the older person, the long-run consequences of current actions may appear closer at hand simply because the units of time the older person uses to make current calculations are so short that even far-removed years still have significant subjective value. Older people, then, in a subjective sense, could be said to have more to lose in terms of years and possibly also in the present discounted value of real income earned.

Seen from that perspective, older people can be said to have a longer time horizon, measured in years, than younger people—up to a point, at least. Young and old people may be equally able to look into the future in terms of how far removed future events are; that is, in how they each perceive time. The difference in their time horizons, as measured by objective standards of days or years, is that the measuring rod is actually longer for the younger person than the older person (just as the measuring rod used by the astronaut twin is longer than the one used by the earthbound twin in the earlier physics example).

Of course, at some point, the prospect of death looms up, and the time horizon over which the older person makes economic calculations begins to shorten. Such a perception of time would lead a person into a savings life cycle with little saving or even dissaving (when inheritance exists) in the early years, followed by a growth in saving until a peak is reached, then by a decline in saving and, finally, by dissaving, a lifetime saving pattern that is fully compatible with the life-cycle saving hypothesis postulated by both Ando and Modigliani (1963) and Friedman (1957).[15]

The delay in savings until middle age and beyond, in my way of thinking, is effectively grounded, albeit partially, in "diminishing marginal utility of income": the people rationally delay saving until their wages increase with years of experience and greater skills—at which time a dollar not spent is worth far less than it is to the young person. Actually, if time does speed up with age, the delay in saving is all the more rational, given that the young person can anticipate his or her rate of pay rising not only with years of experience and skills, but also with the decrease in the length of the time unit. If diminishing marginal utility does play a role, might not marginal utility of income diminish even more with time passing more quickly? This is an intriguing question that can, at this point, have no firm answer.

OTHER WAYS TIME CAN MATTER

The variability of time also may be relevant to a host of other issues. For example, differences in time frames may also add to our understanding of why other groups—not just the old and young but different races—have different saving rates: different groups can see time differently because of, for example, their different rates of metabolism.

I can only imagine that being a part of the downtown Washington order does something to one's view of time. 1 honestly don't know what; all I know is that it seems to screw up the way people act, how they time expenditures and taxes. I remind you of the people in this group who have argued that the "time horizons" of politicians might, because of the institutional setting in Washington, be shorter than the long-term needs of the economy. Clearly, the shorter time frames of elderly people might add to our explanation of why the political balance remains in favor of the elderly when it comes to maintenance of the Social Security system. The elderly might have less time to live and reap the rewards of their political efforts to maintain their benefits, which might be offset in political struggles by their supposedly low opportunity cost and the immediacy of their gains, as conventionally argued. However, it might also be said that their gains are more immediate because their future rewards are more immediate, given their shorter time periods.

Time and distance are inextricably bound, or so it is the case in physics and appears to be the case on a subjective level. People who report time going by slowly when they are young also report that places seemed relatively far away (and bigger). Because of that simple observation, I can't help but believe that a study of time frames might contribute to our understanding of transportation economics. When I mentioned this point to Dwight Lee, he immediately pointed out that the space-time connection might help explain why young people should fly and old people should take the train, and "why young people drive so much faster than old people." They are simply trying to cover what appears to be a long distance in a reasonable amount of time, as they see time. I replied that it only explains why the old people *think* young people are driving so much faster.

Those of us who teach microeconomics have always noted at some point in class that the elasticity of demand is a function of the time period. The longer the time period, the more elastic the demand, everything else constant. You can imagine that if the young experience longer time periods, their demands for any good will *appear* relatively more inelastic than the demands of the old—from the perspective of the external observer judging the behavior of both groups from the perspective of conventional ticks on the clock. This suggests that the inelasticity of young people's demands may not be a reflection of their "urgency" for consumption of any given good, as may have been commonly presumed.[16]

In his new book *Against the Gods*, Peter Bernstein perceptively observes, "Time is the dominant factor in gambling. Risk and time are opposite sides of the same coin, for if there were no tomorrow there would be no risk. Time transforms risk, and the nature of risk is shaped by time horizon: the future is the playing field" (15). That comment is important simply because it forces us to look at risk differently and to take seriously the prospect that time frames matter in the perception of risk and the making of investments. I suspect that a difference between entrepreneurs and the rest of us is not so much a difference in risk aversion, as normally assumed, but in the assessment of time. But the plot thickens, because Bernstein adds that "time matters most when decisions are irreversible. And yet many irreversible decisions must be made on the basis of incomplete information" (15). Bernstein continues with an added explanation for why the young, who are typically more beset with the problem of incomplete information than the old, might delay saving: "Not acting has value. The more uncertain the outcome, the greater may be the value of procrastination. Hamlet had it wrong: he who hesitates is halfway home" (15).

My list of examples so far assumes that time frames change economics, but it might very well be that economics affects time frames. We economists understand that an increase in wages affects people's opportunity cost for doing things such as going to a movie. I can only guess that it has a more profound impact by affecting the way people conceive of time and deal with it. I say that because so many people who are highly paid seem to always be in a rush, which seems to me to imply making more time out of that which they have, as measured by minutes and days.

REASONS FOR TIME DIFFERENCES

Behaviors differ among individuals and groups of people. Some groups save more than other groups, even after adjusting for key factors such as income. A host of external considerations—several of which are typically introduced into the standard econometric analysis—may explain these differences. Economists who assume time is constant, however, would never think to consider differences in subjective time as one of the key variables left out of the analysis—and certainly they do not usually consider forces that may influence people's conception of time.

Differences in subjective time may have several identifiable causes. They may be comparable to the differences in people's assessments of the value of fruit. Some people just view fruit and time differently than do other people. Why? They are different people; the explanation may be no more complicated than that.

However, the sources of perceived time differences are likely to be more fundamental. People may perceive time differently at different ages simply because any given unit of time is an ever-changing proportion of the total amount of time experienced. A year at age one is 100 percent of total time experienced; it is 2 percent at age 50. A year may, in some sense, be a year at all stages of life, but people's assessment of a year, whether in length or value terms, can be distorted by the amount of time that has been experienced.

Sources of differences in the perception of time may also be the consequences of economic and biological considerations. Economists have long argued that people will economize on the use of resources the relative prices of which have risen and vice versa. Automobile makers will use less steel when its price rises relative to other inputs, partly because fewer cars will be sold and partly because the metal "skins" of cars will be made thinner; and students will use less paper (and more of other educational inputs) when the price of paper rises relatively, partly because the available paper will be used more judiciously and intensely. Similarly, wage rate increases can cause people to economize on time, to use the time applied to any endeavor more intensely. People who are paid by the project or whose livelihood is dependent upon the continuing development of their human or physical capital stock—that is, entrepreneurs—may be even more time sensitive than people who are paid by the hour. Entrepreneurs have an economic incentive to find more "time" within any given block of externally measured time (for example, an hour), and the incentive may be strong enough to make them harried, constantly in search for time that, in the absence of the economics of time, would have gone "unused" and unnoticed. Such people may very well see time pass more slowly than people who do not have similar incentives.

As noted, researchers in psychology have found that the experience of "time duration" is a function of the amount and complexity of stimuli received as well as how easily the received stimuli could be coded or organized into a pattern (Ornstein 1969, chapter 4). That is to say, the greater the number and complexity of the stimuli received during a constant measured time period, the longer the subject, on average, thought the time period actually was. The more easily coded the stimuli, the shorter subjects reported duration to be. Time may appear to pass more rapidly with age simply because younger people are faced with a much larger array of stimuli that are relatively new, are fairly complex (given their experience), and are not yet easily coded or organized into a pattern. As people age, they ignore many stimuli as being irrelevant, and they find that many repeated stimuli are no longer difficult to comprehend and to organize into comprehensible patterns. Life, in other words, becomes less complex and more routinized.

Findings in modern biology—specifically, chronobiology, or the "study of temporal processes at all levels of biological organizations" (Hekkens, Kerkhof, and Rietveld 1988)—suggest that differences in the perception of time may be physical, even genetic. One of core deductions of Einsteinian theory is that biological clocks are not necessarily constant, and one of the more interesting facts of animal life is that species tend to have the same average number of heartbeats—about 800 million—no matter how long they live (which, unfortunately, I've been able to document only with reference to its citation on the Public Television program *Nova*). A fly has, on average, approximately the same number of heartbeats as an elephant over their respective lives. The elephant lives longer but has a slower heartbeat than the fly. Chronobiologists have linked species' heart rate to their metabolic rate: the higher the metabolic rate, the higher the heartbeat and the shorter the life span. However, that does not necessarily mean that the fly experiences a shorter life span than the elephant.

Chronobiologists speculate that a specie's metabolic rate affects the its conception of time. A fly, then, perceives time in shorter units (and using our film metaphor, more frames per second) than does an elephant, because of the fly's higher metabolic rate. Such physical linkages (if they do, in fact, exist) can be important to economics because they may offer a potential biological explanation for observed economic behavioral differences. Young people, whose metabolic rates are generally higher, may save less than old people because their metabolic rates are higher.[17]

Accordingly, differences in metabolic rates possibly would explain, at least partially, differences in the rates of saving for different groups and, hence, their level of prosperity.

What is remarkable about this new perspective for time is that it offers the potential for explaining a portion of the standards of living of different ethnic groups. One group or another may be more prosperous today simply because of the group metabolism or other attributes that affect time. If metabolism affects time, diet can affect time. If continual use of computers affects time, so the introduction of ever-more-powerful microprocessors can affect time and, therefore, saving and growth rates. A change in the age composition of the population can have similar affects. Given that exercise can increase a person's metabolic rate and longevity (Poehlman and Danforth 1991; Poehlman et al. 1992; Poehlman, Melby, and Badylak 1991), it is possible that exercise will affect saving in two possibly offsetting ways: first, exercise can increase earnings and savings and postpone the dissaving phase of later life; second, it can lengthen the time units, reducing the inclination to save.

I understand the speculative nature of what I am saying, but I also understand that I may be charting a new course for much new research that, regrettably, I cannot handle. And I don't think my preliminary comments will be the last word that can be written on the many unexplored linkages between physical conditions, the conception of time, and the wealth of nations. One of the luxuries of being able to give this lecture is that I can be somewhat speculative, and I am expected to be so. However, I hasten to insist that my arguments are, very likely, no more speculative than so much of economic analysis that is founded on the claim that time is always and everywhere constant to everyone.

TIME VERSUS DISCOUNT RATES

While few economists have treated the prospects of time as a variable, most have implicitly, if not explicitly, assumed that different people have different discount rates (some measure of the urgency to consume set in percentage terms). They assume that the young typically have higher discount rates than the old. The young, therefore, are less likely than the old to be lured into saving by the reward of market-determined interest rates. Economists often assume that people's discount rates fall as they age, until at some point when the market-based interest rates become an attractive inducement to postpone consumption.

Hypothesized differences in discount rates appear to have exactly the same effect on behavior that the hypothesized differences in time units have. Does it matter, then, which is the focus of analysis? For many purposes, the answer is obviously "no." Predictions of saving behavior over a life cycle will be the same regardless of whether our assumption is that discount rates are falling or that the time units are shortening.

Nevertheless, an assumption that individuals' discount rates vary may be useful as a basis for prediction, but it may be totally wrong as a factual matter. An older person may have exactly the same discount rate as a younger person—just as the earthbound twin may have exactly the same discount rate as his or her sibling in the midst of high-speed space travel. They may behave very differently (or discount future events differently) simply because they have different time frames. Just as it would be descriptively wrong to ascribe differences in the saving behaviors of the twins in the physics example to differences in discount rates, it would be descriptively wrong (at least potentially) to attribute differences in saving behaviors of the young and old people to different discount rates.[18]

To be sure, there are a number of good reasons for looking beyond discount rates and considering the prospect that subjective time units differ. Let us consider several of the more prominent ones.

First, differences in time units could explain the assumed differences in discount rates, extending the completeness, if not the sophistication, of analyses.

Second, different people do profess differences in their time preferences, with some feeling a stronger urge to consume currently and not delay consumption, but they also express different conceptions of time. People readily acknowledge differences in individuals' internal biological clocks. (As noted, older people readily acknowledge that time, for them, has "sped up" as they have aged.) To maintain that it is only discount rates that differ is to deny important information provided by introspection.

Third, behavioral differences may occur when different discount rates combine with different units of time. Two individuals with identical internal discount rates may save at different rates simply because they use different subjective time units That is, in more concrete terms, one teenager may have exactly the same resistance to delaying consumption as another; but they may save at different rates. Their current saving rates could result from their professed differences in subjective time units. Alternatively, one teenager may be able to envision a further removed time horizon than the other because the time units are shorter and because he or she is more adept in evaluating the consequences of current actions on far-removed events. Combining the effects of a discount rate with time units to form one variable, called *the* discount rate, can both obscure useful information and render the analysis less than complete. Using such a composite variable would be tantamount to discussing the effects of nominal price changes without any concern for the potential explanatory value and power of recognizing the independent—at times often conflicting and at other times complementary—real income and substitution effects embedded in the nominal price changes. Discount rates can indeed fall at the same time the time units become longer (just as might be the case when older and older people are sent off into space at faster and faster speeds or when older and older people consume foods that cause their metabolic rates to rise).

Fourth, conceiving of differing time units, whether real or imagined, enables economists to tie into the established findings of physical scientists and then to make predictions that normally would not occur to the physical scientists. Moreover, internal discount rates and time frames may be affected by separate biological and physical factors. As noted earlier, if time units are affected by metabolic rate, as some chronobiologists think, and if the casual linkages are valid in human contexts, then we might expect saving and investment rates to be inversely related to metabolic rates. Chronobiologists would not normally draw that connection; at the same time, economists steeped in the view that time is constant (or nonexistent for modeling purposes) would not normally think to look to biology for grounds to explain differential saving (and growth) rates.

Similarly, physicists steeped in Einsteinian relativity theory understand that speed and gravity are related to time, but they would not normally think to relate the speeds of moving bodies in outer space (or even on this planet) to rates of saving and investment. If the theory of relativity is correct, then it stands to reason that the inhabitants that might exist on fast-moving bodies in space would, from the time perspective of Earth and everything else being equal, have lower saving and investment rates and would be in less advanced stages of development than inhabitants of bodies moving at slower speeds.[19]

I have noted that physicists have, since the days of Einstein, deduced that the astronaut twin on his return to Earth would be younger than his earthbound sibling. However, the two twins would likely differ in far more important ways than age, a point that heretofore does not appear to be recognized by physicists. Everything else being constant, the astronaut twin would likely be less wealthy and less educated than his earthbound sibling. This is because from the perspective of Earth, the astronaut twin would have been earning less (assuming that the pay rate was set according to their individual time frames) and saving and investing at a slower rate in both physical and human capital than his earthbound sibling.[20]

However, there is no reason to believe that high-speed space travel would have affected their lifetime earning, saving, and investing profile. At the same *physical age*, both twins might be equally wealthy and well educated. Then again, we can't be totally sure, given that the astronaut twin would not (likely) be subjected to the same daily and seasonal influences that would influence the earthbound twin's conception of time.

On a more earthly scale, note that gravitational pull varies across the Earth. Its pull depends on latitude and altitude. Generally speaking, the more northern the latitude and the higher the altitude above sea level, the lower the gravitational pull. Perhaps these differences in gravitational pull translate into minute changes in how people perceive time, changes so minute that they may not be economically meaningful within, say, only one generation's time frame. If we allow for the prospect that time varies even a little by geographical location and feature, we may begin to suspect that differences in the way different people perceive time may have resulted in differences in the long-term economic development of different peoples at different locations on Earth. As noted, over the course of many centuries, even small differences in perceived time could translate into significantly different levels of economic development. Granted, gravitational differences may still not be expected to explain more than a minute degree of the development differences on Earth. However, that may not be the case in the cosmos, where the sizes and density of planets may be a large multiple (or small fraction) of the gravitational pull on the Earth.

Naturally, many factors affect the long-term economic development of groups of people. What is being suggested is no different from the suggestion that climate, politics, and political and economic institutions all explain some part of long-term development. Weather, systems of justice, respect for property, and speed and gravitational pull can matter, especially since their effects can be cumulative over very long stretches of time (hundreds of millions if not billions of years) envisioned by physicists.[21]

CONCLUDING COMMENTS

All economic activity takes time, while all static economic analysis assumes away time. In dynamic economic analysis, time is always assumed to be constant across time intervals. The purpose of this lecture has been to help economists break with tradition in economics and recognize time as potentially variable, as it is in physics and in everyday experience. Physicists have documented the variability of time with changes in gravitational pull and speed. That point is important not because such forces might be "large," but only to stress that time is not the physical constant that it is assumed to be by economists. Having acknowledged variable time in physics, economists might be more open to the prospect that time varies for other, more subjective reasons that are more agreeable to the economic way of thinking. One fact stands out: practically everyone admits to the changing nature of time with age. That point suggests the possibility that time is conceived differently in different cultures and perhaps under differing circumstances.

I understand that I have made a claim—that time is variable—that I have not been able to fully document at this time. At the same time, economists have made even less of an effort to document the conventional assumption of constant time. Given that few people would profess that time is always the same, we can only wonder—without further investigation—who stands on firmer conceptual grounds.

If time is indeed a variable, its variability may have important explanatory power (quite apart from the variability of discount rates). While this lecture settles little about the role of time, I submit that it has been unsettling. Its purpose has been to explore a few of the many and varied possible effects of time on economic development by speculating about the effects of differences in both real time and perceived time on key time-based variables—namely, saving, investment, and income growth rates. Given all of the as yet unknown and unexplored linkages between biological and physical forces on people's conception of time, judgments concerning the importance of these forces on saving and investment and economic development must be reserved. Again, at the same time, economists must recognize that their own view of time may be no less speculative and audacious than the one suggested here—and it may, in truth, be misleading and confining.

NOTES

1. For a discussion of the various conceptions of time in physics, biology, physiology, and psychology, see Sorokin (1964, 158–225).
2. They confess that time appears to fly by while they work or when they get into the "flow" of work, as they often describe it (meaning they lose track of time). Sleeping hours do not appear to be as long as waking hours. Time spent at boring tasks seems longer than time at interesting tasks (see Sorokin 1964, 166–67).

3. A simple least squares equation was run using as the dependent variable the number of minutes given by respondents for the perceived length of an hour today relative to what it was when they were eight years of age as the dependent and using age as the independent variable. A negative relationship was found: the older the respondent, the lower the number of minutes. The coefficient on age is significant at the 5 percent level. However, the decline was about 0.4 minutes for each year of age, meaning a 50-year-old person tended to see an hour equal to about 10 percent, or four minutes shorter. The inclusion of the gender of the person in the equation did not materially change the size or statistical significance of the age coefficient. However, the R-squared was only 2 percent.

4. To Newton, time was the great exogenously determined constant. "Absolute, true, and mathematical time of itself and from its own nature, flows equably, without relation to anything external, and by another name is called duration" (Newton [1698] 1934, 6–12).

5. Einstein has explained his theories for laymen (Einstein 1961).

6. These findings were supported by a similar experiment in 1975 and 1976 that involved atomic clocks on the ground and aboard planes that, on several different occasions, circled Chesapeake Bay for 15 hours without stopping. The aircraft flew at an average altitude of 30,000 feet. The clocks on the ground on average were approximately 50-billionths of a second older than the clocks in the air. Theoretically, clocks on the ground were expected to run somewhat slower than clocks at the top of a tower (and at any other height) and much slower than clocks in outer space (as described by Calder 1979, 31).

7. Similarly, because of the immensity of the gravitational pull of black holes, there is some boundary—the event horizon—beyond which nothing, not even light, can escape. Clocks circling the exact edge of the black hole's outer perimeter would stand still, meaning that time itself would stand still, not that the clocks would be broken.

8. Einstein's prediction that speed and time are inversely related was confirmed with an experiment involving muons, which have a two-microsecond life span when stationary but that were sent hurtling around in a circle at 99.94 percent of the speed of light. The speed increased the life span of the muons by a factor of 30 (Calder 1979, 90–91).

9. When Einstein was only 16 years old, he wondered what he would observe if he were to follow a light beam through space. He deduced that he would see a "spatially oscillatory electromagnetic field at rest," which would imply that the laws of electromagnetism would be different for a person at rest than for a person on the move, which could not be true if laws were, as believed at the time, universally applicable. But the deduction led him to the conclusion that something had to give, and that something was assumed to be the "law" regarding the constancy of time (as reported by Clark 1971, chapter 4).

10. However, a light beam transmitted by the person riding the light beam would still move at the speed of light, 186,000 miles a second. If someone riding a light beam were to shine a flashlight out ahead, they would still measure the speed of light at 186,000 miles a second; so would the person observing the flashlight beam from Earth. This is because the person on the beam and on Earth would be measuring the speed of the flashlight beam from different time perspectives.

11. Alternatively, it might be said that if people were going to allocate their risk taking over the course of their lives, they would tend to concentrate risk taking in their later years.

12. A person who envisions their income stream increasing over future years can be expected to stabilize consumption over their life, which implies dissaving early in life, saving in the middle years, and dissaving in the later years of life. See Ando and Modigliani (1963) and Friedman (1957).

13. Admittedly, when faced with actual payoffs of between $5 and $17, the implicit discount rates were lower, but still they declined with greater payoffs and with the length of the time delay in receipt of the award (Thaler 1981, who cites Holcomb and Nelson 1989). This line of research also reveals that people tend to use higher discount rates to delay an award than to delay a penalty (Thaler 1981).

14. It may very well be that a part of the measured saving rate differentials between young and old can be explained by the fact that "saving" has been too narrowly measured.

15. The life-cycle saving pattern, as described, implies two age levels at which any given aging individual has the same planning time horizon—and at which they might be expected to save approximately the same amount.

16. Of course, this means that we may want to rethink addictions to drugs or anything else. Street drugs may affect people by changing their time frame and, thereby, making their demands only appear inelastic to external observers, including the drug pushers.

17. People's basal rate (occurring after extended rest and in the postnutrient absorptive state) tends to decline at a rate of 2 to 3 percent per decade, or 8 to 12 percent over the course of four decades, as determined by cross-sectional and longitudinal studies (Colloway and Zanni 1980; Dill et al. 1967; Keys, Taylor, and Grande, 1973; Poehlman et al. 1992; Robinson et al. 1975; Tzankoff and Norris 1978). It should also be noted that males' metabolism is, on average, higher than females, and the metabolism of black populations tends to be higher than comparable white populations (as reported in Kaplan and Pesce 1989, 527, 785).

18. The mistake would be the same as if physicists were to argue that differences in the saving rates of the twins considered earlier were due solely to differences in discount rates, when in fact they both had exactly the same discount rates. If physicists ignore the possibility and impact of variable time, they would probably predict that the identical twins would save at the same rate, regardless of either twin's perspective. As a factual matter, the twins would be saving at the same rate—within their respective time frames. However, each would observe the other saving at a different rate—from their own time frame.

19. Similarly, inhabitants on bodies near a black hole would be, everything else assumed equal, less advanced than inhabitants far removed from the black hole. Admittedly, everything else is not equal, but our analysis is still applicable: speed and gravitational pulls can affect the rate of economic development, at least as judged from the perspective of Earth and over the course of millennia. Given a choice of two planets of equal sizes and equal distance from other gravitational influences, the more developed economy is likely to be the one moving through space at the slower rate of speed.

    The differences in speed of the two bodies need not be great given the time since they both were hurled outward from the Big Bang. Slight differences in speed, which may make only slight differences in saving and investment rates, can make for very large differences in their current levels of development, given that the Big Bang may have occurred several billion years ago and civilizations may have arisen several million years ago. For much the same reason, the conception of time presented here leads to the conclusion that two different civilizations on different bodies outside the event horizon of a black hole do not have to be far removed from one another to have large differences in their current rates of development of their respective inhabitants.

20. The twins' relative wealth and education levels will, of course, depend upon the time frame chosen for payment of earnings and upon the extent of the communication between the spaceship and Earth. If the astronaut twin is paid at the same rate as the sibling on Earth and according to the time frame of the earthbound twin, then the astronaut twin will actually earn more over the course of life and, therefore, can be expected to save more over the entire course of life. However, communication between the spaceship and Earth will become progressively slower as the speed of light is reached, and then it will be impossible at the speed of light simply because the communication from Earth will not be able to catch up with the spaceship.

21. The analytical problem is complicated, of course, by the fact that physical factors can, through their impact on perceived time, affect people's inclination to adopt given political and economic institutions. To observers/analysts/economists—most of whom consider discount rates the only factor of consequence because time is constant and unaffected by physical factors—such thought may appear to be heresy.

REFERENCES

Ando, A., and F. Modigliani. 1963. "The 'Life Cycle' Hypothesis of Saving: Aggregate Implications and Tests." *American Economic Review* 54: 55–84.

Benzion, U., A. Rapoport, and J. Yagil. 1989. "Discount Rates Inferred from Decisions: An Experimental Study." *Management Science* 35 (March): 270–84.

Bernstein, Peter L. 1996. *Against the Gods: The Remarkable Story of Risk*. New York: John Willey & Sons.

Calder, N. 1979. *Einstein's Universe*. New York: Avon Books.

Calloway, D. H., and E. Zanni. 1980. "Energy Requirements and Energy Expenditure of Elderly Men." *American Journal of Clinical Nutrition* 33: 2088–92.

Courant, P., E. Gramlich, and J. Laitner. 1986. "A Dynamic Microestimate of the Life-Cycle Model." In H. G. Aaron and G. Burbles (eds.), *Retirement and Economic Behavior*, 279–309. Washington, DC: Brookings Institution.

Dill, D. B., C. Robins, and J. C. Ross. 1967. "A Longitudinal Study of 16 Champion Runners." *Journal of Sports Medicine* 7: 4–27.

Einstein, Albert. 1961. *Relativity: The Special and General Theory*. New York: Crown Trade Paperbacks.

Friedman, M. 1957. *A Theory of the Consumption Function*. Princeton, NJ: Princeton University Press.

Hall, R., and F. Mishkin. 1982. "The Sensitivity of Consumption in Transitory Income: Estimates from Panel Data on Households." *Econometrica* 50: 461–81.

Hekkens, W. Th. J. M., G. A. Kerkhof, and W. J. Rietyeld. 1988. "Preface." In Hekkens, Kerkhof, and Rietyeld (eds.), *Trends in Chronobiology*. New York: Pergamon Press.

Holcomb, J. H., and P. K. Nelson. 1989. "An Experimental Investigation of Individual Time Preference." Working Paper, Economics Department, University of Texas–El Paso.

Kaplan, L. A., and A. J. Pesce. 1989. *Clinical Chemistry: Theory, Analysis, and Correlation*, 2nd ed. St Louis: C. V. Mosby.

Keys, A., H. L. Taylor, and F. Grande. 1973. "Basal Metabolism and Age of Adult Men." *Metabolism* 22: 579–87.

Loewenstein, G. 1989. "Frames of Mind in Intertemporal Choice." *Management Science* 34: 200–214.

Mises, Ludwig von. 1963. *Human Action: A Treatise on Economics*. Chicago: Henry Regnery.

Modigliani, F. 1988. "The Role of Intergenerational Transfers." *Journal of Economic Perspectives* 2 (Spring): 15–40.

Newton, Isaac. [1689] 1934. *Philosophiae Naturalis Principia Mathematica*, Bk. 1. Trans. Andrew Motte (1729), rev. Florian Cajori. Berkeley: University of California Press.

Ornstein, R. E. 1969. *On the Experience of Time*. Baltimore: Penguin Books.

Poehlman, E. T., E. M. Berke, J. R. Joseph, A. W. Gardner, S. M. Katzman-Rooks, and M. I. Goran. 1992. "Influence of Aerobic Capacity, Body Composition, and Thyroid Hormones on the Age-Related Decline in Resting Metabolic Rate." *Metabolism* 41: 915–21.

Poehlman, E. T., and E. Danforth Jr. 1991. "Endurance Training Increases Metabolic Rate and Norepinephrine Rate in Older Individuals." *American Physiological Society* 261: E233–E239.

Poehlman, E. T., C. L. Melby, and S. F. Badylak. 1991. "Relation of Age and Physical Exercise Status on Metabolic Rate in Younger and Older Healthy Men." *Journal of Gerontology* 46: B54–B58.

Robinson, S., D. B. Dill, S. P Tzankoff, J. A. Wagner, and R. D. Robinson. 1975. "Longitudinal Studies of Aging in 37 Men." *Journal of Applied Physiology* 38: 263–67.

Shefrin, H., and R. H. Thaler. 1988. "The Behavioral Life-Cycle Hypothesis." *Economic Inquiry* 26 (October): 609–43.

Smith, T. Alexander. 1988. *Time and Public Policy*. Knoxville: University of Tennessee Press.

Sorokin, Pilgrim A. 1964. *Sociocultural Causality, Space, Time: A Study of Referential Principles of Sociology and Social Science*. New York: Russell & Russell.

Thaler, R. H. 1981. "Some Empirical Evidence on Dynamic Inconsistency." *Economic Letters* 8: 201–07.

———. 1992. *The Winner's Curse: Paradoxes and Anomalies of Economic Life*. New York: Free Press.

Tzankoff, S. P., and A. H. Norris. 1978. "Longitudinal Changes in Basal Metabolism in Man." *Journal of Applied Physiology* 45: 536–39.

5.14
Will Johnny Read Next Year?

EUGENIA F. TOMA

As most in this audience know, persons schooled in the Virginia tradition share a sense of camaraderie akin to that of a large, extended family. I am pleased that since my training at Virginia Tech, I have extended my Virginia schooling by spending sabbatical time at the University of Virginia. Faculty there, including Charles Holt, Bill Johnson, Ed Ofsen, and Roger Sherman, continue to embrace the Virginia tradition. And this year, I am working with a fellow Virginian, Dan Newlon, at the National Science Foundation. I think the lesson here is the Virginia badge is similar to a magnet. You wear it and get sucked into the magnetic field created by fellow Virginians, and there is no escape.

Although I do not intend to walk down memory lane this evening, I want to share with you an experience from my first semester of graduate school at Virginia Tech, because that experience has motivated me for the past 20-odd years. Because I am now 40-something and experiencing memory loss, I cannot recall the exact context in which the experience occurred, but I remember well the event. A certain professor, whose office was located in the Public

Prepared for the Fifteenth Annual Lecture in the Virginia Political Economy Lecture Series, George Mason University, Fairfax, VA, March 18, 1999.

Choice Center, one day rather loudly proclaimed that I was a perfect example of why women were thought to be inferior. Now I shall leave to you to think who might have been so blunt. I must say that at the time, I was devastated and had no idea that this particular professor only made such statements to those he deemed worthy of withstanding criticism. But the statement in the long run has proved to be quite motivating, and I perhaps should say thank you tonight to the individual. Without intent, he has had great influence in my life, and I even like him now. That day in the Public Choice Center, I became a public choice feminist (not an oxymoron). To this day, I view the world with my public choice eyes and with my feminist eyes. And this evening, I shall talk to you from both perspectives.

While the Virginia tradition is often associated with lofty topics such as constitutional designs for democratic societies, I am going to talk to you in terms of a very specific application of public choice models. I shall talk about schooling. Schooling, or education, is a difficult topic to present before a general audience. It is difficult because everyone in the audience is an expert and everyone has an emotional answer to the problems of schools. After all, many of you are parents with children in school. Childless persons are nonetheless experts on education because they once attended school. In spite of my awareness that I stand before a room of experts, I want to share my thoughts on education.

We currently are witnessing a rather dramatic change in the delivery of schooling in this country. Evolution is under way and, with few exceptions, academics are only beginning to take notice of the magnitude of these changes that are being discussed and implemented by the public policymakers. The academy remains entrenched in sometimes mundane estimation and technique issues, while all around us major changes are occurring. I hope to convince you, however, that the academy may very well be following, rather than leading, public opinion and policymakers in asking the interesting, innovative questions about the delivery of schooling. Significant contributions to the debate on education require us to think more radically than many in the economics of education arena have been doing for the past 20 years. Public choice or political economy scholars should be leading the way in this discussion. With this lecture, I am calling for the academy to address rigorously the issues about education structures that policymakers are now addressing. If changes are to be sustained and meaningful, I think the academy must inform the debate so that the optimism and the reform will be warranted and long lasting.

A few in the academy are beginning to notice the changing world and its implications for the delivery of schooling. To demonstrate, I should like to play a guessing game. An economist recently wrote, "Schooling on the surface appears to be a near perfect case for the superiority of private provision (over public provision). . . . The theoretical case of school choice and vouchers compared to the current system in the United States seems overwhelming." I shall give you one hint: the economist who said this is a He, so I have narrowed the field slightly. Was it Milton Friedman? No. Was it E. G. West? No. Was it James Buchanan? No. The quote is from Andrei Shleifer, a Harvard University professor, who claims no lineage to the Virginia School nor to the Chicago School. Precisely because he was trained at MIT and is at Harvard, his argument has attracted attention.

Most economists who have studied education in the last 20 or 30 years have built on a question asked by the great scholar and friend of public choice, James Coleman. The question that has been asked is whether school inputs such as expenditures, class size, and teacher salary influence the production of education. Using different data and different estimating techniques, they sometimes answer yes and sometimes no. Of great importance is that most of the questions and answers have been restricted to effects in public schools.

Educators, some economists, and policymakers are often surprised, or even distraught, when they learn that econometricians have been unable to demonstrate systematically the payoffs over the past 30 years from the infusion of resources into public schools. For persons schooled in political economy, the empirical findings are less puzzling. Nevertheless, even the most jaded among us have difficulty understanding how real spending that has increased from $1,815 per pupil in the school year 1949–1950 to $5,623 in 1994–1995 could yield such few gains in measured achievement. The growth in spending for public schools has been more than triple the growth in GNP in this century. The spending per pupil in public schools today exceeds the tuition of the vast majority of private schools in the country.

There are certain institutional settings where we should expect to find that school inputs matter and others where they will not have the socially desired effect. And it is this line of research that is leading scholars, public choice and otherwise, to agree with the conclusion that Milton Friedman reached over 30 years ago. Vouchers are preferable to the current system of schooling.

Incentives matter whether applied to educators or auto producers, and the incentives at play in our current system are incongruent with the world in which we now live. Because incentives matter, I propose that we begin thinking beyond vouchers and think about a truly private system of delivery of schooling in this country. I shall outline an alternative system in which individual consumers and individual producers will face the incentives necessary for teaching and learning. The system will be one in which producers will be rewarded for innovation in the education enterprise. It will be one in which the changes of the world will be reflected in schooling as the changes happen. But before describing the scheme for a new system of schools, I want to reflect upon our current system and the support that remains for that system. Following this reflection, I shall discuss reasons why I think the time is right for a radically new system that realigns incentives.

A complex system of policy making governs our public schools. The federal, state, and local governments all bear some responsibility for policies regarding the schools and are sources of revenues. At each level of government, elected representatives as well as appointed executives and administrators play a role in decision-making. In addition to those expressly chosen for the educational decision-making positions, others influence the policies of these elected and appointed boards and agencies. Each state has its own affiliates of the national teacher employee organizations, the National Education Association (NEA) and the American Federation of Teachers. Finally, parents and other taxpayers play a role in determining the policies of schools either through influencing the representatives or working directly at the school level.

Public school decision structures, like other democratic organizations, have evolved in such a way to represent all those persons who have a stake in the schools' output, either directly as consumers or producers or indirectly as financiers of the schools. While at first glance this may seem laudable, upon further reflection we can attribute many of the failures of the current system to the diffuse and complex structure of policy making. Precisely because of the representative nature of the educational system, for example, change is slow. It happens only after coalitions of the necessary political interest groups form across the variety of levels of government. If change occurs that advances the level of educational achievement, those responsible for inciting the change often are left without rewards. They remain uncompensated because the process for generating change is so diffuse and obtuse that those who sparked the change often cannot be identified. The incentive to experiment with new pedagogy at the individual classroom level or even the individual school level has been lacking.

Furthermore, the individuals who failed to provide the education also have been exempt from responsibility. Substantive educational policy changes most often have stemmed from the state level of government and from bureaucrats far removed from the production process. The states typically implement change with mandatory requirements applying to all schools. If the pedagogy is not correct or the policy works for some students but not others, we do not learn first with small experiments. Rather, we impose change on a system of schooling, and then success or failure is shared by all. When policies do change, they tend not to be marginal. We switch from phonics to whole-word reading or from old math to new math, and to the classroom teachers these changes appear overnight and without their input. After several years, we often revert to the original plan and, again, the reversion may occur overnight from a teacher's perspective.

The system of change barely resembles change within private organizations. There, a firm discovers a better way of making widgets, institutes the new process, and finally, the industry emulates the successful firm. Those that discover the better widget-making process are rewarded in the form of economic profits. And the firms that stubbornly refuse to adapt their methods of production bear economic losses.

A system of schools that is largely static can perform reasonably well in a society of homogenous individuals with few technological advances. Casual empiricism suggests public schools in the United States functioned at somewhat satisfactory levels in the first half of the 20th century, at least for certain segments of society. The success of this country and, to some extent, the success of schools in educating the public have brought enormous changes to the world. The great advances in transportation alone lowered the costs of trade between states and countries. Similar inventions and discoveries in the telecommunications industry reduced further the costs of trade and created the so-called global economy. What served us reasonably well when our communities were small and relatively homogenous does not serve so well in a large, urban, diverse, and dynamic world.

At the same time that the world has changed, so has the configuration of schools and school districts. Both the size of schools and the districts governing the schools have grown throughout the latter half of this century. The larger constituency served by schools and districts conceivably would generate efficiency gains if all persons were identical in tastes. If anything, tastes and preferences have grown more diverse over this period. In many parts of the United States, the descendants of Western Europe now constitute a minority of the population. With immigrants from Eastern Europe, Asia, Africa, and Central and South America, the culturally determined tastes of parents represented in the political process are clearly not homogenous. The growth in cultural diversity contributes to the diminished ability of schools to satisfy the parents and contributes to falling support for the public system.

The changing composition of the body politic and the radical changes in technology, especially over the last two decades, have greatly increased the cost of a public system of schooling. From a political economy perspective, these external factors are changing the political calculus that has kept the public system in place. Consider just one factor. The benefits from schooling as measured by standard rates of return are greater than at any point in modern history. The earnings of college graduates today exceed by more than 70 percent the individual with the same job experience but who completed high school. A significant portion of the earnings' differential stems from the technological changes that have occurred in the last quarter of this century. As a society, we demand highly trained and highly educated persons to produce more technological innovation.

As the individual monetary rewards to higher education increase, it becomes more costly to support an inefficient delivery structure at the lower levels. The opportunity costs of bad schooling are becoming apparent to individuals and to the collective. With sufficiently high returns to schooling, the costs of enduring a bad system exceed the costs of the free-rider problems associated with collective action. The public tolerance for the inefficiencies of the system for an extended period is related to the fact that the greatest costs of this system have been paid by those in the lowest socioeconomic position. It is the poor in our society who have suffered most from bad schools. Consider that on average, students in private schools in the United States outperform those in public schools. But the statistics that are most revealing relate to income and performance differences. The children who gain the most from enrollment in private schools are those in the lowest socioeconomic category. Broken down into quartiles, the highest socioeconomic groups in the United States perform insignificantly different in the public and private schools. It is the lower socioeconomic groups in the United States whom the system has failed most noticeably over the past three decades. This is the category where dropout rates are greater than graduation rates. In certain inner-city schools such as those of Washington, DC, and Detroit, Michigan, only 36 percent of the students complete four years of high school. It has been shown that certain groups of African American male teenagers in inner cities in the United States face a greater probability of incarceration than of graduation.

Upper-income children, on the other hand, live in nice suburban homes and consume the best the public system has to offer. They get the best buildings, the best teachers, the most rigorous curriculum, and the widest variety of extracurricular activities. The costs borne by the children of university professors are real but are hidden. Relatively to all other children, they do the best. Increasingly, this disparity in benefits from the current system is reflected in polls regarding minorities' support (although not the minority leadership) for vouchers and other alternative delivery systems such as charter schools.

Historically, the persons in the lowest rungs of the socioeconomic distribution have not been the persons who have exercised political power in this country. Today's rapidly changing environment is contributing to a shift in the political calculus of the body politic at large and of this group in particular. Two factors are causing the political participation by the poor to change with respect to schooling decisions. The first is the effect of technology on the returns to schooling. As illustrated earlier, the returns to higher education are increasing tremendously. Individuals who receive bad schooling at the elementary and secondary levels either drop out or do not pursue schooling beyond the high school years. As technological change continues to occur, the wedge between individuals who receive good schooling in the early years and those who receive bad schooling will expand.

The second and related change in terms of the political calculus comes from the public policy arena. The decade of the 1990s has altered the nature of the so-called safety net.[1] The welfare system is shifting to a safety net with term limits. After a specified period of time of receiving welfare benefits, individuals must work. If they must work, it becomes more costly to have skills that generate income below subsistence level. Individuals who previously depended on welfare and now must work to provide the financial support of a family will view the costs of bad schooling to be higher to them than under the previous system of welfare. During this transition period for the welfare program, we are attempting to remedy the failure of past schooling at the elementary and secondary levels by providing adult training that will generate a skill level that is consistent with a minimally acceptable level of income. Under the new welfare regime, we are committed to publicly financing the skill development of those who are insufficiently trained as children. But this is inefficient, for early learning facilitates later learning (Heckman 1998). The lack of quality education in the early years adds costs for the individual and society.

I should note that the policy change in welfare is fundamentally inconsistent with our policies in education. In education, we continue to ignore the individual responsibility part of the social welfare equation. Although they are loosening, limitations still remain on the choice of schools that individuals attend and the curriculum that they study. If we are to emphasize individual responsibility in other policy arenas, then it is logically inconsistent to leave such a fundamentally basic and large arena as education outside the loop. Individual responsibility implies that rewards and punishments flow not only to those consuming the schooling but also to the individuals who provide the learning. Several economists have demonstrated that enrollment choice and, thus, individual responsibility on the consumer side can be introduced via vouchers in the context of the existing delivery system. I argue, however, that individual responsibility on the supply side will be accomplished only through a fundamental restructuring of the means of producing schooling. To this point, I shall return later.

Return now to the issue of political support for the current system. The political calculus that is changing among the poor is accompanied by a quiet shift occurring among the middle class as well. The shift in position by the middle class also has been facilitated by the dramatic technological advances of recent years and is coming in the form of a movement toward homeschooling. Homeschooling has been part of educational culture throughout history. E. G. West tells me that John Stuart Mill was homeschooled. So too were Albert Einstein, Amadeus Mozart, and George Washington. But what is different now from then is the preference for homeschooling given the widespread availability of other types of schools. Limited empirical evidence suggests that the growth in numbers of children being homeschooled can be linked to education of women (Houston 1999). Enrollment of women accounts for a major proportion of the growth in college attendance during World War II. As a consequence of greater educational attainment, women face far greater options in the workforce today than in previous generations. Equally significant, due to the increased educational attainment and the technological changes, parents (usually women) can educate at home with greater efficiency than ever before. A woman with a college education faces lower production costs today for two reasons. First, her own training increases the efficiency with which she can impart knowledge to her child. Second, the computer world has lowered the cost of gaining access to the materials needed to provide the education. While we would not expect to see women with PhDs or MBAs providing schooling for their children at home, it is reasonable to expect the woman with some college training, especially in certain fields, to view the home school as a viable option in today's world.

The education of women is, to some degree, changing the political support for public schools. As more people exit the traditional public system, support for the status quo public system erodes. Persons who are homeschooling have a political advantage in that they have formed organized coalitions through homeschooling associations. One state's recent attempt to regulate homeschooling was soon dropped because of the rapid opposition mounted by the homeschooling association in the state.

Wealthy parents, today and historically, have disproportionately expressed dissatisfaction with the public schools for their own children by using the exit option and having them attend private schools. The proportion of families opting for private schools remains fairly constant at approximately 10 percent of students. Certain parts of the country and in parts of some states, the averages do not hold, but there appears to be no dramatic shift in this sector of schooling.

This constant enrollment in private schooling, in combination with lessened support from the poor and the middle classes, has changed the constraints confronting the publicly provided schools. The public bureaucrats are attempting to slow the erosion of attendance and political support by the middle and upper middle classes. One response has been the creation of schools of special character. In the 1970s these schools began as magnet schools, and today the new wave in public schooling is the charter schools. These schools develop charters that specify the goals and performance standards that will be used to measure their success. In return, they are exempt from many of the regulations applying to the traditional public schools. In addition, limited experiments with vouchers for private school enrollment are occurring in certain cities. And increasingly, districts are beginning to reconsider the residential zoning that has determined enrollment at the public schools.

I want to return to the charter schools a bit later but first talk about vouchers. Vouchers are simply a means by which taxpayers fund all or a portion of the costs of privately provided schooling. They are a means of separating the funding and production decisions in the delivery of schooling. While we may not have a consensus in this audience, economists generally agree that public financing of schooling mitigates the imperfect capital market externality that would exist under a privately produced, privately financed system of schooling. In particular, individuals cannot borrow against future human capital, and there likely will be underinvestment in schooling under a pure market system of schooling. There is an underlying efficiency argument for publicly financed schools.

Some economists have begun to look at different configurations of vouchers that would elicit support from the body politic. Professors Hoyt and Lee have shown that a system of vouchers can be designed that generates wealth gains and, therefore, political support among taxpayers (1998). Because vouchers cause students to leave the public system and enroll in private schools, properly designed vouchers can reduce the overall tax burden for schooling. They have demonstrated that the voucher necessary for public support will differ by state because the level of spending and the relative proportion of the population enrolled in public schools differ. Professors Chen and West have demonstrated more recently that a S3/stem of targeted vouchers will dominate a system of universal vouchers in terms of generating political support from the median voter (2000). Both these papers have focused on political support that arises from a change in the tax price associated with providing schooling. Again, I think these exercises are necessary for the academy if we are to inform the debate on the design of a system of schooling that enhances efficiency.

In a series of papers, Professors Epple and Romano are addressing a second issue that underlies the conceptual debate over vouchers and systemic reform of schooling (1998a and b). This issue is peer effect externalities. Peer effects are the spillover effects on learning that come from mixing with other students. While the evidence is incomplete, the emerging consensus tends to be that low-achieving children gain more from mixing with high-achieving students than high-achieving students lose by mixing with low-achieving students (Zimmer and Toma 2000). Those who oppose vouchers often do so because of the concern that the best schools will "skim the cream" from the public schools and the worst-off students will be left alone in the weakest schools.

To see this externality at the most basic level, suppose Ms. High Class is aware that children from lower socioeconomic households benefit from placement in a classroom with her child. Further, she knows that her precious, precocious child will suffer only small amounts by sharing space with these less advantaged, not-so-bright children. While with a sufficiently big heart, Ms. High Class might be willing to allow some of these advantaged children to associate with her rare, gifted child, it becomes more likely she would do so if she is compensated. There is some pricing scheme, in other words, that would induce Ms. High Class to allow her child to associate with those who are not similarly advantaged.

The peer externalities, however, reinforce the idea articulated by E. G. West and others that vouchers need not be given uniformly to all students. Rather, publicly financed vouchers could be structured to reflect the peer externalities to the extent they are correlated with some observable characteristic of the child or her family. There is a pricing mechanism, in other words, that conceptually would internalize the externalities by encouraging the mix of high- and low-ability students. Epple and Romano have demonstrated that the vouchers could be targeted by school rather than to the individual as a means of addressing the externalities (1998a and b). Their work shows that vouchers could be targeted to address the peer issues raised by academics and policymakers.

Those who oppose vouchers and support the status quo system of schooling on the basis of peer externalities are ignoring the realities of a world in which schools are publicly financed and publicly operated. The zoning patterns of urban life in the United States today do not lend themselves to significant mixing of children by socioeconomic class. To the extent that socioeconomic status and ability are correlated, the system also fails to achieve mixing on the basis of ability. Inner cities disproportionately serve as the home of the poor, while the middle and upper classes live in the suburbs. At least one economist has proposed forced busing as the answer to the peer externalities. Forced busing was not acceptable to the body politic as a means of achieving racial integration, and my strong suspicion is that it will not be acceptable cast in a slightly different way.

So, am I presenting just another case for vouchers this evening? No. I do suggest that vouchers can be designed to alleviate some of the conceptual problems of a pure market system of schooling. And I am suggesting that comparing market outcomes to an ideal world is a different standard than the comparison between the market and our world of publicly provided schooling. Vouchers can address issues of access, of peer externalities, and can grant choice to individual households. With choice will come increased competition and some quality gains to the delivery of schooling. Many economists now agree on these points.

As I shall illustrate with an example applied to charter schools, a shift to vouchers alone leaves intact major obstacles to meaningful, long-run reform and improvement of schools. Consider the state of Florida. The state has passed legislation that allows the establishment of charter schools. As stated earlier, the charter adopted by the school purportedly diminishes the regulations imposed on the school and frees it to adopt a special character. More competitive, more diverse school types are predicted to emerge from the charters. Significantly, some are now predicting that Florida will be one of the first states to adopt statewide vouchers for its schools. Viewed from a public choice perspective, charters are a response to the external threats to the traditional public system.

In Florida, evidence is already accumulating to suggest that the charters will not achieve their stated effect in terms of competition enhancement. A major reason they will fail ultimately to improve schooling can be attributed to an interest group that has a vested interest in prohibiting competition and has stood in the way of proposed reforms across the states. This group is the teacher unions. In Florida, the teacher unions have been involved in pushing legislation that will extend to the charter schools the collective bargaining rules, the teacher certification rules, and other rules that currently apply to the production of education within the traditional public schools.

The problem posed by the teacher unions is simple within a political economy context. The teacher unions and, in particular, the management of the unions, are competing for the rents created by a publicly provided system of schooling. A recent advertisement in the *Washington Post* by the National Education Association illustrated the strength of the continuing opposition to reform by the unions. In the page-long ad, the unions voiced a passionate plea to the public to resist reform and send more money for the continuing support of public schools as we have known them in this century.

The union management is properly concerned that introducing choice via vouchers and charters can reduce the potential rents from the production of public schooling. But as the Florida example illustrates so vividly, the reduction in rents can be reversed by ever-more-stringent rules that guide the inputs into the production process and, thereby, restore the monopoly production system. And under almost any publicly financed system, this problem looms.

So is there no hope for true reform? Quite the contrary; we can accomplish radical reform by realigning incentives. We can create structures so that the incentives of the teachers and their professional organizations coincide with the incentives of the public. To achieve this, I propose first that we implement a system of targeted vouchers. The vouchers will vary across states and across income categories but can be designed to win the political support of the consumers of schooling and the taxpaying public. Although they can be designed to win the support of the median voter and the poor and the rich, vouchers will continue to be opposed by the producers of education or the unions. Designing the correct voucher system does not purchase the support of the unions. The gains that the union reaps as a collective from the system of public schooling exceed the gains they would capture from lower taxes via a voucher system.

The suppliers of schooling do not benefit from vouchers, targeted or not, and as suppliers of a monopoly product they will continue to oppose meaningful reform. To garner political support from the suppliers, I propose that we combine the targeted vouchers with a major structural change: assign private ownership rights over the schools by giving them to the teachers and their unions. Make the teacher unions residual claimants in the strongest sense of the term. By owning the schools, the teachers and union members will face incentives that coincide with the incentives of parents and taxpayers. The benefits from schooling subsequently will be shared by the public and the unions.

The production of education is a very labor-intensive activity. Even with today's advances in computer technology, the high costs of producing schooling are tied to salaries of teachers and administrators. The capital assets required in schooling are minimal. Based on a study that Bill Allen and I conducted in the state of Michigan, the value of owning schools does not lie in the value of any physical capital. In Michigan, in the aggregate, the depreciated value of the buildings and equipment used in the educational enterprise is less than the value of the outstanding debt on these buildings and equipment. Of course, in alternative uses such as nursing homes or retirement villages, these buildings and the land they occupy may carry positive net value. And, under my scheme, many existing buildings may be sold for alternative uses. For the sake of argument, let us separate the issue of physical capital from that of human capital. We can do so by allowing states to assume the net debt liability for the buildings and equipment. Again using Michigan as an example, the outstanding debt for schools is less than the amount spent in one year for operating expenses in the schools. And, approximately 80 percent of the operating costs are for salaries of teachers and administrators.

Abstracting from the issue of physical capital, the shares in schools will have value to the extent they represent a future stream of services that will yield benefits to a group of consumers. A school is valuable because it consists of a team of individuals that collectively delivers an educational output desired by the public. The team has specific human capital and knowledge about the educational process that is unique to each group. Within these teams is a collective wisdom about the production of education that the persons outside the education circles do not possess.

We do not want to institute a massive systemic reform in education that dissipates the collective store of knowledge necessary for producing schooling. Rather, we would want systemic reform that capitalizes on that source of knowledge but uses it in a more productive way than it has been used in the past. A daunting task confronting the teachers in the past has been that they have not had the signals commonly associated with market forces to guide them in the production enterprise known as education. With ownership assigned as in the marketplace, the signals will become available. To think more specifically about this plan, suppose we give each teacher, administrator, and union member ownership rights to the schools in the form of coupons that can be bought and sold, and these shares carry all the rights and responsibilities of ownership of private, for-profit stock. Several things will be apparent virtually overnight. Each set of owners will find the value of their stock differing depending on the school in which they participate as employee. Schools that the public views as good will have higher-valued stock than the schools that the public views as weak. The value of some schools will be sufficiently low that the owners will have to institute immediate changes in the way the school operates if they are to hold stock of positive value.

Of great importance, the teams in unproductive, low-valued schools will face options that offer rewards to them for innovating. Teams of employees that discover productive teaching methods will be rewarded via increases in the stock price of their schooling enterprise. They can then continue to operate the schools and capture the returns from success or they can sell their stocks to other teams interested in participating in a successful enterprise. Teams that fail to educate children will be taken over by other teams who possess the knowledge about teaching that will be necessary for producing good schools. Other schools will copy successful methods and adapt them for the special needs of different groups of students. Some teams may be so productive that they establish franchises. Some owners, or former employees, will decide that they are better off selling their ownership shares to more successful teams and will choose new occupations in the future. Significantly, the market will reveal the value of the stock of knowledge now held by the union members. The market will be the judge.

The union member, who is an owner, confronts different incentives than a union member who is an employee. The "union" no longer shares a common goal. Former union members who achieve success will face different objectives in lobbying than former union members who fail in the productive enterprise. Although my plan does not destroy the incentive that exists in every private industry to use the powers of government to grant itself monopoly rents, it introduces true competition into the supply side of the equation. Now the schools and their owners must compete against one another, and that alone diminishes the bargaining strength of an interest group. In the long run, we would likely see a variety of types of schools competing for students. There would be big schools, little schools, traditional schools, specialized schools, and franchise schools. We would see such variety because the population the schools serve is heterogeneous and likely would demand such schooling types. There might be McDonald's Schools and Kentucky Fried Chicken Schools as well as United Way Schools. But almost surely, there also would be the special little schools owned by an individual and offering a unique recipe cooked in just the most secret little sauce.

Interestingly, we also likely would see nonprofit, charitable, and religious schools continuing to offer education alongside the for-profit schools. Schools could choose whether they wanted to accept students that receive voucher funding. As in higher education, government funding will entail some regulation of the uses of the funds. But the tremendous benefit to this plan is that it would transform the decision-making locus of the schools. Rather than being dispersed across three levels of government and large numbers of agencies and individuals, decisions would be vested in those persons in the best position to judge the school population they serve. The owners would have the authority, the responsibility, and the incentive to introduce new techniques and new materials into the classroom. Although in the long run, teachers may not continue to be owners, they would benefit from any transfer of ownership away from themselves.

This plan fits well in the world in which we find ourselves as we enter the rapidly changing 21st century. Individuals are placed at the center of both decision-making and responsibility. With explicit ownership rights, teachers and administrators will reap the gains and bear the costs of their decisions. Their behavior will change because the new system will provide incentives confronting the owners that will be compatible with change. Precisely because we cannot forecast the future, we need a system of schooling that will adapt continuously and accommodate change as it occurs rather than in lumps and jumps. Precisely because we do not know the future, the system of schools that will accommodate the uncertainty is not one in which a group of elected or appointed officials decide how the schools should change.

Rather, a system in which any new information about the future gets reflected in the value of the learning enterprise today is a preferred system. And only a system of private, for-profit schools can internalize such information. With such a system, the teachers and administrators of the schools will have an incentive to innovate in response to new information. The new information may be as diverse as new discoveries about the brain and how we learn to new insights into technology and its uses for the future. Whatever the information, only the market has the capacity to incorporate it into the production of schooling or learning as the information becomes available. Public schools as we have known them throughout this century cannot change as rapidly as the world around us changes.

From the perspective of the academy, does a private, for-profit plan seem radical? The answer is absolutely yes. Even in today's changing environment, in most economics departments around the country, only a tenured professor who operates in fantasyland or a feminist schooled in the tradition of public choice would dare articulate such ideas to her colleagues. Does this mean that such a plan is not feasible? I think not. We have reached the point within the current system that the cost of marginal changes, including changing the number of dollars or the number of teachers in the classroom, is simply too high. We see too clearly the costs of schools that perform badly for a large segment of our population. It is time for major reform.

And now we come to the question posed in the title. Will Johnny read next year? I think so. I think the changing environment surrounding schools today has already begun to affect the underlying educational structure. And I think the political calculus of the body politic supports fundamental reform. At this point, we need the academy to address seriously the issue of private schooling, and we need the political entrepreneur who will lead a single state to go the next step. We can teach Johnny to read by properly structuring the incentives that face those with a stake in the schools. We need to define explicitly ownership of the schools, and the politically expedient way to do this is to give the schools to the unions.

In closing, I assume that it is abundantly clear that my approach to school reform reflects my training in the Virginia political economy tradition. The Virginia training gives us a license to seek adventure in our academic lives, and I am proud to have been trained in that tradition. For me, being a feminist reinforces the thrill of adventure. And for those of you who may have missed the feminist influence in the plan outlined this afternoon, I would like to remind you that I have just proposed the redistribution of large amounts of wealth in this country. I proposed that we give the schools to the teachers. Yes, teachers are disproportionately women. Thank you for your patience, and enjoy your evening.

NOTE

1. Thanks to Steve Craig, University of Houston, for this point.

REFERENCES

Chen, Zhiqi, and E. G. West. 2000. "Selective versus Universal Vouchers: Modeling Median Voter Preferences in Education." *American Economic Review* 90(5): 1520–34.

Epple, Dennis, and Richard Romano. 1998a. "Competition between Private and Public Schools, Vouchers, and Peer-Group Effects." *American Economic Review* 88(1): 33–62.

———. 1998b. "Educational Vouchers and Cream Skimming." NBER Working Paper No. 9354, National Bureau of Economic Research, Cambridge, MA.

Heckman, James. 1998. "Understanding the Sources of Skill Formation in a Market Economy." Gideon Fishelson Memorial Lecture (December).

Houston, Robert. 1999. "Home Schooling as an Alternative School Choice." PhD diss., University of Kentucky.

Hoyt, William H., and Kangoh Lee. 1998. "Educational Vouchers, Welfare Effects, and Voting." *Journal of Public Economics* 69(2): 211–28.

Zimmer, Ron, and Eugenia Toma. 2000. "Peer Effects in Private and Public Schools across Countries." *Journal of Policy Analysis and Management* 19(1): 75–92.

5.15
Economics and the Medieval Church

ROBERT D. TOLLISON

My lecture is about the economics of religion. The basis of the following remarks is the belief that economics can offer useful insights into religious behavior and institutional practices. As such, the economics of religion is one more example of the expansion of the basic paradigm of economics to a new area. Public choice was, of course, such an expansion, as were law and economics, the economic approach to crime, and still other important applications of basic economic methodology to areas outside of the normal purview of neoclassical/orthodox economics.

The application of the principles of self-interested behavior to religion is based upon the simple conviction that there is no such thing as a "noneconomic" sector of the human universe that is out of bounds for the work of the economist. There are obviously no guarantees that the economic model will explain behavior very well in these new applications, but there is nothing, short of a closed mind, that prevents a creative economist from trying to expand the domain of the economic model. And the proof is clearly in the pudding. We will either obtain new and interesting results about religion, or we will not.

Prepared for the Seventeenth Annual Lecture in the Virginia Political Economy Lecture Series, George Mason University, Fairfax, VA, March 15, 2001.

I will therefore provide an introduction to the economics of religion this afternoon (Iannaccone 1998). The primary vehicle for discussion will be the Catholic Church and its exercise of monopoly power during medieval times. The doctrines of usury and purgatory will provide the primary expository vehicles for discussion, and the latter case of purgatory will be accompanied by a tentative explanation of how various Protestant sects were able to enter the market for religious services in the face of the centuries-old Catholic monopoly (Ekelund, Hebert, and Tollison 1989, 1992, 2000; Ekelund et al. 1996).[1] A positive economic methodology is followed, with an emphasis on stating the argument in testable terms.

For example, Protestant entry was not successful in all geographic areas in Western Europe. Why?

ECONOMICS AND RELIGION

On the eve of the 20th century, the great neoclassical economist Alfred Marshall wrote that "the two great forming agencies of the world's history have been the religious and the economic" (1890, 1). Like most economists, however, Marshall tended to separate the two spheres and eschewed opportunities to analyze religious institutions on economic grounds. Two generations have elapsed since Marshall's death, and in the interim the domain of economics has continually expanded. Were he alive today, Marshall might be surprised at the breadth of modern economics, which runs the gamut of human actions—from "the ordinary business of making a living" (Marshall's own phrase) to lobbying activities in legislatures, to the form of contemporary music, to the sleep patterns of individuals, to the dynamics of family interactions, and so on.[2] By ranging far afield, modern economics promises to increase our understanding of many interesting and varied aspects of human behavior.

In its expanded form as "the science of choice," economics models the human decision nexus as a kind of economy, regardless of scientific domain. It matters little whether the problem is perceived as inherently economic or as anthropological, psychological, sociological, political, legal, or religious. For example, public choice theory applies economic principles to the study of political institutions.

The basic premise underlying these approaches is that economic elements come into play in all human decisions. Economists therefore have something to contribute to our understanding of such decisions. Whether or not economic elements *dominate* each decision is another question, one that cannot be resolved a priori or in a generalized way. Nevertheless, uncovering the economic elements in a decision nexus and applying economic analysis to the interpretation of the decision process should improve our understanding of observed behaviors at the margin.

This study lies outside the long-standing tradition that asserts that religious organizations are principally motivated by "otherworldly" interests (e.g., salvation). In this older intellectual tradition, the internal workings of religious organizations are treated as "epiphenomena," or outside the domain of self-interested maximization, primarily because religious belief is defined as a fundamental, faith-driven commitment to a system of ideas, norms, and values that lies beyond the calculus of rational choice. I employ the alternative approach that treats religious behavior as the product of rational choice. Spiritual considerations notwithstanding, decisions within religious organizations are made by human beings living in a worldly environment. Economists have long recognized that even actions ostensibly based on noneconomic criteria may be satisfying several objectives, both noneconomic and economic, simultaneously. Here I seek to uncover the purely economic aspects of decisions made by agents who, outwardly at least, were trying to satisfy economic and noneconomic goals simultaneously.

STYLIZED FACTS OF MEDIEVAL LIFE

Imagine a world where religion dominates everyday life. The priesthood plays a large role in the functioning of the ordinary economy. Ecclesiastical officials enact and enforce laws governing everyday transactions. Kings, princes, and dukes hold at least part of their power by grace of the religious authorities, who also arbitrate international disputes, maintain armies, and fight wars to promote their organizational ends. The dominant religious organization (the Christian Church) is immensely rich and controls most of the landed property in society. Most of the revenues of the Church flow from voluntary contributions of the faithful, who receive in return both spiritual and secular services. This thumbnail sketch approximately describes medieval Europe, wherein the Roman Catholic Church exerted more power than any single monarch and wielded such authority that historians commonly refer to the West during the Middle Ages as "Christendom."

THE CHRISTIAN CHURCH IN THE MIDDLE AGES

For the first three centuries of its corporate existence, Christianity thrived as a kind of underground movement, loosely organized, highly decentralized, and heavily persecuted. The formal character of the Catholic Church, the single institution that came to embody Christianity in its official capacity, emerged as a result of the Edict of Milan in AD 313.[3] In its early organizational structure, the primary authorities within the Church were bishops, who appointed and supervised priests at the parish level. By the time of Charlemagne, bishops were normally selected by the monarch of the countries in which their dioceses were located. The pope was merely the bishop of Rome over this early period and did not possess the central authority that has since come to be vested in the Vatican. Secular and ecclesiastic governments actively competed for the right to appoint and oversee clerics and Church administrators between the 9th and 12th centuries. Despite attempts by some early popes, such as Nicholas I (856–867), to overturn the practice of lay or secular investiture, the papacy was unable to enforce its "independence" until the 12th century, when Pope Gregory VII successfully wrested from the secular monarchs the authority to appoint bishops. Following this "papal revolution," the pope emerged as the supreme judicial and legislative authority in Western Europe. From the 12th century on, all matters pertaining to the ownership, use, and disposal of Church properties came under his authority. All testamentary cases were adjudicable in Rome, meaning that in the long run, the pope determined the allocation of most property rights in Europe. Henceforth, bishops (who served as heads of regional franchises) were subject to papal approval before assuming their duties, and all monastic orders and new monasteries likewise required the pope's consent.

THE CORPORATE STRUCTURE OF THE MEDIEVAL CHURCH

As the Church became increasingly centralized after the 11th century, its internal organization began to assume many of the aspects of the modern corporation. The type of contemporary organization began to assume many of the aspects of the modern corporation. The type of contemporary organization that the medieval Church resembled most is the multidivisional or "M-form" firm. According to Williamson (1975), this kind of firm is characterized by a central office that controls overall financial allocations and conducts strategic, long-range planning but allows divisional managers (usually regional) a high degree of autonomy in day-to-day operations.

The medieval Catholic Church approximately followed this general pattern, establishing an organizational form that appears to have operated successfully for many centuries in a difficult political and technological environment. The Church assigned operating decisions to essentially self-contained operating divisions, or "quasifirms," consisting of monastic orders, dioceses, and other subentities. The general office maintained an elite staff, the Curia (papal bureaucracy), that advised the pope in his role as chief executive officer (CEO) and also monitored and audited the behavior of the clergy who were attached to the operating divisions (much in the manner of franchises). The general office (Vatican) was the strategic director of Church policy. It planned, evaluated, and controlled Church functions and Church doctrines, without being directly "absorbed in the affairs of the functional parts." Finally, the Vatican allocated resources among competing divisions: for example, it could direct funding to special projects or grant tax exemptions to favored units, such as monasteries or specific established "national" churches.

Unlike General Motors, the medieval Church did not organize its divisions in terms of physically differentiated products. Rather than production of Chevrolets, Pontiacs, and Oldsmobiles, the Church produced services that were all ostensibly aimed at the same religious goal—namely, spiritual salvation. Despite the lack of overt physical differentiation, however, the products generated by separate divisions of the Church were distinguishable. Monasteries catered to the spiritual needs of the more intellectually inclined and to higher-income individuals. At the same time, some monks ministered to the poor, and some served as evangelists on the pagan frontiers of Europe. The cathedral chapters served inhabitants of larger urban areas and attracted pilgrims and other travelers who made monetary contributions to the cathedral.

POWERS OF THE PAPACY

Since the 11th century, the pope of the Catholic Church has been elected to a post conferring lifetime tenure and installed according to Catholic dogma as the direct heir to St. Peter and the representative of Christ on Earth. The "infallibility" postulate, formalized only in the 19th century, is far less sweeping than the term implies, but it does lend an aura of "supreme" authority to the office. Insofar as there is no official, established mechanism for removing a pope for malfeasance or other cause, the nature of the position might suggest that the pope is less a CEO in the modern sense than an absolute monarch. By the standards of conventional business practice, this arrangement would be relatively inefficient because it places the corporate CEO beyond effective accountability to shareholders. But there is reason to believe that the stable security of tenure given to the pope was a reasonable adaptation to medieval circumstances, one that lowered certain transaction costs and provided incentives for efficient papal behavior.

The pope's stable security of office contributed to the efficiency of the medieval Church in several ways. First, it helped to insulate the Holy Office from secular political pressure (e.g., having to face reelection). Prior to the Concordat of Worms, secular rulers often appointed and terminated popes at will for openly political reasons. Restricting the access of temporal rulers to such blatant "papal patronage" not only served to protect Church assets from governmental confiscation, it also raised the costs of rent seeking to potential "replacement" popes and their supporters. Lifetime tenure also reduced potential conflicts of interest on the part of the popes, who felt no compulsion to transfer Church wealth to their own account in anticipation of providing for their retirement years. Likewise, lifetime tenure greatly reduced the pope's incentive to take bribes or yield to intimidation by outside forces. Finally, lifetime tenure also meant that the pope had an incentive to promote the long-run interests over the short-run interests of the Church—the Church itself was a permanent institution that did not have to yield to short-run expediency.

Despite certain advantages, lifetime tenure was not absolute in the Middle Ages. Although tenure was normally quite secure, papal behavior was subject to an informal but effective constraint: the possibility of competition for the position by pretenders who were able to enlist the support of cardinals and bishops discontented with the current regime. In other words, the pope could technically, albeit unofficially, be fired and replaced. In the period between AD 1000 and 1450, 20 different "antipopes" actively claimed the papal office. Most were elected by rebellious cardinals—many with the support of various secular rulers. Some of the pretenders were actually more powerful than those legitimately elected. For instance, at the time of the First Crusade, antipope Clement III occupied the Vatican and commanded the support of most bishops in Germany and Italy. Partly for this reason, Pope Urban II preached the First Crusade from Clermont in southern France. Furthermore, in an era when many officially elected popes held their office for less than a year, several antipopes maintained power for extended periods. Elected as an antipope in 1080, Clement III remained in power until his death in 1100.

The process of competition between popes and antipopes in the Middle Ages was in many respects analogous to proxy fights that take place today between various shareholder groups of a corporation. Bishops, who held effective property rights in Church assets (with various limits on transferability), might elect an antipope to replace an existing pope when they became dissatisfied with the performance of a sitting pope. But only when the general clergy (those with grassroots control of Church assets) supported the usurper could the antipope hope to succeed in wrestling away control. Failing such support, the pretender had no more prospect of deposing the "legitimate" pope than dissident stockholders who lack a voting majority have of replacing an unpopular CEO. Thus, even with lifetime tenure as official Church policy, a pope (theoretically at least) could not engage in significant malfeasance without running the risk of encouraging an outside challenger.

Ultimately, of course, the tenure of a pope was limited by his mortality. Although elected for life, the average age at election was high and the typical period of office brief. Among the 63 legitimate popes who held office between AD 1000 and 1400, the average term in office was about six years. Eighteen of the 63 popes served one year or less. During this same interval, two reigning popes resigned, and three were deposed (albeit by political maneuvers of the emperor rather than by internal censure and removal).

In sum, the supply-side of the church was organized along the lines of a modern corporation, and this organization grew up in response to age-old problems of economic organization. The corporate center of the Church in Rome had to resolve massive agency problems in its field operations, and so on. For example, vertical relations issues had to be addressed, such as the formation of agreements between local operatives and Rome so as to avoid problems of double monopolization. It should also be kept in mind that the Church operated as a not-for-profit entity. This suggests that profits had to be consumed within the Church and that normal expense preference behavior would have been evident in Church operations. It should not be surprising, then, to observe Church investments in facilities and other perquisites for Church employees.

NATURE OF OUTPUT IN THE MULTIDIVISIONAL CHURCH

Given the complex and extensive nature of the medieval Church, it is necessary to distinguish between the institutional Church as a provider of public goods on the one hand and as a supplier of private goods on the other. As a kind of surrogate government, the Church provided a number of social and public goods to medieval society. An entire system of law and courts emerged under Church auspices that supplemented the ramshackle structure of governmental and legal institutions that existed during the Middle Ages. At a time when governmental social welfare programs were virtually nonexistent, the

Church maintained an elaborate system of voluntary institutions and practices designed to aid the poor. The Church also organized and supported educational institutions, which provided the bulk of human capital investment during the Middle Ages. Long before the emergence of strong nation-states, the Church used its transnational influence to limit armed conflict among petty warlords who dominated the political landscape of Western Europe.

As important as these contributions were, it is not my intention to examine in detail the public-goods aspect of the medieval Church. My focus is on the Church as a provider of private goods—that is, goods and services that were "purchased" in something resembling a market context. In this market context, religion is by its nature a service industry. The primary service supplied by the medieval Church to its customers was information about and guidance toward the attainment of eternal salvation. At issue here is not the veracity of the Church's theological claims, nor its ability to guarantee the end product, but rather the fact that whatever knowledge consumers possessed in this regard was provided entirely and exclusively by the Church. An important aspect of this service concerned the afterlife: the idea that the soul continues to exist for all eternity after the death of the body. To a medieval Christian, one's existence on Earth was a tiny part of "life"—while the average person might live a mere 40 or 50 years in the earthly realm, the soul's existence in heaven or hell would be forever. Each Christian therefore looked to the Church for advice and guidance on actions required to gain salvation. In this connection, the clergy provided a vital kind of "brokerage" service for the faithful.

Most people in medieval Christendom accepted the fact that the Church of Rome had a major influence over the disposition of their immortal souls—in other words, whether they went to heaven or hell. This belief is crucial to understanding the medieval Church as an economic organization. By virtue of this fact, the Church was the monopoly provider of a pure credence good. The credibility of Church courts, the validity of canon law, the acceptance of the Church as divinely sanctioned arbiter of earthly disputes, and the ultimate trust in the Church's various commercial commitments all derived from the credibility of the religious doctrines promulgated by the Church of Rome.

Despite some rather obvious limitations—the customer could not take salvation for a test drive, nor get a sneak preview of heaven (or hell) and return to tell about it—some facts of medieval life make a compelling argument for treatment of the Church's product as a credence good. During medieval times (and earlier), the distinction between the worldly and the spiritual was often blurred. For example, the belief in miracles was very widespread. In the minds of the faithful, miracles constituted credible evidence of divine intervention.

Likewise, the intercession of saints in the daily affairs of men was regarded as a way in which God directly effected the "technology" through which affairs in the physical world were manipulable; interpretations of phenomena without otherwise apparent explanation were regarded as "evidence" for the efficacy of the divine.

Moreover, as a producer of a credence good, the Church invested heavily in brand-name capital. This includes cathedrals, relics, liturgy, saints, icons, and so on. Such investments were designed to enhance the value and believability of the Church's control over the route to heaven and the afterlife. This is not unlike the investment of modern firms in advertising, product warranties, and the like.

Just as today's consumer can evaluate the quality-related claims of an automobile by driving it or by hiring a mechanic to inspect it, a medieval Christian could evaluate claims by a parish priest about the powers of God and the saints by monitoring for "miracles" and other manifestations of the efficacy of religion. In contrast to ordinary consumer decisions about tangible goods and services made in the modern economy, the evaluation of quality claims in the case of medieval religion involved a process of mutual determination. The basis of acceptable evidence for divine intervention was founded partially on preexisting theological beliefs.

When economists observe rational individuals voluntarily engaging in some activity or consuming some good, they assume that those individuals continue to behave otherwise. It also seems self-evident that if said individuals continue to behave in like manner—that is, engage in repeat transactions aimed at consuming the same good—it can be concluded that those persons found their ex post gratifications to have met their ex ante expectations. If this economic rationale applies to the consumption of ice cream, automobiles, and television programs, it logically should also apply to the consumption of religion. Axiomatically, people engage in religious pursuits because such actions increase their net utility.

There would be no need to belabor this seemingly obvious principle except for the fact that some modern historians and commentators have often insinuated that the Church reduced net social welfare by impeding the advance of science, encouraging superstition, and dissipating surplus productive resources through wasteful expenditures on cathedrals, shrines, and so forth. This view overlooks the utility-enhancing nature of religious practice and Church membership. It is as if we were to criticize spending by modern consumers at Disneyland by bemoaning the lost opportunities for utilizing the same funds to repair roads or advance new medical cures. Even granting the dubious anticlerical assumptions often made by critics of the Church (e.g., the inhibition of science), Roman Catholicism more than likely generated huge increases in the utility of many religious consumers, and, in all likelihood, produced corresponding gains in consumers' surplus.

As an extensive and pervasive monopolist in medieval society, the Church held a major advantage as producer of the credence good of salvation, which included intercession with God. The monopoly status of the Church, coupled with its great temporal power, reinforced the credibility of its claims concerning the quality of its nontestable product. The Church could convincingly maintain that its temporal position was testament to the veracity of its religious claims. Thus, aspiring entrants to the medieval religious market faced a daunting task: convincing their potential customers that the alternative product they offered was more reliable than that already available from an institution endorsed by an Omnipotent God. Obviously, as the Protestant Reformation eventually revealed, this obstacle was not insurmountable. But before losing market share to new entrants, the Church had persistently and successfully erected and maintained "barriers to entry" for centuries.

This discussion, of course, presumes that the relationship between the Church and its adherents was purely voluntary. An alternative argument would be that these were not voluntary but forced transactions. For example, a local businessperson could not function effectively if he were excommunicated from the Church. In this case the above conclusions do not go through, and the more conventional view of historians that the Church was basically a repressive institution carries more weight. My view is that the large majority of Church members belonged to the Church for voluntary reasons, but a careful study of this issue is warranted.

MARKET STRUCTURE OF THE MEDIEVAL RELIGION "INDUSTRY"

The medieval Church solidified its monopoly position by defining competing entrants (heretics) as criminals to be either imprisoned or executed. If successful in its "prosecution," the personal wealth of a dissenting member or a heathen challenger was subject to confiscation by the Church. Often the Church enlisted the authority of secular officials in this regard and sometimes shared the spoils. The Church even orchestrated massive military expeditions (Crusades) in order to prevent the spread of Islam, a competing religion. Clearly, the One True Church strove for monopoly power in the theological marketplace, but it also enlisted the aid of secular governments to exclude competitors.

The medieval Church was not an unbridled monopoly. On the local level, the relatively high mobility of peasants in medieval Europe implies a substantial amount of migration across parishes, with the resulting "Tiebout effects" restraining the ability of priests and other clerics to act as pure monopolists. Conditions among local Church parishes provided another kind of restraint against abuse of monopoly power. Tithes paid by parishioners constituted a small fraction of corporate Church revenue but represented the major portion of a local priest's income. Inasmuch as the parish priest had essentially no enforcement power against nonpayers (priests were forbidden to withhold sacraments for nonpayment), they had to resort to satisfying the parishioners in order to encourage voluntary compliance. Although in theory a priest could sue for unpaid tithes in ecclesiastical court, in practice this remedy was rarely effective.

In sum, the medieval Church was not an unbridled monopoly in the market for religion, nor did its market power come directly or indirectly from government, as is most often the case with contemporary monopolies. Medieval governments were generally weak, disorganized, and largely unable to provide monopoly rents to special interest groups. The effective monopoly power of the Church came mainly from its unique position in a rather unique market. Even so, it faced a number of practical constraints. These institutional constraints limited the economic power of the medieval Church somewhat, but the fact remains that the "owner-operators" of the medieval Church clearly benefited from a host of effective restrictions on competitive entry. As a result, the Church was able to consolidate its wealth and power over many centuries, reaching its peak during the late Middle Ages.

With this background on the supply- and demand-sides of the Church as an economic organization in mind, I now turn to a discussion of Church policies and how they were related to the monopoly power of the Church.

THE DOCTRINE OF USURY

The price of money, like its analogue, the price of goods, was persistently treated by medieval writers as an ethical issue—they perceived justice rather than efficiency as the appropriate goal of economic policy. Ostensibly, this is consistent with a public-interest theory of behavior. The historical record, however, casts strong shadows on this argument. It shows, for example, that Church officials frequently manipulated the usury doctrine to create or bolster the monopoly power of the Church.

I do not assert that the medieval Church invented the doctrine of usury, or the economic doctrine of just price, for its own economic gain. Rather, I contend that in spite of its original (and perhaps lasting) concern for justice, the Church recognized and acted on the rent-seeking opportunities of the doctrine at a certain juncture in its history. I contend that the medieval Church established de facto dual credit markets. When the Church was a lender, it priced its loans at market rates (or above), thus extracting rents. But when it was a borrower, it enforced the usury doctrine, thereby extracting rents by reducing its cost of credit on certain loans. At other times it used the doctrine to increase contributions and membership. Through selective enforcement, moreover, the Church could increase the supply of loans for (laical) consumption purposes.

This hypothesis is consistent with the activities of a rent-seeking monopoly, and it accommodates both monetary and nonmonetary goals, which were often intertwined in the policies pursued by the medieval Church. The chief monetary goal of the Church was to increase its ability to finance its salvation effort; its main nonmonetary goal was to preserve and extend its doctrinal hegemony—that is, to increase demand and lower demand elasticity for final output. Though fragmentary, Vatican records show a pattern of selective enforcement. When it was in the Church's interest to do so, it enforced the usury prohibition to keep its cost of funds low. When the Church lent money, the usury doctrine was mostly ignored. Moreover, besides the direct use of usury policy to enhance its wealth, the Church made indirect use of it to augment the power of the papal monopoly, including its far-flung bureaucracy.

Scholars have tended to overintellectualize the discussion of the Church and its usury doctrine. By focusing on the application and enforcement of the doctrine, one is better able to see it for what it was: a policy with biblical precedent adapted to the rent-seeking purposes of the Church.

The Church was also involved in the extensive system of price controls that prevailed in medieval towns. Here, I think that the modern interest-group theory of regulation offers a clear explanation for these controls and the attendant regulations governing who could sell in the towns and at what prices. These were not "just" prices; they were "regulated" prices.

THE DOCTRINE OF PURGATORY AND PROTESTANT ENTRY[4]

Most medieval church historians agree that the sale of indulgences by the Catholic Church played a prominent role in encouraging competitive entry by competing religions. Indeed, the proximate case of Martin Luther's successful challenge of the Church's dominant market position is almost universally held to be its record of abuses involving indulgences. In conjunction with this view, part of the explanation for the rise and ultimate success of Protestantism was the attempt by the Catholic Church to extract monopoly rents associated with a plethora of doctrinal penance and indulgences.

As with any monopoly, the aim of the medieval Church was to eliminate competition. Output restrictions and price increases were a consequence of such monopoly behavior. As noted earlier, the medieval Church used various methods to eliminate overall competition in its market, including political and social pressures (e.g., shunning through interdict) against unorthodox rivals, such as Jews and Muslims. It also dealt harshly with heresy, magic, and superstition, which had been practiced from early pre-Christian times, by devising such tools as excommunication, Crusades, and Inquisitions. But since it was always the prerogative of individuals to "self-select" among formal and informal belief systems, the Church had to maintain the quality of its product in order to prevent slippage, and it was required to price its services in such a way as to attract new customers. When product price rose and the reputation of the medieval Church became tarnished as "worldly" and venal, the papacy took steps to retain, attract, or regain members. The lowering of relative prices for certain services provided to members of the English Church provides an example. The English Church was always more independent than its European counterparts. In order to prevent defection (prior to Henry VIII's definitive break), the Church lowered the prices of some services.

The chief price confronted by individual Church members over the first millennium was dictated by a certain type of offer of assurances of eternal salvation. Despite the fact that temporal punishments and other forms of penance were administered through the confessional, in which some sins or infractions were more serious than others, individual penitents exercised discrete choice between eternal salvation and eternal damnation. Before the doctrine of purgatory and its accoutrements, the medieval Church did not offer a continuum of choices, certainly none with a halfway house to salvation. The invention and formulation of a package of new doctrines (without biblical precedent) around the 11th and 12th centuries fundamentally changed the nature of medieval Church doctrine and the customary offer of earlier ages. Taken together, the invention of purgatory, the distinction between venial and mortal sins, auricular confession, and, most importantly, the granting of indulgences, created a continuum of price-behavior choices by which individuals might attain the main religious product: assurance of eternal salvation. In effect, the choice offered by the medieval Church became continuous. These inventions initially lowered the price of sin, but they also created ever-expanding opportunities for rent extraction from Church members.[5]

In its role as gatekeeper of heaven, the medieval Church engaged in activities akin to those that take place in a system of criminal justice. From this perspective, the theory of deterrence of sin may be set out in a straightforward fashion. Imagine a demand for forgiveness of sin. It is negatively sloped and depicts the maximum demand price believers would be willing to pay for forgiveness. The invention of purgatory, the distinction between venial and mortal sins, and other innovations employed by the medieval Church gave form to such a demand function.

In contrast, the supply curve of forgiveness was dependent on the Church's long-run costs of providing a belief structure. This included the costs of formulating doctrine, providing liturgy, establishing enforcement mechanisms in downstream Church "firms" (e.g., "confession"), administering the sacraments, collecting relics, and so on. An equilibrium price of forgiveness is consistent with this market view.

As in the case of the suppression of crime (Becker 1968; Becker and Stigler 1974), some "optimum" may be reached. It has been suggested that in regard to sin, the medieval Church merely engaged in a kind of optimal deterrence that involved setting "efficient" penalties for criminal behavior. The historical record reveals otherwise. The Church did not adhere to a single-price scheme of price discrimination. Deterrence, therefore, was not the overriding objective, because it appears that it was subservient to the practice of inframarginal rent extraction. Basically, the medieval Church stood in the position of a perfectly discriminating monopoly. The goal was to put all sinners on their demand curves for sin and forgiveness, thereby creating a situation in which maximum monopoly rents could be collected. Optimal deterrence would have required the Church to set different prices for different sins, which, in fact, it did not do. Instead, the Church set different prices for different customers based on their income. The medieval Church was a rent extractor, not an agent of optimal deterrence.

From the supply-side, the medieval Church was most likely to resist encroachment of new religions and maintain its incumbent monopoly status in situations where it could effectively continue to appropriate consumer surplus through price discrimination. The conditions necessary for the medieval Church to continue to be successful in its chosen strategy were the following. First, there had to be a large reserve of wealth to tap, which was the case in those societies where feudal institutions maintained a landed class. Second, the prevailing wealth distribution had to be relatively stable, in order to repay the Church's "investment" in information and to keep the transaction costs associated with its pricing strategy relatively low. These two conditions were usually met in tradition-bound, authoritarian societies. In other words, the medieval Church was most likely to preserve its incumbent monopoly status in semifeudal societies that had a lot of low-income people (peasants) who were mild targets of the Church's discriminatory policies and a strong landed class (nobility) who routinely engaged in rent-seeking activity, whereby they sought to cut their own deals with the established Church.

By contrast, the medieval Church found it difficult to continue its practice of price discrimination in societies that encouraged profit seeking or increased market participation by lower economic classes.[6] Where the power of the monarch was relatively weak and the ownership of property was open to many, profit opportunities presented themselves to an expanding middle class. The distribution of wealth in such societies was constantly changing, making it more difficult for the Church to engage in effective price discrimination. Societies in which political and economic power were decentralized rather than centralized therefore presented problems to the ongoing profitability of the medieval Church.

The main point that needs to be emphasized is that through time, doctrine and practice combined under Church direction to extract as much consumer surplus as possible from Church members through the implementation of second and third degrees of price discrimination. The Church, in short, manipulated both the quality and the full price of its product so as to put members on the margin of defection. In crude terms, the cost and complexity of the price scales for "assurances of eternal salvation" forced members to self-select out of Roman Catholicism. In one sense, the Church's price discrimination put many of its members on the no-rent margin so that any lower-priced but similar belief system would have been attractive. Protestantism eschewed to price discrimination by eliminating the priest as "middleman." It featured a return to the lower-cost offer that characterized the early Christian Church, which, after the deprecations of the Church monopoly, would have been an appealing alternative to believers. It also repudiated the formalism and much of the complexity of Catholic dogma. These characteristics were shared by all of the reform movement, whether espoused by Luther, Calvin, Zwingli, or others.

Protestantism established individual conscience as the Christian's guide and reinstated "good works" as sufficient to produce "assurance of eternal salvation." It therefore provided a lower-cost alternative than Catholicism and offered to restore lost consumer surplus to many late, medieval Christians, especially the well heeled. The new religions' diminished emphasis on the institutional Church, with its plethora of rules and regulations, constituted a doctrinal break with established religion, to be sure. But it also offered new economic opportunity inasmuch as it allowed individuals to recapture lost consumer surplus and to obtain assurance of salvation at less cost than before. While tithing and other monetary payment were part of Protestantism, the good works "payment" was essentially an "in-kind" expenditure. Given the state of development of capital markets in these times, the in-kind financing of salvation was surely welcomed by defectors from the Catholic Church.

PROTESTANT ENTRY: SUCCESSES AND FAILURES

The doctrinal history of the Roman Catholic Church reveals that by the end of the Middle Ages it had evolved a complex pricing scheme that discriminated among its members according to wealth and status and extracted most of the consumer surplus derived from religion by its parishioners. It seems likely, therefore, that the single most important economic factor in explaining the appeal of Protestantism over Catholicism is the fact that Protestant doctrine offered a more amenable pricing system than the one that had evolved under Catholic doctrine and institutional practice. The "price" of salvation under the new religious doctrine consisted of payments in kind—the performance of good works—and, by declaring priestly agents unnecessary, eliminated the abuses that had crept into the ecclesiastical bureaucracy. The new religion required no intermediaries between man and God, no confession, no explicit or implicit payments for indulgences, and no halfway houses on the way to salvation (e.g., purgatory). The fundamental appeal of Protestantism is that it offered a simple, direct, and relatively inexpensive path to salvation. However, the new religion did not meet with universal success. To understand the ability of the medieval Church to maintain its incumbent monopoly status in some societies, the supply-side elements of the theory must be invoked.

The medieval Church invested resources in acquiring information about the wealth and utility functions of its high-income members and in devising price lists to guide confessors. It can be inferred that it was costly (menu costs) to acquire and to change such lists. In tradition-bound societies where wealth distribution was uneven but stable and wealth-creation opportunities were limited by institutional constraints, the medieval Church could more easily retain its members and still capture large amounts of consumer surplus. In other words, ceteris paribus, Protestantism was rejected in rent-seeking societies and embraced in profit-seeking societies. Catholicism lost its hold on societies that represented emergent market orders because, ultimately, it was more costly and less profitable to pursue its agenda under such circumstances.

One measure of the economic ossification that enabled the Church to maintain its hegemony is the extent to which restrictive property laws were enforced. Feudal forms of property differ from capitalist forms of property. Some countries practiced primogeniture and some did not. Primogeniture was confined mostly to Europe and was practiced mainly among the upper classes who were entrenched within a centralized power system. The law was intended to concentrate wealth in the hands of a few dynastic families, but by disinheriting all younger children it also caused untold bitterness within the family.

The Church served as a kind of insurer, or employer of last resort, to the landed aristocracy in such cases: younger sons could become retainers through ecclesiastical sinecure, a station that could be relinquished if the eldest son died. Moreover, female children could also find ready "employment" in the Church. Prince-bishops, which is what many of the nobility became, were assured that as high Church officials they could maintain a lifestyle befitting their dynastic station. Ecclesiastical careers did not bar anyone from secular dynastic affairs. As long as one did not advance to the subdiaconate (which required a vow of celibacy that could be nullified only by papal dispensation), noble ecclesiastics had little trouble returning to secular life. The medieval Church, in other words, approved of primogeniture precisely because it promoted the kind of stability of wealth distribution that enabled it to price-discriminate successfully among certain members, and it simultaneously provided an incentive to the heads of dynastic families to remain within the system of established religious practice.

As a preliminary test of this proposition, Ekelund, Hebert, and Tollison (2000) gathered data on the principal entry points of Protestantism, and the acceptance of the new religion was compared with the conditions most likely to encourage its success or failure. In simplified form, the theory predicts that societies enforcing primogeniture would be most likely to remain Catholic, whereas those societies with more fluid property laws (and hence more opportunities for wealth enhancement by a larger strata of society) would find Protestantism more palatable. The findings are favorable to their thesis, because they show that those societies with primogeniture remained Catholic, whereas those with partible inheritance laws embraced Protestantism.

CONCLUSION

Economics offers a way to study religious behavior and institutions. As I said at the beginning, the proof is in the pudding. Does economics offer more discerning insights into Church behavior than alternative analytical methods? For example, it seems unexceptionable to say that the doctrine of purgatory was nothing more and nothing less than a system of price discrimination practiced in a revenue-maximizing way by the Church. The Church is a complex institution that has produced notoriously "good" and "bad" results over time. At its core, though, the Church is susceptible to an economic model, and this paper is a modest attempt to establish this point.

NOTES

1. For background and citations to the historical record covered in this paper, the reader can consult the above-cited works, from which this paper draws heavily. I am indebted to my coauthors for allowing me to use these ideas as the basis of my lecture.
2. Adam Smith, author of *The Wealth of Nations* (1776) and acknowledged founder of economics as a social science, first integrated the study of religious behavior with economics. In a far broader view than that of Marshall and his neoclassical contemporaries—appropriately called political economy—Smith studied the economic problems associated with the provision of religious services. Smith's analysis, while not providing a formal theory of monopoly supply of these services, revolved around incentive failures as characteristic of state-sponsored religious instruction.
3. The Edict of Milan was a formal act of toleration issued by the co-emperors Constantine and Licinius, each sympathetic to monotheism.
4. This section and the next draw heavily on Ekelund, Hebert, and Tollison (2000).
5. Note the contradiction of a public-interest theory here—i.e., a lowering of the price of sin.
6. The argument here is superficially related to Weber's (1958) famous hypothesis about Protestantism and economic growth. The point is, however, that Protestantism offered a lower cost contract for believers, not a more rigorous, less preferred alternative. The advent of Protestantism came about in more rapidly developing areas because the Catholic Church could not compete effectively in those areas for the reasons outlined earlier. Protestantism was (controversially) collinear with economic growth, but for different reasons than those ascribed to Weber.

REFERENCES

Becker, Gary S. 1968. "Crime and Punishment: An Economic Approach." *Journal of Political Economy* 76: 169–217.

Becker, Gary S., and George J. Stigler. 1974. "Law Enforcement, Malfeasance, and Compensation for Enforcers" *Journal of Legal Studies* 3: 1–18.

Ekelund, R. B. Jr., R. F. Hebert, and R. D. Tollison. 1989. "An Economic Model of the Medieval Church: Usury as a Form of Rent Seeking." *Journal of Law, Economics, and Organization* 5: 307–31.

———. 1992. "The Economics of Sin and Redemption: Purgatory as a Market-Pull Innovation?" *Journal of Economic Behavior and Organization* 19: 1–15.

———. 2000. "Catholic Monopoly and Protestant Entry." Unpublished manuscript.

Ekelund, R. B. Jr., R. F. Hebert, R. D. Tollison, G. M. Anderson, and A. B. Davidson. 1996. *Sacred Trust: The Medieval Church as an Economic Firm*. New York: Oxford University Press.

Iannaccone, L. R. 1998. "Introduction to the Economics of Religion." *Journal of Economic Literature* 36: 1465–95.

Marshall, Alfred. 1890. *Principles of Economics*. London: Macmillan.

Smith, Adam. [1776] 1937. *An Inquiry into the Nature and Causes of the Wealth of Nations*. Edited by E. Canaan. New York: Random House.

Weber, Max. 1958. *The Protestant Ethic and the Spirit of Capitalism*. New York: Scribner's.

Williamson, Oliver E. 1975. *Markets and Hierarchies*. New York. Free Press.

SECTION 6

THE KNIGHTIAN CONVERSATION

6.0 Introduction

PETER J. BOETTKE AND ALAIN MARCIANO

For Buchanan, what we propose to call the "Knightian conversation" refers to the debates and conversations that take place within the realm of politics. Basically this refers to the idea, crucial for Buchanan, that politics is a conversation or a process—indeed, Buchanan had a deontological approach to politics—but also that this conversation is not aimed at reaching an absolute, definitive, and indisputable truth. Politics as a Knightian conversation is a search for relatively absolute absolutes. This is what we are going to discuss in this introduction, and it will be illustrated in the papers reprinted in this section.

BACK TO "POLITICS"

In the previous parts of this book, we have already discussed "politics." Let us go back to politics, but from a different perspective. We would like to analyze how Buchanan defined "politics." It took time before Buchanan started to really explain what he meant by "politics" or "political decisions." From the 1950s there are only a few references—very few, indeed—that may help us to understand how he defined politics. One of them can be found in a paper already mentioned in this book, "Positive Economics, Welfare Economics and Political Economy" (Buchanan 1959). In this article, Buchanan did not only explain why his approach was positive and did not only give the conditions for a positive political economy. He also explained to what politics corresponds, namely the "observable behavior of individuals *in their capacities as collective decision-makers*" (128, emphasis in original). This definition is simple and short and does not seem particularly enlightening. It does, however, perfectly encapsulate what Buchanan thought of politics. And, let us repeat, it came from his pen in the late 1950s.

This definition has three crucial dimensions that are worth emphasizing. The first one may be the simplest because it relates to an element that is quite well known about Buchanan: his individualism and his opposition to "organicism" (Buchanan 1949). "Organicism" is the idea that groups, societies, and collective entities of any kind do not exist as such, but exist only as the sum and composition or result of the individuals who belong to them. From this perspective, it appears that a political decision is a collective decision, but it is necessarily made by individuals. The second dimension is also worth emphasizing: Buchanan equates politics with what individuals are observed to do—their actual behaviors and not the choices they should make. In other words, Buchanan viewed politics from a positive and not from a normative perspective. One can thus oppose a positive conception of politics that is based on what individuals do to a normative conception of politics based on what individuals should do to reach a certain, predefined decision. Hence, the third dimension that is important to emphasize—perhaps the least visible, but that will be justified by what Buchanan wrote later—corresponds to the fact that Buchanan did *not* define politics by its outcome or result. Implicitly, Buchanan was explaining that politics is a process and that this process is not aimed at reaching a specific goal.

NO TRUTH-JUDGMENTS IN POLITICS

One could argue that this is a far-fetched interpretation of what Buchanan could have thought. However, Buchanan came back to these ideas a few years later to make them explicit. In a paper he wrote in 1967, "Politics and Science: Reflections on Knight's Critique of Polanyi," Buchanan gave a really clear and unambiguous definition of politics and, more specifically, of its goals and objectives. He would come back later, as in some of the articles reprinted here, to his conception—a conception he claimed to have inherited from his mentor at Chicago, Frank H. Knight.

Buchanan had a deontological approach to "politics"—and complementarily he rejected a consequentialist view of politics. He thus defined politics in terms of process and not in terms of a specific goal, outcome, or decision that politics should try to reach. Politics, he wrote, is "the process through which divergent interests are compromised" (Buchanan 1967, 306) or "politics is the process through which the initial preferences are expressed, discussed, compromised, and, finally, resolved in some fashion" (ibid.). Of course, the goal of politics is to make choices—"politics is the collective counterpart to individual choice" (ibid.)—but one cannot tell anything about these choices. One cannot say that one choice is better than another. Or, to put it in other words, one cannot say whether these choices are the right ones—"true"—or the wrong ones—"false." They are the choices that have been made. The explanation, and this is particularly important, is that politics can only be defined as a process because *no* truth-judgment is possible in politics that could allow individuals to qualify the collective choices that have been made. Alternatively, to use the terms that Buchanan used, borrowing from Knight, no absolute judgment can be made in politics.[1]

More precisely, one must distinguish between two levels. First, there is what could be called the basic level, "the level of operational decisions" (Buchanan 1967, 308), which corresponds to the *postconstitutional* level of daily decisions. At this level, the difference with science is the most important and the clearest. Indeed, science is "a process of discovery, of exploration, and success is measured by agreed-on criteria of 'truth'" (ibid.). In science, individuals can discuss and confront their arguments to let emerge a certain consensus about what is true or false. This is not the case in politics. Indeed, individuals are different in the sense that they have different preferences—Buchanan wrote, "Economists summarize this by saying that utility functions differ" (ibid., 306)—and disagree in the ranking of goods and the ordering of alternatives. Now, at this postconstitutional, operational level, these individual preferences are "givens." They have to be taken as "relatively absolute" (Buchanan 1996, 71).

In addition, one cannot say that one preference is better than another one; each preference is as good as any other. This is the normative context in which, according to Buchanan, postconstitutional and operational choices are made. This means that, in this normative context, one cannot impose a choice as being the best one—or the right one. There exists no process that could allow one to impose such a choice, for the simple reason that it does not exist. As a corollary, this means that the disagreements that exist between individuals because of their differences cannot disappear and cannot be narrowed down. Therefore, one could not envisage that discussion or deliberation could lead to a complete agreement on an outcome or a decision or a choice that would be considered as true—in the sense of admitted by everyone. Political choices are accepted by individuals, but their preferences are not modified. Politics, therefore, implies "an overruling of some preferences in favor of others" and also implies that "those whose preferences are overruled acquiesce in the collective outcome" (Buchanan 1967, 306). It implies that individuals "agree to disagree."

There is a second (and higher) level that corresponds to the level of constitutional decisions—the level of decisions about the rules of the social game. At this level, Buchanan totally accepted the possibility of a form of convergence and even agreement on which rules should be adopted that would frame individual interactions. Indeed, at the constitutional level, the normative context changes. Preferences can no longer be taken as given. There is room for improvement because the idea that there exist "better" preferences than others makes sense. But, let us stress, it is only at this constitutional level that this is acceptable—Buchanan goes as far as to say that "it is at this level, and this level only that the exercise of moral passion must be practiced" and can lead to "severe criticisms of the preferences that are observed" (Buchanan 1996, 72). As a consequence, the disagreements between individuals regarding what are the best preferences and accordingly the right choices may disappear or at least be reduced. However, this is only possible with two caveats in mind. First, this is possible only because discussions are not guided by "self-interest of the narrow sort" because narrow self-interest is relegated to a "subsidiary role" (ibid.). Political discussions about the constitutional rules should not be guided by "personal values" but instead by the "predicted working properties of alternative rules" (Buchanan 1967, 308). It is—or it should be—as if individuals are under "some Rawls-like veil of ignorance" (Buchanan 1996, 72). When the constitutional rules are chosen, Buchanan insisted, "there must remain great uncertainty as to how particular rules will advance particular interests" (Buchanan 1967, 307). Then, and this is the second caveat, one must keep in mind that such narrowing down of disagreements and such convergence toward "better" preferences should not be "conceived as a search for a single 'truth,' waiting to be discovered" (Buchanan 1996, 72) and therefore should not be viewed as trying to promote one specific vision of the "good" society. Indeed, there is no unique definition of what a "good society" is. Once again, Buchanan insisted, even at the constitutional level there is no truth-judgment in politics. The objectives that are promoted through constitutional rules, the preferences that are chosen as the best ones, are not "absolutes." They are "relatively absolute absolutes" (ibid., 71).

THE MESSAGE OF TOLERANCE OF CLASSICAL LIBERALISM

Buchanan's message that politics, whether at the constitutional or at the post-constitutional level, is *not* about revealing, discovering, or unveiling a "truth" that exists is obviously a message of tolerance, of mutual respect, and a message of defense of individual liberty and freedom. This is the message carried by classical liberalism.

Indeed, one easily understands that if there does not exist any "truth" to be discovered, then there exists nothing to impose on others. To put it differently, by claiming that any preference is as good as any other, or that preferences are "relatively absolute absolutes," Buchanan also claimed that no one could be right or wrong, nor could his or her preferences be better than the preferences of others. That is, everybody has the right to pursue his or her own objectives and satisfy his or her own preferences. Also (this is important and not infrequently forgotten), everybody should refrain from believing they are right and thinking others are wrong. All values, tastes, and preferences must be tolerated. To put it in other words, all individuals should be considered as "equals" or, more specifically, as "natural equals." Individuals are different—the differences between the philosopher and the porter can be "observed" and "readily explained"—but the empirical differences between individuals are "normatively irrelevant for purposes of discussing the organization of society" (Buchanan 2003).

By contrast, those who consider that the role of politics is to reveal a certain truth, whatever it is, also tend to think "that certain political 'truths' have already been discovered" (Buchanan 1967, 310). These individuals are intolerant because they do not only claim that they have discovered the truth but also "claim the 'right' to impose 'truth' on those who refuse, with apparent ignorance, stubbornness, or blindness, to recognize error" (ibid.). This is quite a natural and consistent behavior: If one believes oneself to have found the truth, why would he not try to impose it on others? Individuals who are convinced of being right cannot but be convinced that others are wrong.

To Buchanan, this attitude was typical of a certain category of individuals, whom he called the "left" (Buchanan 1967) or the "modern" (Buchanan 1968) liberal. The latter are, broadly speaking, all the individuals who believe that their personal views are "right" and that the values of others are "wrong"—more specifically, the modern liberal is the academic liberal of America who is no longer a classical liberal; indeed, Buchanan targeted the professors, faculty, and staff in academia. Thus, he wrote, "This attitude of intolerance seems especially to characterize the modern American left-liberal who dominates the academic setting and to whom there must always exist a set of prevailing 'truths,' politically determined, and from which open dissent becomes, somehow, 'immoral'" (Buchanan 1967, 310).

THE INSTITUTIONS OF FREEDOM AND TOLERANCE: A CONSTITUTIONAL DEMOCRACY

Then there is the question of the range and domain of politics. When do individuals have to make collective and political choices? Or, to put it differently, what should be the institutions of a free and tolerant society? What should be the institutions that would make room for all the individuals' values and preferences? Those are the institutions of what Buchanan called a constitutional democracy, putting the accent on constitutional—"the 'constitutional' qualifier is as important, if not more so, than the noun 'democracy'" (Buchanan 2003).

At the postconstitutional level, Buchanan defended the market as the only political institution that would let individuals pursue their own goals and make choices according to their (given) preferences without being disturbed or coerced by others. Indeed, as was demonstrated by classical liberals, the "market organization, to the extent that it is operative, replaces hierarchical organization" (Buchanan 1996, 7). No sovereign authority that imposes its choices on individuals is required. Individuals engage in market transactions as autonomous and responsible persons: they are not constrained to do so, and, complementarily, they acknowledge others as their equals in the transaction. In markets, free individuals interact freely and in mutual respect with other free individuals. Therefore, and this is what the eighteenth-century scholars discovered, "free markets . . . spontaneously coordinate the activities of persons within a minimally protective legal order independently of detailed government control" (Buchanan 1981, 14). This is precisely why it can be said that markets play a "political role" (Buchanan 1996) or perform a "political function" (Buchanan 1981, 14). This view is perfectly consistent with the idea, presented earlier, that politics is only a process aimed at making choices that are not good or just, right or wrong. They are legitimate as long as the individuals who engage in market transactions do so freely and uncoerced.

Of course, one could say, arguing that markets have a *political* role is misleading and reflects that the political role of markets is limited to the situations in which there is no political decision to make because it is only private transactions that take place in markets. This would not be exact. By emphasizing the role of markets, Buchanan was claiming that one should favor the institutional solutions based on decentralized markets and that markets should have the first and primary role; politics and collective decisions should be subsidiary. In fact, the importance of markets as a political device working at the postconstitutional level implies that politics becomes "limited to the construction and maintenance of the parametric framework for exchange processes" (Buchanan 2003). Thus, Buchanan defended a constitutional democracy as a combination of markets and constitutional politics. But why is constitutional politics necessary? And how can it work? This is something that Buchanan explained very well and very clearly in the documents presented in this section. It can be summarized as follows.

Politics, as collective decisions, is necessary. Indeed, as we have shown in the first section of this volume, Buchanan accepted the idea that markets are not always operative, that they may fail, and do not always allocate resources efficiently. Or, to use other words that he employed quite frequently, there are circumstances in which no gains from trade can be made. In those cases, collective—that is, political—choices must be made. These decisions can be made through elections, but actually the existence of elections and the nature of electoral rules are not what matter the most. What is the most important here is that democracy should not be "unlimited" democracy—that is, a form of democracy that "would presumably allow voting majorities or pluralities, either through plebiscites, referenda, or actions of elected assemblies, to do what they please, when they please, and to whomever they choose" (Buchanan 1981, 1). Democracy must be limited and, more precisely, constitutionally limited. Indeed, what matters the most to Buchanan, from the perspective of how far a democracy is democratic, is the control and limitation of government activities. He insisted that "imposing . . . constitutional limits on the range of governmental powers' does not limit democracy," in contrast to what certain economists—including Paul Samuelson (Buchanan 1981, 12)—believe. In fact, a constitutional—and limited—democracy is much more tolerant than an unlimited democracy. A constitution, first, constrains governments and limits their encroachment on individual rights. Second, it allows each individual to pursue their private goals; and complementarily, no one is in a position to impose their views on others. Within the limits defined by the constitution, "Each man and each group in this community exercise[s] the freedom to carry his own or its own objectives as privately conceived" (Buchanan 1968, 675).

Thus, Buchanan told us that he remained committed to the respect and tolerance of the values of others and was interested in markets and constitutions because they were means to accommodate the differences between individuals. From this perspective, the real domain of collective action—of politics—is determined by what is not done by markets. Market organization is the primary political institution precisely because it allows each individual to pursue their own values, respecting them, and not trying to impose any values on them. What is not covered by markets should be done via collective or political decisions, as long as they take place within constitutional rules.

NOTE

1. This clearly echoes his conception of how academia should function and how academic research should be produced, as described in section 5. However, one must note the major difference between science and politics. In science, truth-judgments are possible.

REFERENCES

Buchanan, J. M. 1949. "The Pure Theory of Government Finance: A Suggested Approach." *Journal of Political Economy* 57(6): 496–505.

———. 1959. "Positive Economics, Welfare Economics, and Political Economy." *Journal of Law and Economics* 2: 124–38.

———. 1967. "Politics and Science: Reflections on Knight's Critique of Polanyi." *Ethics* 77(4): 303–10.

———. 1968. "Student Revolts, Academic Liberalism, and Constitutional Attitudes." *Social Research* 35(4): 666–80.

———. 1981. "Democracy: Limited or Unlimited." Presented at the November 1981 Regional Meeting, Mont Pelerin Society, Viña del Mar, Chile. Box 63, Mont Pelerin Society Archives.

———. 1996. "The Morality of Capitalism: Comment on Peter Koslowski, *The Ethics of Capitalism*." In Peter Koslowski, *Ethics of Capitalism and Critique of Sociobiology: Two Essays with a Comment by James M. Buchanan*, 65–74. Berlin: Springer-Verlag.

———. 2003. "Politics as Tragedy in Several Acts." *Economics & Politics* 15(2): 181–91.

6.1 Democracy

Limited or Unlimited

JAMES M. BUCHANAN

I. INTRODUCTION

In preparing a paper on the topic assigned in the title, my primary reaction is wonderment that anyone might seriously support "unlimited democracy" in any form or fashion. Taken literally, "unlimited democracy" would presumably allow voting majorities or pluralities, either through plebiscites, referenda, or actions of elected assemblies, to do what they please, when they please, and to whomever they choose. The totalitarian thrust of unlimited democracy, defined and interpreted in this sense, has been recognized at least since the early Greek writers on politics. Although political theory has retrogressed in our times, and notably since the 18th century, I do not think it would be possible, even in 1981, to locate a willful defender of totally unconstrained majoritarian rule.

The critical debate for our time, for the 1980s and beyond, does not turn on the desirability or undesirability of unlimited democracy. The debate does turn on the degree and kind of limits that are minimally necessary to ensure

Prepared for presentation at Regional Meeting, Mont Pelerin Society, Viña del Mar, Chile, November 1981.

the viability of a society in which individuals can maintain personal liberties, and, more instrumentally, on how any such limits can be made effective in the mind-set of the late 20th century.

I shall develop my argument in several parts. In part II, I emphasize the difference in political structure and through this the potential difference in the procedural restrictions on the reach of government, between parliamentary democracies and republics, as reflected in the comparison and contrast between European-style parliamentary government and the US system. In part III, I discuss briefly the philosophical foundations of the democratic precept, embodied in the principle of political equality. In part IV, I examine the implications of this principle of political equality for the limits of government. I demonstrate, in particular, that the value of political equality for the individual increases with the range and scope of governmental activity, while at the same time generating the paradox that satisfaction of the principle becomes more difficult. Part V distinguishes between limits on democratic procedures for making governmental decisions and limits on the range of governmental activities. This distinction is often overlooked in academic as well as popular treatments. In part VI, I offer a reason for the confusion in modern political thought, summarized in the term "the electoral fallacy." In part VII, I suggest that modern developments in the theory of public choice and related areas of inquiry provide a basis for getting political thinking straight.

II. LIMITS INHERENT IN POLITICAL STRUCTURE

The institutional-organizational structure of government itself indirectly affects the boundaries, the frequency, the direction, and the magnitude of governmental actions. Each country, with its own history out of which its political institutions have emerged from evolution, revolution, accident, and design, is characterized by unique internal constraints. Clearly, my competence does not extend to a nation-by-nation descriptive catalog. I want, however, to stress the important differences between all governments organized nominally as *parliamentary democracies* and those structures in which powers of governance are divided among independent agencies, branches, or levels, which I shall call *republics*.

Those of my generation who grew up in the United States will recall the near-universal opinion of academic political science of the middle third of this century. The United States' federal republic was held to be grossly inefficient, and parliamentary democracy (notably the British model) was held up as the ideal to be emulated. As students of "civics," we were led to believe that all would indeed be well if only the "checks and balances" inherent in the "separation of powers" structure could be eliminated if the central government could override the parochial interests of the states, of the federalism, if "democracy" could be fully realized, subject only to the constitutional guarantees of the basic freedoms.

This academic denigration of the US political heritage was effective in stimulating much of the centralization and concentration of political power that we have observed in my country since the 1930s. The "checks and balances" that once kept our "compound republic" viable by holding government within relatively narrow limits of action have now been very substantially eroded. I should, nonetheless, argue that the structure that remains still possesses procedural constraints on political excess that are almost totally absent in parliamentary democracies, whose characteristic features combine executive and legislative powers in a single level of government subject to weak or nonexistent judicial review. In the republican structure, there are built-in *procedural* restrictions on the abilities of governments to act that do not exist in parliamentary regimes. In other words, "democracy is limited" to an extent not present in parliamentary structures.

Recognition of this basic difference in political structure does not, of course, imply that only parliamentary regimes require explicit constitutional limits and that republican forms are in themselves sufficient to keep political powers in check. There is no suggestion here that the procedural constraints in existing republican structures are optimal or efficient; quite the contrary. Somewhat paradoxically, we actually find more, not less, discussion of constitutional limits in the United States than in parliamentary societies. In part, such a paradox is explained by the prevalent "constitutional attitude" that has surely been fostered by the very republican institutions noted. To say that "democracy is limited" somewhat more by ordinary procedures in republican structures than in parliamentary regimes does suggest that the need for direct and explicit nonprocedural limits on governmental activities is more urgent in the latter case than in the former.

III. DEMOCRACY AND POLITICAL EQUALITY

I shall not attempt any exegetical analysis of what "democracy" has meant to learned scholars through the ages. And I shall surely not bother to discuss the gross distortions of meaning that we witness each and every day in news reports from various "democratic" regimes throughout the world. At its very simplest dictionary definition, democracy is government "by the people." A secondary element of definition opposes democracy to any form of government by an elite, whether in the form of an aristocracy, a hereditary monarchy, a ruling class, or ruling committee.

How can meaningful content be put on the phrase "government by the people"? This basic requirement has often been taken to mean that democracy is equivalent to rule by the majority. But it takes little or no sophisticated analytics to suggest that rule by a majority, to those who are ruled, is no different from rule by any other group. A majority is not "the people," and there is nothing sacrosanct in simple majority rule, whether this be in terms of direct or representative processes.

In its most fundamental sense, democracy means that governmental decisions, affecting *all* members of the polity, are reached through processes of discussion and decision-making in which *all* members participate, actually or potentially, on equal terms. Ideally, the processes of discussion and participation produce *agreement* by *all* persons on the collectively determined option to be chosen. Failing agreement, the process should be expected to generate appropriate rules through which all persons agree to disagree, majority voting being only one from among many possible rules that might be selected for certain types of collective-choice options (others might be random selection, plurality voting, qualified majority voting, unanimity, or binding arbitration by appointed third parties).

The characteristic feature that does have operational meaning is *political equality* among all persons who qualify for membership in the polity. Each person stands equal before the law of the land, and each person is given equal weight in the ultimate determination of how the law shall be changed, law being defined both in terms of the higher law (constitutional rules) and legislation of the ordinary variety. Each person has the franchise, which he may exercise or not exercise as and if he chooses.

What is the value of political equality to an individual? This question cannot be answered independently of some specification of the range of decisions that are to be made collectively rather than individually. To take an extreme model, suppose that all collective decisions are fully analogous to zero-sum games; politics consists of pure transfers from losers to gainers. Even if ideally realized, political equality, defined as an equal chance to influence the transfer outcome, would be equivalent to being in a pure lottery. Ex ante, each person has an equal chance of being a loser or gainer from politics. Ex post, politics itself generates gainers and losers, violating any precept of "political equality." In this setting, surely the individual will place a negative value on ex ante political equality if he is still at all risk averse, provided that the benchmark for comparison is with the setting in which no zero-sum collective decisions are made at all.

On the other hand, and in sharp contrast, if the individual finds himself necessarily present in a polity in which extensive collective action in the form of pure transfers is predicted to occur (with no explicit limits on such actions), political equality will be valued equivalently to membership in a gigantic lottery with no opportunity to withdraw or exist from the game voluntarily. It is precisely in this setting where individuals may, quite literally, fight to get in on the mutual despoliation that the fully politicized pure transfer society represents.

At the opposing end of the spectrum, consider the setting in which collective decisions are all potentially positive-sum and are expected to generate gains to all persons in the polity. The "public good" embodied in governmental-legal protection of personal and property rights along with the enforcement of voluntary contracts perhaps comes closest to this model. The role of government is described in "protective state" or "minimal state" terms. The value of political equality in this setting becomes analogous to the value to a player of having a part in choosing the referee for a game he is playing and in choosing the allocation of shares in the costs of hiring the referee who is finally chosen. In the net, the political "game" is expected to be beneficial for all players, regardless of whose choice for referee dominates and regardless of the arrangement for sharing the net costs. No person, regardless of the ex post outcome of these collectively determined choices, will seek voluntarily to leave the game. Political equality will clearly be a valuable attribute of the social structure, but clearly it will be much less valuable (and considered much less "necessary") than in the fully politicized transfer society.

IV. THE PARADOX OF UNLIMITED PARTICIPATORY DEMOCRACY

Modern governments are best described as mixtures of transfer and productive-protective states, falling descriptively somewhere along the spectrum between the two extreme models discussed earlier. A particularly relevant feature of modern "democratic" politics is the institutions for making transfers indirectly rather than directly, through the provision in-kind of goods and services rather than through cash payments. These institutions ensure that the political transfer game becomes negative-sum, as opposed to the idealized zero-sum limit in a direct money transfer setting.

The institutions of indirect transfer are preferred by politicians because these institutions allow transfers to be passed off as "productive" activities on the part of ruling political coalitions. A program designed to provide benefits to a selective subgroup in the polity is publicly described as in the "public interest," and modern governments have become past masters in this art of misrepresentation. The objective is, of course, to conceal or to hide the pure transfer aspects of the programs. To the extent that this objective is met, however, the possible satisfaction of the ideal of political equality, even in some *ex ante* sense, is undermined.

An individual or group that finds himself or itself unable to share as a potential member in the compulsory transfer lottery could, at least, recognize what is happening and put up an argument for an equal chance to get at the spoils. In a highly complicated and complex mix of in-kind transfers (with possibly some externality-correction aspects included), it becomes almost impossible for the individual or group to assess his or its position relative to that of other persons and groups in the polity. As the number and size of such transfer programs increase, who is and who is not a member of the lottery scheme and on what terms simply cannot be determined.

Paradoxically, then, the extension of the number and size of governmental-politicized activities in which the individual might expect to participate has the effect of making the value of participation itself increasingly difficult to measure in any direct manner.

V. LIMITS ON GOVERNMENT AND LIMITS ON DEMOCRACY

There is a critical and necessary distinction to be made between (1) the range and scope of governmental-political activities, and (2) the extent of satisfaction of democratic precepts in decision-making for those activities defined to fall within the allowed range and scope of government. If the ultimate objective in organizing and reforming the political structure is that of ensuring and protecting individual liberties, the first of those characteristics may be much more important than the second, even though, as indicated earlier, the second may be intrinsically of value. That is to say, a governmental-political structure that is limited constitutionally to a well-defined range of activities, even if governmental decisions within this range are made nondemocratically, may well be preferred to an open-ended and unlimited governmental-political structure in which decisions are made democratically (by legislative-parliamentary majorities).

This point may be illustrated with the aid of a simple treelike diagram, as in figure 6.1.1, which shows that the basic structural "choice" made at A may be much more important than the structural "choice" made at B. It seems

Figure 6.1.1.

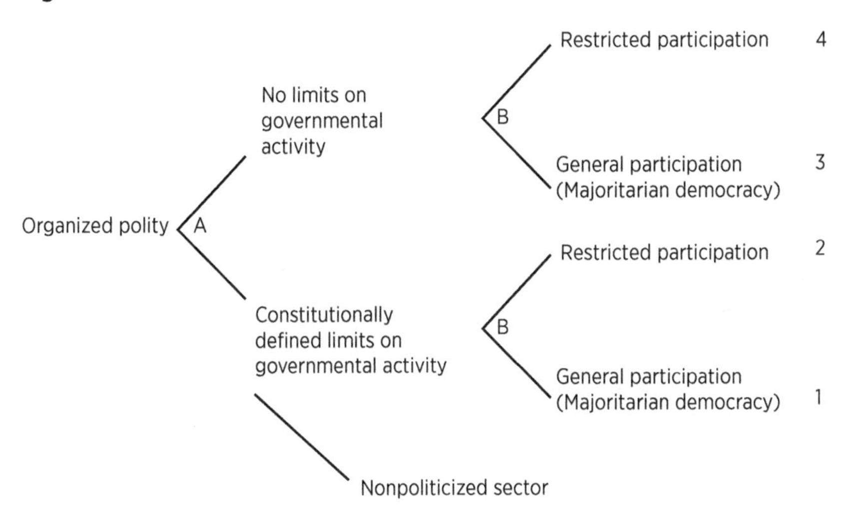

reasonable to suggest that the individual, postulated to be behind some appropriately defined veil of ignorance and/or uncertainty about his own position, would rank order the political structures from 1 to 4, as indicated. This ranking suggests that the individual (any individual) would prefer a constitutionally limited, restricted participation regime to a nonlimited, fully majoritarian regime. The difference in value between 1 and 2 as a set and 3 and 4 as a set may be much more than the difference in value between the two members of either set.

A somewhat different way of stating the argument here is to emphasize that placing limits on the range of governmental powers and/or activities is wholly distinct, actually and conceptually, from placing limits on the exercise of democracy within a defined range. For any *given* institutional means of making collective decisions (majority or plurality voting rules, rule by a restricted committee, junta, or elite), there are alternative allowable limits (ranging from highly restricted to totally unconstrained) on the exercise of governmental-political powers, and there are alternative institutional means of reaching collective decisions.

The central point seems elementary, but it has been the source of major intellectual confusion. There has come to be a widespread acceptance of the notion that any reform effort aimed at imposing new constitutional limits on the range of governmental powers must, at the same time, limit "democracy" in the reaching of collective decisions. This confusion is not confined to uncritical law discussion. It is encountered in such eminent scholars as Nobel laureate

Paul A. Samuelson. In a March 1981 address, Samuelson made this surprising statement: "Only ruminate about Proposition 19 [*sic*] and Proposition 2 1/2. If democracy cannot be trusted, write once and forever that capitalism must be the law of the land. Don't think this scenario can end with the comforting words 'And they lived happily ever afterwards.' I could write a book, a long book, on the evils and instabilities of fascism" (Samuelson 1981, 44).

Proposition 13 and Proposition 2 1/2 (there is and has been no Proposition 19) were constitutional amendments in California and Massachusetts, approved through fully democratic referenda, that placed limits on the powers of legislative majorities in those states to impose taxes. Samuelson seems to suggest that any constitutional limit on powers of legislative majorities are fascistic in tendency, regardless of the procedures through which such limits might be chosen. The elementary "by the people" meaning of "democracy" seems to have been replaced by "by legislative majorities." The most sympathetic reading of the cited passage suggests that Samuelson's whole position fails to recognize the essential distinction stressed in this part of my paper. He does not sense the categorical difference between *rules* within which activity is allowed to take place and *activity within rules*. Samuelson clearly lacks the "constitutional attitude" noted earlier.

VI. THE ELECTORAL FALLACY

Neither the academic nor the practical political philosophers of the 18th century (Montesquieu, Hume, Smith, Madison, Jefferson, and others) made the elementary mistakes of late nineteenth- and twentieth-century political "scientists," both academic and practical. The eighteenth-century wisdom incorporated a highly skeptical attitude toward government and toward persons placed in agency roles to act in the name of collective units. By almost natural progression, this attitude engendered emphasis on the necessity for constitutional limits or controls on the powers and authority of government. The great eighteenth-century discovery that free markets could spontaneously coordinate the activities of persons within a minimally protective legal order independently of detailed governmental control was understood, in part at least, as offering a means through which the range of governmental powers could be checked. The *political function* of the market economy was widely appreciated.

From our vantage point in time, from 1981, when we can appreciate the vastly superior political-philosophical understanding of these eighteenth-century men by any sort of comparison with their twentieth-century counterparts, we are forced to speculate on how and why such widely shared wisdom was lost and on how and why elementary errors in political theory were initially made and came to be almost universally accepted for a century. I am not a specialist in the history of ideas, but I suggest that intellectual confusion emerged, in part, from the juxtaposition of historical events in economics and in politics somewhere after the mid-19th century. The emphasis of classical political economy on the market's political function in minimizing the potential coercion of the state came to be mistaken for the explicitly political liberal objective of minimizing the role for the absolutist or aristocratic state, somehow giving birth to the almost totally unexamined presumption that, once the state becomes "fully democratic," with free and open elections, and with universal suffrage, the eighteenth-century argument for the minimization of potential governmental coercion vanishes.

I have often referred to this misperception as "the electoral fallacy," the misperception that is summarized by the statement that, so long as politicians and parties are required to compete one with another in periodic, free elections, subject to majority or plurality voting under a universally franchised electorate, there is no need for overt limitation on the range and scope of governmental activity. From this misperception, there follows directly the view that constitutional limits on the exercise of governmental authority, *in any form*, must be undesirable. Hence, there arose the twentieth-century praise for the relatively unconstrained parliamentary structure of government, in which the combined legislative-executive majority operates more or less at will, as opposed to the cumbersome and hidebound federalized republic on the United States model.

It is difficult to treat the misperception here as seriously as it must be taken if we are to begin to understand and to appreciate how and why so many brilliant modern minds went so far astray. As I noted at the start of this paper, if explicitly queried, almost none of these thinkers would accept the full implication that *no* constitutional checks should be imposed on majoritarian democracy. But the fact that this is a logically consistent implication of the position taken, and one that is so often overlooked, in itself suggests the dominating influence of the "electoral fallacy." This fallacy, at a deep level of consciousness, has had the effect of lulling social scientists and social philosophers into the notion that they need not concern themselves too much about political limits; they can busy themselves directly with advising legislative majorities on how to go about their social engineering.

VII. GOVERNMENTAL FAILURE, PUBLIC CHOICE, AND PROSPECTS FOR THE 21ST CENTURY

A familiar refrain says, "The times, they are a-changin'," a refrain that is surely descriptive of the attitudes toward the subject matter of this paper. In the relatively short span of three decades, 1950 to 1981, we have witnessed profound shifts in the ways that both academic scholars and ordinary citizens view government and governmental processes. This basic shift in perspective is not parochial; it is shared in many nations of the world (with France apparently offering a possible exception). The socialist god has failed and, more importantly, is now seen to have failed, both in the total and the partial experiments that have been observed. The shift in public attitudes, the demonstrable loss of faith in governmental-political efficacy, must be largely attributable to the observed results that have been historically experienced.

I should emphasize, however, that empirical observations become meaningful only in the context of a paradigm or mind-set that offers coherent analytical explanation. And here I should argue that developments in ideas have also been very important over the postwar decades; only with the emergence of the new analytical framework offered by public choice, broadly defined, can the observed reality of governmental failures be plausibly incorporated into an understandable philosophical context.

I cannot summarize the developments in public choice here. Let me suggest only a few dramatic highlights. Until the early 1950s, the proponents of unlimited majoritarian democracy could proceed blindly along, unaware that majority voting rules often fail to produce equilibrium solutions and generate, instead, a never-ending cycle (option A being preferred by a majority to option B, which is preferred by another majority to option C, which is then, in turn, preferred by yet another majority to option A). Only with the work of Kenneth Arrow and Duncan Black were the empty conceptual foundations of majoritarian institutions exposed. Until Gordon Tullock and I wrote our book, *The Calculus of Consent* (1962), there had been no attempt to analyze the logical foundations of constitutionally limited government grounded squarely on the interests of individual citizens. Until the late 1960s and early 1970s, with the work of Tullock, Downs, and notably Niskanen, no one had tried to model the behavior of bureaucrats in ordinary utility-maximizing terms, making the bureaucrats ordinary men like the rest of us. Until the middle of the 1970s, no one had really examined the institutions of government with a view toward locating the sources of agenda control.

"Public choice" is a positive analysis, totally divorced from ideological precommitment. But once the scholar puts on his public choice eyeglasses to look at the complex world of politics, he necessarily sees things as they are when actors are modeled as human beings and not as angels. A public choice perspective must suggest the efficacy of *limits* on the exercise of majoritarian democracy.

The design, construction, and practical implementation of the appropriate set of limits (the set of constitutional rules) stand as the challenges of our times. These limits may differ from country to country, each of which emerges from its own unique institutional history, but limits there must be if any country is to preserve a social order in which individuals retain personal liberties. Attention must be paid to the potential enforceability of any constitutional constraints that are laid down. The extent to which citizens share what I have called "the constitutional attitude" becomes a critical element in making any set of limits effective. There is much, much work to be done by those of us in the academies in reversing the gross misperceptions of more than a century.

In the United States, we shall celebrate the bicentennial of our constitution in 1987. I have suggested that this decade be devoted to a "constitutional dialogue," one that would look toward shoring up the flaws that have allowed modern governments to expand far beyond the bounds envisaged by our founding fathers. We are in urgent need of constitutional reform, of new limits on the overreach of the Leviathan that has grown despite the presence of procedural constraints.

Let me end on a note of hope. The process of reform has commenced; Howard Jarvis shocked the world in 1978, when he generated California's approval of Proposition 13; Ronald Reagan started the whole process by his unsuccessful attempt with Proposition 1 in 1973. Both the academic and the political climate is more receptive to constitutional ideas in 1981 than at any time during my active career. This interest does not seem parochial to my own country. Audiences in Europe, Latin America, and Japan have seemed responsive to my own attempts at persuasion during the last two years.

Professor Hayek (1979) has suggested that the last two decades of this century are critically important; he suggests that if these two decades can be somehow got through without total loss of liberties, the state of the 21st century offers brighter prospects. Hayek's perception is based on his conviction that the younger generations are not likely to commit the intellectual follies of their elders. I want to suggest that we have got through two or three years since Hayek made these statements surprisingly well; there has been notable improvement in the way the public thinks about politics. My precautionary warning to members of this society is directed against possible "electoral complacency." We should not be lulled to sleep by temporary electoral victories of politicians and parties that share our own ideological precommitments. In a real sense, such victories tend to distract attention away from the more fundamental issues of imposing new rules for limiting government, rules that will remain operative regardless of which parties or which politicians are installed for short terms of office. Temporary periods of office by leaders who share our ideological precommitments can be—and must be—put to good use by using the scarce time to design and to implement new rules that will at least be quasipermanent elements of the social fabric.

REFERENCES

Buchanan, James M., and Gordon Tullock. 1962. *The Calculus of Consent*. Ann Arbor: University of Michigan Press.

Hayek, F. A. 1979. *The Political Order of a Free People*. Chicago: University of Chicago Press.

Samuelson, Paul A. 1981. "The World at Century's End." *Bulletin of the American Academy of Arts and Sciences* 34 (May): 35–44.

6.2
Federalism and Individual Sovereignty

JAMES M. BUCHANAN

I. INTRODUCTION

I have been both surprised and disturbed by two sources of opposition to the move toward federalist structures in which political authority is divided between levels of government. I refer, first, to the opposition in Europe, mainly in Britain, to movements toward effective European federalism. And secondly, I refer to the successful agitation that blocked the proposed Conference of the States in the United States in 1995. What is disturbing about these sources of opposition to the very idea of political federalism is that both emerge from groups that are identified variously to be right wing, conservative, or libertarian. We should not, of course, be surprised at all by socialist-inspired opposition to the federalist idea and ideal. Socialists have been and remain forthright in their desire to extend the range of politicized control over the lives and liberties of persons. But why should conservatives, classical liberals, or libertarians join socialists in opposing structural reforms that embody federalist principles?

I suggest that a coherent classical liberal must be generally supportive of federal political structures since any division of authority must, necessarily, tend to limit the potential range of political coercion. Those persons and groups who oppose the devolution of authority from the central government

Preliminary draft prepared for presentation, Mt. Pelerin Regional Meeting, Cancún, Mexico, January 1996.

to the states in the United States and those who oppose any limits on the separate single nation-states in modern Europe are, by these commitments, placing other values above those of the liberty or sovereignty of individuals.

The incoherence in values that such antifederalist ambivalence reflects is not widely acknowledged to be present. The relationships between federalist political structure and the sovereignty of the individual must be carefully examined, particularly in terms of the implications for current discussions in Europe, Mexico, and the United States.

In section II, I summarize the theory of competitive federalism. My treatment can be brief because I have, along with others, discussed this subject at length in other papers. In section III, I examine the relationship between the engagement-participation of the individual in politics and the size of the political unit. In summary terms, the theory of competitive federalism places emphasis on the prospects for exit, both internal and external, as constraints on political control over the individual, whereas by contrast the theory of what we might call "partitioned sovereignty federalism" places emphasis on the prospects for the exercise of voice in limiting political excesses.

In section IV, I introduce moral elements that may emerge in arguments for federal political structures, and I relate these arguments to observed crises in modern welfare states. Finally, in section V, I apply the analysis more directly to discussion of movements toward federalist structures in several parts of the world.

II. COMPETITIVE FEDERALISM

The normative theory of competitive federalism is congenial to economists in particular, since it is simply the extension of the principles of the market economy to the organization of the political structure. The market economy produces high levels of value from which all participants secure benefits, because persons are legally guaranteed rights of entry into and exit from production and exchange relationships one with another. If a good or service offered by a producer-seller is "bad" by comparison with goods offered by other producer-sellers, the prospective purchaser-consumer simply exercises the exit option and shifts her custom to an alternative supplier. And the facts that profits are promised by marketing "good goods" rather than "bad goods" ensures that scarce resources will flow toward those uses that yield relatively high values. Suppliers remain always in competition among themselves, faced with the knowledge that demanders have available the continuing prospect of exiting from any ongoing economic relationship.

Normatively, the political structure should be complementary to the market in the sense that the objective for its operation is the generation of results that are valued by citizens. By its nature, however, politics is coercive; all members of a political unit must be subjected to the same decisions. The prospect of exit, which is so important in imposing discipline in market relationships, is absent from politics unless it is deliberately built in by the constitution of a federalized structure.

Consider a large economy, described by liberty of resource flows and trade throughout the territory—liberty that is enforced by a political unit, a government, that is coincident in extent with the effective size of the market. If politics could be restricted to the exercise of these minimal or protective state functions (the night watchman state), little or no concern need be expressed about coercive political intrusions on the liberties of citizens. As the experience of this century surely demonstrates, however, politics is almost certain to extend beyond any such limits. (We need not argue here about whether or not and to what extent expansions in the domain of politics are justifiable). The problem becomes one of organizing the beyond-minimal politics of the "productive" and the "transfer" state so as to minimize the potential for political coercion, or, stated conversely, to maximize the protected sphere of individual sovereignty.

It is here that the prospects for organizing the polity in accordance with federalist principles become exceedingly attractive. Federalism offers a means of introducing essential features of the market into politics. Consider, for example, a setting in which the central or federal government is constitutionally restricted to the exercise of minimal or protective state functions, while all other functions are carried out by separated state or provincial units. The availability of the exit option, guaranteed by the central government, would effectively place limits on the ability of state-provincial governments to exploit citizens, quite independently of how political choices within these units might be made. Localized politicians and coalitions would be unable to depart significantly from overall efficiency standards in their taxing, spending, and regulatory politics. And note that the feedback effect of potential exit need exert itself only on a relatively small share of economic decision takers. Even those citizens who might never consider migration in some Tiebout-like regime would be protected by the acknowledged existence of those few citizens who might be marginally sensitive to differential political treatment (see Tiebout 1956). Federalism served the dual purposes of allowing the range or scope for the central government activity to be curtailed and, at the same time, limited the potential for citizen exploitation by state-provincial units.

III. PARTITIONED SOVEREIGNTY FEDERALISM: THE EXERCISE OF VOICE

The efficacy of competitive federalism depends directly on the operative strength of the exit option. The ability of persons to migrate and to shift investment and trade across boundaries serves to limit political exploitation. Recall, however, that in his seminal emphasis, A. E. Hirschman (1970) placed "voice" alongside "exit" in his examination of control institutions. In the market, exit is the dominant means through which persons indirectly exercise control, and, as indicated earlier, federalism incorporates this means into politics. But the exercise of voice is also important, especially perhaps in politics, and this feature lends independent support for federal structures.

The basic logic is straightforward. If the concern is for the protection and maintenance of individual sovereignty against the potential coercion that may be imposed by political or collective action, the size of the political unit, measured by the number of members, becomes a relevant variable, quite separately from the presence or absence of an exit opportunity. And political authority may be deliberately shared between a central government and component units, with effective sovereignty partitioned among levels.[1]

Consider, again, a large economy in which a central government, coincident in size with the economy, is limited to the carrying out of protective or minimal state functions. How should the extensions of political activity beyond these limits be organized? How should the public-goods and welfare state activities be structurally designed?

Even if citizens are predicted to remain locationally fixed and hence within a single jurisdiction so that exit is not a potentially effective means of institutional control at all, there remains a strong normative argument to be made for establishing relatively small and coexisting political units, all of which may be geographically contained within the inclusive boundaries of the economic interaction and the territorial reach of the central government. If persons are, for any reason, either unable or unwilling to exercise the exit option, actually or potentially, they may be able to exercise "voice," defined here as activity that is participatory in determining political choices. And voice is more effective in small than in large political units. One vote is more likely to be decisive in an electorate of a hundred than in an electorate of a thousand or a million. It is easier for one person or a small group to organize a potentially winning political coalition in the localized community than in a large and complex polity.

But voice is more than a vote in some precise mathematical formula for measuring potential influence over political outcomes. Neither the set of alternatives among which political choices are made nor the preferences of citizens-voters are exogenous to the processes of political discussion. And it is self-evident that the influence of any person in a discussion process varies inversely with the size of the group.

Even if exit, as such, is nonexistent in reality, what we may label as "virtual exit" may be important and relevant in the internal discussion-choice process. The mere fact that coexisting units of government exist and can be observed to do things differently exerts spillover effects on internal political actions. As a practical example, even though exit was of some importance, especially in Germany, the *observations* of Western economies, culture, and politics by citizens of Central and Eastern Europe were independently critical in effecting the genuine political revolutions that occurred in 1989–1991. As an additional imaginary experiment, think about how much less vulnerable the Communist regimes would have been in a setting where all of Europe would have been under Communist domination. Or, as yet another thought, consider how prospects for the revolution might have fared in a world without television.

Note that the normative arguments for federalizing political authority made to this point have not included any consideration of the relative economic efficiency of public goods delivery by the different levels of government. These arguments suggest that, even if productive welfare state functions could, in some ideal sense, be best carried out by the central government, there are offsetting grounds, based on what we may call "political efficiency" for partitioning political choice.[2]

IV. HOMOGENEITY, MORAL CAPACITY, AND FEDERALIZATION

The effects of community size on the individual's protection against political exploitation discussed to this point are independent of any consideration of the homogeneity or heterogeneity of the constituent members of the separated state or provincial units. Even if the inclusive polity is made up of similar persons, there remains a normative argument for partitioning effective political sovereignty between central and state-provincial units of governance. If, however, we now introduce prospects for heterogeneity in the inclusive constituency, the argument for federalization is surely strengthened. Small units, defined geographically or territorially, are likely to be more homogenous in makeup than larger units, and the individual is more likely to share preferences for political action with peers than would be the case where political interaction must include persons who are considered to be "foreign," whether the lines here be drawn racially, ethnically, religiously, economically, or otherwise.

If the end objective is the minimization of politically orchestrated coercion, the individual will personally feel under less potential threat in a community of similarly situated peers than in a large community that embodies groups with differing characteristics.

Quite apart from the objectively identifiable characteristics that might allow an outside observer to classify persons into groups, the size of the community also becomes relevant in its direct relationship to the moral capacity of the individual to share values with others. That is to say, homogeneity in values among persons may itself be related to social and locational distance. And these values may include community bonding that may be expressed in terms of utility interdependence. A person may feel genuine empathy for other persons whom she classifies, internally, as members of her moral community, the boundaries of which are determined in part by numbers and by proximity. For example, I may share a common concern for the plight of persons who are citizens of Montgomery County, Virginia, or more inclusively for the plight of the citizens of Virginia, a concern that is either absent or much attenuated with reference to the citizens of Kern County, California, or of California itself.

In a paper I presented at the meetings of the American Economic Association several years ago (Buchanan 1978), I argued that each of us has only a limited moral capacity. It is surely easier and more natural to feel sympathy for and care about others who are members of the same small community than it is to care for members of a large polity. I suggested, further, that a major factor in generating the breakdown of the welfare state was the shift of transfer activities to the central government and away from local communities in which political action might well embody a greater sense of interdependence. I suggested that the shift of political activities that must incorporate moral elements to levels of interaction that extend well beyond our moral capacities can only serve to exacerbate the emergence of raw self-seeking by groups of potential clients on the one hand and by those who feel unduly exploited on the other.

The argument here is, of course, related closely to Hayek's continued emphasis on our genetic heritage, which is basically tribal and leads us to classify other persons into two groups—"us" and "them," or "neighbors" and "strangers." Hayek perceptively noted that only as these genetic dispositions came to be transcended by the culturally evolved norms for generalized reciprocity in interactions did the "great society," defined by the extended market order, become possible (Hayek 1979). We must recognize, however, that politicization in itself explicitly encourages the reemergence of tribal identities. Political action, regardless of how decisions are made, involves choices that are made for and coercively imposed on *all* members of the relevant political economy. Anyone who is a participant is, almost by necessity, required to classify their own interests in juxtaposition against the imagined interests of others in the polity. Federalized structures allow for some partial mapping of politics with tribal identities. At the very least, federalized structures reduce the extent to which tribal identities in politics must be grossly transcended. This consideration assumes relatively more importance if and as the moral linkages are located in the sense discussed earlier, rather than being strictly genetic.

V. FEDERALISM AS AN IDEAL POLITY AND FEDERALISM IN REALITY[3]

It is relatively easy to describe the ideal structure of politics for a large community, defined by territory or by numbers of citizens, if the overriding objective is the projection of individual sovereignty against political coercion. A central government authority should be constitutionally restricted to the enforcement of openness of the whole nexus of economic interaction. Within this scope, the central authority must be strong, but it should not be allowed to extend beyond the limits constitutionally defined. Other political-collective activities should be carried out, if at all, by separate state-provincial units that exist side by side, as competitors of sorts, in the inclusive polity.

The definition of the idealized federalism is useful only because it offers a concrete objective toward which reforms in political arrangements may be directed. In reality, no existing political structure comes close to the ideal. Any constructive effort must therefore commence with an understanding of and appreciation for the politics that is observed to exist. "We start from here and now." This elementary fact should always be prefatory to any discussion of reform.

With reference to the common federalist ideal, however, we may observe categorically different starting places. The situation may be represented by the spectrum in figure 6.2.1, where a federal political structure stands halfway between a regime of fully autonomous states on the one hand and a monolithic, all-powerful central authority on the other.

Figure 6.2.1.

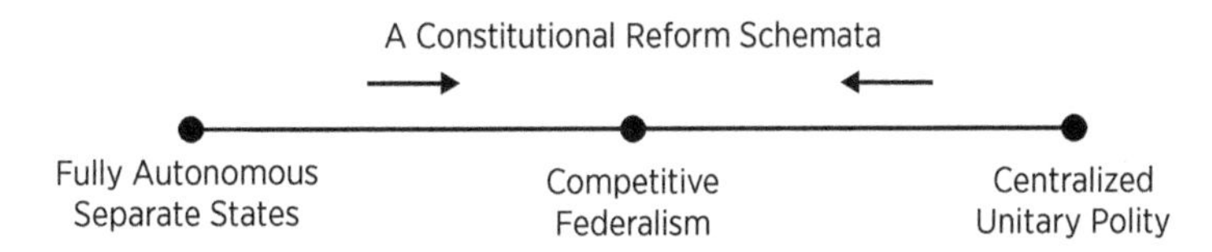

Individual protection against political exploitation is increased as we move toward the center of the spectrum from starting points either left or right of center. In 1787, James Madison sought to increase the authority of the central government; he located the status quo under the Articles of Confederation somewhere to the left of center in figure 6.2.1. He sought to increase the authority of the federal government as a means of placing limits on the authority of the separate states. We know, now, that US history has destroyed Madison's vision. As a result of the destructive Civil War in the 1860s, secession was permanently eliminated as an effective extraconstitutional check on the progressive increase in central government authority. And, in the 20th century, constitutional guarantees against federal encroachment on the authority of states were undermined by executive, legislative, and judicial departures from established principles. At the century's end, therefore, the status quo is clearly on the right side of the spectrum in figure 6.2.1. Effective reform must embody devolution of power from the central government to the states—change that is in the opposite direction from that which Madison accomplished in 1787.

In Mexico, the situation is similar with respect to the direction of change, despite the categorically different history of the country. Reform in the direction of securing effective federalism must incorporate a devolution of authority toward the states and away from the central government.

With Europe, however, matters become quite different. Here the status quo exhibits some features that are analogous to those assessed by Madison 1787. The opportunity has existed, and still exists, to organize European politics so as to put in place a genuine federal structure with many elements of the ideal set out earlier. The Europe-wide economy has been substantially integrated, with historically unprecedented liberties of resource flows and trade across traditional national boundaries. Reform requires the establishment of a strong, but limited, central authority, empowered to enforce the openness of the economy, along with the other minimal state functions. In this way, and only in this way, can the vulnerability of the individual European to exploitation by national political units be reduced. At the same time, however, the extension of the central authority's powers beyond such minimal limits must be rigidly opposed. The separate nation-states, as members of the federal union, most zealously protect the whole range of subminimal political activities.

Opposition to the federalist idea, especially as expressed in arguments by some UK political leaders, stems from an imagined fear of a monolithic central authority in Brussels—a fear that has been fueled in part by the residual vestiges of the socialist mentality among some influential nominal supporters of the federal structure. Both attitudes here fail to understand that federalism and socialism are contradictory systems of political order. Federalism is a means of reducing political power overall and of dividing the power that exists. Socialism is opposed on both counts.

The opposition to federalism that comes from those who otherwise seem sympathetic to classical liberalism apparently reflects a failure to understand that federalism offers protection against the excesses of the autonomous nation-state. Or could it be that the genuine end objective of those who oppose reforms toward federalism is not individual liberty, but rather the preservation of national political sovereignty? It is as if the United Kingdom antifederalists are saying, "We do not mind being politically coerced, so long as it is done by the British parliament."

The position of those zealots in the United States who successfully thwarted the organization of the Conference of the States in 1995 is even more bizarre and surely borders on paranoia. The initiative behind the conference was aimed almost exclusively toward designing ways and means through which effective political authority could be devolved from the federal government to the separate states. How could those persons and groups who mouth slogans about liberty and oppose such initiatives be other than dishonest or ignorant?

APPENDED NOTE ON "INDIVIDUAL SOVEREIGNTY AND INDIVIDUAL LIBERTY"

Note that my title is "Federalism and Individual Sovereignty" rather than "Federalism and Individual Liberty." It may be useful to clarify the distinction. What is the ultimate maximand when the individual considers the organization of the political structure? Unless one is a genuine anarchist who thinks that private and voluntary action can be efficacious over the whole social space (including basic protections to person, property, and contract), this maximand cannot be summarized as the maximization of (equal) individual liberty from political-collective action. Implementation of such an objective would, to many of us, represent a leap backward into the Hobbesian jungle.

A more meaningful maximand is summarized as the maximization of (equal) individual sovereignty. This objective allows for the establishment of political-collective institutions but implies that these institutions be organized so as to minimize political coercion of the individual. Coercion is defined as being required to do things or to submit to things others do to you that you do not, or would not, voluntarily agree to do yourself or to have done to you. A person may give up her liberty to steal from others and pay taxes to support the enforcement of laws against theft provided others are subjected to the same general constraints. So long as her agreement to such political action is voluntary, the individual's sovereignty is protected, even though liberty is restricted (see Buchanan and Lomasky 1984).

NOTES

1. In a monograph concentrated on European prospects, Vaubel (1995) makes several of the same points that I emphasize here. Notably, Vaubel also used the "exit' and "voice" metaphors in the federalist context.
2. For further elaboration, see Brennan and Buchanan (1980, chapter 9).
3. The discussion in this section closely parallels that in my paper (Buchanan 1995), presented at a conference on federalism in Querétaro, Mexico.

REFERENCES

Brennan, Geoffrey, and James M. Buchanan. 1980. *The Power to Tax: Analytical Foundations of a Fiscal Constitution*. Cambridge: Cambridge University Press.

Buchanan, James M. 1978. "Markets, States and the Extent of Morals." *American Economic Review* 68 (May): 364–68.

———. 1995. "Federalism as an Ideal Political Order and an Objective for Constitutional Reform." *Publius: Journal of Federalism* 25(2): 1–9.

Buchanan, James M., and Loren Lomasky. 1984. "The Matrix of Contractarian Justice." *Social Philosophy* 2 (Autumn): 12–32

Hayek, F. A. 1979. *The Political Order of a Free People*. Vol. 3: *Law, Legislation and Liberty*. Chicago: University of Chicago Press.

Hirschman, Albert E. 1970. *Exit, Voice, and Loyalty*. Cambridge, MA: Harvard University Press.

Tiebout, Charles M. 1956. "A Pure Theory of Local Expenditures." *Journal of Political Economy* 60 (October): 416–24.

Vaubel, Roland. 1995. "The Centralisation of Western Europe." Hobart Paper No. 127, Institute of Economic Affairs, London.

SECTION 7

POSTCRISIS ECONOMICS

7.0 Introduction

PETER J. BOETTKE AND ALAIN MARCIANO

The formative years of Buchanan's political economy were the decades following World War II, when—with a few exceptions, including Buchanan himself, obviously—economists focused on formalism and were completely desensitized to the role of institutions and to comparative institutional analysis. This, however, progressively changed in the last quarter of the 20th century. Economists now admitted that economic activities were not taking place in an institutional vacuum and that institutions matter. And the last decades of Buchanan's career saw a general recognition of the role of institutions in determining economic performance.

Also of crucial importance for Buchanan's career was the political economy reality of the 1990s and the first decade of the 21st century. In those decades, most of the pressing questions in the world under examination were defined by tremendous institutional changes that challenged social scientists in general and economists in particular. The increase in the pace of institutional integration in Europe with the 1991 Maastricht Treaty was one, and the collapse of socialism after the fall of the Berlin Wall in 1989 was another, as was the 2008 financial crisis.

As a political economist, Buchanan could not ignore and felt perfectly legitimate to address such challenges. He wrote a little bit about Europe (Buchanan 1990, 1996) and about postsocialism (Buchanan 1991, 1993; Buchanan and Yoon 2014). He also wrote a few papers after and about the crisis. These were his very last academic works, which we present in this section. Buchanan dealt with these major questions: Were economists to blame for the crisis? If yes, why, and who were exactly the economists to blame? If some economists were not to blame, what would be or would have been the solution to the crisis? These are the questions we discuss in this introduction.

ARE ECONOMISTS TO BLAME?

After the financial crisis, economists were almost the first to be blamed. Their fault was that they had not been able to predict the crisis—although a few of them did. "Why Economists Failed to Predict the Financial Crisis," asked an article published and posted on the website of the Wharton School from the University of Pennsylvania (Knowledge @ Wharton 2009). The queen of England visited the London School of Economics in November 2009 and asked the same question—"Why had nobody noticed that the credit crunch was on its way?" Some gave a general answer that involved all the profession. For instance, the Dahlem report spoke of "The Financial Crisis and the Systemic Failure of Academic Economics" (Colander et al. 2009). Others—most of the critiques—were more specific. They targeted a specific approach: the free-market economics of Chicago.

Some voices raised to defend Chicago-style economics—especially Chicago economists themselves. Robert Lucas wrote an article, "In Defense of the Dismal Science" (Lucas 2009). During the 2009 conference organized about "The Future of Markets," Eugene Fama also stuck to the theory that markets are efficient (Cassidy 2010b). For his part, Gary Becker admitted in an interview, "The last twelve months have shown that free markets sometimes don't do a very good job. There's no question, financial markets in the United States and elsewhere didn't do a good job over this period of time" (Cassidy 2010a). He nonetheless added that "if I take the first proposition of Chicago economics—that free markets generally do a good job—I think that still holds" (ibid.). Similarly, another Nobel laureate, James Heckman, admitted that parts of the "Chicago influence . . . still stand up" (ibid.). Other references could be given.

At Chicago, however, the perception of the role played by Chicago ideas was not homogenous. This was evidenced, in particular, by an article written by Michael Fitzgerald entitled "Chicago Schooled: The Visible Hand of the Recession Has Revitalized Critics of the Chicago School of Economics" (Fitzgerald 2009). That article is of particular interest for us because it is the one that "stimulated" Buchanan's comments about "the events of 2007–9" (Buchanan 2010, 2) and about the role played by the Chicago School of

Economics. Fitzgerald concluded that, at least partly, the blame should be borne by Chicago economists. Buchanan, although his "own reaction to the magazine piece was not favorable" (ibid., 1) eventually reached the same conclusion about the blame to place on some of the Chicago economists. He gave this claim a more general turn in a 2011 talk, concluding that he agreed "in placing major blame for the Great Recession on the academic economists" (Buchanan 2011a, 10).[1]

This leads to three questions: Are all economists to blame? Specifically, were Chicago economists to blame? If they were to blame, why?

OLD AND NEW CHICAGO SCHOOLS OF ECONOMICS

If Buchanan agreed to blame some Chicago economists, he certainly did not agree to blame all of them. To understand who was to blame, Buchanan introduced in his analysis and insisted on a distinction between the "new" and "old" Chicago School of Economics.[2]

The distinction has now been discussed and is relatively clearly admitted, between two traditions at Chicago. The first, and old one, is the one of Frank Knight and Jacob Viner. Buchanan added the name of Henry Simons but did not change much about the old school. He insisted that he was himself "a representative adherent" (Buchanan 2010, 5) of this tradition. Then, there is the second new and modern school of thinking at Chicago to which the names of Friedman, Stigler, Becker, or Coase are usually attached. Here, Buchanan departed from the now admitted categorization. He did not really include these economists in the new school. To him, they belong to an intermediary category. They did contribute to the shift from the old to the new way of viewing economists. They departed from the old tradition (ibid., 6–7) but remained, in one way or the other, connected to the old Chicago thinking and cannot be viewed as new Chicago economists.

The main difference between these ways of envisaging economics is discussed in the articles reprinted below. They refer to arguments Buchanan repeated many times during his career. The old Chicago School of Economics does not ignore the role of institutions, especially when it comes to discussing the efficiency of markets. To Buchanan, the old Chicago economists did not believe that markets always work or that they never fail; that is, "if left alone, the market order will work satisfactorily under any and all sets of constraints" (Buchanan 2010, 5)—a quotation that embodies a twofold claim: markets may fail and institutions matter, and both are related. Thus, Buchanan wrote, "The 'old' Chicago School thinking embodied the evaluative judgment that the market does indeed work, in the sense that crises are neither necessary nor inevitable, but only on the supposition that the required encompassing monetary-financial rules are in place" (ibid). To him, Henry Simons could be cited as one of the best examples of the old Chicago School. Simons pleaded for a "positive program for laissez faire" and, accordingly, never argued for "unconstrained economic anarchy" (ibid.). This is precisely why Buchanan viewed himself as belonging to this tradition. Buchanan always insisted that no game could be played without rules. Or, as he repeated in one of the articles reprinted here, "To secure efficiency in the institutions of the market, an additional level of exchanges must be implemented, those among the inclusive, or collective, set of potential beneficiaries in some imagined Wicksellian process of agreement" (ibid., 10).

For their part, the new Chicago economists are those who believe that markets are defined as mechanisms, meaning that an efficient allocation of resources where "efficient" corresponds to a static competitive equilibrium. This corresponds to and echoes what Buchanan had always written, in particular in 1959, about "presumptive efficiency" (Buchanan 1959). New Chicago thinking consists in assuming a definition of efficiency and using it to evaluate the functioning of markets.[3] And, quite surprisingly, in such an approach, markets never fail to allocate resources efficiently. Markets "fail to meet efficiency norms *only when artificial constraints are imposed*" (Buchanan 2010, 10, emphasis added)—which means that no failure, that is no crisis, can be anticipated. Otherwise, "if left alone and with open entry, the activity of potential arbitrageurs suffices" (ibid.). Then, and this is a main difference with the old Chicago thinking, the consequence is that rules do not matter: whatever are the rules within which markets and arbitrageurs operate, an efficient equilibrium will be reached. This is a view that Buchanan had already put forward, of course, about what he had then named "the standard theory of choice in markets," for which "there is little or no concern with the constitution of the choice environment" (Buchanan 1987, 247).

That is not all. Buchanan wrote, "Some contributors to the broadly defined new Chicago tradition were willing to stop at this point" (Buchanan 2010, 9). They pushed their reasoning in terms of efficiency and applied it to institutions. The latter "themselves were . . . considered as arbitrage-like responses that helped to insure the continuing and inclusive efficiency of the network of markets" (ibid.). This is the approach that Buchanan called the "'markets work' mind-set" (ibid.), an approach that applies the same concept of efficiency to the working of markets for private and partitionable goods and also to "the rules, constraints, or conventions within which ordinary market dealings occur" (ibid., 10). In this frame, there is no difference between the rules that frame the social game and the rules that emerge during the game. Then, accordingly and consistently, this approach applies the same criterion to evaluate those rules. It also assumes that the rules that result from the functioning of markets are as efficient as markets themselves. Hence, this approach assumes that "'the market' can generate its own rules" (Buchanan 2011a, 1) but also that these rules are efficient.

Hence, Buchanan concluded that a "mind-set" that proposes "a defense of the unqualified statement that 'markets work,' . . . must share some of the blame for the failure reflected in the crises of 2007–9" (Buchanan 2010, 11). He repeated, in 2011, that the problem came from these economist's "overly enthusiastic extension of the efficient markets models, those that lend credence to the 'markets work' slogan that allows for dismissal of potential criticisms" (Buchanan 2011a, 10). This is crucial to understand Buchanan's "diagnosis" about the origin and nature of the crisis.

THE NATURE OF THE CRISIS: A "CONSTITUTIONAL FAILURE"

Following the previous reasoning, it becomes clear that the main issue with the 2008 financial crisis was not in the financial crisis itself. That was, of course, one of the main issues that was discussed after the crash. Where did the problem come from? What were the causes of the crisis? Some claim that the regulation of markets was not sufficient. Others—as was the case of the economists who answered the queen of England in 2009—argued that "the failure to foresee the timing, extent and severity of the crisis and to head it off, while it had many causes, was principally a failure of the collective imagination of many bright people, both in this country and internationally, to understand the risks to the system as a whole" (Besley and Hennessy 2009).

Interestingly, Buchanan did not disagree with either of these positions. The financial crisis was primarily a constitutional or institutional failure to structure the incentives within which markets operate. Certainly there was a form of regulation in these markets. Rules had emerged during and from the functioning of the market—"Clearly there are elements of institutions best conceived as having emerged anarchistically in modern financial extensions of exchanges" (Buchanan 2010, 8). But economists could not understand the problem because of a lack of "imagination." Indeed, economists could not depart from their position about competitive equilibrium, about markets as mechanisms for allocating scarce resources, or about efficiency. Hence, they could not understand that these rules that had emerged from the functioning of markets were not and *could* not organize efficiently the financial markets: "The main point of our argument is that the processes that guarantee the efficiency of ordinary markets do not operate here, . . . The rules and institutions that emerge in the quasi-anarchy of modern financial markets do not pass muster under any process test for efficiency" (Buchanan 2011a, 8).

Hence, the crisis is the consequence of the belief—characteristic of the new Chicago thinking as summarized earlier—that markets can generate their own rules and that these rules will be efficient. The "New" Chicago School, Buchanan argues, had proceeded in their analysis of financial markets and the macroeconomy as a whole as if institutions didn't matter and the invisible hand of the market economy could be relied upon to guide markets on the right path independent of the framework of rules governing the economic game. Now, these rules "cannot be positively evaluated by standard efficiency criteria" (Buchanan 2011a, 9). Indeed, they are produced by entrepreneurs looking for profit as if they were private goods, which they are not. They are pure public goods, what Buchanan also named "nonpartitionable goods" (ibid., 7). The problem is that "these rules, such as are observed to exist, are generated by entrepreneurs who are motivated by promised differential rents . . . *without consideration of inclusive norms for efficiency*" (ibid., 8, emphasis added). Hence, "there is no decentralized process that allows 'efficiency' to be evaluated deontologically, akin to the evaluation of a market" (Buchanan 1987, 247).

This is where lies the mistake made by the economists and the origin of the financial crisis. They ignored that dysfunctions in the institutional framework could distort the operation of the market economy leading up to a global financial crisis—simply because they ignore constitutional rules. And, of course, economists have to be blamed for this. They "should never have expected that the rules, conventions, practices, and institutions generally that emerged in the quasi-anarchy of the financial sector would meet efficiency norms" (Buchanan 2011a, 2). The very fact "that the rules or constraints on the operation of markets are best classified as 'public goods' in the Samuelson taxonomy . . . does not give economists license to claim that efficient rules are generated as if by magic from within-market behavior. The 'invisible hand,' even as properly interpreted, remains inoperative at the level of choices among rules" (ibid., 10).

The reason is straightforward. Rules matter. Basic economic reasoning from the time of Adam Smith up to James Buchanan stressed that the self-interest hypothesis must be squared with the invisible-hand postulate not through a set of additional behavioral postulates but through a thoroughgoing institutional analysis. It is true that the butcher, the baker, and the brewer provide our dinner not due to feelings of solidarity and benevolence but as a result of their pursuit of self-interest. The point, however, is that their self-interest guides them to coordinate the division of labor so we can enjoy our dinner precisely because they operate within a system of property, prices, and profit/loss. Absent the three p's of property, prices, and profit/loss, individuals will be devoid of the incentives and information required to continually innovate and coordinate their plans to realize the gains from trade and the gains from innovation.

A CONSTITUTIONAL SOLUTION

Now we know what should not have been expected—namely that financial markets were efficient simply because there are rules. However, these rules had never been established at the constitutional level. What would have been a solution proposed by "old Chicago thinkers"? Clearly, since the problem is institutional, so should be the solution.

To understand it, we should start by asking how alternative rules and institutions should be evaluated—any rule, constitutional and postconstitutional ones. More specifically, should we abandon any claim for efficiency when discussing rules? Yes and no. Buchanan did not directly answer the question in his last works. He had already answered by the negative in the 1980s, when he insisted that "there is no criterion through which policy may be *directly* evaluated" (Buchanan 1987, 247) that is evaluated by the results they generate. However, an *indirect* evaluation of these rules is possible, implying that we move "the focus of evaluative attention to the process itself, as contrasted with end-state or outcome patterns" (ibid.). Indeed, "that normative evaluation cannot be *directly* applied to results, either for market or collective action. . . . In collective action, the emphasis on applying evaluative criteria to process rather than end-states is even more important than in market exchange" (Buchanan 2015, 141).

Now, in terms of process, efficiency should depend on how well individual preferences are respected: "An indirect evaluation may be based on some measure of the degree to which the political process facilitates the translation of expressed individual preferences into observed political outcomes" (Buchanan 1987, 247). And then, the criterion of "efficiency" is agreement, unanimity or quasi-unanimity: the "analogue to decentralized trading among individuals . . . is agreement among the individuals who participate. The unanimity rule for collective choice is the political analogue to freedom of exchange of partitionable goods in markets" (ibid.). Hence, markets should have been regulated differently—not necessarily *more*, of course. And, as mentioned above, a "positive program for laissez faire" à la Simon should have been adopted. That is part of the Wicksellian solution Buchanan defended since his very first works and repeated until the very end of his career.

If we slightly depart from the question of the financial crisis, then this solution would find a direct application in terms of fiscal policy. It is a slight departure because the fiscal situation in America in the 2010s was not independent from the crisis. To Buchanan, "America's fiscal tragedy" (Buchanan 2015) was a consequence of the fact that fiscal policy had been left in the hands of politicians. The latter were no benevolent despots. Their decisions were made to satisfy "the demands of constituencies, voters, interest groups, and bureaucracies, who always prefer government spending to taxing" (ibid., 138). It resulted in a "bias toward relatively excessive rates of spending" (ibid., 139) that could hardly be viewed as satisfying individual preferences. An institutional reform was necessary that in particular required a linkage between spending and taxation. That was what Wicksell, according to Buchanan himself, suggested (Buchanan 1987, 248). However, Buchanan went beyond Wicksell. Indeed,

> Wicksell did not consciously extend his analysis to constitutional choice, to the choice of the rules within which ordinary politics is to be allowed to operate. His suggested reforms were, of course, constitutional, since they were aimed to improve the process of decision making. But his evaluative criterion was restricted to the matching of individual preferences with political outcomes in particularized decisions, rather than over any sequence. (Buchanan 1987, 247–48)

Unsurprisingly, Buchanan suggested to modify Wicksell's perspective by adding a constitutional level: "To secure efficiency in the institutions of the market, an additional level of exchanges must be implemented, those among the inclusive, or collective, set of potential beneficiaries in some imagined Wicksellian process of agreement" (Buchanan 2010, 10). In other words, Buchanan's solution to the crisis—the old Chicago thinking solution—would not only have consisted of adopting another criterion to evaluate postconstitutional rules but also to add constitutional rules. And, at the constitutional level, agreement should have been reached under a Rawls-like "veil of uncertainty" (Buchanan 2011a, 9).

The collapse of Soviet Communism in the late 1980s and the collapse of the house of cards that constituted modern finance in the 2000s have demonstrated the necessity of the institutional framework in any political economy analysis of our world. Markets operate in a "socially efficient" manner if and only to the extent they are embedded in a set of rules that guides them in that direction. Absent a framework of rules concerning property, contract, and consent, the market system is likely to be dysfunctional. The financial crisis of 2008 demonstrates not that the invisible hand can slap, but that even the most robust and capable hand cannot function if the skeletal structure is broken or absent.

NOTES

1. A different version of this paper was published in Buchanan (2011b).
2. The history of the term "Chicago School of Economics" is not totally clear. It seems that one of the first to refer to a Chicago School was Lawrence Miller in 1962. Then, Samuelson (1988) made the distinction between a "first" and a "second" school. In 1997, Lawrence Lessig referred to "the New Chicago School" (cited in Rosen 1997). Then, in 1998, Deirdre McCloskey seems to have introduced a reference to the "old" Chicago School (McCloskey 1998). The term became more widely used after Medema used it (Medema 2009, 2018).
3. One of the interesting and important consequences is that, when such an equilibrium is reached, there are "no unexploited gains from trade, no uncaptured or unexplained profit opportunities" (Buchanan 2011a, 8). This equilibrium is stable. Nothing should change: in this competitive adjustment process, after a change, prices and quantities will return to the same level as before.

REFERENCES

Besley, T., and P. Hennessy. 2009. "Letter to the Queen." July 22. https://wwwf.imperial.ac.uk/~bin06/M3A22/queen-lse.pdf.

Buchanan, J. M. 1959. "Positive Economics, Welfare Economics, and Political Economy." *Journal of Law & Economics* 2: 124–38.

———. 1987. "The Constitution of Economic Policy." *American Economic Review* 77(3): 243–50.

———. 1990. "Europe's Constitutional Opportunity." In J. M. Buchanan, *Europe's Constitutional Future*. London: Institute of Economic Affairs.

———. 1991. "Economics in the Post-Socialist Century." *Royal Economic Society* 101(404): 15–21.

———. 1993. "Public Choice after Socialism." *Public Choice* 77(1): 67–74.

———. 1996. "Europe as Social Reality." *Constitutional Political Economy* 7(4): 253–56.

———. 2010. "Chicago School Thinking: Old and New." Preliminary draft, Summer Institute for the Preservation of the History of Economic Thought, Richmond, VA.

———. 2011a. "Ideology or Error: Economists and the Great Recession." Summer Institute for the Preservation of the History of Economic Thought, Richmond, VA.

———. 2011b. "The Limits of Market Efficiency." *Rationality, Markets and Morals: Studies at the Intersection of Philosophy and Economics* 2: 1–7.

———. 2015. "Institutional Sources of America's Fiscal Tragedy." In J. M. Buchanan and Y. J Yoon (eds.), *Individualism and Political Disorder*, 137–44. Northampton, MA: Edward Elgar.

Buchanan, J. M., and Y. J. Yoon. 2014. "The Cost of Civilization, Per Se." *Public Choice* 159(3/4): 321–26.

Cassidy, J. 2010a. "The Chicago Interviews." *New Yorker*, January.

———. 2010b. "Interview with Eugene Fama." *New Yorker*, January 13.

Colander, D., H. Follmer, A. Haas, M. D. Goldberg, K. Juselius, A. Kirman, T. Lux, and B. Sloth. 2009. "The Financial Crisis and the Systemic Failure of Academic Economics." Department of Economics Discussion Paper No. 09-03, University of Copenhagen.

Fitzgerald, M. 2009. "Chicago Schooled: The Visible Hand of the Recession Has Revitalized Critics of the Chicago School of Economics." *University of Chicago Magazine*, September–October.

Knowledge @ Wharton. 2009. "Why Economists Failed to Predict the Financial Crisis." May 13. https://knowledge.wharton.upenn.edu/article/why-economists-failed-to-predict-the-financial-crisis/.

Lucas, R. 2009. "In Defense of the Dismal Science." *Economist*, August 8.

McCloskey, D. 1998. "The Good Old Coase Theorem and the Good Old Chicago School: A Comment on Zerbe and Medema." In S. Medema (ed.), *Coasean Economics: Law and Economics and the New Institutional Economics*, 239–48. New York: Springer.

Medema, S. G. 2009. *The Hesitant Hand: Taming Self-Interest in the History of Economic Ideas*. Princeton, NJ: Princeton University Press.

———. 2018. "Identifying a 'Chicago School' of Economics: On the Origins, Diffusion, and Evolving Meanings of a Famous Brand Name." *History of Recent Economics Conference 2018 Series*, September 26.

Rosen, J. 1997. "The Social Police." *New Yorker*, October.

Samuelson, P. A. 1988. "The Passing of the Guard in Economics." *Eastern Economic Journal* 14(4): 319–29.

7.1
Chicago School Thinking
Old and New

JAMES M. BUCHANAN

I. INTRODUCTION

"Is Chicago School Thinking to Blame?" This question in bold print dominates the cover of the September–October 2009 issue of the *University of Chicago Magazine* and directs attention to the feature article by Michael Fitzgerald (2009), which discusses the Chicago School of Economics as it relates to the crises of 2007–2009. The focus is almost exclusively on the new, or modern, Chicago School emphasis in the development and extensions of the efficient markets models, culminating in the "markets work" mind-set that did permeate much economic thinking, in Chicago and beyond, before the unpredicted events. Since the origins of this mind-set can, with some legitimacy, be located in Chicago, the answer to the question posed seems to be "yes, in part."

My own reaction to the magazine piece was not favorable. My objection was to the neglect through no more than passing reference to Chicago School thinking before the presumed extensions of rational choice logic captured the position of dominance. I was tempted to write a letter to the editor suggesting that there did exist a Chicago School of Economics before the "markets work everywhere" models came into fashion.

Preliminary draft, talk at Summer Institute, Richmond, VA, June 20, 2010.

And, importantly, Chicago thinking pre-Lucas, and even pre-Friedman, pre-Stigler, pre- Becker, pre-Coase, would never have worked under the delusion that markets work within any and all constraints or rules, even in some quasi-anarchistic absence of rules altogether. Although directly stimulated by Fitzgerald's article, these comments offer the opportunity to follow my earlier diagnoses that the events of 2007–2009 provide evidence of "constitutional failure," rather than any breakdown in within-market behavior as such.

My claim here is that the "old" Chicago School would never have countenanced, explicitly or implicitly, any presumption that markets generate efficiency while remaining also invulnerable to collapse independent of constraining rules and institutions. The postcrises inference should never have been that "capitalism failed." The appropriate question should have been, "Did capitalism, or the market order, fail under the set of rules within which economic decision makers were allowed to operate?" The working of markets under alternative sets of rules—this is the proper subject matter for economists, an acknowledged emphasis here on my own promotion of what we call constitutional political economy.

I shall first, in section II, summarize my understanding of Chicago School economics at midcentury, when I was a graduate student, and before the intrusion of Keynesian macroeconomics, Friedman positivism, Stigler empiricism, and the varying rational choice extensions associated with Becker, Coase, and, importantly, Lucas. In section III I discuss the transition between the old and new Chicago School economics, and in section IV I examine more carefully the new Chicago School. Section V concludes the paper.

II. CHICAGO SCHOOL ECONOMICS AT MIDCENTURY

Perhaps the best way to summarize the relevant Chicago School thinking at midcentury or, more specifically, in the immediate post–World War II years, is to call on my own remembered mind-set as I left Chicago in 1948, after two and one-half years of intensive intellectual grounding in economic understanding. I had learned how a market economy could work to resolve Knight's familiar five functions: setting the value scale, organizing production, distributing the product, providing for the future, and adjusting supply to demand in short periods. I had, indeed, come to understand how the market works, but "the market" was treated as an abstracted element of the actual or potential reality that is observable. This conceptualization of economic process was derivative from Frank Knight, whom I later realized was strongly influenced by Max Weber. Note that no claim is advanced to the effect that the market works, warts and all.

The most articulate expositor of the "old" Chicago School was Henry Simons, although there was a sense that the views expressed were fully shared, particularly by Frank Knight and Lloyd Mints. In general terms, the efficacy of the market in allocating valued resource inputs, as exemplified in Simons' rent problems, was taken for granted (Simons 1934). But there was little or no bridge between the models of markets, presented in stylized neoclassical processes, and the economy, as observed.

In those immediate postwar years, macroeconomics was emerging as a quasi-separate area of inquiry. We did learn the formal structure of macroeconomics from Jacob Marshak, which included the mastering of Modigliani's seminal paper on the Keynesian model. But we were not, at Chicago, affected by the Harvard–MIT syndrome that led us to proceed as if we were called to be advisers to politicians. Jacob Viner, who left Chicago one term after I arrived, had famously said that the task of economists was to expose fallacies in the arguments of politicians rather than to offer positive advice (Viner 1950).

Almost by necessity, the Chicago mind-set embodied a critique of political behavior. To be sure, there was an implicit presumption that, if, by some magic, Chicago economics could be applied, then value could be dramatically enhanced. But there was no explicit emphasis on micromanagement of the complex national economy.

What about the business cycle, subject matter that had occupied the attention of so many economists prior to Keynes? Here I rely primarily on my personal interpretation of the Chicago position rather than on any hard evidence. But if the appropriate rules and institutions are in place—that is, if the constitutional constraints are properly set so as to allow the "game" to be played within the rules—there is nothing inherent in a market economy that would generate cycles, whether these be short, medium, or long in duration.

There may be shifts, of course, in demand and supply—conditions that generate fluctuations in particular industries or sectors. But the only linkage among parts of the whole economy involves the common usage through the numeraire of the monetary-financial framework. It then follows directly that, if the value of money is predictable, there need be no transference or transmission of shifts in one industry, location, or sector to others. Admittedly, this result requires, more or less as a side constraint, that the economy be sufficiently decentralized or competitive enough so as to ensure that no particular firm or industry be deemed too big to fail or too vital for other reasons to be exposed to market forces.

There is nothing in this stance that suggests that, if left alone, the market order will work satisfactorily under any and all sets of constraints, or the absence thereof, and especially in the financial-monetary structure. In particular, the emergence of institutions that allow for and encourage shifts among various near monies can only create the potential for cascading asset values, in either direction.

The "old" Chicago School thinking embodied the evaluative judgment that the market does indeed work, in the sense that crises are neither necessary nor inevitable, but only on the supposition that the required encompassing monetary-financial rules are in place. As so stated, there was really no argument to be settled. Hence, this Chicago School vision involved little or no attention paid to the possible matching of observed political-economic reality with the stylized models. Of course, the old Chicago School advocate would say, the market is the superior allocator of value, provided competition is secured by appropriate constraints on concentrations of authority and provided that monetary predictability is descriptive of observed institutional reality.

This "old" Chicago School thinking, of which I consider myself to remain a representative adherent, would never claim that the grubby complex of economic interaction that can be empirically examined becomes a manifestation of behavior that exhausts all of the gains from trade, and, further, that all exchange dealings tend to eliminate rather than create or protect rents. This Chicago School thinking is perhaps best summarized in Henry Simons's 1934 monograph, which laid out a "Positive Program for Laissez Faire," rather than any argument for unconstrained economic anarchy (Simons 1934).

III. TRANSITION

The basic contrast between the "old" and "new" Chicago School thinking can be summarized in terms of two stylized attitudes, located at the two ends of an imagined spectrum. In the first stance, outlined in section II, the role of the economist is to offer an understanding of the workings of an idealized model of economic interaction—an understanding that, once achieved, allows the use of criteria for evaluating alternative constraints, a step that is necessarily grounded in a normative foundation. The role of the economist in this "old" Chicago thinking was not primarily that of describing economic reality in some manner akin to the activity of the practitioners of the hard sciences.

The "new" Chicago thinking, by comparison, embodied scientific thrust. Clearly, the disciplinary reach was extended. Important transition contributions to this half-century shift in thinking were made by Milton Friedman, George Stigler, Gary Becker, and Ronald Coase, each of whom variously stressed the explanatory power of models based on rational choice behavior—models that could yield falsifiable hypotheses.

Friedman, in particular, remained linked to the "old" way of thinking, especially in his popular writing. He did not succumb to the temptation seemingly offered by evolutionary analogues to institutional development. At the same time, however, he joined Stigler in the emphasis on the relevance of empirical testing. Becker's transitional role was to push out the frontiers of behavior amenable to economic explanation, under the often implicit rationality postulate. The impact of Coase's emphasis on the behavioral implications of nonexhausted gains from trade extended well beyond the applications in law. There is relatively little distance from the positions associated with these intellectual-analytical "giants" in the inclusive Chicago tradition to that stylized here as the "new" Chicago School.

IV. NEW CHICAGO SCHOOL THINKING

Several elements may be identified as contributing to the shift in the paradigmatic vision of the market process. First, as already noted, there was the emphasis on the putative scientific status of economics as a discipline. Friedman was instrumental in his insistence that economic analysis focus on the development of empirically refutable hypotheses, which, when accepted, allowed for the expansion of the explanatory frontier. The technological revolution that made possible the dramatic reductions in costs of data collection and processing facilitated the scientific research thrust.

A second and more subtle element involved the increased incorporation of general equilibrium thinking as opposed to the Marshallian dominance of attention on market adjustment from disequilibrium positions. This shift was, itself, causally related to the increased formalization of general equilibrium models of the inclusive market interaction process. The mathematics of general equilibrium were intellectually fascinating. And, when focused on observed market results, data points became putatively reflective of general equilibrium solutions.

In the general equilibrium of an economy, there exist no unexploited gains from trade, no uncaptured or unexplained profit opportunities. It follows that, in this vision, no particular investment yields above or below normal returns. Who should have been surprised, therefore, when empirical results seemed to show that one random walk down Wall Street was as good as another?

Efficiency does require effectively competitive markets for all goods, as valued by participants, and including goods that are defined temporally.

Exchanges extend to contracts involving projected flows of services in periods subsequent to the economy as now observed. The introduction of exceptional elements into the basic analysis can now be seen as a natural extension of inquiry.

For homogenous units of currently dated goods and services, equilibrium prices are identical over all exchanges. This characteristic of the end-states was ensured by the supposed activity of ever-present arbitrageurs. Again, the imagined activity of intertemporal arbitrageurs became a natural extension of the basic models. Predictable influences on the demand-supply conditions are incorporated in current-period equilibrium prices for future-period goods.

The necessary consequence must be the attribution of efficiency to the observed prices of temporally dated goods. The old cobweb theorem, based on some vague empirical recognition of apparent corn-hog cycles, was relegated by economists, in Chicago and elsewhere, to the dustbins of intellectual history. Markets fail to meet efficiency norms only when artificial constraints are imposed. If left alone and with open entry, the activity of potential arbitrageurs suffices.

From this vision of economic interaction, the movement from the attribution of efficiency in the market for a single good to the macroeconomy through time seemed relatively straightforward. Participants are to be modeled as rational choosers in all aspects of their behavior. Rational expectation models captured the interests of economists. Only genuinely exogenous and hence unpredictable shocks could create inefficient results. The implication here is that government cannot, itself, take economy-wide corrective action to stabilize the macroeconomy if this action is predictable.

Some contributors to the broadly defined new Chicago tradition were willing to stop at this point. Others were not so limited. As the technology of information processing and transmission developed, new institutions emerged, notably in the financial sector. These institutions were, themselves, considered as arbitrage-like responses that helped to ensure the continuing and inclusive efficiency of the network of markets. Acquiescence in the development of these new institutions along with accompanying failure to examine and analyze them critically represents a failure of economists generally, but perhaps with a concentration in the modern Chicago School.

The transference of the efficient markets way of thinking from analysis of the separate goods and services to the institutions within which market transactions are implemented involved two misconceptions that were complementary in facilitating implicit acceptance of a "markets work" mind-set. There was a failure to recognize that the rational choice bases upon which the efficient markets construction rests cannot be applied to the rules, constraints, or conventions within which ordinary market dealings occur. As noted, the attribution of efficiency to markets, as reflected in current prices, requires the presumption that profit-seeking arbitrageurs continuously monitor potential departures from equilibrium values. These arbitrageurs make buyer or seller contracts in partitionable goods and services, contracts that allow for concentrated gains or losses to direct participants, without discernible spillover effects.

With institutions, described as rules, constraints, or conventions within which the market "games" are played, no comparable partitionability remains at all descriptive. "Publicness," in the Samuelsonian sense of nonexcludability, is a necessary feature of the parametric framework within which exchanges take place. Institutions are themselves valued only because they are commonly—that is, publicly—used. Prospective arbitrageurs, who may identify a potential profit from some institutional change, cannot secure concentrated benefits analogous to those secured by comparable trading in partitionable goods (Samuelson 1964). (The basic Samuelsonian taxonomy was extended to apply to laws and institutions, by me and others, but we did not follow through and examine the implications.)

Recognition of the publicness of institutional parameters implies that participants, including possible arbitrageurs, may remain in positions that are individually rational while operating within institutional limits that are, in themselves, inefficient in the Pareto sense. To secure efficiency in the institutions of the market, an additional level of exchanges must be implemented, those among the inclusive, or collective, set of potential beneficiaries in some imagined Wicksellian process of agreement. Any claim to the effect that an observed institution, rule, or convention emerging from a market environment is itself efficient because it remains grounded in the rational choice behavior of participants rests on much weaker foundations than the limited attribution of efficiency to results of exchanges in partitionable goods, with the necessary proviso "within existing institutions."

Adherents of the new Chicago School thinking need not, however, agree to the seemingly required extension of the gains-from-trade logic to Wicksellian large number of complex exchanges. An apparently available fallback defense of institutional efficiency incorporates the survival argument from evolutionary biology. This emphasis, which owes much to the influence of Stigler, as supplemented by Becker, and, from outside the narrow limits of Chicago, by Hayek, is rarely carried to its absurd limits, which assigns efficiency to institutions by their very existence. "That which is, is efficient"—few Chicago economists would go so far. But a presumptive normative bias toward the institutions—perhaps especially the new instruments in the financial sector that emerge from the complex exchange process—is descriptive of the attitudes of many economists prior to the crises.

In part, this bias may have been implanted by a failure to sense the foundational difference between the efficiency and survival properties assigned to end-states. The whole neoclassical general equilibrium exercise is teleological in the sense that the objective end-state, the maximal satisfaction of the preferences of participants, is defined independent of its own existence. By comparison, the statement that an institution is efficient because it survives becomes tautological if the criterion for efficiency is itself survival.

V. SUMMATION

To the extent that the "new," or modern, Chicago School thinking involved, either directly or indirectly, an extension of the efficient markets hypotheses to the rules, constraints, and conventions that describe the institutions of the market—that is, to a defense of the unqualified statement that "markets work"—this mind-set must share some of the blame for the failure reflected in the crises of 2007–2009. Implicit acceptance of the framing of inquiry rather than direct exposition may have fostered tragic neglect of attention.

Even if I were competent to make the argument, my purpose here is not that of developing a critique, either of the "markets work" hypotheses or of the centrality of these hypotheses in current Chicago School thinking. My purpose is to use this discussion that contrasts the "old" and the "new" Chicago School thinking as a vehicle for reiterating my plea to fellow economists, everywhere, to look to the "laws and institutions," the constitutional-institutional framework, within which exchange takes place. It is at this level, and only at this level, that effective reforms can be made.

It is indeed sobering to recognize how little our disciple—"economics" or "political economy"—has advanced beyond Adam Smith. His critique of the "man of system," who concentrates on end-states rather than the process through which these are generated, remains as appropriate in 2010 as it did in 1776 (Smith [1776] 1937).

NOTE

These comments were prepared for oral presentation, without specific references. After completing the draft, my attention was called to a paper by Steven Medema (2009) that, although differently focused, has several parallels with my discussion.

REFERENCES

Fitzgerald, M. 2009. "Chicago Schooled: The Visible Hand of the Recession Has Revitalized Critics of the Chicago School of Economics." *University of Chicago Magazine*, September–October.

Medema, Steven G. 2009. "Adam Smith and the Chicago School." In Jeffrey T. Young (ed.), *The Elgar Companion to Adam Smith*, 346–57. Northhampton, MA: Edward Elgar.

Samuelson, Paul A. 1964. "The Pure Theory of Public Expenditure." *Review of Economics and Statistics* 36(4): 387–89.

Simons, Henry C. 1934. "A Positive Program for Laissez-Faire: Some Proposals for a Liberal Economic Policy." Public Policy Pamphlet No. 15, University of Chicago Press, Chicago.

Smith, Adam. [1776] 1937. *An Inquiry into the Nature and Causes of the Wealth of Nations*. Edited by E. Canaan. New York: Random House.

Viner, Jacob. 1950. *The Customs Union Issue*. New York: Carnegie Endowment for International Peace.

7.2
Ideology or Error
Economists and the Great Recession

JAMES M. BUCHANAN

In his book *Capitalism, 4.0*, and even more succinctly in his short entry in the *Economist* 2011 prospective issue, Anatole Kaletsky (2010, 2011) places major blame for the 2007–2008 crises (the Great Recession) on the academic economists, and particularly on their ideology, which Kaletsky and others reference as a market fundamentalist mind-set. The characteristic feature is the presumption that markets are efficient and pervasive over all sources of value. Neither Kaletsky nor other critics have identified causes for what they consider to be this ideologically motivated overextension and misuse of the central efficient market hypothesis that dominated much economic analysis for several decades.

In an earlier effort (Buchanan 2010), I suggested that the undue concentration of economists' attention on stylized models of market processes finds its source not in ideology but in basic analytical error. If this suggestion is valid, there is a basis for a convergence of scientific judgments, an element missing in discourse that moves too hurriedly toward ideological dispute.

Economists, generally, have failed to distinguish between exchange interactions that take place within institutional constraints, or rules, and the origins

Summer Institute Talk 24, June 2011.

and generation of such rules. I suggested further that there is no legitimacy in any claim that "the market" can generate its own rules, at least to the extent that emergent rules meet efficiency criteria.

The familiar logic of welfare economics applies. Once we recognize that the constraints or rules within which persons and firms interact in markets qualify as "public goods" in the classic Samuelson taxonomy (Samuelson 1954), the processes that generate efficient results in "private goods" are absent. Economists should never have expected that the rules, conventions, practices, and institutions generally that emerged in the quasi anarchy of the financial sector would meet efficiency norms. So long as we acknowledge that some sets of rules or constraints are better than others, we are nonetheless invoking an evaluative standard of some sort. It is necessary, however, to go beyond the Samuelson taxonomy and to treat, specifically, the publicness characteristics of rules. This short paper addresses and elaborates the argument as outlined.

THE LOGIC OF EFFICIENT MARKETS

The explanatory value of the efficient market hypotheses rests on an acceptance of the presumption that ever-alert entrepreneurs will take advantage of any unexploited exchange opportunities. To do so, they must be able to give up and deliver values that can be separately identified as designated for end uses. This potential for one-on-one exchange is not available, by definition, in a setting with Samuelsonian "public goods." Prospective end users may place value on a good in this set, but the full value may not come into being. The free-rider dilemma, as generalized, may prevent the full exploitation of the imagined gains from trade, especially in large communities.

The standard efficient market models implicitly define all goods to be fully partitionable—that is, private in the Samuelson taxonomy, both rivalrous and excludable. But, even within these restrictions, why does the activity of prospective entrepreneurs in exploiting opportunities for beneficial exchange produce results that can be classified to be efficient? The answer is that efficiency is itself defined by the process through which it is attained (Buchanan 1982). The values that are relevant are those placed on goods by participants in the exchange process; it becomes misleading to represent these values as existing independent of the sources from which they must emerge.

Economists are thereby able to define as efficient the outcomes that emerge from the stylized limits of voluntary exchange. This definition is in effect little more than a generalization of the economists' basic message that there exist mutual gains from trade. But such gains cannot be aggregated for purposes of making comparisons with alternative institutional arrangements. In this understanding, market failures are identified through departures from the stylized classification of goods in the classic Samuelson taxonomy. The existence of externalities or spillovers of value, positive or negative, outside the trading process becomes the basis for correction.

If, however, "the market" is itself conceived as a means toward the achievement of some end, such as the maximization of some aggregate value, it becomes necessary to have some externally defined scalar against which "the market" and alternative organizational arrangements can be compared. Classical utilitarianism did provide such a scalar, but at the expense of abandoning the voluntary exchange foundations, quite apart from the enormous epistemological requirements for any implementation. As they came to recognize these limits, economists were left with nothing of normative import beyond the boundaries suggested by Pareto.

But need our understanding of "the market"—as an abstractly defined organizational-institutional setting for exchange interaction between and among persons and firms—be ultimately grounded on such implied teleological bases that might be provided by any aggregative measure? Perhaps Adam Smith led economists down the wrong path with his search for and failure to find some ultimate measure of value. And perhaps Lionel Robbins sowed methodological confusion rather than enlightenment when he defined economics, inclusively, as the science of allocation of scarce means among alternative ends. Perhaps Paul Samuelson aided and abetted the developing ambiguity when he stated that all of economics could be brought within the explanatory scope of a maximizing paradigm.

BEYOND PARETO

"The market," even as stylized, cannot in itself "choose" among possible sets of constraints. Whatever set that emerges will of course delineate possible locations on the Pareto optimality surface. No position in this defined set of outcomes dominates all other positions, within those attainable under observed rules or constraints or outside these limits. But if the evaluation of possible outcomes is to be based on efficiency criteria, post-Pareto, there is nothing that directly warrants the elevation of one alternative set of constraints over any other.

Given the restricted scope for derivation of normative judgments under the Pareto limits, it is not at all surprising that political economists exerted efforts to define a meaningful "social welfare function" that would facilitate an ordering among "social states." And much modern policy evaluation proceeds to reintroduce utilitarianism under a "social welfare function" rubric.

SOCIAL AND MARKET ORDERING

The derivation of an ordering of end-states, or patterns of end-states, even within the calculus of the person making the effort, is conceptually different from the imputed order that may be said to describe market choices. In the latter, the individual, to the extent that an ordering takes place, considers the alternatives independent of any orderings and subsequent choices of other participants in the inclusive exchange nexus. In the stylized limit, the individual is neither affected by nor affects the orderings of others in any direct sense. Choice action in the market consequent upon such ordering exerts no externality, positive or negative, on other parties in the inclusive exchange nexus.

Compare this calculus of ordering and the derived market choice with that which explicitly extends beyond the stylized independence that describes pure market exchange. Both by definition and institutional reality, the individual who participates in the ultimate determination of some outcome exerts effects on others, an interdependence that may be recognized when the possible alternatives are ordered prior to choice itself. Within an organizational framework that allows for extensions beyond stylized limits but still operates as a network of exchanges, behavior has been modeled as if the spillover effects, or externalities, exert no influence on the participants' ordering of the alternatives. This domain of inquiry, often labeled as that of Pigovian welfare economics, identifies "market failure" that may warrant collective corrective intervention. The research program does not, however, normally include consideration of possible inclusive alternatives to markets.

As attention is shifted to goods that are defined to fall within the other, or nonpartitionable category in the Samuelson taxonomy, markets may not emerge at all, although substitutes within marketlike activity may be produced. Somewhat surprisingly, relatively little attention has been given to the welfare characteristics of markets that produce and distribute goods that become substitutes for nonpartitionable counterparts. The Coasian critique of Samuelson's lighthouse example is an exception here (Coase 1974). By logical construction, however, any such markets in valued items or services that serve as substitutes for genuinely nonpartitionable goods do not warrant the attribution of efficiency. There must exist a shortfall between the value generated in the markets for substitutes and the value that can be recognized under full exploitation of the potential surplus.

To the extent that goods which serve as substitutes for genuinely nonpartitionable goods are produced in markets, their production must be motivated by profit- or rent-seeking entrepreneurs, whose strictly pecuniary objectives may be differently directed from any stylized ideal provision under some benevolent and omniscient collectivity.

Indeed, in extreme cases, the market response to the demand for the basic services involved here may be welfare reducing rather than welfare enhancing. We think of Viner's early treatment of customs unions (Viner 1950).

The essential point to be made is that the markets that might be observed to emerge and produce valued items that substitute for nonpartitionable goods cannot be classified as "efficient," at least in any sense comparable to the markets in partitionable goods. In a direct comparison with collectivized operation, of course, the markets in the substitutes for nonpartitionable goods may possibly exploit a relatively larger share of potential surplus.

RULES AS NONPARTITIONABLE GOODS

There is almost universal acceptance of the proposition that order is preferred to anarchy. From this it follows that the institutions of order, the rules, the law, and constraints within which interactions among persons take place are "goods" in the sense that they command positive evaluation by participants. Further, in nominally nondiscriminatory societies, these "goods" simultaneously meet the basic criteria for "publicness" in the Samuelson taxonomy. The game metaphor is helpful here: all players must play by the same rules.

What makes up the optimal or efficient set of rules or constraints on economic interaction? Two questions immediately emerge. Since the process criteria that are operative in markets for partitionable goods are not applicable, what scalar may be introduced to assess the possible efficiency of a particular rule or constraint? And relatedly, if no rule is present, what will describe the quasi anarchy to be observed? (What is the institutionalized equivalent of the Coasian lighthouse?)

The second of these questions may be addressed first. And perhaps our usage of the term "quasi anarchy" requires elaboration. The setting we seek to analyze embodies ordered markets in partitionable goods, which are protected by the political-legal structure, as are contractual exchanges in these rights. We do not propose to examine the possible efficiency or inefficiency of this basic political-legal structure. Our concern is with the rules (conventions, practices, institutions) that develop as economic interaction takes place beyond the stylized limits that involve fully partitionable goods, especially as the inclusive exchange nexus becomes increasingly complex. Clearly there are elements of institutions best conceived as having emerged anarchistically in modern financial extensions of exchanges. Once established, the rules emplaced are not contestable by alert entrepreneurs.

The main point of our argument is that the processes that guarantee the efficiency of ordinary markets do not operate here. The result becomes akin to Nozick's model of the emergence of the single dominant protective association (Nozick 1974). The rules and institutions that emerge in the quasi anarchy of modern financial markets do not pass muster under any process test for efficiency. These rules, such as are observed to exist, are generated by entrepreneurs who are motivated by promised differential rents, without consideration of inclusive norms for efficiency. At best, the rules that come into being serve as substitutes for alternatives that might be adjudged superior through some evaluative process. (The rules that are in being may be the analog of the Coasian lighthouse.)

THE EVALUATION OF ALTERNATIVE RULES

If we accept that rules that have emerged from quasi anarchy cannot be positively evaluated by standard efficiency criteria, what can be the basis for comparison? We must face up to the necessity of responding to the first of the two questions posed earlier. Economists' neglect of this question stems, of course, from the error in classification that we emphasize.

My purpose in this paper is not to develop a definitive defense of any particular criterion for assessing the preferability of one set of rules over others. However, to the extent that individual preferences are to enter into any such comparison, the basic relationship between rules (constraints) and interaction within rules must be recognized. The individual, as a participant in the choice among alternative sets of rules, will be conscious of the "publicness" that is necessarily involved. The set of rules that emerges from the selection process, however this may be organized, must be generally imposed on the behavior of all participants.

The ordering of individual preferences among sets of rules differs in important respects from the ordering among end items of consumption. The non-rivalry attribute of rules removes critical aspects of distributional conflict, thereby making potential agreement on rules among participants relatively less difficult to achieve. In *The Calculus of Consent*, Tullock and I (1962) suggest that agreement on rules becomes relatively easier to achieve than agreement on specific allocation-distribution alternatives within existing rules because the sequential extension of rules necessarily places the individual participant behind a "veil of uncertainty," akin to the normatively grounded position behind a "veil of ignorance," made familiar by Rawls (1971).

The implication, as translated into the terms of the midcentury discussion of Samuelson's seminal taxonomy, is that for choices among rules or constraints on the behavior of participants in markets, the standard free-rider barrier to the full exploitation of value-enhancing opportunities becomes relatively much less severe. Elaboration of this distinction is, of course, merely an alternative means of stating that the distributional conflict among potential beneficiaries is substantially lessened as attention shifts to choices among rules, as opposed to choices among end-states.

Embodiment of a recognition that the rules or constraints on the operation of markets are best classified as "public goods" in the Samuelson taxonomy, while at the same time general agreement on the collective provision and dimensional characteristics of such goods is relatively more attainable than like agreement on postrule allocation-distribution of value, does not give economists license to claim that efficient rules are generated as if by magic from within-market behavior. The "invisible hand," even as properly interpreted, remains inoperative at the level of choices among rules. Far-seeing entrepreneurs cannot expect to secure differential rents, at least to the same degree as those promised by exchanges in partitionable goods.

The limits to the efficiency generation possibility of operative markets in setting rules must be recognized. But, at the same time, and perhaps more importantly, the efficiency producing working of markets for partitionable goods, within rules that are accepted by participants, must not be overlooked.

SUMMATION

We agree with Kaletsky in placing major blame for the Great Recession on the academic economists, and specifically on their overly enthusiastic extension of the efficient markets models, those that lend credence to the "markets work" slogan that allows for dismissal of potential criticisms. We differ from Kaletsky and other critics, however, in that we locate the source in analytical or scientific error rather than in any market fundamentalist ideology. Markets do indeed work, but only within effectively designed rules or constraints that cannot, themselves, emerge from marketlike behavior.

To the extent that error rather than ideology explains the stance of the academic economists, there should be relatively more prospect for productive discussion and dialogue. Ideology should not be called upon too early for its potential explanatory influence, especially if in so doing the basic error we identify continues to be overlooked.

I again emphasize that the aim in this short paper is not to offer evaluations of specific rules or of possible structural reforms. The attention is exclusively on the basic understandings that must be achieved prior to any productive discourse on the constitution of the market economy.

REFERENCES

Buchanan, James M. 1982. "Order Defined in the Process of Its Emergence." *Literature of Liberty* (Winter): 5.

———. 2011. "The Limits of Market Efficiency." *Rationality, Markets and Morals: Studies at the Intersection of Philosophy and Economics* 2 (January 31): 1–7.

Buchanan, James M., and Gordon Tullock. 1962. *The Calculus of Consent: Logical Foundations of Constitutional Democracy*. Ann Arbor: University of Michigan Press.

Coase, R. H. 1974. "The Lighthouse in Economics." *Journal of Law and Economics* 17(2): 357–76.

Kaletsky, Anatole. 2010. *Capitalism, 4.0: The Birth of a New Economy*. New York: Public Affairs Press.

———. 2011. "Wrong, INET?: A Challenge to Economic Orthodoxy." *Economist: The World in 2011* (25-Year Special Edition): 156.

Nozick, Robert. 1974. *Anarchy, State, and Utopia*. New York: Basic Books.

Rawls, John. 1971. *A Theory of Justice*. Cambridge, MA: Harvard University Press.

Samuelson, Paul A. 1964. "The Pure Theory of Public Expenditure." *Review of Economics and Statistics* 36(4): 387–89.

Viner, Jacob. 1950. *The Customs Union Issue*. New York: Carnegie Endowment for International Peace.

Conclusion

PETER J. BOETTKE AND ALAIN MARCIANO

In the introduction of one of his collections of essays, *Ethics and Economics Progress*, Buchanan wrote that the first chapters bore on "closely related themes, which may be summarized under the generalized title, 'Ethics and Economics Progress,' or, less inclusively, 'The Economics of Ethics,' or, even more descriptively, 'The Economic Value of Ethical Norms.' As these titles may suggest, the subject matter reflects my disciplinary qualifications; the core discipline here is economics, not ethics" (Buchanan 1997, 1).

Buchanan was an economist, indeed, who made particularly important technical contributions to public economics. He was also an economist—and insisted on that—whenever he discussed topics in nonmarket decision-making such as crime or political decision makers or ethics. However, despite what he said, we can argue that he was not just an economist, at least in the standard sense of the word. He was a social philosopher—as evidenced by his contributions to social philosophy. Or, as we have explained in this book, he was a political economist and, more precisely, one of the rare modern economists to reach back to the project of the Scottish Enlightenment thinkers such as Hume and Smith. This is what this book is about: Buchanan's political economy. This was crucial in 1957 when he established the Thomas Jefferson Center. It was crucial in 1963, when he delivered his presidential address on "What Should Economists Do?" (see Buchanan 1964). This is still crucial, since economics has not deviated much from its tendency to be technical and specialized, and it is difficult to give advice as to what is a "good society."

The reference to a "good society," which he viewed as central in political economy, has clearly a normative dimension. There does exist a normative thrust of classical political economy. However, we must insist that this normativeness is not *absolute*, but rather a relatively absolute absolute in the following twofold meaning: first, no characterization of a good society could be absolute (truth does not exist, except in science); and second, the role of the political economists should be limited to present alternatives to the individuals, not to impose his own values to others. In other words, the role of a positive political economist was to understand the functioning of the economy, to get at the root cause of social and political phenomena—including social and political ills—and to propose to let individuals choose. The choice remains a choice made by individuals.

Hence, Buchanan's message was one of tolerance and of humility, which he never ceased to defend and promote, although the periods during which he did so were not particularly favorable. Hence, Buchanan's message was also radical, not to say revolutionary. Buchanan was a dissenting economist (Boettke 1998), not a mere critic—that is, he was "one who both challenges the mainstream view and begins or assists in the process of reconstruction or the development of an alternative approach" (Medema 2008, 430). He asked questions and challenged conventional wisdom. He was a non-Keynesian when Keynesianism was in vogue; he opposed Samuelson when the latter was triumphing; he developed a subjective research program when the majority of the profession lost sight of the subjective roots of the neoclassical revolution; he rejected the formal models of utility maximization and perfect competition when these models represented the tool kit of any respectable economist; he reintroduced moral concern in economics at a time when economists ignored human frailties; he tried to promote increasing returns when almost all the profession had assumed them away; and he pleaded a form of humility when economists were convinced that they could cure the ills a society or economy was suffering from. The list could even be longer. But he nonetheless won the Nobel Prize in Economics, which is a recognition that his approach was not totally useless or wrong.

At the same time, adopting a deontological approach did not imply that Buchanan defended any outcome and any situation. Humility is not to counsel despair nor fatalism. Buchanan's teacher Frank Knight would say that to call a situation hopeless is to call it ideal. Since the world is far from ideal, the situation must not be hopeless. Reform is therefore possible, and the political economist does have an important role in reform efforts even in the Buchanan framework of the humbled worldly philosopher. Humility and political economy reform need not conflict with one another. We can give but a few examples developed in this book. In the early 1950s, and again in the 1970s, he argued in favor of a rule of fiscal justice to limit the negative consequences of spatial competition and mobility. Later, he argued that a society in which individuals adopt ethical behaviors—that is, take into account the consequences of their actions on others and do not ignore the interdependencies that exist with them—was more preferable than a society in which individuals treat others as means and try to satisfy what he called "naked preferences" or "narrow self-interest." Buchanan even admitted that if individuals were behaving in such unregarding ways, they should be coerced.

Buchanan's liberalism was not extreme, as some try to caricature it. He was not a conservative either—because "the conservative seeks to maintain in being whatever is in being" (Buchanan 1965, 1), and Buchanan was not interested in trying to "conserve" anything. This can be seen in his treatment of the status quo and his deployment of the compensation principle. The status quo is not accorded any normative standing in his analysis beyond the simple point that it defines the starting state of all analysis of social change. Actually, he preferred to be called a right-liberal (ibid., 2).

Our demonstration combines analysis with the publication of rarely printed articles and unpublished, original material. The decision to use already published pieces was not only based on the difficulty in finding them. Our objective was to put them in perspective and complement the new and original pieces that come from the Buchanan archives. Obviously, the archives are much richer than the simple overview we give here. We are just making a first stab at mining these archives to further the ongoing conversation that constitutes technical economics, the broader art of political economy, and the social philosophy of the liberal democratic society.

REFERENCES

Boettke, P. J. 1998. "James M. Buchanan and the Rebirth of Political Economy." Reprinted from Richard P. F. Holt and Steven Pressman (eds.), *Economics and Its Discontent: Dissent in 20th Century Economics*, 21–39. Northampton, MA: Edward Elgar.

Buchanan, J. M. 1964. "What Should Economists Do?" *Southern Economic Journal* 30(3): 213–22.

———. 1965. "A Note on Semantics." *Exchange* 26: 5–6.

———. 1997. *Ethics and Economics Progress*. Norman: University of Oklahoma Press.

Medema, S. G. 2008. "Ronald Coase as a Dissenting Economist." *Studie note di economia* 13(3): 427–48.

Contributors

Peter Bernholz is a professor emeritus of economics at the University of Basel, Basel, Switzerland.

Peter J. Boettke is the University Professor of Economics and Philosophy, George Mason University and director of the F. A. Hayek Program for Advanced Study in Philosophy, Politics, and Economics, Mercatus Center at George Mason University, Fairfax, Virginia, USA.

William Breit was the Vernon F. Taylor Distinguished Professor of Economics and professor emeritus at Trinity College, San Antonio, Texas, USA.

Geoffrey Brennan is a professor emeritus at the Centre for Moral, Social and Political Theory at the Australian National University, Canberra, Australia.

Edgar K. Browning is a professor emeritus of economics at Texas A&M University, College Station, Texas, USA.

James M. Buchanan was the Distinguished Professor Emeritus of Economics at George Mason University, Fairfax, Virginia, USA. He received the Sveriges Riksbank Prize in Economic Sciences in Memory of Alfred Nobel in 1986.

Lynn Eaton is the director of the Special Collections Research Center at the George Mason University Libraries.

Frank A. Geldard was a professor emeritus of psychology at Princeton University, Princeton, New Jersey, USA.

Charles J. Goetz is the Joseph M. Hartfield Professor of Law Emeritus at the University of Virginia School of Law, Charlottesville, Virginia, USA.

Hartmut Kliemt is a visiting professor for behavioral and institutional economics at the Justus Liebig University Gießen, Gießen, Hesse, Germany.

Dwight R. Lee is an Affiliate Visiting Faculty Fellow at the Institute for the Study of Political Economy, Miller College of Business, Ball State University, Muncie, Indiana, USA.

Robert J. Mackay is an affiliated consultant with NERA Economic Consulting.

Alain Marciano is a professor of economics, University of Montpellier, Montpellier, France.

Richard B. McKenzie is the Walter B. Gerken Professor of Enterprise and Society Emeritus in the Paul Merage School of Business at the University of California, Irvine, California, USA.

Dennis C. Mueller is a professor emeritus of economics at the University of Vienna, Vienna, Austria.

Mancur Olson was a distinguished university professor of economics at the University of Maryland, College Park, Maryland, USA.

Robert D. Tollison was the cofounder of the Clemson Institute for the Study of Capitalism and the J. Wilson Newman Professor Emeritus in the Department of Economics at Clemson University, Clemson, South Carolina, USA.

Eugenia F. Toma is a university research professor and the Wendell H. Ford Professor of Public Policy in the Martin School of Public Policy and Administration at the University of Kentucky, Lexington, Kentucky, USA.

Thomas D. Willett is the Horton Professor of Economics in the Department of Economic Sciences at Claremont Graduate University and the director of the Claremont Institute for Economic Policy Studies at Claremont Graduate University, Claremont, California, USA.

Leland Yeager was the Ludwig von Mises Distinguished Professor Emeritus at Auburn University, Auburn, Alabama, USA.

John G. Zenelis is dean of libraries and University Librarian of the George Mason University Libraries.

Index

Page numbers in *italics* refer to figures and tables.

CPSIA information can be obtained
at www.ICGtesting.com
Printed in the USA
BVHW040345130321
601893BV00004B/5